# THE BOOK OF DISCIPLINE
## OF
# THE UNITED METHODIST CHURCH

"The Book Editor, the Secretary of the General Conference, the Publisher of The United Methodist Church, and the Committee on Correlation and Editorial Revision shall be charged with editing the *Discipline*. These editors, in the exercise of their judgment, shall have the authority to make changes in phraseology as may be necessary to harmonize legislation without changing its substance. The editors, in consultation with the Judicial Council, shall also have authority to delete provisions of the *Discipline* which have been ruled unconstitutional by the Judicial Council."

—Plan of Organization and Rules of Order of the General Conference, 2000

*See* Judicial Council Decision 96, which declares the *Discipline* to be a book of law.

Harriett Jane Olson
Book Editor of The United Methodist Church

Carolyn M. Marshall
Secretary of the General Conference

Neil M. Alexander
Publisher of The United Methodist Church

The Committee on Correlation and Editorial Revision
Naomi G. Bartle, Chairperson
Clelia D. Hendrix, Vice Chairperson
Eradio Valverde, Secretary
Richard L. Evans

# THE
# BOOK OF DISCIPLINE
# OF THE
# UNITED METHODIST
# CHURCH
## *2000*

The United Methodist Publishing House
Nashville, Tennessee

ISBN 0-687-03141-9

Leather Edition ISBN 0-687-03151-6
CD-ROM Edition ISBN 0-687-34130-2
Korean Edition ISBN 0-687-02951-1
Spanish Edition ISBN 0-687-02961-9

00 01 02 03 04 05 06 07 08 09 -- 10 9 8 7 6 5 4 3 2 1
PRINTED IN THE UNITED STATES OF AMERICA

# EPISCOPAL GREETINGS

To all people and pastors of United Methodism:
"Grace and peace to you from God our Father and the Lord Jesus
Christ."
—1 Corinthians 1:3

The *Discipline* is the book of law of The United Methodist Church.
It is the product of over 200 years of the General Conferences of the
denominations which now form The United Methodist Church.

The *Discipline* as the instrument for setting forth the laws, plan,
polity, and process by which United Methodists govern themselves
remains constant. Each General Conference amends, perfects, clari-
fies, and adds its own contribution to the *Discipline*. We do not see the
*Discipline* as sacrosanct or infallible, but we do consider it a document
suitable to our heritage. It is the most current statement of how
United Methodists agree to live their lives together. It reflects our
understanding of the Church and of what is expected of its laity and
clergy as they seek to be effective witnesses in the world as a part of
the whole body of Christ.

This book of covenant sets forth the theological grounding of The
United Methodist Church in biblical faith, and affirms that we go forward as "loyal heirs to all that [is] best in the Christian past." It
makes clear that The United Methodist Church is an inclusive society
without regard to ethnic origin, economic condition, gender, age, or
the disabilities of its constituents. It asserts that all who are baptized
and confirmed are ministers of Jesus Christ. It affirms the conciliar
principle and connectionalism as distinctive marks of United
Methodist ecclesiology, makes clear the global character of the

v

Church's mission, and declares interdependence with other Christian bodies both in spirit and cooperation. It affirms with John Wesley that solitary religion is invalid and that Christ lays claim upon the whole life of those who accept him as Lord and Savior.

We therefore commend this *Discipline* to all in our constituency and to friends beyond our bounds who would seek to understand what it means to be a United Methodist. Communication is essential for understanding what the Church is and does. We expect the *Discipline* to be found in libraries of local churches, colleges, universities, and seminaries, as well as in the homes of ordained, diaconal, and licensed ministers and lay members of The United Methodist Church. We pray that it will enable all persons to celebrate God's grace, exalt the meaning of faithful discipleship, and inspire on the part of many a deeper desire to be more effective witnesses for the Head of the Church, even Jesus Christ our Lord.

The Council of Bishops
William B. Oden, President
Sharon Zimmerman Rader,
Secretary

# CONTENTS

**Note:** The basic unit in *The Book of Discipline* is the paragraph ( ¶ ) rather than page, chapter, or section. The paragraphs are numbered consecutively within each chapter or section, but many numbers are skipped between parts, chapters, and sections in order to allow for future enactments and to fit with the following plan:

## PART I
## THE CONSTITUTION
### ¶¶ 1–59

## PART II
## DOCTRINAL STANDARDS AND OUR THEOLOGICAL TASK
### ¶¶ 101–104

## PART III
## THE MINISTRY OF ALL CHRISTIANS
### ¶¶ 120–141

*CONTENTS*

# PART IV
# SOCIAL PRINCIPLES
## ¶¶ 160–166

# PART V
# ORGANIZATION AND ADMINISTRATION
## ¶¶ 201–2719

## Chapter One
## THE LOCAL CHURCH

# CONTENTS

## Chapter Two
### THE MINISTRY OF THE ORDAINED

## Chapter Three
### THE SUPERINTENDENCY

### Chapter Four
### THE CONFERENCES

CONTENTS

Chapter Five
ADMINISTRATIVE ORDER

CONTENTS

Chapter Six
CHURCH PROPERTY

Chapter Seven
JUDICIAL ADMINISTRATION

# UNITED METHODIST BISHOPS

*A List Compiled for* The Book of Discipline
*by the Council of Bishops*

| NAME | ELECTED | NAME | ELECTED |
|---|---|---|---|
| Thomas Coke | 1784 | Osman Cleander Baker | 1852 |
| Francis Asbury | 1784 | Edward Raymond Ames | 1852 |
| Richard Whatcoat | 1800 | Lewis Davis | 1853 |
| Phillip William Otterbein | 1800 | George Foster Pierce | 1854 |
| Martin Boehm | 1800 | John Early | 1854 |
| Jacob Albright | 1807 | Hubbard Hinde Kavanaugh | 1854 |
| William M'Kendree | 1808 | Francis Burns | 1858 |
| Christian Newcomer | 1813 | William W. Orwig | 1859 |
| Enoch George | 1816 | Jacob Markwood | 1861 |
| Robert Richford Roberts | 1816 | Daniel Shuck | 1861 |
| Andrew Zeller | 1817 | John Jacob Esher | 1863 |
| Joseph Hoffman | 1821 | Davis Wasgatt Clark | 1864 |
| Joshua Soule | 1824 | Edward Thomson | 1864 |
| Elijah Hedding | 1824 | Calvin Kingsley | 1864 |
| Henry Kumler Sr. | 1825 | Jonathan Weaver | 1865 |
| John Emory | 1832 | William May Wightman | 1866 |
| James Osgood Andrew | 1832 | Enoch Mather Marvin | 1866 |
| Samuel Heistand | 1833 | David Seth Doggett | 1866 |
| William Brown | 1833 | Holland Nimmons McTyeire | 1866 |
| Beverly Waugh | 1836 | John Wright Roberts | 1866 |
| Thomas Asbury Morris | 1836 | John Dickson | 1869 |
| Jacob Erb | 1837 | John Christian Keener | 1870 |
| John Seybert | 1839 | Reuben Yeakel | 1871 |
| Henry Kumler Jr. | 1841 | Thomas Bowman | 1872 |
| John Coons | 1841 | William Logan Harris | 1872 |
| Joseph Long | 1843 | Randolph Sinks Foster | 1872 |
| Leonidas Lent Hamline | 1844 | Isaac William Wiley | 1872 |
| Edmund Storer Janes | 1844 | Stephen Mason Merrill | 1872 |
| John Russel | 1845 | Edward Gayer Andrews | 1872 |
| Jacob John Glossbrenner | 1845 | Gilbert Haven | 1872 |
| William Hanby | 1845 | Jesse Truesdell Peck | 1872 |
| William Capers | 1846 | Rudolph Dubs | 1875 |
| Robert Paine | 1846 | Thomas Bowman | 1875 |
| David Edwards | 1849 | Milton Wright | 1877 |
| Henry Bidleman Bascom | 1850 | Nicholas Castle | 1877 |
| Levi Scott | 1852 | Henry White Warren | 1880 |
| Matthew Simpson | 1852 | Cyrus David Foss | 1880 |

1

| NAME | ELECTED | NAME | ELECTED |
|---|---|---|---|
| John Fletcher Hurst | 1880 | Elijah Embree Hoss | 1902 |
| Erastus Otis Haven | 1880 | Henry Burns Hartzler | 1902 |
| Ezekiel Boring Kephart | 1881 | William Franklin Heil | 1902 |
| Alpheus Waters Wilson | 1882 | Joseph Flintoft Berry | 1904 |
| Linus Parker | 1882 | Henry Spellmeyer | 1904 |
| John Cowper Granbery | 1882 | William Fraser McDowell | 1904 |
| Robert Kennon Hargrove | 1882 | James Whitford Bashford | 1904 |
| William Xavier Ninde | 1884 | William Burt | 1904 |
| John Morgan Walden | 1884 | Luther Barton Wilson | 1904 |
| Willard Francis Mallalieu | 1884 | Thomas Benjamin Neely | 1904 |
| Charles Henry Fowler | 1884 | Isaiah Benjamin Scott | 1904 |
| William Taylor | 1884 | William Fitzjames Oldham | 1904 |
| Daniel Kumler Flickinger | 1885 | John Edward Robinson | 1904 |
| William Wallace Duncan | 1886 | Merriman Colbert Harris | 1904 |
| Charles Betts Galloway | 1886 | William Marion Weekley | 1905 |
| Eugene Russell Hendrix | 1886 | William Melvin Bell | 1905 |
| Joseph Stanton Key | 1886 | Thomas Coke Carter | 1905 |
| John Heyl Vincent | 1888 | John James Tigert III | 1906 |
| James Newbury FitzGerald | 1888 | Seth Ward | 1906 |
| Isaac Wilson Joyce | 1888 | James Atkins | 1906 |
| John Philip Newman | 1888 | Samuel P. Spreng | 1907 |
| Daniel Ayres Goodsell | 1888 | William Franklin Anderson | 1908 |
| James Mills Thoburn | 1888 | John Louis Nuelsen | 1908 |
| James W. Hott | 1889 | William Alfred Quayle | 1908 |
| Atticus Greene Haygood | 1890 | Charles William Smith | 1908 |
| Oscar Penn Fitzgerald | 1890 | Wilson Seeley Lewis | 1908 |
| Wesley Matthias Stanford | 1891 | Edwin Holt Hughes | 1908 |
| Christian S. Haman | 1891 | Robert McIntyre | 1908 |
| Sylvanus C. Breyfogel | 1891 | Frank Milton Bristol | 1908 |
| William Horn | 1891 | Collins Denny | 1910 |
| Job S. Mills | 1893 | John Carlisle Kilgo | 1910 |
| Charles Cardwell McCabe | 1896 | William Belton Murrah | 1910 |
| Joseph Crane Hartzell | 1896 | Walter Russell Lambuth | 1910 |
| Earl Cranston | 1896 | Richard Green Waterhouse | 1910 |
| Warren Akin Candler | 1898 | Edwin DuBose Mouzon | 1910 |
| Henry Clay Morrison | 1898 | James Henry McCoy | 1910 |
| David Hastings Moore | 1900 | William Hargrave Fouke | 1910 |
| John William Hamilton | 1900 | Uriah Frantz Swengel | 1910 |
| Edwin Wallace Parker | 1900 | Homer Clyde Stuntz | 1912 |
| Francis Wesley Warne | 1900 | William Orville Shepard | 1912 |
| George Martin Mathews | 1902 | Theodore Sommers | |
| Alexander Coke Smith | 1902 | Henderson | 1912 |

2

| NAME | ELECTED | NAME | ELECTED |
|------|---------|------|---------|
| Naphtali Luccock | 1912 | Robert Elijah Jones | 1920 |
| Francis John McConnell | 1912 | Matthew Wesley Clair | 1920 |
| Frederick DeLand Leete | 1912 | Arthur R. Clippinger | 1921 |
| Richard Joseph Cooke | 1912 | William Benjamin Beauchamp | 1922 |
| Wilbur Patterson Thirkield | 1912 | James Edward Dickey | 1922 |
| John Wesley Robinson | 1912 | Samuel Ross Hay | 1922 |
| William Perry Eveland | 1912 | Hoyt McWhorter Dobbs | 1922 |
| Henry Harness Fout | 1913 | Hiram Abiff Boaz | 1922 |
| Cyrus Jeffries Kephart | 1913 | John Francis Dunlap | 1922 |
| Alfred Taylor Howard | 1913 | George Amos Miller | 1924 |
| Gottlieb Heinmiller | 1915 | Titus Lowe | 1924 |
| Lawrence Hoover Seager | 1915 | George Richmond Grose | 1924 |
| Herbert Welch | 1916 | Brenton Thoburn Badley | 1924 |
| Thomas Nicholson | 1916 | Wallace Elias Brown | 1924 |
| Adna Wright Leonard | 1916 | Arthur Biggs Statton | 1925 |
| Matthew Simpson Hughes | 1916 | John S. Stamm | 1926 |
| Charles Bayard Mitchell | 1916 | Samuel J. Umbreit | 1926 |
| Franklin Elmer Ellsworth Hamilton | 1916 | Raymond J. Wade | 1928 |
| Alexander Priestly Camphor | 1916 | James Chamberlain Baker | 1928 |
| Eben Samuel Johnson | 1916 | Edwin Ferdinand Lee | 1928 |
| William H. Washinger | 1917 | Grant D. Batdorf | 1929 |
| John Monroe Moore | 1918 | Ira David Warner | 1929 |
| William Fletcher McMurry | 1918 | John W. Gowdy | 1930 |
| Urban Valentine Williams Darlington | 1918 | Chih Ping Wang | 1930 |
| Horace Mellard DuBose | 1918 | Arthur James Moore | 1930 |
| William Newman Ainsworth | 1918 | Paul Bentley Kern | 1930 |
| James Cannon, Jr. | 1918 | Angie Frank Smith | 1930 |
| Matthew T. Maze | 1918 | George Edward Epp | 1930 |
| Lauress John Birney | 1920 | Joshwant Rao Chitamber | 1930 |
| Frederick Bohn Fisher | 1920 | Juan Ermete Gattinoni | 1932 |
| Charles Edward Locke | 1920 | Junius Ralph Magee | 1932 |
| Ernest Lynn Waldorf | 1920 | Ralph Spaulding Cushman | 1932 |
| Edgar Blake | 1920 | Elmer Wesley Praetorius | 1934 |
| Ernest Gladstone Richardson | 1920 | Charles H. Stauffacher | 1934 |
| Charles Wesley Burns | 1920 | Jarrell Waskom Pickett | 1935 |
| Harry Lester Smith | 1920 | Roberto Valenzuela Elphick | 1936 |
| George Harvey Bickley | 1920 | Wilbur Emery Hammaker | 1936 |
| Frederick Thomas Keeney | 1920 | Charles Wesley Flint | 1936 |
| Charles Larew Mead | 1920 | Garfield Bromley Oxnam | 1936 |
| Anton Bast | 1920 | Alexander Preston Shaw | 1936 |
| | | John McKendree Springer | 1936 |
| | | F. H. Otto Melle | 1936 |

| NAME | ELECTED | NAME | ELECTED |
|---|---|---|---|
| Ralph Ansel Ward | 1937 | John Wesley Edward Bowen | 1948 |
| Victor Otterbein Weidler | 1938 | Lloyd Christ Wicke | 1948 |
| Ivan Lee Holt | 1938 | John Wesley Lord | 1948 |
| William Walter Peele | 1938 | Dana Dawson | 1948 |
| Clare Purcell | 1938 | Marvin Augustus Franklin | 1948 |
| Charles Claude Selecman | 1938 | Roy Hunter Short | 1948 |
| John Lloyd Decell | 1938 | Richard Campbell Raines | 1948 |
| William Clyde Martin | 1938 | Marshall Russell Reed | 1948 |
| William Turner Watkins | 1938 | Harry Clifford Northcott | 1948 |
| James Henry Straughn | 1939 | Hazen Graff Werner | 1948 |
| John Calvin Broomfield | 1939 | Glenn Randall Phillips | 1948 |
| William Alfred Carroll Hughes | 1940 | Gerald Hamilton Kennedy | 1948 |
| Lorenzo Houston King | 1940 | Donald Harvey Tippett | 1948 |
| Bruce Richard Baxter | 1940 | Jose Labarrete Valencia | 1948 |
| Shot Kumar Mondol | 1940 | Sante Uberto Barbieri | 1949 |
| Clement Daniel Rockey | 1941 | Raymond Leroy Archer | 1950 |
| Enrique Carlos Balloch | 1941 | David Thomas Gregory | 1950 |
| Z. T. Kaung | 1941 | Frederick Buckley Newell | 1952 |
| Wen Yuan Chen | 1941 | Edgar Amos Love | 1952 |
| George Carleton Lacy | 1941 | Matthew Wesley Clair Jr. | 1952 |
| Fred L. Dennis | 1941 | John Warren Branscomb | 1952 |
| Dionisio Deista Alejandro | 1944 | Henry Bascom Watts | 1952 |
| Fred Pierce Corson | 1944 | D. Stanley Coors | 1952 |
| Walter Earl Ledden | 1944 | Edwin Edgar Voigt | 1952 |
| Lewis Oliver Hartman | 1944 | Francis Gerald Ensley | 1952 |
| Newell Snow Booth | 1944 | Alsie Raymond Grant | 1952 |
| Willis Jefferson King | 1944 | Julio Manuel Sabanes | 1952 |
| Robert Nathaniel Brooks | 1944 | Friedrich Wunderlich | 1953 |
| Edward Wendall Kelly | 1944 | Odd Arthur Hagen | 1953 |
| William Angie Smith | 1944 | Ferdinand Sigg | 1954 |
| Paul Elliott Martin | 1944 | Reuben Herbert Mueller | 1954 |
| Costen Jordan Harrell | 1944 | Harold Rickel Heininger | 1954 |
| Paul Neff Garber | 1944 | Lyle Lynden Baughman | 1954 |
| Charles Wesley Brashares | 1944 | Prince Albert Taylor Jr. | 1956 |
| Schuyler Edward Garth | 1944 | Eugene Maxwell Frank | 1956 |
| Arthur Frederick Wesley | 1944 | Nolan Bailey Harmon | 1956 |
| John Abdus Subhan | 1945 | Bachman Gladstone Hodge | 1956 |
| John Balmer Showers | 1945 | Hobart Baumann Amstutz | 1956 |
| August Theodor Arvidson | 1946 | Ralph Edward Dodge | 1956 |
| Johann Wilhelm Ernst Sommer | 1946 | Mangal Singh | 1956 |
| | | Gabriel Sundaram | 1956 |
| | | Paul E. V. Shannon | 1957 |

| NAME | ELECTED |
|---|---|
| John Gordon Howard | 1957 |
| Hermann Walter Kaebnick | 1958 |
| W. Maynard Sparks | 1958 |
| Paul Murray Herrick | 1958 |
| Bowman Foster Stockwell | 1960 |
| Fred Garrigus Holloway | 1960 |
| William Vernon Middleton | 1960 |
| William Ralph Ward Jr. | 1960 |
| James Kenneth Mathews | 1960 |
| Oliver Eugene Slater | 1960 |
| William Kenneth Pope | 1960 |
| Paul Vernon Galloway | 1960 |
| Aubrey Grey Walton | 1960 |
| Kenneth Wilford Copeland | 1960 |
| Everett Walter Palmer | 1960 |
| Ralph Taylor Alton | 1960 |
| Edwin Ronald Garrison | 1960 |
| Torney Otto Nall Jr. | 1960 |
| Charles Franklin Golden | 1960 |
| Noah Watson Moore Jr. | 1960 |
| Marquis LaFayette Harris | 1960 |
| James Walton Henley | 1960 |
| Walter Clark Gum | 1960 |
| Paul Hardin Jr. | 1960 |
| John Owen Smith | 1960 |
| Paul William Milhouse | 1960 |
| Pedro Ricardo Zottele | 1962 |
| James Samuel Thomas | 1964 |
| William McFerrin Stowe | 1964 |
| Walter Kenneth Goodson | 1964 |
| Dwight Ellsworth Loder | 1964 |
| Robert Marvin Stuart | 1964 |
| Edward Julian Pendergrass Jr. | 1964 |
| Thomas Marion Pryor | 1964 |
| Homer Ellis Finger Jr. | 1964 |
| Earl Gladstone Hunt Jr. | 1964 |
| Francis Enmer Kearns | 1964 |
| Lance Webb | 1964 |
| Escrivao Anglaze Zunguze | 1964 |
| Robert Fielden Lundy | 1964 |
| Harry Peter Andreassen | 1964 |

| NAME | ELECTED |
|---|---|
| John Wesley Shungu | 1964 |
| Alfred Jacob Shaw | 1965 |
| Prabhakar Christopher Benjamin Balaram | 1965 |
| Stephen Trowen Nagbe | 1965 |
| Franz Werner Schäfer | 1966 |
| Benjamin I. Guansing | 1967 |
| Lineunt Scott Allen | 1967 |
| Paul Arthur Washburn | 1968 |
| Carl Ernst Sommer | 1968 |
| David Frederick Wertz | 1968 |
| Alsie Henry Carleton | 1968 |
| Roy Calvin Nichols | 1968 |
| Arthur James Armstrong | 1968 |
| William Ragsdale Cannon | 1968 |
| Abel Tendekayi Muzorewa | 1968 |
| Cornelio M. Ferrer | 1968 |
| Paul Locke A. Granadosin | 1968 |
| Joseph R. Lance | 1968 |
| Ram Dutt Joshi | 1968 |
| Eric Algernon Mitchell | 1969 |
| Federico Jose Pagura | 1969 |
| Armin E. Härtel | 1970 |
| Ole Edvard Borgen | 1970 |
| Finis Alonzo Crutchfield Jr. | 1972 |
| Joseph Hughes Yeakel | 1972 |
| Robert E. Goodrich Jr. | 1972 |
| Carl Julian Sanders | 1972 |
| Ernest T. Dixon Jr. | 1972 |
| Don Wendell Holter | 1972 |
| Wayne K. Clymer | 1972 |
| Joel Duncan McDavid | 1972 |
| Edward Gonzalez Carroll | 1972 |
| Jesse Robert DeWitt | 1972 |
| James Mase Ault | 1972 |
| John B. Warman | 1972 |
| Mack B. Stokes | 1972 |
| Jack Marvin Tuell | 1972 |
| Melvin E. Wheatley Jr. | 1972 |
| Edward Lewis Tullis | 1972 |
| Frank Lewis Robertson | 1972 |

| NAME | ELECTED | NAME | ELECTED |
|------|---------|------|---------|
| Wilbur Wong Yan Choy | 1972 | Ernest A. Fitzgerald | 1984 |
| Robert McGrady Blackburn | 1972 | R. Kern Eutsler | 1984 |
| Emilio J. M. de Carvalho | 1972 | J. Woodrow Hearn | 1984 |
| Fama Onema | 1972 | Walter L. Underwood | 1984 |
| Mamidi Elia Peter | 1972 | Richard B. Wilke | 1984 |
| Bennie de Quency Warner | 1973 | J. Lloyd Knox | 1984 |
| J. Kenneth Shamblin | 1976 | Neil L. Irons | 1984 |
| Alonzo Monk Bryan | 1976 | Roy Isao Sano | 1984 |
| Kenneth William Hicks | 1976 | Lewis Bevel Jones III | 1984 |
| James Chess Lovern | 1976 | Forrest C. Stith | 1984 |
| Leroy Charles Hodapp | 1976 | Ernest W. Newman | 1984 |
| Edsel Albert Ammons | 1976 | Woodie W. White | 1984 |
| C. Dale White | 1976 | Robert Crawley Morgan | 1984 |
| Ngoy Kimba Wakadilo | 1976 | David J. Lawson | 1984 |
| Almeida Penicela | 1976 | Elias Gabriel Galvan | 1984 |
| LaVerne D. Mercado | 1976 | Rueben Philip Job | 1984 |
| Hermann Ludwig Sticher | 1977 | Leontine T. Kelly | 1984 |
| Shantu Kumar A. Parmar | 1979 | Judith Craig | 1984 |
| Thomas Syla Bangura | 1979 | Rüdiger Rainer Minor | 1986 |
| John Alfred Ndoricimpa | 1980 | Jose Castro Gamboa Jr. | 1986 |
| William Talbot Handy Jr. | 1980 | Thomas Barber Stockton | 1988 |
| John Wesley Hardt | 1980 | Harold Hasbrouck | |
| Benjamin Ray Oliphint | 1980 | Hughes Jr. | 1988 |
| Louis Wesley | | Richard Carl Looney | 1988 |
| Schowengerdt | 1980 | Robert Hitchcock Spain | 1988 |
| Melvin George Talbert | 1980 | Susan Murch Morrison | 1988 |
| Paul Andrews Duffey | 1980 | R. Sheldon Duecker | 1988 |
| Edwin Charles Boulton | 1980 | Joseph Benjamin Bethea | 1988 |
| John William Russell | 1980 | William B. Oden | 1988 |
| Fitz Herbert Skeete | 1980 | Bruce P. Blake | 1988 |
| George Willis Bashore | 1980 | Charles Wilbourne | |
| Roy Clyde Clark | 1980 | Hancock | 1988 |
| William Boyd Grove | 1980 | Clay Foster Lee Jr. | 1988 |
| Emerson Stephen Colaw | 1980 | Sharon A. Brown | |
| Marjorie Swank Matthews | 1980 | Christopher | 1988 |
| Carlton Printess | | Dan E. Solomon | 1988 |
| Minnick Jr | 1980 | William B. Lewis | 1988 |
| Calvin Dale McConnell | 1980 | William W. Dew Jr. | 1988 |
| Kainda Katembo | 1980 | Moises Domingos Fernandes | 1988 |
| Emerito P. Nacpil | 1980 | Joao Somane Machado | 1988 |
| Arthur Flumo Kulah | 1980 | Walter Klaiber | 1989 |
| Felton Edwin May | 1984 | Heinrich Bolleter | 1989 |

6

| NAME | ELECTED | NAME | ELECTED |
|------|---------|------|---------|
| Hans Växby | 1989 | J. Lawrence McCleskey | 1996 |
| Alfred Lloyd Norris | 1992 | Ernest S. Lyght | 1996 |
| Joe Allen Wilson | 1992 | Janice Riggle Huie | 1996 |
| Robert Eugene Fannin | 1992 | Marion M. Edwards | 1996 |
| Amelia Ann B. Sherer | 1992 | C. Joseph Sprague | 1996 |
| Albert Frederick Mutti | 1992 | Peter E. Weaver | 1996 |
| Raymond Harold Owen | 1992 | Jonathan D. Keaton | 1996 |
| Joel Neftali Martinez | 1992 | Ray Chamberlain | 1996 |
| Donald Arthur Ott | 1992 | John L. Hopkins | 1996 |
| Kenneth Lee Carder | 1992 | Michael J. Coyner | 1996 |
| Hae Jong Kim | 1992 | Edward W. Paup | 1996 |
| William Wesley Morris | 1992 | Ntambo Nkulu Ntanda | 1996 |
| Marshall Leroy Meadors Jr | 1992 | Larry M. Goodpaster | 2000 |
| Charles Wesley Jordan | 1992 | Rhymes H. Moncure Jr | 2000 |
| Sharon Zimmerman Rader | 1992 | Beverly J. Shamana | 2000 |
| S. Clifton Ives | 1992 | Violet L. Fisher | 2000 |
| Mary Ann Swenson | 1992 | Gregory V. Palmer | 2000 |
| Done Peter Dabale | 1992 | William W. Hutchinson | 2000 |
| Joseph Humper | 1992 | B. Michael Watson | 2000 |
| Christopher Jokomo | 1992 | D. Max Whitfield | 2000 |
| Daniel C. Arichea Jr. | 1994 | Benjamin Roy Chamness | 2000 |
| G. Lindsey Davis | 1996 | Linda Lee | 2000 |
| Joseph E. Pennel Jr. | 1996 | James R. King | 2000 |
| Charlene Payne Kammerer | 1996 | Bruce R. Ough | 2000 |
| Alfred Johnson | 1996 | Warner H. Brown Jr | 2000 |
| Cornelius L. Henderson | 1996 | José Quipungo | 2000 |
| Susan Wolfe Hassinger | 1996 | Gaspar Joao Domingos | 2000 |

# HISTORICAL STATEMENT

On April 23, 1968, The United Methodist Church was created when Bishop Reuben H. Mueller, representing The Evangelical United Brethren Church, and Bishop Lloyd C. Wicke of The Methodist Church joined hands at the constituting General Conference in Dallas, Texas. With the words, "Lord of the Church, we are united in Thee, in Thy Church and now in The United Methodist Church," the new denomination was given birth by two churches that had distinguished histories and influential ministries in various parts of the world.

Theological traditions steeped in the Protestant Reformation and Wesleyanism, similar ecclesiastical structures, and relationships that dated back almost two hundred years facilitated the union. In the Evangelical United Brethren heritage, for example, Philip William Otterbein, the principal founder of the United Brethren in Christ, assisted in the ordination of Francis Asbury to the superintendency of American Methodist work. Jacob Albright, through whose religious experience and leadership the Evangelical Association was begun, was nurtured in a Methodist class meeting following his conversion.

## Roots, 1736–1816

The United Methodist Church shares a common history and heritage with other Methodist and Wesleyan bodies. The lives and ministries of John Wesley (1703–1791) and of his brother, Charles (1707–1788), mark the origin of their common roots. Both John and Charles were Church of England missionaries to the colony of Geor-

9

gia, arriving in March 1736. It was their only occasion to visit America. Their mission was far from an unqualified success, and both returned to England disillusioned and discouraged, Charles in December 1736, and John in February 1738.

Both of the Wesley brothers had transforming religious experiences in May 1738. In the years following, the Wesleys succeeded in leading a lively renewal movement in the Church of England. As the Methodist movement grew, it became apparent that their ministry would spread to the American colonies as some Methodists made the exhausting and hazardous Atlantic voyage to the New World.

Organized Methodism in America began as a lay movement. Among its earliest leaders were Robert Strawbridge, an immigrant farmer who organized work about 1760 in Maryland and Virginia, Philip Embury and his cousin, Barbara Heck, who began work in New York in 1766, and Captain Thomas Webb, whose labors were instrumental in Methodist beginnings in Philadelphia in 1767.

To strengthen the Methodist work in the colonies, John Wesley sent two of his lay preachers, Richard Boardman and Joseph Pilmore, to America in 1769. Two years later Richard Wright and Francis Asbury were also dispatched by Wesley to undergird the growing American Methodist societies. Francis Asbury became the most important figure in early American Methodism. His energetic devotion to the principles of Wesleyan theology, ministry, and organization shaped Methodism in America in a way unmatched by any other individual. In addition to the preachers sent by Wesley, some Methodists in the colonies also answered the call to become lay preachers in the movement.

The first conference of Methodist preachers in the colonies was held in Philadelphia in 1773. The ten who attended took several important actions. They pledged allegiance to Wesley's leadership and agreed that they would not administer the sacraments because they were laypersons. Their people were to receive the sacraments of baptism and the Lord's Supper at the local Anglican parish church. They emphasized strong discipline among the societies and preachers. A system of regular conferences of the preachers was inaugurated similar to those Wesley had instituted in England to conduct the business of the Methodist movement.

The American Revolution had a profound impact on Methodism. John Wesley's Toryism and his writings against the revolutionary cause did not enhance the image of Methodism among many who supported independence. Furthermore, a number of Methodist preachers refused to bear arms to aid the patriots.

When independence from England had been won, Wesley recognized that changes were necessary in American Methodism. He sent Thomas Coke to America to superintend the work with Asbury. Coke brought with him a prayer book titled *The Sunday Service of the Methodists in North America,* prepared by Wesley and incorporating his revision of the Church of England's Thirty-Nine Articles of Religion. Two other preachers, Richard Whatcoat and Thomas Vasey, whom Wesley had ordained, accompanied Coke. Wesley's ordinations set a precedent that ultimately permitted Methodists in America to become an independent church.

In December 1784, the famous Christmas Conference of preachers was held in Baltimore at Lovely Lane Chapel to chart the future course of the movement in America. Most of the American preachers attended, probably including two African Americans, Harry Hosier and Richard Allen. It was at this gathering that the movement became organized as The Methodist Episcopal Church in America.

In the years following the Christmas Conference, The Methodist Episcopal Church published its first *Discipline* (1785), adopted a quadrennial General Conference, the first of which was held in 1792, drafted a Constitution in 1808, refined its structure, established a publishing house, and became an ardent proponent of revivalism and the camp meeting.

As The Methodist Episcopal Church was in its infancy, two other churches were being formed. In their earliest years they were composed almost entirely of German-speaking people. The first was founded by Philip William Otterbein (1726–1813) and Martin Boehm (1725–1812). Otterbein, a German Reformed pastor, and Boehm, a Mennonite, preached an evangelical message and experience similar to the Methodists. In 1800 their followers formally organized the Church of the United Brethren in Christ. A second church, The Evangelical Association, was begun by Jacob Albright (1759–1808), a Lutheran farmer and tilemaker in eastern Pennsylvania who had been converted and nurtured under Methodist teaching. The Evangelical Association was officially organized in 1803. These two churches were to unite with each other in 1946 and with The Methodist Church in 1968 to form The United Methodist Church.

By the time of Asbury's death in March 1816, Otterbein, Boehm, and Albright had also died. The churches they nurtured had survived

11

the difficulties of early life and were beginning to expand numerically and geographically.

## The Churches Grow, 1817–1843

The Second Great Awakening was the dominant religious development among Protestants in America in the first half of the nineteenth century. Through revivals and camp meetings sinners were brought to an experience of conversion. Circuit riding preachers and lay pastors knit them into a connection. This style of Christian faith and discipline was very agreeable to Methodists, United Brethren, and Evangelicals, who favored its emphasis on the experiential. The memberships of these churches increased dramatically during this period. The number of preachers serving them also multiplied significantly.

Lay members and preachers were expected to be seriously committed to the faith. Preachers were not only to possess a sound conversion and divine calling but were also to demonstrate the gifts and skills requisite for an effective ministry. Their work was urgent and demanding. The financial benefits were meager. But, as they often reminded one another, there was no more important work than theirs.

The deep commitment of the general membership was exhibited in their willingness to adhere to the spiritual disciplines and standards of conduct outlined by their churches. Methodists, for example, were to be strictly guided by a set of General Rules adopted at the Christmas Conference of 1784 and still printed in United Methodism's *Book of Discipline*. They were urged to avoid evil, to do good, and to use the means of grace supplied by God. Membership in the church was serious business. There was no place for those whom Wesley called the "almost Christians."

The structure of the Methodist, United Brethren, and Evangelical Association churches allowed them to function in ways to support, consolidate, and expand their ministries. General Conferences, meeting quadrennially, proved sufficient to set the main course for the church. Annual Conferences under episcopal leadership provided the mechanism for admitting and ordaining clergy, appointing itinerant preachers to their churches, and supplying them with mutual support. Local churches and classes could spring up wherever a few women and men were gathered under the direction of a class leader and were visited regularly by the circuit preacher, one who had a circuit of preaching placed under his care. This system effectively served the needs of city, town, village, or frontier outpost. The churches were able to go to the people wherever they settled.

The earlier years of the nineteenth century were also marked by the spread of the Sunday school movement in America. By 1835 Sunday schools were encouraged in every place where they could be started and maintained. The Sunday school became a principal source of prospective members for the church.

The churches' interest in education was also evident in their establishment of secondary schools and colleges. By 1845 Methodists, Evangelicals, and United Brethren had also instituted courses of study for their preachers to ensure that they had a basic knowledge of the Bible, theology, and pastoral ministry.

To supply their members, preachers, and Sunday schools with Christian literature, the churches established publishing operations. The Methodist Book Concern, organized in 1789, was the first church publishing house in America. The Evangelical Association and United Brethren also authorized the formation of publishing agencies in the early nineteenth century. From the presses of their printing plants came a succession of hymnals, *Disciplines*, newspapers, magazines, Sunday school materials, and other literature to nurture their memberships. Profits were usually designated for the support and welfare of retired and indigent preachers and their families.

The churches were also increasingly committed to missionary work. By 1841 each of them had started denominational missionary societies to develop strategies and provide funds for work in the United States and abroad. John Stewart's mission to the Wyandots marked a beginning of the important presence of Native Americans in Methodism.

The founding period was not without serious problems, especially for the Methodists. Richard Allen (1760–1831), an emancipated slave and Methodist preacher who had been mistreated because of his race, left the church and in 1816 organized The African Methodist Episcopal Church. For similar reasons, The African Methodist Episcopal Zion Church was begun in 1821. In 1830 another rupture occurred in The Methodist Episcopal Church. About 5,000 preachers and laypeople left the denomination because it would not grant representation to the laity or permit the election of presiding elders (district superintendents). The new body was called The Methodist Protestant Church. It remained a strong church until 1939, when it united with

The Methodist Episcopal Church and The Methodist Episcopal Church, South, to become The Methodist Church.

## The Slavery Question and Civil War, 1844–1865

John Wesley was an ardent opponent of slavery. Many of the leaders of early American Methodism shared his hatred for this form of human bondage. As the nineteenth century progressed, it became apparent that tensions were deepening in Methodism over the slavery question. In this matter, as in so many others, Methodism reflected a national ethos because it was a church with a membership that was not limited to a region, class, or race. Contention over slavery would ultimately split Methodism into separate northern and southern churches.

The slavery issue was generally put aside by The Methodist Episcopal Church until its General Conference in 1844, when the pro-slavery and anti-slavery factions clashed. Their most serious conflict concerned one of the church's five bishops, James O. Andrew, who had acquired slaves through marriage. After acrimonious debate the General Conference voted to suspend Bishop Andrew from the exercise of his episcopal office so long as he could not, or would not, free his slaves. A few days later dissidents drafted a Plan of Separation, which permitted the annual conferences in slaveholding states to separate from The Methodist Episcopal Church in order to organize their own ecclesiastical structure. The Plan of Separation was adopted, and the groundwork was prepared for the creation of The Methodist Episcopal Church, South.

Delegates from the southern states met in Louisville, Kentucky, in May 1845, to organize their new church. Their first General Conference was held the following year in Petersburg, Virginia, where a *Discipline* and hymnbook were adopted. Bitterness between northern and southern Methodists intensified in the years leading to Abraham Lincoln's election in 1860 and then through the carnage of the Civil War. Each church claimed divine sanction for its region and prayed fervently for God's will to be accomplished in victory for its side.

## Reconstruction, Prosperity, and New Issues, 1866–1913

The Civil War dealt an especially harsh blow to The Methodist Episcopal Church, South. Its membership fell to two-thirds its prewar strength. Many of its churches lay in ruins or were seriously damaged. A number of its clergy had been killed or wounded in the conflict. Its educational, publishing, and missionary programs had been disrupted. Yet new vitality stirred among southern Methodists, and over the next fifty years its membership grew fourfold to more than two million.

The African American membership of The Methodist Episcopal Church, South, had declined significantly during and after the war. In 1870 its General Conference voted to transfer all of its remaining African American constituency to a new church. The Colored Methodist Episcopal Church (now called The Christian Methodist Episcopal Church) was the product of this decision.

It was during this period that Alejo Hernandez became the first ordained Hispanic preacher in Methodism, although Benigno Cardenas had preached the Methodist message in Spanish in Santa Fe, New Mexico, as early as 1853.

The Methodist Episcopal Church did not suffer as harshly as southern Methodism did during the war. By the late 1860s it was on the verge of major gains in membership and new vigor in its program. Between 1865 and 1913 its membership also registered a 400 percent increase to about four million. Methodist Protestants, United Brethren, and Evangelicals experienced similar growth. Church property values soared, and affluence reflected generally prosperous times for the churches. Sunday schools remained strong and active. Publishing houses maintained ambitious programs to furnish their memberships with literature. Higher educational standards for the clergy were cultivated, and theological seminaries were founded.

Mission work, both home and overseas, was high on the agendas of the churches. Home mission programs sought to Christianize the city as well as the Native American. Missionaries established schools for former slaves and their children. Missions overseas were effective in Asia, Europe, Africa, and Latin America. Women formed missionaries societies that educated, recruited, and raised funds for these endeavors. Missionaries like Isabella Thoburn, Susan Bauernfeind, and Harriett Brittan, and administrators like Bell Harris Bennett and Lucy Rider Meyer, motivated thousands of church women to support home and foreign missions.

Significant Methodist ministries among Asian Americans were instituted during this period, especially among Chinese and Japanese immigrants. A Japanese layman, Kanichi Miyama, was ordained and given full clergy rights in California in 1887.

Two critical issues that caused substantial debate in the churches during this period were lay representation and the role of women. First, should laity be given a voice in the General Conference and the annual conference? The Methodist Protestants had granted the laity representation from the time they organized in 1830. The clergy in The Methodist Episcopal Church, The Methodist Episcopal Church, South, The Evangelical Association, and the Church of the United Brethren in Christ were much slower in permitting the laity an official voice in their affairs. It was not until 1932 that the last of these churches granted laity these rights. Even more contentious was the question of women's right to ordination and eligibility for lay offices and representation in the church. The United Brethren General Conference of 1889 approved ordination for women, but The Methodist Episcopal Church and The Methodist Episcopal Church, South, did not grant full clergy rights until well after their reunion in 1939. The Evangelical Association never ordained women. Laity rights for women were also resisted. Women were not admitted as delegates to the General Conferences of The Methodist Protestant Church until 1892, the United Brethren until 1893, The Methodist Episcopal Church until 1904, and The Methodist Episcopal Church, South, until 1922.

The period between the Civil War and World War I also was marked by other theological developments and controversies. The holiness movement, the rise of liberal theology, and the Social Gospel movement were sources of considerable theological debate. The Methodist Episcopal Church demonstrated its regard for social issues by adopting a Social Creed at its 1908 General Conference. Social problems were also a spur in the movement toward ecumenism and interchurch cooperation. Each of the denominations now included in The United Methodist Church became active in the Federal Council of Churches, the first major ecumenical venture among American Protestants. The era closed with the world on the threshold of a great and horrible war.

## World War and More Change, 1914–1939

In the years immediately prior to World War I, there was much sympathy in the churches for negotiation and arbitration as visible alternatives to international armed conflict. Many church members and clergy openly professed pacifism. However, when the United

States officially entered the war in 1917, pacifism faded. The antecedent churches of United Methodism were not unlike other American denominations in expressing their national loyalties.

When the war ended, the churches were again free to expend their energies in other directions. One of their perennial concerns was temperance, and they were quick to recognize it among their highest priorities. They published and distributed large amounts of temperance literature. Members were asked to pledge that they would abstain from alcoholic beverages. The United Methodist Church still encourages such abstinence.

There was significant theological ferment during this period. Liberal Protestant theology, an important school of thought in the late nineteenth and early twentieth centuries, was questioned. It was attacked by a militant fundamentalism and later by neo-orthodoxy, which accused it of undermining the very essence of the Christian message. Since all three of these theological parties—liberal, fundamentalist, and neo-orthodox—were well represented in the forerunners of United Methodism, it is not surprising that heated doctrinal disputes were present in these churches.

Despite the internal theological differences that the churches experienced, they continued to cooperate with other denominations and acted to heal schisms that had taken place earlier in their own histories. For example, a division that had occurred in The Evangelical Association in 1894 was repaired in 1922, when two factions united as The Evangelical Church. A more important union, at least by statistical measurement, took place among three Methodist bodies—The Methodist Episcopal Church, The Methodist Protestant Church, and The Methodist Episcopal Church, South. Representatives of these churches began meeting in 1916 to forge a plan of union. By the 1930s their proposal included partitioning the united church into six administrative units called jurisdictions. Five of these were geographical; the sixth, the Central Jurisdiction, was racial. It included African American churches and annual conferences wherever they were geographically located in the United States. African American Methodists and some others were troubled by this prospect and opposed the plan of a racially segregated jurisdiction.

The majority of Methodist Protestants favored the union, although it meant accepting episcopal government, which they had not had since their church was organized in 1830. Following overwhelming approvals at the General Conferences and annual confer-

17

ences of the three churches, they were united in April 1939, into The Methodist Church. At the time of its formation the new church included 7.7 million members.

## Movement Toward Union, 1940–1967

Although Methodists, Evangelicals, and United Brethren each had published strong statements condemning war and advocating peaceful reconciliation among the nations, the strength of their positions was largely lost with American involvement in the hostilities of World War II. Nevertheless, throughout the war many churches continued to express their disdain for violence and their support for conscientious objection.

As the war ended, the churches actively worked to secure world peace and order. Many laypeople, pastors, bishops, and church agencies supported the establishment of a world organization to serve as a forum for the resolution of international social, economic, and political problems. In April 1945, their labors contributed to the founding of the United Nations.

During this era, 1940–1967, there were at least three other important matters that occupied the attention of the churches that now compose United Methodism. First, they maintained their concern for ecumenicity and church union. On November 16, 1946, in Johnstown, Pennsylvania, The Evangelical Church and The United Brethren Church were united into The Evangelical United Brethren Church, after twenty years of negotiation. At the time of union, the new church included about 700,000 members. The Methodist Church was also interested in closer ties with other Methodist and Wesleyan bodies. In 1951 it participated in the formation of the World Methodist Council, successor to the Ecumenical Methodist Conferences that were begun in 1881. As expressions of their wider ecumenical commitment, Methodists and the Evangelical United Brethren became active members of the World Council of Churches, founded in 1948, and the National Council of Churches, founded in 1950. These assemblies provided a means for their members to engage in cooperative mission and other ministries. The two churches also cooperated with seven other Protestant denominations in forming the Consultation on Church Union in 1960.

Second, the churches demonstrated growing uneasiness with the problem of racism in both the nation and the church. Many

Methodists were especially disturbed by the manner in which racial segregation was built into the fabric of their denominational structure. The Central Jurisdiction was a constant reminder of racial discrimination. Proposals to eliminate the Central Jurisdiction were introduced at the General Conferences from 1956 to 1966. Finally, plans to abolish the Central Jurisdiction were agreed upon with the contemplated union with the Evangelical United Brethren in 1968, although a few African American annual conferences continued for a short time thereafter.

Third, clergy rights for women were debated by the churches. The issue was especially critical in the creation of The Evangelical United Brethren Church. The Evangelical Church had never ordained women. The United Brethren had ordained them since 1889. In order to facilitate the union of these two churches, the United Brethren accepted the Evangelical practice, and women lost their right to ordination. Methodists debated the issue for several years after their unification in 1939. Full clergy rights for women were finally granted in 1956, but it took a decade more before the number of women in seminaries and pulpits began to grow significantly. When Methodists and the Evangelical United Brethren united in 1968, the right of women to full clergy status was included in the plan of union.

As this period ended, negotiations between The Methodist Church and The Evangelical United Brethren Church were proceeding toward their anticipated union into The United Methodist Church.

## Developments and Changes Since 1968

When The United Methodist Church was created in 1968, it had approximately 11 million members, making it one of the largest Protestant churches in the world.

Since its birth, United Methodism has experienced a number of changes in its life and structure. It has become increasingly aware of itself as a world church with members and conferences in Africa, Asia, Europe, and the United States. While its membership in Europe and the United States has declined noticeably since 1968, membership in Africa and Asia has grown significantly.

An increasing number of women have been admitted to the ordained ministry, appointed to the district superintendency, elected to positions of denominational leadership, and consecrated as bishops. In 1980 Marjorie Matthews was the first woman elected to the Church's episcopacy.

The Church has endeavored to become a community in which all persons, regardless of racial or ethnic background, can participate in every level of its connectional life and ministry.

United Methodism has struggled with a number of critical issues. It has created and refined theological and mission statements. It has discussed and acted on matters of social importance such as nuclear power and world peace, human sexuality, the environment, abortion, AIDS, evangelism, and world mission.

The Church has been concerned with the faithfulness and vitality of its worship. It published a hymnal in 1989, which included a new Psalter and revised liturgies for baptism, the Lord's Supper, weddings, and funerals. Its 1992 General Conference authorized a new *Book of Worship*. A Spanish language hymnal, *Mil Voces Para Celebrar*, was published in 1996.

The United Methodist Church represents the confluence of three streams of tradition: Methodism, the Church of the United Brethren in Christ, and The Evangelical Association. With other churches that are also members of the body of Christ, it humbly and gratefully offers up its praise to God through Jesus Christ and the Holy Spirit for creating and sustaining grace. It seeks further grace as its ministers to the world.

*Part I*

# THE CONSTITUTION

### PREAMBLE

The church is a community of all true believers under the Lordship of Christ. It is the redeemed and redeeming fellowship in which the Word of God is preached by persons divinely called, and the sacraments are duly administered according to Christ's own appointment. Under the discipline of the Holy Spirit the church seeks to provide for the maintenance of worship, the edification of believers, and the redemption of the world.

The church of Jesus Christ exists in and for the world, and its very dividedness is a hindrance to its mission in that world.

The prayers and intentions of The Methodist Church and The Evangelical United Brethren Church have been and are for obedience to the will of our Lord that his people be one, in humility for the present brokenness of the Church and in gratitude that opportunities for reunion have been given. In harmony with these prayers and intentions, these churches do now propose to unite, in the confident assurance that this act is an expression of the oneness of Christ's people.

Conversations concerning union between the two churches and their constituent members have taken place over a long period of years, and the churches have a long and impressive history of fellowship and cooperation.

Therefore, we, the Commissions on Church Union of The Methodist Church, and of The Evangelical United Brethren Church, holding that these churches are essentially one in origin, in belief, in

21

spirit, and in purpose, and desiring that this essential unity be made actual in organization and administration in the United States of America and throughout the world, do hereby propose and transmit to our respective General Conferences the following Plan of Union and recommend to the two churches its adoption by the processes which they respectively require.[1]

## DIVISION ONE—GENERAL

¶ **1.** *Article I. Declaration of Union*—The Evangelical United Brethren Church and The Methodist Church shall be united in one Church. The united Church, as thus constituted, is, and shall be, the successor of the two uniting churches.[2]

¶ **2.** *Article II. Name*—The name of the Church shall be The United Methodist Church. The name of the Church may be translated freely into languages other than English as the General Conference may determine.

¶ **3.** *Article III. Articles of Religion and the Confession of Faith*—The Articles of Religion and the Confession of Faith shall be those currently held by The Methodist Church and The Evangelical United Brethren Church respectively.

¶ **4.** *Article IV. Inclusiveness of the Church*—The United Methodist Church is a part of the church universal, which is one Body in Christ. Therefore all persons, without regard to race, color, national origin, status,[3] or economic condition, shall be eligible to attend its worship services, to participate in its programs, and, when they take the appropriate vows, to be admitted into its membership in any local church in the connection. In The United Methodist Church no conference or other organizational unit of the Church shall be structured so as to exclude any member or any constituent body of the Church because of race, color, national origin, status, or economic condition.[4]

---

1. The Constitution was adopted in Chicago, Illinois, on Nov. 11, 1966, by the General Conferences of The Evangelical United Brethren Church and The Methodist Church and thereafter by the requisite vote in the annual conferences of the two churches. The Plan of Union was made effective by the Uniting Conference in Dallas, Texas, on April 23, 1968.

2. Amended 1984.

3. Amended 1992.

4. *See* Judicial Council Decisions 242, 246, 340, 351, 362, 377, 398, 594, and Decisions 4 and 5, Interim Judicial Council.

¶ **5.** *Article V. Ecumenical Relations*—As part of the church universal, The United Methodist Church believes that the Lord of the church is calling Christians everywhere to strive toward unity; and therefore it will seek, and work for, unity at all levels of church life: through world relationships with other Methodist churches and united churches related to The Methodist Church or The Evangelical United Brethren Church, through councils of churches, and through plans of union and covenantal relationships[5] with churches of Methodist or other denominational traditions.

¶ **6.** *Article VI. Title to Properties*—Titles to properties in The Evangelical United Brethren Church and The Methodist Church shall, upon consummation of the union, be held and administered in accordance with the *Book of Discipline*.[6] Nothing in the Plan of Union at any time after the union is to be construed so as to require any local church or any other property owner of the former The Evangelical United Brethren Church or the former The Methodist Church to alienate or in any way to change the title to property contained in its deed or deeds at the time of union, and lapse of time or usage shall not affect said title or control.

## DIVISION TWO—ORGANIZATION

### Section I. Conferences

¶ **7.** *Article I.*—There shall be a General Conference for the entire Church with such powers, duties, and privileges as are hereinafter set forth.

¶ **8.** *Article II.*—There shall be jurisdictional conferences for the Church in the United States of America, with such powers, duties, and privileges as are hereinafter set forth;[7] *provided* that in The United Methodist Church there shall be no jurisdictional or central conference based on any ground other than geographical and regional division.

¶ **9.** *Article III.*—There shall be central conferences for the church outside the United States of America and, if necessary, provisional central conferences, all with such powers, duties, and privileges as are hereinafter set forth.

---

5. Amended 1996.
6. Amended 1984.
7. *See* Judicial Council Decision 128.

¶ **10.** *Article IV.*—There shall be annual conferences as the fundamental bodies of the Church and, if necessary, provisional annual conferences, with such powers, duties, and privileges as are hereinafter set forth.[8]

¶ **11.** *Article V.*—There shall be a charge conference for each church or charge with such powers, duties, and privileges as are hereinafter set forth.[9]

### Section II. General Conference

¶ **12.** *Article I.*—1. The General Conference shall be composed of not less than 600 nor more than 1,000 delegates, one half of whom shall be clergy and one half lay members, to be elected by the annual conferences. The missionary conferences shall be considered as annual conferences for the purpose of this article.[10]

2. Delegates shall be elected by the annual conferences except that delegates may be elected by other autonomous Methodist churches if and when the General Conference shall approve concordats with such other autonomous Methodist churches for the mutual election and seating of delegates in each other's highest legislative conferences.

3. In the case of The Methodist Church in Great Britain, mother church of Methodism, provision shall be made for The United Methodist Church to send two delegates annually to the British Methodist Conference, and The Methodist Church in Great Britain to send four delegates quadrennially to The United Methodist General Conference, the delegates of both conferences having vote and being evenly divided between clergy and laity.[11]

¶ **13.** *Article II.*—The General Conference shall meet in the month of April or May once in four years at such time and in such place as shall be determined by the General Conference or by its duly authorized committees.

A special session of the General Conference, possessing the authority and exercising all the powers of the General Conference, may be called by the Council of Bishops, or in such other manner as

---

8. *See* Judicial Council Decision 354.
9. *See* Judicial Council Decision 516.
10. Amended 1976.
11. Amended 1996.

the General Conference may from time to time prescribe, to meet at such time and in such place as may be stated in the call. Such special session of the General Conference shall be composed of the delegates to the preceding General Conference or their lawful successors, except that when a particular annual conference or missionary conference[12] shall prefer to have a new election it may do so.[13] The purpose of such special session shall be stated in the call, and only such business shall be transacted as is in harmony with the purpose stated in such call unless the General Conference by a two-thirds vote shall determine that other business may be transacted.[14]

¶ **14.** *Article III.*—The General Conference shall fix the ratio of representation in the General, jurisdictional, and central conferences from the annual conferences, missionary conferences,[15] and the provisional annual conferences, computed on a two-factor basis: (1) the number of clergy members of the annual conference and the missionary conference,[16] and (2) the number of church members in the annual conference and the missionary conference;[17] *provided* that each annual conference, missionary conference,[18] or provisional annual conference shall be entitled to at least one clergy and one lay delegate in the General Conference and also in the jurisdictional or central conference.[19]

¶ **15.** *Article IV.*—The General Conference shall have full legislative power over all matters distinctively connectional, and in the exercise of this power shall have authority as follows:[20]

1. To define and fix the conditions, privileges, and duties of Church membership, which shall in every case be without reference to race or status.[21]

2. To define and fix the powers and duties of elders, deacons, supply preachers, local preachers, exhorters, and deaconesses.[22]

---

12. Amended 1976.
13. *See* Judicial Council Decisions 221, 226, 228, 238, 302.
14. *See* Judicial Council Decision 227.
15. Amended 1976.
16. Amended 1976.
17. Amended 1976.
18. Amended 1976.
19. *See* Judicial Council Decision 403.
20. *See* Judicial Council Decisions 96, 232, 236, 318, 325, 544.
21. *See* Judicial Council Decision 558.
22. *See* Judicial Council Decisions 58, 313.

3. To define and fix the powers and duties of annual conferences, provisional annual conferences, missionary conferences and missions, and of central conferences, district conferences, charge conferences, and congregational meetings.[23]

4. To provide for the organization, promotion, and administration of the work of the Church outside the United States of America.[24]

5. To define and fix the powers, duties, and privileges of the episcopacy, to adopt a plan for the support of the bishops, to provide a uniform rule for their retirement, and to provide for the discontinuance of a bishop because of inefficiency or unacceptability.[25]

6. To provide and revise the hymnal and ritual of the Church and to regulate all matters relating to the form and mode of worship, subject to the limitations of the first and second Restrictive Rules.

7. To provide a judicial system and a method of judicial procedure for the Church, except as herein otherwise prescribed.

8. To initiate and to direct all connectional enterprises of the Church and to provide boards for their promotion and administration.[26]

9. To determine and provide for raising and distributing funds necessary to carry on the work of the Church.[27]

10. To fix a uniform basis upon which bishops shall be elected by the jurisdictional conferences and to determine the number of bishops that may be elected by central conferences.[28]

11. To select its presiding officers from the bishops, through a committee; *provided* that the bishops shall select from their own number the presiding officer of the opening session.[29]

12. To change the number and the boundaries of jurisdictional conferences upon the consent of a majority of the annual conferences in each jurisdictional conference involved.[30]

13. To establish such commissions for the general work of the Church as may be deemed advisable.

---

23. *See* Judicial Council Decision 411.
24. *See* Judicial Council Decision 182; amended 1976.
25. *See* Judicial Council Decisions 35, 114, 312, 365, 413.
26. *See* Judicial Council Decisions 214, 364, 411.
27. *See* Judicial Council Decision 30.
28. *See* Judicial Council Decisions 598, 735.
29. *See* Judicial Council Decision 126.
30. *See* Judicial Council Decisions 55, 56, 215.

14. To secure the rights and privileges of membership in all agencies, programs, and institutions in The United Methodist Church regardless of race or status.[31]

15. To allow the annual conferences to utilize structures unique to their mission, other mandated structures notwithstanding. [32]

16. To enact such other legislation as may be necessary, subject to the limitations and restrictions of the Constitution of the Church.[33]

## Section III. Restrictive Rules

¶ **16.** *Article I.*—The General Conference shall not revoke, alter, or change our Articles of Religion or establish any new standards or rules of doctrine contrary to our present existing and established standards of doctrine.[34]

*Article II.*—The General Conference shall not revoke, alter, or change our Confession of Faith.

¶ **17.** *Article III.*—The General Conference shall not change or alter any part or rule of our government so as to do away with episcopacy or destroy the plan of our itinerant general superintendency.

¶ **18.** *Article IV.*—The General Conference shall not do away with the privileges of our clergy of right to trial by a committee and of an appeal; neither shall it do away with the privileges of our members of right to trial before the church, or by a committee, and of an appeal.[35]

¶ **19.** *Article V.*—The General Conference shall not revoke or change the General Rules of Our United Societies.[36]

¶ **20.** *Article VI.*—The General Conference shall not appropriate the net income of the publishing houses, the book concerns, or the Chartered Fund to any purpose other than for the benefit of retired or disabled preachers, their spouses, widows, or widowers, and children or other beneficiaries of the ministerial pension systems.[37]

---

31. *See* Decisions 4, 5, Interim Judicial Council; Judicial Council Decisions 427, 433, 442, 451, 540, 558, 567, 588, 594.
32. *See* Judicial Council Decision 825; amended 1996.
33. *See* Judicial Council Decision 215.
34. *See* Judicial Council Decisions 86, 142, 243, 358, 847, 871.
35. *See* Judicial Council Decisions 351, 522, 557, 595.
36. *See* Judicial Council Decisions 358, 468, 847, 871.
37. *See* Judicial Council Decisions 322, 330.

## Section IV. Jurisdictional Conferences

¶ **21.** *Article I.*—The jurisdictional conferences shall be composed of as many representatives from the annual conferences and missionary conferences[38] as shall be determined by a uniform basis established by the General Conference. The missionary conferences shall be considered as annual conferences for the purpose of this article.[39]

¶ **22.** *Article II.*—All jurisdictional conferences shall have the same status and the same privileges of action within the limits fixed by the Constitution. The ratio of representation of the annual conferences and missionary conferences[40] in the General Conference shall be the same for all jurisdictional conferences.

¶ **23.** *Article III.*—The General Conferences shall fix the basis of representation in the jurisdictional conferences; *provided* that the jurisdictional conferences shall be composed of an equal number of clergy and lay delegates to be elected by the annual conferences, the missionary conferences,[41] and the provisional annual conferences.

¶ **24.** *Article IV.*—Each jurisdictional conference shall meet at the time determined by the Council of Bishops or its delegated committee, each jurisdictional conference convening on the same date as the others and at a place selected by the jurisdictional committee on entertainment, appointed by its College of Bishops unless such a committee has been appointed by the preceding jurisdictional conference.

¶ **25.** *Article V.*—The jurisdictional conferences shall have the following powers and duties and such others as may be conferred by the General Conferences:

1. To promote the evangelistic, educational, missionary, and benevolent interests of the Church and to provide for interests and institutions within their boundaries.[42]

2. To elect bishops and to cooperate in carrying out such plans for their support as may be determined by the General Conference.

3. To establish and constitute jurisdictional conference boards as auxiliary to the general boards of the Church as the need may appear and to choose their representatives on the general boards in such manner as the General Conference may determine.[43]

---

38. Amended 1976.
39. Amended 1976.
40. Amended 1976.
41. Amended 1976.
42. *See* Judicial Council Decision 67.
43. *See* Judicial Council Decision 183.

4. To determine the boundaries of their annual conferences; *provided* that there shall be no annual conference with a membership of fewer than fifty clergy in full connection, except by the consent of the General Conference; and *provided* further that this provision shall not apply to annual conferences of the former Evangelical United Brethren Church during the first three quadrenniums after union.[44]

5. To make rules and regulations for the administration of the work of the Church within the jurisdiction, subject to such powers as have been or shall be vested in the General Conference.

6. To appoint a committee on appeals to hear and determine the appeal of a traveling preacher of that jurisdiction from the decision of a trial committee.

## Section V. Central Conferences

¶ **26.** *Article I.*—There shall be central conferences for the work of the Church outside the United States of America[45] with such duties, powers, and privileges as are hereinafter set forth. The number and boundaries of the central conferences shall be determined by the Uniting Conference. Subsequently the General Conference shall have authority to change the number and boundaries of central conferences. The central conferences shall have the duties, powers, and privileges hereinafter set forth.

¶ **27.** *Article II.*—The central conferences shall be composed of as many delegates as shall be determined by a basis established by the General Conference. The delegates shall be clergy and lay in equal numbers.[46]

¶ **28.** *Article III.*—The central conferences shall meet within the year succeeding the meeting of the General Conference at such times and places as shall have been determined by the preceding respective central conferences or by commissions appointed by them or by the General Conference. The date and place of the first meeting succeeding the Uniting Conference shall be fixed by the bishops of the respective central conferences, or in such manner as shall be determined by the General Conference.

---

44. *See* Judicial Council Decision 447.
45. Amended 1976.
46. Amended 1992.

¶ **29.** *Article IV.*—The central conferences shall have the following powers and duties and such others as may be conferred by the General Conference:

1. To promote the evangelistic, educational, missionary, social-concern, and benevolent interests and institutions of the Church within their own boundaries.

2. To elect the bishops for the respective central conferences in number as may be determined from time to time, upon a basis fixed by the General Conference, and to cooperate in carrying out such plans for the support of their bishops as may be determined by the General Conference.[47]

3. To establish and constitute such central conference boards as may be required and to elect their administrative officers.[48]

4. To determine the boundaries of the annual conferences within their respective areas.

5. To make such rules and regulations for the administration of the work within their boundaries including such changes and adaptations of the General Discipline as the conditions in the respective areas may require, subject to the powers that have been or shall be vested in the General Conference.[49]

6. To appoint a judicial court to determine legal questions arising on the rules, regulations, and such revised, adapted, or new sections of the central conference *Discipline* enacted by the central conference.

7. To appoint a committee on appeals to hear and determine the appeal of a traveling preacher of that central conference from the decision of a committee on trial.[50]

### Section VI. Annual Conferences

¶ **30.** *Article I.*—The annual conference shall be composed of clergy members as defined by the General Conference, together with a lay member elected by each charge, the diaconal ministers, the active deaconesses under episcopal appointment within the bounds of the annual conference,[51] the conference president of United Methodist Women, the conference president of United Methodist

---

47. *See* Judicial Council Decision 370.
48. *See* Judicial Council Decision 69.
49. *See* Judicial Council Decisions 142, 147, 313.
50. *See* Judicial Council Decision 595.
51. Amended 1996.

Men, the conference lay leader, district lay leaders, the president or equivalent officer of the conference young adult organization, the president of the conference youth organization, the chair of the annual conference college student organization,[52] and two young persons under twenty-five years of age from each district to be selected in such a manner as may be determined by the annual conference.[53] In the annual conferences of the central conferences, the four-year participation and the two-year membership requirements may be waived by the annual conference for young persons under twenty-five years of age. Such persons must be members of The United Methodist Church and active participants at the time of election.[54] Each charge served by more than one clergy shall be entitled to as many lay members as there are clergy members. The lay members shall have been for the two years next preceding their election members of The United Methodist Church[55] and shall have been active participants in The United Methodist Church for at least four years next preceding their election.[56]

If the lay membership should number less than the clergy members of the annual conference, the annual conference shall, by its own formula, provide for the election of additional lay members to equalize lay and clergy membership of the annual conference.[57]

¶ 31. *Article II.*—The annual conference is the basic body in the Church and as such shall have reserved to it the right to vote on all constitutional amendments, on the election of clergy and lay delegates to the General and the jurisdictional or central conferences, on all matters relating to the character and conference relations of its clergy members, and on the ordination of clergy and such other rights as have not been delegated to the General Conference under the Constitution, with the exception that the lay members may not vote on matters of ordination, character, and conference relations of clergy except that the lay members of the conference board of ordained ministry may vote on matters of ordination, character, and conference relations of clergy, with the further exception that

---

52. Amended 1996.
53. Amended 1968, 1970, 1980, 1984.
54. Amended 1988.
55. Amended 1972.
56. Amended 1976.
57. *See* Judicial Council Decisions 24, 113, 129, 349, 378, 479, 495, 511, 553, 561; and Decision 7, Interim Judicial Council.

lay members of the district committee on ordained ministry be full participating members of the district committee on ordained ministry with vote.[58] It shall discharge such duties and exercise such powers as the General Conference under the Constitution may determine.[59]

¶ 32. *Article III.*—The annual conference shall elect clergy and lay delegates to the General Conference and to its jurisdictional or central conference in the manner provided in this section, Articles IV and V.[60] The persons first elected up to the number determined by the ratio for representation in the General Conference shall be representatives in that body. Additional delegates shall be elected to complete the number determined by the ratio for representation in the jurisdictional or central conference, who, together with those first elected as above, shall be delegates in the jurisdictional or central conference. The additional delegates to the jurisdictional or central conference shall in the order of their election be the reserve delegates to the General Conference.[61] The annual conference shall also elect reserve clergy and lay delegates to the jurisdictional or central conference as it may deem desirable. These reserve clergy and lay delegates to the jurisdictional or central conferences may act as reserve delegates to the General Conference when it is evident that not enough reserve delegates are in attendance at the General Conference.[62]

¶ 33. *Article IV.*—The ordained[63] ministerial delegates to the General Conference and to the jurisdictional or central conference shall be elected by and from[64] the ministerial members in full connection with the annual conference or provisional annual conference.[65]

¶ 34. *Article V.*—The lay delegates to the General and jurisdictional or central conferences shall be elected by the lay members of the annual conference or provisional annual conference without regard to

---

58. Amended 1996.
59. *See* Judicial Council Decisions 78, 79, 132, 405, 406, 415, 524, 532, 534, 552, 584, 690, 742, 782, 862.
60. *See* Judicial Council Decision 592.
61. *See* Judicial Council Decision 352.
62. Amended 1992.
63. Amended 1996.
64. Amended 1996.
65. *See* Judicial Council Decisions 1, 308, 403, 473, 531, 534, 875.

age; *provided* such delegates[66] shall have been members of The United Methodist Church for at least two years next preceding their election, and shall have been active participants in The United Methodist Church for at least four years next preceding their election,[67] and are members thereof within the annual conference electing them at the time of holding the General and jurisdictional or central conferences.[68]

### Section VII. Boundaries

¶ **35.** *Article I.*—The United Methodist Church shall have jurisdictional conferences made up as follows:

Northeastern—Connecticut, Delaware, District of Columbia, Maine, Maryland, Massachusetts, New Hampshire, New Jersey, New York, Pennsylvania, Rhode Island, Vermont, the Virgin Islands,[69] West Virginia.[70]

Southeastern—Alabama, Florida, Georgia, Kentucky, Mississippi, North Carolina, South Carolina, Tennessee, Virginia.

North Central—Illinois, Indiana, Iowa, Michigan, Minnesota, North Dakota, Ohio, South Dakota, Wisconsin.

South Central—Arkansas, Kansas, Louisiana, Missouri, Nebraska, New Mexico, Oklahoma, Texas.

Western—Alaska, Arizona, California, Colorado, Hawaii and the territory of the United States in the Pacific region,[71] Idaho, Montana, Nevada, Oregon, Utah, Washington, Wyoming.

¶ **36.** *Article II.*—The work of the Church outside the United States of America[72] may be formed into central conferences, the number and boundaries of which shall be determined by the Uniting Conference, the General Conference having authority subsequently to make changes in the number and boundaries.

¶ **37.** *Article III.*—Changes in the number, names, and boundaries of the jurisdictional conferences may be effected by the General Conference upon the consent of a majority of the annual conferences of each of the jurisdictional conferences involved.[73]

---

66. Amended 1972.
67. Amended 1976.
68. *See* Judicial Council Decisions 403, 887.
69. Amended 1980.
70. Amended 1976.
71. Amended 1980.
72. Amended 1976.
73. *See* Judicial Council Decisions 55, 56, 85, 215.

¶ **38.** *Article IV.*—Changes in the number, names, and boundaries of the annual conferences and episcopal areas may be effected by the jurisdictional conferences in the United States of America[74] and by the central conferences outside the United States of America according to the provisions under the respective powers and pursuant to the respective structures[75] of the jurisdictional and the central conferences.[76]

¶ **39.** *Article V. Transfer of Local Churches*—1. A local church may be transferred from one annual conference to another in which it is geographically located upon approval by a two-thirds vote of those present and voting in each of the following:

   *a)* the charge conference;

   *b)* the congregational meeting of the local church;

   *c)* each of the two annual conferences involved.

The vote shall be certified by the secretaries of the specified conferences or meetings to the bishops having supervision of the annual conferences involved, and upon their announcement of the required majorities the transfer shall immediately be effective.

2. The vote on approval of transfer shall be taken by each annual conference at its first session after the matter is submitted to it.

3. Transfers under the provisions of this article shall not be governed or restricted by other provisions of this Constitution relating to changes of boundaries of conferences.

## Section VIII. District Conferences

¶ **40.** *Article I.*—There may be organized in an annual conference, district conferences composed of such persons and invested with such powers as the General Conference may determine.

## Section IX. Charge Conferences

¶ **41.** *Article I.*—There shall be organized in each charge a charge conference composed of such persons and invested with such powers as the General Conference shall provide.

---

74. Amended 1976.

75. Amended 1992.

76. *See* Judicial Council Decisions 28, 85, 217, 525, 541, 735; and Decisions 1, 2, Interim Judicial Council.

¶ **42.** *Article II. Election of Church Officers*—Unless the General Conference shall order otherwise, the officers of the church or churches constituting a charge shall be elected by the charge conference or by the members of said church or churches at a meeting called for that purpose, as may be arranged by the charge conference, unless the election is otherwise required by local church charters or state or provincial laws.

## DIVISION THREE—EPISCOPAL SUPERVISION

¶ **43.** *Article I.*—There shall be a continuance of an episcopacy in The United Methodist Church of like plan, powers, privileges, and duties as now exist in The Methodist Church and in The Evangelical United Brethren Church in all those matters in which they agree and may be considered identical; and the differences between these historic episcopacies are deemed to be reconciled and harmonized by and in this Plan of Union and Constitution of The United Methodist Church and actions taken pursuant thereto so that a unified superintendency and episcopacy is hereby created and established of, in, and by those who now are and shall be bishops of The United Methodist Church; and the said episcopacy shall further have such powers, privileges, and duties as are herein set forth.[77]

¶ **44.** *Article II.*—The bishops shall be elected by the respective jurisdictional and central conferences and consecrated in the historic manner at such time and place as may be fixed by the General Conference for those elected by the jurisdictions and by each central conference for those elected by such central conference.[78]

¶ **45.** *Article III.*—There shall be a Council of Bishops composed of all the bishops of The United Methodist Church. The council shall meet at least once a year and plan for the general oversight and promotion of the temporal and spiritual interests of the entire Church and for carrying into effect the rules, regulations, and responsibilities prescribed and enjoined by the General Conference and in accord with the provisions set forth in this Plan of Union.[79]

¶ **46.** *Article IV.*—The bishops of each jurisdictional and central conference shall constitute a College of Bishops, and such College of Bishops shall arrange the plan of episcopal supervision of the annual

---

77. *See* Judicial Council Decisions 4, 114, 127, 363.
78. *See* Judicial Council Decision 21.
79. *See* Judicial Council Decision 424.

conferences, missionary[80] conferences, and missions within their respective territories.[81]

¶ 47. *Article V.*—The bishops shall have residential and presidential supervision in the jurisdictional or central conferences[82] in which they are elected or to which they are transferred. Bishops may be transferred from one jurisdiction to another jurisdiction for presidential and residential supervision under the following conditions: (1) The transfer of bishops may be on either of two bases: *(a)* a jurisdiction that receives a bishop by transfer from another jurisdiction may transfer to that jurisdiction or to a third jurisdiction one of its own bishops eligible for transfer, so that the number transferred in by each jurisdiction shall be balanced by the number transferred out; or *(b)* a jurisdiction may receive a bishop from another jurisdiction and not transfer out a member of its own College of Bishops. (2) No bishop shall be transferred unless that bishop shall have specifically consented. (3) No bishop shall be eligible for transfer unless the bishop shall have served one quadrennium in the jurisdiction that elected the bishop to the episcopacy. (4) All such transfers shall require the approval by a majority vote of the members present and voting of the jurisdictional committees on episcopacy of the jurisdictions that are involved.[83] After the above procedures have been followed, the transferring bishop shall become a member of the receiving College of Bishops and shall be subject to residential assignment by that jurisdictional conference.

A bishop may be assigned by the Council of Bishops for presidential service or other temporary service in another jurisdiction than that which elected the bishop; *provided* that the request is made by a majority of the bishops in the jurisdiction of the proposed service.

In the case of an emergency in any jurisdiction or central conference through the death or disability of a bishop or other cause, the Council of Bishops may assign a bishop from another jurisdiction or central conference to the work of the said jurisdiction or central conference, with the consent of a majority of the bishops of that jurisdiction or central conference.

---

80. Amended 1976.
81. *See* Judicial Council Decisions 517, 735.
82. Amended 1980.
83. Amended 1992.

¶ **48.** *Article VI.*—The bishops, both active and retired, of The Evangelical United Brethren Church and of The Methodist Church at the time union is consummated shall be bishops of The United Methodist Church.

The bishops of The Methodist Church elected by the jurisdictions, the active bishops of The Evangelical United Brethren Church at the time of union, and bishops elected by the jurisdictions of The United Methodist Church shall have life tenure. Each bishop elected by a central conference of The Methodist Church shall have such tenure as the central conference electing him shall have determined.[84]

The jurisdictional conference shall elect a standing committee on episcopacy to consist of one clergy and one lay delegate from each annual conference, on nomination of the annual conference delegation. The committee shall review the work of the bishops, pass on their character and official administration, and report to the jurisdictional conference its findings for such action as the conference may deem appropriate within its constitutional warrant of power. The committee shall recommend the assignments of the bishops to their respective residences for final action by the jurisdictional conference.

¶ **49.** *Article VII.*—A bishop presiding over an annual, central, or jurisdictional conference shall decide all questions of law coming before the bishop in the regular business of a session;[85] *provided* that such questions be presented in writing and that the decisions be recorded in the journal of the conference.

Such an episcopal decision shall not be authoritative except for the pending case until it shall have been passed upon by the Judicial Council. All decisions of law made by each bishop shall be reported in writing annually, with a syllabus of the same, to the Judicial Council, which shall affirm, modify, or reverse them.

¶ **50.** *Article VIII.*—The bishops of the several jurisdictional and central conferences shall preside in the sessions of their respective conferences.[86]

¶ **51.** *Article IX.*—In each annual conference there shall be one or more district superintendents who shall assist the bishop in the

---

84. *See* Judicial Council Decisions 4, 303, 361, 709.
85. *See* Judicial Council Decision 33.
86. See Judicial Council Decision 395.

administration of the annual conference and shall have such responsi-bilities and term of office as the General Conference may determine.[87]

¶ **52.** *Article X.*—The bishops shall appoint, after consultation with the district superintendents, ministers to the charges; and they shall have such responsibilities and authorities as the General Conference shall prescribe.

## DIVISION FOUR—THE JUDICIARY

¶ **53.** *Article I.*—There shall be a Judicial Council. The General Conference shall determine the number and qualifications of its members, their terms of office, and the method of election and the filling of vacancies.

¶ **54.** *Article II.*—The Judicial Council shall have authority:

1. To determine the constitutionality of any act of the General Conference upon an appeal of a majority of the Council of Bishops or one-fifth of the members of the General Conference and to determine the constitutionality of any act of a jurisdictional or central conference upon an appeal of a majority of the bishops of that jurisdictional or central conference or upon the appeal of one-fifth of the members of that jurisdictional or central conference.

2. To hear and determine any appeal from a bishop's decision on a question of law made in the annual conference when said appeal has been made by one-fifth of that conference present and voting.

3. To pass upon decisions of law made by bishops in annual conferences.

4. To hear and determine the legality of any action taken therein by any General Conference board or jurisdictional or central conference board or body, upon appeal by one-third of the members thereof, or upon request of the Council of Bishops or a majority of the bishops of a jurisdictional or a central conference.

5. To have such other duties and powers as may be conferred upon it by the General Conference.

6. To provide its own methods of organization and procedure.

¶ **55.** *Article III.*—All decisions of the Judicial Council shall be final. When the Judicial Council shall declare unconstitutional any act of the General Conference then in session, that decision shall be reported back to that General Conference immediately.

---

87. *See* Judicial Council Decisions 368, 398.

¶ **56.** *Article IV.*—The General Conference shall establish for the Church a judicial system that shall guarantee to our clergy a right to trial by a committee and an appeal, and to our members a right to trial before the Church, or by a committee, and an appeal.[88]

## DIVISION FIVE—AMENDMENTS

¶ **57.** *Article I.*—Amendments to the Constitution shall be made upon a two-thirds majority of the General Conference present and voting and a two-thirds affirmative vote of the aggregate number of members of the several annual conferences present and voting, except in the case of the first and second Restrictive Rules, which shall require a three-fourths majority of all the members of the annual conferences present and voting. The vote, after being completed, shall be canvassed by the Council of Bishops, and the amendment voted upon shall become effective upon their announcement of its having received the required majority.[89]

¶ **58.** *Article II.*—Amendments to the Constitution may originate in either the General Conference or the annual conferences.

¶ **59.** *Article III.*—A jurisdictional or central conference[90] may by a majority vote propose changes in the Constitution of the Church, and such proposed changes shall be submitted to the next General Conference. If the General Conference adopts the measure by a two-thirds vote, it shall be submitted to the annual conferences according to the provision for amendments.

---

88. *See* Judicial Council Decision 522.
89. *See* Judicial Council Decisions 154, 243, 244, 349, 483, 884; amended 1976.
90. Amended 1980.

## *Part II*
# DOCTRINAL STANDARDS AND OUR THEOLOGICAL TASK[1]

### ¶ 101. SECTION 1—OUR DOCTRINAL HERITAGE

United Methodists profess the historic Christian faith in God, incarnate in Jesus Christ for our salvation and ever at work in human history in the Holy Spirit. Living in a covenant of grace under the Lordship of Jesus Christ, we participate in the first fruits of God's coming reign and pray in hope for its full realization on earth as in heaven.

Our heritage in doctrine and our present theological task focus upon a renewed grasp of the sovereignty of God and of God's love in Christ amid the continuing crises of human existence.

Our forebears in the faith reaffirmed the ancient Christian message as found in the apostolic witness even as they applied it anew in their own circumstances.

Their preaching and teaching were grounded in Scripture, informed by Christian tradition, enlivened in experience, and tested by reason.

Their labors inspire and inform our attempts to convey the saving gospel to our world with its needs and aspirations.

### Our Common Heritage as Christians

United Methodists share a common heritage with Christians of every age and nation. This heritage is grounded in the apostolic witness

---

1. The Judicial Council ruled in 1972 that all sections of Part II except ¶ 103 were "legislative enactments and neither part of the Constitution nor under the Restrictive Rules" (*see* Judicial Council Decision 358).

41

to Jesus Christ as Savior and Lord, which is the source and measure of all valid Christian teaching.

Faced with diverse interpretations of the apostolic message, leaders of the early church sought to specify the core of Christian belief in order to ensure the soundness of Christian teaching.

The determination of the canon of Christian Scripture and the adoption of ecumenical creeds such as the formulations of Nicaea and Chalcedon were of central importance to this consensual process. Such creeds helped preserve the integrity of the church's witness, set boundaries for acceptable Christian doctrine, and proclaimed the basic elements of the enduring Christian message. These statements of faith, along with the Apostles' Creed, contain the most prominent features of our ecumenical heritage.

The Protestant reformers of the sixteenth and seventeenth centuries devised new confessional statements that reiterated classical Christian teaching in an attempt to recover the authentic biblical witness. These documents affirmed the primacy of Scripture and provided formal doctrinal standards through their statements of essential beliefs on matters such as the way of salvation, the Christian life, and the nature of the church.

Many distinctively Protestant teachings were transmitted into United Methodist understandings through doctrinal formulations such as the Articles of Religion of the Church of England and the Heidelberg Catechism of the Reformed tradition.

Various doctrinal statements in the form of creeds, confessions of belief, and articles of faith were officially adopted by churches as standards of Christian teaching. Notwithstanding their importance, these formal doctrinal standards by no means exhausted authoritative Christian teaching.

The standards themselves initially emerged from a much wider body of Christian thought and practice, and their fuller significance unfolded in the writings of the church's teachers. Some writings have proved simply to be dated benchmarks in the story of the church's continuing maturation.

By contrast, some sermons, treatises, liturgies, and hymns have gained considerable practical authority in the life and thought of the church by virtue of their wide and continuing acceptance as faithful expositions of Christian teaching. Nonetheless, the basic measure of authenticity in doctrinal standards, whether formally established or received by tradition, has been their fidelity to the apostolic faith grounded in Scripture and evidenced in the life of the church through the centuries.

## Basic Christian Affirmations

With Christians of other communions we confess belief in the triune God—Father, Son, and Holy Spirit. This confession embraces the biblical witness to God's activity in creation, encompasses God's gracious self-involvement in the dramas of history, and anticipates the consummation of God's reign.

The created order is designed for the well-being of all creatures and as the place of human dwelling in covenant with God. As sinful creatures, however, we have broken that covenant, become estranged from God, wounded ourselves and one another, and wreaked havoc throughout the natural order. We stand in need of redemption.

**We hold in common with all Christians a faith in the mystery of salvation in and through Jesus Christ.** At the heart of the gospel of salvation is God's incarnation in Jesus of Nazareth. Scripture witnesses to the redeeming love of God in Jesus' life and teachings, his atoning death, his resurrection, his sovereign presence in history, his triumph over the powers of evil and death, and his promised return. Because God truly loves us in spite of our willful sin, God judges us, summons us to repentance, pardons us, receives us by that grace given to us in Jesus Christ, and gives us hope of life eternal.

**We share the Christian belief that God's redemptive love is realized in human life by the activity of the Holy Spirit, both in personal experience and in the community of believers.** This community is the church, which the Spirit has brought into existence for the healing of the nations.

Through faith in Jesus Christ we are forgiven, reconciled to God, and transformed as people of the new covenant.

"Life in the Spirit" involves diligent use of the means of grace such as praying, fasting, attending upon the sacraments, and inward searching in solitude. It also encompasses the communal life of the church in worship, mission, evangelism, service, and social witness.

**We understand ourselves to be part of Christ's universal church when by adoration, proclamation, and service we become conformed to Christ.** We are initiated and incorporated into this community of faith by Baptism, receiving the promise of the Spirit that re-creates and transforms us. Through the regular celebration of Holy

Communion, we participate in the risen presence of Jesus Christ and are thereby nourished for faithful discipleship.

We pray and work for the coming of God's realm and reign to the world and rejoice in the promise of everlasting life that overcomes death and the forces of evil.

**With other Christians we recognize that the reign of God is both a present and future reality.** The church is called to be that place where the first signs of the reign of God are identified and acknowledged in the world. Wherever persons are being made new creatures in Christ, wherever the insights and resources of the gospel are brought to bear on the life of the world, God's reign is already effective in its healing and renewing power.

We also look to the end time in which God's work will be fulfilled. This prospect gives us hope in our present actions as individuals and as the Church. This expectation saves us from resignation and motivates our continuing witness and service.

**We share with many Christian communions a recognition of the authority of Scripture in matters of faith, the confession that our justification as sinners is by grace through faith, and the sober realization that the church is in need of continual reformation and renewal.**

We affirm the general ministry of all baptized Christians who share responsibility for building up the church and reaching out in mission and service to the world.

With other Christians, we declare the essential oneness of the church in Christ Jesus. This rich heritage of shared Christian belief finds expression in our hymnody and liturgies. Our unity is affirmed in the historic creeds as we confess one holy, catholic, and apostolic church. It is also experienced in joint ventures of ministry and in various forms of ecumenical cooperation.

Nourished by common roots of this shared Christian heritage, the branches of Christ's church have developed diverse traditions that enlarge our store of shared understandings. Our avowed ecumenical commitment as United Methodists is to gather our own doctrinal emphases into the larger Christian unity, there to be made more meaningful in a richer whole.

If we are to offer our best gifts to the common Christian treasury, we must make a deliberate effort as a church to strive for critical self-understanding. It is as Christians involved in ecumenical partnership that we embrace and examine our distinctive heritage.

## Our Distinctive Heritage as United Methodists

The underlying energy of the Wesleyan theological heritage stems from an emphasis upon practical divinity, the implementation of genuine Christianity in the lives of believers.

Methodism did not arise in response to a specific doctrinal dispute, though there was no lack of theological controversy. Early Methodists claimed to preach the scriptural doctrines of the Church of England as contained in the Articles of Religion, the Homilies, and the *Book of Common Prayer*.

Their task was not to reformulate doctrine. Their tasks were to summon people to experience the justifying and sanctifying grace of God and encourage people to grow in the knowledge and love of God through the personal and corporate disciplines of the Christian life.

The thrust of the Wesleyan movement and of the United Brethren and Evangelical Association was "to reform the nation, particularly the Church, and to spread scriptural holiness over the land."

Wesley's orientation toward the practical is evident in his focus upon the "scripture way of salvation." He considered doctrinal matters primarily in terms of their significance for Christian discipleship.

The Wesleyan emphasis upon the Christian life—faith and love put into practice—has been the hallmark of those traditions now incorporated into The United Methodist Church. The distinctive shape of the Wesleyan theological heritage can be seen in a constellation of doctrinal emphases that display the creating, redeeming, and sanctifying activity of God.

### Distinctive Wesleyan Emphases

Although Wesley shared with many other Christians a belief in grace, justification, assurance, and sanctification, he combined them in a powerful manner to create distinctive emphases for living the full Christian life. The Evangelical United Brethren tradition, particularly as expressed by Phillip William Otterbein from a Reformed background, gave similar distinctive emphases.

Grace pervades our understanding of Christian faith and life. By grace we mean the undeserved, unmerited, and loving action of God in human existence through the ever-present Holy Spirit. While the grace of God is undivided, it precedes salvation as "prevenient

45

grace," continues in "justifying grace," and is brought to fruition in "sanctifying grace."

We assert that God's grace is manifest in all creation even though suffering, violence, and evil are everywhere present. The goodness of creation is fulfilled in human beings, who are called to covenant partnership with God. God has endowed us with dignity and freedom and has summoned us to responsibility for our lives and the life of the world.

In God's self-revelation, Jesus Christ, we see the splendor of our true humanity. Even our sin, with its destructive consequences for all creation, does not alter God's intention for us—holiness and happiness of heart. Nor does it diminish our accountability for the way we live.

Despite our brokenness, we remain creatures brought into being by a just and merciful God. The restoration of God's image in our lives requires divine grace to renew our fallen nature.

**Prevenient Grace**—We acknowledge God's prevenient grace, the divine love that surrounds all humanity and precedes any and all of our conscious impulses. This grace prompts our first wish to please God, our first glimmer of understanding concerning God's will, and our "first slight transient conviction" of having sinned against God.

God's grace also awakens in us an earnest longing for deliverance from sin and death and moves us toward repentance and faith.

**Justification and Assurance**—We believe God reaches out to the repentant believer in justifying grace with accepting and pardoning love. Wesleyan theology stresses that a decisive change in the human heart can and does occur under the prompting of grace and the guidance of the Holy Spirit.

In justification we are, through faith, forgiven our sin and restored to God's favor. This righting of relationships by God through Christ calls forth our faith and trust as we experience regeneration, by which we are made new creatures in Christ.

This process of justification and new birth is often referred to as conversion. Such a change may be sudden and dramatic, or gradual and cumulative. It marks a new beginning, yet it is part of an ongoing process. Christian experience as personal transformation always expresses itself as faith working by love.

Our Wesleyan theology also embraces the scriptural promise that we can expect to receive assurance of our present salvation as the Spirit "bears witness with our spirit that we are children of God."

**Sanctification and Perfection**—We hold that the wonder of God's acceptance and pardon does not end God's saving work, which continues to nurture our growth in grace. Through the power of the Holy Spirit, we are enabled to increase in the knowledge and love of God and in love for our neighbor.

New birth is the first step in this process of sanctification. Sanctifying grace draws us toward the gift of Christian perfection, which Wesley described as a heart "habitually filled with the love of God and neighbor" and as "having the mind of Christ and walking as he walked."

This gracious gift of God's power and love, the hope and expectation of the faithful, is neither warranted by our efforts nor limited by our frailties.

**Faith and Good Works**—We see God's grace and human activity working together in the relationship of faith and good works. God's grace calls forth human response and discipline.

Faith is the only response essential for salvation. However, the General Rules remind us that salvation evidences itself in good works. For Wesley, even repentance should be accompanied by "fruits meet for repentance," or works of piety and mercy.

Both faith and good works belong within an all-encompassing theology of grace, since they stem from God's gracious love "shed abroad in our hearts by the Holy Spirit."

**Mission and Service**—We insist that personal salvation always involves Christian mission and service to the world. By joining heart and hand, we assert that personal religion, evangelical witness, and Christian social action are reciprocal and mutually reinforcing.

Scriptural holiness entails more than personal piety; love of God is always linked with love of neighbor, a passion for justice and renewal in the life of the world.

The General Rules represent one traditional expression of the intrinsic relationship between Christian life and thought as understood within the Wesleyan tradition. Theology is the servant of piety, which in turn is the ground of social conscience and the impetus for social action and global interaction, always in the empowering context of the reign of God.

**Nurture and Mission of the Church**—Finally, we emphasize the nurturing and serving function of Christian fellowship in the Church. The personal experience of faith is nourished by the worshiping community.

For Wesley there is no religion but social religion, no holiness but social holiness. The communal forms of faith in the Wesleyan tradition not only promote personal growth; they also equip and mobilize us for mission and service to the world.

The outreach of the church springs from the working of the Spirit. As United Methodists, we respond to that working through a connectional polity based upon mutual responsiveness and accountability. Connectional ties bind us together in faith and service in our global witness, enabling faith to become active in love and intensifying our desire for peace and justice in the world.

## Doctrine and Discipline in the Christian Life

No motif in the Wesleyan tradition has been more constant than the link between Christian doctrine and Christian living. Methodists have always been strictly enjoined to maintain the unity of faith and good works through the means of grace, as seen in John Wesley's *Nature, Design, and General Rules of the United Societies* (1743). The coherence of faith with ministries of love forms the discipline of Wesleyan spirituality and Christian discipleship.

The General Rules were originally designed for members of Methodist societies who participated in the sacramental life of the Church of England. The terms of membership in these societies were simple: "a desire to flee from the wrath to come and to be saved from their sins."

Wesley insisted, however, that evangelical faith should manifest itself in evangelical living. He spelled out this expectation in the three-part formula of the Rules:

"It is therefore expected of all who continue therein that they should continue to evidence their desire of salvation,

"First: By doing no harm, by avoiding evil of every kind . . . ;

"Secondly: By . . . doing good of every possible sort, and, as far as possible, to all . . . ;

"Thirdly: By attending upon all the ordinances of God" (*see* ¶ 103).

Wesley's illustrative cases under each of these three rules show how the Christian conscience might move from general principles to specific actions. Their explicit combination highlights the spiritual spring of moral action.

Wesley rejected undue reliance upon these rules. Discipline was not church law; it was a way of discipleship. Wesley insisted that true religion is "the knowledge of God in Christ Jesus," "the life which is hid with Christ in God," and "the righteousness that [the true believer] thirsts after."

## General Rules and Social Principles

Upon such evangelical premises, Methodists in every age have sought to exercise their responsibility for the moral and spiritual quality of society. In asserting the connection between doctrine and ethics, the General Rules provide an early signal of Methodist social consciousness.

The Social Principles (¶¶ 160–166) provide our most recent official summary of stated convictions that seek to apply the Christian vision of righteousness to social, economic, and political issues. Our historic opposition to evils such as smuggling, inhumane prison conditions, slavery, drunkenness, and child labor was founded upon a vivid sense of God's wrath against human injustice and wastage.

Our struggles for human dignity and social reform have been a response to God's demand for love, mercy, and justice in the light of the Kingdom. We proclaim no *personal gospel* that fails to express itself in relevant social concerns; we proclaim no *social gospel* that does not include the personal transformation of sinners.

It is our conviction that the good news of the Kingdom must judge, redeem, and reform the sinful social structures of our time.

*The Book of Discipline* and the General Rules convey the expectation of discipline within the experience of individuals and the life of the Church. Such discipline assumes accountability to the community of faith by those who claim that community's support.

Support without accountability promotes moral weakness; accountability without support is a form of cruelty.

A church that rushes to punishment is not open to God's mercy, but a church lacking the courage to act decisively on personal and social issues loses its claim to moral authority. The church exercises its discipline as a community through which God continues to "reconcile the world to himself."

## Conclusion

These distinctive emphases of United Methodists provide the basis for "practical divinity," the experiential realization of the gospel of Jesus Christ in the lives of Christian people. These emphases have been preserved not so much through formal doctrinal declarations as through the vital movement of faith and practice as seen in converted lives and within the disciplined life of the Church.

Devising formal definitions of doctrine has been less pressing for United Methodists than summoning people to faith and nurturing them in the knowledge and love of God. The core of Wesleyan doctrine that informed our past rightly belongs to our common heritage as Christians and remains a prime component within our continuing theological task.

## ¶ 102. SECTION 2—OUR DOCTRINAL HISTORY

The pioneers in the traditions that flowed together into The United Methodist Church understood themselves as standing in the central stream of Christian spirituality and doctrine, loyal heirs of the authentic Christian tradition. In John Wesley's words, theirs was "the old religion, the religion of the Bible, the religion . . . of the whole church in the purest ages." Their gospel was grounded in the biblical message of God's self-giving love revealed in Jesus Christ.

Wesley's portrayal of the spiritual pilgrimage in terms of "the scripture way of salvation" provided their model for experiential Christianity. They assumed and insisted upon the integrity of basic Christian truth and emphasized its practical application in the lives of believers.

This perspective is apparent in the Wesleyan understanding of "catholic spirit." While it is true that United Methodists are fixed upon certain religious affirmations, grounded in the gospel and confirmed in their experience, they also recognize the right of Christians to disagree on matters such as forms of worship, structures of church government, modes of Baptism, or theological explorations. They believe such differences do not break the bond of fellowship that ties Christians together in Jesus Christ. Wesley's familiar dictum was, "As to all opinions which do not strike at the root of Christianity, we think and let think."

But, even as they were fully committed to the principles of religious toleration and theological diversity, they were equally confident that there is a "marrow" of Christian truth that can be identified and that must be conserved. This living core, as they believed, stands revealed in Scripture, illumined by tradition, vivified in personal and corporate experience, and confirmed by reason. They were very much aware, of course, that God's eternal Word never has been, nor can be, exhaustively expressed in any single form of words.

They were also prepared, as a matter of course, to reaffirm the ancient creeds and confessions as valid summaries of Christian truth. But they were careful not to set them apart as absolute standards for doctrinal truth and error.

Beyond the essentials of vital religion, United Methodists respect the diversity of opinions held by conscientious persons of faith. Wesley followed a time-tested approach: "In essentials, unity; in non-essentials, liberty; and in all things, charity."

The spirit of charity takes into consideration the limits of human understanding. "To be ignorant of many things and to be mistaken in some," Wesley observed, "is the necessary condition of humanity." The crucial matter in religion is steadfast love for God and neighbor, empowered by the redeeming and sanctifying work of the Holy Spirit.

## The Wesleyan "Standards" in Great Britain

In this spirit, the British Methodists under the Wesleys never reduced their theology to a confessional formula as a doctrinal test. Methodism was a movement within the Church of England, and John Wesley constantly maintained that he taught the scriptural doctrines contained in the Thirty-Nine Articles, the Homilies, and the *Book of Common Prayer* of his national church. The Bible, of course, constituted for him the final authority in all doctrinal matters.

As the movement grew, Wesley provided his people with published sermons and a Bible commentary for their doctrinal instruction. His *Sermons on Several Occasions* (1746–60) set forth those doctrines which, he said, "I embrace and teach as the essentials of true religion." In 1755, he published *Explanatory Notes Upon the New Testament* as a guide for Methodist biblical exegesis and doctrinal interpretation.

As occasional controversies arose, the need for a standard measure of Methodist preaching became evident. In 1763, Wesley produced a "Model Deed" for Methodist properties, which stipulated that the trustees for each preaching house were responsible for ensuring that the preachers in their pulpits "preach no other doctrine than is contained in Mr. Wesley's *Notes Upon the New Testament* and four volumes of *Sermons*."

These writings, then, contained the standard exposition of Methodist teaching. They provide a model and measure for adequate preaching in the Wesleyan tradition. The primary norm for Wesley's writings was Scripture, as illumined by historic traditions and vital faith. Wesley put forth no summary of biblical revelation for the British Methodists because the Thirty-Nine Articles of the Church of England were already available.

The Wesley brothers also composed hymns that were rich in doctrinal and experiential content. The hymns, especially those of Charles Wesley, not only are among the best-loved within Methodism but also are major resources for doctrinal instruction.

Furthermore, John Wesley specified various disciplines and rules, such as the General Rules, to implement in personal and communal life the practical divinity he proclaimed.

In addition to these writings, Wesley established the conference to instruct and supervise the Methodist preachers. He produced Minutes to ensure their fidelity to the doctrines and disciplines of the Methodist movement. These writings and structures filled out the Wesleyan understanding of the church and the Christian life.

## Doctrinal Standards in American Methodism

As long as the American colonies were primarily under British control, the Methodists could continue as part of the sacramental community of the Church of England. The early conferences, under the leadership of British preachers, declared their allegiance to the Wesleyan principles of organization and doctrine. They stipulated that the Minutes of the British and American conferences, along with the *Sermons* and *Notes* of Wesley, contained their basic doctrine and discipline.

After the formal recognition of American independence in 1783, Wesley realized that the Methodists in America were free of English control, religious as well as civil, and should become an independent Methodist church. Wesley then furnished the American Methodists with a liturgy (*The Sunday Service of the Methodists in North America*) and a doctrinal statement (*The Articles of Religion*). The *Sunday Service* was Wesley's abridgment of the *Book of Common Prayer*; the *Articles of Religion* were his revision of the Thirty-Nine Articles.

The American Methodist preachers, gathered at Baltimore in December 1784, adopted the Sunday Service and the Articles of Religion as part of their actions in forming the new Methodist Episcopal Church. This "Christmas Conference" also accepted a hymnbook that Wesley had prepared (1784) and adopted a slightly modified version of the General Rules as a statement of the Church's nature and discipline. The conference spent most of its time adapting the British "Large Minutes" to American conditions. Subsequent editions of this document came to be known as the *Doctrines and Discipline of the Methodist Episcopal Church* (the *Book of Discipline*).

The shift from "movement" to "church" had changed the function of doctrinal norms within American Methodism. Rather than prescribing doctrinal emphases for preaching within a movement, the Articles outlined basic norms for Christian belief within a church, following the traditional Anglican fashion.

The preface to the first separate publication of the Articles states, "These are the doctrines taught among the people called Methodists. Nor is there any doctrine whatever, generally received among that people, contrary to the articles now before you."

American Methodists were not required to subscribe to the Articles after the Anglican manner, but they were accountable (under threat of trial) for keeping their proclamation of the gospel within the boundaries outlined therein. For generations, the *Doctrines and Discipline* cited only the Articles as the basis for testing correct doctrine in the newly formed church: The charge of doctrinal irregularity against preachers or members was for "disseminating doctrines contrary to our Articles of Religion." In this manner, the church protected its doctrinal integrity against the heresies that were prevalent at the time— Socinianism, Arianism, and Pelagianism (*see* Articles I, II, and IX).

The Articles of Religion, however, did not guarantee adequate Methodist preaching; they lacked several Wesleyan emphases, such as assurance and Christian perfection. Wesley's *Sermons* and *Notes*, therefore, continued to function as the traditional standard exposition of distinctive Methodist teaching.

The General Conference of 1808, which provided the first Constitution of The Methodist Episcopal Church, established the Articles of Religion as the Church's explicit doctrinal standards. The first Restrictive Rule of the Constitution prohibited any change, alteration, or addition to the Articles themselves, and it stipulated that no new standards or rules of doctrine could be adopted that were contrary to the "present existing and established standards of doctrine."

Within the Wesleyan tradition, then as now, the *Sermons* and

*Notes* furnished models of doctrinal exposition. Other documents have also served American Methodism as vital expressions of Methodist teaching and preaching. Lists of recommended doctrinal resources vary from generation to generation but generally acknowledge the importance of the hymnbook, the ecumenical creeds, and the General Rules. Lists of such writings in the early nineteenth century usually included John Fletcher's *Checks Against Antinomianism* and Richard Watson's *Theological Institutes.*

The doctrinal emphases of these statements were carried forward by the weight of tradition rather than the force of law. They became part of the heritage of American Methodism to the degree that they remained useful to continuing generations.

During the great frontier revivals of the nineteenth century, the influence of European theological traditions waned in America. Preaching focused on "Christian experience," understood chiefly as "saving faith in Christ." Among the Methodists there was a consistent stress on free will, infant baptism, and informal worship, which led to protracted controversies with the Presbyterians, Baptists, and Episcopalians, respectively.

Methodist interest in formal doctrinal standards remained secondary to evangelism, nurture, and mission. The Wesleyan hymnody served in practice as the most important single means of communicating and preserving the doctrinal substance of the gospel.

By the end of the nineteenth century, Methodist theology in America had become decidedly eclectic, with less specific attention paid to its Wesleyan sources.

The force of the Articles of Religion underwent several shifts. For a time, the first Restrictive Rule was exempted from the process of constitutional amendment, thus allowing no consideration of change in doctrinal standards. Mention of the Articles of Religion was included in the membership vows of The Methodist Episcopal Church, South.

At the beginning of the twentieth century, however, the waning force of doctrinal discipline and the decreasing influence of the Wesleyan theological heritage among the American Methodists, along with minor but significant changes in the wording of the *Book of Discipline* regarding doctrinal standards, led to a steady dilution of the force of the Articles of Religion as the Church's constitutional standards of doctrine.

During this same period, theologians and church leaders began to explore ways of expressing the gospel that were in keeping with developing intellectual currents. These leaders also began to rethink the historical social compassion of the Wesleyan tradition in the midst of the emerging industrial, urban civilization. They deepened our awareness of the systemic nature of evil and the urgency to proclaim the gospel promise of social redemption. Consequently, theologies supportive of the social gospel found fertile soil within the Methodist traditions.

These years were times of theological and ethical controversy within Methodism as new patterns of thought clashed with the more familiar themes and styles of the previous two centuries.

In recent decades there has been a strong recovery of interest in Wesley and in the more classic traditions of Christian thought. This recovery has been part of a broad resurgence of Reformation theology and practice in Europe and America, renewing the historical legacy of Protestantism in the context of the modern world. These trends have been reinforced in North America by the reaffirmation of evangelical piety.

The ecumenical movement has brought new appreciation for the unity as well as the richness and diversity of the church catholic.

Currents of theology have developed out of Black people's struggle for freedom, the movement for the full equality of women in church and society, and the quest for liberation and for indigenous forms of Christian existence in churches around the world.

The challenge to United Methodists is to discern the various strands of these vital movements of faith that are coherent, faithful understandings of the gospel and the Christian mission for our times.

The task of defining the scope of our Wesleyan tradition in the context of the contemporary world includes much more than formally reaffirming or redefining standards of doctrine, although these tasks may also be involved. The heart of our task is to reclaim and renew the distinctive United Methodist doctrinal heritage, which rightly belongs to our common heritage as Christians, for the life and mission of the whole church today.

### Doctrinal Traditions in The Evangelical Church and The United Brethren Church

The unfolding of doctrinal concerns among Jacob Albright's Evangelical Association and Phillip William Otterbein's United

Brethren in Christ roughly parallels Methodist developments. Differences emerged largely from differing ecclesiastical traditions brought from Germany and Holland, together with the modified Calvinism of the Heidelberg Catechism.

In the German-speaking communities of America, Albright and Otterbein considered evangelism more important than theological speculation. Although they were not doctrinally indifferent, they stressed conversion, "justification by faith confirmed by a sensible assurance thereof," Christian nurture, the priesthood of all believers in a shared ministry of Christian witness and service, and entire sanctification as the goal of Christian life.

As with Wesley, their primary source and norm for Christian teaching was Scripture. Otterbein enjoined his followers "to be careful to preach no other doctrine than what is plainly laid down in the Bible." Each new member was asked "to confess that he received the Bible as the Word of God." Ordinands were required to affirm without reserve the plenary authority of Scripture.

Matched with these affirmations was the conviction that converted Christians are enabled by the Holy Spirit to read Scripture with a special Christian consciousness. They prized this principle as the supreme guide in biblical interpretation.

Jacob Albright was directed by the conference of 1807 to prepare a list of Articles of Religion. He died before he could attempt the task.

George Miller then assumed the responsibility. He recommended to the conference of 1809 the adoption of the German translation of the Methodist Articles of Religion, with the addition of a new one, "Of the Last Judgment." The recommendation was adopted. This action affirms a conscious choice of the Methodist Articles as normative. The added article was from the Augsburg Confession, on a theme omitted in the Anglican Articles.

In 1816, the original twenty-six Articles were reduced to twenty-one by omitting five polemical articles aimed at Roman Catholics, Anabaptists, and sixteenth-century sectaries. This act of deletion reflected a conciliatory spirit in a time of bitter controversy.

In 1839, a few slight changes were made in the text of 1816. It was then stipulated that "the Articles of Faith . . . should be constitutionally unchangeable among us."

In the 1870s, a proposal to revise the Articles touched off a flurry of debate, but the conference of 1875 decisively rejected the proposal.

In later action the twenty-one Articles were reduced to nineteen by combining several, but without omitting any of their original content.

These nineteen were brought intact into the Evangelical United Brethren union of 1946.

Among the United Brethren in Christ, a summary of normative teaching was formulated in 1813 by Christian Newcomer and Christopher Grosch, colleagues of Otterbein. Its first three paragraphs follow the order of the Apostles' Creed. Paragraphs four and five affirm the primacy of Scripture and the universal proclamation of "the biblical doctrine . . . of man's fall in Adam and his deliverance through Jesus Christ." An added section commends "the ordinances of baptism and the remembrance of the Lord" and approves foot washing as optional.

The first General Conference of the United Brethren in Christ (1815) adopted a slight revision of this earlier statement as the denomination's Confession of Faith. A further revision was made in 1841, with the stipulation that there be no further changes: "No rule or ordinance shall at any time be passed to change or do away with the Confession of Faith as it now stands." Even so, agitation for change continued.

In 1885, a church commission was appointed to "prepare such a form of belief and such amended fundamental rules for the government of this church in the future as will, in their judgment, be best adapted to secure its growth and efficiency in the work of evangelizing the world."

The resulting proposal for a new Confession of Faith and Constitution was submitted to the general membership of the Church, the first such referendum on a Confession of Faith in United Brethren history, and was then placed before the General Conference of 1889. Both the general membership and the conference approved the Confession by preponderant majorities. It was thereupon enacted by episcopal "proclamation." However, this action was protested by a minority as a violation of the Restrictive Rule of 1841 and became a basic cause for a consequent schism, resulting in the formation of The United Brethren Church (Old Constitution).

The Confession of Faith of 1889 was more comprehensive than any of its antecedents, with articles on depravity, justification, regeneration and adoption, sanctification, the Christian Sabbath, and the future state. The article on sanctification, though brief, is significant

in its reflection of the doctrine of holiness of the Heidelberg Catechism. The 1889 Confession was brought by the United Brethren into
the union with the Evangelicals in 1946.

## The Evangelical United Brethren Confession of Faith

The *Discipline* of the new Evangelical United Brethren Church
(1946) contained both the Evangelical Articles and the United
Brethren Confession. Twelve years later the General Conference of
the united church authorized its board of bishops to prepare a new
Confession of Faith.

A new Confession, with sixteen articles, of a somewhat more
modern character than any of its antecedents, was presented to the
General Conference of 1962 and adopted without amendment. The
Evangelical article, "Entire Sanctification and Christian Perfection," is
reflected in this confession as a distinctive emphasis. The Confession
of Faith replaced both former Articles and Confession and was
brought over intact into the *Discipline* of The United Methodist
Church (1968).

## Doctrinal Standards in The United Methodist Church

In the Plan of Union for The United Methodist Church, the preface to the Methodist Articles of Religion and the Evangelical United
Brethren Confession of Faith explains that both were accepted as doctrinal standards for the new church. Additionally, it stated that
although the language of the first Restrictive Rule never has been formally defined, Wesley's *Sermons* and *Notes* were understood specifically to be included in our present existing and established standards
of doctrine. It also stated that the Articles, the Confession, and the
Wesleyan "standards" were "thus deemed congruent if not identical
in their doctrinal perspectives and not in conflict." This declaration
was accepted by subsequent rulings of the Judicial Council.[2]

The Constitution of The United Methodist Church, in its Restrictive Rules (*see* ¶¶ 16–20), protects both the Articles of Religion and
the Confession of Faith as doctrinal standards that shall not be
revoked, altered, or changed. The process of creating new "standards
or rules of doctrine" thus continues to be restricted, requiring either

---

2. *See* Judicial Council Decision 358.

that they be declared "not contrary to" the present standards or that they go through the difficult process of constitutional amendment.

The United Methodist Church stands continually in need of doctrinal reinvigoration for the sake of authentic renewal, fruitful evangelism, and ecumenical dialogue. In this light, the recovery and updating of our distinctive doctrinal heritage—catholic, evangelical, and reformed—is essential.

This task calls for the repossession of our traditions as well as the promotion of theological inquiry both within the denomination and in our ecumenical efforts. All are invited to share in this endeavor to stimulate an active interest in doctrinal understanding in order to claim our legacy and to shape that legacy for the Church we aspire to be.

## ¶ 103. SECTION 3—OUR DOCTRINAL STANDARDS AND GENERAL RULES

### THE ARTICLES OF RELIGION OF THE METHODIST CHURCH[3]

[Bibliographical Note: The Articles of Religion are here reprinted from the *Discipline* of 1808 (when the first Restrictive Rule took effect), collated against Wesley's original text in *The Sunday Service of the Methodists* (1784). To these are added two Articles: "Of Sanctification" and "Of the Duty of Christians to the Civil Authority," which are legislative enactments and not integral parts of the document as protected by the Constitution (*see* Judicial Council Decisions 41, 176).]

### Article I—Of Faith in the Holy Trinity

There is but one living and true God, everlasting, without body or parts, of infinite power, wisdom, and goodness; the maker and preserver of all things, both visible and invisible. And in unity of this Godhead there are three persons, of one substance, power, and eternity—the Father, the Son, and the Holy Ghost.

---

3. Protected by Restrictive Rule 1 (¶ 16).

## Article II—Of the Word, or Son of God, Who Was Made Very Man

The Son, who is the Word of the Father, the very and eternal God, of one substance with the Father, took man's nature in the womb of the blessed Virgin; so that two whole and perfect natures, that is to say, the Godhead and Manhood, were joined together in one person, never to be divided; whereof is one Christ, very God and very Man, who truly suffered, was crucified, dead, and buried, to reconcile his Father to us, and to be a sacrifice, not only for original guilt, but also for actual sins of men.

## Article III—Of the Resurrection of Christ

Christ did truly rise again from the dead, and took again his body, with all things appertaining to the perfection of man's nature, wherewith he ascended into heaven, and there sitteth until he return to judge all men at the last day.

## Article IV—Of the Holy Ghost

The Holy Ghost, proceeding from the Father and the Son, is of one substance, majesty, and glory with the Father and the Son, very and eternal God.

## Article V—Of the Sufficiency of the Holy Scriptures for Salvation

The Holy Scripture containeth all things necessary to salvation; so that whatsoever is not read therein, nor may be proved thereby, is not to be required of any man that it should be believed as an article of faith, or be thought requisite or necessary to salvation. In the name of the Holy Scripture we do understand those canonical books of the Old and New Testament of whose authority was never any doubt in the church. The names of the canonical books are:

Genesis, Exodus, Leviticus, Numbers, Deuteronomy, Joshua, Judges, Ruth, The First Book of Samuel, The Second Book of Samuel, The First Book of Kings, The Second Book of Kings, The First Book of Chronicles, The Second Book of Chronicles, The Book of Ezra, The Book of Nehemiah, The Book of Esther, The Book of Job, The Psalms, The Proverbs, Ecclesiastes or the Preacher, Cantica or Songs of Solomon, Four Prophets the Greater, Twelve Prophets the Less.

All the books of the New Testament, as they are commonly received, we do receive and account canonical.

### Article VI—Of the Old Testament

The Old Testament is not contrary to the New; for both in the Old and New Testament everlasting life is offered to mankind by Christ, who is the only Mediator between God and man, being both God and Man. Wherefore they are not to be heard who feign that the old fathers did look only for transitory promises. Although the law given from God by Moses as touching ceremonies and rites doth not bind Christians, nor ought the civil precepts thereof of necessity be received in any commonwealth; yet notwithstanding, no Christian whatsoever is free from the obedience of the commandments which are called moral.

### Article VII—Of Original or Birth Sin

Original sin standeth not in the following of Adam (as the Pelagians do vainly talk), but it is the corruption of the nature of every man, that naturally is engendered of the offspring of Adam, whereby man is very far gone from original righteousness, and of his own nature inclined to evil, and that continually.

### Article VIII—Of Free Will

The condition of man after the fall of Adam is such that he cannot turn and prepare himself, by his own natural strength and works, to faith, and calling upon God; wherefore we have no power to do good works, pleasant and acceptable to God, without the grace of God by Christ preventing us, that we may have a good will, and working with us, when we have that good will.

### Article IX—Of the Justification of Man

We are accounted righteous before God only for the merit of our Lord and Saviour Jesus Christ, by faith, and not for our own works or deservings. Wherefore, that we are justified by faith, only, is a most wholesome doctrine, and very full of comfort.

### Article X—Of Good Works

Although good works, which are the fruits of faith, and follow after justification, cannot put away our sins, and endure the severity of God's judgment; yet are they pleasing and acceptable to God in Christ, and spring out of a true and lively faith, insomuch that by them a lively faith may be as evidently known as a tree is discerned by its fruit.

### Article XI—Of Works of Supererogation

Voluntary works—besides, over and above God's commandments—which they call works of supererogation, cannot be taught without arrogancy and impiety. For by them men do declare that they do not only render unto God as much as they are bound to do, but that they do more for his sake than of bounden duty is required; whereas Christ saith plainly: When you have done all that is commanded you, say, We are unprofitable servants.

### Article XII—Of Sin After Justification

Not every sin willingly committed after justification is the sin against the Holy Ghost, and unpardonable. Wherefore, the grant of repentance is not to be denied to such as fall into sin after justification. After we have received the Holy Ghost, we may depart from grace given, and fall into sin, and, by the grace of God, rise again and amend our lives. And therefore they are to be condemned who say they can no more sin as long as they live here; or deny the place of forgiveness to such as truly repent.

### Article XIII—Of the Church

The visible church of Christ is a congregation of faithful men in which the pure Word of God is preached, and the Sacraments duly administered according to Christ's ordinance, in all those things that of necessity are requisite to the same.

### Article XIV—Of Purgatory[4]

The Romish doctrine concerning purgatory, pardon, worshiping, and adoration, as well of images as of relics, and also invocation of

---

4. For the contemporary interpretation of this and similar articles (i.e., Articles XIV, XV, XVI, XVIII, XIX, XX, and XXI) in consonance with our best ecumenical insights and judgment, *see* "Resolution of Intent—With a View to Unity" (*The Book of Resolutions*, 2000, p. 236).

saints, is a fond thing, vainly invented, and grounded upon no warrant of Scripture, but repugnant to the Word of God.

## Article XV—Of Speaking in the Congregation in Such a Tongue as the People Understand

It is a thing plainly repugnant to the Word of God, and the custom of the primitive church, to have public prayer in the church, or to minister the Sacraments, in a tongue not understood by the people.

## Article XVI—Of the Sacraments

Sacraments ordained of Christ are not only badges or tokens of Christian men's profession, but rather they are certain signs of grace, and God's good will toward us, by which he doth work invisibly in us, and doth not only quicken, but also strengthen and confirm, our faith in him.

There are two Sacraments ordained of Christ our Lord in the Gospel; that is to say, Baptism and the Supper of the Lord.

Those five commonly called sacraments, that is to say, confirmation, penance, orders, matrimony, and extreme unction, are not to be counted for Sacraments of the Gospel; being such as have partly grown out of the *corrupt* following of the apostles, and partly are states of life allowed in the Scriptures, but yet have not the like nature of Baptism and the Lord's Supper, because they have not any visible sign or ceremony ordained of God.

The Sacraments were not ordained of Christ to be gazed upon, or to be carried about; but that we should duly use them. And in such only as worthily receive the same, they have a wholesome effect or operation; but they that receive them unworthily, purchase to themselves condemnation, as St. Paul saith.

## Article XVII—Of Baptism

Baptism is not only a sign of profession and mark of difference whereby Christians are distinguished from others that are not baptized; but it is also a sign of regeneration or the new birth. The Baptism of young children is to be retained in the Church.[5]

---

5. *See* Judicial Council Decision 142.

### Article XVIII—Of the Lord's Supper

The Supper of the Lord is not only a sign of the love that Christians ought to have among themselves one to another, but rather is a sacrament of our redemption by Christ's death; insomuch that, to such as rightly, worthily, and with faith receive the same, the bread which we break is a partaking of the body of Christ; and likewise the cup of blessing is a partaking of the blood of Christ.

Transubstantiation, or the change of the substance of bread and wine in the Supper of our Lord, cannot be proved by Holy Writ, but is repugnant to the plain words of Scripture, overthroweth the nature of a sacrament, and hath given occasion to many superstitions.

The body of Christ is given, taken, and eaten in the Supper, only after a heavenly and spiritual manner. And the mean whereby the body of Christ is received and eaten in the Supper is faith.

The Sacrament of the Lord's Supper was not by Christ's ordinance reserved, carried about, lifted up, or worshiped.

### Article XIX—Of Both Kinds

The cup of the Lord is not to be denied to the lay people; for both the parts of the Lord's Supper, by Christ's ordinance and commandment, ought to be administered to all Christians alike.

### Article XX—Of the One Oblation of Christ, Finished upon the Cross

The offering of Christ, once made, is that perfect redemption, propitiation, and satisfaction for all the sins of the whole world, both original and actual; and there is none other satisfaction for sin but that alone. Wherefore the sacrifice of masses, in the which it is commonly said that the priest doth offer Christ for the quick and the dead, to have remission of pain or guilt, is a blasphemous fable and dangerous deceit.

### Article XXI—Of the Marriage of Ministers

The ministers of Christ are not commanded by God's law either to vow the estate of single life, or to abstain from marriage; therefore it is lawful for them, as for all other Christians, to marry at their own discretion, as they shall judge the same to serve best to godliness.

## Article XXII—Of the Rites and Ceremonies of Churches

It is not necessary that rites and ceremonies should in all places be the same, or exactly alike; for they have been always different, and may be changed according to the diversity of countries, times, and men's manners, so that nothing be ordained against God's Word. Whosoever, through his private judgment, willingly and purposely doth openly break the rites and ceremonies of the church to which he belongs, which are not repugnant to the Word of God, and are ordained and approved by common authority, ought to be rebuked openly, that others may fear to do the like, as one that offendeth against the common order of the church, and woundeth the consciences of weak brethren.

Every particular church may ordain, change, or abolish rites and ceremonies, so that all things may be done to edification.

## Article XXIII—Of the Rulers of the United States of America

The President, the Congress, the general assemblies, the governors, and the councils of state, *as the delegates of the people,* are the rulers of the United States of America, according to the division of power made to them by the Constitution of the United States and by the constitutions of their respective states. And the said states are a sovereign and independent nation, and ought not to be subject to any foreign jurisdiction.

## Article XXIV—Of Christian Men's Goods

The riches and goods of Christians are not common as touching the right, title, and possession of the same, as some do falsely boast. Notwithstanding, every man ought, of such things as he possesseth, liberally to give alms to the poor, according to his ability.

## Article XXV—Of a Christian Man's Oath

As we confess that vain and rash swearing is forbidden Christian men by our Lord Jesus Christ and James his apostle, so we judge that the Christian religion doth not prohibit, but that a man may swear when the magistrate requireth, in a cause of faith and charity, so it be done according to the prophet's teaching, in justice, judgment, and truth.

[The following Article from the Methodist Protestant *Discipline* is placed here by the Uniting Conference (1939). It was not one of the Articles of Religion voted upon by the three churches.]

## Of Sanctification

Sanctification is that renewal of our fallen nature by the Holy Ghost, received through faith in Jesus Christ, whose blood of atonement cleanseth from all sin; whereby we are not only delivered from the guilt of sin, but are washed from its pollution, saved from its power, and are enabled, through grace, to love God with all our hearts and to walk in his holy commandments blameless.

[The following provision was adopted by the Uniting Conference (1939). This statement seeks to interpret to our churches in foreign lands Article XXIII of the Articles of Religion. It is a legislative enactment but is not a part of the Constitution. (*See* Judicial Council Decisions 41, 176, and Decision 6, Interim Judicial Council.)]

## Of the Duty of Christians to the Civil Authority

It is the duty of all Christians, and especially of all Christian ministers, to observe and obey the laws and commands of the governing or supreme authority of the country of which they are citizens or subjects or in which they reside, and to use all laudable means to encourage and enjoin obedience to the powers that be.

## THE CONFESSION OF FAITH
## OF THE EVANGELICAL UNITED BRETHREN CHURCH[6]

[Bibliographical Note: The text of the Confession of Faith is identical to that of its original in *The Discipline of The Evangelical United Brethren Church* (1963).]

## Article I—God

We believe in the one true, holy and living God, Eternal Spirit, who is Creator, Sovereign and Preserver of all things visible and invisible. He is infinite in power, wisdom, justice, goodness and love,

---

6. Protected by Restrictive Rule 2 (¶ 16).

and rules with gracious regard for the well-being and salvation of men, to the glory of his name. We believe the one God reveals himself as the Trinity: Father, Son and Holy Spirit, distinct but inseparable, eternally one in essence and power.

### Article II—Jesus Christ

We believe in Jesus Christ, truly God and truly man, in whom the divine and human natures are perfectly and inseparably united. He is the eternal Word made flesh, the only begotten Son of the Father, born of the Virgin Mary by the power of the Holy Spirit. As ministering Servant he lived, suffered and died on the cross. He was buried, rose from the dead and ascended into heaven to be with the Father, from whence he shall return. He is eternal Savior and Mediator, who intercedes for us, and by him all men will be judged.

### Article III—The Holy Spirit

We believe in the Holy Spirit who proceeds from and is one in being with the Father and the Son. He convinces the world of sin, of righteousness and of judgment. He leads men through faithful response to the gospel into the fellowship of the Church. He comforts, sustains and empowers the faithful and guides them into all truth.

### Article IV—The Holy Bible

We believe the Holy Bible, Old and New Testaments, reveals the Word of God so far as it is necessary for our salvation. It is to be received through the Holy Spirit as the true rule and guide for faith and practice. Whatever is not revealed in or established by the Holy Scriptures is not to be made an article of faith nor is it to be taught as essential to salvation.

### Article V—The Church

We believe the Christian Church is the community of all true believers under the Lordship of Christ. We believe it is one, holy, apostolic and catholic. It is the redemptive fellowship in which the Word of God is preached by men divinely called, and the sacraments are duly administered according to Christ's own appointment. Under the discipline of the Holy Spirit the Church exists for the maintenance of worship, the edification of believers and the redemption of the world.

### Article VI—The Sacraments

We believe the Sacraments, ordained by Christ, are symbols and pledges of the Christian's profession and of God's love toward us. They are means of grace by which God works invisibly in us, quickening, strengthening and confirming our faith in him. Two Sacraments are ordained by Christ our Lord, namely Baptism and the Lord's Supper.

We believe Baptism signifies entrance into the household of faith, and is a symbol of repentance and inner cleansing from sin, a representation of the new birth in Christ Jesus and a mark of Christian discipleship.

We believe children are under the atonement of Christ and as heirs of the Kingdom of God are acceptable subjects for Christian Baptism. Children of believing parents through Baptism become the special responsibility of the Church. They should be nurtured and led to personal acceptance of Christ, and by profession of faith confirm their Baptism.

We believe the Lord's Supper is a representation of our redemption, a memorial of the sufferings and death of Christ, and a token of love and union which Christians have with Christ and with one another. Those who rightly, worthily and in faith eat the broken bread and drink the blessed cup partake of the body and blood of Christ in a spiritual manner until he comes.

### Article VII—Sin and Free Will

We believe man is fallen from righteousness and, apart from the grace of our Lord Jesus Christ, is destitute of holiness and inclined to evil. Except a man be born again, he cannot see the Kingdom of God. In his own strength, without divine grace, man cannot do good works pleasing and acceptable to God. We believe, however, man influenced and empowered by the Holy Spirit is responsible in freedom to exercise his will for good.

### Article VIII—Reconciliation Through Christ

We believe God was in Christ reconciling the world to himself. The offering Christ freely made on the cross is the perfect and sufficient sacrifice for the sins of the whole world, redeeming man from all sin, so that no other satisfaction is required.

### Article IX—Justification and Regeneration

We believe we are never accounted righteous before God through our works or merit, but that penitent sinners are justified or accounted righteous before God only by faith in our Lord Jesus Christ.

We believe regeneration is the renewal of man in righteousness through Jesus Christ, by the power of the Holy Spirit, whereby we are made partakers of the divine nature and experience newness of life. By this new birth the believer becomes reconciled to God and is enabled to serve him with the will and the affections.

We believe, although we have experienced regeneration, it is possible to depart from grace and fall into sin; and we may even then, by the grace of God, be renewed in righteousness.

### Article X—Good Works

We believe good works are the necessary fruits of faith and follow regeneration but they do not have the virtue to remove our sins or to avert divine judgment. We believe good works, pleasing and acceptable to God in Christ, spring from a true and living faith, for through and by them faith is made evident.

### Article XI—Sanctification and Christian Perfection

We believe sanctification is the work of God's grace through the Word and the Spirit, by which those who have been born again are cleansed from sin in their thoughts, words and acts, and are enabled to live in accordance with God's will, and to strive for holiness without which no one will see the Lord.

Entire sanctification is a state of perfect love, righteousness and true holiness which every regenerate believer may obtain by being delivered from the power of sin, by loving God with all the heart, soul, mind and strength, and by loving one's neighbor as one's self.

Through faith in Jesus Christ this gracious gift may be received in this life both gradually and instantaneously, and should be sought earnestly by every child of God.

We believe this experience does not deliver us from the infirmities, ignorance, and mistakes common to man, nor from the possibilities of further sin. The Christian must continue on guard against spiritual pride and seek to gain victory over every temptation to sin. He must respond wholly to the will of God so that sin will lose its power over him; and the world, the flesh, and the devil are put under his feet. Thus he rules over these enemies with watchfulness through the power of the Holy Spirit.

### Article XII—The Judgment and the Future State

We believe all men stand under the righteous judgment of Jesus Christ, both now and in the last day. We believe in the resurrection of the dead; the righteous to life eternal and the wicked to endless condemnation.

### Article XIII—Public Worship

We believe divine worship is the duty and privilege of man who, in the presence of God, bows in adoration, humility and dedication. We believe divine worship is essential to the life of the Church, and that the assembling of the people of God for such worship is necessary to Christian fellowship and spiritual growth.

We believe the order of public worship need not be the same in all places but may be modified by the church according to circumstances and the needs of men. It should be in a language and form understood by the people, consistent with the Holy Scriptures to the edification of all, and in accordance with the order and *Discipline* of the Church.

### Article XIV—The Lord's Day

We believe the Lord's Day is divinely ordained for private and public worship, for rest from unnecessary work, and should be devoted to spiritual improvement, Christian fellowship and service. It is commemorative of our Lord's resurrection and is an emblem of our eternal rest. It is essential to the permanence and growth of the Christian Church, and important to the welfare of the civil community.

## Article XV—The Christian and Property

We believe God is the owner of all things and that the individual holding of property is lawful and is a sacred trust under God. Private property is to be used for the manifestation of Christian love and liberality, and to support the Church's mission in the world. All forms of property, whether private, corporate or public, are to be held in solemn trust and used responsibly for human good under the sovereignty of God.

## Article XVI—Civil Government

We believe civil government derives its just powers from the sovereign God. As Christians we recognize the governments under whose protection we reside and believe such governments should be based on, and be responsible for, the recognition of human rights under God. We believe war and bloodshed are contrary to the gospel and spirit of Christ. We believe it is the duty of Christian citizens to give moral strength and purpose to their respective governments through sober, righteous and godly living.

## THE STANDARD SERMONS OF WESLEY

[Bibliographical Note: The Wesleyan "standards" have been reprinted frequently. The critical edition of Wesley's *Sermons* is included in *The Works of John Wesley,* vols. 1–4 (Nashville: Abingdon Press, 1984–87).]

## THE EXPLANATORY NOTES UPON THE NEW TESTAMENT

[Bibliographical Note: *The Explanatory Notes Upon the New Testament* (1755) is currently in print (Schmul Publishing Company's 1975 edition) and is forthcoming as vols. 5–6 of *The Works of John Wesley.*]

## THE GENERAL RULES OF THE METHODIST CHURCH[7]

[Bibliographical Note: The General Rules are printed here in the text of 1808 (when the fifth Restrictive Rule took effect), as subsequently amended by constitutional actions in 1848 and 1868.]

---

7. Protected by Restrictive Rule 5 (¶ 19).

## The Nature, Design, and General Rules of Our United Societies

In the latter end of the year 1739 eight or ten persons came to Mr. Wesley, in London, who appeared to be deeply convinced of sin, and earnestly groaning for redemption. They desired, as did two or three more the next day, that he would spend some time with them in prayer, and advise them how to flee from the wrath to come, which they saw continually hanging over their heads. That he might have more time for this great work, he appointed a day when they might all come together, which from thenceforward they did every week, namely, on Thursday in the evening. To these, and as many more as desired to join with them (for their number increased daily), he gave those advices from time to time which he judged most needful for them, and they always concluded their meeting with prayer suited to their several necessities.

This was the rise of the **United Society,** first in Europe, and then in America. Such a society is no other than "a company of men having the *form* and seeking the *power* of godliness, united in order to pray together, to receive the word of exhortation, and to watch over one another in love, that they may help each other to work out their salvation."

That it may the more easily be discerned whether they are indeed working out their own salvation, each society is divided into smaller companies, called **classes,** according to their respective places of abode. There are about twelve persons in a class, one of whom is styled the **leader.** It is his duty:

1. To see each person in his class once a week at least, in order: (1) to inquire how their souls prosper; (2) to advise, reprove, comfort or exhort, as occasion may require; (3) to receive what they are willing to give toward the relief of the preachers, church, and poor.

2. To meet the ministers and the stewards of the society once a week, in order: (1) to inform the minister of any that are sick, or of any that walk disorderly and will not be reproved; (2) to pay the stewards what they have received of their several classes in the week preceding.

There is only one condition previously required of those who desire admission into these societies: "a desire to flee from the wrath to come, and to be saved from their sins." But wherever this is really fixed in the soul it will be shown by its fruits.

It is therefore expected of all who continue therein that they should continue to evidence their desire of salvation,

*First*: By doing no harm, by avoiding evil of every kind, especially that which is most generally practiced, such as:

The taking of the name of God in vain.

The profaning the day of the Lord, either by doing ordinary work therein or by buying or selling.

Drunkenness: buying or selling spirituous liquors, or drinking them, unless in cases of extreme necessity.

Slaveholding; buying or selling slaves.

Fighting, quarreling, brawling, brother going to law with brother; returning evil for evil, or railing for railing; the using many words in buying or selling.

The buying or selling goods that have not paid the duty.

The giving or taking things on usury—i.e., unlawful interest.

Uncharitable or unprofitable conversation; particularly speaking evil of magistrates or of ministers.

Doing to others as we would not they should do unto us.

Doing what we know is not for the glory of God, as:

The putting on of gold and costly apparel.

The taking such diversions as cannot be used in the name of the Lord Jesus.

The singing those songs, or reading those books, which do not tend to the knowledge or love of God.

Softness and needless self-indulgence.

Laying up treasure upon earth.

Borrowing without a probability of paying; or taking up goods without a probability of paying for them.

It is expected of all who continue in these societies that they should continue to evidence their desire of salvation,

*Secondly*: By doing good; by being in every kind merciful after their power; as they have opportunity, doing good of every possible sort, and, as far as possible, to all men:

To their bodies, of the ability which God giveth, by giving food to the hungry, by clothing the naked, by visiting or helping them that are sick or in prison.

To their souls, by instructing, reproving, or exhorting all we have any intercourse with; trampling under foot that enthusiastic doctrine that "we are not to do good unless *our hearts be free to it.*"

By doing good, especially to them that are of the household of faith or groaning so to be; employing them preferably to others; buying one of another, helping each other in business, and so much the more because the world will love its own and them only.

By all possible diligence and frugality, that the gospel be not blamed.

By running with patience the race which is set before them, denying themselves, and taking up their cross daily; submitting to bear the reproach of Christ, to be as the filth and offscouring of the world; and looking that men should say all manner of evil of them *falsely*, for the Lord's sake.

It is expected of all who desire to continue in these societies that they should continue to evidence their desire of salvation,

*Thirdly:* By attending upon all the ordinances of God; such are:

The public worship of God.

The ministry of the Word, either read or expounded.

The Supper of the Lord.

Family and private prayer.

Searching the Scriptures.

Fasting or abstinence.

These are the General Rules of our societies; all of which we are taught of God to observe, even in his written Word, which is the only rule, and the sufficient rule, both of our faith and practice. And all these we know his Spirit writes on truly awakened hearts. If there be any among us who observe them not, who habitually break any of them, let it be known unto them who watch over that soul as they who must give an account. We will admonish him of the error of his ways. We will bear with him for a season. But then, if he repent not, he hath no more place among us. We have delivered our own souls.

## ¶ 104. SECTION 4—OUR THEOLOGICAL TASK

Theology is our effort to reflect upon God's gracious action in our lives. In response to the love of Christ, we desire to be drawn into a deeper relationship with the "author and perfecter of our faith." Our theological explorations seek to give expression to the mysterious reality of God's presence, peace, and power in the world. By so doing, we attempt to articulate more clearly our understanding of the divine-human encounter and are thereby more fully prepared to participate in God's work in the world.

The theological task, though related to the Church's doctrinal expressions, serves a different function. Our doctrinal affirmations assist us in the discernment of Christian truth in ever-changing contexts. Our theological task includes the testing, renewal, elaboration, and application of our doctrinal perspective in carrying out our calling "to spread scriptural holiness over these lands."

While the Church considers its doctrinal affirmations a central feature of its identity and restricts official changes to a constitutional process, the Church encourages serious reflection across the theological spectrum.

As United Methodists, we are called to identify the needs both of individuals and of society and to address those needs out of the resources of Christian faith in a way that is clear, convincing, and effective. Theology serves the Church by interpreting the world's needs and challenges to the Church and by interpreting the gospel to the world.

## The Nature of Our Theological Task

**Our theological task is both critical and constructive.** It is *critical* in that we test various expressions of faith by asking: Are they true? Appropriate? Clear? Cogent? Credible? Are they based on love? Do they provide the Church and its members with a witness that is faithful to the gospel as reflected in our living heritage and that is authentic and convincing in the light of human experience and the present state of human knowledge?

Our theological task is *constructive* in that every generation must appropriate creatively the wisdom of the past and seek God in their midst in order to think afresh about God, revelation, sin, redemption, worship, the church, freedom, justice, moral responsibility, and other significant theological concerns. Our summons is to understand and receive the gospel promises in our troubled and uncertain times.

**Our theological task is both individual and communal.** It is a feature in the ministry of *individual* Christians. It requires the participation of all who are in our Church, lay and ordained, because the mission of the Church is to be carried out by everyone who is called to discipleship. To be persons of faith is to hunger to understand the truth given to us in Jesus Christ.

Theological inquiry is by no means a casual undertaking. It requires sustained disciplines of study, reflection, and prayer.

Yet the discernment of "plain truth for plain people" is not limited to theological specialists. Scholars have their role to play in assisting the people of God to fulfill this calling, but all Christians are called to theological reflection.

Our theological task is *communal*. It unfolds in conversations open to the experiences, insights, and traditions of all constituencies that make up United Methodism.

This dialogue belongs to the life of every congregation. It is fostered by laity and clergy, by the bishops, by the boards, agencies, and theological schools of the Church.

Conferences speak and act for United Methodists in their official decisions at appropriate levels. Our conciliar and representative forms of decision-making do not release United Methodists as individuals from the responsibility to develop sound theological judgment.

**Our theological task is contextual and incarnational.** It is grounded upon God's supreme mode of self-revelation—the incarnation in Jesus Christ. God's eternal Word comes to us in flesh and blood in a given time and place, and in full identification with humanity. Therefore, theological reflection is energized by our incarnational involvement in the daily life of the Church and the world, as we participate in God's liberating and saving action.

**Our theological task is essentially practical.** It informs the individual's daily decisions and serves the Church's life and work. While highly theoretical constructions of Christian thought make important contributions to theological understanding, we finally measure the truth of such statements in relation to their practical significance. Our interest is to incorporate the promises and demands of the gospel into our daily lives.

Theological inquiry can clarify our thinking about what we are to say and do. It presses us to pay attention to the world around us.

Realities of intense human suffering, threats to the survival of life, and challenges to human dignity confront us afresh with fundamental theological issues: the nature and purposes of God, the relations of human beings to one another, the nature of human freedom and responsibility, and the care and proper use of all creation.

## Theological Guidelines: Sources and Criteria

As United Methodists, we have an obligation to bear a faithful Christian witness to Jesus Christ, the living reality at the center of the Church's life and witness. To fulfill this obligation, we reflect critically on our biblical and theological inheritance, striving to express faithfully the witness we make in our own time.

Two considerations are central to this endeavor: the sources from which we derive our theological affirmations and the criteria by which we assess the adequacy of our understanding and witness.

Wesley believed that the living core of the Christian faith was revealed in Scripture, illumined by tradition, vivified in personal experience, and confirmed by reason.

Scripture is primary, revealing the Word of God "so far as it is necessary for our salvation." Therefore, our theological task, in both its critical and constructive aspects, focuses on disciplined study of the Bible.

To aid his study of the Bible and deepen his understanding of faith, Wesley drew on Christian tradition, in particular the Patristic writings, the ecumenical creeds, the teachings of the Reformers, and the literature of contemporary spirituality.

Thus, tradition provides both a source and a measure of authentic Christian witness, though its authority derives from its faithfulness to the biblical message.

The Christian witness, even when grounded in Scripture and mediated by tradition, is ineffectual unless understood and appropriated by the individual. To become our witness, it must make sense in terms of our own reason and experience.

For Wesley, a cogent account of the Christian faith required the use of reason, both to understand Scripture and to relate the biblical message to wider fields of knowledge. He looked for confirmations of the biblical witness in human experience, especially the experiences of regeneration and sanctification, but also in the "common sense" knowledge of everyday experience.

The interaction of these sources and criteria in Wesley's own theology furnishes a guide for our continuing theological task as United Methodists. In that task Scripture, as the constitutive witness to the wellsprings of our faith, occupies a place of primary authority among these theological sources.

In practice, theological reflection may also find its point of departure in tradition, experience, or rational analysis. What matters most is that all four guidelines be brought to bear in faithful, serious, theological consideration. Insights arising from serious study of the Scriptures and tradition enrich contemporary experience. Imaginative and critical thought enables us to understand better the Bible and our common Christian history.

## Scripture

United Methodists share with other Christians the conviction that Scripture is the primary source and criterion for Christian doctrine. Through Scripture the living Christ meets us in the experience of redeeming grace. We are convinced that Jesus Christ is the living Word of God in our midst whom we trust in life and death.

The biblical authors, illumined by the Holy Spirit, bear witness that in Christ the world is reconciled to God. The Bible bears authentic testimony to God's self-disclosure in the life, death, and resurrection of Jesus Christ as well as in God's work of creation, in the pilgrimage of Israel, and in the Holy Spirit's ongoing activity in human history.

As we open our minds and hearts to the Word of God through the words of human beings inspired by the Holy Spirit, faith is born and nourished, our understanding is deepened, and the possibilities for transforming the world become apparent to us.

The Bible is sacred canon for Christian people, formally acknowledged as such by historic ecumenical councils of the Church. Our doctrinal standards identify as canonical thirty-nine books of the Old Testament and the twenty-seven books of the New Testament.

Our standards affirm the Bible as the source of all that is "necessary" and "sufficient" unto salvation (Articles of Religion) and "is to be received through the Holy Spirit as the true rule and guide for faith and practice" (Confession of Faith).

We properly read Scripture within the believing community, informed by the tradition of that community. We interpret individual texts in light of their place in the Bible as a whole.

We are aided by scholarly inquiry and personal insight, under the guidance of the Holy Spirit. As we work with each text, we take into account what we have been able to learn about the original context and intention of that text. In this understanding we draw upon the careful historical, literary, and textual studies of recent years, which have enriched our understanding of the Bible.

Through this faithful reading of Scripture, we may come to know the truth of the biblical message in its bearing on our own lives and the life of the world. Thus, the Bible serves both as a source of our faith and as the basic criterion by which the truth and fidelity of any interpretation of faith is measured.

While we acknowledge the primacy of Scripture in theological reflection, our attempts to grasp its meaning always involve tradition, experience, and reason. Like Scripture, these may become creative vehicles of the Holy Spirit as they function within the Church. They quicken our faith, open our eyes to the wonder of God's love, and clarify our understanding.

The Wesleyan heritage, reflecting its origins in the catholic and reformed ethos of English Christianity, directs us to a self-conscious use of these three sources in interpreting Scripture and in formulating faith statements based on the biblical witness. These sources are, along with Scripture, indispensable to our theological task.

The close relationship of tradition, experience, and reason appears in the Bible itself. Scripture witnesses to a variety of diverse traditions, some of which reflect tensions in interpretation within the early Judeo-Christian heritage. However, these traditions are woven together in the Bible in a manner that expresses the fundamental unity of God's revelation as received and experienced by people in the diversity of their own lives.

The developing communities of faith judged them, therefore, to be an authoritative witness to that revelation. In recognizing the interrelationship and inseparability of the four basic resources for theological understanding, we are following a model that is present in the biblical text itself.

## Tradition

The theological task does not start anew in each age or each person. Christianity does not leap from New Testament times to the present as though nothing were to be learned from that great cloud of witnesses in between. For centuries Christians have sought to interpret the truth of the gospel for their time.

In these attempts, tradition, understood both in terms of process and form, has played an important role. The passing on and receiving of the gospel among persons, regions, and generations constitutes a dynamic element of Christian history. The formulations and practices that grew out of specific circumstances constitute the legacy of the corporate experience of earlier Christian communities.

These traditions are found in many cultures around the globe. But the history of Christianity includes a mixture of ignorance, misguided zeal, and sin. Scripture remains the norm by which all traditions are judged.

The story of the church reflects the most basic sense of tradition, the continuing activity of God's Spirit transforming human life. Tradition is the history of that continuing environment of grace in and by which all Christians live, God's self-giving love in Jesus Christ. As such, tradition transcends the story of particular traditions.

In this deeper sense of tradition, all Christians share a common history. Within that history, Christian tradition precedes Scripture, and yet Scripture comes to be the focal expression of the tradition. As United Methodists, we pursue our theological task in openness to the richness of both the form and power of tradition.

The multiplicity of traditions furnishes a richly varied source for theological reflection and construction. For United Methodists, certain strands of tradition have special importance as the historic foundation of our doctrinal heritage and the distinctive expressions of our communal existence.

We are now challenged by traditions from around the world that accent dimensions of Christian understanding that grow out of the sufferings and victories of the downtrodden. These traditions help us rediscover the biblical witness to God's special commitment to the poor, the disabled, the imprisoned, the oppressed, the outcast. In these persons we encounter the living presence of Jesus Christ.

These traditions underscore the equality of all persons in Jesus Christ. They display the capacity of the gospel to free us to embrace the diversity of human cultures and appreciate their values. They reinforce our traditional understanding of the inseparability of personal salvation and social justice. They deepen our commitment to global peace.

A critical appreciation of these traditions can compel us to think about God in new ways, enlarge our vision of shalom, and enhance our confidence in God's provident love.

Tradition acts as a measure of validity and propriety for a community's faith insofar as it represents a consensus of faith. The various traditions that presently make claims upon us may contain conflicting images and insights of truth and validity. We examine such conflicts in light of Scripture, reflecting critically upon the doctrinal stance of our Church.

It is by the discerning use of our standards and in openness to emerging forms of Christian identity that we attempt to maintain fidelity to the apostolic faith.

At the same time, we continue to draw on the broader Christian tradition as an expression of the history of divine grace within which Christians are able to recognize and welcome one another in love.

## Experience

In our theological task, we follow Wesley's practice of examining experience, both individual and corporate, for confirmations of the realities of God's grace attested in Scripture.

Our experience interacts with Scripture. We read Scripture in light of the conditions and events that help shape who we are, and we interpret our experience in terms of Scripture.

All religious experience affects all human experience; all human experience affects our understanding of religious experience.

On the personal level, experience is to the individual as tradition is to the church: It is the personal appropriation of God's forgiving and empowering grace. Experience authenticates in our own lives the truths revealed in Scripture and illumined in tradition, enabling us to claim the Christian witness as our own.

Wesley described faith and its assurance as "a sure trust and confidence" in the mercy of God through our Lord Jesus Christ, and a steadfast hope of all good things to be received at God's hand. Such assurance is God's gracious gift through the witness of the Holy Spirit.

This "new life in Christ" is what we as United Methodists mean when we speak of "Christian experience." Christian experience gives us new eyes to see the living truth in Scripture. It confirms the biblical message for our present. It illumines our understanding of God and creation and motivates us to make sensitive moral judgments.

Although profoundly personal, Christian experience is also corporate; our theological task is informed by the experience of the church and by the common experiences of all humanity. In our attempts to understand the biblical message, we recognize that God's gift of liberating love embraces the whole of creation.

Some facets of human experience tax our theological understanding. Many of God's people live in terror, hunger, loneliness, and degradation. Everyday experiences of birth and death, of growth and life in the created world, and an awareness of wider social relations also belong to serious theological reflection.

A new awareness of such experiences can inform our appropriation of scriptural truths and sharpen our appreciation of the good news of the kingdom of God.

As a source for theological reflection, experience, like tradition, is richly varied, challenging our efforts to put into words the totality of the promises of the gospel. We interpret experience in the light of scriptural norms, just as our experience informs our reading of the biblical message. In this respect, Scripture remains central in our efforts to be faithful in making our Christian witness.

### Reason

Although we recognize that God's revelation and our experiences of God's grace continually surpass the scope of human language and reason, we also believe that any disciplined theological work calls for the careful use of reason.

By reason we read and interpret Scripture.

By reason we determine whether our Christian witness is clear.

By reason we ask questions of faith and seek to understand God's action and will.

By reason we organize the understandings that compose our witness and render them internally coherent.

By reason we test the congruence of our witness to the biblical testimony and to the traditions that mediate that testimony to us.

By reason we relate our witness to the full range of human knowledge, experience, and service.

Since all truth is from God, efforts to discern the connections between revelation and reason, faith and science, grace and nature, are useful endeavors in developing credible and communicable doctrine. We seek nothing less than a total view of reality that is decisively informed by the promises and imperatives of the Christian gospel, though we know well that such an attempt will always be marred by the limits and distortions characteristic of human knowledge.

Nevertheless, by our quest for reasoned understandings of Christian faith we seek to grasp, express, and live out the gospel in a way that will commend itself to thoughtful persons who are seeking to know and follow God's ways.

In theological reflection, the resources of tradition, experience, and reason are integral to our study of Scripture without displacing Scripture's primacy for faith and practice. These four sources—each making distinctive contributions, yet all finally working together—guide our quest as United Methodists for a vital and appropriate Christian witness.

## The Present Challenge to Theology in the Church

In addition to historic tensions and conflicts that still require resolution, new issues continually arise that summon us to fresh theological inquiry. Daily we are presented with an array of concerns that challenge our proclamation of God's reign over all of human existence.

Of crucial importance are concerns generated by great human struggles for dignity, liberation, and fulfillment—aspirations that are inherent elements in God's design for creation. These concerns are borne by theologies that express the heart cries of the downtrodden and the aroused indignation of the compassionate.

The perils of nuclear destruction, terrorism, war, poverty, violence, and injustice confront us. Injustices linked to race, gender, class, and age are widespread in our times. Misuse of natural resources and disregard for the fragile balances in our environment contradict our calling to care for God's creation. Secularism pervades high-technology civilizations, hindering human awareness of the spiritual depths of existence.

We seek an authentic Christian response to these realities that the healing and redeeming work of God might be present in our words and deeds. Too often, theology is used to support practices that are unjust. We look for answers that are in harmony with the gospel and do not claim exemption from critical assessment.

A rich quality of our Church, especially as it has developed in the last century, is its global character. We are a Church with a distinctive theological heritage, but that heritage is lived out in a global community, resulting in understandings of our faith enriched by indigenous experiences and manners of expression.

We affirm the contributions that United Methodists of varying ethnic, language, cultural, and national groups make to one another and to our Church as a whole. We celebrate our shared commitment to clear theological understanding and vital missional expression.

United Methodists as a diverse people continue to strive for consensus in understanding the gospel. In our diversity, we are held together by a shared inheritance and a common desire to participate in the creative and redemptive activity of God.

Our task is to articulate our vision in a way that will draw us together as a people in mission.

In the name of Jesus Christ we are called to work within our diversity while exercising patience and forbearance with one another. Such patience stems neither from indifference toward truth nor from an indulgent tolerance of error but from an awareness that we know only in part and that none of us is able to search the mysteries of God except by the Spirit of God. We proceed with our theological task, trusting that the Spirit will grant us wisdom to continue our journey with the whole people of God.

## Ecumenical Commitment

Christian unity is founded on the theological understanding that through faith in Jesus Christ we are made members-in-common of the one body of Christ. Christian unity is not an option; it is a gift to be received and expressed.

United Methodists respond to the theological, biblical, and practical mandates for Christian unity by firmly committing ourselves to the cause of Christian unity at local, national, and world levels. We invest ourselves in many ways by which mutual recognition of churches, of members, and of ministries may lead us to sharing in Holy Communion with all of God's people.

Knowing that denominational loyalty is always subsumed in our life in the church of Jesus Christ, we welcome and celebrate the rich experience of United Methodist leadership in church councils and consultations, in multilateral and bilateral dialogues, as well as in other forms of ecumenical convergence that have led to the healing of churches and nations.

We see the Holy Spirit at work in making the unity among us more visible.

Concurrently, we have entered into serious interfaith encounters and explorations between Christians and adherents of other living faiths of the world. Scripture calls us to be both neighbors and witnesses to all peoples. Such encounters require us to reflect anew on our faith and to seek guidance for our witness among neighbors of other faiths. We then rediscover that the God who has acted in Jesus Christ for the salvation of the whole world is also the Creator of all humankind, the One who is "above all and through all and in all" (Ephesians 4:6).

As people bound together on one planet, we see the need for a self-critical view of our own tradition and accurate appreciation of other traditions. In these encounters, our aim is not to reduce doctrinal differences to some lowest common denominator of religious agreement, but to raise all such relationships to the highest possible level of human fellowship and understanding.

We labor together with the help of God toward the salvation, health, and peace of all people. In respectful conversations and in practical cooperation, we confess our Christian faith and strive to display the manner in which Jesus Christ is the life and hope of the world.

## Conclusion

Doctrine arises out of the life of the Church—its faith, its worship, its discipline, its conflicts, its challenges from the world it would serve.

Evangelism, nurture, and mission require a constant effort to integrate authentic experience, rational thought, and purposeful action with theological integrity.

A convincing witness to our Lord and Savior Jesus Christ can contribute to the renewal of our faith, bring persons to that faith, and strengthen the Church as an agent of healing and reconciliation.

This witness, however, cannot fully describe or encompass the mystery of God. Though we experience the wonder of God's grace at work with us and among us, and though we know the joy of the present signs of God's kingdom, each new step makes us more aware of the ultimate mystery of God, from which arises a heart of wonder and an attitude of humility. Yet we trust that we can know more fully what is essential for our participation in God's saving work in the world, and we are confident in the ultimate unfolding of God's justice and mercy.

In this spirit we take up our theological task. We endeavor through the power of the Holy Spirit to understand the love of God given in Jesus Christ. We seek to spread this love abroad. As we see more clearly who we have been, as we understand more fully the needs of the world, as we draw more effectively upon our theological heritage, we will become better equipped to fulfill our calling as the people of God.

Now to God
who by the power at work within us
is able to do far more abundantly
than all that we ask or think,
to God be glory in the church
and in Christ Jesus to all generations,
for ever and ever. Amen.
—Ephesians 3:20-21 (based on RSV)

## Part III

# THE MINISTRY OF ALL CHRISTIANS

## THE MISSION AND MINISTRY OF THE CHURCH

### Section I. The Churches

¶ **120.** *The Mission*—The mission of the Church is to make disciples of Jesus Christ. Local churches provide the most significant arena through which disciple-making occurs.

¶ **121.** *Rationale for Our Mission*—The mission of the Church is to make disciples of Jesus Christ by proclaiming the good news of God's grace and thus seeking the fulfillment of God's reign and realm in the world. The fulfillment of God's reign and realm in the world is the vision Scripture holds before us. The United Methodist Church affirms that Jesus Christ is the Son of God, the Savior of the world, and the Lord of all. We respect persons of all religious faiths and we defend religious freedom for all persons. Jesus' words in Matthew 28:19–20 provide the Church with our mission: "Go therefore and make disciples of all nations, baptizing them in the name of the Father and of the Son and of the Holy Spirit, and teaching them to obey everything that I have commanded you."

This mission is our grace-filled response to the Reign of God in the world announced by Jesus. God's grace is active everywhere, at all times, carrying out this purpose as revealed in the Bible. It is *expressed* in God's covenant with Abraham and Sarah, in the Exodus of Israel from Egypt, and in the ministry of the prophets. It is fully *embodied* in the life, death, and resurrection of Jesus Christ. It is *experienced* in the ongoing creation of a new people by the Holy Spirit.

John Wesley, Phillip Otterbein, Jacob Albright, and our other spiritual forebears understood this mission in this way. Whenever United Methodism has had a clear sense of mission, God has used our Church to save persons, heal relationships, transform social structures, and spread scriptural holiness, thereby changing the world. In order to be truly alive, we embrace Jesus' mandate to make disciples of all peoples.

¶ 122. *The Process for Carrying Out Our Mission*—We make disciples as we:

—proclaim the gospel, seek, welcome and gather persons into the body of Christ;

—lead persons to commit their lives to God through baptism and profession of faith in Jesus Christ;

—nurture persons in Christian living through worship, the sacraments, spiritual disciplines, and other means of grace, such as Wesley's Christian conferencing;

—send persons into the world to live lovingly and justly as servants of Christ by healing the sick, feeding the hungry, caring for the stranger, freeing the oppressed, and working to develop social structures that are consistent with the gospel; and

—continue the mission of seeking, welcoming and gathering persons into the community of the body of Christ.

¶ 123. *The Global Nature of Our Mission*—The Church seeks to fulfill its global mission through the Spirit-given servant ministries of all Christians, both lay and clergy. Faithfulness and effectiveness demand that all ministries in the Church be shaped by the mission of making disciples of Jesus Christ.

¶ 124. *Our Mission in the World*—God's self-revelation in the life, death, and resurrection of Jesus Christ summons the church to ministry in the world through witness by word and deed in light of the church's mission. The visible church of Christ as a faithful community of persons affirms the worth of all humanity and the value of interrelationship in all of God's creation.

In the midst of a sinful world, through the grace of God, we are brought to repentance and faith in Jesus Christ. We become aware of the presence and life-giving power of God's Holy Spirit. We live in confident expectation of the ultimate fulfillment of God's purpose.

We are called together for worship and fellowship and for the upbuilding of the Christian community. We advocate and work for the unity of the Christian church. We call all persons into discipleship under the Lordship of Jesus Christ.

As servants of Christ we are sent into the world to engage in the struggle for justice and reconciliation. We seek to reveal the love of God for men, women, and children of all ethnic, racial, cultural, and national backgrounds and to demonstrate the healing power of the gospel with those who suffer.

## Section II. The Ministry of All Christians

¶ **125.** *The Heart of Christian Ministry*—The heart of Christian ministry is Christ's ministry of outreaching love. Christian ministry is the expression of the mind and mission of Christ by a community of Christians that demonstrates a common life of gratitude and devotion, witness and service, celebration and discipleship. All Christians are called through their baptism to this ministry of servanthood in the world to the glory of God and for human fulfillment. The forms of this ministry are diverse in locale, in interest, and in denominational accent, yet always catholic in spirit and outreach.

¶ **126.** *The Ministry of the Community*—The church as the community of the new covenant has participated in Christ's ministry of grace across the years and around the world. It stretches out to human needs wherever love and service may convey God's love and ours. The outreach of such ministries knows no limits. Beyond the diverse forms of ministry is this ultimate concern: that all persons will be brought into a saving relationship with God through Jesus Christ and be renewed after the image of their creator (Colossians 3:10). This means that all Christians are called to minister wherever Christ would have them serve and witness in deeds and words that heal and free.

¶ **127.** *Ministry as Gift and Task*—This ministry of all Christians in Christ's name and spirit is both a gift and a task. The gift is God's unmerited grace; the task is unstinting service. Entrance into the church is acknowledged in baptism and may include persons of all ages. In this sacrament the church claims God's promise, the seal of the Spirit (Ephesians 1:13). Baptism is followed by nurture and the consequent awareness by the baptized of the claim to ministry in Christ placed upon their lives by the church. Such a ministry is ratified in confirmation, where the pledges of baptism are accepted and renewed for life and mission. Entrance into and acceptance of ministry begin in a local church, but the impulse to minister always moves one beyond the congregation toward the whole human community. God's gifts are richly diverse for a variety of services; yet all have dignity and worth.

¶ **128.** *Faithful Ministry*—The people of God, who are the church made visible in the world, must convince the world of the reality of the gospel or leave it unconvinced. There can be no evasion or delegation of this responsibility; the church is either faithful as a witnessing and serving community, or it loses its vitality and its impact on an unbelieving world.

¶ **129.** *The Unity of Ministry in Christ*—There is but one ministry in Christ, but there are diverse gifts and evidences of God's grace in the body of Christ (Ephesians 4:4-16). The ministry of all Christians is complementary. No ministry is subservient to another. All United Methodists are summoned and sent by Christ to live and work together in mutual interdependence and to be guided by the Spirit into the truth that frees and the love that reconciles.

¶ **130.** *The Journey of a Connectional People*—Connectionalism in the United Methodist tradition is multi-leveled, global in scope, and local in thrust. Our connectionalism is not merely a linking of one charge conference to another. It is rather a vital web of interactive relationships.

We are connected by sharing a common tradition of faith, including our Doctrinal Standards and General Rules (¶ 103); by sharing together a constitutional polity, including a leadership of general superintendency; by sharing a common mission, which we seek to carry out by working together in and through conferences that reflect the inclusive and missional character of our fellowship; by sharing a common ethos that characterizes our distinctive way of doing things.

## Section III. Servant Ministry and Servant Leadership

¶ **131.** *Mission as Active Expectancy*—The ministry of all Christians consists of service for the mission of God in the world. The mission of God is best expressed in the prayer that Jesus taught his first disciples: Thy kingdom come; thy will be done, on earth as in heaven. All Christians, therefore, are to live in active expectancy: faithful in service of God and their neighbor; faithful in waiting for the fulfillment of God's universal love, justice, and peace on earth as in heaven.

Pending this time of fulfillment, the ministry of all Christians is shaped by the teachings of Jesus. The handing on of these teachings is entrusted to leaders who are gifted and called by God to appointed offices in the church: some apostles, some prophets, some evangelists, some pastors and teachers, to equip the saints for the work of ministry, for building up the body of Christ (Ephesians 4:11-12). For these persons to lead the church effectively, they must embody the teachings of Jesus in servant ministries and servant leadership. Through these ministries and leadership, congregations of the church are faithfully engaged in the forming of Christian disciples and vitally involved in the mission of God in the world.

¶ **132.** *Calling and Gifts of Leadership*—The United Methodist Church has traditionally recognized these gifts and callings in the ordained offices of elder and deacon. The United Methodist tradition has recognized that laypersons as well as ordained persons are gifted and called by God to lead the Church. The servant leadership of these persons is essential to the mission and ministry of congregations. They help to form Christian disciples in covenant community within the local congregation through spiritual formation and guidance for Christian living in the world.

## Section IV. Servant Ministry

¶ **133.** *Christian Discipleship*—The ministry of all Christians consists of privilege and obligation. The privilege is a relationship with God that is deeply spiritual. The obligation is to respond to God's call to holy living in the world. In the United Methodist tradition these two dimensions of Christian discipleship are wholly interdependent.

¶ **134.** *Our Relationship with God: Privilege*—Christians experience growth and transition in their spiritual life just as in their physical and emotional lives. While this growth is always a work of grace, it does not occur uniformly. Spiritual growth in Christ is a dynamic process marked by awakening, birth, growth, and maturation. This process requires careful and intentional nurture for the disciple to reach perfection in the Christian life. There are stages of spiritual growth and transition: Christian beginnings; Christian birth; Christian growth; and Christian maturity. These require careful and intentional nurture for the disciple to come to maturity in the Christian life and to engage fully in the ministry of all Christians.

¶ **135.** *Our Relationship with Christ in the World: Obligation*—The ministry of all Christians in the United Methodist tradition has always been energized by deep religious experience, with emphasis on how ministry relates to our obligation to Jesus Christ. The early Methodists developed a way of life that fostered reliability, and their methodical discipleship is best expressed in the General Rules that John Wesley first published in 1743, which remain in the United Methodist *Book of Discipline,* pages 71–74.

### Section V. Servant Leadership

¶ **136.** *Leadership Privileges and Responsibilities*—Within The United Methodist Church, there are those called to servant leadership, lay and ordained. Such callings are evidenced by special gifts, evidence of God's grace, and promise of usefulness. God's call to servant leadership is inward as it comes to the individual and outward through the discernment and validation of the Church. The privilege of servant leadership in the Church is the call to share in the preparation of congregations and the whole Church for the mission of God in the world. The obligation of servant leadership is the forming of Christian disciples in the covenant community of the congregation. This involves discerning and nurturing the spiritual relationship with God that is the privilege of all servant ministers. It also involves instructing and guiding Christian disciples in their witness to Jesus Christ in the world through acts of worship, devotion, compassion, and justice under the guidance of the Holy Spirit. John Wesley described this as "watching over one another in love."

¶ **137.** *Ordained Ministry*—Ordained ministers are called by God to a lifetime of servant leadership in specialized ministries among the people of God. Ordained ministers are called to interpret to the Church the needs, concerns, and hopes of the world and the promise of God for creation. Within these specialized ministries, deacons are called to ministries of Word and Service, and elders are called to ministries of Service, Word, Sacrament, and Order (¶ 323). Through these distinctive functions ordained ministers devote themselves wholly to the work of the Church and to the upbuilding of the ministry of all Christians. They do this through the careful study of Scripture and its faithful interpretation; through effective proclamation of the gospel and responsible administration of the sacraments; through diligent pastoral leadership of their congregations for fruitful discipleship;

and by following the guidance of the Holy Spirit in witnessing beyond the congregation in the local community and to the ends of the earth. The ordained ministry is defined by its faithful commitment to servant leadership following the example of Jesus Christ, by its passion for the hallowing of life, and by its concern to link all local ministries with the widest boundaries of the Christian community.

## Section VI. Called to Inclusiveness

¶ 138. We recognize that God made all creation and saw that it was good. As a diverse people of God who bring special gifts and evidences of God's grace to the unity of the Church and to society, we are called to be faithful to the example of Jesus' ministry to all persons.

Inclusiveness means openness, acceptance, and support that enables all persons to participate in the life of the Church, the community, and the world. Thus, inclusiveness denies every semblance of discrimination.

The mark of an inclusive society is one in which all persons are open, welcoming, fully accepting, and supporting of all other persons, enabling them to participate fully in the life of the church, the community, and the world. A further mark of inclusiveness is the setting of church activities in facilities accessible to persons with disabilities.

In The United Methodist Church inclusiveness means the freedom for the total involvement of all persons who meet the requirements of The United Methodist *Book of Discipline* in the membership and leadership of the Church at any level and in every place. In the spirit of this declaration, United Methodist seminaries will make all efforts to meet Americans with Disabilities (ADA) accessibility standards by the year 2011. Exemptions for historical or existing buildings are not allowed under this requirement.

## Section VII. The Fulfillment of Ministry Through The United Methodist Church

¶ 139. *The Church*—Affirming the spiritual dimensions of the ministry of all Christians, as proclaimed in ¶¶ 120–141 of this *Book of Discipline*, it is recognized that this ministry exists in the secular world and that civil authorities may seek legal definition predicated on the nature of The United Methodist Church in seeking fulfillment of this ministry. Accordingly, it is appropriate that the meaning of "The United Methodist Church," "the general Church," "the entire Church," and "the Church" as used in the *Book of Discipline* should now be stated consistently with the traditional self-understanding of United Methodists as to the meaning of these words.

These terms refer to the overall denomination and connectional relation and identity of its many local churches, the various conferences and their respective councils, boards, and agencies, and other Church units, which collectively constitute the religious system known as United Methodism. Under the Constitution and disciplinary procedures set forth in this *Book of Discipline*, "The United Methodist Church" as a denominational whole is not an entity, nor does it possess legal capacities and attributes. It does not and cannot hold title to property, nor does it have any officer, agent, employee, office, or location. Conferences, councils, boards, agencies, local churches, and other units bearing the name "United Methodist" are, for the most part, legal entities capable of suing and being sued and possessed of legal capacities.

¶ **140.** *Definition of* Clergy—*Clergy* in The United Methodist Church are individuals who serve as commissioned ministers, deacons, elders, and local pastors under appointment of a bishop (full- and part-time), who hold membership in an annual conference, and who are commissioned, ordained, or licensed.

¶ **141.** *Employment Status of Clergy*—Ministry in the Christian church is derived from the ministry of Christ (¶ 301). Jesus makes it clear to us that he is a shepherd and not a hireling (John 10:11-15). Similarly, United Methodist clergy appointed to local churches are not employees of the local church or the annual conference. It is recognized that for certain limited purposes such as taxation, benefits, and insurance, governments and other entities may classify clergy as employees. Such classifications are not to be construed as affecting or defining United Methodist polity, including the historic covenants that bind annual conferences, clergy, and congregations, episcopal appointive powers and procedures, or other principles set forth in the Constitution or the *Book of Discipline* (*see e.g.*, ¶¶ 301; 319–320; 324–325; 329; 331). In addition, any such classifications should be accepted, if at all, only for limited purposes, as set forth above, and with the full recognition and acknowledgment that it is the responsibility of the clergy to be God's servants.

## Part IV
# SOCIAL PRINCIPLES

### PREFACE

The United Methodist Church has a long history of concern for social justice. Its members have often taken forthright positions on controversial issues involving Christian principles. Early Methodists expressed their opposition to the slave trade, to smuggling, and to the cruel treatment of prisoners.

A social creed was adopted by The Methodist Episcopal Church (North) in 1908. Within the next decade similar statements were adopted by The Methodist Episcopal Church, South, and by The Methodist Protestant Church. The Evangelical United Brethren Church adopted a statement of social principles in 1946 at the time of the uniting of the United Brethren and The Evangelical Church. In 1972, four years after the uniting in 1968 of The Methodist Church and The Evangelical United Brethren Church, the General Conference of The United Methodist Church adopted a new statement of Social Principles, which was revised in 1976 (and by each successive General Conference).

The Social Principles are a prayerful and thoughtful effort on the part of the General Conference to speak to the human issues in the contemporary world from a sound biblical and theological foundation as historically demonstrated in United Methodist traditions. They are intended to be instructive and persuasive in the best of the prophetic spirit. The Social Principles are a call to all members of The United Methodist Church to a prayerful, studied dialogue of faith and practice. (*See* ¶ 509.)

## PREAMBLE

We, the people called United Methodists, affirm our faith in God our Creator and Father, in Jesus Christ our Savior, and in the Holy Spirit, our Guide and Guard.

We acknowledge our complete dependence upon God in birth, in life, in death, and in life eternal. Secure in God's love, we affirm the goodness of life and confess our many sins against God's will for us as we find it in Jesus Christ. We have not always been faithful stewards of all that has been committed to us by God the Creator. We have been reluctant followers of Jesus Christ in his mission to bring all persons into a community of love. Though called by the Holy Spirit to become new creatures in Christ, we have resisted the further call to become the people of God in our dealings with each other and the earth on which we live.

Grateful for God's forgiving love, in which we live and by which we are judged, and affirming our belief in the inestimable worth of each individual, we renew our commitment to become faithful witnesses to the gospel, not alone to the ends of earth, but also to the depths of our common life and work.

## ¶ 160.　　I. THE NATURAL WORLD

All creation is the Lord's, and we are responsible for the ways in which we use and abuse it. Water, air, soil, minerals, energy resources, plants, animal life, and space are to be valued and conserved because they are God's creation and not solely because they are useful to human beings. God has granted us stewardship of creation. We should meet these stewardship duties through acts of loving care and respect. Economic, political, social, and technological developments have increased our human numbers, and lengthened and enriched our lives. However, these developments have led to regional defoliation, dramatic extinction of species, massive human suffering, overpopulation, and misuse and overconsumption of natural and nonrenewable resources, particularly by industrialized societies. This continued course of action jeopardizes the natural heritage that God has entrusted to all generations. Therefore, let us recognize the responsibility of the church and its members to place a high priority on changes in economic, political, social, and technological lifestyles to support a more ecologically equitable and sustainable world leading to a higher quality of life for all of God's creation.

A) *Water, Air, Soil, Minerals, Plants*—We support and encourage social policies that serve to reduce and control the creation of industrial byproducts and waste; facilitate the safe processing and disposal of toxic and nuclear waste and move toward the elimination of both; encourage reduction of municipal waste; provide for appropriate recycling and disposal of municipal waste; and assist the cleanup of polluted air, water, and soil. We call for the preservation of old-growth forests and other irreplaceable natural treasures, as well as preservation of endangered plant species. We support measures designed to maintain and restore natural ecosystems. We support policies that develop alternatives to chemicals used for growing, processing, and preserving food, and we strongly urge adequate research into their effects upon God's creation prior to utilization. We urge development of international agreements concerning equitable utilization of the world's resources for human benefit so long as the integrity of the earth is maintained.

B) *Energy Resources Utilization*—Affirming the inherent value of nonhuman creation, we support and encourage social policies that are directed toward rational and restrained transformation of parts of the nonhuman world into energy for human usage and that de-emphasize or eliminate energy-producing technologies that endanger the health, the safety, and even the existence of the present and future human and nonhuman creation. Further, we urge wholehearted support of the conservation of energy and responsible development of all energy resources, with special concern for the development of renewable energy sources, that the goodness of the earth may be affirmed.

C) *Animal Life*—We support regulations that protect the life and health of animals, including those ensuring the humane treatment of pets and other domestic animals, animals used in research, and the painless slaughtering of meat animals, fish, and fowl. We encourage the preservation of all animal species including those threatened with extinction.

D) *Space*—The universe, known and unknown, is the creation of God and is due the respect we are called to give the earth.

E) *Science and Technology*—We recognize science as a legitimate interpretation of God's natural world. We affirm the validity of the claims of science in describing the natural world, although we preclude science from making authoritative claims about theological issues. We recognize technology as a legitimate use of God's natural world when such use enhances human life and enables all of God's children to develop their God-given creative potential without violating our ethical convictions about the relationship of humanity to the natural world.

In acknowledging the important roles of science and technology, however, we also believe that theological understandings of human experience are crucial to a full understanding of the place of humanity in the universe. Science and theology are complementary rather than mutually incompatible. We therefore encourage dialogue between the scientific and theological communities and seek the kind of participation that will enable humanity to sustain life on earth and, by God's grace, increase the quality of our common lives together.

*F) Food Safety*—We support policies that protect the food supply and that ensure the public's right to know the content of the foods they are eating. We call for rigorous inspections and controls on the biological safety of all foodstuffs intended for human consumption. We urge independent testing for chemical residues in food, and the removal from the market of foods contaminated with potentially hazardous levels of pesticides, herbicides, or fungicides; drug residues from animal antibiotics, steroids, or hormones; contaminants due to pollution that are carried by air, soil, or water from incinerator plants or other industrial operations. We call for clear labeling of all processed or altered foods, with premarket safety testing required. We oppose weakening the standards for organic foods. We call for policies that encourage and support a gradual transition to sustainable and organic agriculture.

## ¶ 161.　　　II. THE NURTURING COMMUNITY

The community provides the potential for nurturing human beings into the fullness of their humanity. We believe we have a responsibility to innovate, sponsor, and evaluate new forms of community that will encourage development of the fullest potential in individuals. Primary for us is the gospel understanding that all persons are important—because they are human beings created by God and loved through and by Jesus Christ and not because they have merited significance. We therefore support social climates in which human communities are maintained and strengthened for the sake of all persons and their growth. We also encourage all individuals to be sensitive to others by using appropriate language when referring to all persons. Language of a derogatory nature (with regard to race, nationality, ethnic background, gender, sexuality, and physical differences) does not reflect value for one another and contradicts the gospel of Jesus Christ.

*A) The Family*—We believe the family to be the basic human community through which persons are nurtured and sustained in mutual love, responsibility, respect, and fidelity. We understand the family as encompassing a wider range of options than that of the two-generational unit of parents and children (the nuclear family), including the extended family, families with adopted children, single parents, stepfamilies, and couples without children. We affirm shared responsibility for parenting by men and women and encourage social, economic, and religious efforts to maintain and strengthen relationships within families in order that every member may be assisted toward complete personhood.

*B) Other Christian Communities*—We further recognize the movement to find new patterns of Christian nurturing communities such as Koinonia Farms, certain monastic and other religious orders, and some types of corporate church life. We urge the Church to seek ways of understanding the needs and concerns of such Christian groups and to find ways of ministering to them and through them.

*C) Marriage*—We affirm the sanctity of the marriage covenant that is expressed in love, mutual support, personal commitment, and shared fidelity between a man and a woman. We believe that God's blessing rests upon such marriage, whether or not there are children of the union. We reject social norms that assume different standards for women than for men in marriage.

*D) Divorce*—When a married couple is estranged beyond reconciliation, even after thoughtful consideration and counsel, divorce is a regrettable alternative in the midst of brokenness. It is recommended that methods of mediation be used to minimize the adversarial nature and fault-finding that are often part of our current judicial processes.

Although divorce publicly declares that a marriage no longer exists, other covenantal relationships resulting from the marriage remain, such as the nurture and support of children and extended family ties. We urge respectful negotiations in deciding the custody of minor children and support the consideration of either or both parents for this responsibility in that custody not be reduced to financial support, control, or manipulation and retaliation. The welfare of each child is the most important consideration.

Divorce does not preclude a new marriage. We encourage an intentional commitment of the Church and society to minister compassionately to those in the process of divorce, as well as members of divorced and remarried families, in a community of faith where God's grace is shared by all.

*E) Single Persons*—We affirm the integrity of single persons, and we reject all social practices that discriminate or social attitudes that are prejudicial against persons because they are single.

*F) Women and Men*—We affirm with Scripture the common humanity of male and female, both having equal worth in the eyes of God. We reject the erroneous notion that one gender is superior to another, that one gender must strive against another, and that members of one gender may receive love, power, and esteem only at the expense of another. We especially reject the idea that God made individuals as incomplete fragments, made whole only in union with another. We call upon women and men alike to share power and control, to learn to give freely and to receive freely, to be complete and to respect the wholeness of others. We seek for every individual opportunities and freedom to love and be loved, to seek and receive justice, and to practice ethical self-determination. We understand our gender diversity to be a gift from God, intended to add to the rich variety of human experience and perspective; and we guard against attitudes and traditions that would use this good gift to leave members of one sex more vulnerable in relationships than members of another.

*G) Human Sexuality*—We recognize that sexuality is God's good gift to all persons. We believe persons may be fully human only when that gift is acknowledged and affirmed by themselves, the church, and society. We call all persons to the disciplined, responsible fulfillment of themselves, others, and society in the stewardship of this gift. We also recognize our limited understanding of this complex gift and encourage the medical, theological, and social science disciplines to combine in a determined effort to understand human sexuality more completely. We call the Church to take the leadership role in bringing together these disciplines to address this most complex issue. Further, within the context of our understanding of this gift of God, we recognize that God challenges us to find responsible, committed, and loving forms of expression.

Although all persons are sexual beings whether or not they are married, sexual relations are only clearly affirmed in the marriage bond. Sex may become exploitative within as well as outside marriage.

We reject all sexual expressions that damage or destroy the humanity God has given us as birthright, and we affirm only that sexual expression that enhances that same humanity. We believe that sexual relations where one or both partners are exploitative, abusive, or promiscuous are beyond the parameters of acceptable Christian behavior and are ultimately destructive to individuals, families, and the social order.

We deplore all forms of the commercialization and exploitation of sex, with their consequent cheapening and degradation of human personality. We call for strict global enforcement of laws prohibiting the sexual exploitation or use of children by adults and encourage efforts to hold perpetrators legally and financially responsible. We call for the establishment of adequate protective services, guidance, and counseling opportunities for children thus abused. We insist that all persons, regardless of age, gender, marital status, or sexual orientation, are entitled to have their human and civil rights ensured.

We recognize the continuing need for full, positive, age-appropriate and factual sex education opportunities for children, young people, and adults. The Church offers a unique opportunity to give quality guidance and education in this area.

Homosexual persons no less than heterosexual persons are individuals of sacred worth. All persons need the ministry and guidance of the church in their struggles for human fulfillment, as well as the spiritual and emotional care of a fellowship that enables reconciling relationships with God, with others, and with self. Although we do not condone the practice of homosexuality and consider this practice incompatible with Christian teaching, we affirm that God's grace is available to all. We implore families and churches not to reject or condemn their lesbian and gay members and friends. We commit ourselves to be in ministry for and with all persons.[1]

*H) Family Violence and Abuse*—We recognize that family violence and abuse in all its forms—verbal, psychological, physical, sexual—is detrimental to the covenant of the human community. We encourage the Church to provide a safe environment, counsel, and support for the victim. While we deplore the actions of the abuser, we affirm that person to be in need of God's redeeming love.

*I) Sexual Harassment*—We believe human sexuality is God's good gift. One abuse of this good gift is sexual harassment. We define sexual harassment as any unwanted sexual comment, advance or

---

1. *See* Judicial Council Decision 702.

demand, either verbal or physical, that is reasonably perceived by the recipient as demeaning, intimidating, or coercive. Sexual harassment must be understood as an exploitation of a power relationship rather than as an exclusively sexual issue. Sexual harassment includes, but is not limited to, the creation of a hostile or abusive working environment resulting from discrimination on the basis of gender.

Contrary to the nurturing community, sexual harassment creates improper, coercive, and abusive conditions wherever it occurs in society. Sexual harassment undermines the social goal of equal opportunity and the climate of mutual respect between men and women. Unwanted sexual attention is wrong and discriminatory. Sexual harassment interferes with the moral mission of the Church.

*J) Abortion*—The beginning of life and the ending of life are the God-given boundaries of human existence. While individuals have always had some degree of control over when they would die, they now have the awesome power to determine when and even whether new individuals will be born. Our belief in the sanctity of unborn human life makes us reluctant to approve abortion. But we are equally bound to respect the sacredness of the life and well-being of the mother, for whom devastating damage may result from an unacceptable pregnancy. In continuity with past Christian teaching, we recognize tragic conflicts of life with life that may justify abortion, and in such cases we support the legal option of abortion under proper medical procedures. We cannot affirm abortion as an acceptable means of birth control, and we unconditionally reject it as a means of gender selection. We oppose the use of late-term abortion known as dilation and extraction (partial-birth abortion) and call for the end of this practice except when the physical life of the mother is in danger and no other medical procedure is available, or in the case of severe fetal anomalies incompatible with life. We call all Christians to a searching and prayerful inquiry into the sorts of conditions that may warrant abortion. We commit our Church to continue to provide nurturing ministries to those who terminate a pregnancy, to those in the midst of a crisis pregnancy, and to those who give birth. Governmental laws and regulations do not provide all the guidance required by the informed Christian conscience. Therefore, a decision concerning abortion should be made only after thoughtful and prayerful consideration by the parties involved, with medical, pastoral, and other appropriate counsel.

*K) Adoption*—Children are a gift from God to be welcomed and received. We recognize that some circumstances of birth make the rearing of a child difficult. We affirm and support the birth parent(s) whose choice it is to allow the child to be adopted. We recognize the agony, strength, and courage of the birth parent(s) who choose(s) in hope, love, and prayer to offer the child for adoption. In addition, we affirm the receiving parent(s) desiring an adopted child. When circumstances warrant adoption, we support the use of proper legal procedures. We commend the birth parent(s), the receiving parent(s), and the child to the care of the Church, that grief might be shared, joy might be celebrated, and the child might be nurtured in a community of Christian love.

*L) Faithful Care of the Dying*—We applaud medical science for efforts to prevent disease and illness and for advances in treatment that extend the meaningful life of human beings. At the same time, care for the dying is part of our stewardship of the divine gift of life. The use of medical technologies to prolong terminal illnesses requires responsible judgment about when life-sustaining treatments truly support the goals of life, and when they have reached their limits. There is no moral or religious obligation to use these when they impose undue burdens or only extend the process of dying. Dying persons and their families thus have the liberty to discontinue treatments when they cease to be of benefit to the patient.

We recognize the agonizing personal and moral decisions faced by the dying, their physicians, their families, and their friends. We urge that decisions faced by the dying be made with thoughtful and prayerful consideration by the parties involved, with medical, pastoral, and other appropriate counsel. Even when one ceases to resist death, the church and society must continue to provide faithful care, including pain relief, companionship, support, and spiritual nurture for the dying person in the hard work of preparing for death.

*M) Suicide*—We believe that suicide is not the way a human life should end. The church has an obligation to see that all persons have access to needed pastoral and medical care and therapy in those circumstances that lead to loss of self-worth, suicidal despair, and/or the desire to seek physician-assisted suicide. We encourage the church to provide education to address the biblical, theological, social, and ethical issues related to suicide, including United Methodist theological seminary courses focusing on issues of suicide.

A Christian perspective on suicide begins with an affirmation of faith that nothing, including suicide, separates us from the love of

God (Romans 8:38-39). Therefore, we deplore the condemnation of people who take their own lives, and we consider unjust the stigma that so often falls on surviving family and friends.

We encourage pastors to address this issue through preaching and teaching. We urge pastors to provide pastoral care to attempters, survivors, and their families, and to those families who have lost loved ones to suicide, seeking always to remove the oppressive stigma around suicide. The Church does not endorse the enlistment of medical providers, who are charged to cure and to care, to assist people in taking their own lives.

## ¶ 162.          III. THE SOCIAL COMMUNITY

The rights and privileges a society bestows upon or withholds from those who comprise it indicate the relative esteem in which that society holds particular persons and groups of persons. We affirm all persons as equally valuable in the sight of God. We therefore work toward societies in which each person's value is recognized, maintained, and strengthened. We support the basic rights of all persons to equal access to housing, education, employment, medical care, legal redress for grievances, and physical protection. We deplore acts of hate or violence against groups or persons based on race, ethnicity, gender, sexual orientation, religious affiliation, or economic status.

*A) Rights of Racial and Ethnic Persons—Racism* is the combination of the power to dominate by one race over other races and a value system that assumes that the dominant race is innately superior to the others. Racism includes both personal and institutional racism. Personal racism is manifested through the individual expressions, attitudes, and/or behaviors that accept the assumptions of a racist value system and that maintain the benefits of this system. Institutional racism is the established social pattern that supports implicitly or explicitly the racist value system. Racism plagues and cripples our growth in Christ, inasmuch as it is antithetical to the gospel itself. White people are unfairly granted privileges and benefits that are denied to persons of color. Therefore, we recognize racism as sin and affirm the ultimate and temporal worth of all persons. We rejoice in the gifts that particular ethnic histories and cultures bring to our total life. We commend and encourage the self-awareness of all racial and ethnic groups and oppressed people that leads them to demand their just and equal rights as members of society. We assert the obligation of society and groups within the society to implement compensatory programs that redress long-standing, systemic social deprivation of racial and ethnic people. We further assert the right of members of racial and ethnic groups to equal opportunities in employment and promotion; to education and training of the highest quality; to nondiscrimination in voting, in access to public accommodations, and in housing purchase or rental; to credit, financial loans, venture capital, and insurance policies; and to positions of leadership and power in all elements of our life together. We support affirmative action as one method of addressing the inequalities and discriminatory practices within our Church and society.

B) *Rights of Religious Minorities*—Religious persecution has been common in the history of civilization. We urge policies and practices that ensure the right of every religious group to exercise its faith free from legal, political, or economic restrictions. We condemn all overt and covert forms of religious intolerance, being especially sensitive to their expression in media stereotyping. We assert the right of all religions and their adherents to freedom from legal, economic, and social discrimination.

C) *Rights of Children*—Once considered the property of their parents, children are now acknowledged to be full human beings in their own right, but beings to whom adults and society in general have special obligations. Thus, we support the development of school systems and innovative methods of education designed to assist every child toward complete fulfillment as an individual person of worth. All children have the right to quality education, including full sex education appropriate to their stage of development that utilizes the best educational techniques and insights. Christian parents and guardians and the Church have the responsibility to ensure that children receive sex education consistent with Christian morality, including faithfulness in marriage and abstinence in singleness. Moreover, children have the rights to food, shelter, clothing, health care, and emotional well-being as do adults, and these rights we affirm as theirs regardless of actions or inactions of their parents or guardians. In particular, children must be protected from economic, physical, emotional, and sexual exploitation and abuse.

D) *Rights of Young People*—Our society is characterized by a large population of young people who frequently find full participation in society difficult. Therefore, we urge development of policies that encourage inclusion of young people in decision-making processes and that eliminate discrimination and exploitation. Creative and appropriate employment opportunities should be legally and socially available for young people.

*E) Rights of the Aging*—In a society that places primary emphasis upon youth, those growing old in years are frequently isolated from the mainstream of social existence. We support social policies that integrate the aging into the life of the total community, including sufficient incomes, increased and nondiscriminatory employment opportunities, educational and service opportunities, and adequate medical care and housing within existing communities. We urge social policies and programs, with emphasis on the unique concerns of older women and ethnic persons, that ensure to the aging the respect and dignity that is their right as senior members of the human community. Further, we urge increased consideration for adequate pension systems by employers, with provisions for the surviving spouse.

*F) Rights of Women*—We affirm women and men to be equal in every aspect of their common life. We therefore urge that every effort be made to eliminate sex-role stereotypes in activity and portrayal of family life and in all aspects of voluntary and compensatory participation in the Church and society. We affirm the right of women to equal treatment in employment, responsibility, promotion, and compensation. We affirm the importance of women in decision-making positions at all levels of Church life and urge such bodies to guarantee their presence through policies of employment and recruitment. We support affirmative action as one method of addressing the inequalities and discriminatory practices within our Church and society. We urge employers of persons in dual career families, both in the Church and society, to apply proper consideration of both parties when relocation is considered.

*G) Rights of Persons with Disabilities*—We recognize and affirm the full humanity and personhood of all individuals with disabilities as full members of the family of God. We also affirm their rightful place in both the church and society. We affirm the responsibility of the Church and society to be in ministry with children, youth, and adults with mental, physical, developmental, and/or psychological disabilities whose particular needs in the areas of mobility, communication, intellectual comprehension, or personal relationships might make more challenging their participation or that of their families in the life of the Church and the community. We urge the Church and society to recognize and receive the gifts of persons with disabilities to enable them to be full participants in the community of faith. We call the Church and society to be sensitive to, and advocate for, programs of rehabilitation, services, employment, education, appropriate housing, and transportation. We call on the Church and society to protect the civil rights of persons with disabilities.

*H) Equal Rights Regardless of Sexual Orientation*—Certain basic human rights and civil liberties are due all persons. We are committed to supporting those rights and liberties for homosexual persons. We see a clear issue of simple justice in protecting their rightful claims where they have shared material resources, pensions, guardian relationships, mutual powers of attorney, and other such lawful claims typically attendant to contractual relationships that involve shared contributions, responsibilities, and liabilities, and equal protection before the law. Moreover, we support efforts to stop violence and other forms of coercion against gays and lesbians. We also commit ourselves to social witness against the coercion and marginalization of former homosexuals.

*I) Population*—Since the growing worldwide population is increasingly straining the world's supply of food, minerals, and water and sharpening international tensions, the reduction of the rate of consumption of resources by the affluent and the reduction of current world population growth rates have become imperative. People have the duty to consider the impact on the total world community of their decisions regarding childbearing and should have access to information and appropriate means to limit their fertility, including voluntary sterilization. We affirm that programs to achieve a stabilized population should be placed in a context of total economic and social development, including an equitable use and control of resources; improvement in the status of women in all cultures; a human level of economic security, health care, and literacy for all. We oppose any policy of forced abortion or forced sterilization.

*J) Alcohol and Other Drugs*—We affirm our long-standing support of abstinence from alcohol as a faithful witness to God's liberating and redeeming love for persons. We support abstinence from the use of any illegal drugs. Since the use of alcohol and illegal drugs is a major factor in crime, disease, death, and family dysfunction, we support educational programs encouraging abstinence from such use.

Millions of living human beings are testimony to the beneficial consequences of therapeutic drug use, and millions of others are testimony to the detrimental consequences of drug misuse. We encourage wise policies relating to the availability of potentially beneficial or potentially damaging prescription and over-the-counter drugs; we urge that complete information about their use and misuse be readily available to both doctor and patient. We support the strict administration of laws regulating the sale and distribution of all opiates. We support regulations that protect society from users of drugs of any kind where it can be shown that a clear and present social danger exists. Drug-dependent persons and their family members are individuals of infinite human worth deserving of treatment, rehabilitation, and ongoing life-changing recovery. Misuse should be viewed as a symptom of underlying disorders for which remedies should be sought. We commit ourselves to assisting those who have become dependent, and their families, in finding freedom through Jesus Christ and in finding good opportunities for treatment, for ongoing counseling, and for reintegration into society.

K) Tobacco—We affirm our historic tradition of high standards of personal discipline and social responsibility. In light of the overwhelming evidence that tobacco smoking and the use of smokeless tobacco are hazardous to the health of persons of all ages, we recommend total abstinence from the use of tobacco. We urge that our educational and communication resources be utilized to support and encourage such abstinence. Further, we recognize the harmful effects of passive smoke and support the restriction of smoking in public areas and workplaces.

L) Medical Experimentation—Physical and mental health has been greatly enhanced through discoveries by medical science. It is imperative, however, that governments and the medical profession carefully enforce the requirements of the prevailing medical research standard, maintaining rigid controls in testing new technologies and drugs utilizing human beings. The standard requires that those engaged in research shall use human beings as research subjects only after obtaining full, rational, and uncoerced consent.

M) Genetic Technology—The responsibility of humankind to God's creation challenges us to deal carefully with the possibilities of genetic research and technology. We welcome the use of genetic technology for meeting fundamental human needs for health, a safe environment, and an adequate food supply. We oppose the cloning of humans and the genetic manipulation of the gender of an unborn child.

Because of the effects of genetic technologies on all life, we call for effective guidelines and public accountability to safeguard against any action that might lead to abuse of these technologies, including political or military ends. We recognize that cautious, well-intended use of genetic technologies may sometimes lead to unanticipated harmful consequences.

Human gene therapies that produce changes that cannot be passed to offspring (somatic therapy) should be limited to the alleviation of suffering caused by disease. Genetic therapies for eugenic choices or that produce waste embryos are deplored. Genetic data of individuals and their families should be kept secret and held in strict confidence unless confidentiality is waived by the individual or by his or her family, or unless the collection and use of genetic identification data is supported by an appropriate court order. Because its long-term effects are uncertain, we oppose genetic therapy that results in changes that can be passed to offspring (germ-line therapy).

*N) Rural Life*—We support the right of persons and families to live and prosper as farmers, farm workers, merchants, professionals, and others outside of the cities and metropolitan centers. We believe our culture is impoverished and our people deprived of a meaningful way of life when rural and small-town living becomes difficult or impossible. We recognize that the improvement of this way of life may sometimes necessitate the use of some lands for nonagricultural purposes. We oppose the indiscriminate diversion of agricultural land for nonagricultural uses when nonagricultural land is available. Further, we encourage the preservation of appropriate lands for agriculture and open space uses through thoughtful land use programs. We support governmental and private programs designed to benefit the resident farmer rather than the factory farm and programs that encourage industry to locate in nonurban areas.

We further recognize that increased mobility and technology have brought a mixture of people, religions, and philosophies to rural communities that were once homogeneous. While often this is seen as a threat to or loss of community life, we understand it as an opportunity to uphold the biblical call to community for all persons. Therefore, we encourage rural communities and individuals to maintain a strong connection to the earth and to be open to: offering mutual belonging, caring, healing, and growth; sharing and celebrating cooperative leadership and diverse gifts; supporting mutual trust; and affirming individuals as unique persons of worth, and thus to practice shalom.

*O) Sustainable Agriculture*—A prerequisite for meeting the nutritional needs of the world's population is an agricultural system which uses sustainable methods, respects ecosystems, and promotes a livelihood for people that work the land.

We support a sustainable agricultural system that will maintain and support the natural fertility of agricultural soil, promote the diversity of flora and fauna, and adapt to regional conditions and structures—a system where agricultural animals are treated humanely and where their living conditions are as close to natural systems as possible. We aspire to an effective agricultural system where plant, livestock, and poultry production maintains the natural ecological cycles, conserves energy, and reduces chemical input to a minimum.

Sustainable agriculture requires a global evaluation of the impact of agriculture on food and raw material production, the preservation of animal breeds and plant varieties, and the preservation and development of the cultivated landscape.

World trade of agricultural products needs to be based on fair trade and prices, based on the costs of sustainable production methods, and must consider the real costs of ecological damage. The needed technological and biological developments are those that support sustainability and consider ecological consequences.

*P) Urban–Suburban Life*—Urban–suburban living has become a dominant style of life for more and more persons. For many it furnishes economic, educational, social, and cultural opportunities. For others, it has brought alienation, poverty, and depersonalization. We in the Church have an opportunity and responsibility to help shape the future of urban-suburban life. Massive programs of renewal and social planning are needed to bring a greater degree of humanization into urban–suburban lifestyles. Christians must judge all programs, including economic and community development, new towns, and urban renewal, by the extent to which they protect and enhance human values, permit personal and political involvement, and make possible neighborhoods open to persons of all races, ages, and income levels. We affirm the efforts of all developers who place human values at the heart of their planning. We must help shape urban–suburban development so that it provides for the human need to identify with and find meaning in smaller social communities. At the same time, such smaller communities must be encouraged to assume responsibilities for the total urban–suburban community instead of isolating themselves from it.

*Q) Media Violence and Christian Values*—The unprecedented impact the media (principally television and movies) are having on Christian and human values within our society becomes more apparent each day. We express disdain at current media preoccupation with dehumanizing portrayals, sensationalized through mass media "entertainment" and "news." These practices degrade humankind and violate the teachings of Christ and the Bible.

United Methodists, along with those of other faith groups, must be made aware that the mass media often undermine the truths of Christianity by promoting permissive lifestyles and detailing acts of graphic violence. Instead of encouraging, motivating, and inspiring its audiences to adopt lifestyles based on the sanctity of life, the entertainment industry often advocates the opposite, painting a cynical picture of violence, abuse, greed, profanity, and a constant denigration of the family. The media must be held accountable for the part they play in the decline of values we observe in society today. Many in the media remain aloof to the issue, claiming to reflect rather than to influence society. For the sake of our human family, Christians must work together to halt this erosion of moral and ethical values in the world community by:

1) encouraging local congregations to support and encourage parental responsibility to monitor their children's viewing and listening habits on TV, movies, radio and the Internet,

2) encouraging local congregations, parents and individuals to express their opposition to the gratuitous portrayal of violent and sexually indecent shows by writing to the stations that air them and the companies that sponsor them,

3) encouraging individuals to express their opposition to the corporate sponsors of these shows by the selection and purchase of alternate products.

*R) The Internet*—Development of the Internet and other electronic means of communication is radically changing the way in which many people communicate. The Internet provides creative opportunities for human advancement drawing upon vast resources around the world. The positive consequences of the Internet continue to expand: adults and children can contact their peers anywhere, utilize the resources of the world to nurture their minds and spirits, and look for ways to attain their goals. Therefore, the church should promote positive uses of the Internet, and equal access to it. However, the Internet also exposes users to grave dangers. Therefore, the Internet must be managed responsibly, especially for children, in order to maximize its benefits, while minimizing the risk of exposure to inappropriate and illegal materials. Religious and civic groups should work together to make the Internet a safer place for all.

S) *Persons Living with HIV and AIDS*—Persons diagnosed as positive for Human Immune Virus (HIV) and with Acquired Immune Deficiency Syndrome (AIDS) often face rejection from their families and friends and various communities in which they work and interact. In addition, they are often faced with a lack of adequate health care, especially toward the end of life.

All individuals living with HIV and AIDS should be treated with dignity and respect.

We affirm the responsibility of the Church to minister to and with these individuals and their families regardless of how the disease was contracted. We support their rights to employment, appropriate medical care, full participation in public education, and full participation in the Church.

We urge the Church to be actively involved in the prevention of the spread of AIDS by providing educational opportunities to the congregation and the community. The Church should be available to provide counseling to the affected individuals and their families.

T) *Right to Health Care*—Health is a condition of physical, mental, social, and spiritual well-being, and we view it as a responsibility—public and private. Health care is a basic human right. Psalm 146 speaks of the God "who executes justice for the oppressed;/ who gives food to the hungry./ The LORD sets the prisoners free;/ the LORD opens the eyes of the blind." It is unjust to construct or perpetuate barriers to physical wholeness or full participation in community.

We encourage individuals to pursue a healthy lifestyle and affirm the importance of preventive health care, health education, environmental and occupational safety, good nutrition, and secure housing in achieving health. We also recognize the role of governments in ensuring that each individual has access to those elements necessary to good health.

U) *Organ Transplantation and Donation*—We believe that organ transplantation and organ donation are acts of charity, *agape* love, and self-sacrifice. We recognize the life-giving benefits of organ and other tissue donation and encourage all people of faith to become organ and tissue donors as a part of their love and ministry to others in need. We urge that it be done in an environment of respect for deceased and living donors and for the benefit of the recipients, and following protocols that carefully prevent abuse to donors and their families.

## ¶ 163.    IV. THE ECONOMIC COMMUNITY

We claim all economic systems to be under the judgment of God no less than other facets of the created order. Therefore, we recognize the responsibility of governments to develop and implement sound fiscal and monetary policies that provide for the economic life of individuals and corporate entities and that ensure full employment and adequate incomes with a minimum of inflation. We believe private and public economic enterprises are responsible for the social costs of doing business, such as employment and environmental pollution, and that they should be held accountable for these costs. We support measures that would reduce the concentration of wealth in the hands of a few. We further support efforts to revise tax structures and to eliminate governmental support programs that now benefit the wealthy at the expense of other persons.

A) *Property*—We believe private ownership of property is a trusteeship under God, both in those societies where it is encouraged and where it is discouraged, but is limited by the overriding needs of society. We believe that Christian faith denies to any person or group of persons exclusive and arbitrary control of any other part of the created universe. Socially and culturally conditioned ownership of property is, therefore, to be considered a responsibility to God. We believe, therefore, governments have the responsibility, in the pursuit of justice and order under law, to provide procedures that protect the rights of the whole society as well as those of private ownership.

B) *Collective Bargaining*—We support the right of public and private (including farm, government, institutional, and domestic) employees and employers to organize for collective bargaining into unions and other groups of their own choosing. Further, we support the right of both parties to protection in so doing and their responsibility to bargain in good faith within the framework of the public interest. In order that the rights of all members of the society may be maintained and promoted, we support innovative bargaining procedures that include representatives of the public interest in negotiation and settlement of labor-management contracts, including some that may lead to forms of judicial resolution of issues. We reject the use of violence by either party during collective bargaining or any labor/management disagreement. We likewise reject the permanent replacement of a worker who engages in a lawful strike.

C) *Work and Leisure*—Every person has the right to a job at a living wage. Where the private sector cannot or does not provide jobs for all who seek and need them, it is the responsibility of government to provide for the creation of such jobs. We support social measures that ensure the physical and mental safety of workers, that provide for the equitable division of products and services, and that encourage an increasing freedom in the way individuals may use their leisure time. We recognize the opportunity leisure provides for creative contributions to society and encourage methods that allow workers additional blocks of discretionary time. We support educational, cultural, and recreational outlets that enhance the use of such time. We believe that persons come before profits. We deplore the selfish spirit that often pervades our economic life. We support policies that encourage the sharing of ideas in the workplace, cooperative and collective work arrangements. We support rights of workers to refuse to work in situations that endanger health and/or life without jeopardy to their jobs. We support policies that would reverse the increasing concentration of business and industry into monopolies.

D) *Consumption*—Consumers should exercise their economic power to encourage the manufacture of goods that are necessary and beneficial to humanity while avoiding the desecration of the environment in either production or consumption, and avoid purchasing products made in conditions where workers are being exploited because of their age, gender, or economic status.

Consumers should evaluate their consumption of goods and services in the light of the need for enhanced quality of life rather than unlimited production of material goods. We call upon consumers, including local congregations and Church-related institutions, to organize to achieve these goals and to express dissatisfaction with harmful economic, social, or ecological practices through such appropriate methods as boycott, letter writing, corporate resolution, and advertisement. For example, these methods can be used to influence better television and radio programming.

E) *Poverty*—In spite of general affluence in the industrialized nations, the majority of persons in the world live in poverty. In order to provide basic needs such as food, clothing, shelter, education, health care, and other necessities, ways must be found to share more equitably the resources of the world. Increasing technology, when accompanied by exploitative economic practices, impoverishes many persons and makes poverty self-perpetuating. Therefore, we do not hold poor people morally responsible for their economic state. To begin to alleviate poverty, we support such policies as: adequate income maintenance, quality education, decent housing, job training, meaningful employment opportunities, adequate medical and hospital care, and humanization and radical revisions of welfare programs. Since low wages are often a cause of poverty, employers should pay their employees a wage that does not require them to depend upon government subsidies such as food stamps or welfare for their livelihood.

*F) Migrant Workers*—Migratory and other farm workers, who have long been a special concern of the Church's ministry, are by the nature of their way of life excluded from many of the economic and social benefits enjoyed by other workers. Many of the migrant laborers' situations are aggravated because they are racial and ethnic minority persons who have been oppressed with numerous other inequities within the society. We advocate for the rights of all migrants and applaud their efforts toward responsible self-organization and self-determination. We call upon governments and all employers to ensure for migratory workers the same economic, educational, and social benefits enjoyed by other citizens. We call upon our churches to seek to develop programs of service to such migrant people who come within their parish and support their efforts to organize for collective bargaining.

*G) Gambling*—Gambling is a menace to society, deadly to the best interests of moral, social, economic, and spiritual life, and destructive of good government. As an act of faith and concern, Christians should abstain from gambling and should strive to minister to those victimized by the practice. Where gambling has become addictive, the Church will encourage such individuals to receive therapeutic assistance so that the individual's energies may be redirected into positive and constructive ends. The Church should promote standards and personal lifestyles that would make unnecessary and undesirable the resort to commercial gambling—including public lotteries—as a recreation, as an escape, or as a means of producing public revenue or funds for support of charities or government.

*H) Family Farms*—The value of family farms has long been affirmed as a significant foundation for free and democratic societies.

In recent years, the survival of independent farmers worldwide has been threatened by various factors, including the increasing concentration of all phases of agriculture into the hands of a limited number of transnational corporations. The concentration of the food supply for the many into the hands of the few raises global questions of justice that cry out for vigilance and action.

We call upon the agribusiness sector to conduct itself with respect for human rights primarily in the responsible stewardship of daily bread for the world, and secondarily in responsible corporate citizenship that respects the rights of all farmers, small and large, to receive a fair return for honest labor. We advocate for the rights of people to possess property and to earn a living by tilling the soil.

We call upon our churches to do all in their power to speak prophetically to the matters of food supply and the people who grow the food for the world.

*I) Corporate Responsibility*—Corporations are responsible not only to their stockholders, but also to other stakeholders: their workers, suppliers, vendors, customers, the communities in which they do business, and for the earth, which supports them. We support the public's right to know what impact corporations have in these various arenas, so that people can make informed choices about which corporations to support.

We applaud corporations that voluntarily comply with standards that promote human well-being and protect the environment.

## ¶ 164.     V. THE POLITICAL COMMUNITY

While our allegiance to God takes precedence over our allegiance to any state, we acknowledge the vital function of government as a principal vehicle for the ordering of society. Because we know ourselves to be responsible to God for social and political life, we declare the following relative to governments:

*A) Basic Freedoms and Human Rights*—We hold governments responsible for the protection of the rights of the people to free and fair elections and to the freedoms of speech, religion, assembly, communications media, and petition for redress of grievances without fear of reprisal; to the right to privacy; and to the guarantee of the rights to adequate food, clothing, shelter, education, and health care. The form and the leaders of all governments should be determined by exercise of the right to vote guaranteed to all adult citizens. We also strongly reject domestic surveillance and intimidation of political opponents by governments in power and all other misuses of elective or appointive offices. The use of detention and imprisonment for the harassment and elimination of political opponents or other dissidents violates fundamental human rights. Furthermore, the mistreatment or torture of persons by governments for any purpose violates Christian teaching and must be condemned and/or opposed by Christians and churches wherever and whenever it occurs. For the same reason, we oppose capital punishment and urge its elimination from all criminal codes.

The Church regards the institution of slavery as an infamous evil. All forms of enslavement are totally prohibited and shall in no way be tolerated by the Church.

B) *Political Responsibility*—The strength of a political system depends upon the full and willing participation of its citizens. We believe that the state should not attempt to control the church, nor should the church seek to dominate the state. Separation of church and state means no organic union of the two, but it does permit interaction. The church should continually exert a strong ethical influence upon the state, supporting policies and programs deemed to be just and opposing policies and programs that are unjust.

C) *Freedom of Information*—Citizens of all countries should have access to all essential information regarding their government and its policies. Illegal and unconscionable activities directed against persons or groups by their own governments must not be justified or kept secret, even under the guise of national security.

D) *Education*—We believe responsibility for education of the young rests with the family, the church, and the government. In our society, this function can best be fulfilled through public policies that ensure access for all persons to free public elementary and secondary schools and to post-secondary schools of their choice. Persons in our society should not be precluded by financial barriers from access to church-related and other independent institutions of higher education. We affirm the right of public and independent colleges and universities to exist, and we endorse public policies that ensure access and choice and that do not create unconstitutional entanglements between church and state. The state should not use its authority to promote particular religious beliefs (including atheism), nor should it require prayer or worship in the public schools, but it should leave students free to practice their own religious convictions. The state should not prohibit the free exercise of voluntary prayer in public schools or at other public occasions. It is vital that we not misinterpret the rightful separation of church and state as the abolition of all religious expression from public view.

*E) Civil Obedience and Civil Disobedience*—Governments and laws should be servants of God and of human beings. Citizens have a duty to abide by laws duly adopted by orderly and just process of government. But governments, no less than individuals, are subject to the judgment of God. Therefore, we recognize the right of individuals to dissent when acting under the constraint of conscience and, after having exhausted all legal recourse, to resist or disobey laws that they deem to be unjust or that are discriminately enforced. Even then, respect for law should be shown by refraining from violence and by being willing to accept the costs of disobedience. We do not encourage or condone, under any circumstances, any form of violent protest or action against anyone involved in the abortion dilemma. We offer our prayers for those in rightful authority who serve the public, and we support their efforts to afford justice and equal opportunity for all people. We assert the duty of churches to support those who suffer because of their stands of conscience represented by nonviolent beliefs or acts. We urge governments to ensure civil rights, as defined by the International Covenant on Civil and Political Rights, to persons in legal jeopardy because of those nonviolent acts.

*F) Criminal and Restorative Justice*—To protect all persons from encroachment upon their personal and property rights, governments have established mechanisms of law enforcement and courts. A wide array of sentencing options serves to express community outrage, incapacitate dangerous offenders, deter crime, and offer opportunities for rehabilitation. We support governmental measures designed to reduce and eliminate crime that are consistent with respect for the basic freedom of persons.

We reject all misuse of these mechanisms, including their use for the purpose of revenge or for persecuting or intimidating those whose race, appearance, lifestyle, economic condition, or beliefs differ from those in authority. We reject all careless, callous or discriminatory enforcement of law that withholds justice from all non-English speaking persons and persons with disabilities. We further support measures designed to remove the social conditions that lead to crime, and we encourage continued positive interaction between law enforcement officials and members of the community at large.

In the love of Christ, who came to save those who are lost and vulnerable, we urge the creation of a genuinely new system for the care and restoration of victims, offenders, criminal justice officials, and the community as a whole. Restorative justice grows out of biblical authority, which emphasizes a right relationship with God, self, and community. When such relationships are violated or broken through crime, opportunities are created to make things right.

Most criminal justice systems around the world are retributive. These retributive justice systems profess to hold the offender accountable to the state and use punishment as the equalizing tool for accountability. In contrast, restorative justice seeks to hold the offender accountable to the victimized person, and to the disrupted community. Through God's transforming power, restorative justice seeks to repair the damage, right the wrong, and bring healing to all involved, including the victim, the offender, the families, and the community. The Church is transformed when it responds to the claims of discipleship by becoming an agent of healing and systemic change.

*G) Military Service*—We deplore war and urge the peaceful settlement of all disputes among nations. From the beginning, the Christian conscience has struggled with the harsh realities of violence and war, for these evils clearly frustrate God's loving purposes for humankind. We yearn for the day when there will be no more war and people will live together in peace and justice. Some of us believe that war, and other acts of violence, are never acceptable to Christians. We also acknowledge that most Christians regretfully realize that, when peaceful alternatives have failed, the force of arms may be preferable to unchecked aggression, tyranny and genocide. We honor the witness of pacifists who will not allow us to become complacent about war and violence. We also respect those who support the use of force, but only in extreme situations and only when the need is clear beyond reasonable doubt, and through appropriate international organizations. We urge the establishment of the rule of law in international affairs as a means of elimination of war, violence, and coercion in these affairs.

We reject national policies of enforced military service as incompatible with the gospel. We acknowledge the agonizing tension created by the demand for military service by national governments. We urge all young adults to seek the counsel of the Church as they reach a conscientious decision concerning the nature of their responsibility as citizens. Pastors are called upon to be available for counseling with all young adults who face conscription, including those who conscientiously refuse to cooperate with a system of conscription.

We support and extend the ministry of the Church to those persons who conscientiously oppose all war, or any particular war, and who therefore refuse to serve in the armed forces or to cooperate with systems of military conscription. We also support and extend the Church's ministry to those persons who conscientiously choose to serve in the armed forces or to accept alternative service.

## ¶165.      VI. THE WORLD COMMUNITY

God's world is one world. The unity now being thrust upon us by technological revolution has far outrun our moral and spiritual capacity to achieve a stable world. The enforced unity of humanity, increasingly evident on all levels of life, presents the Church as well as all people with problems that will not wait for answer: injustice, war, exploitation, privilege, population, international ecological crisis, proliferation of arsenals of nuclear weapons, development of transnational business organizations that operate beyond the effective control of any governmental structure, and the increase of tyranny in all its forms. This generation must find viable answers to these and related questions if humanity is to continue on this earth. We commit ourselves as a Church to the achievement of a world community that is a fellowship of persons who honestly love one another. We pledge ourselves to seek the meaning of the gospel in all issues that divide people and threaten the growth of world community.

*A) Nations and Cultures*—As individuals are affirmed by God in their diversity, so are nations and cultures. We recognize that no nation or culture is absolutely just and right in its treatment of its own people, nor is any nation totally without regard for the welfare of its citizens. The Church must regard nations as accountable for unjust treatment of their citizens and others living within their borders. While recognizing valid differences in culture and political philosophy, we stand for justice and peace in every nation.

*B) National Power and Responsibility*—Some nations possess more military and economic power than do others. Upon the powerful rests responsibility to exercise their wealth and influence with restraint. We affirm the right and duty of people of all nations to determine their own destiny. We urge the major political powers to use their nonviolent power to maximize the political, social, and economic self-determination of other nations rather than to further their own special interests. We applaud international efforts to develop a more just international economic order in which the limited resources of the earth will be used to the maximum benefit of all nations and peoples. We urge Christians in every society to encourage the governments under which they live and the economic entities within their societies to aid and work for the development of more just economic orders.

C) War and Peace—We believe war is incompatible with the teachings and example of Christ. We therefore reject war as a usual instrument of national foreign policy and insist that the first moral duty of all nations is to resolve by peaceful means every dispute that arises between or among them; that human values must outweigh military claims as governments determine their priorities; that the militarization of society must be challenged and stopped; that the manufacture, sale, and deployment of armaments must be reduced and controlled; and that the production, possession, or use of nuclear weapons be condemned. Consequently, we endorse general and complete disarmament under strict and effective international control.

D) Justice and Law—Persons and groups must feel secure in their life and right to live within a society if order is to be achieved and maintained by law. We denounce as immoral an ordering of life that perpetuates injustice. Nations, too, must feel secure in the world if world community is to become a fact.

Believing that international justice requires the participation of all peoples, we endorse the United Nations and its related bodies and the International Court of Justice as the best instruments now in existence to achieve a world of justice and law. We commend the efforts of all people in all countries who pursue world peace through law. We endorse international aid and cooperation on all matters of need and conflict. We urge acceptance for membership in the United Nations of all nations who wish such membership and who accept United Nations responsibility. We urge the United Nations to take a more aggressive role in the development of international arbitration of disputes and actual conflicts among nations by developing binding third-party arbitration. Bilateral or multilateral efforts outside of the United Nations should work in concert with, and not contrary to, its purposes. We reaffirm our historic concern for the world as our parish and seek for all persons and peoples full and equal membership in a truly world community.

## ¶ 166.        VII. OUR SOCIAL CREED

We believe in God, Creator of the world; and in Jesus Christ, the Redeemer of creation. We believe in the Holy Spirit, through whom we acknowledge God's gifts, and we repent of our sin in misusing these gifts to idolatrous ends.

We affirm the natural world as God's handiwork and dedicate ourselves to its preservation, enhancement, and faithful use by humankind.

We joyfully receive for ourselves and others the blessings of community, sexuality, marriage, and the family.

We commit ourselves to the rights of men, women, children, youth, young adults, the aging, and people with disabilities; to improvement of the quality of life; and to the rights and dignity of racial, ethnic, and religious minorities.

We believe in the right and duty of persons to work for the glory of God and the good of themselves and others and in the protection of their welfare in so doing; in the rights to property as a trust from God, collective bargaining, and responsible consumption; and in the elimination of economic and social distress.

We dedicate ourselves to peace throughout the world, to the rule of justice and law among nations, and to individual freedom for all people of the world.

We believe in the present and final triumph of God's Word in human affairs and gladly accept our commission to manifest the life of the gospel in the world. Amen.

*(It is recommended that this statement of Social Principles be continually available to United Methodist Christians and that it be emphasized regularly in every congregation. It is further recommended that "Our Social Creed" be frequently used in Sunday worship.)*

# Part V
# ORGANIZATION AND ADMINISTRATION

## Chapter One
## THE LOCAL CHURCH

### Section I. The Church and Pastoral Charge

¶ **201.** *Definition of a Local Church*—The **local church** provides the most significant arena through which disciple-making occurs. It is a community of true believers under the Lordship of Christ. It is the redemptive fellowship in which the Word of God is preached by persons divinely called and the sacraments are duly administered according to Christ's own appointment. Under the discipline of the Holy Spirit, the church exists for the maintenance of worship, the edification of believers, and the redemption of the world.

¶ **202.** *The Function of the Local Church*—The church of Jesus Christ exists in and for the world. It is primarily at the level of the local church that the church encounters the world. The local church is a strategic base from which Christians move out to the structures of society. The function of the local church, under the guidance of the Holy Spirit, is to help people to know Jesus Christ personally and to live their daily lives in light of their relationship with God. Therefore, the local church is to minister to persons in the community where the church is located, to provide appropriate training and nurture to all, to cooperate in ministry with other local churches, to defend God's creation and live as an ecologically responsible community, and to participate in the worldwide mission of the church, as minimal expectations of an authentic church.

¶ **203.** *Relation to the Wider Church*—The local church is a connectional society of persons who have professed their faith in Christ, have been baptized, have assumed the vows of membership in The United Methodist Church, and are associated in fellowship as a local United Methodist church in order that they may hear the Word of God, receive the sacraments, praise and worship the triune God, and carry forward the work that Christ has committed to his church. Such a society of believers, being within The United Methodist Church and subject to its *Discipline*, is also an inherent part of the church universal, which is composed of all who accept Jesus Christ as Lord and Savior, and which in the Apostles' Creed we declare to be the holy catholic church.

¶ **204.** *Care of Members*—Each local church shall have a definite evangelistic, nurture, and witness responsibility for its members and the surrounding area and a missional outreach responsibility to the local and global community. It shall be responsible for ministering to all its members, wherever they live, and for persons who choose it as their church.

¶ **205.** *Definition of a Pastoral Charge*—1. A **pastoral charge** shall consist of one or more churches that are organized under and subject to the *Discipline* of The United Methodist Church, with a charge conference, and to which an ordained or licensed minister is or may be duly appointed or appointable as pastor in charge or co-pastor. Where co-pastors are appointed, the bishop may designate for administrative purposes one as pastor in charge.[1]

2. A pastoral charge of two or more churches may be designated a **circuit** or a cooperative parish.

3. A pastoral charge may be designated by the bishop and cabinet as a "teaching parish" when either a local church with a pastor or a cooperative parish with a director is available to serve as a counseling elder for a probationary, local, or student pastor appointed or assigned to the teaching parish. A teaching parish shall have a demonstrable commitment to a cooperative or team ministry style and the training of pastors.

---

1. *See* Judicial Council Decisions 113, 319.

## Section II. Cooperative Parish

¶ **206.** 1. Local churches, with the guidance of the Holy Spirit, may enhance their witness to one another and to the world by showing forth the love of Jesus Christ through forms of mutual cooperation.

2. Annual conferences shall implement a process of cooperative parish development through which cooperative parish ministries are initiated and developed in both urban and town-and-country situations. Where cooperative parish ministries already exist in an annual conference, the conference shall direct the appropriate conference boards and agencies to develop strategies designed to make use of cooperative ministries as means of creating greater effectiveness in the nurture, outreach, and witness ministries of urban, suburban, and town-and-country situations; and the annual conference shall prepare and adopt a formal written policy concerning cooperative parish ministries, including a plan for financial support. Parish development is an intentional plan of enabling congregations, church-related agencies, and pastors in a defined geographic area to develop a relationship of trust and mutuality that results in coordinated church programs and ministry, supported by appropriate organizational structures and policy. A superintendent or director of parish development may be appointed to work with the cabinet(s) in the implementation of these ministries in a conference or an area. In addition, district superintendents shall submit recommendations annually regarding those churches in their districts that would benefit from being included in a cooperative ministry.

3. Cooperative parish ministries may be expressed in forms such as the following: *(a)* Larger parish—a number of congregations working together using a parish-wide parish council and other committees and work groups as the parish may determine; providing representation on boards and committees from all churches; guided by a constitution or covenant; and served by a staff appointed or assigned to the parish and involving a director. *(b)* Multiple charge parish—an intentionally organized group of two or more pastoral charges in which each church continues to relate to its charge conference on the organizational level and also participates in a parish-wide council. The pastors are appointed or assigned to the charges and also to the parish, and a director or coordinator is appointed or assigned by the bishop.[2] *(c)* Blended ministry parish—the merging of

---

2. *See* Judicial Council Decision 556.

the organizations and memberships of churches spread throughout a defined geographical area into one church that intentionally develops two or more worship/program centers at agreed-upon locations, and for which there is one charge conference and one set of committees and other groups of an organized local church, guided by a covenant and served by a staff and a director appointed or assigned to the parish. *(d)* Group ministry—a loosely organized group of two or more pastoral charges in which the pastors are appointed or assigned to charges. The pastors and/or lay council, representing all churches, may designate a coordinator. *(e)* Enlarged charge—two or more congregations, usually on the same circuit and of relatively equal size, that work as a unit with the leadership of one or more pastors. There may be a charge council and necessary committees. *(f)* Extended or shared ministry—a larger membership church sharing ministry with a smaller membership church usually served by one pastor. *(g)* Cluster groups—a group of churches located in the same geographic area with a loosely knit organization that allows the participating congregations and pastoral charges to engage in cooperative programs in varying degree. A district may be divided into cluster groups for administrative purposes. *(h)* Probe staff—composed of the pastors and other staff assigned to a geographic region to explore possibilities for cooperation and developing strategy for improved ministries to persons. *(i)* Cooperative ecumenical parish—formed by a local United Methodist church and one or more local churches of other Christian traditions. *(j)* Shared facilities—two or more United Methodist congregations sharing a building such as those performing ministries in different languages and/or with different racial and ethnic groups. The congregations may enter into a covenant that ensures mutual representation on such bodies as church council, board of trustees, and other committees and work groups.

In order to support the covenant relationship and to ensure the autonomy of the local congregations, the congregations shall identify liaison persons who will represent the local congregations in their respective church council sessions. The congregations shall negotiate a covenant agreement about their use of the facility to ensure mutual support as policies are formulated, programs are developed, and the facility is utilized.

4. Each general board and agency shall arrange for its directors and staff to be trained in cooperative ministry concepts better to provide support resources for annual conferences and local churches.

5. Bishops, district superintendents, conference staff, and other leaders shall become familiar through training with the benefits of cooperative ministries. They shall provide leadership and training opportunities for pastors and local church leaders as to the value of cooperative ministries in moving toward excellence in nurture, outreach, and witness ministries. They are to explore and develop meaningful ministries to persons in congregations, communities, and the global community.

6. Cabinets shall give priority in the appointment process to appointing directors and clergy staff of cooperative ministries, especially cooperative parish ministries, who have been trained in cooperative ministry concepts and who have demonstrated effective ministries of nurture, outreach, and witness. The cabinet shall develop and implement strategies designed to enable and equip pastors presently appointed to cooperative parish ministries to provide effective ministries of nurture, outreach, and witness.

7. Annual conferences and cabinets are urged to assist in the development and strengthening of cooperative ministries by pursuing funding assistance from general Church, annual conference, and other sources for each cooperative ministry, including cooperative parish ministries.

## Section III. Ecumenical Shared Ministries

¶ 207. Local churches, with the guidance of the Holy Spirit, may respond to opportunities for ecumenical resource sharing in their communities by creating ecumenical shared ministries, working with local congregations of other Christian churches to enhance ministry, make wise stewardship of limited resources, and live out the ecumenical spirit in creative ways responsive to the needs of God's peoples as well as to opportunities for expanded mission and ministry.

¶ 208. *Definition*—Ecumenical shared ministries are ecumenical congregations formed by a local United Methodist church and one or more local congregations of other Christian traditions. Forms of ecumenical shared ministries include: *(a)* a federated church, in which one congregation is related to two or more denominations, with persons choosing to hold membership in one or the other of the denominations; *(b)* a union church, in which a congregation with one unified membership roll is related to two denominations; *(c)* a merged church, in which two or more congregations of different denominations form one congregation that relates to only one of the constituent denominations; *(d)* a yoked parish, in which congregations of different denominations share a pastor.

¶ **209.** *Covenanting*—Congregations entering into an ecumenical shared ministry shall develop a clear covenant of mission, set of bylaws, or articles of agreement that address financial and property matters, church membership, denominational askings and apportionments, committee structure and election procedures, terms and provisions of the pastorate, reporting procedures, relationship with the parent denominations, and matters related to amending or dissolving the agreement. In the formation of an ecumenical shared ministry, ¶¶ 242 and 246.1-2 shall be followed in its organization. In an interdenominational local church merger, ¶¶ 2546 and 2547 shall be followed. In the case of federated and union churches, ¶ 2547 shall be followed.

¶ **210.** *Connectional Responsibilities*—Cabinets, conference staff and other leaders shall be expected to work with ecumenical shared ministries at their inception as well as in maintaining avenues of vital relationship and connection to The United Methodist Church, while recognizing that such avenues must also be maintained with the denominational partners in ministry.

¶ **211.** *Cabinet Priority*—Cabinets shall be urged to give priority in the appointment process to the providing of ecumenical shared ministries with pastoral leaders who have demonstrated commitment to ecumenism and who exhibit a clear appreciation for a variety of denominational expressions and polities.

## Section IV. Churches in Transitional Communities

¶ **212.** Since many of the communities in which the local church is located are experiencing transition, special attention must be given to forms of ministry required in such communities. The local church is required to respond to the changes that are occurring in its surrounding community and to organize its mission and ministry accordingly.

1. When the communities where the church is located experience transition especially identified as economic and/or ethnic, the local church shall engage in deliberate analysis of the neighborhood change and alter its program to meet the needs and cultural patterns of the new residents. The local church shall make every effort to

remain in the neighborhood and develop effective ministries to those who are newcomers, whether of a cultural, economic, or ethnic group different from the original or present members.

2. In communities in transition, the local church shall be regarded as a principal base of mission from which structures of society shall be confronted, evangelization shall occur, and a principal witness to the changing community shall be realized.

3. It is recommended that decisions concerning ministry in transitional communities be made after thorough consultation has taken place between structures and agencies in the connection.

4. It is recommended that the commitment of resources in terms of money and personnel to ministries in transitional communities be of sufficient longevity to allow for experimentation, evaluation, and mid-course corrections to ensure an adequate effort in ministry in those situations. Evaluations shall involve those on the local level as well as those at the funding level.

5. The ministry of the local church in transitional areas may be enhanced by review and possible development of some form of cooperative ministry.

¶ **213.** *A Process for Assessment of Local Church Potential*—In static, declining, or changing population areas, local churches may take the opportunity to study their congregation's potential. Upon the request of the congregation the district superintendent shall appoint a study task force to do an extensive study of the past, present, and potential ministry of that local church. Alternatively, the district superintendent may appoint such a task force when the future viability of the congregation is in question or whenever he/she deems it necessary for other reasons. The task force shall be composed of an equal number of lay and clergypersons and shall include persons from that congregation.

1. This study shall include, but not be limited to: *a)* unique missional opportunities and needs of the community; *b)* present ministries of the congregation; *c)* number of leaders and style of leadership; *d)* growth potential of the surrounding community; *e)* fiscal and facilities needs; *f)* distance from other United Methodist churches; *g)* number and size of churches of other denominations in the community; *h)* other items that may impact the church's ability to fulfill the mission of the Church as stated in Chapter One, Section I.

2. The findings shall be published and presented to the congregation with recommendations as to how best to fulfill the local church's

call to ministry and to assist them in determining how they shall serve the community with nurture, outreach, and witness ministries as an organized church (¶¶ 201–204) or cooperative parish ministries (¶ 206) or ecumenical shared ministries (¶ 207); or give special attention to redevelopment, relocation, or discontinuance. Those invited to the presentation shall include: the members of the congregation, the pastor(s), the district superintendent, and members of the district board of church location and building (¶ 2518).

3. The members of the local church shall consider the recommendations and adopt a response to them. The district superintendent shall report the results of the study and the congregation's response to the cabinet, with recommendations for the allocation of conference staff, resourcing, financial support, or other resources needed to undergird the congregation's efforts to reach its recommended potential. Such annual conference support shall be committed no longer than three years.

### Section V. Church Membership

¶ 214. *Eligibility*—The United Methodist Church is a part of the holy catholic (universal) church, as we confess in the Apostles' Creed. In the church, Jesus Christ is proclaimed and professed as Lord and Savior. All people may attend its worship services, participate in its programs, receive the sacraments and become members in any local church in the connection (¶ 4). (In the case of persons whose disabilities prevent them from assuming the vows, their legal guardian[s], themselves members in full covenant relationship with God and the Church, the community of faith, may recite the appropriate vows on their behalf.)

¶ 215. *The Wider Church*—A member of any local United Methodist church is a member of the denomination and the catholic (universal) church.

THE MEANING OF MEMBERSHIP

¶ 216. When persons unite with a local United Methodist church, they, or, if unable to answer for themselves, their parent(s), legal guardian(s), sponsor(s) or godparent(s), profess their faith in God, the Father Almighty, maker of heaven and earth; in Jesus Christ his only Son, and in the Holy Spirit. Thus, they make known their desire to live their daily lives as disciples of Jesus Christ. They covenant together with God and with the members of the local church to keep the vows which are a part of the order of confirmation and reception into the Church:

1. To renounce the spiritual forces of wickedness, reject the evil powers of the world, and repent of their sin;

2. To accept the freedom and power God gives them to resist evil, injustice, and oppression;

3. To confess Jesus Christ as Savior, put their whole trust in his grace, and promise to serve him as their Lord;

4. To remain faithful members of Christ's holy church and serve as Christ's representatives in the world;

5. To be loyal to The United Methodist Church and do all in their power to strengthen its ministries;

6. To faithfully participate in its ministries by their prayers, their presence, their gifts, and their service;

7. To receive and profess the Christian faith as contained in the Scriptures of the Old and New Testaments.

¶ **217.** *Growth in Faithful Discipleship*—Faithful membership in the local church is essential for personal growth and for developing a deeper commitment to the will and grace of God. As members involve themselves in private and public prayer, worship, the sacraments, study, Christian action, systematic giving, and holy discipline, they grow in their appreciation of Christ, understanding of God at work in history and the natural order, and an understanding of themselves.

¶ **218.** *Mutual Responsibility*—Faithful discipleship includes the obligation to participate in the corporate life of the congregation with fellow members of the body of Christ. A member is bound in sacred covenant to shoulder the burdens, share the risks, and celebrate the joys of fellow members. A Christian is called to speak the truth in love, always ready to confront conflict in the spirit of forgiveness and reconciliation.

¶ **219.** *The Call to Ministry of All the Baptized*—All members of Christ's universal church are called to share in the ministry which is committed to the whole church of Jesus Christ. Therefore, each member of The United Methodist Church is to be a servant of Christ on mission in the local and worldwide community. This servanthood is performed in family life, daily work, recreation and social activities, responsible citizenship, the stewardship of property and accumulated resources, the issues of corporate life, and all attitudes toward other persons. Participation in disciplined groups is an expected part of personal mission involvement. Each member is called upon to be a witness for Christ in the world, a light and leaven in society, and a reconciler in a culture of conflict. Each member is to identify with the agony and suffering of the world and to radiate and exemplify the Christ of hope. The standards of attitude and conduct set forth in the Social Principles (Part IV) shall be considered as an essential resource for guiding each member of the Church in being a servant of Christ on mission.

¶ 220. *Accountability*—1. All members are to be held accountable for their faithfulness to their covenant and vows with God and the other members of the Church. Should any member be accused of violating the covenant and failing to keep the vows that the member entered into with God and the other members of the local church as stated in ¶ 216, then it shall be the responsibility of the local church, working through its pastor and its agencies, to minister to that person in compliance with the provisions of ¶ 227 in an effort to enable the member faithfully to perform the vows and covenant of membership.

2. In the event that those efforts fail, then the lay member and the local church may agree to voluntary mediation in which the parties are assisted in reaching a settlement or agreement satisfactory to all parties by a trained, neutral third-party mediator or mediation team.

3. In the further event that those efforts fail to effect reconciliation and reaffirmation of the vows and covenant of ¶ 216 by the lay member, then the members of the church may pursue the procedures set forth in ¶¶ 2702.3, 2706.5, and 2714.

## ADMISSION INTO THE CHURCH

¶ 221. *Non-Local Church Settings*—A duly appointed minister of The United Methodist Church, while serving as chaplain of any organization, institution, or military unit, or as a campus pastor, or while otherwise present where a local church is not available, may receive a person into the membership of The United Methodist Church under the conditions of ¶ 216. Where possible, before the vows of membership have been administered such appointed minister shall consult with the pastor of the local church on the choice of the person concerned; and upon agreement by the pastor, a statement verifying that such vows were made shall be issued. The pastor thereof on receiving such statement shall duly enroll that person as a member on the appropriate roll.

**¶ 222.** *General Church Membership Roll*—When a person is received and/or baptized into the Church by a chaplain endorsed by the Section of Chaplains and Related Ministries and has no local church to which the membership and records may be sent, the chaplain shall send the name, address, and related facts to the General Board of Higher Education and Ministry for recording on the General Church Membership Roll. It is desirable that as soon as possible such people be transferred from the General Church Membership Roll to the appropriate roll of the local United Methodist church of their choice. The name of any person who has been on the General Church Membership Roll for more than eight years and for whom a current mailing address cannot be obtained shall be removed from the General Church Membership Roll.

**¶ 223.** *Outside of Congregational Settings*—Any candidate for church membership who for good reason is unable to appear before the congregation may, at the discretion of the pastor, be received elsewhere in accordance with the Ritual of The United Methodist Church. In any such case lay members should be present to represent the congregation. Names of such persons shall be placed on the church roll, and announcement of their reception shall be made to the congregation.

**¶ 224.** *Transfer from Other Denominations*—A member in good standing in any Christian denomination who has been baptized and who desires to unite with The United Methodist Church may be received as a professing member by a proper certificate of transfer from that person's former church, or by a declaration of Christian faith, and upon affirming willingness to be loyal to The United Methodist Church (*see* ¶¶ 214–216). The pastor will report to the sending church the date of reception of such a member. It is recommended that instruction in the faith, work, and polity of the Church be provided for all such persons. Persons received from churches that do not issue certificates of transfer or letters of recommendation shall be listed as "Received From Other Denominations."

**¶ 225.** *Care of Children and Youth*—1. Because the redeeming love of God revealed in Jesus Christ extends to all persons, and because Jesus explicitly included the children in his kingdom, the pastor of each charge shall earnestly exhort all Christian parents or guardians to present their children to the Lord in baptism at an early age. Before baptism is administered, the pastor shall diligently instruct the parents or guardians regarding the meaning of this sacrament and the vows that they assume. It is expected of parents or guardians who present their children for baptism that they shall use all diligence in bringing them up in conformity to the Word of God and in the fellowship of the Church and to encourage them to participate in preparation for their profession of faith and confirmation at the appropriate time. At least one parent or guardian shall be a member of a Christian church; or sponsor(s) or godparent(s) who are members shall assume the baptismal vows. They shall be admonished of this obligation and be earnestly exhorted to faithfulness therein. At the time of baptism they shall be informed that the Church, with its Christian education program, will aid them in the Christian nurture of their children.

2. The pastor of the church shall, at the time of administering the Sacrament of Baptism, furnish the parents or guardians of the child who is baptized with a certificate of baptism, which shall also clearly state that the child is now enrolled as a **preparatory member** in The United Methodist Church. The pastor shall also admonish members of the congregation of their responsibility for the Christian nurture of the child. The pastor shall be responsible for seeing that the membership secretary adds the full name of the baptized child to the preparatory membership roll of the church. When the baptized child lives in a community not served by the pastor who administers the Sacrament of Baptism, the pastor is responsible for reporting the baptism to a pastor or district superintendent who serves in the area where the baptized child lives in order that the child's name might be properly entered on the preparatory membership roll. (*See* ¶ 223.)

3. The pastor shall keep and transmit to the succeeding pastor an accurate register of the names of all baptized children in the charge, including both those who have been baptized there and those who have been baptized elsewhere. This register of baptized children shall serve as the list of preparatory members for whom the congregation has ongoing responsibility for nurture in the life of discipleship until they become full members and accept God's grace for themselves. It shall give the full name of the child, the date of birth, the date and place of baptism, the names of the parent(s) or guardian(s) and their place of residence and phone number, and the names of the sponsor(s) or godparent(s).

4. It shall be the duty of the pastor, the parent(s), guardian(s), sponsor(s), or godparent(s), the officers and teachers of the church

school, and all members of the congregation to provide training for the children of the Church throughout their childhood that will lead to a personal commitment to Jesus Christ as Lord and Savior, to an understanding of the Christian faith, and to an appreciation of the privileges and obligations of baptism and membership. The pastor shall, building on the preparation that youth have received throughout their childhood, organize them into classes for membership and confirmation (§ 5). This instruction shall be based on materials that the youth have already used and on other resources produced by The United Methodist Church for the purpose of confirmation preparation. When youth so prepared shall give evidence of their own Christian faith and purpose, and understanding of the privileges and obligations of membership, they may be received as full members.

5. Youth who are members of the Church have all rights and responsibilities of membership within the baptismal covenant. (*See* ¶ 255.2.) It is strongly recommended that each local church offer for all senior high youth who are members of the Church an advanced class of instruction in the meaning of the Christian life and discipleship. It is further recommended that this course, taught by or under the guidance of the pastor, diaconal minister, certified Christian educator, youth worker, or other staff, emphasize the doctrines of The United Methodist Church and the nature and mission of the Church, leading to continued growth in the knowledge, grace, and service of our Lord Jesus Christ. It shall be the responsibility of the pastor to participate in the growth process through interaction and ministry with youth.

6. All children shall continually be nurtured as they grow in ability to profess their faith in God and Jesus Christ.

AFFILIATE AND ASSOCIATE MEMBERSHIP

¶ **226.** A member of The United Methodist Church, of an affiliated autonomous Methodist or united church, or of a Methodist church that has a concordat agreement with The United Methodist Church, who resides for an extended period in a city or community at a distance from the member's home church, may on request be enrolled as an **affiliate member** of a United Methodist church located in the vicinity of the temporary residence. The home pastor shall be notified of the affiliate membership. Such membership shall entitle the person to the fellowship of that church, to its pastoral care and oversight, and to participation in its activities, including the holding of office; except such as would allow one to vote in a United Methodist body other than the local church. However, that person shall be counted and reported only as a member of the home church. A member of another denomination may become an **associate member** under the same conditions, but may not become a voting member of the church council.[3] This relationship may be terminated at the discretion of the United Methodist church in which the affiliate or associate membership is held whenever the affiliate or associate member shall move from the vicinity of the United Methodist church in which the affiliate or associate membership is held.

## CARE OF MEMBERS

¶ **227.** 1. The local church shall endeavor to enlist each member in activities for spiritual growth and in participation in the services and ministries of the Church and its organizations. It shall be the duty of the pastor and of the members of the church council by regular visitation, care, and spiritual oversight to provide necessary activities and opportunities for spiritual growth through individual and family worship and individual and group study to connect faith and daily living, and continually to aid the members to keep their vows to uphold the Church by attendance, prayers, gifts, and service. The Church has a moral and spiritual obligation to nurture its nonparticipating and indifferent members and to lead them into an active church relationship.

2. *Care of Members—a)* The pastor in cooperation with the church council may arrange the membership in groups—with a leader for each group—designed to involve the membership of the Church in its ministry to the community. These groups shall be of such size, usually not larger than eight or ten families, as to be convenient and effective for service. Such groups may be especially helpful in evangelistic outreach by contacting newcomers and unreached persons, by visitation, by mobilizing neighbors to meet social issues in the community, by responding to personal and family crises, by holding prayer meetings in the homes, by distributing Christian literature, and by other means. Nonresident members should constitute a special group to be served by correspondence. The groups shall be

---

3. *See* Judicial Council Decision 372.

formed and the leaders appointed by the church council upon recommendation of the pastor.

*b)* While primary responsibility and initiative rests with each member faithfully to perform the vows of the baptismal covenant that have been solemnly assumed, if the member should be neglectful of that responsibility, these procedures shall be followed:

(1) If a member residing in the community is negligent of the vows or is regularly absent from the worship of the church without valid reason, the pastor and the membership secretary shall report that member's name to the church council, which shall do all in its power to reenlist the member in the active fellowship of the church. It shall visit the member and make clear that, while the member's name is on the roll of a particular local church, one is a member of The United Methodist Church as a whole, and that, since the member is not attending the church where enrolled, the member is requested to do one of four things: *(a)* reaffirm the baptismal vows and return to living in the community of the baptismal covenant in the church where the member's name is recorded, *(b)* request transfer to another United Methodist church where the member will return to living in the community of the baptismal covenant (*see* ¶ 238), *(c)* arrange transfer to a particular church of another denomination (*see* ¶ 239), or *(d)* request withdrawal. If the member does not comply with any of the available alternatives over a period of two years, the member's name may be removed. (*See* § [4].)

(2) If a member whose address is known is residing outside the community and is not participating in the worship or activity of the church, the directives to encourage a transfer of the member shall be followed each year until that member joins another church or requests in writing that the name be removed from the roll of professing members; *provided,* however, that if after two years the council has not been able to relate that member to the church at the new place of residence, the name may be removed from the roll of members by the procedure of § (4) below.

(3) If the address of a member is no longer known to the pastor, the membership secretary and the evangelism ministry group chairperson shall make every effort to locate the member, and circulate the list of names throughout the parish. If the member can be located, the directives of either § (1) or § (2) above shall be followed, but if after two years of such efforts the address is still unknown, the

member's name may be removed from the roll of members by the procedure of § (4) below.

(4) If the directives of §§ (1), (2), or (3) above have been followed for the specified number of years without success, the member's name may be removed from the roll of members by vote of the charge conference on recommendation of the pastor and the evangelism ministry chairperson, each name being considered individually; *provided* that the member's name shall have been entered in the minutes of the annual charge conference for two consecutive years. On the roll there shall be entered after the name: "Removed by Charge Conference Action"; and if the action is on the basis of § (3), there shall be added: "Reason: Address Unknown." The record shall be retained[4] in order that upon reaffirmation of the baptismal covenant the person may be restored as a member. Should a transfer of membership be requested, the pastor may, after consultation with the person, issue the certificate of transfer.

(5) Recognizing that the Church has a continuing moral and spiritual obligation to nurture all persons, even those whose names have been removed from the roll of members, it is recommended that a roll of persons thus removed shall be maintained. It shall then become the responsibility of the church council to provide for the review of this roll at least once a year. (*See also* ¶ 233.) After the review has been made, it is recommended that the pastor and/or the commission on evangelism contact those whose names appear on this roll, either in person or by other means, in the most effective and practical manner. The names and addresses of those who have moved outside the local church's area should be sent to local churches in their new communities that those churches may visit and minister to them.

¶ **228.** *Transfer from Discontinued Local Churches*—If a local church is discontinued, the district superintendent shall select another United Methodist church and transfer its members thereto, or to such other churches as the members may select. (*See* ¶ 2548.2.)

### MEMBERSHIP RECORDS AND REPORTS

¶ **229.** *Membership Records*—Each local church shall accurately maintain the following membership rolls:

---

4. *See* Judicial Council Decision 207.

1. Full Membership Roll (¶ 222).

2. Preparatory Membership Roll (¶ 225.2), containing the names and pertinent information of baptized children and youth of the church eighteen years of age and under who are not full members, and other persons who have been enrolled in confirmation preparation.

3. Members Removed by Charge Conference Action (¶ 227.2*b*[4]).

4. Constituency Roll, containing the names and addresses of such persons as are not members of the church concerned, including unbaptized children, dedicated children, church school members, preparatory members who have reached the age of nineteen who have not been received into full membership, and other nonmembers for whom the local church has pastoral responsibility.

5. Affiliate Membership Roll (¶ 226).

6. Associate Membership Roll (¶ 226).

7. In the case of a union or federated church with another denomination, the governing body of such a church may report an equal share of the total membership to each judicatory, and such membership shall be published in the minutes of each church, with a note to the effect that the report is that of a union or federated church, and with an indication of the total actual membership.

¶ 230. *Baptism Records*—For purpose of record, a permanent list of congregational baptisms with dates, birth dates, full names, addresses, full names of parents, godparents, or sponsors, and officiating minister shall be kept by each local church. In the case of transfer to another congregation, death, or withdrawal, notation of this shall be made in the baptismal record.

¶ 231. *Annual Membership Report and Audit*—The pastor shall report to each charge conference the names of persons received into the membership of the church or churches of the pastoral charge and the names of persons removed since the last charge conference, indicating how each was received or removed. The church council shall appoint a committee to audit the membership rolls, submitting the report annually to the charge conference.

¶ 232. *Permanent Records*—The basic membership records in each local church shall consist of: a permanent church register and a card index, a loose-leaf book, or a membership record on an electronic information system (*see* ¶ 244).

1. The **permanent church register** shall be kept on either paper-based or electronic media. If it is on a paper medium, it shall be a vol-

ume of durable material prepared by The United Methodist Publishing House. The format and content of the record forms contained in it and the manner of its binding shall be as approved by the Committee on Official Forms and Records of the General Council on Finance and Administration (*see* ¶ 805.4c). If on a paper medium, the names shall be recorded chronologically as each person is received into the fellowship of that church and without reference to alphabetical order. The names shall be numbered in regular numerical order, and the number of each shall appear on the corresponding card, page, or record in the card index, loose-leaf book, or electronic information system membership record. If it is on an electronic medium, it will not be necessary to maintain a chronological number. The number that is assigned automatically by the computer system is sufficient for this purpose. However, the electronic medium shall meet the following criteria:

*a)* It shall contain all of the information required by the General Council on Finance and Administration.

*b)* Conversion of the information from paper records to an electronic medium shall be followed by a complete audit to ensure the accuracy of the converted records.

*c)* Off-site storage and electronic backup shall be maintained.

2. The **card index, loose-leaf book, or electronic system membership record** shall be kept on a form approved by the General Council on Finance and Administration or, in the case of electronically maintained records, shall contain the same information as required in the approved form with the exception of the sequential number. This record of membership shall be filed in alphabetical order and shall show the number appearing opposite each name on the permanent register. The pastor shall report annually to the annual conference the total membership of the charge as shown on the membership records.

3. When an electronic information system is used for record keeping, printout copies of the membership records and backup electronic media shall be retained in a secure off-site place (*see* ¶ 244).

¶ **233.** *Membership Secretary*—The charge conference shall name a **membership secretary** who, under the direction of the pastor, shall keep accurate records of all membership rolls (*see* ¶ 229) and shall report regularly to the church council.

CHANGES IN CHURCH MEMBERSHIP OR LOCAL CHURCH MEMBERSHIP

¶ **234.** Members in a local church may be removed from the roll by death, transfer, withdrawal, or actions of either the charge conference or trial court (*see* ¶ 2714). It shall be the duty of the pastor of the charge or of the membership secretary to keep an accurate record of all removals of membership and to report to each charge conference the names of all persons whose membership has been removed since the conference preceding, in each instance indicating the reason for such action.

¶ **235.** *Members Who Move*—If a member of a United Methodist church shall move to another community so far removed from the home church that the member cannot participate regularly in its worship and activity, this member shall be encouraged to transfer membership to a United Methodist church in the community of the newly established residence. Whenever possible, the local church of membership is encouraged to use the services of the Moving United Methodist program of the General Commission on United Methodist Men. As soon as the pastor is reliably informed of this change of residence, actual or contemplated, it shall be the pastor's duty and obligation to assist the member to become established in the fellowship of a church in the community of the future home and to send to a United Methodist pastor in such community, or to the district superintendent, or (if neither is known) to the Moving United Methodist office of the General Commission on United Methodist Men, a letter of notification, giving the latest known address of the person or persons concerned and requesting local pastoral oversight.

¶ **236.** *Lay Missionaries in Non-United Methodist Churches*—Laypersons in service outside the United States under the General Board of Global Ministries and assigned to churches other than United Methodist may accept all the rights and privileges, including associate membership, offered them by a local church in their place of residence without impairing their relationship to their home local church.

¶ **237.** *Members Residing at a Distance*—When a pastor discovers a member of The United Methodist Church residing in the community whose membership is in a church so far removed from the place of residence that the member cannot participate regularly in its worship and activity, it shall be the duty and obligation of the pastor to give pastoral oversight to such person and to encourage transfer of membership to a United Methodist church in the community where the member resides.

**¶ 238.** *Transfer to Other United Methodist Churches*—When a pastor receives a request for a transfer of membership from the pastor of another United Methodist church or a district superintendent, that pastor shall send the proper certificate directly to the pastor of the United Methodist church to which the member is transferring, or if there is no pastor, to the district superintendent. On receipt of such a **certificate of transfer,** the pastor or district superintendent shall enroll the name of the person so transferring after public reception in a regular service of worship, or if circumstances demand, public announcement in such a service. The pastor of the church issuing the certificate shall then be notified, whereupon said pastor shall remove the member from the roll.

Certificates of transfer shall be accompanied by two official forms. A "Notice of Transfer of Membership" is to be sent to the member by the pastor who transfers the membership. An "Acknowledgment of Transfer of Membership" is to be sent to the former pastor by the pastor who receives the transferred member.

In case the transfer is not made effective, the pastor shall return the certificate to the pastor of the sending church.

**¶ 239.** *Transfer to Other Denominations*—A pastor, upon receiving a request from a member to transfer to a church of another denomination, or upon receiving such request from a pastor or duly authorized official of another denomination, shall (with the approval of the member) issue a certificate of transfer and, upon receiving confirmation of the member's reception into another congregation, shall properly record the transfer of such person on the membership roll of the local church; and the member's name shall thereby be removed. For the transfer of a member of The United Methodist Church to a church of another denomination, an official "Transfer of Membership to Another Denomination" form shall be used.

**¶ 240.** *Withdrawal Without Notice*—If a pastor is informed that a member has without notice united with a church of another denomination, the pastor shall make diligent inquiry and, if the report is confirmed, shall enter "Withdrawn" after the person's name on the membership roll and shall report the same to the next charge conference.

**¶ 241.** *Withdrawal of Membership*—Persons may be removed from the roll of baptized members by death, transfer, withdrawal or removal for cause, with the understanding that withdrawal or removal for cause in no way abrogates the baptismal covenant from God's side. When a person returns to the church, he or she affirms the baptismal vows and, without rebaptism, becomes a full member.

If a member proposes to withdraw from The United Methodist Church, that member shall communicate the purpose in writing to the pastor of the local church in which membership is held. On receiving such notice of withdrawal, the pastor shall properly record the fact of withdrawal on the membership roll. If requested, the pastor shall give a statement of withdrawal to such member. Such person, upon written request, may be restored to membership on recommendation of the pastor.

## Section VI. Organization and Administration

¶ 242. *Primary Tasks*—The local church shall be organized so that it can pursue its primary task and mission in the context of its own community—reaching out and receiving with joy all who will respond; encouraging people in their relationship with God and inviting them to commitment to God's love in Jesus Christ; providing opportunities for them to seek strengthening and growth in spiritual formation; and supporting them to live lovingly and justly in the power of the Holy Spirit as faithful disciples.

In carrying out its primary task, it shall be organized so that adequate provision is made for these basic responsibilities: (1) planning and implementing a program of nurture, outreach, and witness for persons and families within and without the congregation; (2) providing for effective pastoral and lay leadership; (3) providing for financial support, physical facilities, and the legal obligations of the church; (4) utilizing the appropriate relationships and resources of the district and annual conference; (5) providing for the proper creation, maintenance, and disposition of documentary record material of the local church; and (6) seeking inclusiveness in all aspects of its life.

¶ 243. *Organization*—The basic organizational plan for the local church shall include provision for the following units: a charge conference, a church council, a committee on pastor-parish relations, a board of trustees, a committee on finance, a committee on lay leadership, and such other elected leaders, commissions, councils, committees, and task forces as the charge conference may determine. Every local church shall develop a plan for organizing its administrative and programmatic responsibilities. Each local congregation shall provide a comprehensive program of nurture, outreach, and witness, along with leadership training, and the planning and administration of the congregation's organizational and temporal life, in accordance with the mission of The United Methodist Church (*see* ¶¶ 120–124).

1. The church council and all other administrative and programmatic structures of the local church shall be amenable to the charge conference (*see* ¶ 245). The church council shall function as the executive agency of the charge conference.

2. Alternative plans may be developed in accordance with the provisions of ¶ 246.2. Such alternatives include: nurture, outreach, and witness ministries; administrative council; or administrative board/council on ministries.

3. Members of the church council or alternative structure shall be persons of genuine Christian character who love the church, are morally disciplined, are committed to the mandate of inclusiveness in the life of the church, are loyal to the ethical standards of The United Methodist Church set forth in the Social Principles, and are competent to administer its affairs. It shall include youth members chosen according to the same standards as adults. All shall be members of the local church, except where central conference legislation provides otherwise. The pastor shall be the administrative officer and, as such, shall be an ex officio member of all conferences, boards, councils, commissions, committees, and task forces, unless otherwise restricted by the *Discipline*.[5]

¶ 244. *Information Technology*—Each local church, as it creates or maintains computerized information and data, is strongly encouraged to confer with its annual conference for recommendations and guidelines as it relates to information technology.

## THE CHARGE CONFERENCE

Members of the charge conference shall be persons of genuine Christian character who love the Church, are morally disciplined, are committed to the mandate of inclusiveness in the life of the Church, are loyal to the ethical standards of The United Methodist Church set forth in the Social Principles, and are competent to administer its affairs. It shall include youth members chosen according to the same

---

5. *See* Judicial Council Decisions 469, 500.

standards as adults. All shall be members of the local church, except where central conference legislation provides otherwise. The pastor shall be the administrative officer, and as such shall be an ex officio member of all conferences, boards, councils, commissions, committees, and task forces, unless restricted by the *Discipline*.

¶ **245.** *General Provisions*—1. Within the pastoral charge the basic unit in the connectional system of The United Methodist Church is the **charge conference.** The charge conference shall therefore be organized from the church or churches in every pastoral charge as set forth in the Constitution (¶ 41). It shall meet annually for the purposes set forth in ¶ 246. It may meet at other times as indicated in § 7 below.

2. The membership of the charge conference shall be all members of the church council or other appropriate body, together with retired ordained ministers and retired diaconal ministers who elect to hold their membership in said charge conference and any others as may be designated in the *Discipline*. If more than one church is on the pastoral charge, all members of each church council shall be members of the charge conference.

3. The charge conference may make provision for recognition of the faithful service of members of the church council by electing them honorary members. An honorary member shall be entitled to all the privileges of a member, except the right to vote.

4. The district superintendent shall fix the time of meetings of the charge conference. The charge conference shall determine the place of meeting.

5. The district superintendent shall preside at the meetings of the charge conference or may designate an elder to preside.

6. The members present and voting at any duly announced meeting shall constitute a quorum.

7. Special sessions may be called by the district superintendent after consultation with the pastor of the charge, or by the pastor with the written consent of the district superintendent. The purpose of such special session shall be stated in the call, and only such business shall be transacted as is in harmony with the purposes stated in the call. Any such special session may be convened as a church conference in accordance with ¶ 247.

8. Notice of time and place of a regular or special session of the charge conference shall be given at least ten days in advance by two or more of the following (except as local laws may otherwise pro-

vide): from the pulpit of the church, in its weekly bulletin, in a local church publication, or by mail.

9. A charge conference shall be conducted in the language of the majority, with adequate provision being made for translation.

10. A **joint charge conference** for two or more pastoral charges may be held at the same time and place, as the district superintendent may determine.

¶ **246.** *Powers and Duties*—1. The charge conference shall be the connecting link between the local church and the general Church and shall have general oversight of the church council(s).

2. The charge conference, the district superintendent, and the pastor shall organize and administer the pastoral charge and churches according to the policies and plans herein set forth. When the membership size, program scope, mission resources, or other circumstances so require, the charge conference may, in consultation with and upon the approval of the district superintendent, modify the organizational plans; *provided* that the provisions of ¶ 242 are observed.

3. The primary responsibilities of the charge conference in the annual meeting shall be to review and evaluate the total mission and ministry of the church (¶¶ 120–124), receive reports, and adopt objectives and goals recommended by the church council that are in keeping with the objectives of The United Methodist Church.

4. The charge conference **recording secretary** shall keep an accurate record of the proceedings and shall be the custodian of all records and reports, and with the presiding officer, shall sign the minutes. A copy of the minutes shall be provided for the district superintendent, and a permanent copy shall be retained for church files. When there is only one local church on a charge, the secretary of the church council shall be the secretary of the charge conference. When there is more than one church on a charge, one of the secretaries of the church councils shall be elected by the charge conference to serve as its secretary.

5. *a)* It is strongly recommended that the charge conference elect a **church historian** in order to preserve the history of each local church. The responsibilities of the historian are to keep the **historical records** up to date; serve as chairperson of the committee on records and history, if any; cooperate with the annual conference commission on archives and history or comparable structure, if any; provide an annual report on the care of church records and historical materials to the charge conference; and also provide, with the pastor and the com-

mittee on records and history, if any, for the preservation of all local church records and historical materials no longer in current use. Records and historical materials include all documents, minutes, journals, diaries, reports, letters, pamphlets, papers, manuscripts, maps, photographs, books, audiovisuals, sound recordings, magnetic or other tapes, or any other documentary material, regardless of form or characteristics, made or received pursuant to any provisions of the *Discipline* in connection with the transaction of church business by any local church of The United Methodist Church or any of its constituent predecessors. The church historian may be a member of the church council. This person may also hold another elected position on the council.

*b)* There may be a local church **committee on records and history,** chaired by the church historian, to assist in fulfilling these responsibilities.

6. Each charge is encouraged to be inclusive in the make-up of the council so that all segments of the congregation are represented.

7. The charge conference may establish a limit to the consecutive terms of office for any or all of the elected or appointed officers of the local church, except where otherwise mandated. It is recommended that no officer serve more than three consecutive years in the same office.

8. The charge conference shall examine and recommend to the district committee on ordained ministry, faithfully adhering to the provisions of ¶ 306.3*b*, candidates for the ordained ministry who have been members in good standing of the local church for at least two years; whose gifts, evidence of God's grace, and call to the ministry clearly establish them as candidates; and who have met the educational requirements. It is out of the faith and witness of the congregation that men and women respond to God's call to ordained ministry. Every local church should intentionally nurture candidates for ordained ministry and provide spiritual and some financial support, including the Ministerial Education Fund, for their education and formation as servant leaders for the ministry of the whole people of God.

9. The charge conference shall examine and recommend, faithfully adhering to the provisions of ¶ 307, renewal of candidacy of candidates for the ordained ministry.

10. The charge conference shall examine and recommend to the responsible Church agency any candidates for Church-related vocations.

11. The charge conference shall inquire annually into the gifts, labors, and usefulness of the lay speakers related to the charge and recommend to the district and/or conference committee on lay speaking those persons who have met the standards set forth for a local church lay speaker and/or for certified lay speaker (¶¶ 266–269).

12. The charge conference shall in consultation with the district superintendent set the compensation of the pastor and other staff appointed by the bishop.[6]

13. As soon as practicable after the session of annual conference, each district superintendent or designated agent shall notify each local church in the district what amounts have been apportioned to it for World Service, conference benevolences and other general Church, jurisdictional, and annual conference funds. In preparation for and at the charge conference, it shall be the responsibility of the district superintendent, the pastor, and the lay member(s) of the annual conference and/or the church lay leader(s) to interpret to each charge conference the importance of these apportioned funds, explaining the causes supported by each of them and their place in the total program of the Church. **The World Service Fund** is basic in the financial program of The United Methodist Church. World Service on apportionment represents the minimum needs for the mission and ministry of the Church. **Conference benevolences** represent the minimum needs for mission and ministry in the annual conference. Payment in full of these apportionments by local churches is the first benevolent responsibility of the church (¶ 812).

14. The charge conference shall receive and act on the annual report from the pastor concerning all membership rolls. (*See* ¶ 231.)

15. In those instances where there are two or more churches on a pastoral charge, the charge conference may provide for a charge or parish council, a chargewide or parish treasurer, and such other officers, commissions, committees, and task groups as necessary to carry on the work of the charge.

16. In those instances where there are two or more churches on a pastoral charge, the charge conference may elect a chargewide or parish committee on lay leadership, a chargewide or parish committee on pastor-parish relations, a chargewide or parish committee on finance, and a chargewide or parish board of trustees in such instances where property is held in common by two or more churches

---

6. *See* Judicial Council Decisions 213, 252, 461.

of the charge. All churches of the charge shall be represented on such chargewide or parish committees or boards. Chargewide or parish organization shall be consistent with disciplinary provisions for the local church.

17. In instances of multiple church charges, the charge conference shall provide for an equitable distribution of parsonage maintenance and upkeep expense or adequate housing allowance (if annual conference policy permits) among the several churches.

18. The charge conference shall promote awareness of and concurrence with Policies Relative to Socially Responsible Investments (¶ 716), the Social Principles (¶¶ 160–166), and *The Book of Resolutions of The United Methodist Church.*

19. If any charge conference initiates, joins, monitors, or terminates a boycott, the guidelines in *The Book of Resolutions,* 2000, should be followed. The General Conference is the only body that can initiate, empower, or join a boycott in the name of The United Methodist Church.

20. When authorized by the district superintendent and the district board of church location and building, the charge conference may provide for the sponsoring of satellite congregations.

21. The charge conference shall have such other duties and responsibilities as the general, jurisdictional, or annual conference may duly commit to it.

¶ **247.** *The Church Conference*—To encourage broader participation by members of the church, the charge conference may be convened as the **church conference,** extending the vote to all local church members present at such meetings. The church conference shall be authorized by the district superintendent. It may be called at the discretion of the district superintendent or following a written request to the district superintendent by one of the following: the pastor, the church council, or 10 percent of the membership of the local church. In any case a copy of the request shall be given to the pastor. Additional regulations governing the call and conduct of the charge conference as set forth in ¶¶ 245–246 shall apply also to the church conference. A joint church conference for two or more churches may be held at the same time and place as the district superintendent may determine. A church conference shall be conducted in the language of the majority with adequate provision being made for translation. (For church local conference *see* ¶ 2526.)

¶ **248.** *Election of Leaders*—The charge conference, or church conference authorized by the district superintendent, shall elect upon recommendation by the committee on lay leadership of each local church on the pastoral charge, or by nomination from the floor and by vote of each such local church, at least the following leaders for the four basic responsibilities (¶ 243):

1. Chairperson of the church council.
2. The committee on lay leadership.
3. The committee on pastor-parish relations and its chairperson.
4. A chairperson and additional members of the committee on finance; the financial secretary and the church treasurer(s) if not paid employees of the local church; and the trustees as provided in ¶¶ 2525–2527, unless otherwise required by state law.
5. The lay member(s) of the annual conference and lay leader(s).
6. A recording secretary (*see* ¶ 246.4).
7. Special attention shall be given to the inclusion of women, men, youth, young adults, persons over sixty-five years of age, persons with disabilities, and racial and ethnic persons.
8. All local church offices and all chairs of organizations within the local church may be shared between two persons, with the following exceptions: trustee, officers of the board of trustees, treasurer, lay member of annual conference, member and chairperson of the committee on staff- or pastor-parish relations. When two persons jointly hold a position that entails membership on the church council, both may be members of it.

¶ 249. *Removal of Officers and Filling of Vacancies*—If a leader or officer who has been elected by the charge conference is unable or unwilling to perform the duties reasonably expected of such a leader or officer, the district superintendent may call a special session of the charge conference in accordance with ¶ 245.7. The purpose of such special session shall be stated as "Consideration for the removal of person(s) from office and the election of person(s) to fill vacancy(ies)." The committee on lay leadership (¶¶ 258.1, 246.16) shall meet as soon as possible after the special session of the charge conference has been announced and shall propose person(s) who may be elected if vacancy(ies) occur at the charge conference. If the charge conference votes to remove a person or persons from office, the vacancy(ies) shall be filled in the manner prescribed for elections in accordance with ¶ 248. When a local church trustee is under consideration for removal and the pastoral charge consists of two or more churches, a church local conference shall be called instead of a charge conference, in accordance with ¶ 2525.

¶ **250.** *Duties of Leaders and Members*—1. Out of the general ministry of each local church (¶ 126), there shall be elected by the charge conference a **lay leader** who shall function as the primary lay representative of the laity in that local church and shall have the following responsibilities:

*a*) fostering awareness of the role of laity both within the congregation and through their ministries in the home, workplace, community, and world, and finding ways within the community of faith to recognize all these ministries;

*b*) meeting regularly with the pastor to discuss the state of the church and the needs for ministry;

*c*) membership in the charge conference and the church council, the committee on finance, and the committee on lay leadership, where, along with the pastor, the lay leader shall serve as an interpreter of the actions and programs of the annual conference and the general Church (to be better equipped to comply with this responsibility, it is recommended that a lay leader also serve as a lay member of annual conference);

*d*) continuing involvement in study and training opportunities to develop a growing understanding of the Church's reason for existence and the types of ministry that will most effectively fulfill the Church's mission;

*e*) assisting in advising the church council of opportunities available and the needs expressed for a more effective ministry of the church through its laity in the community;

*f*) informing the laity of training opportunities provided by the annual conference. Where possible, the lay leader shall attend training opportunities in order to strengthen his or her work. The lay leader is urged to become a certified lay speaker.

In instances where more than one church is on a charge, the charge conference shall elect additional lay leaders so that there will be one lay leader in each church. Associate lay leaders may be elected to work with the lay leader in any local church.

2. The **lay member(s)** of the annual conference and one or more alternates shall be elected annually or quadrennially as the annual conference directs. If the charge's lay representative to the annual conference shall cease to be a member of the charge or shall for any reason fail to serve, an alternate member in the order of election shall serve in place.

Both the lay members and the alternates shall have been members in good standing of The United Methodist Church for at least two years and shall have been active participants for at least four years next preceding their election (*see* ¶ 30), except in a newly organized church, which shall have the privilege of representation at the annual conference session.[7] No local pastor shall be eligible as a lay member or alternate.[8] United Methodist churches that become part of an ecumenical shared ministry shall not be deprived of their right of representation by a lay member in the annual conference. The lay member(s) of the annual conference, along with the pastor, shall serve as an interpreter of the actions of the annual conference session. These persons shall report to the local church council on actions of the annual conference as soon as possible, but not later than three months after the close of the conference.

3. The **church council chairperson** shall be elected by the charge conference annually and shall have the following responsibilities:

*a)* leading the council in fulfilling its responsibilities (*see* ¶ 248);

*b)* preparing and communicating the agenda of the council meetings in consultation with the pastor(s), lay leader, and other appropriate persons;

*c)* reviewing and assigning responsibility for the implementation of actions taken by the council;

*d)* communicating with members of the council and others as appropriate to permit informed action at council meetings;

*e)* coordinating the various activities of the council;

*f)* providing the initiative and leadership for the council as it does the planning, establishing of objectives and goals, and evaluating;

*g)* participating in leadership training programs as offered by the annual conference and/or district.

The church council chairperson shall be entitled to attend meetings of all boards and committees of the church unless specifically limited by the *Book of Discipline*. The chairperson is encouraged to attend annual conference.

## THE CHURCH COUNCIL

¶ **251.** 1. *Purpose*—The **church council** shall provide for planning and implementing a program of nurture, outreach, witness, and

---

7. *See* Judicial Council Decision 495.
8. *See* Judicial Council Decisions 170, 305, 328, 342, 469.

resources in the local church. It shall also provide for the administration of its organization and temporal life. It shall envision, plan, implement, and annually evaluate the mission and ministry of the church. The church council shall be amenable to and function as the administrative agency of the charge conference (¶ 243).

2. *Mission and Ministry*—Nurture, outreach, and witness ministries and their accompanying responsibilities include:

*a)* The nurturing ministries of the congregation shall give attention to but not be limited to education, worship, Christian formation, membership care, small groups, and stewardship. Attention must be given to the needs of individuals and families of all ages.

*b)* The outreach ministries of the church shall give attention to local and larger community ministries of compassion, justice, and advocacy. These ministries include church and society, global ministries, higher education and campus ministry, health and welfare, Christian unity and interreligious concerns, religion and race, and the status and role of women.

*c)* The witness ministries of the church shall give attention to developing and strengthening evangelistic efforts of sharing of personal and congregational stories of Christian experience, faith, and service; communications; lay speaking ministries; and other means that give expressions of witness for Jesus Christ.

*d)* The leadership development and resourcing ministries shall give attention to the ongoing preparation and development of lay and clergy leaders for the ministry of the church (¶ 258.1).

3. *Meetings*—a) The council shall meet at least quarterly. The chairperson or the pastor may call special meetings.

*b)* In order for the council to give adequate consideration to the missional purpose of the local church, it is recommended that the first agenda item at each meeting be related to its ministries of nurture, outreach, and witness. The administrative and supportive responsibilities of the church will then be given attention. It is recommended that the council use a consensus/discernment model of decision-making.

4. *Other Responsibilities*—It will also be the responsibility of the church council to:

*a)* review the membership of the local church;

*b)* fill interim vacancies occurring among the lay officers of the church between sessions of the annual charge conference;

*c)* establish the budget on recommendation of the committee on finance and ensure adequate provision for the financial needs of the church;

*d)* recommend to the charge conference the salary and other remuneration of the pastor(s) and staff members after receiving recommendations from the committee on pastor-parish relations (staff-parish relations);

*e)* review the recommendation of the committee on pastor-parish relations regarding provision of adequate housing for the pastor(s), and report the same to the charge conference for approval. Housing provisions shall comply with the annual conference housing policy and parsonage standards. Housing shall not be considered as part of compensation or remuneration.

5. *Membership*—The charge conference will determine the size of the church council. Members of the church council shall be involved in the mission and ministry of the congregation as defined in ¶ 251.2. The membership of the council may consist of as few as eleven persons or as many as the charge conference deems appropriate. The council shall include persons who represent the program ministries of the church as outlined in ¶ 242. The membership shall include but not be limited to the following:

*a)* the chairperson of the church council;

*b)* the lay leader;

*c)* the chairperson and/or a representative of the pastor-parish relations committee;

*d)* the chairperson and/or a representative of the committee on finance;

*e)* the chairperson and/or a representative of the board of trustees;

*f)* the church treasurer;

*g)* a lay member to annual conference;

*h)* the president and/or a representative of the United Methodist Men;

*i)* the president and/or a representative of the United Methodist Women;

*j)* a representative of the United Methodist Youth;

*k)* the pastor(s).

6. *Quorum*—The members present and voting at any duly announced meeting shall constitute a quorum.

SPECIALIZED MINISTRIES

**¶ 252.** *Age-Level, Family, and Specialized-Ministries Coordinators (see also ¶ 251)*—The charge conference may elect annually a **coordinator of children's ministries,** a **coordinator of youth ministries,** a **coordinator of adult ministries,** and a **coordinator of family ministries.** Where young adult and specific age-level ministries would be enhanced, **coordinators of young adult and/or older adult ministries** may be elected. Where there are civic youth-serving agencies or Scouting ministry units present there may be elected a Scouting coordinator. Where needs for specialized areas of ministry arise (for example, single adults or persons with disabilities), coordinators of these areas of ministry may be elected.

**¶ 253.** *Other Ministry Group Coordinators*—In order to fulfill the mission of the local church, the charge conference may elect annually a coordinator or ministry group chairperson for any or all of these areas: Christian unity and interreligious concerns, church and society, community volunteers, education, evangelism, higher education and campus ministry, missions, prayer advocacy, religion and race, status and role of women, earth advocacy, stewardship, and worship.

Where desirable, the charge conference may combine coordinators' or ministry group chairpersons' assignments. Each coordinator or ministry group chairperson, if elected, shall work with the church council (or other appropriate body), pastor(s), and other church leaders to address the needs and opportunities of the particular area, utilizing all appropriate resources and relationships of the district, annual conference, and/or general church.

**¶ 254.** *Church-School Superintendent and Small-Group Coordinator*— The charge conference may elect: (1) a **superintendent of the church school** or Sunday school, and/or a **coordinator of small-group ministries,** who shall be responsible for helping to organize and supervise the total program for nurturing faith, building Christian community, and equipping people of all ages for ministry in daily life through small groups in the church; (2) a **health-and-welfare ministries coordinator,** who shall assist the local church and its people in being involved in direct service to persons in need; and (3) a **communications coordinator,** who shall assist the local church and its members with communication tasks by making available ideas, resources, and skills.

**¶ 255.** *Program Ministries*—The ministries of the local church are offered so that people encounter God's redeeming love for the world and respond by participating in God's action in the world. To achieve this ministry, people need to be involved in a variety of small-group settings. Some will be formed by the church council. Others will emerge with the approval of this body. Another type is historical, expressing itself in organizational structures that are related to counterparts in annual conferences and the general Church. These are referred to as **program ministries** and are related to the church council.

1. *The Church School and Small-Group Ministries*—In each local church there shall be a variety of small-group ministries, including the church school, for supporting the formation of Christian disciples focused on the transformation of the world. These small groups may concentrate on teaching and learning, fellowship, support, community ministries, and accountability. Members of small groups will build their knowledge of the Bible, the Christian faith, The United Methodist Church, and the societal context in which the church finds itself. In addition, small groups, including the church school, shall provide people with opportunities for practicing skills for faithful discipleship, including but not limited to worship, faith sharing, the creation of new faith communities, spiritual discernment, Bible study, theological reflection, prayer, community building, service with the poor and marginalized, and advocacy for peace and justice. Local churches or charges are encouraged to develop a policy to provide for the safety of the infants, children, and youth entrusted to their care.

*a) The Church School*—In each local church there shall be a **church school** for the purpose of accomplishing the church's educational ministry.

The church school is challenged to create communities in which people of all ages experience God's active presence in their lives; foster healthy, nonviolent relationships within the congregation and community; testify to the reconciling love of God through Christ; and live out their faith in the world as witnesses to the coming reign of God.

*b) Classes, Class Leaders, Class Meetings, and Covenant Groups*—A structure for **classes, class leaders, class meetings,** and **covenant groups** may be organized within the local congregation for the purpose of developing mutual accountability for living a disciplined Christian life.

*c) Mission and Ministry Groups*—Christian discipleship is patterned after the servanthood of Jesus, who cared for the sick, fed the hungry, and befriended the outcast. People may participate in small groups in order to serve the needs of the poor and marginalized, advocate for social justice, and demonstrate their faith in all their relationships and whatever setting they find themselves in.

d) *Support Groups*—Where needed, the local church may organize small groups to support particular needs of congregation and community members, including but not limited to care and prayer groups, divorce recovery, grief recovery, parenting groups, and support for people who are suffering from chronic illness.

2. *Young People's Ministries*—The term *young people* is inclusive of all persons from approximately twelve through thirty years of age. The term encompasses both youth and young-adult ministries and allows for age flexibility given the different age definitions for young people in various cultures around the world. The term *youth ministry* is an inclusive title, encompassing all the concerns of the Church and all activities by, with, and for youth. The youth ministry of The United Methodist Church shall include all persons from approximately twelve through eighteen years of age (generally persons in the seventh grade through the twelfth grade, taking into account the grouping of youth in the public schools), who are currently or potentially associated with the church or any of its activities. Youth who are members of the church have all rights and responsibilities of church membership except voting on matters prohibited by state law (*see* ¶ 225.5). The term *young-adult ministry* is an inclusive title, encompassing all the concerns of the Church and all activities by, with, and for young adults. The young-adult ministry of The United Methodist Church shall include all persons from approximately eighteen to thirty who are currently or potentially associated with the church or any of its activities. Young adults who are members of the church have all rights and responsibilities of church membership.

a) The **coordinator of youth ministries and the youth council,** when organized, shall be responsible for recommending to the church council activities, program emphases, and settings for youth. The coordinator and council shall use available resources and means to inform youth concerning the Youth Service Fund and shall cultivate its support; *provided* that prior to this cultivation or as a part of it, the youth shall have been challenged to assume their financial responsibilities in connection with the total program and budget of the local church.

*b)* The local church may designate one of its settings as the **United Methodist Youth Fellowship.**

*c)* In each charge conference there may be a **council for youth empowerment.**

(1) The council shall be made up of no less than three-fourths youth. Nominations for members of the council (both youth and adults) shall come from the youth group (or related structure). The nominations will then be sent to the committee on lay leadership for approval and then to the charge conference for approval. The council shall be composed of:

*(a)* At least one young adult.

*(b)* The coordinator of youth ministries (or related position) and other related staff as ex-officio members with voice but not vote.

*(c)* Any youth serving on a district, conference, jurisdictional, or general Church board or agency.

*(d)* Any adult serving on a district, conference, jurisdictional, or general Church youth council or organization.

(2) All offices of this council shall be held by youth. No member shall serve for more than four consecutive years.

(3) The council shall meet at least semi-annually. It may meet additionally at the request of the pastor, coordinator of youth ministries (or related person), or an officer of the committee.

Responsibilities:

*(a)* To assist the coordinator of youth ministry (or related position) and other related staff in planning and developing activities, program emphases, and settings for youth in the local church.

*(b)* To assist the coordinator of youth ministry (or related position) in finding and encouraging qualified adults and interns to work with youth in the local church.

*(c)* To develop a covenant for all adult volunteer youth workers.

*(d)* To encourage and facilitate the furthering of education for the coordinator of youth ministries (or related position) and related staff.

*(e)* To encourage and educate youth on possible careers in professional ministry and how to consider any vocational calling and opportunity to serve.

*(f)* To be a resource for other churches interested in starting or revitalizing youth ministry within their own local churches.

(g) To further educate youth and adults on The United Methodist Church as a connectional church by encouraging and supporting the participation of youth and adults in district, annual, jurisdictional, and central conferences, and other general Church ministries.

(h) To promote and educate persons about the Youth Service Fund.

(i) To promote the camping and retreat ministries within the local church.

(j) To empower youth to be participants in The United Methodist Church.

(k) To consult with the pastor/staff parish relations committee in: 1) developing written job descriptions; 2) nominating; 3) evaluating the job performance of the coordinator of youth ministries (or related position) and any other volunteer and paid staff related to youth ministry in the local church.

(l) It is strongly recommended that the council develop a program budget for their ministry.

d) The **coordinator of young adult ministries and the young-adult council,** when organized, shall be responsible for recommending to the church council the activities, program emphases, and settings for young adults.

3. Civic youth-serving agencies and Scouting ministries offer another setting for ministry to children, youth, their leaders, and their families. These opportunities would include the Boy Scouts, Girl Scouts, Camp Fire Boys and Girls, 4-H, or other appropriate national organizations. The God and Country award program shall be available to all appropriate age-level participants of the local church education program including the church school, youth ministry, and Scouting ministries. The Scouting coordinator shall relate to the church council, the superintendent of the church school, the coordinator of children's ministries, the coordinator of youth ministries, and the various youth-serving agency structures.

4. *United Methodist Women*—In every local church there shall be an organized unit of **United Methodist Women.** The following is the authorized constitution:

*Article 1. Name*—The name of this organization shall be United Methodist Women.

*Article 2. Relationships*—The unit of United Methodist Women in the local church is directly related to the district and conference organizations of United Methodist Women and to the Women's Division of the General Board of Global Ministries of The United Methodist Church.

*Article 3. Purpose*—The organized unit of United Methodist Women shall be a community of women whose purpose is to know God and to experience freedom as whole persons through Jesus Christ; to develop a creative, supportive fellowship; and to expand concepts of mission through participation in the global ministries of the Church.

*Article 4. Membership*—Membership shall be open to any woman who indicates her desire to belong and to participate in the global mission of the Church through United Methodist Women. The pastor(s) shall be an ex officio member of the local unit and of its executive committee.

*Article 5. Officers and Committees*—The local unit shall elect a president, a vice president, a secretary, a treasurer, and a committee on nominations. Additional officers and committees shall be elected or appointed as needed, in accordance with the plans of the Women's Division as set forth in the bylaws for the local unit of United Methodist Women.

*Article 6. Funds*—*a)* The organized unit of United Methodist Women shall secure funds for the fulfillment of its purpose.

*b)* All funds from whatever source secured by the unit of United Methodist Women belong to the organization and shall be disbursed only in accordance with its constitution and by its order.

*c)* The total budget secured and administered by the organized unit in the local church shall include: (1) pledges and other money for the programs and responsibilities of the Women's Division to be directed through regular channels of finance of United Methodist Women; and (2) funds to be used in mission locally, which shall include amounts for administration and membership development.

*d)* The organized unit in the local church shall make an annual pledge to the total budget of the district or conference organization of United Methodist Women.

*e)* All undesignated funds channeled to the Women's Division shall be appropriated by the division.

*Article 7. Meetings*—The organized unit in the local church shall hold such meetings for implementing the purpose and transacting its business as the unit itself shall decide.

*Article 8. Relationship in the Local Church*—The organized unit of United Methodist Women shall encourage all women to participate in the total life and work of the Church and shall support them in assuming positions of responsibility and leadership.

*Article 9. Amendments*—Proposed amendments to this constitution may be sent to the recording secretary of the Women's Division of the General Board of Global Ministries before the last annual meeting of the division in the quadrennium.

**Note:** For a description of the Women's Division of the General Board of Global Ministries and its subsidiary organizations, *see* ¶¶ 1317–1325.

¶ **256.** *United Methodist Men*—Each church or charge shall have an organized unit of **United Methodist Men** chartered and annually recertified through the General Commission on United Methodist Men to provide a dedicated ministry for building men spiritually and involving men in the total ministry of the Church (¶ 2302).

1. Local church resource material for supporting effective men's ministries shall be provided by the district, conference, and jurisdictional organizations of United Methodist Men and the General Commission on United Methodist Men (¶ 2302).

2. United Methodist Men exists to declare the centrality of Christ in every man's life. Men's ministry leads to the spiritual growth of men and effective discipleship. This purpose is served as men are called to model the servant leadership of Jesus Christ.

3. Individual and group strategies form the foundation of United Methodist Men ministry.

*a*) Enhance Evangelism, Mission, and Spiritual Life (EMS), as men become servant leaders.

*b*) Advocate programs that train men within local churches to promote specific ministries including prayer, missions, stewardship, and civic/youth serving ministries.

*c*) Forge pastoral partnerships by men committed to the effective support and service of clergy and local congregations.

*d*) Enhance organizational strength through effective leadership, resources, membership growth, and financial accountability.

*e*) Assist men in their ever-changing relationships, roles, and responsibilities in the family setting, workplace, and society.

*f*) Understand the organization, doctrines, and beliefs of The United Methodist Church.

*g)* Fulfill the membership vows through the commitment to prayer, presence, gifts, and service in congregational life.

*h)* Fulfill the Great Commission with and through The United Methodist Church as one part of the Body of Christ.

4. Men seeking membership in a local unit of United Methodist Men will be asked to subscribe to the major strategies listed in § 3 above and to these personal objectives:

*a)* To engage daily in Bible study and prayer.

*b)* To bear witness to Christ's way in daily work and in all personal contacts through words and actions.

*c)* To engage in Christian service.

5. United Methodist Men may be organized in one or more components within a local church as needed. Multiple local churches may also form a single unit of United Methodist Men according to their needs.

6. Membership shall be open to any man who indicates his desire to belong and to participate in the ministry of the church through United Methodist Men.

7. The appointed clergy of the local church or charge shall be ex officio member(s) of the unit and its executive committee

¶ 257. *Other Age-Level Councils*—Where the size of the church and the extent of the program indicate the need, the work of the church council (or other appropriate body) may be facilitated by one or more age-level councils and/or a family council, or such other means as fit the needs of the congregation. The membership of these councils shall be elected by the church council (or other appropriate body).

ADMINISTRATIVE COMMITTEES

¶ 258. 1. There shall be elected annually, by the charge conference in each local church, a **committee on lay leadership** that is composed of full members of the local church. The charge of this committee is to identify, develop, deploy, evaluate, and monitor Christian spiritual leadership for the local congregation. Members of the committee shall engage in and be attentive to developing and enhancing their own Christian spiritual life in light of the mission of the Church (Part V, Chapter One, Section 1).

In conducting its work, the committee shall engage in biblical and theological reflections on the mission of the church, the primary task, and ministries of the local church. It shall provide a means of identifying the spiritual gifts and abilities of the membership. The committee shall work with the church council, or alternative administrative bodies, to determine the diverse ministry tasks of the congregation and the skills needed for leadership.

*a*) The committee on lay leadership shall serve throughout the year to guide the church council, or alternative structure, on matters regarding the leadership (other than employed staff) of the congregation so as to focus on mission and ministry as the context for service; guide the development and training of spiritual leaders; recruit, nurture, and support spiritual leaders; and assist the church council, or alternative structure, in assessing the changing leadership needs.

*b*) The committee shall recommend to the charge conference, at its annual session, the names of people to serve as officers and leaders of designated ministries of the church council, or alternative administrative body required for the work of the church and as the law of the church requires or as the charge conference deems necessary to its work.

*c*) This committee is to be composed of not more than nine persons, in addition to the pastor and the lay leader. At least one young adult elected by the charge conference shall serve as a member of the committee. One or more members elected by the charge conference may be youth. The pastor shall be the chairperson. A layperson elected by the committee on lay leadership shall serve as the vice chairperson of the committee.

*d*) In order to secure experience and stability, the membership shall be divided into three classes, one of which shall be elected each year for a three-year term. To begin the process of rotation where such has not been in place, in the first year, one class shall be elected for one year, one class for two years, and one class for three years. Each year's new class, and vacancies at the time of charge conference, shall be elected from nominees, from the floor of the charge conference and/or through the recommendation of the committee on lay leadership. Retiring members of the committee shall not succeed themselves. Only one person from an immediate family residing in the same household shall serve on the committee. When vacancies occur during the year, nominees shall be elected by the church council, or alternative church structure, with the permission of the district superintendent.

*e*) In the identification and selection process, care shall be given that the leadership of ministries reflects inclusivity and diversity.

2. There shall be elected annually by the charge conference in each local church a **committee on pastor-parish relations or staff-parish relations** who are full members of the local church or charge or associate members (¶ 226), except in cases where central conference legislation or local law provides otherwise. People serving on this committee must be engaged in and attentive to their Christian spiritual development so as to give proper leadership in the responsibilities with which the committee is entrusted.

In conducting its work, the committee shall identify and clarify its values for ministry. It shall engage in biblical and theological reflections on the mission of the church, the primary task, and ministries of the local church.

The committee shall reflect biblically and theologically on the role and work of the pastor(s) and staff as they carry out their leadership responsibilities. The committee shall assist the pastor(s) and staff in assessing their gifts and setting priorities for leadership and service. It is the responsibility of the committee to communicate with the committee on lay leadership and/or the church council when there is a need for other leaders or for employed staff to perform in areas where utilization of the gifts of the pastor(s) and staff proves an inappropriate stewardship of time.

*a)* The committee shall be composed of not fewer than five nor more than nine persons representative of the total charge. One of the members shall be a young adult and one member may be a youth. In addition, the lay leader and a lay member of the annual conference shall be members. No staff member or immediate family member of a pastor or staff member may serve on the committee. Only one person from an immediate family residing in the same household shall serve on the committee.

*b)* In order to secure experience and stability, the membership shall be divided into three classes, one of which shall be elected each year for a three-year term. The lay member of the annual conference and the lay leader are exempt from the three-year term. To begin the process of rotation where such a process has not been in place, on the first year one class shall be elected for one year, one class for two years, and one class for three years. Retiring members of the committee shall not succeed themselves. When vacancies occur during the year, nominees shall be elected at the church council (or alternative church structure).

*c)* In those charges where there is more than one church, the committee shall include at least one representative from each local church. The charge conference may appoint a local church **pastoral advisory committee** for those churches desiring such a committee. The advisory committee shall consist of three persons placed in three classes with the chairperson serving as a member of the charge committee. The committee shall meet upon request of the pastor or of the chairperson, and its duties shall be those outlined in § 2*f*(3) and (4). The committee shall meet only with the knowledge of the pastor.

*d)* The committees on pastor-parish relations of charges that are in cooperative parish ministries shall meet together to consider the professional leadership needs of the cooperative parish ministry as a whole. Where churches are organized as a larger parish, the committee on pastor-parish relations shall consist of at least one representative from each church. Individual churches may form pastoral advisory committees as needed.

*e)* The committee shall meet at least quarterly. It shall meet additionally at the request of the bishop, the district superintendent, the pastor, any member of the professional staff, or the chairperson of the committee. To fulfill his or her obligation under ordination, his or her connectional responsibility under appointment, and his or her duty as a pastor, the pastor should be present at each meeting of the committee on pastor-parish relations except where he or she voluntarily excuses himself or herself. The committee shall meet only with the knowledge of the pastor and/or the district superintendent. It may meet with the district superintendent without the pastor being present. However, the pastor or any member of the staff under consideration shall be notified prior to such meeting at which a pastor's or clergy staff member's continued appointment or a lay staff member's employment is discussed and be brought into consultation immediately thereafter. In the event that only one congregation on a charge containing more than one church has concerns it wishes to share, its member(s) in the committee may meet separately with the pastor or any member of the professional staff or the district superintendent, but only with the knowledge of the pastor and/or district superintendent. The committee may meet in closed session upon recommendation of the pastor, any other person accountable to the committee, the chairperson of the committee, or the district superintendent.

*f)* The duties of the committee shall include the following:

(1) To confer with and counsel the pastor(s) and staff on the

matters pertaining to the effectiveness of ministry; relationships with the congregation; conditions that may impede the effectiveness of ministry; and to interpret the nature and function of the ministry.

(2) To confer with, consult, and counsel the pastor(s) and staff on matters pertaining to priorities in the use of gifts, skills, and time and priorities for the demands and effectiveness of the mission and ministry of the congregation.

(3) To provide evaluation at least annually for the use of the pastor(s) and staff in an ongoing effective ministry and for identifying continuing educational needs and plans.

(4) To communicate and interpret to the congregation the nature and function of ministry in The United Methodist Church regarding open itinerancy, the preparation for ordained ministry, and the Ministerial Education Fund.

(5) To develop and approve written job descriptions and titles for associate pastors and other staff members in cooperation with the senior pastor. The term *associate pastor* is used as a general term to indicate any pastoral appointment in a local church other than the pastor in charge (*see* ¶ 330). Committees shall be encouraged to develop specific titles for associate pastors that reflect the job descriptions and expectations.

(6) To consult with the pastor and staff concerning continuing education and spiritual renewal, to arrange with the church council for the necessary time and financial assistance for the attendance of the pastor and/or staff at such continuing education and spiritual renewal events as may serve their professional and spiritual growth, and to encourage staff members to seek professional certification in their fields of specialization.

(7) To enlist, interview, evaluate, review, and recommend annually to the charge conference lay preachers and persons for candidacy for ordained ministry (*see* ¶¶ 246.8 and 305), and to enlist and refer to the General Board of Global Ministries persons for candidacy for missionary service, recognizing that The United Methodist Church affirms the biblical and theological support of persons regardless of gender, race, ethnic origin, or disabilities for these ministries. Neither the pastor nor any member of the committee on pastor-parish relations shall be present during the consideration of a candidacy application or renewal for a member of their immediate family. The committee shall provide to the charge conference a list of students from the charge who are preparing for ordained ministry,

diaconal ministry, and/or missionary service, and shall maintain contact with these students, supplying the charge conference with a progress report on each student.

(8) To interpret preparation for ordained ministry and the Ministerial Education Fund to the congregation.

(9) To confer with the pastor and/or other appointed members of the staff if it should become evident that the best interests of the charge and pastor(s) will be served by a change of pastor(s). The committee shall cooperate with the pastor(s), the district superintendent, and the bishop in securing clergy leadership. Its relationship to the district superintendent and the bishop shall be advisory only.[9] (See ¶¶ 430–433.)

(10) To recommend to the church council, after consultation with the pastor, the professional and other staff positions (whether employee or contract) needed to carry out the work of the church or charge. The committee and the pastor shall recommend to the church council a written statement of policy and procedures regarding the process for hiring, contracting, evaluating, promoting, retiring, and dismissing staff personnel who are not subject to episcopal appointment as ordained clergy. Until such a policy has been adopted, the committee and the pastor shall have the authority to hire, contract, evaluate, promote, retire, and dismiss nonappointed personnel. When persons are hired or contracted, consideration shall be given to the training qualifications and certification standards set forth by the general Church agency to which such positions are related. The committee shall further recommend to the church council a provision for adequate health and life insurance, pension benefits, and severance pay for all lay employees.

(11) To recommend to the charge conference, when the size of the employed staff of the charge makes it desirable, the establishment of a personnel committee. This committee shall be composed of such members of the committee on pastor-parish relations as it may designate and such additional members as the charge conference may determine.

(12) To educate the church community on the value of diversity of selection in clergy and lay staff and develop a commitment to same.

---

9. *See* Judicial Council Decision 701.

(13) Members of the committee on pastor-parish relations (or staff-parish relations) shall keep themselves informed of personnel matters in relationship to the Church's policy, professional standards, liability issues, and civil law. They are responsible for communicating and interpreting such matters to staff. Committee members should make themselves available for educational and training opportunities provided by the conference, district, and/or other arenas that will enable them to be effective in their work.

3. There shall be a **board of trustees,** whose membership and duties are detailed in ¶¶ 2524-2551.

4. There shall be a **committee on finance,** elected annually by the charge conference upon recommendation by the committee on lay leadership or from the floor, composed of the chairperson; the pastor(s); a lay member of the annual conference; the chairperson of the church council; the chairperson or representative of the committee on pastor-parish relations; a representative of the trustees to be selected by the trustees; the chairperson of the ministry group on stewardship; the lay leader; the financial secretary; the treasurer; the church business administrator; and other members to be added as the charge conference may determine. It is recommended that the chairperson of the committee on finance shall be a member of the church council. The financial secretary, treasurer, and church business administrator, if paid employees, shall be members without vote.

Where there is no stewardship ministry area, stewardship shall be the responsibility of a subgroup of the committee on finance or shall be assigned to a task group that shall report to the church council.

All financial askings to be included in the annual budget of the local church shall be submitted to the committee on finance. The committee on finance shall compile annually a complete budget for the local church and submit it to the church council for review and adoption. The committee on finance shall be charged with responsibility for developing and implementing plans that will raise sufficient income to meet the budget adopted by the church council. It shall administer the funds received according to instructions from the church council.

The committee shall carry out the church council's directions in guiding the treasurer(s) and financial secretary.

*a)* The committee shall designate at least two persons not of the immediate family residing in the same household to count the offering. They shall work under the supervision of the financial secretary. A record of all funds received shall be given to the financial secretary and treasurer. Funds received shall be deposited promptly in accordance with the procedures established by the committee on finance. The financial secretary shall keep records of the contributions and payments.

*b)* The **church treasurer(s)** shall disburse all money contributed to causes represented in the local church budget, and such other funds and contributions as the church council may determine. The treasurer(s) shall remit each month to the conference treasurer all World Service and conference benevolence funds then on hand. Contributions to benevolence shall not be used for any cause other than that to which they have been given. The church treasurer shall make regular and detailed reports on funds received and expended to the committee on finance and the church council.[10] The treasurer(s) shall be adequately bonded.

*c)* The committee shall make provision for an annual audit of the records of the financial officers of the local church and all its organizations and shall report to the charge conference.

*d)* The committee shall recommend to the church council proper depositories for the church's funds. Funds received shall be deposited promptly in the name of the local church.

*e)* Contributions designated for specific causes and objects shall be promptly forwarded according to the intent of the donor and shall not be used for any other purpose.

*f)* After the budget of the local church has been approved, additional appropriations or changes in the budget must be approved by the church council.

*g)* The committee shall prepare annually a report to the church council of all designated funds that are separate from the current expense budget.

5. The church council may appoint such other committees as it deems advisable, including: committee on communications, committee on records and history, committee on health and welfare, and committee on memorial gifts.

## Section VII. The Method of Organizing a New Local Church

¶ **259.** 1. **A new local church** or **mission congregation** shall be established only with the consent of the bishop in charge and the cab-

---

10. *See* Judicial Council Decisions 63, 320, 539.

inet and with due consideration of the conference entity assigned the responsibility for congregational development. The bishop shall designate the district within whose bounds the church or mission congregation shall be organized. The district superintendent of that district, or his or her designee, shall be the agent in charge of the project and shall recommend to the district board of church location and building (¶ 2518) the method of organization, and whether a specific site shall be selected or an area of organization be designated. The district superintendent shall avail him/herself of existing demographic, lifestyle and ethnographic information in the process of establishing a new congregation and its location, or shall recommend to the board of trustees of a selected local church that they share their facility with the proposed congregation. If there is a city or district missionary organization, or if funds for the project are anticipated from a conference organization, those bodies shall also be asked to approve the method of organization and location for a new congregation.

2. The bishop may appoint a pastor to launch a new local church, or with the bishop's approval the district superintendent may authorize a local church or group of local churches to launch a new church by gathering interested people in small groups for Bible study, outreach, community building, and worship at a site in an area approved by the district board of church location and building.

3. A pastor of The United Methodist Church, while serving as the pastor of a new church prior to the convening of a constituting conference (¶ 259.7), may receive a person into the membership of The United Methodist Church under the conditions of ¶ 216. When a person is received and/or baptized into the church, the pastor shall send the name, address, and related facts to the annual conference secretary for recording on a general membership roll. These names shall be transferred as soon as possible to the roll of the new church, when constituted, or to another church upon the member's request. If the new church is being sponsored by an existing church, membership may be recorded on the roll of that church.

4. Each annual conference or its equivalent may determine the minimum number of members and other criteria required for the organization of a local United Methodist church.

5. When the number of people interested in being charter members of the new church reaches the number necessary as set by the conference to charter a new church, the district superintendent shall

call the interested people to meet at an appointed time for the purpose of organizing them into a chartered (organized) local church, or may by written authorization designate an elder in the district to call such a meeting. The district superintendent or the designated elder shall preside and shall appoint a secretary to keep a record of the meeting. Following a time of worship, opportunity shall be given to those in attendance to present themselves for membership.

6. People desiring to become members on profession of their faith in Christ shall also be given opportunity to present themselves for membership. Any who have not been baptized shall receive the sacrament of baptism. If they profess their faith and are confirmed, they will be received as members. When the district superintendent or designated elder is satisfied as to the genuineness of their faith and purpose, they shall be received into the membership of the church. Other baptized people are to be entered on the roll of those who are baptized.

7. A list shall be made of all the people received into the membership of the proposed church by transfer and on profession of faith. Those people shall be members of the constituting church conference, and each shall be entitled to vote.

8. The constituting church conference shall then be called to order by the district superintendent or by an elder whom the superintendent designates (*see* ¶ 245.5). A committee on nominations, elected on nominations from the floor as the conference may determine, shall nominate members of the proposed church council. The chairperson of the committee on nominations shall be the appointed pastor (see ¶ 258.1). When the members have been chosen, the district superintendent or the designated elder shall declare the church properly constituted.

9. The district superintendent or an elder whom the superintendent designates shall then adjourn the constituting church conference and call to order the charge conference of the pastoral charge. The membership of the charge conference shall be those newly elected, and any others entitled to membership. The charge conference shall then elect such officers of the church as the *Discipline* requires, including trustees of church property, and shall organize its structure as provided in the *Discipline*. When such officers have been duly elected and such structure put in place, the church is duly organized, and from this point its work shall proceed as described in the *Discipline*, provided that when a newly organized church is attached to a circuit,

the charge conference shall not be held until such time as representatives from all the churches of the charge can be properly assembled for that purpose.

10. The charge conference may take action, at its discretion, authorizing and directing the newly elected trustees to incorporate the newly organized church in accordance with local laws and the provisions of the *Discipline*.

## Section VIII. Transfer of a Local Church

¶ 260. A local church may be transferred from one annual conference to another in which it is geographically located by a two-thirds vote of the members who are present and voting in each of the following: (1) the charge conference, (2) a congregational meeting of the local church, and (3) each of the two annual conferences involved. Upon announcement of the required majorities by the bishop or bishops involved, the transfer shall immediately be effective. The votes required may originate in the local church or either of the annual conferences involved and shall be effective regardless of the order in which taken. In each case a two-thirds vote of those present and voting shall remain effective unless and until rescinded prior to the completion of the transfer by a vote of a majority of those present and voting.

## Section IX. Protection of Rights of Congregations

¶ 261. Nothing in the Plan and Basis of Union at any time after the union is to be construed so as to require any local church of the former Church of the United Brethren in Christ, or of the former The Evangelical Church, or of the former The Evangelical United Brethren Church, or of the former The Methodist Church to alienate or in any way to change the title to property contained in its deed or deeds at the time of union; and lapse of time or usage shall not affect said title or control.

## Section X. Special Sundays

¶ 262. The special Sundays in The United Methodist Church are intended to be illustrative of the nature and calling of the church and are celebrated annually. The special Sundays are placed on the calendar to make clear the calling of the church as the people of God, and to give persons the opportunity of contributing offerings to special programs.

Six special churchwide Sundays provide for churchwide offerings to do deeds expressive of our commitment: Human Relations Day, One Great Hour of Sharing, World Communion Sunday, United Methodist Student Sunday, Peace with Justice Sunday, and Native American Ministries Sunday. Three special Sundays are without offering: Heritage Sunday, Laity Sunday, and Organ and Tissue Donor Sunday. Four churchwide Sundays, Christian Education, Golden Cross, Disability Awareness, and Rural Life Sundays, provide opportunities for annual conference offerings.

The special Sundays approved by General Conference shall be the only Sundays of churchwide emphasis. The program calendar of the denomination shall include only the special Sundays approved by General Conference, special Sundays approved by ecumenical agencies to which The United Methodist Church is officially related, and the days and seasons of the Christian Year.

Because of the diversity of history and heritages experienced by the central conferences, they shall not be required to observe all of the special days listed below. The central conferences are authorized to observe other special days appropriate to their unique history and heritages.

GENERAL PROVISIONS REGARDING
CHURCHWIDE SPECIAL SUNDAYS WITH OFFERINGS

¶ 263. Six special churchwide Sundays with offerings shall be celebrated in each United Methodist Church.

*Purpose*—The purpose of the churchwide offerings shall be determined by General Conference upon recommendation of the General Council on Finance and Administration, after consultation with the Council of Bishops and the General Council on Ministries. The purpose of these funds shall remain constant for the quadrennium, and the net receipts shall be distributed on ratio to the administering agencies by the treasurer of the General Council on Finance and Administration (see ¶ 816.7 and ¶ 806.1*d*). The funds shall be promoted by the General Commission on Communication in cooperation with the agencies responsible for the administration of these funds. (*See* ¶ 1806.12.) Each offering shall be promptly remitted in full by the local church treasurer to the annual conference treasurer, who shall transmit the funds in full, except where noted differently below, to the General Council on Finance and Administration within thirty days of receipt in the office of the annual conference treasurer.

1. *Human Relations Day*—Human Relations Day shall be observed with an offering, preferably on the Sunday before the observance of Martin Luther King Jr.'s birthday. This Sunday occurs during Epiphany, the season of manifesting God's light to the world. Human Relations Day calls the Church to recognize the right of all God's children in realizing their potential as human beings in relationship with each other. The purpose of the day is to further the development of better human relations.

The offering receipts will be allocated and administered as follows:

a) *Community Developers Program:* 57 percent (administered by the General Board of Global Ministries);

b) *United Methodist Voluntary Services Program:* 33 percent (administered by the General Board of Global Ministries);

c) *Youth Offender Rehabilitation Program:* 10 percent (administered by the General Board of Church and Society).

Net receipts of the Human Relations Day offering shall be distributed on ratio to the administering agencies.

2. *One Great Hour of Sharing*—One Great Hour of Sharing shall be observed with an offering, preferably on the Fourth Sunday in Lent. Lent is the season of repentance, self-examination, and awareness of the hurts of the peoples of the world. One Great Hour of Sharing calls the Church to share the goodness of life with those who hurt. The observance shall be under the general supervision of the General Commission on Communication. Insofar as possible, the planning and promotion of the One Great Hour of Sharing shall be done cooperatively with other denominations through the National Council of the Churches of Christ in the U.S.A., it being understood, however, that receipts shall be administered by The United Methodist Church. Net receipts from the offering, after payment of the expenses of promotion, shall be remitted by the treasurer of the General Council on Finance and Administration to the General Board of Global Ministries, to be administered by the United Methodist Committee on Relief.

3. *World Communion Sunday*—World Communion Sunday shall be observed with an offering, preferably on the first Sunday of October.

World Communion Sunday calls the church to be the catholic inclusive church. In connection with World Communion Sunday there shall be a churchwide appeal conducted by the General Commission on Communication in accord with the following directives: Each local church shall be requested to remit as provided in ¶ 816.8 all the communion offering received on World Communion Sunday and such portion of the communion offering received at other observances of the sacrament of the Lord's Supper as the local church may designate.

The receipts shall be divided as follows, with the last two to be administered by the General Board of Higher Education and Ministry:

a) 50 percent for Crusade Scholarships, to be administered by the General Board of Global Ministries, with at least one half of the annual amount for ministries beyond the United States of America;

b) 35 percent for the Ethnic Scholarship Program; and

c) 15 percent for the Ethnic In-Service Training Program.

4. *United Methodist Student Day*—United Methodist Student Day shall be observed with an offering, preferably on the last Sunday in November or another Sunday appropriate to the local church. United Methodist Student Day calls the Church to support students as they prepare for life in uniting faith with knowledge. The offering receipts support the United Methodist scholarships and the United Methodist Student Loan Fund. The funds shall be administered by the General Board of Higher Education and Ministry.

5. *Peace with Justice Sunday*—Peace with Justice Sunday shall be observed with an offering, preferably on the *first* Sunday After Pentecost. Pentecost celebrates the outpouring of the Holy Spirit calling for God's shalom. Peace with Justice witnesses to God's demand for a faithful, just, disarmed, and secure world. The observance of Peace with Justice Sunday shall be under the general supervision of the General Board of Church and Society.

a) The annual conference treasurer shall retain 50 percent of the receipts for Peace with Justice ministries in the annual conference, to be administered by the annual conference board of church and society or equivalent structure.

b) The annual conference treasurer shall remit the remaining 50 percent of the receipts to the General Council on Finance and Administration. The funds shall be administered by the General Board of Church and Society for Peace with Justice ministries.

6. *Native American Ministries Sunday*—Native American Ministries

Sunday shall be observed with an offering, preferably on the Third Sunday of Easter. This Sunday serves to remind the Church of the gifts and contributions made by Native Americans to our society. The observance of Native American Ministries Sunday will be under the general supervision of the General Board of Global Ministries.

*a)* The annual conference treasurer shall retain 50 percent of the receipts for the developing and strengthening of Native American ministries within the annual conference, to be administered by the annual conference committee on Native American ministry.

Should there be no Native American ministries within the annual conference, the annual conference treasurer shall remit this 50 percent to the General Council on Finance and Administration.

*b)* The annual conference treasurer shall report gross receipts and remit the remaining 50 or 100 percent of the receipts as applicable to the General Council on Finance and Administration.

*c)* The funds to be distributed include 50 percent to the General Board of Higher Education and Ministry to provide scholarships for Native Americans attending United Methodist schools of theology and schools of theology approved by the University Senate of The United Methodist Church. The student must agree to serve at least two years in a Native American United Methodist congregation or ministry as a condition of receiving the Native American Ministries Sunday scholarship. Fifty percent of the scholarship will be converted to a loan if the student fails to serve in a Native American congregation or ministry upon graduation.

*d)* The remaining 50 percent of the fund shall be distributed to the General Board of Global Ministries to expand the number of target cities in their Native American Urban Initiative.

GENERAL PROVISIONS REGARDING SPECIAL SUNDAYS
WITHOUT CHURCHWIDE OFFERINGS

¶ **264.** Three special Sundays without churchwide offering shall be approved by General Conference upon recommendation of the General Council on Ministries after consultation with the Council of Bishops. The program functions assigned to the general agencies are carried out by the respective agencies through normal programmatic channels. Special Sundays are not needed for these program functions to be implemented.

1. *Heritage Sunday*—Heritage Sunday shall be observed on April

23, the day in 1968 when The United Methodist Church was created by the union of The Evangelical United Brethren Church and The Methodist Church, or the Sunday following that date. It falls during Eastertide, the season in which we remember the Resurrection and triumph of our Lord. Heritage Sunday calls the Church to remember the past by committing itself to the continuing call of God. The observance of Heritage Sunday shall be under the general supervision of the General Commission on Archives and History. Any general agency of the Church which desires to recommend a theme for a given year for this Sunday may do so one year prior to the observance for which the recommendation is made. This recommendation is to be made to the General Commission on Archives and History, and the decision of the annual theme of this Sunday shall be made by the voting members of the General Commission on Archives and History.

2. *Laity Sunday*—Laity Sunday shall be observed annually, preferably on the third Sunday in October. Laity Sunday calls the Church to celebrate the ministry of all lay Christians, as their lives are empowered for ministry by the Holy Spirit. The observance of Laity Sunday shall be under the general supervision of the General Board of Discipleship. Any general agency of the Church that desires to recommend a theme for a given year for this Sunday may do so two years prior to the observance for which the recommendation is made. This recommendation is to be made to the General Board of Discipleship, and the decision of the annual theme of this Sunday shall be made by the voting members of the General Board of Discipleship.

3. *Organ and Tissue Donor Sunday*—Organ and Tissue Donor Sunday shall be observed annually, preferably on the second Sunday in November since the date is close to Thanksgiving and is viewed as a time to come together around the issues of life and Thanksgiving. Congregations are encouraged to support Organ and Tissue Donor Sunday by including the topic in their worship services. Worship resource materials are available at all of the not-for-profit donor programs in the United States.

¶ **265.** *Approved Sundays for Annual Conference Observation*—Four special Sundays approved by General Conference provide opportunities for annual conference offerings. Local church treasurers shall remit the receipts of the following four offerings to the annual conference treasurer, and receipts will be acknowledged in accordance with the procedure of the annual conference. Local churches shall report the amount of the offering in the manner indicated in the local church report to the annual conference.

1. *Christian Education Sunday*—Christian Education Sunday shall be observed on a date determined by the annual conference. It calls the Church as the people of God to be open to growth and learning as disciples of Jesus Christ. If the annual conference so directs, an offering may be received for the work of Christian education within the annual conference. The observance of Christian Education Sunday shall be under the general supervision of the General Board of Discipleship.

2. *Golden Cross Sunday*—Golden Cross Sunday shall be observed annually on a date determined by the annual conference. If the annual conference so directs, an offering may be received for the work of health and welfare ministries in the annual conference. The observance of Golden Cross Sunday shall be under the general supervision of the General Board of Global Ministries.

3. *Rural Life Sunday*—Rural Life Sunday shall be observed on a date to be determined by the annual conference. Rural Life Sunday shall call the Church to celebrate the rural heritage of The United Methodist Church, to recognize the ongoing crisis occurring in rural areas of the nation and world today, and to affirm the interdependence of rural and urban communities. The observance of Rural Life Sunday shall be under the general supervision of the General Board of Global Ministries. Anyone who desires to recommend a theme for a given year for this Sunday may do so one year prior to the observance for which the recommendation is made. This recommendation is to be made to the General Board of Global Ministries, and the decision of the annual theme of this Sunday shall be made by the voting members of the General Board of Global Ministries. If the annual conference so directs, an offering may be received for the purpose of strengthening the nurture, outreach, and/or witness of congregations in town and rural areas.

4. *Disability Awareness Sunday*—Disability Awareness Sunday shall be observed annually on a date to be determined by the annual conference. Disability Awareness Sunday calls the Church to celebrate the gifts and graces of persons with disabilities and calls the Church and society to full inclusion of persons with disabilities in the community. If the annual conference so directs, an offering may be received and the funds used by the annual conference to promote the work of creating architectural and attitudinal accessibility in local

churches. The observance of Disability Awareness Sunday shall be under the general supervision of the General Board of Global Ministries.

Annual conferences may determine other special Sundays with or without offering. Special Sundays with offering shall be approved by the annual conference upon recommendation of the annual conference council on ministries in consultation with annual conference council on finance and administration. Special Sundays without offering shall be approved by the annual conference upon recommendation of the annual conference council on ministries. Local church treasurers shall remit the receipts of all annual conference Special Sundays with offering to the annual conference treasurer, and receipts will be acknowledged in accordance with procedures of the annual conference. Local churches shall report the amount of the offering in the manner indicated in the Local Church Report to the annual conference.

## Section XI. Lay Speaking Ministries

¶ 266. *Lay Speaking*—1. A **lay speaker** (local church or certified) is a member of a local church or charge who is ready and desirous to serve the Church and who is well informed on and committed to the Scriptures and the doctrine, heritage, organization, and life of The United Methodist Church and who has received specific training to develop skills in witnessing to the Christian faith through spoken communication, church and community leadership, and care-giving ministries. An applicant must be active in the support of the local church or charge.

2. Lay speakers are to serve the local church or charge (or beyond the local church or charge) in any way in which their witness or leadership and service inspires the laity to deeper commitment to Christ and more effective discipleship, including the interpretation of the Scriptures, doctrine, organization, and ministries of the church.

3. Through continued study and training a lay speaker should prepare to undertake one or more of the following functions, giving primary attention to service within the local church or charge.

*a)* To take initiative in giving leadership, assistance, and support to the program emphases of the church.

*b)* To lead meetings for prayer, training, study, and discussion when requested by the pastor, district superintendent, or committee on lay speaking.

*c)* To conduct, or assist in conducting, services of worship, and present sermons and addresses when requested by the pastor, district superintendent, or committee on lay speaking.

*d)* To relate to appropriate committees and ministry areas in providing leadership for congregational and community life and fostering care-giving ministries.

4. Lay speaker training courses shall be those recommended by the General Board of Discipleship or alternates approved by the conference committee on lay speaking. Such training should enable ministries with all language and cultural groups as appropriate.

5. It is recommended that a service of commitment be held for persons recognized as local church or certified lay speakers.

¶ 267. *Local Church Lay Speaker*—1. A candidate may be recognized as a local church lay speaker by the district or conference committee on lay speaking after the candidate has:

*a)* Made application in writing to the appropriate committee and has been recommended by the pastor and the church council or the charge conference of the local church in which membership is held. The district superintendent shall be responsible for reporting the names of applicants to the appropriate committee.

*b)* Completed the basic course for lay speaking.

2. The local church lay speaker shall serve the local church in which membership is held by witness of the spoken word, vital leadership service, and care-giving ministry (*see* ¶ 266.3).

3. To maintain status, a report and reapplication with recommendations must be submitted annually (*see* ¶ 246.11).

¶ 268. *Certified Lay Speaker*—1. A candidate may be recognized as a certified lay speaker by the district or conference committee on Lay Speaking Ministries after the candidate has:

*a)* Made application in writing to the appropriate committee and has been recommended by the pastor and the church council or the charge conference of the local church in which he or she holds membership.

*b)* Completed both basic and one advanced training courses for lay speaking.

*c)* Had his or her qualifications reviewed and approved by the appropriate committee (*see* ¶ 258.2 *f* [7]).

2. The certified lay speaker shall continue to serve the local church in the witness of the spoken word, vital leadership service, and care-giving ministry (*see* ¶ 266.1). In addition, the certified lay

speaker may serve in the district and conference and in local churches other than the local church in which membership is held.

3. Recognition as a certified lay speaker shall be renewed annually by the district or conference committee on Lay Speaking Ministries after the certified lay speaker has:

*a)* Requested in writing the renewal of certification.

*b)* Submitted an annual report to the charge conference and the committee on Lay Speaking Ministries, giving evidence of the satisfactory performance of lay speaking service.

*c)* Been recommended for renewal by the pastor and the church council or charge conference.

*d)* Completed at least once in every three years an advanced course for lay speakers.

¶ 269. *Transfer of Certification by Certified Lay Speakers*—A certified lay speaker who moves may transfer certification to the new district upon receipt of a letter from the previous district's committee on Lay Speaking Ministries confirming current certification and the date of completion of the most recent advanced course taken. Further renewal of certification is in accordance with ¶ 268.

¶ 270. *Provisions for Lay Missioners*—Lay missioners are committed laypersons, mostly volunteers, who are willing to be trained and work in a team with a pastor-mentor to develop faith communities, establish community ministries, develop church school extension programs, and engage in congregational development. All lay missioners must follow the guidelines established by the National Committee on Hispanic Ministries of the National Plan for Hispanic Ministries and may be certified by their annual conference. If annual conferences choose to certify lay missioners, they must do so according to the guidelines. They are accountable to their pastor-mentor as members of the ministry team. The ministry team is accountable to the local congregation or sponsoring body that established the goals for the ministry and assigned the ministry team. The lay missioner is accountable to the policies and procedures of the annual conference where assigned. The concept of lay missioners is theologically based in the ministry of the laity. While lay missioners are engaged in a variety of ministries, their purpose is to complement, not replace, pastors.[11]

---

11. *See* Judicial Council Decision 693.

*Chapter Two*

# THE MINISTRY OF THE ORDAINED

## Section I. The Meaning of Ordination and Conference Membership

¶ **301.** 1. Ministry in the Christian church is derived from the ministry of Christ, who calls all persons to receive God's gift of salvation and follow in the way of love and service. The whole church receives and accepts this call, and all Christians participate in this continuing ministry (*see* ¶¶ 120–138).

2. Within the church community, there are persons whose gifts, evidence of God's grace, and promise of future usefulness are affirmed by the community, and who respond to God's call by offering themselves in leadership as ordained ministers (¶ 302).

¶ **302.** *Ordination and Apostolic Ministry*—The pattern for this response to the call is provided in the development of the early church. The apostles led in prayer and preaching, ordered the spiritual and temporal life of the community, established leadership for the ministry of service, and provided for the proclamation of the gospel to new persons and in new places. The early church, through the laying on of hands, set apart persons with responsibility to preach, to teach, to administer the sacraments, to nurture, to heal, to gather the community in worship, and to send them forth in witness. The church also set apart other persons to care for the physical needs of others, reflecting the concerns for the people of the world. In the New Testament (Acts 6), we see the apostles identifying and authorizing persons to a ministry of service. These functions, though set apart, were never separate from the ministry of the whole people of God. Paul states (Ephesians 4:1-12) that different gifts and ministries are given to all persons.

¶ **303.** *Purpose of Ordination*—1. Ordination to this ministry is a gift from God to the church. In ordination, the church affirms and continues the apostolic ministry through persons empowered by the Holy Spirit. As such, those who are ordained make a commitment to conscious living of the whole gospel and to the proclamation of that gospel to the end that the world may be saved.

2. Ordination is fulfilled in leadership of the people of God

182

through ministries of Service, Word, Sacrament, and Order. The Church's ministry of service is a primary representation of God's love. Those who respond to God's call to lead in service and to equip others for this ministry through teaching, proclamation, and worship and who assist elders in the administration of the sacraments are ordained deacons. Those whose leadership in service includes preaching and teaching the Word of God, administration of the sacraments, ordering the Church for its mission and service, and administration of the *Discipline* of the Church are ordained as elders.

3. Ordained persons exercise their ministry in covenant with all Christians, especially with those whom they lead and serve in ministry. They also live in covenant of mutual care and accountability with all those who share their ordination, especially in The United Methodist Church, with the ordained who are members of the same annual conference and part of the same Order. The covenant of ordained ministry is a lifetime commitment, and those who enter into it dedicate their whole lives to the personal and spiritual disciplines it requires.

4. The effectiveness of the Church in mission depends on these covenantal commitments to the ministry of all Christians and the ordained ministry of the Church. Through ordination and through other offices of pastoral leadership, the Church provides for the continuation of Christ's ministry, which has been committed to the church as a whole. Without creative use of the diverse gifts of the entire body of Christ, the ministry of the church is less effective. Without responsible leadership, the focus, direction, and continuity of that ministry is diminished. It is out of the faith and witness of the congregation that men and women respond to God's call to ordained ministry. Every local church should intentionally nurture candidates for ordained ministry and provide spiritual and financial support for their education, where practical, as servant leaders for the ministry of the whole people of God.

5. In keeping with ancient Christian teaching and our Wesleyan tradition, we affirm that ordination for the same, or equivalent order, is not repeatable.

¶ **304.** *Qualifications for Ordination*—1. Those whom the Church ordains shall be conscious of God's call to ordained ministry, and their call shall be acknowledged and authenticated by the Church. God's call has many manifestations, and the Church cannot structure a single test of authenticity. Nevertheless, the experience of the Church and the needs of its ministry require certain qualities of faith, life, and practice from those who seek ordination as deacons and elders. In order that The United Methodist Church may be assured that those persons who present themselves as candidates for ordained ministry are truly called of God, the Church expects persons seeking ordination to:

*a)* Have a personal faith in Christ and be committed to Christ as Savior and Lord.

*b)* Nurture and cultivate spiritual disciplines and patterns of holiness.

*c)* Acknowledge a call by God to give themselves completely to ordained ministry following Jesus' pattern of love and service.

*d)* Communicate persuasively the Christian faith in both oral and written form.

*e)* Make a commitment to lead the whole Church in loving service to humankind.

*f)* Give evidence of God's gifts for ordained ministry, evidence of God's grace in their lives, and promise of future usefulness in the mission of the Church.

*g)* Be persons in whom the community can place trust and confidence.

*h)* Accept that Scripture contains all things necessary for salvation through faith in God through Jesus Christ; be competent in the disciplines of Scripture, theology, church history, and Church polity; possess the skills essential to the practice of ordained ministry; and lead in making disciples for Jesus Christ.

*i)* Be accountable to The United Methodist Church, accept its Doctrinal Standards and *Discipline* and authority, accept the supervision of those appointed to this ministry, and be prepared to live in the covenant of its ordained ministers.

2. For the sake of the mission of Jesus Christ in the world and the most effective witness to the Christian gospel, and in consideration of the influence of an ordained minister on the lives of other persons both within and outside the Church, the Church expects those who seek ordination to make a complete dedication of themselves to the highest ideals of the Christian life. To this end, they agree to exercise responsible self-control by personal habits conducive to bodily health, mental and emotional maturity, integrity in all personal relationships, fidelity in marriage and celibacy in singleness, social responsibility, and growth in grace and in the knowledge and love of God.

3. While persons set apart by the Church for ordained ministry are subject to all the frailties of the human condition and the pressures of society, they are required to maintain the highest standards of holy living in the world. Since the practice of homosexuality is incompatible with Christian teaching, self-avowed practicing homosexuals[1] are not to be accepted as candidates, ordained as ministers, or appointed to serve in The United Methodist Church.

4. The United Methodist Church entrusts those persons who are in the ordained ministry with primary responsibility for maintaining standards of education and preparation for ordination. Having been originally recommended by a charge conference and by authorization of the ordained members in full connection with the annual conference, according to the procedures set out in the *Book of Discipline* for the examination and approval of candidates for ordination, persons are elected to membership in the annual conference and ordained by the bishop.

5. In all cases where the district committee on ordained ministry, conference boards of ordained ministry, or ordained members in full connection in clergy session vote on granting any status regarding license, ordination, or conference membership, it is understood that the requirements set forth herein are minimum requirements only. Each person voting is expected to vote prayerfully based on personal judgment of the applicant's gifts, evidence of God's grace, and promise of future usefulness for the mission of the Church.

## Section II. Candidacy for Licensed and Ordained Ministry

¶ 305. *Entrance Procedures into Licensed and Ordained Ministry—* The ordained ministry is recognized by The United Methodist Church as a called-out and set-apart ministry. Therefore, it is appropriate that those persons who present themselves as candidates for ordained ministry be examined regarding the authenticity of their call by God to ordered ministry.

*Wesley's Questions for the Examiners—*In order that The United Methodist Church may be assured that those persons who present themselves as candidates for ministry are truly called of God to this

---

1. *"Self-avowed practicing homosexual"* is understood to mean that a person openly acknowledges to a bishop, district superintendent, district committee of ordained ministry, board of ordained ministry, or clergy session that the person is a practicing homosexual. *See* Judicial Council Decisions 702, 708, 722, 725, 764, 844.

order, let those who consider recommending such persons for candidacy as ordained ministers in The United Methodist Church prayerfully and earnestly ask themselves these questions:

1. Do they know God as pardoning God? Have they the love of God abiding in them? Do they desire nothing but God? Are they holy in all manner of conversation?

2. Have they gifts, as well as evidence of God's grace, for the work? Have they a clear, sound understanding; a right judgment in the things of God; a just conception of salvation by faith? Do they speak justly, readily, clearly?

3. Have they fruit? Have any been truly convinced of sin and converted to God, and are believers edified by their service?

As long as these marks occur in them, we believe they are called of God to serve. These we receive as sufficient proof that they are moved by the Holy Spirit.

¶ **306.** *Candidacy for Licensed and Ordained Ministry*—A person, upon hearing and heeding the call to servant leadership through licensed or ordained ministry, shall contact the pastor of the local church, another ordained deacon or elder, or the district superintendent to begin the process as an inquiring candidate.

The following is the process through which a person moves toward licensing and/or ordination and conference membership, and is to be resourced by the General Board of Higher Education and Ministry. All persons entering into this process shall receive written communication about decisions made regarding the different stages of their candidacy.

1. *The Inquiring Candidate* shall contact the pastor in the local church or another ordained deacon or elder; obtain and read the book *The Christian as Minister* and discuss it with the pastor in the local church or another ordained deacon or elder. Inquiring candidates should be encouraged to pursue their education at one of the United Methodist seminaries.

2. *The Exploring Candidate*—Those seeking to explore candidacy for licensed or ordained ministry:

*a)* shall have been a member in good standing of The United Methodist Church for at least two years immediately preceding the application for candidacy, including a year of service in some form of congregational leadership, either in that local church or one agreed to by the district committee on ordained ministry, provided that in the case of an affiliate member, there has been a consultation with and approval by the charge conference of the home church (this paragraph shall become effective at the end of the 2000 General Conference);

*b)* shall apply to the district superintendent in writing for admission to the candidacy studies; and

*c)* shall be assigned as an exploring candidate to a candidacy mentor by the district committee on ordained ministry in consultation with the district superintendent and shall complete the preliminary studies that will focus on the spiritual discernment of the call, after proper registration through the annual conference candidacy registrar and the board of ordained ministry.

3. *Declared Candidate for Licensing or Ordination*—Declared candidates are those who have completed the exploratory process in § 2 and who seek to become certified candidates. They shall:

*a)* consult with the pastor and committee on pastor or staff-parish relations after formulating a written statement reflecting their call to ministry and requesting recommendation for certification. The candidate shall be interviewed by the committee on his or her statement and Wesley's historic questions in ¶ 305;

*b)* be recommended by the charge conference in accordance with the following method: A meeting for the purpose of recommending a candidate for ordained ministry shall be preceded by at least two public announcements and shall be held in the presence of the bishop, district superintendent, or an authorized elder, who shall counsel with those present regarding the ability and qualifications of the applicant and make plain the importance of such recommendation to the candidate for ordination. To be valid such a recommendation shall be: i) voted by written ballot by two-thirds of the charge conference present at this meeting, provided that in the case of an affiliate member there has been a consultation with and approval by the charge conference of the home church, and ii) have been graduated from an accredited high school or received a certificate of equivalency;

*c)* continue the candidacy studies for ordained ministry with a candidacy mentor.

4. *The Certified Candidate*—Candidates who have completed the requirements of § 2–3 and desire to be certified as candidates for ordination shall:

*a)* appear before the district committee on ordained ministry for examination;

*b)* complete the psychological tests required;

*c)* submit a written response providing evidence of under-

187

standing and expectation concerning the following: i) the most formative experiences of your Christian life; ii) God's call to ordained ministry and the role of the church in your call; iii) reflect on your year's experience in leadership in the congregation; iv) your future usefulness as a minister in The United Methodist Church; v) your personal beliefs as a Christian; vi) your personal gifts for ministry; vii) how your personal relationships may affect your future ministry;

*d)* submit a written response providing evidence of understanding the ministry of deacon and the ministry of the elder within The United Methodist Church;

*e)* provide other information as may be required for determining gifts, evidence of God's grace, fruit, and demonstration of the call for the ministry of deacon or elder; and

*f)* agree for the sake of the mission of Jesus Christ in the world and the most effective witness of the gospel, and in consideration of their influence as ministers, to make a complete dedication of themselves to the highest ideals of the Christian life as set forth in ¶¶ 102–104; 160–166. To this end they shall agree to exercise responsible self-control by personal habits conducive to bodily health, mental and emotional maturity, fidelity in marriage and celibacy in singleness, social responsibility, and growth in grace and the knowledge and love of God.[2]

---

2. In adopting the statements in ¶¶ 304.2 and 306.4*f* on the moral and social responsibility of ordained ministers, the General Conference seeks to elevate the standards by calling for a more thoroughgoing moral commitment by the candidate and for a more careful and thorough examination of candidates by district committees and boards of the ministry.

The legislation in no way implies that the use of tobacco is a morally indifferent question. In the light of the developing evidence against the use of tobacco, the burden of proof would be upon all users to show that their use of it is consistent with the highest ideals of the Christian life. Similarly, regarding beverage alcohol, the burden of proof would be upon users to show that their action is consistent with the ideals of excellence of mind, purity of body, and responsible social behavior.

Therefore, the changes here do not relax the traditional view concerning the use of tobacco and beverage alcohol by ordained ministers in The United Methodist Church. Rather they call for higher standards of self-discipline and habit formation in all personal and social relationships. They call for dimensions of moral commitment that go far beyond any specific practices which might be listed. (*See* Judicial Council Decision 318.)

The General Conference, in response to expressions throughout the Church regarding homosexuality and ordination, reaffirms the present language of the *Discipline* regarding the character and commitment of persons seeking ordination and affirms its high standards.

¶ **307.** *Continuation of Candidacy*—The progress of candidates shall be reviewed and candidacy renewed annually. Candidacy may be renewed by the district committee on ordained ministry (¶ 660) on recommendation of the charge conference and on evidence that the candidate's gifts, fruits, and evidence of God's grace continue to be satisfactory and that the candidate is making satisfactory progress in the required studies.

1. A candidate preparing for ordained ministry who is enrolled as a student in a school, college, university, or school of theology recognized by the University Senate shall present annually to the district committee on ordained ministry an official transcript from the school the person is attending.

The transcript shall be considered by the district committee on ordained ministry along with other evidence that the candidate's gifts, evidence of God's grace, and fruit continue to be satisfactory. An annual personal interview with the candidate is recommended.

2. A person who is a certified candidate or who is in the candidacy process may have her or his status or studies accepted by another district committee in the same or another annual conference.

---

For more than 200 years candidates for ordination have been asked Wesley's Questions, including ". . . Have they a clear, sound understanding; right judgment in the things of God; a just conception of salvation by faith? . . ." (¶ 305).

All candidates agree to make a complete dedication of themselves to the highest ideals of the Christian life and to this end agree "to exercise responsible self-control, by personal habits conducive to bodily health, mental and emotional maturity, fidelity in marriage and celibacy in singleness, social responsibility, and growth in grace and the knowledge and love of God" (¶ 304).

The character and commitment of candidates for the ordained ministry is described or examined in six places in the *Book of Discipline* (¶¶ 304, 305, 306.4, 315, 321, and 326). These say in part: "Only those shall be elected to full membership who are of unquestionable moral character and genuine piety, sound in the fundamental doctrines of Christianity and faithful in the discharge of their duties" (¶ 324).

The statement on ordination (¶ 304) states: "*The Church expects those who seek ordination to make a complete dedication of themselves to the highest ideals of the Christian life . . . [and to] agree to exercise responsible self-control by personal habits. . . .*"

There are eight crucial steps in the examination of candidates. They are:

(1) The self-examination of the individual seeking ordination as he or she responds to God's call in personal commitment to Christ and his church.

(2) The decision of the committee on pastor-parish relations, which makes the first recommendation to the charge conference when a member seeks to become a candidate for ordained ministry.

(3) The decision of the charge conference, which must recommend the candidate.

(4) The decision of the district committee on ordained ministry, which must recommend the candidate to the conference board of ordained ministry and, where applicable, the decision of the district conference.

¶ **308.** *Discontinuance and Reinstatement of Certified Candidacy*—1. *Discontinuance of a Certified Candidate*—Certified candidates may be discontinued on their own request, upon severing relationship in The United Methodist Church, or upon action to discontinue by the district committee on ordained ministry. The district committee on ordained ministry shall file with the conference board of ordained ministry a permanent record of the circumstances relating to the discontinuance of the certified candidate.

2. *Reinstatement of Certified Candidate's Status*—Certified candidates whose status has been discontinued by a district committee on ordained ministry of an annual conference of The United Methodist Church shall only be reinstated by the district committee of the district in which they were discontinued. When approved by the district committee on ordained ministry, their certified candidate's credentials shall be reissued and they shall be eligible to continue the process.

---

(5) The decision of the board of ordained ministry, which must recommend deacon's ordination and probationary membership. *See* Judicial Council Decisions 513, 536, 542.

(6) The decision of the clergy members of the annual conference, who must elect candidates to probationary membership.

(7) The recommendation of the board of ordained ministry for deacon's or elder's ordination and full membership.

(8) The election to deacon's or elder's ordination and full membership by the clergy members of the annual conference.

All clergy members of the annual conference are accountable as to character and effectiveness to the annual conference throughout their entire ministry.

The General Conference has made it clear in the "Doctrinal Standards and Our Theological Task" (Part II of the Discipline) that Scripture, tradition, experience, and reason are our guidelines. "United Methodists share with other Christians the conviction that Scripture is the primary source and criterion for Christian doctrine."

In the Social Principles, the General Conference has said that "we do not condone the practice of homosexuality and consider this practice incompatible with Christian teaching." Furthermore, the Principles state that "we affirm the sanctity of the marriage covenant that is expressed in love, mutual support, personal commitment, and shared fidelity between a man and a woman. We believe that God's blessing rests upon such marriage, whether or not there are children of the union. We reject social norms that assume different standards for women than for men in marriage." Also, "we affirm the integrity of single persons, and we reject all social practices that discriminate or social attitudes that are prejudicial against persons because they are single."

The General Conference affirms the wisdom of our heritage expressed in the disciplinary provisions relating to the character and commitment of ordained ministers. The United Methodist Church has moved away from prohibitions of specific acts, for such prohibitions can be endless. We affirm our trust in the covenant community and the process by which we ordain ministers.

In our covenant we are called to trust one another as we recommend, examine, and elect candidates for the ordained ministry and conference membership. *See* Judicial Council Decision 480.

¶ **309.** *Appointment of Certified Candidates*—A certified candidate is eligible for appointment as a local pastor upon completion of License for Pastoral Ministry (¶ 340).

## Section III. Clergy Orders in The United Methodist Church

¶ **310.** *Orders in Relation to the Ministry of All Christians*—Baptism is God's gift of unmerited grace through the Holy Spirit. It is an incorporation into Christ which marks the entrance of each person into the church and its ministry (Romans: 6:3, 4, 18).

The New Testament witness to Jesus Christ makes clear that the primary form of his ministry in God's name is that of service, *diakonia*, in the world. Very early in its history, the church came to understand that all of its members were commissioned in baptism to ministries of love, justice, and service within local congregations and the larger communities in which they lived; all who follow Jesus have a share in the ministry of Jesus, who came not to be served, but to serve. There is thus a general ministry of all baptized Christians (*see* ¶¶ 125–135).

Within the people of God, some persons are called to the ministry of deacon. The words deacon, deaconess, and diaconate all spring from a common Greek root—*diakonos*, or "servant," and *diakonia*, or "service." Very early in its history the church, as an act of worship and praise of God, instituted an order of ordained ministers to personify or focus the servanthood to which all Christians are called. These people were named *deacons*. This ministry exemplifies and leads the Church in the servanthood every Christian is called to live both in the church and the world. The deacon embodies the interrelationship between worship in the gathered community and service to God in the world.

Within the people of God, other persons are called to the ministry of elder. The elders carry on the historic work of the *presbyteros* in the life of the Church. Beginning in some of the very early Christian communities, the *presbyteros* assisted the bishop in leading the gathered community in the celebration of sacraments and the guidance and care of its communal life. The ministry of elder exemplifies and leads the Church in service to God in the world, in remembering and celebrating the gifts of God and living faithfully in response to God's grace.

¶ **311.** *Order of Deacons and Order of Elders*—There shall be in each

191

annual conference an Order of Deacons and an Order of Elders. All persons ordained as clergy in The United Methodist Church upon election to full membership in the annual conference shall be members of and participate in an Order appropriate to their election. An order is a covenant community within the church to mutually support, care for, and hold accountable its members for the sake of the life and mission of the church. These orders, separately or together, seek to respond to the spiritual hunger among clergy for a fulfilling sense of vocation, for support among peers during this stressful time of change in the Church, and for a deepening relationship with God.

¶ **312.** *Purpose of an Order*—The specific and limited function of each Order is to: (1) provide for regular gatherings of ordained deacons and ordained elders for continuing formation in relationship to Jesus Christ through such experiences as Bible study, study of issues facing the church and society, and theological exploration in vocational identity and leadership; (2) assist in plans for individual study and retreat experiences; (3) develop a bond of unity and common commitment to the mission and ministry of The United Methodist Church and the annual conference; (4) enable the creation of relationships that allow mutual support and trust; and (5) hold accountable all members of the Order in the fulfilling of these purposes. All of the functions of the Order(s) shall be fulfilled in cooperation and coordination with the board of ordained ministry and do not replace the normal supervisory processes, the processes of evaluation for ordained ministers, or the responsibilities of the board of ordained ministry, the cabinet, or the clergy session.

¶ **313.** *Organization of an Order*—The bishop shall convene and provide continuing spiritual leadership for the Order, with the support and assistance of the board of ordained ministry. Necessary financial support shall be provided by the annual conference through the budget of the board. The board may also use other appropriate funding sources for this purpose. The board shall nominate from within the Order's membership and the Order shall elect quadrennially a chairperson of the Order who, in cooperation with and under the guidance of the bishop, will provide continuing leadership for the Order. The chairperson will be responsible for implementation of plans and activities of the Order and will represent the Order to the conference board of ordained ministry. The chairperson will serve as a member of the board's executive committee. Activities of the Order and proposals for funding shall be regularly reported to the board.

¶ **314.** *Membership in an Order*—Persons shall become members of the Order of Deacons or Order of Elders following their election to full membership in the annual conference. Acceptance of the status of full membership will constitute a commitment to regular participation in the life of the Order.

### Section IV. The Commissioned Minister as Probationary Member

¶ **315.** *Qualifications for Election to Probationary Membership and Commissioning*—A person shall be eligible for election to probationary membership and commissioning in the annual conference by vote of the clergy session on recommendation of its board of ordained ministry after meeting the following qualifications.

1. *Candidacy Requirement:* Each candidate shall have been a certified candidate for probationary membership and commissioning for at least two years and no more than twelve years.

2. *Service Requirement:* Each candidate shall have had a minimum of two years in a service setting as determined by the district committee on ordained ministry as a condition for probationary membership and commissioning. This required service may be concurrent with academic study, provided there is adequate mentoring and supervision in the theology and practice of servant leadership. A service setting shall be in a position approved by the bishop and cabinet in the conference where the candidacy relationship is held, even if the service setting is outside the bounds of the annual conference.

3. *Undergraduate Requirement:* A candidate for probationary membership and commissioning shall have completed a bachelor's degree from a college or university recognized by the University Senate. Exceptions to the undergraduate degree requirements may be made in consultation with the General Board of Higher Education and Ministry in some instances, for missional purposes, for persons who have a minimum of sixty semester hours of Bachelor of Arts credit and:

*a)* have been prevented from pursuit of the normal course of baccalaureate education,

*b)* are members of a group whose cultural practices and training enhance insight and skills for effective ministry not available through conventional formal education, or

*c)* have graduated with a Bachelor degree or its equivalent from a college not recognized by the University Senate and have completed the Master of Divinity or equivalent first professional degree in a school of theology listed by the University Senate.

4. Graduate Requirement:

*a)* a candidate for ordination as an elder shall have received a Master of Divinity or its equivalent from a school listed by the University Senate.

*b)* a candidate for ordination as a deacon shall have:

(1) received a master's degree from a seminary listed by the University Senate, or

(2) received a master's degree in the area of the specialized ministry in which the candidate will serve, and completed the basic graduate theological studies, in a context which will provide formation as a United Methodist deacon in full connection within a cohesive program developed by the seminary and approved by the General Board of Higher Education and Ministry, documented by a record of completion from that school.

*c)* In all cases candidates shall have completed a minimum of twenty-four semester hours of graduate theological studies in the Christian faith, including the areas of: Old Testament; New Testament; theology; church history; mission of the church in the world; evangelism; worship/liturgy; and United Methodist doctrine, polity and history. These courses can be included within or in addition to a seminary degree.

5. In some instances a candidate who is pursuing ordination to serve as deacon in full connection may fulfill the academic requirements through the following professional certification alternate route:

*a)* shall have reached thirty-five years of age at the time to become a certified candidate;

*b)* completed a bachelor's degree, received professional certification or license in the area of ministry in which the candidate will serve, have completed a minimum of eight semester hours of graduate credit or equivalent quarter hours in the area of specialization, and have been recommended by the conference board of ordained ministry;

*c)* have completed a minimum of twenty-four semester hours of the basic graduate theological studies of the Christian faith including the areas of: Old Testament; New Testament; theology; church history; mission of the church in the world; evangelism; worship/liturgy; and United Methodist doctrine, polity, and history, in a context which will provide a cohesive program and formation as a United Methodist deacon in full connection within a cohesive program developed by the seminary and approved by the General Board of Higher Education and Ministry, documented by a record of completion from that school.

6. Local pastors may fulfill the requirements for probationary membership and commissioning when they have:

*a)* reached forty years of age;

*b)* completed the five-year Course of Study for ordained ministry, of which no more than four courses may be taken by correspondence or Internet; and

*c)* an Advanced Course of Study consisting of thirty-two semester hours of graduate theological study or its equivalent as determined by the General Board of Higher Education and Ministry that shall include the areas of evangelism, and United Methodist history, doctrine, and polity (*see* Judicial Council Decision 823).

7. The board of ordained ministry shall require an official transcript of credits from each school before recognizing any of the applicant's educational claims. In case of doubt, the board may submit a transcript to the General Board of Higher Education and Ministry.

8. Each candidate shall present a satisfactory certificate of good health by a physician on the prescribed form. Disabilities are not to be construed as unfavorable health factors when a person with disability is capable of meeting the professional standards and is able to render effective service as a probationary member and commissioned minister.

9. Each candidate shall respond to a written and oral doctrinal examination administered by the conference board of ordained ministry. The examination shall cover the following:

*a)* Describe your personal experience of God and the understanding of God you derive from biblical, theological, and historical sources.

*b)* What is your understanding of humanity, and the human need for divine grace?

*c)* How do you interpret the statement Jesus Christ is Lord?

*d)* What is your conception of the activity of the Holy Spirit in personal faith, in the community of believers, and in responsible living in the world?

*e)* What is your understanding of the kingdom of God; the Resurrection; eternal life?

*f)* What are the theological tasks of a probationary member and commissioned minister with special reference to Part II of the *Book of Discipline?*

*g)* The United Methodist Church holds that the living core of the Christian faith was revealed in Scripture, illumined by tradition, vivified in personal experience, and confirmed by reason. What is your understanding of this theological position of the Church?

*h)* Describe the nature and mission of the Church. What are its primary tasks today?

*i)* Discuss your understanding of the primary characteristics of United Methodist polity.

*j)* How do you perceive yourself, your gifts, your motives, your role, and your commitment as a probationary member and commissioned minister in The United Methodist Church?

*k)* Describe your understanding of *diakonia*, the servant ministry of the church, and the servant ministry of the probationary member and commissioned minister.

*l)* What is the meaning of ordination in the context of the general ministry of the Church?

*m)* Describe your understanding of an inclusive church and ministry.

*n)* You have agreed as a candidate for the sake of the mission of Jesus Christ in the world and the most effective witness of the gospel, and in consideration of their influence as ministers, to make a complete dedication of yourself to the highest ideals of the Christian life, and to this end agree to exercise responsible self-control by personal habits conducive to bodily health, mental and emotional maturity, integrity in all personal relationships, fidelity in marriage and celibacy in singleness, social responsibility, and growth in grace and the knowledge and love of God. What is your understanding of this agreement?

10. Each candidate shall have been recommended in writing to the conference board of ordained ministry, based on a three-fourths majority vote of the district committee on ordained ministry.

11. Each candidate shall have a personal interview with the conference board of ordained ministry to complete his or her candidacy.

12. Each candidate shall submit on a form provided by the board of ordained ministry a notarized statement detailing any written accusations or convictions for felony, misdemeanor, or incident of sexual misconduct, or certifying that this candidate has neither been accused in writing nor convicted of a felony, misdemeanor, or any incident of sexual misconduct.

13. Each candidate shall file with the board a written, concise, autobiographical statement (in duplicate on a prescribed form) regarding age, health, family status, Christian experience, call to ministry, educational record, formative Christian experiences, and plans for service in the Church.

14. Each candidate shall have been recommended in writing to the clergy session based on at least a two-thirds majority vote of the conference board of ordained ministry.

¶ **316.** *Commissioning*—Commissioning is the act of the church that publicly acknowledges God's call and the response, talents, gifts and training of the candidate. The church invokes the Holy Spirit as the candidate is commissioned to be a faithful servant leader among the people, to lead the church in service, to proclaim the Word of God and to equip others for ministry.

Through commissioning, the church sends persons in leadership and service in the name of Jesus Christ and marks their entrance into a time of probation as they prepare for ordination. Commissioned ministers are probationary clergy members of the annual conference and are accountable to the bishop and the clergy session for the conduct of their ministry.

During probation the clergy session discerns their fitness for ordination and their effectiveness in ministry. After fulfilling all candidacy requirements and upon recommendation of the conference board of ordained ministry, the clergy session shall vote on the probationary membership and commissioning of the candidates. The bishop and secretary of the conference shall provide credentials as a probationary member and a commissioned minister in the annual conference.

The period of commissioned ministry is concluded when the probationary members are received as full members of the annual conference and ordained as either deacon or elder, or a decision is made not to proceed toward ordination and probationary membership is ended.

¶ **317.** *Probationary Service of Commissioned Ministers*—All persons who are commissioned ministers shall be appointed by a bishop (¶ 430) and serve a minimum of three years as a probationary member of the annual conference. During the probationary period, arrangements shall be offered by the board of ordained ministry for all commissioned ministers to be involved in a curriculum that extends theological education by using covenant groups and mentoring to support the practice and work of their ministry as servant leaders, to contemplate the grounding of ordained ministry, and to understand covenant ministry in the life of the conference. The specialized service of probationary members shall be evaluated by the district superintendent and the board of ordained ministry in terms of the probationary member's ability to express and give leadership in servant ministry.

1. The commissioned ministers planning to give their lives as deacons in full connection shall be in ministries of Word and Service the entire probationary period. A commissioned person preparing for ordination as a deacon shall be licensed for the practice of ministry during probationary membership to perform the duties of the ministry of the deacon as stated in ¶ 319.

2. The commissioned ministers planning to give their lives as elders in full connection shall be in ministries of Service, Word, Sacrament, and Order. A commissioned minister preparing for ordination as an elder who serving as pastor of a local church shall be licensed for pastoral ministry (¶ 340).

3. Commissioned ministers who are serving in extension ministries or graduate degree programs shall be accountable to the district superintendent and the board of ordained ministry for the conduct of ministry, and for demonstrating their effectiveness in the ministry of the order to which they seek to be ordained. In every case, they will demonstrate their effectiveness in servant leadership in the local church to the satisfaction of the board of ordained ministry.

¶ **318.** *Eligibility and Rights of Probationary Membership*—Probationary members are on trial in preparation for membership in full connection in the annual conference as deacons or elders. They are on probation as to character, servant leadership, and effectiveness in ministry. The annual conference, through the clergy session, has jurisdiction over probationary members. Annually, the board of ordained ministry shall review and evaluate their relationship and make recommendation to the clergy members in full connection regarding their continuance. No member shall be continued on probation beyond the sixth regular session following their admission to probationary membership and commissioning unless extended, upon recommendation of the board of ordained ministry by a three-fourths vote, by the clergy session. Such extensions shall not be granted beyond three additional years.

1. Probationary members who are preparing for deacon's or

elder's orders may be ordained deacons or elders when they qualify for membership in full connection in the annual conference.

2. Probationary members shall have the right to vote in the annual conference on all matters except the following:

a) constitutional amendments;

b) election of delegates to the general and jurisdictional or central conferences;

c) all matters of ordination, character, and conference relations of clergy.

3. Probationary members may serve on any board, commission, or committee of the annual conference except the board of ordained ministry (¶ 632.1). They shall not be eligible for election as delegates to the General, central, or jurisdictional conferences.

4. Probationary members shall be amenable to the annual conference in the performance of their ministry and are subject to the provisions of the *Book of Discipline* in the performance of their duties. They shall be supervised by the district superintendent under whom they are appointed. They shall also be assigned a deacon or elder as mentor by the board of ordained ministry. Probationary members preparing to become elders shall be eligible for appointment by meeting disciplinary provisions (¶ 340).

5. Probationary members in appointments beyond the local church shall relate themselves to the district superintendent in the area where their work is done. The district superintendent shall give them supervision and report annually to their board of ordained ministry.

6. *Discontinuance from Probationary Membership*—Probationary members may request discontinuance of this relationship or may be discontinued by the annual conference upon recommendation of the board of ordained ministry. When probationary members in good standing withdraw to unite with another denomination or to terminate their membership in The United Methodist Church, their action shall be considered a request for discontinuance of their relationship and their credentials shall be surrendered to a district superintendent. Prior to any final recommendation of discontinuance without consent, a probationary member will be advised of the right to a hearing before the executive committee of the conference board of ordained ministry. A report of the action will be made to the full board. The provisions of fair process (¶ 359.2) shall be observed and there shall be a review by the administrative review committee under ¶ 633 prior to hearing by the annual conference. When this relationship is dis-

continued, they shall no longer be permitted to exercise ministerial functions and shall return their credentials to the district superintendent for deposit with the secretary of the conference, and their membership shall be transferred by the district superintendent to the local church they designate after consultation with the pastor. The board of ordained ministry shall file with the resident bishop and the secretary of the conference a permanent record of the circumstances relating to discontinuance as a probationary member as required in ¶ 632.3d. After discontinuance, probationary members may be classified and approved as local pastors in accordance with the provision of ¶ 341.

### Section V. The Ordained Deacon in Full Connection

¶ 319. *The Ministry of a Deacon*—From among the baptized, deacons are called by God to a lifetime of servant leadership, authorized by the Church, and ordained by a bishop. Deacons fulfill servant ministry in the world and lead the Church in relating the gathered life of Christians to their ministries in the world, interrelating worship in the gathered community with service to God in the world. Deacons give leadership in the Church's life: in the teaching and proclamation of the Word; in worship, and in assisting the elders in the administration of the sacraments of baptism and the Lord's Supper; in forming and nurturing disciples; in conducting marriages and burying the dead; in the congregation's mission to the world; and in leading the congregation in interpreting the needs, concerns, and hopes of the world. It is the deacons, in both person and function, whose distinctive ministry is to embody, articulate, and lead the whole people of God in its servant ministry. From the earliest days of the church, deacons were called and set apart for the ministry of love, justice, and service; of connecting the church with the most needy, neglected, and marginalized among the children of God. This ministry grows out of the Wesleyan passion for social holiness and ministry among the poor.

Deacons lead the congregation in its servant ministry and equip and support all baptized Christians in their ministry. The distinct ministry of the deacon has evolved in United Methodism over many years—the continuing work of the deaconess, the home missionary, and the diaconal minister. The Church, recognizing the gifts and impact of all predecessor embodiments of the diaconate and providing for the continuation of the office of deaconess, affirms that this distinctiveness is made visible and central to the Church's life and ministry through ordination and that the ministry of the deacon is a faithful response of the mission of the Church meeting the emerging needs of the future. Deacons are accountable to the annual conference and the bishop for the fulfillment of their call to servant leadership.

¶ 320. *Ministry, Authority, and Responsibilities of Deacons in Full Connection*—1. Deacons are persons called by God, authorized by the Church, and ordained by a bishop to a lifetime ministry of Word and Service to both the community and the congregation in a ministry that connects the two. Deacons exemplify Christian discipleship and create opportunities for others to enter into discipleship. In the world, the deacon seeks to express a ministry of compassion and justice, assisting laypersons as they claim their own ministry. In the congregation, the ministry of the deacon is to teach and to form disciples, and to lead worship together with other ordained and laypersons.

2. The deacon in full connection shall have the rights of voice and vote in the annual conference where membership is held; shall be eligible to serve as clergy on boards, commissions, or committees of the annual conference and hold office on the same; and shall be eligible for election as a clergy delegate to the General, central, or jurisdictional conference. The deacon in full connection shall attend all the sessions of the annual conference and share with elders in full connection responsibility for all matters of ordination, character, and conference relations of clergy (¶ 325.1).

3. As members of the Order of Deacons, all deacons in full connection are in covenant with all other such deacons in the annual conference and shall participate in the life of their Order.

¶ 321. *Requirements for Ordination as Deacon and Admission to Full Connection*—Probationary members who are applying for admission into full connection and who have been probationary members for at least three years may be admitted into membership in full connection in an annual conference by two-thirds vote of the clergy members in full connection of the annual conference, upon recommendation by two-thirds vote of the board of ordained ministry, after they have qualified as follows:

1. Served under episcopal appointment in a ministry of service the entire probationary period. Upon recommendation of the board of ordained ministry, the annual conference may equate nonsalaried service as meeting this qualification. Such equivalence is to be determined in light of the years of service involved, the quality of that ser-

vice, the maturity of the applicant, and other relevant factors determined by the board. Supervision is to be: (a) by the district superintendent, and (b) by the board of ordained ministry. The applicant's service must be evaluated by the board of ordained ministry as effective according to written guidelines developed by the board and adopted by the clergy members in full connection. Lay persons directly involved in the applicant's servant ministry shall be involved by the board in the annual evaluation.

2. Been previously elected as a probationary member.

3. Responded to a written or oral doctrinal examination administered by the board of ordained ministry. The candidate shall demonstrate the ability to communicate clearly in both oral and written form. The candidate's reflections and the board's response shall be informed by the insights and guidelines of Part II of the *Book of Discipline*. The examination shall also focus upon the covenantal relationship of the applicant to God, to the Church, and to the Order of Deacon, as well as the understanding of *diaconia*, servant leadership, and the interrelatedness of the Church and the world. The applicant shall be able to articulate the call of God to the order of deacon and to relate that call to leadership within the ministry of all Christians, through the setting of their service, the local church, and the annual conference.

4. The following questions are guidelines for the preparation of the examination:

*a*) Theology.

(1) How has the practice of ministry affected your experience and understanding of God?

(2) What effect has the practice of ministry had on your understanding of humanity and the need for divine grace?

(3) What changes has the practice of ministry had on your understanding of (a) the "Lordship of Jesus Christ," and (b) the work of the Holy Spirit?

(4) The United Methodist Church holds that Scripture, tradition, experience, and reason are sources and norms for belief and practice, but that the Bible is primary among them. What is your understanding of this theological position of the Church?

(5) How do you understand the following traditional evangelical doctrines: (a) repentance; (b) justification; (c) regeneration; (d) sanctification? What are the marks of the Christian life?

(6) For the sake of the mission of Jesus Christ in the world and the most effective witness to the Christian gospel, and in consid-

eration of your influence as an ordained minister, are you willing to make a complete dedication of yourself to the highest ideals of the Christian life; and to this end will you agree to exercise responsible self-control by personal habits conducive to physical health, intentional intellectual development, fidelity in marriage and celibacy in singleness, integrity in all personal relationships, social responsibility, and growth in grace and the knowledge of the love of God?[3]

(7) What is the meaning and significance of the sacraments?

(8) Describe the nature and mission of the Church. What are its primary tasks today?

(9) What is your understanding of: (*a*) the kingdom of God; (*b*) the Resurrection; (*c*) eternal life?

*b*) Vocation.

(1) How do you understand your vocation as an ordained deacon?

*c*) The Practice of Ministry.

(1) How has the practice of service ministry during the probationary period affected your understanding of ministry?

(2) Do you offer yourself to be appointed by the bishop to a service ministry?

(3) Describe and evaluate your personal gifts for ministry. What would be your areas of strength and areas in which you need to be strengthened?

(4) Are you willing to relate yourself in ministry to all persons without regard to race, color, ethnicity, national origin, social status, gender, sexual orientation, age, economic condition, or disabilities?

(5) Provide evidence of experience in peace and justice ministries.

*d*) *Historic Examination for Admission into Full Connection and Ordination as Deacon*—The bishop as chief pastor shall engage those seeking to be admitted in serious self-searching and prayer to prepare them for their examination before the conference. At the time of the examination, the bishop shall also explain to the conference the historic nature of the following questions and seek to interpret their spirit and intent. The questions are these and any others which may be thought necessary:

(1) Have you faith in Christ?

(2) Are you going on to perfection?

---

3. *See* Judicial Council Decision 542.

(3) Do you expect to be made perfect in love in this life?

(4) Are you earnestly striving after perfection in love?

(5) Are you resolved to devote yourself wholly to God and God's work?

(6) Do you know the General Rules of our Church?

(7) Will you keep the General Rules of our Church?

(8) Have you studied the doctrines of The United Methodist Church?

(9) After full examination do you believe that our doctrines are in harmony with the Holy Scriptures?

(10) Have you studied our form of Church discipline and polity?

(11) Do you approve our Church government and polity?

(12) Will you support and maintain them?

(13) Will you exercise the ministry of compassion?

(14) Will you diligently instruct the children in every place?

(15) Will you visit from house to house?

(16) Will you recommend fasting or abstinence, both by precept and example?

(17) Are you determined to employ all your time in the work of God?

(18) Are you in debt so as to embarrass you in your work?

(19) Will you observe the following directions?

(a) Be diligent. Never be unemployed. Never be triflingly employed. Never trifle away time; neither spend any more time at any one place than is strictly necessary.

(b) Be punctual. Do everything exactly at the time. And do not mend our rules, but keep them; not for wrath, but for conscience' sake.

5. A probationary member of the annual conference who has completed the requirements for deacon's orders and admission into full membership shall be eligible for election to full membership and ordination as deacon by a bishop.

6. A deacon shall be ordained by a bishop by the laying on of hands, employing the Order of Service for the Ordination of Deacons. The bishops shall be assisted by other deacons and may include laity designated by the bishop representing the Church community and representatives of other Christian communions, in the laying on of hands.

¶ **322.** *Appointment of Deacons in Full Connection to Various*

*Ministries*—1. Deacons in full connection may be appointed to serve as their primary field of service:

a) Through agencies and settings beyond the local church that extend the witness and service of Christ's love and justice in the world by equipping all Christians to fulfill their own calls to Christian service; or

b) Through United Methodist Church-related agencies, schools, colleges, theological schools, ecumenical agencies; or

c) Within a local congregation, charge, or cooperative parish.

2. Deacons in full connection may be appointed to attend school as part of their renewal and personal growth.

3. Deacons in settings that extend the witness and service of Christ's love and justice in the world are amenable to the annual conference of which they are members and insofar as possible should maintain close working relationship with and effective participation in the work of their annual conference, assuming whatever responsibilities they are qualified and requested to assume.

Deacons under appointment beyond the local church shall submit annually to the bishop and the district superintendent, with a copy to their board of ordained ministry, a written report on the official form developed for the Church by the General Council on Finance and Administration for use by the annual conference.

This report shall include a copy of the evaluation by the institution in which the deacon serves. The report and evaluation shall serve as the basis for the evaluation of these deacons in light of the missional needs of the church and the fulfillment of their ordination to be minister of Word and Service. Deacons serving in appointments outside the conference in which they hold membership shall also furnish a copy of their report to the bishop of the area in which they reside and work.

The General Board of Higher Education and Ministry, Section of Deacons and Diaconal Ministries, in order to assist the boards of ordained ministry and cabinets, will provide guidelines to validate the appropriateness in service beyond the local church in special settings and will be available for consultation with bishops and cabinets.

4. When deacons in full connection serve in an agency or setting beyond the local church, the bishop, after consultation with the deacon and the pastor in charge, shall appoint the deacon to a local congregation where they will take missional responsibility for leading other Christians into ministries of service. In this ministry the dea-

cons shall be accountable to the pastor in charge, the charge conference, and other bodies that coordinate the ministry of the local church. In those instances where the appointment is in another episcopal area, the appointment to a local church shall be made in consultation with the bishop of that area.

5. This appointment shall be in a setting that allows one to fulfill the call to specialized ministry and where supervision is provided with goals, evaluation, and accountability acceptable to the bishop, cabinet, and the board of ordained ministry.

6. The appointment of deacons in full connection shall be made by the bishop.

*a)* It may be initiated by the bishop or the district superintendent, individual deacon in full connection, or the agency seeking their service.

*b)* It shall be clarified by a written statement of intentionality of servant leadership in order to establish a clear distinction between the work to which all Christians are called and the work for which deacons in full connection are appropriately prepared and authorized.

*c)* If the bishop and cabinet consider an appointment not to be in the best interest of the Church, the bishop may choose not to make the appointment. In such event, the bishop shall be in consultation with the deacon and the board of ordained ministry. The deacon in full connection shall then seek another appointment, request a leave of absence, relinquish his or her credentials, or be terminated by disciplinary procedures.

*d)* Deacons in full connection at their request or with their consent may be appointed to a nonsalaried position. Such missional appointments will serve to express the Church's concern for social holiness, for ministry among the poor, and for advancing emerging needs of the future. In such cases, the bishop will carefully review plans for expressing this appointed ministry and will consult with the deacon about the well-being and financial security of his or her family.

7. At the request of the deacon in full connection and with the consent of the bishop and cabinet where conference membership is held, the deacon may receive a less than full-time appointment under the following conditions:

*a)* The deacon in full connection shall present a written request to the bishop and the conference board of ordained ministry, giving a rationale for the request at least ninety days prior to the annual conference at which the appointment is to be made.

*b)* Reappointment to less than full-time service shall be requested annually of the bishop by the deacon in full connection.

*c)* The bishop may make an interim appointment of less than full-time service upon request of a deacon in full connection, with the recommendation of the executive committee of the conference board of ordained ministry.

8. With approval and consent of the bishops or other judicatory authorities involved, deacons in full connection from other annual conferences, other Methodist churches, or other denominations may receive appointments in the annual conference while retaining their home conference membership or denominational affiliation. Appointments are to be made by the bishop of the conference in which the deacon in full connection is to serve. Upon the recommendation of the board of ordained ministry, clergy in such appointments may be granted voice but not vote in the annual conference to which they are appointed. Their membership on conference boards and agencies is restricted to the conference of which they are a member. Such appointments are renewable annually.

9. Deacons in full connection with the approval of their bishop and the judicatory authorities of the other denomination may receive an appointment to another denomination while retaining their home conference membership. The appointment may be made in response to exceptional missional needs.

10. Deacons in full connection who are serving outside the bounds of their annual conference will receive an appointment to a local congregation in the area in which their primary appointment is located. This arrangement will be made in consultation between the two bishops. The deacons will be under the supervision of an appropriate district superintendent who will provide a written report to the deacon's bishop.

11. Ordained deacons, after consultation and with the written consent of the pastor in charge, and with the approval of the district superintendent and in consultation with the staff-parish relations committee of a charge conference, shall relate to a charge conference within the bounds of the annual conference in which they shall hold membership and to which they shall submit an annual report. In those instances where the appointment is in another annual conference the deacon will relate also to a charge conference where he or she resides. The deacons shall be held amenable to the annual confer-

ence in which they hold membership for the continuation of their ordination rights.

12. Ordained deacons from other annual conferences of the United Methodist Church may be received by transfer into full membership with the consent of the bishops involved. The process should be initiated by the receiving bishop. Consultation with the chairperson or executive committee of the board of ordained ministry of the receiving conference shall be held prior to transfer.

13. Special provisions will be made for deacons whose primary appointment does not have accountability structures, but whose charge conference will supply this need.

14. Support for deacons under appointment of a bishop.

a) Deacons shall receive their support under the policies and agreements of the setting of their primary field of service.

b) When the deacon's primary field of service is within a local congregation, charge, or cooperative parish, the deacon shall receive a salary from the local church, charge, or cooperative parish (¶ 623.2) not less than the minimum established by the equitable compensation policy of the annual conference for full-time and part-time pastors and shall participate in the denominational pension and benefit plans, programs, and in the health benefit and supplemental programs of his or her annual conference subject to the provisions and standards of those programs as established by the annual conference where health coverage is not provided from another source.

c) The above (§ 10 [a-b]) does not apply to a deacon appointed by a bishop to a nonsalaried position (§ 4[d]).

d) In The United Methodist Church and other employing agencies there shall be an annual review of the deacon's performance no later than ninety days prior to annual conference.

e) Since deacons are not guaranteed a place of employment in the Church, special attention shall be given to termination procedures that allow time for seeking another service appointment. Notification of dismissal shall provide a ninety-day period to final termination of employment unless the contract specifies otherwise or except for causes as listed in ¶ 2702.

## Section VI. The Ordained Elder in Full Connection

¶ **323.** *Ministry of an Elder*—Elders are ordained ministers who, by God's grace, have completed their formal preparation and have been commissioned and served as a probationary member, have been found by the Church to be of sound learning, of Christian character, possessing the necessary gifts and evidence of God's grace, and whose call by God to ordination has been confirmed by the Church. Elders are ordained to a lifetime ministry of Service, Word, Sacrament, and Order. They are authorized to preach and teach the Word of God, to administer the sacraments of baptism and Holy Communion, and to order the life of the Church for mission and ministry. The servant leadership of the elder is expressed by leading the people of God in worship and prayer, by leading persons to faith in Jesus Christ, by exercising pastoral supervision in the congregation, and by leading the Church in obedience to mission in the world.

As members of the Order of Elder, all elders are in covenant with all other elders in the annual conference and shall participate in the life of their Order.

ADMISSION AND CONTINUANCE OF
FULL MEMBERSHIP IN THE ANNUAL CONFERENCE

¶ 324. *Elders in Full Connection*—1. Elders in full connection with an annual conference by virtue of their election and ordination are bound in special covenant with all the ordained elders of the annual conference. In the keeping of this covenant they perform the ministerial duties and maintain the ministerial standards established by those in the covenant. They offer themselves without reserve to be appointed and to serve, after consultation, as the appointive authority may determine. They live with all other ordained ministers in mutual trust and concern and seek with them the sanctification of the fellowship. By entering into the covenant, they accept and subject themselves to the process of clergy discipline, including serving on committees on investigation, trial courts, or appellate committees. Only those shall be elected to full membership who are of unquestionable moral character and genuine piety, sound in the fundamental doctrines of Christianity, and faithful in the discharge of their duties.[4]

2. A probationary member of the annual conference who has completed the requirements for Elder's Orders and admission into

---

4. *See* Judicial Council Decisions 406, 534, 552, 555.

full membership shall be eligible for election to full membership and ordination as elder by a bishop.

3. An elder shall be ordained by a bishop by the laying on of hands, employing the Order of Service for the Ordination of Elders. The bishops shall be assisted by other elders and may include laity designated by the bishop representing the Church community and representatives of other Christian communions in the laying on of hands.

¶ 325. *Ministry, Authority, and Responsibilities of an Elder in Full Connection*—An elder in full connection is authorized to give spiritual and temporal servant leadership in the Church in the following manner:

1. Elders in full connection shall have the right to vote on all matters in the annual conference except in the election of lay delegates to the general and jurisdictional or central conferences (¶ 602.1*a*) and shall share with deacons in full connection responsibility for all matters of ordination, character, and conference relations of clergy. This responsibility shall not be limited by the recommendation or lack of recommendation by the board of ordained ministry, notwithstanding provisions which grant to the board of ordained ministry the right of recommendation.[5] They shall be eligible to hold office in the annual conference and to be elected delegates to the general and jurisdictional or central conferences under the provision of the Constitution (¶ 33, Article IV). Every effective elder in full connection who is in good standing shall be continued under appointment by the bishop.[6]

2. There are professional responsibilities that elders are expected to fulfill and that represent a fundamental part of their accountability and a primary basis of their continued eligibility for annual appointment. These shall include:

*a)* Continuing availability for appointment.

*b)* Growth in vocational competence and effectiveness through continuing formation is expected of conference members. The board of ordained ministry (¶ 632.2*n*) shall set minimal standards and specific guidelines for continuing formation for members of their conference and ensure their availability. Further specificity of priorities for current appointments shall be arranged in consultations with appropriate bodies in that setting.

*c)* Annual participation in a process of evaluation with committees on pastor-parish relations or a comparable body.

---

5. *See* Judicial Council Decision 690.
6. *See* Judicial Council Decisions 462, 473, 492, 534, 552, 555.

*d)* Annual participation in evaluation with his or her district superintendent.

*e)* Willingness to assume supervisory and mentoring responsibilities within the connection.

3. If an elder fails to meet these professional responsibilities, the provisions of ¶ 359.3*c* may be invoked.

4. Clergy who are retired, located, on incapacity leave, or on sabbatical leave may at their own initiative apply to the conference board of ordained ministry for affiliate membership in the annual conference where they reside. By a two-thirds vote of the executive session, such clergy may be received with rights and privileges, including service on conference boards, agencies, task forces, and committees, with voice but without vote. Voting membership shall be retained in the clergy member's home annual conference for the duration of affiliate member relationship. Such persons may serve on the board, agency, task force or committee of only one annual conference at any one time.

¶ 326. *Requirements for Admission to Full Connection and Ordination as Elder*—Probationary members who are candidates for full connection and ordination as elders and have been probationary members for at least three years may be admitted into membership in full connection in an annual conference and approved for elder's ordination by two-thirds vote of the clergy members in full connection of the annual conference, upon recommendation by two-thirds vote of the board of ordained ministry,[7] after they have qualified as follows. They shall have: (1) served full-time under episcopal appointment for at least three full annual conference years following the completion of the educational requirements specified in 3(*b*) below. Upon recommendation of the board of ordained ministry, an annual conference may equate less than full-time to the requirement of full-time service. Such equivalence is to be determined in light of the years of service involved, the quality of that service, the maturity of the applicant, and other relevant factors. Supervision is to be (*a*) personally assumed or delegated by the district superintendent, and (*b*) assumed by a mentor assigned by the board of ordained ministry. Their service shall be evaluated by the board of ordained ministry as effective according to written guidelines developed by the board and adopted by the clergy members in full connection.[8] In rare cases, the board of

---

7. *See* Judicial Council Decisions 157, 344.
8. *See* Judicial Council Decisions 555, 719.

ordained ministry may, by a two-thirds vote, approve years of service in an autonomous Methodist church as meeting this requirement if adequate supervision has been provided; (2) been previously elected as probationary members; (3) met the following educational requirements: (a) graduation with a Bachelor of Arts or equivalent degree from a college or university listed by the University Senate, or demonstrated competency equivalence through a process designed in consultation with the General Board of Higher Education and Ministry; (b) graduation with a Master of Divinity degree from a school of theology listed by the University Senate, or its equivalent as determined by the General Board of Higher Education and Ministry; or (c) met the education requirements of ¶315.6 for local pastors; (d) educational requirements in every case shall include a minimum of two semester or three quarter hours in each of the fields of United Methodist history, doctrine, and polity; provided that a candidate may meet the requirements by undertaking an independent study program provided and administered by the General Board of Higher Education and Ministry (see ¶ 1424.4); (4) satisfied the board regarding physical, mental, and emotional health; (5) prepared and preached at least one written sermon on a biblical passage specified by the board of ordained ministry; (6) presented a plan and outline for teaching a book or books of the Bible; (7) responded to a written or oral doctrinal examination administered by the board of ordained ministry. The candidate should demonstrate the ability to communicate clearly in both oral and written form. The candidate's reflections and the board's response should be informed by the insights and guidelines of Part II of the Discipline. The following questions are guidelines for the preparation of the examination:

a) Theology.

(1) How has the practice of ministry affected your experience and understanding of God?

(2) What effect has the practice of ministry had on your understanding of humanity and the need for divine grace?

(3) What changes has the practice of ministry had on your understanding of: (a) the "Lordship of Jesus Christ," and (b) the work of the Holy Spirit?

(4) The United Methodist Church holds that Scripture, tradition, experience, and reason are sources and norms for belief and practice, but that the Bible is primary among them. What is your understanding of this theological position of the Church?

(5) How do you understand the following traditional evangelical doctrines: *(a)* repentance; *(b)* justification; *(c)* regeneration; *(d)* sanctification? What are the marks of the Christian life?

(6) For the sake of the mission of Jesus Christ in the world and the most effective witness to the Christian gospel and in consideration of your influence as an ordained minister, are you willing to make a complete dedication of yourself to the highest ideals of the Christian life; and to this end will you agree to exercise responsible self-control by personal habits conducive to physical health, intentional intellectual development, fidelity in marriage and celibacy in singleness, integrity in all personal relationships, social responsibility, and growth in grace and the knowledge and love of God?[9]

(7) What is the meaning and significance of the sacraments?

(8) Describe the nature and mission of the Church. What are its primary tasks today?

(9) What is your understanding of: *(a)* the Kingdom of God; *(b)* the Resurrection; *(c)* eternal life?

*b)* Vocation.

(1) How do you conceive your vocation as an ordained minister?

*c)* The Practice of Ministry.

(1) How has the practice of ordained ministry affected your understanding of the expectations and obligations of the itinerant system?

(2) Do you offer yourself without reserve to be appointed and to serve as the appointive authority may determine?

(3) Describe and evaluate your personal gifts for ministry. What would be your areas of strength and areas in which you need to be strengthened?

(4) Are you willing to minister with all persons without regard to race, color, ethnicity, national origin, social status gender, sexual orientation, age, economic condition, or disabilities?

(5) Will you regard all pastoral conversations of a confessional nature as a trust between the person concerned and God?

(6) Provide evidence of experience in peace and justice ministries.

¶ **327.** *Historic Examination for Admission into Full Connection*—The bishop as chief pastor shall engage those seeking to be admitted in serious self-searching and prayer to prepare them for their examina-

9. *See* Judicial Council Decision 542.

tion before the conference. At the time of the examination the bishop shall also explain to the conference the historic nature of the following questions and seek to interpret their spirit and intent. The questions are these and any others that may be thought necessary:

1. Have you faith in Christ?
2. Are you going on to perfection?
3. Do you expect to be made perfect in love in this life?
4. Are you earnestly striving after it?
5. Are you resolved to devote yourself wholly to God and his work?
6. Do you know the General Rules of our Church?
7. Will you keep them?
8. Have you studied the doctrines of The United Methodist Church?
9. After full examination, do you believe that our doctrines are in harmony with the Holy Scriptures?
10. Will you preach and maintain them?
11. Have you studied our form of Church discipline and polity?
12. Do you approve our Church government and polity?
13. Will you support and maintain them?
14. Will you diligently instruct the children in every place?
15. Will you visit from house to house?
16. Will you recommend fasting or abstinence, both by precept and example?
17. Are you determined to employ all your time in the work of God?
18. Are you in debt so as to embarrass you in your work?
19. Will you observe the following directions?

*a)* Be diligent. Never be unemployed. Never be triflingly employed. Never trifle away time; neither spend any more time at any one place than is strictly necessary.

*b)* Be punctual. Do everything exactly at the time. And do not mend our rules, but keep them; not for wrath, but for conscience' sake.[10]

## Section VII. Appointments to Various Ministries

¶ **328.** *General Provisions*—1. All elders in full connection who are in good standing in an annual conference shall be continued under

---

10. These are the questions that every Methodist preacher from the beginning has been required to answer upon becoming a full member of an annual conference. These questions were formulated by John Wesley and have been little changed throughout the years.

appointment by the bishop unless they are granted a sabbatical leave, an incapacity leave (¶ 355), family leave, a leave of absence, retirement, or have failed to meet the requirements for continued eligibility (¶ 325.2).[11]

2. In addition to the ordained elders, persons who have been granted a license as local pastors and who have been approved by vote of the clergy members in full connection may be appointed as pastors in charge under certain conditions, which are specified in ¶¶ 340–343. All clergy members and licensed local pastors to be appointed shall assume a lifestyle consistent with Christian teaching as set forth in the Social Principles.

¶ 329. *The Itinerant System*—The itinerant system is the accepted method of The United Methodist Church by which ordained elders are appointed by the bishop to fields of labor.[12] All ordained elders shall accept and abide by these appointments. Persons appointed to multiple-staff ministries, either in a single parish or in a cluster or larger parish, shall have personal and professional access to the bishop and cabinet, the committee on pastor-parish relations, as well as to the pastor in charge. The nature of the appointment process is specified in ¶¶ 430–434.

1. Full-time service shall be the norm for ordained elders in the annual conference. Full-time service shall mean that the person's entire vocational time, as defined by the district superintendent in consultation with the pastor and the committee on pastor-parish relations, is devoted to the work of ministry in the field of labor to which one is appointed by the bishop.

2. Less than full-time service may be rendered by a clergy member under the conditions stipulated in this paragraph.[13] Less than full-time service shall mean that a specified amount of time less than full-time agreed upon by the bishop and the cabinet, the clergy member, and the annual conference board of ordained ministry is devoted to the work of ministry in the field of labor to which the person is appointed by the bishop. At his or her own initiative, a clergy member may request and may be appointed in one-quarter, one-half, or three-quarter time increments by the bishop to less than full-time service without loss of essential rights or membership in the annual con-

---

11. *See* Judicial Council Decisions 380, 462, 492, 524, 702.
12. *See* Judicial Council Decision 713.
13. *See* Judicial Council Decision 719.

ference. Division of Chaplains and Related Ministries-endorsed appointments beyond the local church may be for less than full-time service. Appointment to less than full-time service is not a guarantee, but may be made by the bishop, provided that the following conditions are met:

a) The ordained elder seeking less than full-time service should present a written request to the bishop and the chairperson of the board of ordained ministry at least three months prior to the annual conference session at which the appointment is made. Exceptions to the three-month deadline shall be approved by the cabinet and the executive committee of the board of ordained ministry.

b) Following appropriate consultation, as established in ¶¶ 329 and 430–434, and upon joint recommendation of the cabinet and the board of ordained ministry, the less than full-time category shall be confirmed by a two-thirds vote of the clergy members in full connection of the annual conference.

c) Reappointment to less than full-time service shall be requested by the ordained elder and approved annually by the bishop and cabinet and shall not be granted for more than a total of eight years, except by a three-fourths vote of the clergy members in full connection of the annual conference.

d) Ordained elders who receive appointment at less than full-time service remain within the itineracy and, as such, remain available, upon consultation with the bishop and cabinet, for appointment to full-time service. A written request to return to full-time appointment shall be made to the bishop and cabinet at least six months prior to the annual conference session at which the appointment is to be made.

e) The bishop may make *ad interim* appointments at less than full-time service upon request of the ordained elder, following consultation as specified in ¶¶ 429–433 and upon recommendation of the cabinet and executive committee of the board of ordained ministry, the same to be acted upon by the next regular session of the annual conference.[14]

3. Interim appointments may be made to charges that have special transitional needs.

a) Ordained ministers and local pastors may be appointed as interim pastors. They will be available for interim assignments of

---

14. *See* Judicial Council Decision 579.

varying lengths. Interim pastors may serve outside the annual conference where membership is held under the provision of ¶ 337.1, with approval and consent of the bishops involved.

*b)* Interim appointments will be for a specified length of time, established in advance following consultation with the district superintendent, the pastor-parish relations committee, and the interim pastor.

¶ **330.** *Definition of a Pastor*—A pastor is an ordained elder, probationary deacon (according to 1992 *Book of Discipline*) or licensed person approved by vote of the clergy members in full connection and may be appointed by the bishop to be in charge of a station, circuit, cooperative parish, extension ministry, ecumenical shared ministry,[15] or to a church of another denomination, or on the staff of one such appointment.

¶ **331.** *Performance Evaluations*—Persons serving as pastors of congregations shall be evaluated in part on the basis of the following list of responsibilities and duties:

*Responsibilities and Duties of a Pastor*—The pastor(s) shall oversee the total ministry of the local church in its nurturing ministries and in fulfilling its mission of witness and service in the world by: (1) giving pastoral support, guidance, and training to the lay leadership in the church, equipping them to fulfill the ministry to which they are sent as servants under the Lordship of Christ; (2) providing ministry within the congregation and to the world; (3) ensuring faithful transmission of the Christian faith; and (4) administering the temporal affairs of the congregation. In the context of these basic responsibilities, the pastor shall give attention to the following specific duties:

1. *Ministering Within the Congregation and to the World*—*a)* To preach the Word, oversee the worship life of the congregation, read

---

15. *Ecumenical shared ministries* are ecumenical congregations formed by a local United Methodist church and one or more local congregations of other Christian traditions. Forms of ecumenical shared ministries include: (a) a federated congregation, in which one congregation is related to two denominations, with persons holding membership in one or the other of the denominations; (b) a union congregation, in which a congregation with one unified membership roll is related to two denominations; (c) a merged congregation, in which two or more congregations of different denominations form one congregation which relates to only one of the constituent denominations; and (d) a yoked parish, in which a United Methodist congregation is yoked with one or more congregations of other denominations.

and teach the Scriptures, and engage the people in study and witness.[16]

*b)* To administer the sacraments of baptism and the Lord's Supper and all the other means of grace. It shall be the duty of all appointed pastors, before baptizing infants or children, to prepare the parents and sponsors by instructing them concerning the significance of Holy Baptism, the responsibilities of the parents and the sponsor(s) for the Christian training of the baptized child, and how these obligations may be properly discharged (*see* ¶ 225.1). All appointed pastors may select and train lay members with appropriate words and actions to immediately deliver the consecrated communion elements to members confined at home, in a nursing home, or in a hospital.

*c)* To encourage reaffirmation of the baptismal covenant and renewal of baptismal vows at different stages of life. The practice of re-baptism does not conform with God's action in baptism and is not consistent with Wesleyan tradition and the historic teaching of the church. Therefore, the pastor should counsel any person seeking re-baptism to participate in a rite of re-affirmation of baptismal vows.

*d)* To give oversight to the total educational program of the church and encourage the distribution and use of United Methodist literature in each local church.

*e)* To provide leadership for the funding ministry of the congregation and to encourage giving as a spiritual discipline.

*f)* To lead the congregation by teaching and example in a ministry with people with disabilities.

*g)* To be involved and to lead the congregation in evangelistic outreach that others might come to know Christ, be baptized, and become members.

*h)* To encourage people baptized in infancy or early childhood to make their profession of faith after instruction so that they might become professing members of the church.

*i)* To perform the marriage ceremony after due counsel with the parties involved. The decision to perform the ceremony shall be the right and responsibility of the pastor. Qualifications for performing marriage shall be in accordance with the laws of the state and The United Methodist Church.

*j)* To counsel those who are under threat of marriage breakdown and explore every possibility for reconciliation.

---

16. *See* Judicial Council Decision 694.

*k)* To counsel bereaved families and conduct appropriate funeral and memorial services.

*l)* To counsel with members of the church and community concerning military service and its alternatives.

*m)* To counsel persons struggling with personal, ethical, or spiritual issues.

*n)* To visit in the homes of the church and community, especially among the sick, aged, and others in need.

*o)* To participate in community, ecumenical, and interreligious concerns and to lead the congregation to become so involved through ministries of service and advocacy, relevant to specific and diverse community contexts; and to pray and labor for the unity of the Christian community.

*p)* To search out from among the membership and constituency men and women for pastoral ministry and other church-related occupations; to help them interpret the meaning of the call of God; to advise and assist when they commit themselves thereto; to counsel with them concerning the course of their preparation; and to keep a careful record of such decisions.

*q)* To give diligent pastoral leadership in ordering the life of the congregation for discipleship in the world.

2. *Equipping and Supervising—a)* To give diligent pastoral leadership ordering the life of the congregation for nurture and care.

*b)* To offer counsel and theological reflection in the following:

(1) The development of goals for fulfilling the missions of the congregation, the annual conference, and the general Church.

(2) The development of plans for implementing the goals of the congregation and a process for evaluating their effectiveness.

(3) The selection, training, and deployment of lay leadership within the congregation and the development of a process for evaluating lay leadership.

*c)* To lead the congregation in experiencing the racial and ethnic inclusiveness of The United Methodist Church and to help prepare it for participation in the itineracy of all ordained men and women.

*d)* To participate in denominational and conference programs and training opportunities and to seek out opportunities for cooperative ministries with other United Methodist pastors and churches.

*e)* To be willing to assume supervisory responsibilities within the connection.

*f)* To lead the congregation in the fulfillment of its mission through full and faithful payment of all apportioned ministerial support, administrative, and benevolent funds.

3. *Administration—a)* To be the administrative officer of the local church and to assure that the organizational concerns of the congregation are adequately provided for.

*b)* To be responsible for the process of goal setting and planning through which the laity take responsibility for ministry in the church and in the world.

*c)* To administer the provisions of the *Discipline* and supervise the working program of the local church.

*d)* To give an account of their pastoral ministries to the charge and annual conference according to the prescribed forms. The care of all church records and local church financial obligations shall be included. The pastor shall certify the accuracy of all financial, membership, and any other reports submitted by the local church to the annual conference for use in apportioning costs back to the church.

¶ **332.** *Unauthorized Conduct*—1. Pastors shall first obtain the written consent of the district superintendent before engaging for an evangelist any person who is not a general evangelist (¶¶ 628.3*f*, 1111.7), a clergy member of an annual conference, a local pastor, or a certified lay speaker in good standing in The United Methodist Church.

2. No pastor shall discontinue services in a local church between sessions of the annual conference without the consent of the charge conference and the district superintendent.

3. No pastor shall arbitrarily organize a pastoral charge. (*See* ¶ 259 for the method of organizing a local church.)

4. No clergy member or local pastor shall hold a religious service within the bounds of a pastoral charge other than the one to which appointed without the consent of the clergy member or local pastor in charge or the district superintendent. If that clergy member or local pastor does not refrain from such conduct, he or she shall then be liable to the provisions of ¶ 359.1 and ¶ 2702.

5. All clergy of The United Methodist Church are charged to maintain all confidences inviolate, including confessional confidences.

6. Ceremonies that celebrate homosexual unions shall not be conducted by our ministers and shall not be conducted in our churches.

¶ **333.** *Support for Elders in Full Connection Appointed to Pastoral Charges*—To strengthen the effectiveness of the connectional system, assumption of the obligations of the itinerant ministry required upon admission to the traveling connection places upon the Church a counter obligation to provide adequate support for the entire ministry of the Church (¶ 618). The Church shall provide, and the ordained minister is entitled to receive, not less than the equitable compensation established by the annual conference for clergy members according to provisions of ¶ 623.3. The annual conference may determine for its clergy members an alternative salary compensation program as an option to the process described in ¶ 246.12 and ¶ 621.

1. *Support for Elders in Full Connection Appointed to Pastoral Charges Who Render Full-Time Service*—Each elder in full connection of an annual conference who is in good standing and who is appointed to full-time service under the provision of ¶ 329.1 shall have a claim upon the conference Equitable Compensation Fund and a right to receive not less than base compensation established by the annual conference for persons in full-time service.[17]

2. *Support for Ordained Elders Appointed to Pastoral Charges Who Render Less than Full-Time Service*—Each elder in full connection who is in good standing and who is appointed by the bishop to less than full-time service under the provisions of ¶ 329.2 shall have a claim upon the conference Equitable Compensation Fund in one-quarter increments according to the guidelines established by the annual conference commission on equitable compensation.

3. Notwithstanding anything herein to the contrary, the benefits provided to ordained ministers, in addition to the cash compensation, under the benefit programs administered by the General Board of Pension and Health Benefits may be different for ordained ministers serving full-time as pastors to local charges and for ordained ministers serving other types of appointments.

4. No pastor shall be entitled to any claim for unpaid base compensation against any church or charge served after pastoral connection with the church or charge has ceased.

### Section VIII. Appointments to Extension Ministries

¶ 334. *Appointments Extending the Ministry of The United Methodist Church*—1. Elders in effective relationship may be appointed to serve in ministry settings beyond the local United Methodist church in the

---

17. *See* Judicial Council Decisions 579, 587.

witness and service of Christ's love and justice. Persons in these appointments remain within the itineracy and shall be accountable to the annual conference. They shall be given the same moral and spiritual support by it as are persons in appointments to pastoral charges.[18] Their effectiveness shall be evaluated in the context of the specific setting in which their ministry is performed.

2. The institution or agency desiring to employ an ordained minister shall, when feasible, through its appropriate official, consult the ordained minister's bishop and secure approval before completing any agreement to employ the ordained minister. If the institution or agency is located in another area, the bishop of that area shall also be consulted.

3. Elders desiring an appointment extending the ministry of the United Methodist church or change of appointment shall consult with their bishop and/or district superintendent prior to any interviews relative to such an appointment.

¶ 335. *Provisions for Appointment to Extension Ministries*—Elders in appointments extending the ministry of the local United Methodist church are full participants in the itinerant system. Therefore, a conference member in an appointment beyond the local United Methodist church must be willing upon consultation to receive an appointment in a pastoral charge. When either the conference member or the annual conference requests appointment to a pastoral charge, the request shall be made in writing to or from the bishop, the cabinet, and the board of ordained ministry. Such a request should be made at least six months prior to annual conference. In both instances, consultation shall give due regard to the individual's special training, experience, skills, and leadership potential.

1. *Categories of Appointment*—In order to establish a clear distinction between the work to which all Christians are called and the tasks for which ordained ministers are appropriately prepared and authorized, the following categories are established for appointments of elders within the itinerary of The United Methodist Church.

*a)* Appointments within the connectional structures of United Methodism:

(1) Appointments for which the annual conference provides for pension contributions to the Ministerial Pension Plan, such as dis-

---

18. *See* Judicial Council Decisions 321, 325, 466, 579.

trict superintendents, staff members of conference councils and boards, treasurers, bishops' assistants, superintendents or directors of parish development, general evangelists, and campus ministers. Only elders in full connection may be appointed district superintendents;

(2) Appointments to a general agency for which the general agency provides pension contributions to the Ministerial Pension Plan;

(3) Appointments to a United Methodist institution or other ministry, such as superintendents or directors of parish development, general evangelists, campus ministers, missionaries, faculty and administrators of United Methodist schools of theology or other educational institutions approved by the University Senate; and

(4) Appointments to an ecumenical agency.

*b)* Appointments to extension ministries of elders in full connection under endorsement by the General Board of Higher Education and Ministry and other ministry settings which the bishop and conference board of ordained ministry may designate.[19] The board shall annually verify the appropriate employment of persons under its endorsement and request their reappointment.

*c)* Elders in service under the General Board of Global Ministries may be appointed to the ministries listed in *a)* and *b)* above. They may be assigned to service either in annual conferences or central conferences, or with affiliated autonomous churches, independent churches, churches resulting from the union of Methodist Churches and other communions, mission institutions, or in other denominational or ecumenical ministries. They may accept such rights and privileges, including affiliate membership, as may be offered them by central conferences or by other churches to which they are assigned without impairing their relationship to their home annual conference.

*d)* Elders may receive appointments beyond the ministry usually extended through the local United Methodist church and other institutions listed above in *a)* and *b)*[20] when considered by the bishop and the annual conference board of ordained ministry to be a true extension of the Christian ministry of the Church. They may be appointed to pastoral ministry in other Christian denominations at

---

19. *See* Judicial Council Decisions 321, 325, 329.
20. *See* Judicial Council Decisions 380, 877.

the request of appropriate judicatory officers of that denomination. These ministries shall be initiated in missional response to the needs of persons in special circumstances and unique situations and shall reflect the commitment of the clergy to intentional fulfillment of their ordination vows to Word, Sacrament, and Order. These appointments may involve clergy with expertise from other vocations. Conference members in such appointments retain conference membership, and the annual conference may choose to extend financial support and benefits for its clergy by vote of the annual conference. (See ¶ 623.3, .5.)

Conference members who serve as staff members of ecumenical agencies or as pastors of non-United Methodist congregations may also be considered as holding an extension ministry, provided their position is approved by the bishop and the conference board of ordained ministry. They shall remain accountable to their vows as members of their annual conference.

The General Board of Higher Education and Ministry, in order to assist boards of ordained ministry, will provide standards to assist in validating the appropriateness of special ministry settings. In addition, it will provide advocacy for persons serving in settings approved under this paragraph and shall encourage the development of emerging ministries that extend the ministry of the Church into the world.

Those seeking such an appointment shall submit to the cabinet, the board of ordained ministry, and the General Board of Higher Education and Ministry a written statement describing in detail the proposed setting for their ministry, sharing a sense of calling to that ministry and their gifts and evidence of God's grace for it, and expressing the intentional fulfillment of their ordination vows. This material will be submitted not later than 120 days before desired appointment to the proposed setting. On recommendation of the cabinet and the board of ordained ministry, such positions are to be confirmed by a two-thirds vote of the clergy members of the annual conference.

The bishop may make *ad interim* appointments in this category after consultation with the cabinet and executive committee of the board of ordained ministry, the position to be formally acted upon by the next session of the annual conference.

2. *Relation to the Annual Conference—a) Accountability to the Annual Conference*—Elders in extension ministries are amenable to the annual conference of which they are members and insofar as possible should

maintain close working relationship with and effective participation in the work of their annual conference, assuming whatever responsibilities they are qualified and requested to assume.

Elders under appointment in extension ministries shall submit annually to the bishop, the district superintendent, and the board of ordained ministry a written report on the official form developed for the Church by the General Council on Finance and Administration for use by the annual conference. This report shall serve as the basis for the evaluation of these clergy in light of the missional needs of the Church and the fulfillment of their ordination to be minister of Service, Word, Sacrament, and Order. Elders formally evaluated by the institutions in which they serve will provide, instead of an evaluation, a narrative report reflecting their ministry. Elders serving in appointments outside the conference in which they hold membership shall furnish a copy of their report also to the bishop of the area in which they serve. Annual conferences shall review the qualifications of persons in extension ministry status and integrate them into the ongoing work of the annual conference.

*b) Responsibility of the Annual Conference*—The bishop, representatives of the cabinet, and an endorsed representative from extension ministries within the board of ordained ministry shall provide an opportunity to meet annually with ordained clergy in extension ministries who perform their ministry within the bounds of annual conference, both of that annual conference and those who hold membership elsewhere. The bishop shall convene the meeting, which is to be planned by the cabinet and the board of ordained ministry. The purpose of this meeting is to gain understanding of one another's role and function in ministry; to report to other ordained ministers appointed to extension ministries and discuss with them matters concerning the overall approach to ministry in the episcopal area; to interpret the role and function of extension ministries to the larger church through the offices of the bishop and his or her representatives; to nurture the development of various ministries as significant in assisting the mission of the Church; and to discuss specific programs and services that the bishop and his or her representatives may initiate, in which the various ordained ministers serving in appointments beyond the local church may be qualified as consultants and supervisors. Using the appropriate resources and personnel of the annual conference, the bishop shall provide for an annual visit to the ministry setting of all persons under appointment in extension ministries assigned within the geographical bounds of the annual conference and shall provide a report of the visit to the bishop of persons from other annual conferences.

3. *Relation to the Local Church—a)* Elders appointed in extension ministries shall establish membership in a charge conference in their home annual conference in consultation with the pastor in charge and with approval of the district superintendent and the bishop. They shall submit to their home charge conference an annual report of pastoral duties and the fulfillment of their ordination through their special appointment, including ministerial activities in the charge where they have an affiliate membership relation and in other units of the Church at large, as well as continuing formation experiences completed and anticipated. This report may be the one submitted to the bishop, district superintendent, and board of ordained ministry (¶ 335.2*a*). District superintendents, because of the nature of their work and the relationship defined in ¶¶ 429.3, 359.1*a*, and 656, shall not be required to have a charge conference affiliation.

All conference members who are elders in full connection, including those in extension ministries, shall be available and on call to administer the sacraments of baptism and the Lord's Supper as required by the *Discipline* (¶ 331.1*b*) and requested by the district superintendent of the district in which the appointment is held.

*b) Affiliate Relation to a Local Church—*Ordained elders under appointment to extension ministries and serving outside of the geographical bounds of their home annual conference shall promptly notify the bishop of the area in which they reside of their names, addresses, and the annual conferences in which their credentials are held. They shall be affiliate members without vote of a charge conference either within the district where they carry out the primary work of their appointment or within the district where they reside. Persons serving outside the geographic bounds of any annual conference are exempt from this requirement. The selection of the charge conference shall be made after consultation between the elder and the pastor of the local United Methodist church.

These ordained elders under appointment in extension ministries and serving outside the geographical boundaries of their home annual conference shall submit to the charge conference of which they are affiliate members a copy of the report submitted to their home charge conference and/or an oral report concerning their ministry and the fulfillment of their ordination. The district superintendent shall be responsible for the notification to these ministers concerning the time and place of the charge conference.

4. *Affiliate Relation to Annual Conference*—Ordained elders appointed to extension ministries outside the boundary of their annual conference may at their own initiative apply to the board of ordained ministry for affiliate membership in the annual conference in which their appointment is located or in which they reside. By a two-thirds vote of the clergy session,[21] such clergy may be received with rights and privileges, including service on conference boards, agencies, task forces, and committees, with voice but without vote. Voting membership shall be retained in the appointee's home annual conference for the duration of affiliate member relationship. Nomination to general Church boards and agencies and election as delegates to general and jurisdictional conferences shall originate in the appointee's home annual conference. Such persons may serve on the board, agency, task force, or committee of only one annual conference at any one time.[22]

5. *General Provisions—a)* These appointments shall be made only to positions related to adequate accountability structures, according to guidelines established by the board of ordained ministry and cabinet in the annual conferences in which membership is held.

*b)* For information regarding pensions, the conference will continue to list the source of annuity claim for each of its clergy.

*c)* All conference secretaries shall submit to the editors of the General Minutes a list of such appointments beyond the local church made in their annual conferences, and there shall be published in the General Minutes a list of ordained ministers in the Church serving in the major categories under these appointments.

*d)* Elders appointed to extension ministries shall attend the annual conference in which membership is held.

*e)* Individual participation in Armed Forces Reserve or National Guard units and part-time employment with the Veteran's Administration shall be reflected in annual conference journals.

¶ **336.** *Provisions for Appointment to Ecumenical Shared Ministries*— United Methodist clergy members in full connection may be appointed annually to churches of other Christian denominations or to ecumenical shared ministries. Persons in these appointments

---

21. *See* Judicial Council Decision 555.
22. *See* Judicial Council Decision 554.

remain in the itineracy and shall be accountable to the annual conference. Their effectiveness shall be evaluated in the context of the specific setting in which their ministry is performed. (*See* ¶ 335.1[*d*].)

### Section IX. Clergy from Other Annual Conferences, Other Methodist and Christian Denominations

¶ 337. *Provisions for Clergy from Outside the Annual Conference—* Ordained clergy or probationary members from other annual conferences and Christian denominations may receive an appointment in the annual conference in the following manner:

1. *Ordained Clergy or Probationary Members from Other Annual Conferences and Other Methodist Denominations*—With approval and consent of the bishops or other judicatory authorities involved, ordained clergy or probationary members of other annual conferences or other Methodist churches may receive appointments in the annual conference while retaining their home conference membership or denominational affiliation. Appointments are to be made by the resident bishop of the conference in which the clergy person is to serve. Upon the recommendation of the board of ordained ministry, clergy in such appointments may be granted voice but not vote in the annual conference to which they are appointed. Their membership on conference boards and agencies is restricted to the conference of which they are a member. They shall be compensated no less than the equitable salary provisions of the annual conference in which they serve and participate in the pension and insurance programs of that annual conference. Such appointments are renewable annually. Furthermore, it shall be the responsibility of the board of pensions of the annual conference in which the appointment is received to enroll such clergy in the Ministerial Pension Plan and the Comprehensive Protection Plan (*see* ¶ 1506.21).[23]

2. *Elders or Ordained Clergy from Other Denominations*—On recommendation of the board of ordained ministry, the clergy members in full connection may approve annually clergy in good standing in other Christian denominations to serve appointments or ecumenical ministries within the bounds of the annual conference while retaining their denominational affiliation; *provided* they present suitable credentials, give assurance of their Christian faith and experience, and other

---

23. *See* Judicial Council Decisions 16, 361, 554.

qualifications. They shall give evidence of their agreement with and willingness to support and maintain United Methodist doctrine, discipline, and polity. Their ordination credentials shall be examined by the bishop and the board of ordained ministry and, upon its recommendation, may be recognized as valid elders in The United Methodist Church while they are under appointment. When the board of ordained ministry certifies that their credentials are at least equal to those of United Methodist elders, they may be accorded the right to vote in the annual conference on all matters except the following: (a) constitutional amendments; (b) election of delegates to the general and jurisdictional or central conferences; (c) all matters of ordination, character, and conference relations of ministers. They may serve on any board, commission, or committee of an annual conference, except the board of ordained ministry and the board of trustees (¶¶ 632.1, 2512.1). They shall not be eligible for election as delegates to the general, jurisdictional, or central conferences. They shall also be subject to the provisions governing sabbatical leave, leave of absence, location, retirement, minimum salary, and pension. They shall not have security of appointment.

3. Between conference sessions, the board of ordained ministry may approve them for appointment pending the recognition of their orders. The bishop may make *ad interim* recognition of valid ordination after consultation with the cabinet and executive committee of the board of ordained ministry, pending recognition by the vote of the clergy members in full connection. In every case, prior examination shall be made of the ordained minister's understanding, acceptance, and willingness to support and maintain United Methodist doctrine, discipline, and polity.[24]

¶ 338. *Transfers*—1. *From Other Annual Conferences*—Ordained clergy or probationary members from other annual conferences of The United Methodist Church may be received by transfer into probationary or full membership with the consent of the bishops involved. Consultation with the chairperson or executive committee of the board of ordained ministry shall be held prior to the transfer.

2. *From Other Methodist Denominations*—a) Ordained elders or ordained clergy from other Methodist churches may be received by transfer into probationary or full conference membership, with the consent of the bishops or other authorities involved, without going

---

24. *See* Judicial Council Decision 444.

through the process required for ministers from other denominations. Prior consultation with the chairperson or executive committee of the board of ordained ministry shall be held in order to determine that the minister meets the standards for conference membership established by the *Discipline* and the annual conference.

*b)* Ordained elders or ordained clergy being transferred from other Methodist churches shall meet the educational requirements of The United Methodist Church, or the equivalent approved by the General Board of Higher Education and Ministry.

*c)* The General Board of Higher Education and Ministry shall certify the satisfaction of educational requirements for conference membership and, in cases where additional education is required, shall develop an educational program in consultation with the board of ordained ministry.

3. *From Other Denominations—a)* On recommendation of the board of ordained ministry, the clergy members in full connection may recognize the orders of elders or ordained clergy from other denominations and receive them as probationary members or local pastors. They shall present their credentials for examination by the bishop and board of ordained ministry and give assurance of their Christian faith and experience. They shall give evidence of their agreement with and willingness to support and maintain United Methodist doctrine, discipline, and polity and present a satisfactory certificate of good health on the prescribed form from a physician approved by the board of ordained ministry. They shall make themselves available for any psychological or aptitude tests the board may require. The board of ordained ministry, in consultation with the General Board of Higher Education and Ministry, shall determine whether they meet the educational requirements for conference membership.

*b)* Ordained elders or ordained clergy from other Christian denominations shall serve as probationary members for at least two years and complete all the requirements of ¶ 326, including courses in United Methodist history, doctrine, and polity, before being admitted into full conference membership.

4. The board of ordained ministry of an annual conference is required to ascertain from an ordained elder or ordained clergyperson seeking admission into its membership on credentials from another denomination whether or not membership in the effective relation was previously held in an annual conference of The United Methodist Church or one of its legal predecessors, and if so, when

and under what circumstances the ordained minister's connection with such annual conference was severed.

5. Ordained elders or ordained clergy seeking admission into an annual conference on credentials from another denomination who have previously withdrawn from membership in the effective relation in an annual conference of The United Methodist Church or one of its legal predecessors shall not be admitted or readmitted without the consent of the annual conference from which they withdrew or its legal successor, or the annual conference of which the major portion of their former conference is a part, such consent to be granted upon recommendation of its board of ordained ministry.

¶ 339. *Recognition of Orders of Clergy from Other Denominations*—1. Clergy from other denominations may have their orders recognized by the clergy members in full connection of the annual conference after examination of their credentials by the bishop and board of ordained ministry. Prior to admission to membership in the annual conference, such recognition of orders may be given upon recommendation of the bishop and board of ordained ministry.

2. When the orders of an ordained minister of another church shall have been duly recognized, the certificates of ordination by said church shall be returned to the minister with the following inscription written plainly on the back:

> *These orders are recognized by the* _____ *Annual Conference of The United Methodist Church, this* _____ *day of* _____ , _____ *[year]* .
>
> _____ , *President*
> _____ , *Secretary*

The ordained minister also will be furnished with a certificate of recognition of orders signed by the bishop.

## Section X. License for Pastoral Ministry

¶ 340. *License for Pastoral Ministry*—All persons not ordained as elders who are appointed to preach and conduct divine worship and perform the duties of a pastor shall have a license for pastoral ministry. The board of ordained ministry (¶ 632.2g) may recommend to the executive session of the annual conference the licensing of those persons who are:

1. Probationary members commissioned by the annual conference, or

2. Local pastors who have completed the following:

   *a)* The conditions for candidacy certification in ¶¶ 306.2–4;

   *b)* The studies for the license as a local pastor as prescribed and supervised by the General Board of Higher Education and Ministry or one-third of their work for a Master of Divinity degree at a school of theology listed by the University Senate;

   *c)* Been examined and recommended by the district committee on ordained ministry;

   *d)* Been approved by the board of ordained ministry (¶ 632.2*g*); and

   *e)* Provided the board with a satisfactory certificate of good health on a prescribed form from a physician approved by that board if being appointed as a full-time local pastor. This process shall be in accordance with the guidelines provided through the General Board of Higher Education and Ministry, Division of Ordained Ministry. The conference may require psychological and/or psychiatric tests and evaluations to provide additional information to qualify for such coverage.

   ¶ **341.** *Authority and Duties of License for Pastoral Ministry*—1. Probationary members approved annually by the board of ordained ministry and local pastors approved annually by the district committee on ordained ministry may be licensed by the bishop to perform all the duties of a pastor (¶ 331), including the sacraments of baptism and Holy Communion as well as the service of marriage (where state laws allow),[25] burial, confirmation, and membership reception, while appointed to a particular charge. For the purposes of these paragraphs the charge will be defined as "people within or related to the community being served." While local pastors are not eligible for appointment to extension ministries, probationary members may be appointed to extension ministries approved by the bishop and the board of ordained ministry.

   2. Such authorization granted by the license may be renewed annually by the district committee or the board of ordained ministry.

   3. The license shall remain valid only so long as the appointment continues and shall be recertified by the bishop when assignments change between sessions of the annual conference.[26]

---

25. *See* Judicial Council Decision 694.
26. *See* Judicial Council Decision 112.

4. A local pastor shall be under the supervision of a district superintendent and a pastoral mentor who shall supervise the local pastor's work in the Course of Study for ordained ministry and give counsel on matters of pastoral responsibility ( ¶¶ 331, 347).

5. Local pastors shall be amenable to the clergy session of the annual conference in the performance of their pastoral duties and shall attend the sessions of the annual conference.

6. The membership of local pastors under full-time and part-time appointment is in the annual conference where they shall have the right to vote on all matters except constitutional amendments, election of delegates to general, jurisdictional, or central conferences, and matters of ordination, character, and conference relations of clergy.

7. Student local pastors (¶ 343.3) may retain their membership in their home church and charge conference or place it in the church where they are appointed, but in the discharge of their ministerial functions they shall be amenable to the district superintendent under whom they serve. They shall have the right to voice, but not vote in the annual conference.

8. All local pastors shall receive written communication about decisions made regarding their relationship with the annual conference.

¶ 342. *Interim License as Local Pastor*—Between sessions of the annual conference, persons who have completed the conditions for licensing listed above may be granted interim license as a local pastor upon recommendation of the cabinet, the district committee on ordained ministry, and executive committee of the conference board of ordained ministry, and may be appointed by the bishop.

¶ 343. *Categories of Local Pastor*—Upon satisfactory completion of the requirements of ¶ 340, the district committee on ordained ministry shall certify the completion of the prescribed studies to the candidates and the board of ordained ministry, and they shall be listed in the journal as eligible to be appointed as local pastors. Award of the license shall not be made until an appointment to a pastoral charge is made in accordance with ¶ 328. In recommending to the annual conference those who have met the requirements to serve as local pastors for the ensuing year, the board of ordained ministry shall classify them in three categories with educational and other requirements of their category. Any person who fails to meet these requirements shall be discontinued as a local pastor. The categories shall be defined as follows:

1. *Full-Time Local Pastors*—Those eligible to be appointed full-time local pastors are persons *(a)* who may devote their entire time to the church in the charge to which they are appointed and its outreach in ministry and mission to the community; *(b)* who receive in cash support per annum from all Church sources a sum equal to or larger than the minimum base compensation established by the annual conference for full-time local pastors; *(c)* who, unless they have completed the Course of Study, shall complete four courses per year in a Course of Study school or the correspondence curriculum prescribed by the General Board of Higher Education and Ministry (¶ 1424.4); *(d)* who, when they have completed the Course of Study, are involved in continuing education(¶ 349);[27] *(e)* who shall not be enrolled as a full-time student in any school.

2. *Part-Time Local Pastors*—Those eligible to be appointed as part-time local pastors are persons *(a)* who have met the provisions of ¶ 340; *(b)* who do not devote their entire time to the charge to which they are appointed; or *(c)* do not receive in cash support per annum from all Church sources a sum equal to or larger than the minimum base compensation established by the annual conference for full-time local pastors; and *(d)* who, unless they have completed the Course of Study, shall complete two courses per year in a Course of Study school or the correspondence curriculum prescribed by the General Board of Higher Education and Ministry. Part-time local pastors may be appointed to small membership churches that are grouped together in a charge under the supervision of a mentor.

3. *Student Local Pastors*—Those eligible to be appointed as student local pastors shall be enrolled as pretheological or theological students in a college, university, or school of theology listed by the University Senate *(a)* who have met the provisions of ¶ 340, and *(b)* who shall make appropriate progress in their educational program as determined by the board of ordained ministry.

4. Upon recommendation of the board of ordained ministry, the clergy members in full connection may vote approval annually for students of other denominations enrolled in a school of theology listed by the University Senate to serve as local pastors for the ensuing year under the direction of the district superintendent; *provided* that they shall indicate to the satisfaction of the board of ordained ministry their agreement to support and maintain the doctrine and polity of The United Methodist Church while under appointment.

---

27. *See* Judicial Council Decisions 343, 572.

5. Local pastors, except student local pastors, may serve on any board, commission, or committee with voice and vote, except on matters of clergy character, qualifications, status, and ordination, except the board of ordained ministry and the district committee on ordained ministry (¶ 632.1). They shall not be eligible to vote on or serve as delegates to the general, jurisdictional, or central conference.

¶ 344. *Continuance as a Local Pastor*—1. Persons licensed as local pastors who are not probationary members shall continue in college, in a program of theological education at an approved seminary, or in the Course of Study.

2. Upon completing each year's education and other qualifications, a local pastor who is not a probationary member may be recommended for continuance by the district committee on ordained ministry. The clergy members in full connection of the annual conference may approve continuance of a local pastor after reference to and recommendation by its board of ordained ministry.

3. A full-time local pastor shall complete the Course of Study curriculum within eight years and a part-time local pastor within twelve, unless a family situation or other circumstance precludes the local pastor's opportunity to meet said requirements. The local pastor may be granted an annual extension beyond the prescribed limit upon a three-fourths vote of the district committee on ordained ministry, recommendation by the conference board of ordained ministry, and the vote of the clergy members in full connection.[28]

4. A local pastor may choose to remain in a local relationship with the annual conference upon having completed the five-year Course of Study.

5. None of the provisions in this legislation shall be interpreted to change or limit authorizations to local pastors ordained as deacon and elder prior to 1996.[29]

¶ 345. *Fellowship of Local Pastors and Associate Members*—Each annual conference may organize a Fellowship of Local Pastors and Associate Members. All licensed local pastors and associate members may be members of and participate in the Fellowship. The Fellowship will provide mutual support for its members for the sake of the life and mission of the church.

---

28. *See* Judicial Council Decisions 436, 439.
29. *See* Judicial Council Decisions 436, 439.

1. The specific and limited function is to:

a) provide for regular gatherings of local pastors and associate members for continuing formation in relationship to Jesus Christ through such experiences as Bible study, study of issues facing the church and society, and theological exploration in vocational identity and leadership;

b) encourage local pastors in continued study beyond the course of study;

c) develop a bond of unity and common commitment to the mission and ministry of The United Methodist Church and the annual conference; and

d) enable the creation of relationships that allow mutual support and trust.

2. The bishop will convene the fellowship and the board of ordained ministry shall coordinate its life and work. Necessary financial support shall be provided by the annual conference through the budget of the board. The Fellowship will elect a chairperson from its membership who, with the guidance and support of the board of ordained ministry, will provide leadership for the Fellowship. Activity of the Fellowship will be reported regularly to the Board of Ordained Ministry.

¶ **346.** *Exiting, Reinstatement, and Retirement of Local Pastors Who Are Not Probationary Members*—1. *Discontinuance of Local Pastor*—Whenever a local pastor retires or is no longer approved for appointment by the annual conference as required in ¶ 343, whenever any local pastor severs relationship with The United Methodist Church, whenever the appointment of a local pastor is discontinued by the bishop, or whenever the district committee on ordained ministry does not recommend continuation of license, license and credentials shall be surrendered to the district superintendent for deposit with the secretary of the conference. After consultation with the pastor, the former local pastor shall designate the local church in which membership shall be held. The board of ordained ministry shall file with the resident bishop a permanent record of the circumstances relating to the discontinuance of local pastor status as required in ¶ 632.3d.

2. *Withdrawal Under Complaints and Charges*—When a local pastor is accused of an offense under ¶ 2702 and desires to withdraw from the Church, the procedures described in ¶ 2719.2 shall apply.

3. *Trial of Local Pastor*—When a local pastor is accused of an offense under ¶ 2702, the procedures described in ¶¶ 2703–2713 shall apply.

4. *Reinstatement of Local Pastor Status*—Local pastors whose

approved status has been discontinued from an annual conference of The United Methodist Church or one of its legal predecessors may be reinstated only by the annual conference that previously approved them, its legal successor, or the annual conference of which the major portion of their former conference is a part, only upon recommendation by the district committee on ordained ministry from which their license was discontinued, the board of ordained ministry, and the cabinet. Persons seeking reinstatement shall provide evidence that they have been members of a local United Methodist church for at least one year prior to their request for reinstatement. The district committee shall require a recommendation from the charge conference where his or her membership is currently held. When approved by the clergy members in full connection as provided in ¶ 328, their license and credentials shall be restored, and they shall be eligible for appointment as pastors of a charge. They shall complete current studies and meet requirements as provided in ¶¶ 340, 343.

Whenever persons whose approval as local pastors has been discontinued by an annual conference are being considered for appointment or temporary employment in another annual conference, the board of ordained ministry where these persons are being considered shall obtain from the board of ordained ministry of the conference where approval has been discontinued verification of their qualifications and information about the circumstances relating to the termination of their approval as local pastors.

5. *Retirement of Local Pastor*—A local pastor who has made satisfactory progress in the course of study as specified in ¶345.1 or .2 may be recognized as a retired local pastor. Retirement provisions for local pastors shall be the same as those for clergy members in ¶ 356.1, .2, .4, with pensions payable in accordance with ¶ 1506.5*a*. Retired local pastors may attend annual conference sessions with voice but not vote. A retired local pastor may be appointed by the bishop to a charge and licensed without any additional claim upon the conference minimum compensation nor further pension credit.

### Section XI. Mentoring and Mentors

¶ 347. *Mentors*—1. Mentors shall be recommended by the cabinet, selected, trained and held accountable by the board of ordained ministry. There are two categories of mentor, each with distinct functions and responsibilities as follows:

*a)* Candidacy mentors are clergy in full connection or associate members trained to provide counsel and guidance related to the candidacy process. Candidates will be assigned a candidacy mentor by the district committee on ordained ministry in consultation with the district superintendent (¶ 306). Candidacy mentors will work with the candidate until that candidate begins serving in an appointive ministry as a local pastor or a commissioned minister.

*b)* Clergy mentors are clergy in full connection trained to provide ongoing oversight and counsel with local pastors and probationary members pursuing ordained ministry. Local pastors will be assigned a clergy mentor by the district committee on ordained ministry in consultation with the district superintendent. Probationary members will be assigned a clergy mentor by the conference board of ordained ministry in consultation with the district superintendent. A candidacy mentor may continue with the same person if trained to serve as a clergy mentor.

2. Mentoring occurs within a relationship where the mentor takes responsibility for creating a safe place for reflection and growth. An effective mentor has a mature faith, models effective ministry, and possesses the necessary skill to help individuals discern their call in ministry. Mentoring is a part of the preparation and growth for inquirers and candidates for ordained ministry, local pastors and probationary members of an annual conference. Mentoring is distinct from the evaluative and supervisory process that is a part of preparation for ministry.

3. The conference board of ordained ministry may assign one mentor to work either with one individual or with a group of local pastors and/or probationary members. Persons transferring from other denominations will also be assigned a clergy mentor (¶338.3.b).

4. Clergy mentoring begins when a person receives an appointment as a local pastor or as a commissioned minister entering probationary service.

### Section XII. Evaluation for Continuing Formation for Full Members and Local Pastors

¶ 348. *Evaluation*—Evaluation is a continuous process for formation in servant ministry and servant leadership that must take place in a spirit of understanding and acceptance. Evaluation serves as a process for pastors to assess their effectiveness in ministry and to discern God's call to continue in ordained ministry.

1. The district superintendent, in consultation with the pastor-parish relations committee, will evaluate annually the pastors' effectiveness for ministry (¶¶ 325.2c, 421, 632.2n, q), using criteria, processes, and training developed by the cabinet and the board of ordained ministry. The pastors in local churches shall participate annually in an evaluation with the committee on pastor-parish relations for use in an ongoing effective ministry and for identifying continuing education needs and plans (¶ 258.2f[3]), using criteria, processes, and training developed by the board of ordained ministry and the cabinet.

2. Clergy serving in appointments to extension ministries will undergo annual evaluation by their immediate supervisors, engage in annual self-evaluation, and include copies of these evaluations in the annual report submitted to their bishop, district superintendent, and the board of ordained ministry (¶ 335.2a). When possible, they shall have a conversation with their district superintendent about their ministry.

¶ 349. *Continuing Education and Spiritual Growth*—1. Throughout their careers, clergy shall engage in continuing education for ministry, professional development, and spiritual formation and growth in order to lead the church in fulfilling the mission of making disciples for Jesus Christ. This shall include carefully developed personal programs of study augmented periodically by involvement in organized educational and spiritual growth activities.

2. A clergy member's continuing education and spiritual growth program should include such leaves at least one week each year and at least one month during one year of every quadrennium. Such leaves shall not be considered as part of the ministers' vacations and shall be planned in consultation with their charges or other agencies to which they are appointed as well as the bishop, district superintendent, and annual conference continuing education committee.

3. A clergy member may request a formational and spiritual growth leave of up to six months while continuing to hold an appointment in the local church. Such leaves are available to clergy members who have held full-time appointments for at least six years. Such a leave shall be with the approval of the committee on pastor-parish relations, the church council, and the district superintendent. Annual conferences are encouraged to assist with pulpit supply and other temporary support for such leaves.

4. Financial arrangements for continuing education as part of

one's professional development, formation, and spiritual growth shall be negotiated in the following manner: *(a)* for elders and local pastors it shall be done in consultation with the district superintendent and the committee on pastor-parish relations; *(b)* for deacons, with an appropriate supervisory body; *(c)* for district superintendents, with the district committee on superintendency; *(d)* for conference staff, with the appropriate supervisory body; *(e)* for others in extension ministries, with the appropriate persons in their agency.

5. Clergy shall be asked by the district superintendent in the charge conference to report on their programs of continuing education, formation, and spiritual growth for the past year and plans for the year to come. The district superintendent shall also ask the local church to describe its provision for time and financial support of continuing education for ministry, professional development, formation and spiritual growth for the pastors, diaconal ministers and deacons serving their primary appointment in that local church.

6. Clergy in extension ministries shall give evidence of their continuing formation and spiritual growth program and future plans in their annual reports (¶ 335.2*a*).

¶ **350.** *Sabbatical Leave*—A sabbatical leave should be allowed for a program of study or travel approved by the conference board of ordained ministry. Associate members or clergy members in full connection who have been serving in a full-time appointment for six consecutive years from the time of their reception into full or associate membership may be granted a sabbatical leave for up to one year. Whenever possible, the compensation level of the last appointment served before the leave should be maintained in the appointment made at the termination of the leave. The appointment to sabbatical leave is to be made by the bishop holding the conference, upon the vote of the annual conference after recommendation by the board of ordained ministry. Associate members and clergy members in full connection shall submit a written request for a sabbatical leave, including plans for study or travel, to the board of ordained ministry, with copies to the bishop and district superintendent, ordinarily six months before the opening session of the annual conference. To be eligible for an additional sabbatical leave, associate members and clergy members in full connection shall have served six consecutive years under full-time appointment following the previous sabbatical leave.[30]

---

30. *See* Judicial Council Decision 473.

## Section XIII. Changes of Conference Relationship

¶ **351.** *Provision for Change in Conference Relationship*—When ordained ministers sense that God is calling them to seek a change in conference relationship, either for a short or long term, they are urged to review this with colleagues, the district superintendent, and the bishop. Probationary and associate members and members in full connection seeking a change in conference relationship shall make written request to their board of ordained ministry stating the reasons for the requested change of relationship. In addition, the board of ordained ministry may request personal interviews with the probationary or associate members and members in full connection requesting the change in relationship, except where personal appearance results in undue hardship.[31] Clergy appointed to a general agency of the United Methodist Church shall be covered by the policies of the agency in relation to family leave, maternity or paternity leave, and incapacity leave.

¶ **352.** *Leave of Absence*—1. This relationship is granted to clergy who are probationary, associate, and full members, who because of sufficient reason are unable to or who choose temporarily to cease to perform their ministerial duties. This relationship may be initiated by clergypersons as a voluntary leave of absence or by district superintendents as an involuntary leave of absence through the board of ordained ministry and granted or renewed by the vote of the clergy session of members in full connection with the annual conference upon the board's recommendation. Between sessions of the annual conference, leave of absence may be granted or terminated, with the approval of the bishop and district superintendents, by the executive committee of the board of ordained ministry.[32] This interim action shall be subject to the approval of the clergy session of members in full connection with the annual conference at its next session.[33] This leave shall be counted as a part of the six-year limit for probationary members (¶ 318), unless the six-year limit is extended by the clergy session of members in full connection with the annual conference upon the recommendation of the board of ordained ministry. Should there be complaints or charges pending at the time of a request for leave of absence, they should be placed in the file of the clergyperson.

---

31. *See* Judicial Council Decisions 524, 530.
32. *See* Judicial Council Decision 689.
33. *See* Judicial Council Decision 689.

All subsequent actions concerning such entries should be duly noted and placed in the file. Clergypersons on leaves of absence shall have no claim on the conference funds. However, in exceptional circumstances, on the recommendation of the district superintendents, salary and/or other benefits may be granted to an elder or associate member by vote of the clergy session of members in full connection with the annual conference. In an interim between sessions of the annual conference, by vote of the bishop, cabinet, and executive committee of the board of ordained ministry, salary and/or benefits may be granted. Clergypersons on leaves of absence shall not be eligible for membership on annual, jurisdictional, central, or general conference agencies and may not be elected or serve as delegates to general or jurisdictional conferences.

a) *Voluntary Leave of Absence*—The written request for this relationship should be made at least ninety days prior to the annual conference session, giving specific reasons for the request.[34] Representatives of the annual conference board of ordained ministry may interview the clergy member to determine sufficient cause.[35] This relationship shall be approved annually upon written request of the clergy member and shall not be granted for more than five years in succession, except by a two-thirds vote of the clergy members in full connection.[36]

b) *Involuntary Leave of Absence*—The district superintendents may request an involuntary leave of absence without the consent of the probationary, associate, or full member, at least ninety days prior to the annual conference session. They shall give to the probationary, associate, or full member and the board of ordained ministry in writing specific reasons for the request. The fair process for administrative hearings as set forth in ¶ 359.2 shall be followed in any involuntary leave of absence procedure. The clergyperson has the right to a hearing before the bishop, district superintendents, and executive committee of the board of ordained ministry prior to being placed on involuntary leave of absence. Written notice of the board's action should be sent to the respondent and the administrative review committee's chairperson. Involuntary leaves of absence shall be approved by two-thirds vote of the clergy session of members in full connection

---

34. *See* Judicial Council Decision 689.
35. *See* Judicial Council Decision 782.
36. *See* Judicial Council Decisions 581, 782.

with the annual conference.[37] By two-thirds vote of the clergy session of members in full connection with the annual conference, upon recommendation of the bishop, district superintendents, and board of ordained ministry, the ninety-day notice requirement may be waived. This relation shall be approved annually upon written request of the district superintendents and shall not be approved for more than three years in succession.

The administrative review committee (¶ 633) shall ensure that the disciplinary procedures for involuntary leave of absence were properly followed. The entire process leading to the recommendation for involuntary leave of absence shall be reviewed by the administrative review committee, and it shall report its findings to the clergy session of members in full connection with the annual conference.

2. After consultation and with the written consent of the pastor in charge, and with the approval of the district superintendent and the staff-parish relations committee of a local church, clergy members shall designate a charge conference within the bounds of the annual conference in which they shall hold membership and to which they shall submit an annual report. The exercise of their ministry shall be limited to the charge conference in which their membership is held and with the written permission of the pastor in charge unless special permission is granted by the bishop of the conference where membership is held. They shall report all marriages performed, baptisms administered, funerals conducted and other ministerial activities to the charge conference, pastor in charge, and board of ordained ministry, and they shall be held amenable to the annual conference for their conduct and the continuation of their ordination rights. In case of failure to report to the board of ordained ministry, the clergy session of the annual conference may locate or terminate the clergy member without further process.

3. Probationary, associate, or full members on voluntary leave of absence may, with the permission of the charge conference in which membership is held, and with the approval of the Section of Chaplains and Related Ministries, continue to hold an existing reserve commission as an armed forces chaplain, but may not voluntarily serve on extended active duty.

4. When an end to the leave of absence is requested by the probationary, associate, or full member in the case of a voluntary leave of

---

37. *See* Judicial Council Decision 782.

absence, and by the district superintendents in the case of an involuntary leave of absence, it shall be by written request at least six months prior to the session of annual conference.[38] The board of ordained ministry shall review the circumstances surrounding the granting of the relationship for the purpose of determining whether those circumstances have been alleviated or resolved. When the board has determined that the circumstances of the voluntary leave have not been alleviated or resolved and the request is denied, the board must promptly begin a process to place the clergyperson on involuntary leave of absence, administrative location, involuntary incapacity leave, or involuntary retirement[39] or such other action as is deemed appropriate.

5. When probationary, associate, or full members on voluntary leave of absence do not request an extension of the leave of absence annually during the five-year period or do not indicate willingness to return to the itinerant ministry at the end of the five-year period following documented efforts to make contact with the clergyperson, the board of ordained ministry may recommend to the clergy session of members in full connection with the annual conference that the clergyperson be located or terminated. If the district superintendents do not intend to extend the involuntary leave of absence, they shall notify both the board of ordained ministry and the clergyperson at least six months prior to the session of the annual conference to permit clergypersons to exercise their options. The clergyperson shall have the right to request a change to a voluntary leave of absence or termination of leave of absence. Any consecutive combination of voluntary and involuntary leaves of absence shall be counted in the total of five years for purposes of ¶¶ 352, 359.[40]

¶ 353. *Family Leave*—1. This relationship is granted to diaconal ministers, clergy who are local pastors, probationary members, associate members, and clergy members in full connection who, because of an immediate family member's need for full-time care, are temporarily unwilling or unable to perform the duties of a full-time itinerant ministry. This relationship may be initiated by the clergy member through the board of ordained ministry and granted or renewed by the vote of the clergy members in full connection upon

---

38. *See* Judicial Council Decision 721.
39. *See* Judicial Council Decision 689.
40. *See* Judicial Council Decisions 450, 459, 473, 508, 524, 530.

the board's recommendation. Between sessions of the annual conference, this relationship may be granted or terminated with the approval of the bishop, district superintendents, and executive committee of the board of ordained ministry. This interim action shall be subject to the approval of the annual conference at its next session. This relationship shall be approved annually upon written request of the probationary, associate, or full member and shall not be granted for more than five years in succession, except by a two-thirds vote of the clergy members in full connection. The written request for this relationship shall be made at least ninety days prior to annual conference. This leave shall not count as a part of the six-year limit for probationary members unless the board of ordained ministry recommends otherwise. After consultation and with the written consent of the pastor in charge, and with the approval of the district superintendent and the staff-parish relations committee of a local church, ordained ministers on family leave shall designate a charge conference in which they shall hold membership and to which they shall submit an annual report. Outside their charge conference, under the supervision of the district superintendent, the ordained clergy on family leave may preach, teach, perform marriages and baptisms, and administer the sacraments. They shall report all ministerial functions performed to their charge conference. They shall be held amenable for their conduct and the continuation of their ordination rights to the annual conference. Probationary, associate, and full members on family leave who affiliate with a charge conference outside the geographical boundaries of their home annual conference shall follow the procedures outlined in ¶ 335.3b. In case of failure to report to the charge conference, the annual conference may locate them without their consent. They shall have no claim on conference funds, except by vote of the clergy members in full connection. They may participate in the conference health program through their own contributions. They shall be eligible for membership on conference committees, commissions, or boards.

2. Persons on family leave may, with the permission of the charge conference in which membership is held and with the approval of the Division of Chaplains and Related Ministries, continue to hold an existing reserve commission as an armed forces chaplain, but may not voluntarily serve on extended active duty.

3. When a member requests to terminate the family leave, it shall be by written request to the board of ordained ministry at least ninety days prior to the session of annual conference.

4. When probationary, associate, or full members do not request an extension of the family leave annually during the five-year period or do not indicate willingness to return to the itinerant ministry at the end of the five-year period, the provisions of ¶ 359 shall be invoked.

¶ 354. *Maternity or Paternity Leave*—Maternity or paternity leave, not to exceed one fourth of a year, will be available and shall be granted by the bishop and the cabinet, and the executive committee of the board of ordained ministry to any local pastor, probationary member, associate member, or clergy member in full connection who so requests it at the birth or arrival of a child into the home for purposes of adoption.

1. Persons desiring maternity or paternity leave should file their request with the committee on pastor-parish relations after consulting with the district superintendent at least ninety days prior to its beginning to allow adequate pastoral care for the churches involved to be developed.

2. During the leave, the clergy member's annual conference relations will remain unchanged, and the health and welfare benefit plans will remain in force.

3. A maternity or paternity leave of up to one quarter of a year will be considered as an uninterrupted appointment for pension purposes.

4. Compensation will be maintained for no less than the first eight weeks of leave.

5. During the leave time, pastoral responsibility for the church or churches involved will be handled through consultation with the committee on pastor-parish relations of the local church(es) and the district superintendent.

6. Special arrangements shall be made for district superintendents, bishops, and those under special appointment.

¶ 355. *Incapacity Leave Resulting From Health Matters and Disabling Conditions*—1. When clergy who are members of an annual conference (¶ 365) are unable to perform their ministerial work because of incapacity due to health matters and disabling conditions, upon recommendations of the conference board of ordained ministry and the conference board of pensions, and by a majority vote of the executive session of clergy members in full connection with the annual conference who are present and voting, they may be granted annual incapacity leave without losing their relationship to the annual conference; *provided*, however, that such leave may be granted or renewed only after a thorough investigation of the case by the joint committee on incapacity of the annual conference, which will report its findings to the conference board of ordained ministry and the conference board of pensions. This relationship may be initiated by the clergy member or cabinet with or without the consent of the clergy member through the board of ordained ministry. When incapacity leave is given without the clergy member's consent, reasonable accommodation shall be offered whenever possible. When a clergy member is granted incapacity leave by the annual conference, if the medical evidence has not yet met the standards for the receipt of benefits as set forth in the Comprehensive Protection Plan, section 5.04, the conference board of pensions may authorize payment of the benefits in the amount that would otherwise be payable from the Comprehensive Protection Plan. The payments shall be made by the General Board of Pension and Health Benefits as a charge to the annual conference granting the incapacity leave. If payments from the Comprehensive Protection Plan are subsequently approved, the annual conference will be reimbursed for benefits already paid, not to exceed the amount otherwise payable from the Comprehensive Protection Plan. Each incapacity leave granted by the annual conference shall be recorded in the conference minutes.

2. When clergy who are members of an annual conference are unable to perform their ministerial work between sessions of the annual conference on account of health matters and disabling conditions, with the approval of a majority of the district superintendents, after consultation with the executive committee of the conference board of ordained ministry and the executive committee of the conference board of pensions, an incapacity leave may be granted by the bishop for the remainder of the conference year; *provided,* however, that such leave may be granted only after a thorough investigation of the case including accommodation provisions by the joint committee on incapacity of the annual conference; which will report its findings to the conference board of ordained ministry and the conference board of pensions. When a clergy member is granted incapacity leave by the bishop, if the medical evidence has not yet met the standards for receipt of benefits as set forth in the Comprehensive Protection Plan, section 5.04, the conference board of pensions may authorize payment of the benefits in the amount that would otherwise be payable from the Comprehensive Protection Plan. The payments shall be made by the General Board of Pension and Health Benefits as a

charge to the annual conference granting the incapacity leave. If payments from the Comprehensive Protection Plan are subsequently approved, the annual conference will be reimbursed for benefits already paid, not to exceed the amount otherwise payable from the Comprehensive Protection Plan.

3. When clergy members on incapacity leave provide medical evidence that they have recovered sufficiently to resume ministerial work, or are able to return through reasonable accommodation, they may receive an appointment from a bishop between sessions of the annual conference, thereby terminating the incapacity leave. Such appointment shall be reported immediately by the cabinet to the conference board of pensions and to the General Board of Pension and Health Benefits. Such termination of leave, together with the effective date, shall also be recorded in the minutes of the annual conference at its next regular session.[41]

¶ 356. *Retirement*—Retired clergy members are those who have been placed in the retired relation either at their own request or by action of the clergy session upon recommendation of the board of ordained ministry.[42] (*See* ¶¶ 1506–1509 and the Ministerial Pension Plan for pension information.) Requests for retirement shall be stated in writing to the bishop, cabinet, and board of ordained ministry at least one hundred twenty days prior to the date on which retirement is to be effective. The board of ordained ministry shall provide guidance and counsel to the retiring member and family as they begin a new relationship in the local church.

1. *Mandatory Retirement*—Every clergy member of an annual conference who will have attained age seventy on or before July 1 in the year in which the conference is held shall automatically be retired.[43]

2. *Voluntary Retirement*—a) *With Twenty Years of Service*—Any clergy members of the annual conference who have completed twenty years or more of service under appointment as ordained ministers or as local pastors with pension credit for service before 1982 or with full participation in the Comprehensive Protection Plan since 1981 prior to the opening date of the session of the conference may request the annual conference to place them in the retired relation with the privilege of receiving their pensions for the number of approved

41. *See* Judicial Council Decision 473.
42. *See* Judicial Council Decisions 87, 88, 531.
43. *See* Judicial Council Decisions 7, 165, 413, 578.

years served in the annual conference or conferences and such other benefits as the final annual conference may provide, payment to begin the first of any month after the ordained minister attains age sixty-two.[44] If pension begins prior to the age at which retirement under ¶ 356.2c could have occurred, then the provisions of ¶ 1506.4i shall apply.

b) *With Thirty-five Years of Service or at Age Sixty-two*—At their own request and by vote of the clergy members in full connection, any clergy members who will have attained age sixty-two on or before July 1 in the year in which the session of the annual conference is held or will have completed thirty-five years of service under appointment as an ordained minister, or a local pastor with pension credit for service before 1982 or with full participation in the Comprehensive Protection Plan since 1981, as of the conference session may be placed in the retired relation with an annuity claim for an actuarially reduced pension (*see* ¶ 1506.4i).[45]

c) *With Forty Years of Service or at Age Sixty-five*—At their own request and by vote of the clergy members in full connection, any clergy members who will have attained age sixty-five on or before July 1 in the year in which the session of the conference is held or will have completed forty years of service under appointment as an ordained minister, or as a local pastor with pension credit for service before 1982 or with full participation in the Comprehensive Protection Plan since 1981, as of the conference session may be placed in the retired relation with the privilege of making an annuity claim.[46]

d) The dates specified in ¶ 356.1 and .2a-c notwithstanding, between sessions of the annual conference any member who attains the age and/or number of years of service specified in those sections may, upon the member's own request and with the approval of the bishop, cabinet, and executive committee of the board of ordained ministry, be granted the retired relation *ad interim*, with applicable annuity claim, subject to the approval of the clergy members in full connection at the next annual conference session.

e) The annual conference, at its discretion, upon joint recommendation of the board of ordained ministry and the conference board of pensions, may designate any time within the ensuing con-

---

44. *See* Judicial Council Decision 717.
45. *See* Judicial Council Decision 428.
46. *See* Judicial Council Decision 379.

ference year as the effective date of retirement of a clergy member who is placed in the retired relation under the provisions of § 2b or § 2c above.[47]

3. *Involuntary Retirement*—By a two-thirds vote of those present and voting, the clergy members in full connection may place any clergy members in the retired relation with or without their consent and irrespective of their age if such relation is recommended by the board of ordained ministry and the cabinet.[48] The procedures for fair process in administrative hearings shall be followed in any involuntary retirement procedure. Written notice of the intended action shall be given to such member by the board of ordained ministry at least one hundred and eighty days prior to annual conference. Written notice also should be given to the chairperson of the administrative review committee.

The administrative review committee (¶ 633) shall ensure that the disciplinary procedures for involuntary retirement were properly followed. The entire process leading to the recommendation for involuntary retirement shall be reviewed by the administrative review committee, and it shall report its findings to the clergy session of members in full connection of the annual conference. Any clergy member who is placed in the retired relationship under this subparagraph shall be entitled to the privilege of receiving his or her pension for the number of approved years served in the annual conference or conferences and such other benefits as the final annual conference may provide, payment to begin the first of any month after the ordained minister attains age sixty-two. If pension begins prior to the age at which retirement under ¶ 356.2c could have occurred, then the provisions of ¶ 1506.4i shall apply.

4. *Preretirement Counseling*—The board of ordained ministry in cooperation with the conference board of pensions shall offer to all clergy members anticipating retirement preconsultation at least five years prior to the date of anticipated retirement (¶ 632.2n). The purpose of the consultation will be to assist the clergy and spouses to plan and to prepare for the adjustments associated with retirement as well as providing guidance and counsel for their return to a new relationship in the local church. In preretirement counseling the board of ordained ministry and the conference board of pensions may relate to

---

47. *See* Judicial Council Decision 769.
48. *See* Judicial Council Decisions 522, 769.

the annual conference association of retired ministers or similar organization where it exists. The boards shall take initiative in assisting retirees to establish such organizations.

5. *Charge Conference Membership*—*a)* All retired clergy members who are not appointed as pastors of a charge, after consultation with the pastor and the district superintendent, shall have a seat in the charge conference and all the privileges of membership in the church where they elect to hold such membership except as set forth in the *Discipline.* They shall report to the charge conference and to the pastor all marriages performed, baptisms administered, and other pastoral functions. If they reside outside the bounds of the conference, they shall forward annually to the conference where membership is held a report of their Christian and ministerial conduct, together with an account of the circumstances of their families, signed by the district superintendent or the pastor of the charge within the bounds of which they reside. Without this report, the conference, after having given thirty days' notice, may locate them without their consent.

6. *Appointment of Retired Ordained Ministers*—A retired ordained minister shall be eligible to receive an appointment when requested by the bishop and cabinet. A retired ordained minister appointed to a pastoral charge shall have neither a claim upon minimum compensation, nor further pension credit. Retired ordained ministers may serve on conference agencies.[49]

7. *Return to Effective Relationship*—A clergy member who has retired under the provisions of ¶ 356.2 may at his or her own request be made an effective member upon recommendation of the board of ordained ministry, the bishop and cabinet, and by majority vote of the clergy members in full connection of the annual conference and thereby be eligible for appointment so long as he or she remains in the effective relation or until ¶ 356.1 applies. Each clergy member requesting return to effective relationship after voluntary retirement must meet the following conditions: (1) presentation of their certificate of retirement; (2) a satisfactory certificate of good health on the prescribed form from a physician approved by the board of ordained ministry. However, any pension being received through the General Board of Pension and Health Benefits shall be discontinued upon their return to the effective relationship. The pension shall be reinstated upon subsequent retirement.

---

49. *See* Judicial Council Decisions 87, 88, 531, 558.

8. This paragraph shall be effective at the conclusion of the 1996 General Conference, except for matters that have already proceeded to the Joint Review Committee.

¶ 357. *Honorable Location*—1. An annual conference may grant clergy members in full connection certificates of honorable location at their own request; *provided* that the board of ordained ministry shall have first examined their character and found them in good standing; and *provided* that the clergy session shall also pass on their character after the request is made; and *provided* further, that this relation shall be granted only to one who intends to discontinue service in the itinerant ministry. The board of ordained ministry shall provide guidance and counsel to the locating member and family as they return to a new relationship in the local church.[50] Upon recommendation of the board of ordained ministry, an annual conference may offer transition assistance.

2. Location shall be certified by the presiding bishop. Associate members or clergy members in full connection located according to the provisions of this paragraph shall not continue to hold membership in the annual conference. After consultation and with the written consent of the pastor in charge, and with the approval of the district superintendent and the staff-parish relations committee of a local church, located clergy members shall designate the local church in which they shall hold membership. Documentation of this consent and approvals shall be filed with the board of ordained ministry. As clergy members of the charge conference, they shall be permitted to exercise ministerial functions only with the written permission of the pastor in charge. They shall have all the privileges of membership in the church where they elect to hold charge conference membership, except as set forth in the *Book of Discipline*. When approved by the executive committee of the board of ordained ministry, a person on honorable location may be appointed *ad interim* by the bishop as a local pastor. A copy of the annual report to the charge conference shall be forwarded to the registrar of the board of ordained ministry in order for location to be continued. They shall report to the charge conference and the pastor all marriages performed, baptisms administered, and funerals conducted and shall be held amenable for their conduct and the continuation of their ordination rights to the annual conference within which the charge conference membership is held.

---

50. *See* Judicial Council Decision 366.

Failure to submit the report for two consecutive years may result in termination of orders upon recommendation of the board of ordained ministry and vote of the clergy session. The provisions of this paragraph shall not apply to persons granted involuntary location prior to the General Conference of 1976. The names of located members after the annual passage of their character shall be printed in the journal.

3. Ordained ministers on honorable location may request the annual conference to grant them the status of honorable location—retired.[51] Requests for retired status shall be stated in writing to the bishop, cabinet, and registrar of the board of ordained ministry at least ninety days prior to the annual conference session. Those granted honorable location retired status shall be accountable for all ministerial services performed to the charge conference in which they hold membership. If such services have been performed, they shall report to that charge conference and exercise their ministry under the supervision of the pastor in charge therein as outlined in ¶ 357.2. They shall continue to be held amenable for their conduct, through accountability to their charge conference, to the annual conference in which charge conference membership is held.

¶ **358.** *Withdrawal*—1. *Withdrawal to Unite with Another Denomination*[52]—When ordained members in good standing withdraw to unite with another denomination or to terminate their membership in the denomination, their credentials shall be deposited with the conference secretary, and if they desire it and the conference authorizes it, the credentials may be returned with the following inscription written plainly across their face:

*A. B. has this day been honorably dismissed by the* _____ *Annual Conference from the ministry of The United Methodist Church.*

Dated: _____

_____ , *President*

_____ , *Secretary*

2. *Withdrawal from the Ordained Ministerial Office*—Ordained members of an annual conference in good standing who desire to leave their ministerial office and withdraw from the conference may be

---

51. *See* Judicial Council Decision 717.
52. *See* Judicial Council Decision 696.

allowed to do so by the annual conference at its session. The ordained minister's credentials shall be given to the district superintendent for deposit with the secretary of the conference, and his or her membership may be transferred to a church which he or she designates, after consultation with the pastor, as the local church in which he or she will hold membership.[53]

3. *Withdrawal Under Complaints or Charges*—When clergy members are accused of an offense under ¶ 2702 and desire to withdraw from the membership of the annual conference, it may permit them to withdraw under the provisions of ¶ 2719.2. The clergy member's credentials shall be surrendered to the district superintendent for deposit with the secretary of the conference, and their membership may be transferred to a local church that they designate, after consultation with the pastor.[54]

4. *Withdrawal Between Conferences*[55]—In the event that withdrawal by surrender of the ministerial office, to unite with another denomination, or under complaints or charges, should occur in the interval between sessions of an annual conference, the clergy member's credentials shall be surrendered to the bishop or district superintendent along with a letter of withdrawal from the ordained ministry. Both the credentials and the letter of withdrawal shall be deposited with the secretary of the conference. This action shall be reported by the board of ordained ministry to the annual conference at its next session.[56] The effective date of withdrawal shall be the date of the letter of withdrawal.[57]

### Section XIV. Complaints

¶ **359.** *Complaint Procedures*—1. *General Provisions*—Ordination and membership in an annual conference in The United Methodist Church is a sacred trust. The qualifications and duties of local pastors, associate members, probationary members, and full members are set forth in the *Book of Discipline* of The United Methodist Church, and we believe they flow from the gospel as taught by Jesus the Christ and proclaimed by his apostles. Whenever a person in any of

---

53. *See* Judicial Council Decision 552.
54. *See* Judicial Council Decisions 552, 691.
55. *See* Judicial Council Decision 696.
56. *See* Judicial Council Decision 552.
57. *See* Judicial Council Decision 691.

the above categories, including those on leaves of all types, honorable or administrative location, or retirement, is accused of violating this trust, the membership of his or her ministerial office shall be subject to review.

This review shall have as its primary purpose a just resolution of any violations of this sacred trust, in the hope that God's work of justice, reconciliation and healing may be realized in the body of Christ.

*a) Supervision*—In the course of the ordinary fulfillment of the superintending role, the bishop or district superintendent may receive or initiate complaints about the performance or character of a clergyperson.[58] A complaint is a written and signed statement claiming misconduct or unsatisfactory performance of ministerial duties.[59] The person filing the complaint and the clergyperson shall be informed by the district superintendent or bishop of the process for filing the complaint and its purpose.[60]

*b) Supervisory Response*—The supervisory response is pastoral and administrative and shall be directed toward a just resolution among all parties. It is not part of any judicial process. At any meetings no verbatim record shall be made; no legal counsel shall be present; the person against whom the complaint was made may choose another person to accompany him or her with the right to voice; the person making the complaint shall have the right to choose a person to accompany him or her with the right to voice.[61]

The supervisory response should be carried out by the bishop and district superintendent in a confidential and timely manner, with attention to communication to all parties regarding the complaint and the process. At the determination of the bishop, persons with qualifications and experience in assessment, intervention, or healing may be selected to assist in the supervisory response. The bishop also may consult with the committee on pastor-parish relations for pastors, the district committee on superintendency for the district superintendents, appropriate personnel committee or other persons who may be helpful. The supervisory response also may include mediation in which the parties are assisted in an agreement satisfactory to all parties by a trained, neutral third party mediator or mediation team.[62]

---

58. *See* Judicial Council Decision 685.
59. *See* Judicial Council Decisions 763, 777.
60. *See* Judicial Council Decision 751.
61. *See* Judicial Council Decision 836.
62. *See* Judicial Council Decisions 691, 700, 751, 763, 768.

c) *Suspension*—When deemed appropriate, to protect the well-being of the person making the complaint, the church, and/or clergy, the bishop, with the recommendation of the executive committee of the board of ordained ministry, may suspend the person from all clergy responsibilities, but not from an appointment, for a period not to exceed sixty days. During the suspension, salary, housing, and benefits provided by a pastoral charge will continue at a level no less than on the date of suspension.[63] The person so suspended shall retain all rights and privileges as stated in ¶ 325. The cost of supply of a pastor during the suspension will be borne by the annual conference.

d) *Referral of a Complaint*—If the supervisory response does not achieve a resolution , the bishop may refer the complaint[64] as judicial or administrative based on the following criteria:

(1) *Judicial Complaint*—If the bishop determines that the complaint is based on allegations of one or more offenses listed in ¶ 2702.1, the bishop may refer the complaint to the counsel for the Church, who shall be appointed by the bishop. The counsel for the Church shall be a clergyperson in full connection and shall have the right to choose one assistant counsel without voice who may be an attorney. The counsel for the Church shall draft and sign a judicial complaint, attaching as exhibits all relevant written materials, including but not limited to information from the supervisory process and a suggested list of witnesses as deemed appropriate, forward the judicial complaint to the committee on investigation and represent the Church in the judicial process. The statute of limitations in ¶ 2702.4 should be considered prior to the referral of a judicial complaint.

(2) *Administrative Complaint*—If the bishop determines that the complaint is based on allegations of incompetence, ineffectiveness, or unwillingness or inability to perform ministerial duties, he or she may refer the complaint as an administrative complaint to the board of ordained ministry for its consideration of remedial or other action[65] (*see* ¶ 359.3*a*).

e) *Supervisory Follow-up*—The bishop and cabinet shall provide a process for healing within the congregation if there has been signifi-

---

63. *See* Judicial Council Decision 776.
64. *See* Judicial Council Decision 700.
65. *See* Judicial Council Decision 763.

cant disruption to congregational life by the complaint. This process may include sharing of information by the bishop and/or cabinet about the nature of the complaint without disclosing alleged facts, which may compromise any possible forthcoming administrative or judicial process. This may include a mediation process for unresolved conflicts, support for victims, and reconciliation for parties involved.[66]

2. *Fair Process in Administrative Hearings*—The following procedures are presented for the protection of the rights of individuals and for the protection of the Church in administrative hearings. The process set forth in this paragraph commences upon referral of a matter as an administrative complaint. Special attention should be given to the timely disposition of all matters and to ensuring racial, ethnic, and gender diversity in the committee hearing the complaint.

*a)* In any administrative proceeding the respondent (the person against whom the administrative complaint has been filed) shall have a right to be heard before any final action is taken.

*b)* Notice of any hearing shall advise the respondent of the reason for the proposed procedures with sufficient detail to allow the respondent to prepare a response. Notice shall be given not less than twenty days prior to the hearing.

*c)* The respondent shall have a right to be accompanied by a clergyperson in full connection to any hearing, in accordance with the appropriate disciplinary provisions. The clergyperson accompanying the respondent shall have the right to voice.

*d)* In any administrative hearing, under no circumstances shall one party, in the absence of the other party, discuss substantive issues with members of the pending hearing body. Questions of procedure may be raised with the presiding officer of the hearing body.

*e)* The respondent shall have access to all records relied upon in the determination of the outcome of the administrative process.

*f)* In the event that a clergyperson fails to appear for supervisory interviews, refuses mail, refuses to communicate personally with the bishop or district superintendent, or otherwise fails to respond to supervisory requests or requests from official administrative committees, such actions or inactions shall not be used as an excuse to avoid or delay any Church processes, and such processes may continue without the participation of such individual.

---

66. *See* Judicial Council Decision 763.

*g)* In order to preserve the integrity of the Church's administrative process and ensure full participation in it at all times, the bishop, cabinet, board of ordained ministry, witnesses, advocates, administrative review committee, clergy in full connection voting in executive session, and all others who participate in the Church's administrative process shall have immunity from prosecution of complaints brought against them related to their role in a particular administrative process, unless they have committed a chargeable offense in conscious and knowing bad faith. The complainant/plaintiff in any proceeding against any such person related to their role in a particular judicial process shall have the burden of proving, by clear and convincing evidence, that such person's actions constituted a chargeable offense committed knowingly in bad faith. The immunity set forth in this provision shall extend to civil court proceedings, to the fullest extent permissible by the civil laws.

3. *Disposition of Administrative Complaints*—When a complaint has been received, the board of ordained ministry shall develop a response in a timely manner. The complaint shall be referred to a committee of the board that deals with matters of conference relations (other than the executive committee) and this committee shall conduct an administrative hearing following the fair process provisions of § 2. The bishop or a cabinet representative shall present the administrative complaint to the committee. The respondent shall be given an opportunity to address the administrative complaint in person, in writing and with the assistance of a clergyperson in full connection, with voice. Once the committee has heard the cabinet representative, the respondent, and others as determined by the chairperson of the committee, it may recommend remedial action, discontinuance, leave of absence, administrative location, dismissal of the complaint or such other action that it deems appropriate, to the board of ordained ministry. The board may accept or amend the recommendations of the committee, or it may dismiss the complaint. In rare instances, the board may refer the complaint back to the bishop for possible referral as a judicial complaint. The board's response will be shared with the clergyperson, the bishop, the cabinet, and the person bringing the original complaint.

*a) Remedial Action*—In cooperation with the cabinet and in consultation with the clergyperson, the board of ordained ministry may choose or recommend one or more of the following options for a program of remedial action, subject to regular oversight by the board and annual review:

(1) Program of continuing education (¶ 349);

(2) Leave of absence, voluntary or involuntary (¶ 352);

(3) Early retirement (¶ 356.2) or involuntary retirement (¶ 356.3);

(4) Sabbatical leave (¶ 350);

(5) Honorable location (¶ 357);

(6) Surrender of ordained ministerial office (¶ 358.2);

(7) Personal counseling or therapy;

(8) Program of career evaluation;

(9) Peer support and supervision;

(10) Private reprimand: a letter signed by the chairperson of the board of ordained ministry and the clergyperson's district superintendent, addressed to the clergyperson with a file copy in the permanent file of the board of ordained ministry (¶ 606.6) stating the appropriateness of the complaint, the specific remedial action required, and the conditions under which the reprimand shall be withdrawn. A report of the reprimand and the remedial action taken shall remain in the personnel file of the respondent once the reprimand has been withdrawn.

(11) Administrative location.

*b)* Clergy residing beyond the bounds of the conference—Any clergy members residing beyond the bounds of the conference in which membership is held shall be subject to administrative complaints or process exercised by the appropriate officers or committees of the conference of which he or she is a member, unless the presiding bishops of the two annual conferences and the clergy member subject to the process agree that fairness would be better served by having the process carried out in the annual conference in which he or she is serving under appointment, or if retired, currently residing.

*c)* Recommendation to Administrative Location—(1) Upon recommendation of the board of ordained ministry, the annual conference may place members on administrative location when, in the judgment of the annual conference, members have demonstrated a pattern of being unable effectively and competently to perform the duties of itinerant ministry; provided that the annual conference shall have first examined their character and found them in good standing. The requirements of fair process as set forth in ¶ 359.2 shall be followed in any administrative location procedure.

(2) The board of ordained ministry shall notify the clergy

member, chairperson of the administrative review committee, bishop, district superintendent, and the complainant of the recommendation to administrative location at least sixty days before the opening of the next annual conference.

The notice to the clergy member shall also inform the member of the right to a hearing before the bishop, cabinet, and executive committee of the board of ordained ministry prior to the recommendation being forwarded to the executive session of the clergy members in full connection of the annual conference for consideration and action. Such choice by the ordained member must be made and notification of the choice sent to the bishop and the chairperson of the board of ordained ministry within thirty days following receipt of notice from the board.[67] The chairperson of the board of ordained ministry shall preside at such a hearing. The recommendation of the board of ordained ministry shall be acted upon by the clergy session of members in full connection with the annual conference.

(3) The administrative review committee (¶ 633) shall ensure that the disciplinary procedures for administrative location were properly followed. The entire process leading up to the recommendation to administrative location shall be reviewed by the administrative review committee, and it shall report its findings to the clergy session of members in full connection with the annual conference.

(4) The provisions of ¶ 359.3 c above apply to administrative location, except that a person on administrative location may not be given *ad interim* appointments by the bishop. Upon recommendation of the board of ordained ministry, an annual conference may offer financial assistance from conference resources in this transition.

d) *Recommendation to Discontinue Probationary Membership*—The board of ordained ministry shall recommend the discontinuance of a probationary member in keeping with the provisions of ¶ 318.6.

### Section XV. Readmission to Conference Relationship

¶ **360.** *Readmission to Probationary Membership*—Persons who have been discontinued as probationary members under the provisions of ¶ 318.6 from an annual conference of The United Methodist Church or one of its legal predecessors may be readmitted by the annual conference in which they held previously such membership and from

---

67. *See* Judicial Council Decisions 384, 485.

which they requested discontinuance or were discontinued, or its legal successor, or the annual conference of which the major portion of their former conference is a part, upon their request and recommendation by the district committee on ordained ministry, the board of ordained ministry, and the cabinet after review of their qualifications, as required in ¶ 315, and the circumstances relating to their discontinuance. When reinstated by vote of the clergy members in full connection, their probationary membership in the conference shall be restored, they shall serve a minimum of three years of probation according to ¶ 317 prior to ordination, and they shall be authorized by licensing and/or commissioning to perform those ministerial functions for which they are qualified.

¶ 361. *Readmission after Honorable or Administrative Location*— Associate members or clergy members in full connection requesting readmission after honorable or administrative location must meet the following conditions:

1. Presentation of their certificate of location.

2. A satisfactory report and recommendation by the charge conference and pastor of the local church in which their membership is held.

3. A satisfactory certificate of good health on the prescribed form from a physician approved by the board of ordained ministry. The board of ordained ministry should require psychological evaluation.

4. Recommendation by the district committee on ordained ministry, the board of ordained ministry, and the cabinet after review of their qualifications, the circumstances relating to their location and conduct during the period of time while on location. When reinstated by vote of the clergy members in full connection of the annual conference that granted the location, their membership in the conference shall be restored, and they shall be authorized to perform all ministerial functions. The conference board of ordained ministry may require at least one year of service as a local pastor prior to readmission to conference membership.

¶ 362. *Readmission After Leaving the Ministerial Office*—Associate members or clergy members in full connection who have left the ministerial office under the provisions of ¶ 358 to an annual conference of The United Methodist Church or one of its legal predecessors may be readmitted by the annual conference in which they held previously such membership and to which they surrendered the ministerial office, or its legal successor, or the annual conference of which the major portion of the former conference is a part, upon their request and recommendation by the district committee on ordained ministry, the board of ordained ministry, and the cabinet after review of their qualifications and the circumstances relating to the surrender of their ministerial office. A period of at least two years service as a local pastor shall be required prior to readmission to conference membership. This service may be rendered in any annual conference of The United Methodist Church with the consent of the board of ordained ministry of the annual conference in which members previously held membership. When reinstated by vote of the clergy members in full connection, their membership in the conference and their credentials shall be restored, and they shall be authorized to perform all ministerial functions.[68]

¶ **363.** *Readmission After Termination by Action of the Annual Conference*—Persons who have been terminated by an annual conference of The United Methodist Church or one of its legal predecessors may seek full membership in the annual conference in which they previously held membership and from which they were terminated, or its legal successor, or the annual conference of which the major portion of their former conference is a part, upon recommendation of the cabinet and completion of all requirements for full membership, including all requirements for election to candidacy and probationary membership. The provisions of this paragraph shall apply to all persons terminated or involuntarily located prior to General Conference of 1976.

¶ **364.** *Readmission After Involuntary Retirement*—Clergy members of an annual conference desiring to return to effective relationship after having been placed in involuntary retirement (¶ 356.3) must meet the following conditions:

1. Submit a written request for reinstatement to the board of ordained ministry.

2. The board of ordained ministry and the cabinet shall review the member's qualifications and the circumstances relating to his or her retirement.

3. Recommendation by the board of ordained ministry, the bishop, cabinet, and a two-thirds vote of the clergy members in full connection of the annual conference that granted the involuntary retirement. A period of at least two years of service as a local pastor shall be required prior to readmission to conference membership.

---

68. *See* Judicial Council Decisions 515, 552.

4. Presentation of the certificate of retirement.

5. Presentation of satisfactory certificate of good health on the prescribed form from a physician approved by the board of ordained ministry. The board of ordained ministry may require a psychological evaluation. Any pension being received through the General Board of Pension and Health Benefits shall be discontinued upon their return to effective relationship. The pension shall be reinstated upon subsequent retirement.

### Section XVI. General Provisions

¶ 365. 1. The annual conference is the basic body of The United Methodist Church. The clergy membership of an annual conference shall consist of deacons and elders in full connection (¶¶ 320, 324), probationary members (¶ 318), associate members, affiliate members (¶¶ 335.4, 559.4), and local pastors under full-time and part-time appointment to a pastoral charge (¶ 342). All clergy are amenable to the annual conference in the performance of their duties in the positions to which they are appointed.[69]

2. Both men and women are included in all provisions of the *Discipline* that refer to the ordained ministry.[70]

3. In all cases where district committees on ordained ministry, boards of ordained ministry, or clergy in executive session vote on granting any status regarding license, ordination, or conference membership, it is understood that the requirements set forth herein are minimum requirements only. Each person voting is expected to vote prayerfully based on his or her personal judgment of the applicant's gifts, evidence of God's grace, and promise of future usefulness for the mission of the Church.

4. All clergy members mentioned in ¶ 365.1 shall receive written communication about decisions made regarding their relationship with the annual conference.

5. There shall be an annual meeting of this covenant body, in executive session of clergy members in full connection with the annual conference, including both deacons and elders, at the site of the regular session of the annual conference to consider questions relating to matters of ordination, character, and conference relations (¶¶ 605.6, 633.2).

---

69. *See* Judicial Council Decisions 327, 371.
70. *See* Judicial Council Decisions 317, 155.

6. A special session of the annual conference may be held at such time and at such place as the bishop shall determine, after consultation with the cabinet and the executive committee of the board of ordained ministry. A special clergy session shall have only such powers as stated in the call.

¶ **366.** *Transitional Provisions for Those Beginning Candidacy Before January 1, 1997*—1. All persons having begun candidacy for diaconal ministry, deacon's and elder's ordination and conference membership, or full-time local pastors prior to January 1, 1997, will be allowed to proceed under the provisions of the 1992 *Book of Discipline* (¶¶ 305–306, 419–421). These continuing procedures must be completed under the provisions set forth in the 1992 *Book of Discipline* prior to December 31, 2008, after which date the provisions of the current *Book of Discipline* will govern the process by which persons enter ministry. All persons continuing as diaconal ministers will be cared for under ¶¶ 305–317 of the 1992 *Book of Discipline*.

2. Persons with the status of associate members in good standing as of January 1, 1997, may, upon the recommendation of the conference board of ordained ministry and election by a two-thirds vote of the clergy session, be elected full members of the annual conference and ordained elders. This option shall be available until December 31, 2004. The following qualifications shall be fulfilled prior to the board's recommendation to the clergy session:

*a)* Fulfilled the provisions of ¶ 304.

*b)* Received the recommendation of the cabinet.

*c)* Have completed or demonstrated that they have completed a minimum of twenty-four semester hours of the basic graduate theological studies of the Christian faith, including the areas of: Old Testament; New Testament; theology; church history; mission of the church in the world; worship/liturgy; and United Methodist doctrine, polity, and history. This requirement may be fulfilled in either a school of theology approved by the University Senate or in a special course of study provided by the General Board of Higher Education and Ministry.

*d)* Provide a written statement demonstrating an understanding of the theology of the ordination of deacons and elders and a willingness to fulfill the purposes of those ordinations.

3. Diaconal ministers who are in good standing with the annual conference and have completed a minimum of three years in an

approved service appointment may become ordained deacons in full connection provided the following requirements are completed:

*a)* Applied in writing to the conference board of ordained ministry for the transfer of their credentials to ordained deacon in full connection.

*b)* Completed a continuing formation and education program developed by the General Board of Higher Education and Ministry. This program shall include an understanding of the meaning of appointment by a bishop, ordination, and the interrelatedness of worship and the world.

*c)* Demonstrated an understanding of the call to the order of deacon, and whose ministry fulfills and exemplifies the definition and description of the ordained deacon (¶¶ 319, 320), and who has either met the educational requirements of the diaconate (¶ 321), or whose competence and experience is determined to be equivalent by the board of ordained ministry through the Division of Deacons, if constituted.

*d)* Received a two-thirds positive vote of the clergy session.

The bishop shall ordain these persons by the laying on of hands at the service of ordination of the annual conference and shall provide deacon's credentials to these deacons in full connection.

Diaconal ministers who seek to become ordained deacons in full connection shall apply before December 31, 2004.

4. The work of the former conference boards of diaconal ministry will be cared for by the conference boards of ordained ministry effective January 1, 1997.

## Chapter Three

# THE SUPERINTENDENCY

## Section I. The Nature of Superintendency

¶ **401.** *Task*—The task of superintending in The United Methodist Church resides in the office of bishop and extends to the district superintendent, with each possessing distinct and collegial responsibilities. The mission of the Church is to make disciples of Jesus Christ (*see* Chapter One, Section I). From apostolic times, certain ordained persons have been entrusted with the particular tasks of superintending. The purpose of superintending is to equip the Church in its disciple-making ministry. Those who superintend carry primary responsibility for ordering the life of the Church. It is their task to enable the gathered Church to worship and to evangelize faithfully.

It is also their task to facilitate the initiation of structures and strategies for the equipping of Christian people for service in the Church and in the world in the name of Jesus Christ and to help extend the service in mission. It is their task, as well, to see that all matters, temporal and spiritual, are administered in a manner that acknowledges the ways and the insights of the world critically and with understanding while remaining cognizant of and faithful to the mandate of the Church. The formal leadership in The United Methodist Church, located in these superintending offices, is an integral part of the system of an itinerant ministry.[1]

¶ **402.** *Guidelines for Superintending in this Age*—The demands of this age on the leadership of bishops and district superintendents in The United Methodist Church can be seen in mode, pace, and skill:

1. *Mode*—Leaders need to be able to facilitate consensus and integrate it into a living tradition, to be open to the prophetic word, to be skilled in team-building, and to be effective in negotiation. The style of leadership should rise out of nurtured and cultivated spiritual disciplines and patterns of holiness, for the Spirit is given to the community and its members to the extent that they participate.

---

1. *See* Judicial Council Decision 524.

2. *Pace*—Beyond formal systems of accountability, leaders need to open themselves to forms of accountability that they cultivate for themselves through a support group. Such a group can listen, can help, and can clarify, as well as participate with the leader, as he or she thinks through time demands and constraints in the process of sorting out of priorities. Appropriate time must be taken for reflection, study, developing friendships, and self-renewal.

3. *Skill*—Among the skills needed by leaders are spiritual discipline, theological reflection, building the unique inclusive community of the Church and of the larger community as well. Reading the signs of the times, analyzing, designing strategy, assessing needs, organizing a wide range of resources, and evaluating programs and personnel are yet other skills crucial for leaders.

## Section II. Offices of Bishop and District Superintendent

¶ 403. *Special Ministry, Not Separate Order*—The offices of **bishop** and **district superintendent** exist in The United Methodist Church as particular ministries. Bishops are elected and district superintendents are appointed from the group of elders who are ordained to be ministers of Service, Word, Sacrament, and Order and thereby participate in the ministry of Christ, in sharing a royal priesthood that has apostolic roots (1 Peter 2:9; John 21:15-17; Acts 20:28; 1 Peter 5:2-3; 1 Timothy 3:1-7).

¶ 404. *Duties of Bishops and District Superintendents*—Bishops and superintendents share in the full ministry as ordained elders. The body of Christ is one; yet many members with differing functions are all joined together in the one body (1 Corinthians 12:28).

1. Bishops are elders in full connection who are elected from the elders and set apart for a ministry of general oversight and supervision (¶ 401). As followers of Jesus Christ called to servant leadership, bishops are authorized to guard the faith, order, liturgy, doctrine, and discipline of the Church; to seek and be a sign of the unity of the faith; to exercise the discipline of the whole Church; to supervise and support the Church's life, work, and mission throughout the world; and to lead all persons entrusted to their oversight in worship, in the celebration of the sacraments, and in their mission of witness and service in the world. Bishops carry a primary responsibility to support and encourage the ministry of all Christians. They share with other bishops in the supervision of the whole Church, encouraging and

supporting all baptized people in the exercising of their gifts and ministries, praying for them, and proclaiming and interpreting to them the gospel of Christ. Bishops are to be prophetic voices and courageous leaders in the cause of justice for all people. Bishops are also authorized to appoint ordained clergy to their responsibilities, consecrate, ordain, and commission persons in ministry to the Church and world.

2. District superintendents are elders in full connection appointed by the bishop to the cabinet and assigned to responsibilities of oversight and supervision within a district and in the entire annual conference (¶ 401). A servant leader who serves as an extension of the oversight of the bishop, the district superintendent is authorized to fulfill those responsibilities designated in the *Book of Discipline* under the supervision of the resident bishop.

### Section III. Election, Assignment, and Termination of Bishops

¶ **405.** *Provisions for Episcopal Areas in Jurisdictions*—1. In central conferences, the number of bishops shall be determined on the basis of missional needs, as approved by the General Conference on recommendation of the Commission on Central Conference Affairs.

2. In all other conferences, the number of bishops shall be determined on the following basis:

*a*) Each jurisdiction having 500,000 church members or fewer shall be entitled to six bishops, and each jurisdiction having more than 500,000 church members shall be entitled to one additional bishop for each 320,000 church members or major fraction thereof; provided, however, that in those jurisdictions where this requirement would result in there being an average of more than 55,000 square miles per episcopal area, such jurisdiction shall be entitled to six bishops for the first 400,000 church members or fewer and for each additional 290,000 church members or two-thirds thereof shall be entitled to one additional bishop.

*b*) A jurisdiction shall not have the number of bishops to which it is entitled reduced until and unless the number of its church members shall have decreased by at least ten percent below the number of church members which had previously entitled the jurisdiction to its number of bishops.

*c*) If the number of church members in a jurisdiction shall have decreased by at least ten percent below the number of church members which had previously entitled the jurisdiction to its number of bishops, then the number of bishops to which it shall be entitled shall be determined on the basis of missional needs, as approved by the General Conference on the recommendation of the Interjurisdictional Committee on Episcopacy; provided however that said jurisdiction shall be entitled to no less than the number of bishops to which it would be entitled under subparagraph *a)* above.

*d)* If a jurisdiction, as a result of the provisions of this paragraph, shall have the number of bishops to which it had previously been entitled reduced, then the reduction in the number of bishops to which it is entitled shall be effective as of September 1 of the fourth calendar year after said reduction has been determined by the General Conference.

3. This legislation shall take effect immediately upon adjournment of the 2000 General Conference.

¶ **406.** *Election and Consecration of Bishops*—1. *Nomination*—An annual conference, in the session immediately prior to the next regular session of the jurisdictional or central conference, may name one or more nominees for episcopal election. Balloting at jurisdictional and central conferences shall not be limited to nominees of annual conferences nor shall any jurisdictional or central conference delegate be bound to vote for any specific nominee. Each jurisdictional or central conference shall develop appropriate procedures for furnishing information about nominees from annual conferences. This shall be done at least two weeks prior to the first day of the jurisdictional or central conference. Similar procedures shall be developed for persons nominated by ballot who receive ten votes, or 5 percent of the valid votes cast, and the information shall be made available to the delegates at the site of the conference.

2. *Process*—*a)* Jurisdictional and central conference delegates, in electing bishops, shall give due consideration to the inclusiveness of The United Methodist Church with respect to sex, race, and national origin. In addition, consideration shall be given to the nature of superintendency as described in ¶¶ 401–402.

*b)* The jurisdictional and central conferences are authorized to fix the percentage of votes necessary to elect a bishop. It is recommended that at least 60 percent of those present and voting be necessary to elect.

*c)* Consecration of bishops may take place at the session of the conference at which election occurs or at a place and time designated by the conference. The consecration service may include bishops from other jurisdictional and central conferences. It is strongly urged that the consecration service also include representatives from other Christian communions (see ¶¶ 124, 427.2, 1901).

¶ 407. *Assignment Process*—1. *Jurisdictional Committee on Episcopacy*—The jurisdictional committee on episcopacy, after consultation with the College of Bishops, shall recommend the assignment of the bishops to their respective residences for final action by the jurisdictional conference; it shall not reach any conclusion concerning residential assignments until all elections of bishops for that session are completed and all bishops have been consulted. A bishop may be recommended for assignment to the same residence for a third quadrennium only if the jurisdictional committee on episcopacy on a two-thirds vote and the jurisdictional conference by a two-thirds vote determines such assignment to be in the best interest of the jurisdiction.

The date of assignment for all bishops is September 1 following the jurisdictional conference.[2]

A newly elected bishop shall be assigned to administer an area other than that within which his or her membership was most recently held, unless by a two-thirds vote the jurisdictional committee shall recommend that this restriction be ignored and by majority vote the jurisdictional conference shall concur.[3]

2. *Central Conference Committee on Episcopacy*—The central conference committee on episcopacy, after consultation with the College of Bishops, shall recommend the assignment of the bishops to their respective residences for final action by the central conference.[4]

3. *Special Assignments*—The Council of Bishops may, with consent of the bishop and the concurrence of the jurisdictional or central conference committee on episcopacy, assign one of its members for one year to some specific churchwide responsibility deemed of sufficient importance to the welfare of the total Church. In this event, a bishop shall be released from the presidential responsibilities within the episcopal area for that term. Another bishop or bishops, active or retired, and not necessarily from the same jurisdictional or central conference, shall be named by the Council of Bishops on recommendation of the

---

2. *See* Judicial Council Decision 781.
3. *See* Judicial Council Decisions 48, 57, 416, 538.
4. *See* Judicial Council Decision 248.

College of Bishops of the jurisdiction involved to assume presidential responsibilities during the interim. In the event that more than one retired bishop is assigned to fulfill presidential responsibilities in one episcopal area, the Episcopal Fund shall be responsible only for the difference between the pensions paid the retired bishops and the remuneration of one active bishop. This assignment may be renewed for a second year by a two-thirds vote of the Council of Bishops and majority vote of the jurisdictional or central committee on episcopacy, and the consent of the bishop and the College of Bishops involved. The bishop so assigned shall continue to receive regular salary and support.

¶ **408.** *Vacancy in the Office of Bishop*—A vacancy in the office of bishop may occur due to death, retirement (¶ 409.1, .2, .3), resignation (¶ 409.4), judicial procedure (¶ 2712), leave of absence (¶ 411.1), or incapacity (¶ 411.4). In case assignment of a bishop to presidential supervision of an episcopal area is terminated by any of the above causes, the vacancy shall be filled by the Council of Bishops on nomination of the College of Bishops of the jurisdiction or central conference concerned; or, if the vacancy should occur within twenty-four months of the episcopal assumption of presidential supervision of that area, the College of Bishops of the jurisdiction or central conference concerned may call a special session of the jurisdictional or central conference as provided in ¶ 519.2.

¶ **409.** *Termination of Office*—An elder who is serving as a bishop up to the time of retirement shall have the status of a retired bishop.[5]

1. *Mandatory Retirement*—*a)* A bishop shall be retired on August 31 next following the regular session of the jurisdictional conference if the bishop's sixty-sixth birthday has been reached on or before July 1 of the year in which the jurisdictional conference is held.[6]

*b)* Pension as approved by the General Conference shall be payable on September 1 following the close of the jurisdictional conference.

*c)* If, however, the retired bishop accepts any one of the following assignments of churchwide responsibility, the General Council on Finance and Administration, after consultation with the Council of Bishops, shall set a level of compensation not to exceed a maximum determined by the General Conference on recommendation of the General Council on Finance and Administration: (1) assignment of a

---

5. *See* Judicial Council Decisions 361, 407.
6. *See* Judicial Council Decisions 413, 578.

special nature with direct relationship and accountability to the Council of Bishops, or (2) assignment to a general agency or United Methodist Church-related institution of higher education. Only the difference between the compensation as established and the continuing pension shall be paid from the Episcopal Fund. Assignment of retired bishops to United Methodist Church-related institutions of higher education must be at the initiative of the institutions, with service not to exceed the mandatory retirement ages of the institutions.

If a bishop is assigned to a general agency or United Methodist Church-related institution of higher education, that agency or United Methodist Church-related institution of higher education shall participate by payment of 50 percent of the difference between the compensation herein established and the pension of the bishop. The general agency or United Methodist Church-related institution of higher education shall further assume all responsibility for the bishop's operational and travel expenses related to the assignment.

Compensation for any special assignment shall cease after the bishop has reached the mandatory age of retirement for all ordained ministers (¶ 356.1) or completes the assignment, whichever comes first. No assignment to a jurisdiction, central conference, annual conference, or non-United Methodist agency shall qualify for additional compensation from the Episcopal Fund under the provisions of this paragraph. The status of a retired bishop on special assignment shall, for purposes of housing and other benefits, be that of a retired bishop.

2. *Voluntary Retirement—a)* Bishops who have completed twenty years or more of service under full-time appointment as ordained ministers or as local pastors with pension credit prior to the opening date of the session of the jurisdictional conference, including at least one quadrennium as bishop, may request the jurisdictional conference or central conference to retire them with the privilege of receiving their pension as determined by the General Council on Finance and Administration, payment of which may begin the first of any month when such payments would be permissible under the provisions of the Ministerial Pension Plan. If the bishop has not reached age sixty-five or completed forty years of service at the time of retirement, the pension benefit for years of service prior to January 1, 1982, may be actuarially reduced as provided under guidelines adopted by the General Conference.

*b)* Bishops who have attained age sixty-two or have completed thirty-five years of service under full-time appointment as an elder or bishop may request the jurisdictional or central conference to place them in the retired relation with the privilege of receiving their pension as determined by the General Council on Finance and Administration.

c) Any bishop who seeks a voluntary retired status shall notify the president of the Council of Bishops at least six months prior to the General Conference.

d) A bishop may seek voluntary retirement for health reasons and shall be so retired by the jurisdictional or central conference committee on episcopacy upon recommendation by the involved College of Bishops and upon presentation of satisfactory medical evidence. Such bishops shall receive their pensions as provided by the General Council on Finance and Administration in consultation with the jurisdictional or central conference committee on episcopacy.

e) Pension as approved by the General Conference shall be payable on September 1 following the close of the jurisdictional conference.

3. *Involuntary Retirement*—a) A bishop may be placed in the retired relation regardless of age by a two-thirds vote of the jurisdictional or central conference committee on episcopacy if, after not less than a thirty-day notice in writing is given to the affected bishop and hearing held, such relationship is found by said committee to be in the best interests of the bishop and/or the Church. Appeal from this action may be made to the Judicial Council with the notice provisions being applicable as set forth in ¶ 2716.

b) A bishop, for health reasons, may be retired between sessions of the jurisdictional or central conference by a two-thirds vote of the jurisdictional or central conference committee on episcopacy upon the recommendation of one third of the membership of the involved College of Bishops. The affected bishop, upon request, shall be entitled to a review of his or her health condition by a professional diagnostic team prior to action by the involved College of Bishops. Notification of action to retire shall be given by the chairperson and secretary of the jurisdictional or central conference committee on episcopacy to the secretary of the Council of Bishops and the treasurer of the Episcopal Fund. Appeal from this action may be made to the Judicial Council with the notice provisions being applicable as set forth in ¶ 2716. Upon such retirement, the bishop shall receive a pension as determined by the General Council on Finance and Administration. *See also* 2d above.

4. *Resignation*—A bishop may voluntarily resign from the episcopacy at any time. A bishop may resign from the office by submitting his or her resignation to the Council of Bishops. The Council of Bishops shall have authority to take appropriate actions concerning matters relating to the resignation, including the appointment of an acting bishop to act until a successor is elected and assigned. The consecration papers of a bishop in good standing so resigning shall be properly inscribed by the secretary of the Council of Bishops and returned. He or she shall be furnished with a certificate of resignation, which shall entitle him or her to membership as a traveling elder in the annual conference (or its successor) in which membership was last held. Notification of this action shall be given by the secretary of the Council of Bishops to the chairperson and secretary of the jurisdictional or central conference committee on episcopacy. When the resigned bishop or surviving spouse and dependent children become conference claimants, the Episcopal Fund shall pay a pension as determined by the General Council on Finance and Administration.

¶ **410.** *Status of Retired Bishops*—A retired bishop is a bishop of the Church in every respect and continues to function as a member of the Council of Bishops in accordance with the Constitution and other provisions of the *Discipline*.

1. Retired bishops may participate in the Council of Bishops and its committees, but without vote. They may preside over sessions of an annual conference, provisional annual conference, or mission if requested to do so by the bishop assigned to that conference, or in the event of that bishop's incapacity, by the president of the College of Bishops to which the conference is related. A retired bishop elected by the Council of Bishops may serve as the ecumenical officer of the Council (term to begin September 1, 1996). In emergency situations, where the resident bishop is unable to preside, the College of Bishops shall assign an effective or retired bishop to preside over the sessions of the annual conference (¶ 46). They may not make appointments or preside at the jurisdiction or central conference. However, when a retired bishop is appointed by the Council of Bishops to a vacant episcopal area or parts of an area under the provisions of ¶¶ 410.3, 411.1, or 411.3, that bishop may function as a bishop in the effective relationship.[7]

---

7. *See* Judicial Council Decision 248.

2. A retired bishop may be considered a member of an annual conference, without vote, for purposes of appointment to a local charge within the said conference.

3. A bishop retired under ¶ 409.1, .2 above may be appointed by the Council of Bishops upon recommendation of the involved College of Bishops to presidential responsibility for temporary service in an area in the case of death, resignation, disability, or procedure involving a resident bishop (¶ 2703.1). This appointment shall not continue beyond the next jurisdictional or central conference.

¶ 411. *Leaves*—1. *Leave of Absence*—A bishop may be granted a leave of absence for a justifiable reason for not more than six months in consultation with the area committee on episcopacy and with the approval of the College of Bishops, the jurisdictional or central conference committee on episcopacy, and the executive committee of the Council of Bishops. During the period for which the leave is granted, the bishop shall be released from all episcopal responsibilities, and another bishop chosen by the executive committee of the Council of Bishops shall preside in the episcopal area. Salary and other benefits shall be continued through the Episcopal Fund.

2. *Renewal Leave*—Every bishop in the active relationship shall take up to three months' leave from his or her normal episcopal responsibilities for purposes of reflection, study, and self-renewal during each quadrennium. The College of Bishops, in consultation with the appropriate jurisdictional or central conference committee on episcopacy, shall coordinate details pertaining to such leaves.

3. *Sabbatical Leave*—A bishop who has served for at least two quadrennia may be granted a sabbatical leave of not more than one year for a program of study or renewal in consultation with the area committee on episcopacy and with the approval of the College of Bishops, the jurisdictional or central conference committee on episcopacy, and the executive committee of the Council of Bishops. During the period for which the sabbatical leave is granted, the bishops shall be released from the presidential responsibilities within the episcopal area, and another bishop or bishops shall be designated by the Council of Bishops to assume the presidential duties. The bishop shall receive one-half salary and, where applicable, housing allowance for the period of the leave.

4. *Incapacity Leave*—Bishops who by reason of impaired health are temporarily unable to perform full work may be released by the jurisdictional or central conference committee on episcopacy from the

obligation to travel through the connection at large. They may choose a place of residence, and the Council of Bishops shall be at liberty to assign them to such work as they may be able to perform. Salary and other benefits shall be continued through the Episcopal Fund.

¶ 412. *Expiration of Terms in Central Conferences*—In a central conference where term episcopacy prevails, bishops whose term of office expires prior to the time of compulsory retirement because of age and who are not reelected by the central conference shall be returned to membership as traveling elders in the annual conference (or its successor) of which they ceased to be a member when elected bishop. Their term of office shall expire at the close of the central conference at which their successor is elected, and they shall therefore be entitled to participate as a bishop in the consecration of the successor. The credentials of office as bishop shall be submitted to the secretary of the central conference, who shall make thereon the notation that the bishop has honorably completed the term of service for which elected and has ceased to be a bishop of The United Methodist Church.[8]

¶ 413. *Complaints Against Bishops*—1. Episcopal leadership in The United Methodist Church shares with all other ordained persons in the sacred trust of their ordination. The ministry of bishops as set forth in *The Book of Discipline of The United Methodist Church* also flows from the gospel as taught by Jesus the Christ and proclaimed by his apostles (¶ 403). Whenever a bishop violates this trust or is unable to fulfill appropriate responsibilities, continuation in the episcopal office shall be subject to review. This review shall have as its primary purpose a just resolution of any violations of this sacred trust, in the hope that God's work of justice, reconciliation, and healing may be realized.

2. Any complaint concerning the effectiveness, competence, or one or more of the offenses listed in ¶ 2702 shall be submitted to the president of the College of Bishops in that jurisdictional or central conference. If the complaint concerns the president, it shall be submitted to the secretary of the College of Bishops. A complaint is a written statement claiming misconduct, unsatisfactory performance of ministerial duties, or one or more of the offenses listed in ¶ 2702.[9] For the purposes of this paragraph, the United Methodist bishops of the central conferences shall constitute one college of bishops.

---

8. *See* Judicial Council Decisions 61, 236, 370.
9. *See* Judicial Council Decision 751.

3. After receiving a complaint as provided in § 1, the president and the secretary of the College of Bishops, or the secretary and another member of the college if the complaint concerns the president (or the president and another member of the college if the complaint concerns the secretary), in consultation with a lay and clergy member of the jurisdictional or central conference committee on episcopacy appointed by the chair of the jurisdictional or central conference committee on episcopacy, shall make a supervisory response. This response shall be directed toward a just resolution among all parties and may include consultation with the jurisdictional committee on episcopacy or voluntary mediation in which the parties are assisted in reaching a settlement or agreement satisfactory to all parties by a trained neutral third party mediator or mediation team.[10] When deemed appropriate to protect the well-being of the complainant, the Church and/or bishop, the College of Bishops, in consultation with the jurisdictional or central conference committee on episcopacy, may suspend the bishop from all episcopal responsibilities for a period not to exceed sixty days. During the suspension, salary, housing and benefits will continue. The supervisory response is pastoral and administrative and shall be directed toward a just resolution. It is not a part of any judicial process. The supervisory response should be carried out in a confidential and timely manner, with attention to communication to all parties regarding the complaint and the process. No verbatim record shall be made and legal counsel shall not be present, although the bishop against whom the complaint was made may choose another bishop or clergyperson to accompany him or her, with the right to voice. At the determination of the president (secretary), persons with qualifications and experience in assessment, intervention, or healing may be selected to assist in the supervisory responses. Others may be consulted as well. The supervisory response also may include mediation, in which the parties are assisted in reaching an agreement satisfactory to all parties by a trained, neutral third-party mediator or mediation team. If the supervisory response does not result in resolution of the matter, the president or secretary of the College of Bishops may refer the matter as follows:

*a) Judicial Complaint*—If a complaint is based on allegations of one or more offenses listed in ¶ 2702, the president and secretary of the College of Bishops (or the two members of the College who are handling

---

10. *See* Judicial Council Decision 763.

the complaint) may refer the complaint to a bishop from another jurisdictional or central conference, or to an elder in full connection within the same jurisdictional or central conference, who shall serve as counsel for the Church. Counsel for the Church shall represent the interests of the Church in pressing the claims of the person making the complaint. Counsel for the Church shall have the right to choose one assistant counsel without voice who may be an attorney. The counsel for the Church shall draft and sign the complaint as a judicial complaint, forward it to the jurisdictional or central conference committee on investigation (¶ 2704), and represent the Church in the judicial process. The fair process provisions in ¶ 2701 shall apply to this judicial process. The statue of limitations in ¶ 2702 should be considered prior to the referral of a judicial complaint.[11]

*b) Administrative Complaint*—If the complaint is based on allegations of incompetence, ineffectiveness, or unwillingness or inability to perform episcopal duties, the president and secretary of the College of Bishops (or the two members of the college who are handling the complaint) may refer the complaint to the jurisdictional or central conference committee on episcopacy.[12] The committee may recommend involuntary retirement (¶ 409.3), disability leave (¶ 411.4), remedial measures (¶ 359), other appropriate action, or it may dismiss the complaint. In rare instances when the jurisdictional or central conference committee on episcopacy deems the matter serious enough and when one or more offenses listed in ¶ 2702 are involved, the committee may refer the complaint back to the president and secretary of the College of Bishops (or the two members of the college who are handling the complaint) for referral as a judicial complaint to the jurisdictional or central conference committee on investigation. The provisions of ¶ 358.2 for fair process in administrative hearings shall apply to this administrative process.

4. Any actions of the jurisdictional or central conference committee taken on a complaint shall be reported to the next session of the jurisdictional or central conference.

---

11. The statute of limitations for bishops went into effect as law on a prospective basis on April 27, 1996. All alleged offenses that occurred prior to this date are time-barred. *See* Judicial Council Decisions 691, 704, and 761.

12. *See* Judicial Council Decision 784.

## Section IV. Specific Responsibilities of Bishops

¶ **414.** *Leadership—Spiritual and Temporal*—1. To lead and oversee the spiritual and temporal affairs of The United Methodist Church which confesses Jesus Christ as Lord and Savior, and particularly to lead the Church in its mission of witness and service in the world.

2. To strengthen the local church, giving spiritual leadership to both laity and clergy; and to build relationships with people of local congregations of the area.

3. To guard, transmit, teach, and proclaim, corporately and individually, the apostolic faith as it is expressed in Scripture and tradition, and, as they are led and endowed by the Spirit, to interpret that faith evangelically and prophetically.

4. To travel through the connection at large as the Council of Bishops (¶ 427) to implement strategy for the concerns of the Church.

5. To teach and uphold the theological traditions of The United Methodist Church.

6. To provide liaison and leadership in the quest for Christian unity in ministry, mission, and structure and in the search for strengthened relationships with other living faith communities.

7. To organize such missions as shall have been authorized by the General Conference.

8. To promote and support the evangelistic witness of the whole Church.

9. To discharge such other duties as the *Discipline* may direct.

10. To convene the Order of Deacons and the Order of Elders and work with the elected chairperson of each order.

¶ **415.** *Presidential Duties*—1. To preside in the general, jurisdictional, central, and annual conferences.[13]

2. To provide general oversight for the fiscal and program operations of the annual conference(s). This may include special inquiry into the work of agencies to ensure that the annual conference and general church policies and procedures are followed.

3. To ensure fair process for clergy and laity as set forth in ¶ 2701 in all involuntary administrative and judicial proceedings through monitoring the performance of annual conference officials, boards, and committees charged with implementing such procedures.

---

13. *See* Judicial Council Decision 395.

4. To form the districts after consultation with the district superintendents and after the number of the same has been determined by vote of the annual conference.[14]

5. To appoint the district superintendents annually (¶¶ 417–418).

6. To consecrate bishops, to ordain elders and deacons, to consecrate diaconal ministers, to commission deaconesses and missionaries, and to see that the names of the persons commissioned and consecrated are entered on the journals of the conference and that proper credentials are furnished to these persons. As these services are acts of the whole Church, text and rubrics are to be used as approved by the General Conference.

7. To fix the appointments of deaconesses and missionaries and to see that the names and appointments are printed in the journals of the conference.

¶ 416. *Working with Ordained, Licensed, Consecrated, and Commissioned Personnel*—1. To make and fix the appointments in the annual conferences, provisional annual conferences, and missions as the *Discipline* may direct (¶¶ 430–434).

2. To divide or to unite a circuit(s), station(s), or mission(s) as judged necessary for missional strategy and then to make appropriate appointments.

3. To announce the appointments of deaconesses, diaconal ministers, home missionaries, and laypersons in service under the General Board of Global Ministries.

4. To fix the charge conference membership of all ordained ministers appointed to ministries other than the local church in keeping with ¶ 335.

5. To transfer, upon the request of the receiving bishop, clergy member(s) of one annual conference to another; *provided* said member(s) agrees to said transfer; and to send immediately to the secretaries of both conferences involved, to the conference boards of ordained ministry, and to the clearing house of the General Board of Pension and Health Benefits, written notices of the transfer of members and of their standing in the course of study if they are undergraduates.[15]

6. To appoint associate members, probationary members, or full members to attend any school, college, or theological seminary listed

---

14. *See* Judicial Council Decision 422.
15. *See* Judicial Council Decisions 114, 254, 554.

by the University Senate, or to participate in a program of Clinical Pastoral Education in a setting accredited by the Association for Clinical Pastoral Education. Such appointments are not to be considered as extension ministry appointments.

7. To keep and maintain appropriate supervisory records on all district superintendents and other records on ministerial personnel as determined by the bishop or required by the *Discipline* or action of the annual conference. When a district superintendent is no longer appointed to the cabinet, the bishop shall give that person's supervisory file to the superintendent of record. Supervisory records shall be kept under guidelines approved by the General Council on Finance and Administration. The supervisory records maintained by the bishop are not the personnel records of the annual conference.

## Section V. Selection, Assignment, and Term of District Superintendents

¶ **417.** *Selection and Assignment*—Inasmuch as the district superintendency is an extension of the general superintendency, the bishop shall appoint elders to serve as district superintendents. Prior to each appointment, the bishop shall consult with the cabinet and the committee on district superintendency of the district to which the new superintendent will be assigned (¶ 431) for the purpose of determining leadership needs of the annual conference and the district (¶¶ 401–402). In the selection of superintendents, bishops shall give due consideration to the inclusiveness of The United Methodist Church with respect to sex, race, national origin, physical challenge, and age, except for the provisions of mandatory retirement.

¶ **418.** *Limitations on Years of Service*—The normal term for a district superintendent shall be up to six years, but this may be extended to no more than up to eight years at the discretion of the bishop, in consultation with the cabinet and the district committee on superintendency. No superintendent shall serve for more than eight years in any consecutive eleven years. No elder shall serve as district superintendent more than twelve years. In addition, consideration shall be given to the nature of superintendency as described in ¶¶ 401–402.[16]

16. *See* Judicial Council Decisions 368, 512.

## Section VI. Specific Responsibilities of District Superintendents

¶ 419. The district superintendent shall oversee the total ministry of the clergy and of the churches in the communities of the district in their missions of witness and service in the world: (a) by giving priority to the scheduling of time and effort for spiritual leadership, pastoral support, supervision, and encouragement to the clergy and to the churches of the district; (b) by encouraging their personal, spiritual, and professional growth; (c) by encouraging their personal commitment to the mandate of inclusiveness in the life of the church; (d) by nominating persons to serve as guides for the ministry inquiring process; (e) by nominating clergy in full connection to serve in the ministry of mentoring candidates, commissioned ministers, local pastors and other probationary members; (f) by participating with the bishops in the appointment-making process; (g) by enabling programs throughout the district that may assist local churches to build and extend their ministry and mission with their people and to the community; (h) by working in cooperation with appropriate district and annual conference agencies to explore long-range, experimental, ecumenical, multicultural, multiracial, and cooperative ministries; (i) to provide representation and leadership in the district in the quest for Christian unity in ministry and mission, encouraging local congregations in the development of an understanding and relationship with other living faith communities and in working with ecumenical agencies and coalitions in the sharing of resources, and, where appropriate, serving as an ecumenical liaison with other living faith communities; (j) by assisting the bishop in the administration of the annual conference. In the fulfillment of this ministry, the superintendent shall consult at least annually (¶ 663.3) with the committee on district superintendency. In the context of these basic responsibilities, the district superintendent shall give attention to the following specific tasks.[17]

¶ 420. *Spiritual and Pastoral Leadership*—The district superintendent is responsible for giving spiritual leadership to clergy and laity in the churches of the district. The district superintendent should model and encourage spiritual formation through the practices of personal prayer, Bible study, communal worship, service, and frequent participation in the sacraments of baptism and Holy Communion.

---

17. *See* Judicial Council Decision 398.

1. To give pastoral support and care to the ordained, licensed, consecrated, and commissioned personnel and their families by traveling through the district, preaching, visiting, and maintaining the connectional order of the *Discipline*.

2. To counsel with clergy and with consecrated and commissioned personnel concerning matters affecting their ministry and personal life.

3. To encourage the building of covenantal community among the clergy and among consecrated and commissioned personnel for mutual support and discipline; to build systems of mutual support for clergy and diaconal families.

¶ 421. *Supervision*—1. To work with elders, deacons, local pastors, diaconal ministers, and charge conferences in formulating statements of purpose for congregations in fulfilling their mission and with committees on pastor-parish relations to clarify the priorities for the ministry of clergy and diaconal ministers.

2. To establish a clearly understood process of supervision for clergy of the district, including observation of all aspects of ministry, direct evaluation, and feedback to the clergy involved.

3. To consult with committees on pastor-parish relations to update their profiles for appointment in accordance with ¶ 432.1 and with pastors to update their profiles for appointment in accordance with ¶ 432.2.[18]

4. To make specific provision for the supervision of probationary members and local pastors appointed within the district.

5. To receive annually from each clergyperson a report of his or her program of continuing education and spiritual growth, to give counsel concerning future plans, and to encourage congregations to give time and financial support for such programs.

¶ 422. *Personnel*—1. To work with pastors and diaconal ministers, committees on pastor-parish relations, and congregations in interpreting the meaning of ministry and in identifying and enlisting candidates of the highest quality for ordained ministry, with special concern for the inclusiveness of the Church with respect to gender, race, national origin, and disabilities; to encourage candidates to attend United Methodist seminaries in preparation for their leadership in the church.

2. To work with the district committee on ordained ministry in

---

18. *See* Judicial Council Decision 701.

enabling a meaningful and appropriate examination of candidates into ordained ministry; to issue and renew licenses to preach when authorized (¶ 340); to keep careful records of all such candidates; to maintain regular communication with all candidates in order to advise and encourage them in spiritual and academic preparation for their ministry. The district superintendent shall not serve as chairperson of the district committee on ordained ministry.

3. To work with the bishop and cabinet in the process of appointment and assignment for ordained ministers.

4. To cooperate with the board of ordained ministry in its efforts to provide or arrange support services and liaison for pastors at times of changing conference relationships or termination (¶¶ 350–358, 359–360).

¶ **423.** *Administration*—1. To schedule and preside, or authorize an elder to preside, in each annual charge conference or church conference within the district (¶¶ 245, 247).

2. To administer the district office, including supervision of support staff (¶¶ 612.1*a*; 663.4*a*).

3. To develop adequate compensation for all clergy, including provision for housing, utilities, travel, and continuing education.

4. To keep and maintain appropriate supervisory records on all ministerial personnel appointed or related to charges within the district. Supervisory records shall be kept under guidelines approved by the General Council on Finance and Administration. At the time of appointment change, supervisory records shall be given to the superintendent of record. The bishop shall be the superintendent of record for the district superintendents.

5. To cooperate with the district board of church location and building and local church boards of trustees or building committees in arranging acquisitions, sales, transfers, and mortgages of property; and to ensure that all charters, deeds, and other legal documents conform to the *Discipline* and to the laws, usages, and forms of the county, state, territory, or country within which such property is situated and to keep copies thereof.

6. To ensure that an investigation be made and a plan of action be developed for the future missional needs of The United Methodist Church or the community prior to consenting to the proposed action to sell or transfer any United Methodist local church property.

7. To keep accurate and complete records for one's successor, including:

  *a)* All abandoned church properties and cemeteries within the bounds of the district;

  *b)* All church properties being permissively used by other religious organizations, with the names of the local trustees thereof;

  *c)* All known endowments, annuities, trust funds, investments, and unpaid legacies belonging to any pastoral charge or organization connected therewith in the district and an accounting of their management;

  *d)* Membership of persons from churches that have been closed.

  8. To receive a plan for the cultivation of giving from each congregation that includes promotion for current and deferred financial support in local churches for district, conference, and denominational causes.

  9. To develop with appropriate district committees strategies that give careful attention to the needs of churches of small membership and to the formation of cooperative ministries.

  10. To transfer members of a discontinued church to another United Methodist church of their choice or to such other churches as members may elect.

  11. To recommend to the bishop for approval, after consultation with the churches involved, any realignment of pastoral charge lines and report them to the annual conference.

  12. To serve within the district as acting administrator of any pastoral charge in which a pastoral vacancy may develop or where no pastor has been appointed.[19]

  13. To see that the provisions of the *Discipline* are observed and to interpret and decide all questions of Church law and discipline raised by the churches in the district, subject to affirmation, modification, or reversal by the president of the annual conference.

  14. To secure an annual audit report of any and all district funds and send a copy to the district conference or annual conference council on finance and administration.

  ¶ **424.** *Program*—1. To oversee the programs of the Church within the bounds of the district in cooperation with pastors and congregations, working with and through the district council on ministries where it exists.

  2. To work cooperatively with the conference council on ministries or alternative structure and its staff in all program concerns of the Church; may serve as a member of the annual conference council on ministries.

---

  19. *See* Judicial Council Decision 581.

3. To give leadership within the district in the quest for Christian unity and interreligious relationships as an extension of the episcopal office.

4. To establish long-range planning that is responsive to ecumenical and racially inclusive perspectives and to initiate new and vital forms of ministry.

5. To participate with the cabinet in submitting to the annual conference a report reflecting the state of the conference, with recommendations for greater effectiveness.

¶ 425. *Renewal and Study Leave*—A district superintendent may take up to three months' leave from his or her normal superintendent responsibilities for purposes of reflection, study, and self-renewal once during his or her term as superintendent. The bishop and cabinet, in consultation with the committee on district superintendency, shall coordinate details pertaining to such leaves.

## Section VII. Expressions of Superintendency

¶ **426.** *Relationship Between Bishops and District Superintendents*— The offices of bishop and district superintendent are linked with each other in ways described elsewhere (¶ 403). The interdependence of the offices calls for a collegial style of leadership. However, both the office of bishop and that of district superintendent are embedded in their own contexts.

¶ **427.** *Council of Bishops*—1. Bishops, although elected by jurisdictional or central conferences, are elected general superintendents of the whole Church. As all ordained ministers are first elected into membership of an annual conference and subsequently appointed to pastoral charges, so bishops become through their election members first of the Council of Bishops before they are subsequently assigned to areas of service. By virtue of their election and consecration, bishops are members of the Council of Bishops and are bound in special covenant with all other bishops. In keeping with this covenant, bishops fulfill their servant leadership and express their mutual accountability. The Council of Bishops is a faith community of mutual trust and concern responsible for the faith development and continuing well-being of its members.

2. The Council of Bishops is thus the collegial expression of episcopal leadership in the Church and through the Church into the world. The Church expects the Council of Bishops to speak to the

Church and from the Church to the world and to give leadership in the quest for Christian unity and interreligious relationships.

3. In order to exercise meaningful leadership, the Council of Bishops is to meet at stated intervals. The Council of Bishops is charged with the oversight of the spiritual and temporal affairs of the whole Church, to be executed in regularized consultation and cooperation with other councils and service agencies of the Church.

4. The Council of Bishops may assign one of its members to visit another episcopal area or Methodist-related church. When so assigned, the bishop shall be recognized as the accredited representative of the Council of Bishops, and when requested by the resident bishop or president in that area or Church, may exercise therein the functions of episcopacy.

¶ 428. *Conference of Methodist Bishops*—There may be a conference of Methodist bishops, composed of all the bishops elected by the jurisdictional and central conferences and one bishop or chief executive officer from each affiliated autonomous Methodist or united church, which shall meet on call of the Council of Bishops after consultation with other members of the conference of Methodist bishops. The travel and other necessary expense of bishops of affiliated autonomous Methodist or united churches related to the meeting of the Conference of Methodist Bishops shall be paid on the same basis as that of bishops of The United Methodist Church.

¶ 429. *Cabinet*—1. District superintendents, although appointed to the cabinet and assigned to districts, are also to be given conference-wide responsibilities. As all ordained ministers are first elected into membership of an annual conference and subsequently appointed to pastoral charges, so district superintendents become through their selection members first of a cabinet before they are subsequently assigned by the bishop to service in districts.

2. The cabinet under the leadership of the bishop is the expression of superintending leadership in and through the annual conference. It is expected to speak to the conference and for the conference to the spiritual and temporal issues that exist within the region encompassed by the conference.

3. The cabinet is thus also the body in which the individual district superintendents are held accountable for their work, both for conference and district responsibilities.[20]

---

20. *See* Judicial Council Decision 763.

4. In order to exercise meaningful leadership, the cabinet is to meet at stated intervals. The cabinet is charged with the oversight of the spiritual and temporal affairs of a conference, to be executed in regularized consultation and cooperation with other councils and service agencies of the conference.

5. The cabinet is to consult and plan with the district committee and conference board of ordained ministry in order to make a horough analysis of the needs of the district for clergy, implementing this planning with a positive and conscious effort to fill these needs (¶ 632.2*a*).

6. When the cabinet considers matters relating to coordination, implementation, or administration of the conference program, and other matters as the cabinet and Director of Council on Ministries, or equivalent, may determine, the director shall be present.

7. The cabinet shall assume leadership responsibility for ascertaining those places where ecumenical shared ministry would be an effective way of expressing the United Methodist presence in a community.

## Section VIII. Appointment-Making

¶ **430.** *Responsibility*—1. Clergy shall be appointed by the bishop, who is empowered to make and fix all appointments in the episcopal area of which the annual conference is a part. Appointments are to be made with consideration of the gifts and evidence of God's grace of those appointed, to the needs, characteristics, and opportunities of congregations and institutions, and with faithfulness to the commitment to an open itineracy. Open itineracy means appointments are made without regard to race, ethnic origin, gender, color, disability, marital status, or age, except for the provisions of mandatory retirement. The concept of itineracy is important, and sensitive attention should be given in appointing clergy with physical challenges to responsibilities and duties that meet their gifts and graces. Through appointment-making, the connectional nature of the United Methodist system is made visible.

2. Appointment-making across conference lines shall be encouraged as a way of creating mobility and open itineracy. The jurisdictional committee on ordained ministry will cooperate with bishops and cabinets in providing information on supply and demand within the jurisdiction.

¶ **431.** *Consultation and Appointment-Making*—Consultation is the process whereby the bishop and/or district superintendent confer with the pastor and committee on pastor-parish relations, taking into consideration the criteria of ¶ 432, a performance evaluation, needs of the appointment under consideration, and mission of the Church. Consultation is not merely notification. Consultation is not committee selection or call of a pastor. The role of the committee on pastor-parish relations is advisory. Consultation is both a continuing process and a more intense involvement during the period of change in appointment.[21]

1. The process of consultation shall be mandatory in every annual conference.

2. The Council of Bishops shall inquire annually of their colleagues about the implementation of the process of consultation in appointment-making in their respective areas.[22]

¶ **432.** *Criteria*—Appointments shall take into account the unique needs of a charge, the community context, and also the gifts and evidence of God's grace of a particular pastor. To assist bishops, cabinets, pastors, and congregations to achieve an effective match of charges and pastors, criteria must be developed and analyzed in each instance and then shared with pastors and congregations.

1. *Congregations*—The district superintendent shall develop with the pastor and the committees on pastor-parish relations of all churches profiles that reflect the needs, characteristics, and opportunities for mission of the charge consistent with the Church's statement of purpose (¶ 421.1). These profiles shall be reviewed annually and updated when appropriate to include:

*a)* The general situation in which a congregation finds itself in a particular setting: size, financial condition, quality of lay leadership, history.

*b)* The convictional stance of the congregation: theology; prejudices, if any; spiritual life.

*c)* The ministry of the congregation among its people for the sake of the community: service programs, basis for adding new members, reasons for losing members, mission to community and world, forms of witness.

*d)* The qualities and functions of pastoral ministry needed to fulfill the mission and goals of the congregation.

---

21. *See* Judicial Council Decisions 101, 501.
22. *See* Judicial Council Decision 701.

2. *Pastors*—The district superintendent annually shall develop with the pastor profiles reflecting the pastor's gifts, evidence of God's grace, professional experience and expectations, and also the needs and concerns of the pastor's spouse and family. These profiles shall be reviewed annually and updated when appropriate to include:

a) *Spiritual and personal sensibility:* personal faith, call and commitment to ordained ministry, work through the institutional church, integration of vocation with personal and family well-being, lifestyle.

b) *Academic and career background:* nature of theological stance, experience in continuing education, professional experience, record of performance.

c) *Skills and abilities:* in church administration, leadership development, worship and liturgy, preaching and evangelism, teaching and nurturing, counseling and group work, ability to work in cooperation, ability in self-evaluation, and other relational skills.

d) *Community context:* the ability of the pastor to relate effectively to his or her community setting, such as rural, town, urban, suburban, and so forth.

e) *Family situation.*

3. *Community Context*—The district superintendent may develop community profiles with the pastor and the committee on pastor-parish relations. Sources of information for these profiles could include: neighborhood surveys; local, state, and national census data; information from annual conference committees on parish and community development; and research data from the General Council on Ministries and other Church agencies. Profiles may be reviewed annually and updated when appropriate to include:

a) General demographic data and trends including age, sex, and racial-ethnic composition of the community.

b) Economic trends, including the incidence of poverty.

c) Projected community changes.

d) Other sociological, economic, political, historical, and ecumenical aspects of the community surrounding the church.

¶ 433. *Process of Appointment-Making*—The process used in appointment-making shall include:[23]

1. A change in appointment may be initiated by a pastor, a committee on pastor-parish relations, a district superintendent, or a bishop.

---

23. *See* Judicial Council Decision 701.

2. The bishop and the cabinet shall consider all requests for change of appointment in light of the profile developed for each charge and the gifts and evidence of God's grace, professional experience, and family needs of the pastor.

3. When a change in appointment has been determined, the district superintendent should meet together or separately with the pastor and the committee on pastor-parish relations where the pastor is serving, for the purpose of sharing the basis for the change and the process used in making the new appointment.

4. All appointments shall receive consideration by the bishop, the district superintendent(s), and the cabinet as a whole until a tentative decision is made.

5. The process used in making the new appointment shall include:

*a)* The district superintendent shall confer with the pastor about a specific possible appointment (charge) and its congruence with gifts, evidence of God's grace, professional experience and expectations, and the family needs of the pastor, identified in consultation with the pastor (¶ 432.2).

*b)* If the appointment is to a cooperative parish ministry or to a charge that is part of a cooperative parish ministry, the following shall be included in the consultation process:

(1) The prospective appointee shall be informed prior to the appointment that the charge under consideration is part of a cooperative parish ministry.[24]

(2) The coordinator or director of the cooperative ministry, or, if there is no coordinator or director, a representative of the staff of the cooperative ministry, shall be conferred with concerning the prospective appointment and shall have the opportunity to meet with the prospective appointee prior to the appointment being made.[25]

(3) The prospective appointee shall have demonstrated skills in cooperative Christian mission or show potential for the same to ensure that the cooperative venture is strengthened during the time of the appointee's leadership.

*c)* If the appointment is to a position other than pastor in charge, the following shall be included in the consultation process:

---

24. *See* Judicial Council Decision 556.
25. *See* Judicial Council Decision 556.

(1) The prospective appointee shall be informed prior to the appointment that the position under consideration is part of a multiple-staff ministry and shall be furnished an initial written job description approved by the committee on pastor-parish relations.

(2) The pastor in charge shall be conferred with concerning the prospective appointee.

(3) The prospective appointee and pastor in charge shall meet for discussion of the job description and mutual expectations.

6. The district superintendent shall confer with the receiving committee on pastor-parish relations about pastoral leadership (¶ 432.1).

7. When appointments are being made to less than full-time ministry, the district superintendent shall consult with the clergy person to be appointed and the committee on pastor-parish relations regarding proportional time, salary, and pension credit and benefit coverage.

8. If during this consultative process it is determined by the bishop and cabinet that this decision should not be carried out, the process is to be repeated until the bishop, basing his or her decision on the information and advice derived from consultation, makes and fixes the appointment.

9. A similar process of consultation shall be available to persons in appointments beyond the local church.

10. When the steps in the process have been followed and completed, the announcement of that decision shall be made to all parties directly involved in the consultative process, that is, the appointment cabinet, the pastor, and the committee on pastor-parish relations, before a public announcement is made.

¶ 434. *Frequency*—While the bishop shall report all pastoral appointments to each regular session of an annual conference, appointments to charges may be made at any time deemed advisable by the bishop and cabinet. Appointments are made with the expectation that the length of pastorates shall respond to the long-term pastoral needs of charges, communities, and pastors. The bishop and cabinet should work toward longer tenure in local church appointments to facilitate a more effective ministry.

¶ 435. *Appointment of Deacons in Full Connection*—The deacons shall be appointed by the bishop in the annual conference where they are members in full connection. Appointments of the deacons are to be made in consideration of the gifts and evidence of God's grace of the deacon, needs of the community, and the gifts of the congregation and institutions. The appointment shall reflect the nature of the ministry of the deacon as a faithful response of the mission of the church meeting the emerging needs in the world (¶ 322). It may be initiated by the individual deacon in full connection, the agency seeking their service, the bishop, or the district superintendent.

*Chapter Four*

# THE CONFERENCES

The United Methodist Church is a connectional structure maintained through its chain of conferences.

## Section I. The General Conference

¶ **501.** *Definition of Powers*—The General Conference has full legislative power over all matters distinctively connectional (*see* ¶ 15, Division Two, Section II, Article IV, The Constitution). It has no executive or administrative power.

¶ **502.** *Composition*—1. The voting membership of the **General Conference** shall consist of:

*a)* An equal number of clergy and lay delegates elected by the annual conferences as provided in the *Discipline*. The missionary conferences and provisional annual conferences shall be considered as annual conferences for the purposes of this paragraph.

*b)* Delegates from The Methodist Church in Great Britain and other autonomous Methodist churches with which concordat agreements have been established providing for mutual election and seating of delegates in each other's highest legislative conferences (¶¶ 12.2, 12.3; 552).

2. The number of delegates to which an annual conference is entitled shall be computed on a two-factor basis: the number of clergy members of the annual conference, and the number of members of local churches in the annual conference.[1]

The term *clergy members* as used in this paragraph shall refer to both active and retired members of the annual conference (¶ 602.1).

3. The secretary of the General Conference shall calculate the number of delegates to be elected by each annual conference, based on the factors specified above, as follows:

*a)* One clergy delegate for the first 375 clergy members of the annual conference and one clergy delegate for each additional 140 clergy members or major fraction thereof,[2] and

---

1. *See* Judicial Council Decisions 109, 333, 592.
2. *See* Judicial Council Decisions 327, 558.

*b)* One clergy delegate for the first 26,000 members of local churches of the annual conference and one clergy delegate for each additional 44,000 local church members or major fraction thereof, and

*c)* A number of lay delegates equal to the total number of clergy delegates authorized as above.

*d)* Every annual conference shall be entitled to at least one clergy and one lay delegate.

*e)* This formula is designated to comply with the Constitution, Division Two, Section II, Article I (¶ 12), which defines the minimum and maximum number of delegates to a General Conference. Should the computations provided in the paragraph result in a figure below the prescribed minimum or above the prescribed maximum for delegates, the secretary of the General Conference shall be authorized to remedy the situation by adjusting up or down the numbers of clergy members and members of local churches of the annual conference necessary to entitle an annual conference to elect delegates, any such adjustment to be proportionally the same for the two factors.[3]

4. Delegates to the General Conference shall be elected at the session of the annual conference held in the calendar year preceding the session of the General Conference. At least thirty days prior to the beginning of that calendar year, the secretary of the General Conference shall notify the bishop and the secretary of each annual conference of the number of delegates to be elected by that annual conference.

5. The secretary of each annual conference, using the certificate of election form supplied by the secretary of the General Conference, shall report to the secretary of the General Conference the names, addresses, and such other information as may be required for delegates and reserves elected by the annual conference.

6. The secretary of the General Conference shall prepare and send to each annual conference secretary credentials to be signed and distributed to the delegates and reserves elected by the annual conference.

¶ 503. *Presiding Officers*—The bishops shall be the presiding officers at the General Conference.

¶ 504. *Election of Secretary-Designate*—1. The Council of Bishops shall present a nomination from the ordained ministry or lay membership of The United Methodist Church for secretary-designate. Other nominations shall be permitted from the floor. The election, if there be two or more nominees, shall be by ballot.

---

3. *See* Judicial Council Decision 687.

2. *Assumption of Office*—The secretary-designate shall assume the responsibilities of the office of secretary as soon after the adjournment of the General Conference as all work in connection with the session has been completed, including the corrections to the *Daily Christian Advocate,* which serves as the official journal of the General Conference. The exact date of the transfer of responsibility to the secretary-designate shall be determined by the Commission on the General Conference, but shall not be later than December 31, following the adjournment of the General Conference.

3. *Assigned Duties*—The secretary, in cooperation with the General Commission on the General Conference, shall initiate procedures to prepare delegates from central conferences for full participation in the General Conference by providing information concerning both the operation of the General Conference and materials it will consider. As far as possible, the materials should be provided in the languages of the delegates. After consultation with the Council of Bishops and the General Commission on Christian Unity and Interreligious Concerns, the secretary shall issue invitations to ecumenical representatives.

¶ 505. *Rules of Order*—The Plan of Organization and Rules of Order of the General Conference shall be the Plan of Organization and Rules of Order as approved by the preceding General Conference until they have been altered or modified by the action of the General Conference.

¶ 506. *Quorum*—When the General Conference is in session, it shall require the presence of a majority of the whole number of delegates to the General Conference to constitute a quorum for the transaction of business; but a smaller number may take a recess or adjourn from day to day in order to secure a quorum, and at the final session may approve the journal, order the record of the roll call, and adjourn *sine die.*

¶ 507. *Petitions to General Conference*—Any organization, clergy member, or lay member of The United Methodist Church may petition the General Conference in the following manner:

1. The petition must be sent to the secretary of the General Conference or a designated petitions secretary in a format determined by the secretary of the General Conference.

2. Each petition must address only one issue if the *Discipline* is not affected; if the *Discipline* is affected, each petition must address only one paragraph of the *Discipline,* except that, if two or more para-

graphs in the *Discipline* are so closely related that a change in one affects the others, the petition may call for the amendment of those paragraphs also to make them consistent with one another.

3. Each petition must be signed by the person submitting it, accompanied by appropriate identification, such as address, local church, or United Methodist board or agency relationship. Each petition submitted by fax or electronic mail must identify the individual submitting it, accompanied by identification as above, and must contain a valid electronic mail return address or return fax number by which the submitter can be reached. Electronic signatures will be accepted in accordance with common business practice.

4. All petitions submitted to the General Conference, except those submitted by individual members of The United Methodist Church and local church groups, which call for the establishment of new programs or the expansion of existing programs will be invalid unless accompanied by supporting data that address the issue of anticipated financial requirements of the program.

5. Petitions must be postmarked by a national postal service no later than 150 days prior to the opening session of the General Conference.

6. If petitions are transmitted by a means other than a national postal service, they must be in the hands of the petitions secretary no later than 150 days prior to the opening session of the General Conference. Exceptions to the time limitations shall be granted for petitions originating from an annual conference session held between 150 and 45 days prior to the opening session of the General Conference, and for other petitions at the discretion of the Committee on Reference.

7. Petitions adopted and properly submitted by annual conferences, jurisdictional and central conferences, the United Methodist Youth Organization, or general agencies or councils of the Church, and petitions properly submitted by individual members (either clergy or lay) of The United Methodist Church and local church groups, *provided* that they have been received by the petitions secretary or secretary of the General Conference no later than 150 days before the opening of General Conference, shall be printed in the Advance Edition of the *Daily Christian Advocate*.

8. Petitions and/or resolutions not printed in the Advance Edition of the *Daily Christian Advocate* shall be printed or copied and provided to all delegates. Where the content of petitions is essentially the same, the petition will be printed once, with the first author named and the number of additional copies received printed.

9. The secretary of the General Conference shall arrange for electronic access to all petitions, including General Conference action and the resulting impact on *The Book of Discipline of The United Methodist Church*, throughout the General Conference session. This access shall be available until the publication of the new edition of *The Book of Discipline of The United Methodist Church*. Implementation shall be according to guidelines established by the Committee on Plan of Organization and Rules of Order.

¶ **508.** *Legislation Effective Date*—All legislation of the General Conference of The United Methodist Church shall become effective January 1 following the session of the General Conference at which it is enacted, unless otherwise specified (¶ 537.22).

¶ **509.** *Speaking for the Church*—1. No person, no paper, no organization, has the authority to speak officially for The United Methodist Church, this right having been reserved exclusively to the General Conference under the Constitution. Any written public policy statement issued by a general Church agency shall clearly identify either at the beginning or at the end that the statement represents the position of that general agency and not necessarily the position of The United Methodist Church (¶ 717).[4]

2. Any individual member called to testify before a legislative body to represent The United Methodist Church shall be allowed to do so only by reading, without elaboration, the resolutions and positions adopted by the General Conference of The United Methodist Church.

¶ **510.** *Duties of the Secretary*—The secretary of the General Conference shall be responsible for the permanent record of the General Conference, which shall include:

1. Corrections to the *Daily Christian Advocate*. The editor will then file with the Commission on Archives and History two bound copies of the *Daily Christian Advocate* and corrections as the official record of General Conference. Bound copies shall also be made available at cost by The United Methodist Publishing House.

2. A *Book of Resolutions* to be edited by The United Methodist Publishing House. The book shall contain all valid resolutions of the General Conference. The preface of the *Book of Resolutions* shall include the guidelines for writing resolutions.

---

4. *See* Judicial Council Decision 458.

a) Resolutions and positions adopted by the General Conference of The United Methodist Church are valid until they are specifically rescinded, amended, or superseded by action of subsequent sessions of the General Conference. All valid resolutions and positions of the General Conference of The United Methodist Church, beginning with those adopted by the 1968 Uniting Conference, shall be listed in each edition of the *Book of Resolutions*. There shall be a complete subject index to all valid resolutions of the General Conference of The United Methodist Church in each edition of the *Book of Resolutions*. Resolutions shall be considered official expressions of The United Methodist Church for eight years following their adoption, after which time they shall be deemed to have expired unless readopted. Those that have expired shall not be printed in subsequent editions of the *Book of Resolutions*.

b) The General Council on Ministries and the program boards and agencies shall review all valid resolutions and recommend to the General Conference the removal of time-dated material.

3. The Advance Edition of the *Daily Christian Advocate* and the *Daily Christian Advocate*.

4. All original documents of a General Conference shall be filed with the General Commission on Archives and History.

## Section II. The Jurisdictional Conference

¶ **511.** *Interjurisdictional Committee on Episcopacy*—1. There shall be an **Interjurisdictional Committee on Episcopacy** elected by the General Conference consisting of the persons nominated by their annual conference delegations to serve on the several jurisdictional committees on episcopacy.[5] The committee shall meet not later than the fifth day of the conference session and at the time and place set for their convening by the president of the Council of Bishops and shall elect from their number a chairperson, vice chairperson, and secretary. The function of this joint committee shall be to discuss the possibility of transfers of bishops across jurisdictional lines at the forthcoming jurisdictional conferences for residential and presidential responsibilities in the ensuing quadrennium; and to review on the basis of missional needs an application from a jurisdiction which, by number of its church members as provided in ¶ 405, would experience a reduc-

---

5. *See* Judicial Council Decision 472.

tion in the number of its bishops, and recommend the number of bishops to which that jurisdiction should be entitled to the General Conference for determination by the General Conference.

It shall elect an executive committee consisting of the officers named above and two clergy and two laypersons from the nominees to each jurisdictional committee, elected by that committee to conduct consultations with bishops and others interested in possible episcopal transfers. The executive committee shall be responsible to the interjurisdictional committee.

2. A bishop may be transferred across jurisdictional lines only when that bishop has consented to such transfer and has served at least one quadrennium in or under assignment by the jurisdiction in which the bishop was elected. Such a transfer shall be concluded when the committee on episcopacy of each jurisdiction involved has approved the transfer(s) by a majority vote of those present and voting, insofar as the transfer(s) affects those jurisdictions. (See ¶ 47, Article V.)6

3. The Interjurisdictional Committee on Episcopacy shall be recognized as the official body through which cross-jurisdictional transfers shall be arranged. Should a bishop request transfer, the bishop has the option to identify the receiving jurisdiction. A jurisdiction may request that a specific bishop be transferred or may indicate a willingness to accept a bishop transferring from another jurisdiction. Request for transfer from either a bishop or jurisdictional committees on episcopacy shall be received by the Interjurisdictional Committee on Episcopacy by April 1 of the year preceding the year of jurisdictional conferences. The Interjurisdictional Committee on Episcopacy will arrange consultation between bishop(s) requesting transfer and the appropriate jurisdictional committee(s) on episcopacy by January 1 of the year of jurisdictional conference(s). Once the jursidictional committee(s) on episcopacy has taken action, jurisdictional conference secretaries shall inform the Interjurisdictional Committee on Episcopacy not later than August 1 following jurisdictional conferences.7

4. The Interjurisdictional Committee on Episcopacy will report to each General Conference the action taken during the previous quadrennium.

---

6. See Judicial Council Decision 745.
7. See Judicial Council Decision 745.

¶ **512.** *Equal Status*—All jurisdictional conferences shall have the same status and the same privileges of action within the limits fixed by the Constitution.

¶ **513.** *Membership*—The membership of each jurisdictional conference shall consist of an equal number of clergy and lay delegates elected by the annual conferences as provided in the *Discipline*. Consideration shall be given to electing an inclusive delegation (¶¶ 124, 138). The number of delegates to which an annual conference is entitled shall be twice the number of its General Conference delegates.

¶ **514.** *Election of Delegates*—The clergy and lay delegates and reserves to the jurisdictional conferences shall be elected by ballot in accordance with the provisions of the Constitution.

¶ **515.** *Deliberations*—The clergy and lay delegates shall deliberate in one body.

¶ **516.** *Convening Date*—Each jurisdictional conference shall meet within the period prescribed by the Constitution at such time and place as shall have been determined by the preceding jurisdictional conference or by its properly constituted committee.

¶ **517.** *Rules of Order*—The jurisdictional conference shall adopt its own procedure, rules, and plan of organization. It shall take a majority of the whole number of delegates elected to make a quorum for the transaction of business; however, a smaller number may take a recess or adjourn from day to day and at the final session may approve the journal, order the record of the roll call, and adjourn *sine die*.

¶ **518.** *Expenses*—The jurisdictional conference shall provide for the expenses of its sessions.

¶ **519.** *Special Sessions*—1. The jurisdictional conference may order a special session in such manner as it shall determine.

2. The College of Bishops of a jurisdiction by a two-thirds vote shall have authority to call a special session of the jurisdictional conference when necessary; *provided*, however, that if an episcopal area is left vacant by reason of death, retirement, or other cause within twenty-four months of the close of the preceding jurisdictional conference, the College of Bishops may by majority vote convene within three months, after giving not less than thirty days' notice, a special session of the jurisdictional conference for the purpose of electing and consecrating a bishop and of considering any other matters specified in the call; and *provided* further, that in such case the standing committee on episcopacy may recommend to the conference reassignment of one or more of the previously elected bishops.

3. The delegates to a special session of the jurisdictional conference shall be the delegates last elected by each annual conference.

4. A called session of the jurisdictional conference cannot transact any other business than that indicated in the call.

¶ 520. *Presiding Bishops*—The jurisdictional conference shall be presided over by the bishops of the jurisdiction or a bishop of another jurisdiction or of a central conference. In case no bishop of the jurisdiction is present, the conference may elect a president from the clergy delegates.

¶ 521. *Accountability*—Bishops elected by or administering in a jurisdictional conference shall be amenable for their conduct to their jurisdictional conference. Any bishop shall have the right of appeal to the Judicial Council.

¶ 522. *Jurisdictional Committee on Episcopacy*—1. There shall be a **jurisdictional committee on episcopacy** consisting of one clergy and one lay delegate to the jurisdictional conference from each annual conference elected by the jurisdictional conference upon nomination of their respective annual conference delegations.

The committee shall be convened by the president of the College of Bishops at the close of the jurisdictional conference to which the delegates have been elected. It shall serve through the succeeding jurisdictional conference.

The committee shall elect from its members a chairperson, a vice chairperson, and a secretary. It shall meet at least biennially.

Should there be a vacancy in an annual conference's elected representation on the jurisdictional committee on episcopacy by death, resignation, election to the episcopacy, cessation of membership in the annual conference from which one is elected, or for other reasons that the annual conference delegation may determine, the annual conference delegation shall nominate another person to fill the vacancy. That person may begin to serve on the committee as a nominee until the jurisdictional conference can elect.

2. The jurisdictional conference shall provide funding for the expenses of the jurisdictional committee on episcopacy.

3. The jurisdictional committee on episcopacy shall:

   *a)* Review the work of the bishops, pass on their character and official administration, and report to the jurisdictional conference its findings for such action as the conference may deem appropriate within its constitutional warrant of power.

*b)* Recommend boundaries of the episcopal areas and the assignments of the bishops.[8]

*c)* Be available to the Council and College of Bishops for consultation on matters of mutual concern.

*d)* Determine the number of effective bishops eligible for assignment.

*e)* Receive and act upon requests for possible voluntary and involuntary retirement of bishops.

*f)* Consult with the conference committees on episcopacy with respect to the needs for episcopal leadership and how best they can be fulfilled.

*g)* Establish a consultation process with each bishop regarding his or her episcopal assignment.

*h)* Prepare a report of its decisions, activities, and recommendations to be transmitted to its successor through the office of the secretary of the jurisdictional conference. The report shall be made available to delegates of the jurisdictional conference prior to the jurisdictional conference.

¶ **523.** *Powers and Duties of Jurisdictional Conference*—The **jurisdictional conference** shall have powers and duties as described in the Constitution. It shall also have such other powers and duties as may be conferred by the General Conference. It shall act in all respects in harmony with the policy of The United Methodist Church with respect to elimination of discrimination based upon race.

¶ **524.** *Definition of Church Members*—In all elections in a jurisdictional conference that are based on the number of church members within that jurisdiction, the number counted shall include lay members, clergy members, and bishops assigned to that jurisdiction.

¶ **525.** *Annual Conference Journals*—The jurisdictional conference shall have authority to examine and acknowledge the journals of the annual conferences within its bounds and shall make such rules for the drawing up of the journals as may seem necessary.

¶ **526.** *Jurisdictional Conference Journals*—The jurisdictional conference shall keep an official journal of its proceedings, duly signed by the secretary and president or secretary of the College of Bishops, which shall be deposited in accordance with ¶ 1711.3 *j, k* and with the secretary of the General Conference. The printing shall be done at the expense of the jurisdiction.

---

8. *See* Judicial Council Decision 517.

JURISDICTIONAL AGENCIES

¶ **527.** *Agencies*—The jurisdictional conference shall have the authority to appoint or elect such agencies as the General Conference may direct or as it deems necessary for its work. Insofar as possible, the membership on councils, boards, and agencies of the jurisdictional conference shall include one-third clergy, one-third laywomen, and one-third laymen in keeping with the policies for general Church agencies, except for the board of ordained ministry and the jurisdictional committee on episcopacy. Special attention shall be given to the inclusion of clergywomen, youth, young adults, older adults, single adults, persons with disabilities, persons from churches of small membership, and racial and ethnic persons. (*See* ¶ 710.8 *a–c.*)

¶ **528.** *Coordination of Programs*—In each jurisdiction of The United Methodist Church there may be a **jurisdictional council on ministries** or **jurisdictional administrative council,** or alternative structure, organized as the jurisdiction shall determine and with the authority to coordinate the programs of the general agencies within the jurisdiction.

¶ **529.** *Program Agencies*—In each jurisdiction there may be jurisdictional program agencies related to the general program agencies and the appropriate annual conference program agencies organized as the jurisdictional conference shall determine.

¶ **530.** *Archives and History*—1. There may be a **jurisdictional commission on archives and history,** auxiliary to the general commission, to be composed of the chairperson of each annual conference commission on archives and history or the historian of each annual conference, the president of the jurisdictional historical society, and at least five members at large to be elected by the jurisdictional commission, or composed in a way the jurisdictional conference determines.

2. The jurisdictional commission may organize and promote a jurisdictional historical society.

¶ **531.** *Jurisdictional Youth Ministry Organization Convocation*— There shall be a **jurisdictional youth ministry organization convocation** to be held at least once every other year in each jurisdiction (alternating years with the United Methodist Youth Organization Convocation, ¶ 1205). Among the membership of the convocation for the purpose of the election of steering committee members, there shall be four voting representatives from each conference: the conference coordinator of youth ministries or designate; the conference council on youth ministry chairperson or designate; two youth at large, to be elected as shall be determined by the conference council on youth ministry. It is recommended that at least two members from each annual conference be racial and ethnic minority persons. Each youth shall be a member (full or preparatory) of The United Methodist Church. Other persons may be added by jurisdictions according to their respective operational guidelines, *provided* that the above categories are cared for and the recommended fifty-fifty racial and ethnic minority representation is observed. The expenses of the jurisdictional youth ministry organization convocation shall be borne by the participating annual conferences or the jurisdiction.

There shall be a **jurisdictional youth coordinator** who shall be accountable to the jurisdictional council on ministries and the jurisdictional youth ministry organization. This coordinator may or may not be the same person as the adult representative to the United Methodist Youth Organization Steering Committee (¶ 1206). This decision is to be determined by the representatives of the jurisdictional youth ministry organization convocation, or the jurisdictional youth ministry organization.

A responsibility of the jurisdictional youth ministry organization shall be to elect three youth members and one adult member to the United Methodist Youth Organization Steering Committee (*see* ¶ 1206). At least one of the youth shall be a racial and ethnic minority youth. All youth elected to the steering committee shall be at the time of their election entering into the eleventh grade or under, or their age shall be sixteen or younger. Nominations shall come from annual conference councils on youth ministry. The nominating process followed by the conference councils on youth ministry shall include the solicitation of nominations from local churches, subdistricts, and districts. As far as possible, members of the United Methodist Youth Organization Steering Committee from each jurisdiction shall be from four different annual conferences in that jurisdiction.

In addition to enabling the election of its two steering committee youth members, the following are suggested responsibilities for the jurisdictional youth ministry organization:

1. To initiate and support jurisdictional events (camps, conferences, workshops, and so forth).

2. To recommend priorities, concerns, and/or policies to the United Methodist Youth Organization Steering Committee.

3. To promote the establishment and awareness of racial and eth-

nic minority needs, concerns, issues, and so forth, through caucuses, camps, consultations, and so forth.

4. To promote the spiritual growth of participants in the jurisdictional youth ministry organization convocation.

5. To promote an evangelistic outreach to and through youth.

6. To provide training and supportive experiences for conference youth personnel.

7. To enable communication between general and conference levels of youth ministry.

8. To nominate the jurisdictional youth member to the General Council on Ministries (¶ 907.1a[5]) in the years that jurisdictional conference meets.

9. An additional responsibility of the jurisdictional youth ministry organization convocation will be to elect a steering committee or executive body to carry out the functions and suggested responsibilities of the convocation during the interval between convocations. The convocation shall determine the representation of such body, the manner of election, any funding thereof, and the relationship of the body to the annual conferences and to the jurisdictional council on ministries or equivalent.

¶ 532. *Committee on Ordained Ministry*—There may be a **jurisdictional committee on ordained ministry**. This committee shall be comprised of the chair of the conference boards of ordained ministry or their representatives, the deans/presidents of the United Methodist seminaries in the jurisdiction, two representatives from the college of bishops and three members at large, named by the committee to insure inclusivity. Deacons and laypersons shall be represented in the committee. When a jurisdictional board of higher education and ministry exists, this board may be a part of that structure. The duties of the committee may include: providing information on supply and demand and encouraging mobility across conference lines; to create a forum for the discussion of issues related to representative ministry; to deal with matters of enlistment and recruitment; to create dialogue with seminaries serving the jurisdiction; to enable ethnic ministries in the jurisdictions. Funding shall be provided through the jurisdictional conference and the annual conference boards of ordained ministry.

¶ 533. **Constitution of United Methodist Women in the Jurisdiction**—*Article 1. Name*—In each jurisdiction there shall be a jurisdiction organization named United Methodist Women, auxiliary to the Women's Division of the General Board of Global Ministries.

Article 2. *Authority*—Each jurisdiction organization of United Methodist Women shall have authority to promote its work in accordance with the program and policies of the Women's Division of the General Board of Global Ministries.

Article 3. *Membership*—The jurisdiction organization of United Methodist Women shall be composed of the members of the core planning group; six delegates from each conference organization, all of whom shall be conference officers; members of the Women's Division living within the jurisdiction; a representative of the jurisdictional association of deaconesses and home missionaries; and all the bishops of the jurisdiction.

Article 4. *Meetings and Elections*—*a)* There shall be a meeting of the jurisdiction organization of United Methodist Women during the last year of the quadrennium. At that time the jurisdiction president and other Core Planning Group officers shall be elected, and directors of the Women's Division shall be elected according to the *Discipline* (¶¶ 644.6*d*, 1324).

*b)* There may be other meetings as needed.

Article 5. *Amendments*—Proposed amendments to the constitution shall be sent to the recording secretary of the Women's Division prior to the last annual meeting of the division in the quadrennium.

¶ 534. *Committee on United Methodist Men*—In each jurisdiction there shall be a **jurisdictional committee on United Methodist Men,** auxiliary to the General Commission on United Methodist Men (¶ 2301).

The membership of the jurisdictional committee on United Methodist Men shall be composed of the elected officers, committee chairpersons, and ministry coordinators as defined by the organizations' bylaws as well as the conference president of United Methodist Men of each annual conference organization within the boundary of the jurisdiction.

Each jurisdictional committee on United Methodist Men shall have authority to promote its work in accordance with the policies and programs of the General Commission on United Methodist Men.

The jurisdictional committee on United Methodist Men shall elect the jurisdictional president during the last year of the quadrennium. The jurisdictional committee on United Methodist Men shall nominate to the jurisdictional conference, for election, the jurisdictional members of the General Commission on United Methodist Men. The nomination shall be four persons and shall include among the four at least one clergy, one woman, ethnic representation, and the jurisdictional president of United Methodist Men. Special consideration should be given to include one male under the age of thirty-five (*see* ¶ 2303.1). This legislation shall take effect upon the adjournment of the 2000 General Conference. There may be meetings, retreats, and cooperative training events held by the jurisdictional committee on United Methodist Men.

**Section III. Central Conferences**

¶ **535.** *Authorization*—1. In territory outside the United States, annual conferences, provisional annual conferences, missionary conferences, mission conferences, and missions, in such numbers as the General Conference by a two-thirds vote shall determine, may be organized by the General Conference into central conferences or provisional central conferences, with such duties, privileges, and powers as are hereinafter set forth and as the General Conference by a two-thirds vote shall prescribe.[9]

2. There shall be such **central conferences** as have been authorized or shall be hereafter authorized by the General Conference; *provided* that a central conference shall have a total of at least thirty clergy and thirty lay delegates on the basis of representation as set forth in this section, except as the General Conference may fix a different number. A central conference in existence at the time of union may be continued with a lesser number of delegates for reasons deemed sufficient by the Uniting Conference.

3. The United Methodist Church shall have central conferences with ministries in the following countries:

*a) Africa Central Conference:* Angola, Botswana, Burundi, Kenya, Malawi, Mozambique, Namibia, Rwanda, South Africa, Sudan, Uganda, Zambia, Zimbabwe;

*b) Central and Southern Europe Central Conference:* Albania, Algeria, Austria, Bosnia, Bulgaria, Croatia, Czech Republic, France, Hungary, Republic of Macedonia, Poland, Slovak Republic, Switzerland, Tunisia, (Carpathian) Ukraine, FR Yugoslavia;

*c) Congo Central Conference:* Congo, Congo Brazzaville, Democratic Republic of Congo, Tanzania, Zambia;

*d) Germany Central Conference:* Germany;

---

9. *See* Judicial Council Decision 549.

*e) Northern Europe Central Conference:* Denmark, Estonia, Finland, Latvia, Lithuania, Norway, Russia, Sweden, Ukraine;

*f) Philippines Central Conference:* Philippines;

*g) West Africa Central Conference:* Guinea, Liberia, Nigeria, Senegal, Sierra Leone.

**¶ 536.** *Organization*—1. The **central conference** shall be composed of clergy and lay members in equal numbers, the clergy members elected by the clergy members of the annual conference and the lay members by the lay members thereof. Their qualifications and the manner of election shall be determined by the central conference itself, subject only to constitutional requirements. Each annual conference and provisional annual conference shall be entitled to at least two clergy and two lay delegates, and no other selection of delegates shall be authorized that would provide for more than one clergy delegate for every six clergy members of an annual conference; except that a majority of the number fixed by a central conference as the ratio of representation shall entitle an annual conference to an additional clergy delegate and to an additional lay delegate. Each missionary conference and mission is authorized to elect and send one of its members to the central conference concerned as its representative, said representative to be accorded the privilege of sitting with the committees of the central conference, with the right to speak in the committees and in the regular sessions of the central conference, but without the right to vote. Representatives of missionary conferences or missions shall have the same claim for payment of expenses as is allowed to members of the central conference.[10]

2. The first meeting of a central conference shall be called by the bishop or bishops in charge at such time and place as they may elect, to which members of the annual conferences, provisional annual conferences, missionary conferences, and missions concerned shall be elected on the basis of representation as provided herein. The time and place of future meetings shall be determined by the central conference or its executive committee.

3. Each central conference shall meet within the year succeeding the session of the General Conference at such time and place as the central conference itself or its bishops may determine, with the right to hold such adjourned sessions as it may determine. The sessions of said conference shall be presided over by the bishops. In case no

---

10. *See* Judicial Council Decision 371.

bishop is present, the conference shall elect a temporary president from among its own members. The bishops resident in a central conference or a majority of them, with the concurrence of the executive committee or other authorized committee, shall have the authority to call an extra session of the central conference to be held at the time and place designated by them.[11]

4. The Council of Bishops may assign one or more of its number to visit any central conference or provisional central conference. When so assigned, the bishop shall be an accredited representative of the general Church, and when requested by a majority of the bishops resident in that conference may exercise therein the functions of the episcopacy.

5. The presiding officer of the central conference shall decide questions of order, subject to an appeal to the central conference, and shall decide questions of law, subject to an appeal to the Judicial Council, but questions relating to the interpretation of the rules and regulations made by the central conference for the governing of its own session shall be decided by the central conference.[12]

6. Each central conference within the bounds of which the General Board of Global Ministries has work shall maintain a cooperative and consultative relationship with the said board through a duly constituted executive committee, executive board, or council of cooperation; but the legal distinction between the General Board of Global Ministries and the organized church on the field shall always be kept clear.

7. The journal of the proceedings of a central conference, duly signed by the president and secretary, shall be sent for examination to the General Conference through its secretary.

8. A provisional central conference may become a central conference upon the fulfillment of the necessary requirements and upon the authorization of the General Conference.

9. In the case of a central conference, the rule of proportionate representation shall be applied by each annual conference, and in the case of the delegates to the Central Conference of Central and Southern Europe, the rule shall be applied to delegates coming from the annual conference of Switzerland/France.

---

11. *See* Judicial Council Decision 371.
12. *See* Judicial Council Decisions 375, 376, 381.

¶ **537.** *Powers*—1. To a central conference shall be committed for supervision and promotion, in harmony with the *Discipline* and interdenominational contractual agreements, the missionary, educational, evangelistic, industrial, publishing, medical, and other connectional interests of the annual conferences, provisional annual conferences, missionary conferences, and missions within its territory and such other matters as may be referred to it by said bodies or by order of the General Conference; and it shall provide suitable organizations for such work and elect the necessary officers for the same.

2. A central conference, when authorized by a specific enabling act of the General Conference, may elect one or more bishops from among the traveling elders of The United Methodist Church. The number of bishops to be elected by each central conference shall be determined from time to time by the General Conference.

3. When a central conference shall have been authorized to elect bishops, such elections shall be conducted under the same general procedure as prevails in the jurisdictional conferences for the election of bishops. A central conference shall have power to fix the tenure of bishops elected by the said central conference.[13]

4. A central conference shall participate in the General Episcopal Fund on payment of its apportionment on the same percentage basis as that fixed for annual conferences in jurisdictional conferences. When the total estimated support, including salaries and all allowances for the bishops elected by it, and the estimated receipts on apportionment have been determined by a central conference, a statement of these amounts in itemized form shall be submitted to the General Council on Finance and Administration. This council, after consideration of the relative cost of living in various central conferences, shall determine the amount to be paid from the General Episcopal Fund in meeting the budget, after which the treasurer of the General Episcopal Fund shall pay the amount established to the bishop concerned, or as the central conference may determine.

5. An ordained minister who has served a term or part of a term as a bishop in a central conference where term episcopacy has prevailed shall, upon retirement from the effective relation in the ministry, be paid an allowance from the General Episcopal Fund in such sum as the General Council on Finance and Administration shall determine for the years during which the ordained minister served as a bishop.[14]

---

13. *See* Judicial Council Decisions 311, 430.
14. *See* Judicial Council Decision 394.

6. A central conference, in consultation with the bishops of that central conference, shall fix the episcopal areas and residences and make assignments to them of the bishops who are to reside in that central conference. The bishops of a central conference shall arrange the plan of episcopal visitation within its bounds.

7. The secretary of a central conference in which one or more bishops have been chosen shall report to the secretary of the General Conference the names of the bishop or bishops and the residences to which they have been assigned by the central conference.

8. A central conference shall have authority to elect and support general officers in all departments of the work of the Church within the boundaries of the central conference but may not determine the number of bishops.

9. A central conference shall have power to make such changes and adaptations of the *Book of Discipline* as the special conditions and the mission of the church in the area require, especially concerning the organization and administration of the work on local church, district, and annual conference levels; *provided* that no action shall be taken that is contrary to the Constitution and the General Rules of The United Methodist Church; and *provided* that the spirit of connectional relationship is kept between the local and the general church. Subject to this restriction, a central conference may delegate to an annual conference within its boundaries the power to make one or the other of the changes and adaptations referred to in this paragraph, upon the request of such annual conference.[15]

10. A central conference shall fix the boundaries of the annual conferences, provisional annual conferences, missionary conferences, and missions within its bounds, proposals for changes first having been submitted to the annual conferences concerned as prescribed in the *Discipline* of The United Methodist Church. No annual conference shall be organized with fewer than thirty-five clergy members except as provided by an enabling act for the quadrennium, which shall not reduce the number below twenty-five. Nor shall an annual conference be continued with fewer than twenty-five clergy members except as provided by an enabling act for the quadrennium.[16]

11. A central conference may advise its annual conferences and

---

15. *See* Judicial Council Decision 313.
16. *See* Judicial Council Decisions 525, 541, 549.

provisional annual conferences to set standards of character and other qualifications for admission of lay members.

12. A central conference shall have power to make changes and adaptations in procedure pertaining to the annual, district, and charge conferences within its territory and to add to the business of the annual conference supplementary questions considered desirable or necessary to meet its own needs.

13. A central conference shall have authority to examine and acknowledge the journals of the annual conferences, provisional annual conferences, missionary conferences, and missions located within its bounds and to make rules for the drawing up of the journals as may seem necessary.

14. A central conference may have a standing **committee on women's work.** This committee should preferably be composed of the women delegates and such other persons as the central conference may elect. The duty of this committee shall be to study the relation of women to the Church and to devise ways and means of developing this portion of the Church membership, to the end that it may assume its rightful responsibilities in the extension of the Kingdom. The committee shall make recommendations to the central conference regarding women's organizations within its areas. A central conference organization may become a member of the World Federation of Methodist Women and may elect a representative to the World Federation of Methodist Women within the provisions of the federation.

15. A central conference may organize a women's unit, after consultation with the committee on women's work, in connection with any annual conference or provisional annual conference within its bounds and provide a constitution and bylaws for it.

16. A central conference shall have authority to adopt rules of procedure governing the investigation and trial of its clergy, including bishops, and lay members of the Church and to provide the necessary means and methods of implementing the said rules; *provided*, however, that the ordained ministers shall not be deprived of the right of trial by a clergy committee, and lay members of the Church of the right of trial by a duly constituted committee of lay members; and *provided* also, that the rights of appeal shall be adequately safeguarded.[17]

17. A central conference is authorized to prepare and translate simplified or adapted forms of such parts of the Ritual as it may deem

---

17. *See* Judicial Council Decisions 310, 595.

necessary, such changes to require the approval of the resident bishop or bishops of the central conference.

18. A central conference shall have the power to conform the detailed rules, rites, and ceremonies for the solemnization of marriage to the statute laws of the country or countries within its jurisdiction.

19. Subject to the approval of the bishops resident therein, a central conference shall have the power to prescribe courses of study, including those in the vernaculars, for its ministry, both foreign and indigenous, including local preachers, lay speakers, Bible women, deaconesses, teachers—both male and female—and all other workers whatsoever, ordained or lay. It shall also make rules and regulations for examination in these courses.

20. A central conference shall have authority to edit and publish a central conference *Discipline,* which shall contain in addition to the Constitution of the Church such sections from the general *Discipline* of The United Methodist Church as may be pertinent to the entire Church and also such revised, adapted, or new sections as shall have been enacted by the central conference concerned under the powers given by the General Conference.

21. In a central conference or provisional central conference using a language other than English, legislation passed by a General Conference shall not take effect until twelve months after the close of that General Conference in order to afford the necessary time to make adaptations and to publish a translation of the legislation that has been enacted, the translation to be approved by the resident bishop or bishops of the central conference. This provision, however, shall not exclude the election of delegates to the General Conference by annual conferences within the territory of central conferences or provisional central conferences.

22. A central conference is authorized to interpret Article XXIII of the Articles of Religion (*page 65*) so as to recognize the governments of the country or countries within its territory.

23. A central conference shall have power to authorize the congregations in a certain state or country to form special organizations in order to receive the acknowledgment of the state or country according to the laws of that state or country. These organizations shall be empowered to represent the interests of the Church to the authorities of the state or country according to the rules and principles of The United Methodist Church, and they shall be required to give regular reports of their activities to their respective annual conferences.

24. A central conference may, with the consent of the bishops resident in that conference, enter into agreements with churches or missions of other denominations for the division of territory or of responsibility for Christian work within the territory of the central conference.

25. A central conference shall have the right to negotiate with other Protestant bodies looking toward the possibility of church union; *provided* that any proposals for church union shall be submitted to the General Conference for approval before consummation.[18]

26. A central conference, where the laws of the land permit, shall have the power to organize and incorporate one or more executive committees, executive boards, or councils of cooperation, with such membership and such powers as may have been granted by the central conference for the purpose of representing it in its property and legal interests and for transacting any necessary business that may arise in the interval between the sessions of the central conference or that may be committed to said boards or committees by the central conference.

27. A central conference, through a duly incorporated property-holding body or bodies, shall have authority to purchase, own, hold, or transfer property for and on behalf of all the unincorporated organizations of The United Methodist Church within the territory of that central conference or on behalf of other organizations of The United Methodist Church that have entrusted their property to that central conference.

28. A central conference shall have authority to make the necessary rules and regulations for the holding and management of such properties; *provided*, however, that *(a)* all procedure shall be subject to the laws of the country or countries concerned; *(b)* no transfer of property shall be made from one annual conference to another without the consent of the conference holding title to such property; and *(c)* the status of properties held by local trustees or other holding bodies shall be recognized.

29. A central conference shall not directly or indirectly, through its incorporated property-holding body or bodies, alienate property or proceeds of property without due consideration of its trusteeship for local churches, annual conferences, the General Board of Global Ministries, and other organizations, local or general, of the Church.

---

18. *See* Judicial Council Decision 350.

30. A central conference or any of its incorporated organizations shall not involve the General Board of Global Ministries or any organization of the Church in any financial obligation without the official approval of said board or organization. All invested funds, fiduciary trusts, or property belonging to an annual conference, a provisional annual conference, a missionary conference, or a mission, or any of its institutions, acquired by bequest, donation, or otherwise and designated for a specific use, shall be applied to the purpose for which they were designated. They shall not be diverted to any other purpose, except by the consent of the conference or mission involved and with the approval of the central conference concerned and civil court action when necessary. The same rule shall apply to similar funds or properties acquired by a central conference for specific objects. In cases involving the diversion of trust funds and properties within the territory of a central conference, the central conference concerned shall determine the disposition of the interests involved, subject to an appeal to the judicial court of the central conference.

31. When former central conferences of The United Methodist Church become or have become autonomous churches or entered into church unions, retired bishops therein shall continue to have membership in the Council of Bishops if the retired bishops involved so desire.

32. A central conference that adapts and edits the *Discipline* as provided in ¶ 537.21 shall establish a **judicial court**, which in addition to other duties that the central conference may assign to it shall hear and determine the legality of any action of the central conference taken under the adapted portions of the *Discipline* or of a decision of law by the presiding bishop of the central conference pertaining to the adapted portions of the *Discipline*, upon appeal by the presiding bishop or by one-fifth of the members of the central conference. Further, the judicial court shall hear and determine the legality of any action of an annual conference taken under the adapted portions of the *Discipline* or of a decision of law by the presiding bishop of the annual conference pertaining to the adapted portion of the *Discipline*, upon appeal of the presiding bishop or of such percentage of the members of the annual conference as may be determined by the central conference concerned.

## Section IV. Provisional Central Conferences

¶ **538.** Annual conferences, provisional annual conferences, missionary conferences, and missions outside the United States that are

317

not included in central conferences or in the territory of affiliated autonomous churches and that, because of geographical, language, political, or other considerations, have common interests that can best be served thereby, may be organized into provisional central conferences as provided in ¶ 535.1.[19]

¶ 539. *Organization*—The organization of provisional central conferences shall conform to the regulations prescribed for central conferences insofar as they are considered applicable by the bishop in charge.

¶ 540. *Powers*—The General Conference may grant to a provisional central conference any of the powers of a central conference except that of electing bishops.[20]

¶ 541. Ad Interim *Provisions*—In the interval between General Conferences, the General Board of Global Ministries, upon the recommendation of the bishops in charge and after consultation with the annual conferences, provisional annual conferences, missionary conferences, and missions concerned, may make changes in the boundaries of a provisional central conference and may grant to a provisional central conference or to any of its component parts any of the powers of a central conference except that of electing bishops. All changes in boundaries and all grants of powers authorized by the General Board of Global Ministries shall be reported to the ensuing session of the General Conference and shall expire at the close of that session unless renewed by the General Conference.

¶ 542. *Lay Membership*—An annual conference or a provisional annual conference in the field of a provisional central conference shall have the power to set standards of character and other qualifications for admission of its lay members.

¶ 543. Ad Interim *Provisions for Conferences Outside the United States*—To annual conferences, provisional annual conferences, missionary conferences, and missions that are outside the United States and are not included in central conferences or provisional central conferences, the General Conference may grant any of the powers of central conferences except that of electing bishops; and in the interval between General Conferences, the General Board of Global Ministries may grant such powers when requested to do so by the bishop in charge and by the annual conference, provisional annual conference, missionary conference, or mission concerned.

---

19. *See* Judicial Council Decision 525.
20. *See* Judicial Council Decision 403.

¶ **544.** *Episcopal Supervision*—The General Conference shall make provision for the episcopal supervision of work in the territory outside the United States that is not now included in central conferences.

¶ **545.** The Council of Bishops may provide, if and when necessary, for episcopal visitation of mission fields not included in central or provisional central conferences.

**Section V. Autonomous Methodist Churches,
Affiliated Autonomous Methodist Churches,
Affiliated United Churches, Covenanting Churches,
Concordat Churches**

¶ **546.** *Autonomous Methodist Churches*—1. A self-governing Methodist church in whose establishment The United Methodist Church or one of its constituent members (The Evangelical United Brethren Church and The Methodist Church) has assisted, but which has not entered into the Act of Covenanting with The United Methodist Church, shall be known as an **autonomous Methodist church.**

2. When the requirements of such a Methodist church for its ministry are comparable to those of The United Methodist Church, clergy may be transferred between its properly constituted ministerial bodies and the annual and provisional annual conferences of The United Methodist Church, with the approval and consent of the appointive authorities involved.

3. A program of visitation may be mutually arranged by the Council of Bishops in cooperation with the equivalent leadership of the autonomous Methodist church and/or united church.

4. If desired by the autonomous Methodist church, the Council of Bishops, in consultation with the General Board of Global Ministries, shall work out plans of cooperation with that church. The General Board of Global Ministries shall serve as the agent of The United Methodist Church for a continuing dialogue looking to the establishment of mission priorities with special reference to matters of personnel and finance.

5. An autonomous Methodist church or other church of the Wesleyan tradition may enter into the Act of Covenanting with The United Methodist Church under the provisions of ¶ 549.

¶ **547.** *Affiliated Autonomous Methodist Churches*—A self-governing church in whose establishment The United Methodist Church or one

319

of its constituent members (The Evangelical United Brethren Church and The Methodist Church) has assisted and which by mutual agreement has entered into a covenant of relationship or an Act of Covenanting (see ¶ 549) with The United Methodist Church shall be known as an **affiliated autonomous Methodist church.**

Such an agreement shall include the following provisions:

1. Certificates of church membership given by clergy in one church shall be accepted by clergy in the other church.

2. Clergy may be transferred between annual and provisional annual conferences of The United Methodist Church and of affiliated autonomous Methodist churches and their ordination(s) recognized as valid, with the approval and consent of the bishops or other appointive authorities involved.

3. Each affiliated autonomous Methodist church shall be entitled to two delegates, one clergy and one layperson, to the General Conference of The United Methodist Church in accordance with ¶ 2403.1*b*. They shall be entitled to all the rights and privileges of delegates, including membership on committees, except the right to vote. Such a church having more than 70,000 full members shall be entitled to one additional delegate. At least one of the three delegates shall be a woman. The bishop or president of the affiliated autonomous Methodist churches may be invited by the Council of Bishops to the General Conference.

4. A program of mutual visitation may be arranged by the Council of Bishops in cooperation with the equivalent leadership of the affiliated autonomous church. The Council of Bishops may assign one or more of its members for visitation to such churches.

5. Other provisions shall be as mutually agreed upon by the two churches.

6. The Council of Bishops, in consultation with the General Board of Global Ministries, shall work out plans of cooperation with that church. The General Board of Global Ministries shall serve as the agent of The United Methodist Church for a continuing dialogue looking to the establishment of mutual mission priorities, including, but not limited to, the exchange of personnel and financial resources.[21]

---

21. *See* Judicial Council Decision 692.

BECOMING AN AFFILIATED AUTONOMOUS METHODIST OR UNITED CHURCH

¶ **548.** When conferences outside the United States that are parts of The United Methodist Church desire to become an **affiliated autonomous Methodist** or **affiliated united church,** approval shall first be secured from the central conference involved and this decision be ratified by the annual conferences within the central conference by two-thirds majority of the aggregate votes cast by the annual conferences.[22]

1. The conference shall prepare a historical record with reasons why autonomy is requested and shall consult with the Commission on Central Conference Affairs (¶ 2201) on proceedings for autonomy.

2. The Commission on Central Conference Affairs and the conferences involved shall mutually agree on the confession of faith and the constitution of the new church. These shall be prepared with care and shall be approved by the conferences.

3. Preparation of its *Discipline* is the responsibility of the conference(s) desiring autonomy.

4. Upon recommendation of the Commission on Central Conference Affairs, when all disciplinary requirements for affiliated autonomous relationship have been met, the General Conference through an enabling act shall approve of and grant permission for the conference(s) involved to become an affiliated autonomous Methodist or united church.

5. Then the central conference involved shall meet, declare the present relationship between The United Methodist Church and the conference(s) involved dissolved, and reorganize as an affiliated autonomous Methodist or affiliated united church in accordance with the enabling act granted by the General Conference. The Commission on Central Conference Affairs shall assist in this process and, when the plans are consummated, report to the Council of Bishops. The proclamation of affiliated autonomous status shall then be signed by the president of the Council of Bishops and the secretary of the General Conference.

6. A plan of cooperation shall be developed in accordance with ¶ 547.6 above.

BECOMING A COVENANTING CHURCH

¶ **549.** *A Covenanting Church*—1. There may be established with autonomous Methodist churches, affiliated autonomous Methodist

---

22. *See* Judicial Council Decision 548.

321

churches, affiliated united churches, or with other Christian churches and The United Methodist Church a covenanting relationship whose elements are described in the 1988 *Book of Resolutions* or otherwise developed.

    *a)* The purpose of an **Act of Covenanting** with another Christian church is to encourage a new sense of global common cause, mutual support, mutual spiritual growth, common study of Scripture and culture, creative interaction as ministers in the mission of God's church, cross-fertilization of ideas about ways to be in that mission, sharing of resources, and exploration of new forms of service directed at old and emerging needs.

    *b)* An Act of Covenanting will include recognition of our respective baptisms as different facets of the one baptism; recognition of one another as authentic expressions of the one holy, catholic, and apostolic church of Jesus Christ; recognition of the ordained ministries of the two churches; commitment to systematic participation in full eucharistic fellowship; commitment to function in new ways of partnership, visitations, and programs.

    *c)* For The United Methodist Church, oversight of the covenantal relationships is the responsibility of the Council of Bishops, with the assistance of the General Commission on Christian Unity and Interreligious Concerns, while participation in specific projects is the responsibility of the appropriate general agency or agencies.

    2. The Council of Bishops shall represent The United Methodist Church in developing an Act of Covenanting with a prospective partner church. The Council of Bishops shall make recommendations to General Conference as to the specific covenanting agreements. When approved by General Conference and by the chief legislative body of the partner church, the Act of Covenanting becomes effective when signed by the president of the Council of Bishops and the secretary of the General Conference of The United Methodist Church and by the authorized persons in the covenanting church. The text of each Act of Covenanting as adopted shall be printed in the appropriate General Conference journal.[23]

    ¶ **550.** *Affiliated United Churches*—An affiliated united church shall have the same relationship and privileges as affiliated autonomous Methodist churches in accordance with ¶¶ 547–548 above.

---

23. *See* Judicial Council Decision 692.

BECOMING AN AUTONOMOUS METHODIST OR UNITED CHURCH

¶ **551.** When conferences in nations other than the United States that are parts of The United Methodist Church desire to become an **autonomous Methodist** or **united church,** approval shall first be secured from the central conference involved and this decision be ratified by the annual conferences within the central conference by two-thirds majority of the aggregate votes cast by the annual conferences.

1. The conference shall prepare a historical record with reasons why autonomy is requested and shall consult with the Commission on Central Conference Affairs (¶ 2201) on proceedings for autonomy.

2. The Commission on Central Conference Affairs and the conferences involved shall mutually agree on the confession of faith and the constitution of the new church. These shall be prepared with care and shall be approved by the conferences.

3. Preparation of its *Discipline* is the responsibility of the conference(s) desiring autonomy.

4. Upon recommendation of the Commission on Central Conference Affairs, when all disciplinary requirements for autonomous relationship have been met, the General Conference through an enabling act shall approve of and grant permission for the conference(s) involved to become an autonomous Methodist or united church.

5. Then the central conference involved shall meet, declare the present relationship between The United Methodist Church and the conference(s) involved dissolved, and reorganize as an autonomous Methodist or united church in accordance with the enabling act granted by the General Conference. The Commission on Central Conference Affairs shall assist in this process and, when the plans are consummated, report to the Council of Bishops. The proclamation of autonomous status shall then be signed by the president of the Council of Bishops and the secretary of the General Conference.

6. A plan of cooperation shall be developed in accordance with ¶ 547.6 above.

¶ **552.** *Concordat Agreements*—1. There may be **concordats** with other Methodist churches in accordance with ¶ 12.2 and for The Methodist Church of Great Britain in accordance with ¶ 12.3.

2. The purposes of such concordats are:

*a)* to manifest the common Methodist heritage,

*b)* to affirm the equal status of the two churches and express mutual acceptance and respect, and *c)* to create opportunities for closer fellowship between the two churches, especially on the leadership level.

3. With the exception of The Methodist Church of Great Britain, such concordats may be established by the following procedure:

*a)* The Methodist church shall, through its major decision-making body, request a concordat relationship with The United Methodist Church through the Council of Bishops. Concordats may also be initiated by The United Methodist Church acting through the Council of Bishops who shall, in cooperation with the Methodist church in question, ascertain that all disciplinary conditions are met and then prepare the necessary enabling legislation for adoption by the General Conference.

*b)* When such concordat agreement has been approved by the General Conference, the Council of Bishops shall prepare a statement of the concordat agreement to be signed by the president of the Council of Bishops, the secretary of the General Conference, and two representatives of the Methodist church with whom the concordat agreement is made. Such concordats shall be printed in the *Daily Christian Advocate* of that General Conference.

4. Such concordat agreement shall entitle the two churches to the following rights and privileges:

*a)* The two churches shall each elect two delegates, one clergy and one lay, to be seated in each other's General Conference or equivalent bodies with all rights and privileges, except the right to vote. Agreements in existing concordats shall be honored.

*b)* The host church shall make provisions for full hospitality, including room and board, for the delegates of the other concordat church. Travel and other expenses shall be the responsibility of the visiting church.

*c)* A program of mutual visitation may be arranged by the Council of Bishops in cooperation with the equivalent leadership of the other concordat church. The Council of Bishops may assign one or more of its members for episcopal visitation to concordat churches.

*d)* Clergy may be transferred between the two churches in accordance with ¶¶ 338.2*b* and 547.2.

## BECOMING PART OF THE UNITED METHODIST CHURCH

**¶ 553.** 1. An autonomous Methodist church or affiliated autonomous Methodist church outside the United States may become a part of The United Methodist Church when all of the following requirements are fulfilled:

*a)* Said church shall accept and approve the Constitution, Articles of Faith, *Discipline,* and polity of The United Methodist Church.

*b)* Said church, if it is within the boundaries of a central or provisional central conference, shall apply for membership in that conference. Such application shall be approved by the central or provisional central conference and by the General Conference. In the event that said church is not within the boundaries of an existing central or provisional conference, then its membership application shall be reviewed by the Council of Bishops and shall be approved by the General Conference.

*c)* Said church shall declare its own constitution and church order null and void.

*d)* The Commission on Central Conference Affairs shall advise and assist said church in this process and prepare the necessary enabling act for approval by the General Conference.

*e)* The General Conference shall approve legislation authorizing the necessary adjustments in the organization of the central or provisional central conference involved. In the event that said church is not within the boundaries of an existing central or provisional central conference, then legislation shall be approved to either change boundaries of a contiguous conference or to establish a new central or provisional central conference.

*f)* The Commission on Central Conference Affairs shall assist said church in the process of becoming a part of The United Methodist Church, determine when all requirements are met, and report to the General Conference.

2. Other churches outside the United States may become a part of The United Methodist Church by following the same procedure.

## Section VI. Provisional Annual Conferences

¶ **554. A provisional annual conference** is a conference that, because of its limited membership, does not qualify for annual conference status.

¶ **555.** *Provisions*—Any missionary conference or mission established under the provisions of the *Discipline* may be constituted as a provisional annual conference by the General Conference, in consultation with the central conference, provisional central conference, or jurisdictional conference within which the missionary conference or mission is located; *provided* that:

1. No provisional annual conference shall be organized with fewer than ten clergy members or be continued with fewer than six clergy members.

2. The total financial support from the General Board of Global Ministries, including the Advance, shall not exceed an appropriate percentage as determined in consultation with the board.

3. The membership and contributions of the conference have shown a reasonable increase during the previous quadrennium and give evidence of an aggressive program for continued progress in both areas.

¶ 556. *Organization*—A provisional annual conference shall be organized in the same manner and have the same powers and functions as an annual conference, subject to the approval of the presiding bishop; and its members shall share *pro rata* in the proceeds of The United Methodist Publishing House with members of the annual conferences, with the following exceptions:

1. The bishop having episcopal supervision of a provisional annual conference in a foreign or a home mission field may appoint a representative as **superintendent,** to whom may be committed specific responsibility for the representation of the General Board of Global Ministries in its relation to the indigenous church and also in cooperation with other recognized evangelical missions. Such duties shall be exercised so as not to interfere with the work of the district superintendent. This superintendent may also be a district superintendent; *provided* the superintendent is a member of the said conference. The superintendent shall be responsible directly to the bishop appointed to administer the work in that episcopal area and shall make adequate reports of the work and needs of the field to the bishop and to the secretaries of the General Board of Global Ministries immediately concerned.

2. A provisional annual conference shall meet annually at the time appointed by the bishop. If there is no bishop present, the superintendent shall preside. In the absence of both, the presidency shall be determined as in an annual conference (¶ 603.6). The conference or a committee thereof shall select the place for holding the conference.

3. In a provisional annual conference receiving major funding from the General Board of Global Ministries, the assigned staff of the board shall provide consultation and guidance in setting up the

annual budget and Advance projects within the conference and in the promotion of new mission projects. The conference, in making requests for appropriations for support, including grants and loans for building projects, shall submit to the General Board of Global Ministries a statement of the proposed annual budget and proposed financial plan for new mission and building plans. Items involving increased appropriations from the General Board of Global Ministries or increased askings from the Advance shall be subject to modifications by the General Board of Global Ministries.

4. A provisional annual conference shall elect one ordained minister and one layperson as delegates with full voting and other rights to the General Conference and to the jurisdictional conference. Delegates to central conferences shall be elected in accordance with ¶ 536.1.

¶ 557. *Board of Global Ministries*—In a provisional annual conference in the United States, Puerto Rico, or the Virgin Islands, there shall be a conference board of global ministries constituted as in an annual conference and having the same duties and powers.

### Section VII. The Missionary Conference

¶ 558. *Definition*—A conference is a **missionary conference** because of its particular mission opportunities, its limited membership and resources, its unique leadership requirements, its strategic regional or language considerations, and ministerial needs. The General Board of Global Ministries shall provide administrative guidance and major financial assistance, including attention to the distinctive property matters.

¶ 559. *Organization*—A missionary conference shall be organized in the same manner and with the same rights and powers as an annual conference (¶¶ 601–604), but with the following exceptions:

1. The College of Bishops shall provide episcopal supervision for any missionary conference(s) within its jurisdictional boundaries as are organized. The bishop thus placed in charge and having episcopal supervision within the respective episcopal area in cooperation with the General Board of Global Ministries shall appoint a conference superintendent and/or district superintendents. Such conference and/or district superintendent(s) shall be an elder(s) and shall be subject to the same limitations on years of service as district superintendents (¶ 418). Years of service may be either consecutive or nonconsecutive. Years of service as a conference and/or district

superintendent in a missionary conference shall be counted toward the total of twelve years permitted in a regular annual conference.[24]

2. The General Board of Global Ministries shall give close supervision and guidance in setting up the administrative and promotional budgets and Advance projects within the conference and in the promotion of new mission projects. The conference, in making requests for appropriations for support and grants and loans for building projects, shall submit to the General Board of Global Ministries a statement of the proposed annual promotional and administrative budget and the proposed financial plan for new mission and building projects. New work and building projects involving increased appropriations from the General Board of Global Ministries shall first have the approval of the General Board of Global Ministries.

3. Missionary conferences shall elect clergy and lay delegates to General and jurisdictional conference on the same basis as annual conferences as provided in ¶¶ 502 and 513.

4. *a) Membership*—A missionary conference shall determine by majority vote whether it will establish the right of full ministerial membership.

*b)* An ordained minister in full connection with an annual conference who is appointed to a missionary conference that has previously voted to include full membership under § 4a may choose either to request the bishop of the missionary conference to seek the transfer of his or her membership into full membership with the missionary conference or retain his or her membership in a home conference and be considered in an affiliated relationship to the missionary conference. Affiliated relationship shall entitle the ordained minister to the fellowship of the conference, to full participation in its activities, including holding office and representing the missionary conference in general and jurisdictional conferences. An affiliate member of a missionary conference shall not vote in his or her annual conference while retaining the affiliate relationship to a missionary conference. Such affiliate relationship to a missionary conference shall be only for the duration of the ordained minister's appointment to the conference.

An affiliate member elected to a general or jurisdictional conference from a missionary conference shall not be eligible to be elected to such position from the conference where his or her membership is held.

---

24. *See* Judicial Council Decisions 448, 512.

*c)* A missionary conference may elect into full ministerial membership those persons desiring full membership in accordance with ¶ 561.

*d)* A pastor under full-time appointment in a missionary conference, upon consultation with and the approval of the bishop and conference or district superintendent or cabinet, may waive his or her claim upon the conference minimum salary. This waiver is to be reviewed annually and is to be effective until the time of subsequent appointment.

5. A missionary conference may include in its membership representation of such mission agencies within its boundaries as it deems advisable; *provided,* however, such representation shall not exceed a number equal to one-third of the total membership of the missionary conference and that such representatives shall be members of The United Methodist Church in accordance with constitutional requirements.[25]

6. In order to provide traditional and experimental ministries, the bishop of the missionary conference may appoint an effective elder to other than full-time pastoral appointment combined with secular employment. This will in no way affect the conference relationship. Pension and other benefits shall be provided in consultation with the parties involved and with the approval of the missionary conference.

7. A missionary conference that has not established the right of full ministerial membership may ordain indigenous racial and ethnic persons as deacons who, although they are not associate members, shall be accorded all the rights and privileges of associate membership in the missionary conference; *provided* that they have completed all of the necessary requirements for candidacy and such other requirements the missionary conference may establish. Further, these persons have the right to pursue transfer of their ministerial relationship to another annual conference as an associate member and to pursue a relationship of full connection under the guidance of that annual conference.

¶ **560.** Only the General Conference can create a missionary conference or change a missionary conference to a provisional annual conference or an annual conference. A petition to the General Conference for change in status from a missionary conference shall set forth details of the history and status of the conference and shall be accom-

---

25. *See* Judicial Council Decision 511.

panied by a report and recommendation of the General Board of Global Ministries.

**¶ 561.** *Rights and Privileges*—Missionary conferences shall have the same rights as those given to the central conferences in ¶ 537.9, .10 to make such changes and adaptations regarding the ministry and ordination of ordained ministers as the effective use of indigenous leadership in the missionary conference may require; *provided* that no action shall be taken that is contrary to the Constitution and the General Rules of The United Methodist Church.

**Section VIII. Mission**

**¶ 562.** *Definition*—A **mission** is an administrative body for a field of work inside or outside the structures of any annual conference, provisional annual conference, or missionary conference that is under the care of the General Board of Global Ministries and exercises in a general way the functions of a district conference.

The purpose of a mission is to provide ministry with a particular group or region whose needs cannot be fully met with the existing structures and resources of the annual conference(s). It may also be the initial stage in moving toward the formation of a provisional or missionary conference.

The establishment of a mission may involve special considerations in areas of leadership, language resources, and/or property.

**¶ 563.** *Establishment and Administration of a Mission*—1. The General Board of Global Ministries, in consultation with the presiding bishop or bishops (¶ 414.6) of an annual conference(s), shall determine the need and set the boundaries for the mission established within an annual conference, across conference lines, or for another extended region or constituency.

2. A mission shall be made up of all regularly appointed missionaries, both lay and clergy, mission traveling preachers, and other lay members. The mission shall determine the number of lay members and the method of their selection. In so doing, it shall ensure that all aspects of the mission's work are represented.[26]

3. When the mission lies within the bounds of one episcopal area, the resident bishop shall preside over the mission. When the mission

---

26. *See* Judicial Council Decision 341.

crosses the boundaries of one or more episcopal areas or jurisdictions, the College(s) of Bishops shall assign a bishop to the mission.

The bishop assigned to a mission, in consultation with the general secretary of the General Board of Global Ministries, may appoint one or more superintendents of the mission as may be determined and for whom support has been provided. The bishop shall decide which groups or charges the respective superintendents shall supervise.

4. A mission shall meet annually at the time and place designated by the bishop in charge, who shall preside. In the absence of the bishop, a superintendent of the mission shall preside. The presiding officer shall bring forward the regular business of the meeting and arrange the work.

5. The annual meeting shall have the power to certify candidates for the ordained ministry, to pass on the character of clergy who are not members of an annual conference, to receive mission traveling preachers, and to recommend to an annual conference proper persons for probationary membership and ordination. The examination of local pastors shall be held by the mission and certified to an annual conference.

Mission traveling preachers are members of the mission without being members of an annual conference. The mission shall determine the requirements for a mission traveling preacher in order to most effectively utilize the indigenous leadership. Mission traveling preachers are limited in their itineration to the bounds of the mission.

6. The bishop shall, at the annual meeting, assign the missionaries and mission traveling preachers to the several charges for the ensuing year; *provided* that transfer of missionaries related to the General Board of Global Ministries shall be completed only after consultation with the board.

7. Administration, initiation, and coordination of a mission shall be in the General Board of Global Ministries.

### Section IX. The Annual Conference

¶ 601. *Purpose*—The purpose of the annual conference is to make disciples for Jesus Christ by equipping its local churches for ministry and by providing a connection for ministry beyond the local church; all to the glory of God.

¶ 602. *Composition and Character*—1. The clergy membership of an annual conference (¶ 365) shall consist of deacons and elders in full connection (¶ 324), probationary members (¶ 318), associate members, affiliate members (¶¶ 335.4, 559.4), and local pastors under full-time and part-time appointment to a pastoral charge (¶ 342).[27] (*See also* ¶ 30.)

*a)* Clergy members in full connection shall have the right to vote on all matters in the annual conference except in the election of lay delegates to the general and jurisdictional or central conferences and shall have sole responsibility for all matters of ordination, character, and conference relations of clergy.[28]

*b)* Probationary clergy members shall have the right to vote in the annual conference on all matters except constitutional amendments, election of clergy delegates to the general and jurisdictional or central conferences, and matters of ordination, character, and conference relations of clergy.

*c)* Associate and affiliate clergy members shall have the right to vote in the annual conference on all matters except constitutional amendments, election of clergy delegates to the general and jurisdictional or central conferences, and matters of ordination, character, and conference relations of clergy.

*d)* Full-time and part-time local pastors under appointment to a pastoral charge shall have the right to vote in the annual conference on all matters except constitutional amendments; election of delegates to the general and jurisdictional or central conferences; and matters of ordination, character, and conference relations of clergy.[29]

2. Persons who enter candidacy for diaconal ministry prior to January 1, 1997, shall be allowed to complete candidacy, and those consecrated will serve as lay members of the annual conference as long as they maintain this status in The United Methodist Church.

3. Persons who become associate members prior to January 1, 1997, shall be allowed to continue in this relationship and serve under the provision of the 1992 *Book of Discipline* as long as they hold this status.

4. The lay membership of the annual conference shall consist of a lay member elected by each charge, diaconal ministers, deaconesses, the conference president of United Methodist Women, the conference president of United Methodist Men, the conference lay leader, district

---

27. *See* Judicial Council Decisions 341, 371, 477, 552, 584.
28. *See* Judicial Council Decision 690.
29. *See* Judicial Council Decision 862.

lay leaders, the conference director of Lay Speaking Ministries, the president or equivalent officer of the conference young adult organization, the president of the conference youth organization, the chair of the annual conference college student organization, one young person between the ages of twelve and seventeen and one young person between the ages of eighteen and thirty from each district to be selected in such a manner as may be determined by the annual conference. If the lay membership should number less than the clergy members of the annual conference, the annual conference shall, by its own formula, provide for the election of additional lay members to equalize lay and clergy membership of the annual conference.

Each charge served by more than one clergy member under appointment (including deacons in full connection for whom this is their primary appointment) shall be entitled to as many lay members as there are clergy members under appointment. The lay members shall have been members of The United Methodist Church for the two years preceding their election and shall have been active participants in The United Methodist Church for at least four years preceding their election (¶¶ 30, 250.2).

*a)* In the annual conference or the central conferences, the four-year participation and the two-year membership requirements may be waived for young persons under twenty-five years of age. Such persons must be members of The United Methodist Church and active participants at the time of election.

*b)* By authorization of a central conference, national diaconal ministers may be given the same privileges as a diaconal minister.[30]

5. The lay member or alternate, whoever was last seated in the annual conference, shall be seated in a special session of the annual conference when convened; *provided* that no local charge shall be deprived of its lay member due to death, serious illness, or cessation of membership. Under such circumstances, another lay member may be elected by the charge conference.[31] (*See* ¶ 30.)

6. The lay members of the annual conference shall participate in all deliberations and vote upon all measures except on the granting or validation of license, ordination, reception into full conference membership, or any question concerning the character and official conduct of ordained ministers, except those who are lay members of

---

30. *See* Judicial Council Decision 505.
31. *See* Judicial Council Decision 319.

the board of ordained ministry. Lay members shall serve on all committees except those on ministerial relations and for the trial of clergy.[32]

7. When at any time a lay member is excused by the annual conference from further attendance during the session, the alternate lay member, if present, shall be seated. The lay member or the alternate shall be the lay member of the annual conference, and it shall be the duty of the lay member to report to the local church on actions of the annual conference.

8. It is the duty of every member and all probationers and local pastors of the annual conference to attend its sessions and furnish such reports in such form as the *Discipline* may require. Any such person unable to attend shall report by letter to the conference secretary, setting forth the reason for the absence. Should any ordained minister in active service be absent from the session of the annual conference without a satisfactory reason for the absence, the matter shall be referred by the conference secretary to the board of ordained ministry.

9. The following shall be seated in the annual conference and shall be given the privilege of the floor without vote: official representatives from other denominations, especially from member churches of the Consultation on Church Union, invited by the annual conference; missionaries regularly assigned by the General Board of Global Ministries and serving within the bounds of the annual conference; lay missionaries regularly appointed by the General Board of Global Ministries in nations other than the United States and certified lay missionaries from nations other than the United States serving within the bounds of the annual conference.

10. If not otherwise a voting member of the annual conference, the conference chancellor shall be seated in the annual conference and shall be given the privilege of the floor without vote.

¶ 603. *Organization*—1. Annual conferences may become severally bodies corporate, whenever practicable, under the law of the countries, states, and territories within whose bounds they are located.[33]

2. The bishops shall appoint the times for holding the annual conferences.

---

32. *See* Judicial Council Decisions 109, 505, 592.
33. *See* Judicial Council Decision 108.

3. The annual conference or a committee thereof shall select the place for holding the conference, but should it become necessary for any reason to change the place of meeting, a majority of the district superintendents, with the consent of the bishop in charge, may change the place.

4. The annual conference sessions shall be held in places that are accessible to people with disabilities.

5. A special session of the annual conference may be held at such time and in such place as shall have been determined by the annual conference after consultation with the bishop, or by the bishop with the concurrence of three-fourths of the district superintendents. A special session of the annual conference shall have only such powers as are stated in the call.[34]

6. The bishop assigned shall preside over the annual conference or, in case of inability, shall arrange for another bishop to preside. In the absence of a bishop, the conference shall by ballot, without nomination or debate, elect a president *pro tempore* from among the traveling elders. The president thus elected shall discharge all the duties of a bishop except ordination.[35]

7. The annual conference at the first session following the General Conference or jurisdictional or central conferences (or, if it may desire, at the last session preceding the general, jurisdictional, or central conferences) shall elect a secretary and statistician to serve for the succeeding quadrennium. In the case of a vacancy in either office in the interim of the sessions, the bishop, after consultation with the district superintendents, shall appoint a person to act until the next session of the annual conference. (*See* ¶ 617 for election of the treasurer.)

8. The annual conference may designate as chancellor a layperson who is a member in good standing in one of the local churches or a clergyperson who is a member of the annual conference in the episcopal area, and who is a member of the appropriate bar or bars in the episcopal area. The chancellor, who shall be nominated by the bishop and elected by the annual conference, shall serve as legal adviser to the bishop and the annual conference.

9. *a)* **The conference lay leader** is the elected leader of conference laity. The lay leader will have responsibility for fostering awareness of the role of the laity both within the congregation and through their

---

34. *See* Judicial Council Decision 397.
35. *See* Judicial Council Decisions 367, 373.

ministries in the home, workplace, community, and world in achieving the mission of the Church and for enabling and supporting lay participation in the planning and decision-making processes of the annual conference, district, and local church in cooperation with the bishop, district superintendents, and pastors. The lay leader shall be a member of the annual conference, the conference council on ministries, the conference committee on nominations, the conference committee on episcopacy, the executive committee, if any, of the conference council on ministries; and the committee planning annual conference sessions; and may be designated by virtue of office to membership on any conference agency by the annual conference.

*b)* The conference lay leader shall be the chairperson of the conference board of laity, or its equivalent, and shall relate to the organized lay groups in the conference such as Lay Speaking Ministries, United Methodist Men, United Methodist Women, and United Methodist Youth and support their work and help them coordinate their activities. The conference lay leader shall also have the general responsibility in: (1) developing the advocacy role for laity in the life of the Church; (2) increasing the participation of laity in the sessions and structure of the annual conference; and (3) encouraging laypersons in the general ministry of the Church.

*c)* The conference lay leader shall be elected by the annual conference as the annual conference may determine. The method of nomination and term of office shall be determined by the annual conference. Associate lay leader(s), to work with the conference lay leader, may be elected by the annual conference as it may determine.

¶ 604. *Powers and Duties*—1. The annual conference, for its own government, may adopt rules and regulations not in conflict with the *Discipline* of The United Methodist Church; *provided* that in exercise of its powers, each annual conference shall act in all respects in harmony with the policy of The United Methodist Church with respect to elimination of discrimination on the basis of race.[36]

2. An annual conference cannot financially obligate any organizational unit of The United Methodist Church except the annual conference itself.[37]

---

36. *See* Judicial Council Decisions 43, 74, 109, 141, 318, 323, 367, 373, 418, 432, 435, 476, 536, 584, 590, 592, 688, 699, 876.

37. *See* Judicial Council Decision 707.

3. The annual conference may admit into clergy membership only those who have met all the disciplinary requirements for membership and only in the manner prescribed in the *Discipline*.[38]

4. The annual conference shall have power to make inquiry into the moral and official conduct of its clergy members. Subject only to the provisions of ¶¶ 2701–2719, the annual conference shall have power to hear complaints against its clergy members and may try, reprove, suspend, deprive of clergy office and credentials, expel, or acquit any against whom charges may have been preferred. The annual conference shall have power to locate a clergy member for failure to perform effectively and competently the duties of itinerant ministry.[39]

5. The status of a clergy member and of a probationer and the manner and conditions of a transfer of a clergy member from one annual conference to another are governed by the section on the ordained ministry (Chapter Two).

6. Transfers of traveling preachers are conditioned on the passing of their character by the conference to which they are amenable. The official announcement that a preacher is transferred changes the preacher's membership so that all rights and responsibilities in the conference to which that preacher goes begin from the date of transfer. Such member of an annual conference shall not vote twice on the same constitutional question, nor be counted twice in the same year in the basis for election of delegates, nor vote twice in the same year for delegates to the general, jurisdictional, or central conferences.

7. Whenever clergy members, whether on probation or in full connection, are transferred to another annual conference, either in connection with a transfer of the pastoral charge to which they are appointed or by reason of the dissolution or merger of the annual conference, they shall have the same rights and obligations as the other members of the conference to which they are transferred.

8. The annual conference shall have power to make inquiry into the financial status of the local churches, and where there is a deficit in finances, it may require the pastor and the lay member to appear before the appropriate committee and make explanation. Based upon its findings, it shall provide counsel to help the church overcome such a deficit position.

---

38. *See* Judicial Council Decision 440.
39. *See* Judicial Council Decisions 534, 782.

9. The annual conference shall have the power to make inquiry into the membership status of the local churches, and where no members have been received on confession of faith during the year, it may require the pastor and the lay member to appear before the appropriate agency and make explanation.

10. The annual conference shall give recognition to any new churches that have been organized during the year and shall, through the presiding bishop and the secretary, send to each new church a certificate of organization, which the district superintendent shall, on behalf of the conference, present to the new church in an appropriate ceremony.

11. The annual conference shall secure, during the course of its annual session, the answers to the questions for conducting annual conference sessions, and the secretary to the annual conference shall include the answers to these questions in the conference journal and in the report to the council on finance and administration.

12. If any annual conference initiates, joins, monitors, or terminates a boycott, the guidelines in *The Book of Resolutions*, 2000, should be followed. The General Conference is the only body that can initiate, empower, or join a boycott in the name of The United Methodist Church.

13. The annual conference may choose to adopt a conference-wide plan for compensation of pastors. Such a plan shall provide the method for setting and funding the salaries, and/or other compensation elements as specified in the plan, of the pastors appointed to the charges of the annual conference.

14. *Closed Sessions*—In the spirit of openness and accountability, all meetings of official boards, agencies, commissions, and committees of the annual conference, including sub-unit meetings and teleconferences, shall be open. Portions of a meeting may be closed for consideration of specific subjects if such a closed session is authorized by an affirmative public vote of at least three-fourths of the voting members present. The vote shall be taken in public session and recorded in the minutes. Documents distributed in open meetings shall be considered public.

Great restraint shall be used in closing meetings; closed sessions should be used as seldom as possible. Subjects that may be considered in closed session are limited to real-estate matters; negotiations, when general knowledge could be harmful to the negotiation process; personnel matters; issues related to the accreditation or approval of institutions; discussions relating to litigation or collective bargaining; deployment of security personnel or devices; and negotiations involving confidential third-party information.

A report on the results of a closed session shall be made immediately upon its conclusion or as soon thereafter as is practicable.

¶ 605. *Business of the Conference*—1. The session shall open with a period of devotion, followed by a call of the roll, including the roll of the local pastors.

2. The annual conference, to expedite the transaction of its business, may adopt an agenda as a basis of its procedure. Such agenda shall be prepared by the bishop, the district superintendents, the conference lay leader, and such others as the conference may name and shall be submitted to the conference for adoption.

3. Members for all standing committees, boards, and commissions of the annual conference shall be selected in such manner as the *Book of Discipline* may specifically require or as the annual conference may determine.[40] Attention shall be given to inclusiveness (¶¶ 124, 138).

For the purpose of adjusting tenure, a certain number of members may be elected or appointed for particular terms. Members shall hold office until their successors are elected. For the annual conference agencies provided for by the *Discipline, see* ¶ 608.1; and for the agencies established by the annual conference itself, *see* ¶ 608.2.

4. The business of the annual conference shall include receiving and acting upon reports from district superintendents, officers, standing and special committees, boards, commissions, and societies and also making such inquiries as the Council of Bishops shall recommend by the provision of a supplemental guide.[41]

5. The agenda of the annual conference shall provide time for an address or report that shall be the responsibility of the conference lay leader.

6. The annual conference shall make inquiry into the moral and official conduct of its ordained ministers and local pastors. In response to the inquiry whether all such persons are blameless in their life and official administration, the district superintendent may answer for all the preachers in the district in one answer, or the board of ordained ministry may make inquiry of each district superintendent about each ordained minister in the district and make one report

---

40. *See* Judicial Council Decision 559.
41. *See* Judicial Council Decision 367.

to the bishop and the conference in open session.[42] Questions relating to matters of ordination, character, and conference relations of clergy shall be the business of the clergy session. The actions of the clergy session shall be for and on behalf of the annual conference. The provisions of the *Book of Discipline* applicable to an annual conference shall also be applicable to the clergy session. All clergy members (¶¶ 601.1, 602.1) of the annual conference and the lay members of the board of ordained ministry may attend and shall have voice in the clergy session. Only the ordained clergy in full connection and the lay members of the board of ordained ministry may vote (¶ 602.1*a*). Others may be admitted by express action of the clergy session, but shall not have vote, nor, unless specifically granted by the clergy session, shall have voice (¶ 324).[43]

7. At the conclusion of the examination of the standing of the ordained ministers and local pastors in the conference or at such later times as the bishop may designate, the presiding bishop may call to the bar of the conference the class to be admitted into full connection and receive them into conference membership after asking the questions to be found in ¶ 327. This examination of the ordained ministers and the passing of their characters may be the business of one session.

¶ 606. *Records and Archives*—1. The annual conference shall keep an exact record of its proceedings according to the forms provided by the general, jurisdictional, and central conferences. If there are no archives of the annual conference, the secretary shall keep the bound copy or copies to be handed on to the succeeding secretary. The conference shall send to its jurisdictional conference or central conference copies of the minutes of the quadrennium for examination.

2. Each annual conference shall send to the General Council on Finance and Administration two printed copies of its annual journal and one printed copy to the General Council on Ministries and to United Methodist Communications.[44]

3. The annual conference journal shall include the following divisions, in the following order:

　　*a)* Officers of annual conference,

　　*b)* Boards, commissions, committees; rolls of conference members,

---

42. *See* Judicial Council Decisions 42, 406, 534, 555.
43. *See* Judicial Council Decisions 686, 690, 769, 782.
44. *See* Judicial Council Decision 481.

c) Daily proceedings,

d) Business of the annual conference report (formerly known as the disciplinary questions),

e) Appointments,

f) Reports as ordered by the annual conference,

g) Memoirs as ordered by the annual conference,

h) Roll of dead—deceased clergy members,

i) Historical,

j) Miscellaneous,

k) Pastoral record (including the records of accepted local pastors in such manner as the conference may determine),

l) Statistics,

m) Index.

4. An annual conference in the United States and Puerto Rico shall include in its journal a list of the deaconesses and missionaries, clergy and lay, active and retired, who have gone from the conference into mission service or who are presently serving in such capacity within the bounds of the annual conference.

5. The annual conference journal shall include a listing of the consecrated diaconal ministers and their service records.

6. The secretary, treasurer, or other administrative officer named by the annual conference shall keep a complete service record of ordained and diaconal ministry personnel in the annual conference. Service records shall include but not be limited to biographical information supplied by the individual, a list of appointments, and a record of annual conference actions with regard to conference relationships. In addition to service records, the secretary, treasurer, or other administrative officer named by the annual conference shall keep descriptions of circumstances related to changes in conference relationships, credentials surrendered to the bishop or district superintendent, and confidential trial records.

7. The local church report to the annual conference shall be submitted on the prescribed forms no later than thirty days following the close of the calendar year. If the annual conference sets an earlier deadline for receiving the reports, the earlier deadline shall apply.

8. All records of secretaries, statisticians, and treasurers shall be kept according to the forms prepared by the General Council on Finance and Administration so that all statistical and financial items shall be handled alike in all conferences and that uniformity of reporting shall be established as a churchwide policy.

9. All records of candidates and ordained and diaconal ministry personnel maintained by the conference secretary, treasurer, or other administrative officer named by the annual conference, board of ordained ministry, board of pensions, and the district committee on ordained ministry are to be kept on behalf of the annual conference in conformity with guidelines provided by the General Council on Finance and Administration, in consultation with the General Board of Higher Education and Ministry and the General Board of Pension and Health Benefits, and the following principles:

*a)* The annual conference is the owner of its personnel records and files;

*b)* Individuals in whose name a record is kept shall have access to the information contained in a record or file, with the exception of surrendered credentials and information for which a right-of-access waiver has been signed;

*c)* Access to unpublished records by persons other than the bishop, district superintendent, conference secretary, treasurer, or other administrative officer or the board of ordained ministry, through its chair, board of pensions, through its chair, the district committee on ordained ministry, through its chair, counsel for the Church, and committee on investigation, through its chair, shall require written consent of the person in whose name a record is kept; access to trial records shall be governed by the provisions of ¶ 2712.5, 2713,5.[45]

¶ 607. *Connectional Ministries*—Each annual conference is responsible to focus and guide the mission and ministry of The United Methodist Church within its boundaries by: 1. envisioning the ministries necessary to live out the mission of the church in and through the annual conference; 2. creating and nurturing relationships and connections among the local, district, annual conference, and general church ministries; 3. providing encouragement, coordination, and support for the ministries of nurture, outreach, and witness in districts and congregations for the transformation of the world; 4. ensuring the alignment of the total resources of the annual conference to its mission; 5. developing and strengthening ethnic ministries, including ethnic local churches and concerns; 6. providing for advocacy and monitoring functions to ensure that the church is consistent with its stated values.

---

45. *See* Judicial Council Decisions 751, 765.

It is recommended that each annual conference have **a director of connectional ministries** or designated person to focus and guide the mission and ministry of The United Methodist Church within the annual conference.

*a)* The director may be lay or clergy.

*b)* The director shall serve as an officer of the annual conference and shall sit with the cabinet when the cabinet considers matters relating to coordination, implementation, or administration of the conference program, and other matters as the cabinet and director may determine.

*c)* In partnership with the bishop and cabinet and the elected leadership of the conference, the director of connectional ministries shall have the following primary responsibilities:

(1) to serve as steward of the vision of the annual conference, including the development, clarification, interpretation, and embodiment of the vision;

(2) to serve as leader of the continuous process of transformation and renewal necessary for the annual conference to be faithful to our Christian identity in a changing world;

(3) to ensure alignment of the total resources of the conference to its vision;

(4) to ensure the connections among the local, district, annual conference, and general church ministries for the purpose of networking, resourcing, and communicating their shared ministry.

### CONFERENCE AGENCIES

¶ **608.** The annual conference is responsible for structuring its ministries and administrative procedures in order to accomplish its purpose (¶ 601). In so doing it shall provide for the connectional relationship of the local church, district, and conference with the general agencies. It will monitor to ensure inclusiveness—racial, gender, age, and people with disabilities—in the annual conference.

1. An annual conference shall provide for the functions and General Conference connections with all general agencies provided by the *Discipline* as follows: *a)* There shall be clear connections between the General Conference agencies, annual conference program and administrative entities, and the local congregation; *b)* There shall be clear checks and balances regarding program functions and financial/administration functions within the annual conference. In doing

this, the annual conference may organize units so long as the functions of ministry are fulfilled and the connectional relationships are maintained.[46]

2. The annual conference may appoint additional committees for the purpose of promoting the work of The United Methodist Church within the bounds of the said annual conference and may prescribe their membership and their powers and duties.

3. Each annual conference may make its agencies of such size as its work may require; *provided* that consideration shall be given to the inclusion of lay and clergypersons from small membership churches. All local pastors serving charges are eligible for election or appointment to such agencies, except those dealing with qualifications, orders, and status of clergy and local pastors.

4. Whenever possible, meetings scheduled by the annual conference and its districts, boards, or committees should be held in places that are accessible to persons with disabilities even if this means scheduling meetings outside church-related facilities.

5. In the nomination and election of the membership on councils, boards, and agencies of the annual conference, special attention shall be given to the inclusion of clergywomen, youth (¶ 255.2.), young adults, older adults, persons from churches with small memberships, people with disabilities, and racial and ethnic persons, in keeping with policies for general Church agencies. It is further recommended that the membership of such agencies, except for the Board of Ordained Ministry, include one-third clergy, one-third laywomen, and one-third laymen, who are professing members of local churches. [47]

6. Members of general agencies (¶ 701) shall serve as ex officio members of the corresponding annual conference agency or its equivalent structure (*see* ¶ 710.4, .5). If this results in a person being a member of more than one annual conference agency in violation of either annual conference policy or another provision of the *Book of Discipline*, the person shall choose the annual conference agency on which to serve.

7. It is strongly recommended that the annual conference provide for child and dependent care both during the sessions of the annual conference and meetings of the annual conference boards and agencies.

---

46. *See* Judicial Council Decisions 827, 835, 848, 878.
47. *See* Judicial Council Decisions 446, 558.

THE CONFERENCE COUNCIL ON FINANCE AND ADMINISTRATION

¶ 609. In each annual conference there shall be a **conference council on finance and administration,** hereinafter called the council, or other structure to provide for the functions of this ministry and maintain the connectional relationships (¶ 608.1).

¶ 610. The council's purpose, membership, organization, and relationships shall be as follows:

1. *Purpose*—The purpose of the council shall be to develop, maintain, and administer a comprehensive and coordinated plan of fiscal and administrative policies, procedures, and management services for the annual conference.

2. *Membership—a)* Each annual conference shall elect, at its session next succeeding the General Conference or jurisdictional conference, a conference council on finance and administration composed of not less than five nor more than twenty-one members; in every case there shall be at least one layperson more than clergy included on the council.[48] Persons shall be nominated for membership in a manner determined by the conference in accordance with ¶ 608.5. Churches of less than two hundred members shall be represented on the conference council on finance and administration. The term of office shall begin with the adjournment of the annual conference session at which they are elected and shall be for a period of four years and until their successors are elected. No member or employee of any conference agency and no employee, trustee, or director of any agency or institution participating in the funds of any conference budget shall be eligible for voting membership on the council.[49] Any vacancy shall be filled by action of the council until the next conference session, at which time the annual conference shall fill the vacancy.

*b)* The following shall be ex officio members of the council in addition to the number set by the annual conference under ¶ 610.2*a:* (1) the conference treasurer/director of administrative services, without vote; (2) any members of the General Council on Finance and Administration who reside within the bounds of the conference, with vote unless voting membership is in conflict with another provision of the *Book of Discipline,* in which case their membership shall be without vote; in either case, they shall not be eligible to serve on an agency receiving funding; (3) the presiding bishop, without vote; (4) a

---

48. *See* Judicial Council Decision 441.
49. *See* Judicial Council Decisions 10, 493.

district superintendent chosen by the cabinet, without vote; and (5) the director of connectional ministries or equivalent, or another representative of the conference council on ministries, without vote.

c) The executive director of the conference or area United Methodist foundation may be included in the membership, without vote.

3. *Officers*—The council shall elect from its voting membership a president, a vice president, a secretary, and such other officers as it may deem necessary. Consideration shall be given to inclusiveness (¶¶ 124, 138). The conference treasurer/director of administrative services (¶ 617) shall be the treasurer of the council. The treasurer/director of administrative services shall not be eligible for voting membership on the council and shall not be eligible for election to any of those offices that are to be filled by voting members of the council.

4. No member of the council shall vote on or take part in deliberations on significant matters directly or indirectly affecting her or his business, income, or employment, or the business, income, or employment of his or her immediate family.

5. *Organization*—a) The council may establish committees and task forces and define their duties and authority as it deems necessary for fulfilling its purpose and responsibilities.

b) The annual conference may enact bylaws governing meetings, quorum, and other matters of procedure for the council, or it may authorize the council to enact such bylaws; in any event, such bylaws shall not be in conflict with the *Book of Discipline*.

c) If deemed necessary for the fulfillment of its functions and if so authorized by the annual conference, the council may be incorporated.

6. *Amenability*—The council shall be amenable and report directly to the annual conference.[50]

7. *Relationships*—a) The council and the annual conference council on ministries shall cooperate in the development of the conference benevolences budget (¶ 612.3). b) In the interest of developing and implementing coordinated annual conference policies in the areas of fiscal management and administrative services, the council shall serve in a liaison role among conference agencies with responsibilities in these areas. It shall be authorized to convene representatives of

---

50. *See* Judicial Council Decisions 551, 560.

annual conference administrative and clergy support agencies for the purpose of consulting on matters of mutual concern, such as the coordination of fiscal management, fundraising activities, and administrative services in the annual conference.

¶ **611.** *Responsibilities*—The council shall have authority and responsibility to perform the following functions:

1. To recommend to the annual conference for its action and determination budgets of anticipated income and proposed expenditures for all funds that provide for annual conference clergy support, annual conference administrative expenses, and annual conference benevolence and program causes (¶ 612).[51]

2. To receive, consider, report, and make recommendations to the annual conference regarding the following prior to final decision by the annual conference: *(a)* any proposal to raise capital funds for any purpose; *(b)* funding considerations related to any proposal that may come before the conference; *(c)* any requests to conduct a special conference-wide financial appeal, whether by special collections, campaigns, or otherwise in the local churches of the conference.

3. To recommend to the annual conference for its action and decision the methods or formulas by which apportionments to churches, charges, or districts for duly authorized general, jurisdictional, conference, and district funds shall be determined (¶ 613).

4. To consult and cooperate with the commission on communication in providing district superintendents, pastors, and appropriate officers of the local churches and charge conferences with interpretive aids or other materials to assist in gaining understanding and support of the conference budget and other approved conference causes.

5. To develop policies governing the investment of conference funds (except for pension funds as provided in ¶ 1508), whether in debt or equity, short-term or long-term instruments, with the aim of maximizing funds available for mission in a manner consistent with the preservation of capital, the Policies Relative to Socially Responsible Investments (¶ 716), and the Social Principles of the Church. A statement of such policies shall be printed in the conference journal at least once in each quadrennium.

6. To recommend to the annual conference procedures for funding local churches and assisting them in making their church buildings, facilities, and programs accessible.

---

51. *See* Judicial Council Decisions 521, 744.

7. To recommend to the annual conference for its action procedures for dealing responsibly with situations in which budgeted funds, as approved by the annual conference, are inadequate to meet emerging missional needs or unforeseen circumstances.[52]

8. To review at least quarterly and to account to the annual conference for the disbursement of funds in accordance with budgets approved by the conference.

9. To recommend to the annual conference for its action and determination the conditions under which it may borrow funds for current expense purposes and the maximum amount of such borrowing.

10. To have authority and supervision over the conference treasurer/director of administrative services subject to ¶ 617; to establish policies governing the treasurer/director's work.

11. To work in cooperation with other annual conference agencies for the design and implementation of a plan by which the annual conference may designate the conference treasury as a central treasury for funds designated for any or all conference agencies participating in conference funds.

12. To establish uniform and equitable policies and practices in the employment and compensation of personnel, in consultation and cooperation with other conference agencies that employ staff, unless the annual conference has designated another agency to carry this responsibility. These policies and practices shall be in accordance with the Social Principles (¶ 162 A, E, F, and G).

13. To cooperate with the General Council on Finance and Administration and with the General Board of Discipleship in promoting and standardizing the financial recording and reporting system in the local churches of the conference.

14. In cooperation with the General Council on Finance and Administration, related annual conference agencies and institutions, and local churches, to make recommendations to the annual conference regarding the development, promotion, and review of a broad general program of insurance protection, except for employee benefit programs.

15. To cooperate with the General Council on Finance and Administration in order to provide leadership, training, and encouragement in the areas of church business administration for individuals

---

52. *See* Judicial Council Decision 551.

and organizations of The United Methodist Church by: (1) distributing information regarding certification as a church business administrator; and (2) listing in the council's report to the annual conference the names of persons certified as church business administrators by the General Council on Finance and Administration who are employed within the bounds of the annual conference.

16. To make recommendations to the annual conference for its action and determination regarding plans to initiate or cause to be organized a foundation or similar organization for the purpose of securing, conserving, or expending funds for the direct or indirect benefit or support of the annual conference, or of any conference agency, or any of its programs or work. The council shall have opportunity to make its recommendations regarding such plans if the foundation or similar organization is: (1) proposed to be organized by the annual conference itself, whether acting alone or in concert with other annual conferences; (2) proposed to be organized by any conference council, board, commission, committee, or other agency; (3) to make use of the name *United Methodist* in its title or solicitation; or (4) proposed for the purpose of soliciting gifts primarily from the United Methodist constituency.

17. To perform such other administrative and fiscal functions and services as the annual conference may assign.

18. To ensure that no apportioned conference funds are expended for the use of alcoholic beverages.

¶ 612. *Budgets*—The council shall recommend to the annual conference for its action and determination budgets of anticipated income and proposed expenditures for all funds to be apportioned to the churches, charges, or districts.[53]

Prior to each regular session of the annual conference, the council shall make a diligent and detailed study of the needs of all the conference agencies and causes asking to be included in the budget of any conference fund. The chairperson of each conference agency, or other duly authorized representative, shall have opportunity to represent the claims of that agency before the council.

1. *Clergy Support Budgets—a)* It shall be the duty of the council, unless otherwise provided, to estimate the total amount necessary to furnish a sufficient and equitable support for the district superintendents of the conference, including base compensation, travel, staff,

---

53. *See* Judicial Council Decisions 551, 560, 744.

office, and housing. The council shall report specific recommendations to the annual conference for conference action (¶¶ 423.2, 663.4a).[54]

*b)* The council shall report to the annual conference at each session the percentage approved by the General Conference as the basis for the Episcopal Fund apportionment to the annual conference and shall include in its recommended clergy support budget the amount determined by the treasurer of the General Council on Finance and Administration as necessary to meet this apportionment.

*c)* Based on recommendations from the episcopal residence committee (¶ 636.4d), the council shall recommend the amount to be raised as the annual conference share of the cost of the bishop's housing.

*d)* After consultation with the conference board of pensions, the council shall report to the annual conference the amounts computed by that agency as necessary to meet the needs for pensions and benefit programs of the conference. Such amounts need not be derived solely from apportionments.

*e)* It shall recommend to the annual conference an amount determined in consultation with the commission on equitable compensation to be used for compliance with the approved schedule of equitable base compensation for pastors (¶ 623.3).

*f)* It shall recommend to the annual conference estimates of the amounts needed for any other programs of clergy support the conference may adopt, such as a Sustentation Fund (¶ 624) or provision for the moving expenses of pastors.

2. *Administration Budget—a)* The council shall recommend to the annual conference estimates of the amounts needed for administrative expenses of the conference, including its own expenses and those of the conference treasurer's office. It shall consult with the conference agencies and officers to be included in the administrative budget regarding the estimated budgets of their expenses and base its conference administration budget recommendations on information thus received.

*b)* It shall include in its estimates recommendations regarding the conference's share of an area expense fund, if any, and apportionments for administration properly made by the jurisdictional conference and the General Conference (¶ 811.5).

---

54. *See* Judicial Council Decisions 44, 584, 590, 591, 818.

3. *Conference Benevolences Budget—a)* In preparing the conference benevolences budget, the council, working together with the conference council on ministries or alternative structure as provided in ¶ 612.3*b*, shall make diligent effort to secure full information regarding all conference benevolence and service causes that none may be neglected, jeopardized, or excluded. Basing its judgment of needs upon the information secured, the council shall recommend to the annual conference for its action and determination the total amount to be apportioned for the conference benevolences budget. After receiving the recommendations of the conference council on ministries or alternative structure, the council shall also recommend the amount or the percentage of the total of the conference benevolences budget that shall be allocated to each cause included in the said budget. Such recommendations should reflect agreement with the conference council on ministries or alternative structure on program agency allocations as specified below.[55]

*b)* The council on finance and administration and the annual conference council on ministries shall work together to establish and follow a procedure that shall preserve the following principles:

(1) It is the responsibility of the conference council on finance and administration to establish the total amount to be recommended to the annual conference as the conference benevolences budget and, within that amount, the total sum to be recommended for distribution among the conference program agencies. It is likewise the responsibility of the council to study the budget requests for any agencies or causes to be included in the conference benevolences budget other than the conference program agencies, including the requests of the conference council on ministries, and to give the chairpersons or other authorized representatives of such agencies and causes opportunity to represent their claims before the council.[56]

(2) It is the responsibility of the conference council on ministries to study the budget requests of the conference program agencies and to recommend to the conference council on finance and administration amounts to be allocated from the conference benevolences budget to each such agency, within the total established by the conference council on finance and administration.[57]

---

55. *See* Judicial Council Decisions 400, 521, 551, 582.
56. *See* Judicial Council Decisions 521, 551.
57. *See* Judicial Council Decisions 521, 551.

(3) It is the responsibility of the conference council on finance and administration to present the conference benevolences budget recommendations to the annual conference. The recommended allocations to conference program agencies should reflect agreement between the council and the conference council on ministries or alternative structure.[58]

c) The term *conference benevolences* shall include those conference allocations and expenditures directly associated with the program, mission, and benevolent causes of annual conference program agencies and institutions. Annual conference program agencies and institutions shall be defined as those agencies with responsibilities parallel to those of the program-related general agencies (¶ 703) and institutions whose work is within the field of responsibility of one or more of those agencies. Administrative expenses that are directly related to the program, mission, and benevolent causes of conference program agencies, including the expenses of the conference council on ministries or alternative structure, may also be included in the conference benevolences budget. The term *conference benevolences* shall not include allocations and expenditures for other conference agencies and officers whose work is primarily administrative. It shall likewise not include annual conference clergy support funds as set forth in ¶¶ 618–626, allocations and expenditures of conference agencies responsible for administering clergy support funds, or apportionments made to the annual conference by the general or jurisdictional conferences.

d) The council, on receiving from the treasurer of the General Council on Finance and Administration a statement of the amount apportioned that annual conference for World Service, may recommend that the conference combine the total World Service apportionment, without reduction for the quadrennium, and the approved conference benevolences budget (¶ 612.3a). If combined the sum of these two amounts shall be known as **World Service and Conference Benevolences,** and the combined budget thus established shall include a statement of the percentage for World Service and the percentage for conference benevolences.[59] (*See also* ¶ 612.)

4. *Other Apportioned Causes*—The council shall include in its budget recommendations specific amounts recommended for all other

58. *See* Judicial Council Decision 551.
59. *See* Judicial Council Decision 348.

funds properly apportioned to the annual conference for the support of duly authorized general or other connectional funds. The budget recommendations shall likewise include any other amounts to be apportioned to the districts, charges, or churches by the annual conference for conference or district causes of any kind.

5. *Special Appeals*—*a)* No annual conference agency or interest, including any related agency or institution such as a school, college, university, hospital, home, housing project, or other service institution, shall make a special conference-wide appeal to the local churches for funds without the approval of the annual conference upon recommendation of the council, except in case of an extreme emergency, when such approval may be given by a two-thirds vote of the district superintendents and of the council, acting jointly. Neither shall special conference-wide appeals to local churches for funds be made by such boards, interests, agencies, or institutions that are not related to the annual conference in which the appeal is to be made, unless approval for such an appeal is granted by the annual conference upon recommendation of the council. The annual conference approvals specified in this paragraph shall not be required for special churchwide financial appeals that have been approved under the provisions of ¶ 811.4, for solicitations that have been approved under the provisions of ¶ 812.3, or for any other general fund promotion or appeal authorized by the General Conference or approved and conducted under other provisions of the *Book of Discipline.*

*b)* When application is made to the council for the privilege of a special conference-wide financial appeal, whether by special collections, campaigns, or otherwise, the council shall investigate the application and its possible relation to other obligations of the conference and in the light of the facts make recommendations to the conference for its action and determination. If application for privilege of a special appeal is made directly to the conference, the application shall be referred to the council before final action is taken.

*c)* The council may include in its budget recommendations to the annual conference amounts to be considered as goals for special appeals or other nonapportioned causes.

6. The council shall make its budget recommendations to the annual conference in a format based on guidelines suggested by the General Council on Finance and Administration.

¶ **613.** *Apportionments*—The council shall recommend to the annual conference for its action and determination the methods or formulas by which the approved budgeted amounts for clergy support, administration, World Service, Conference Benevolences, and other apportioned causes (¶¶ 612.1–.4) shall be apportioned to the districts, churches, or charges of the conference.

1. The council, on receiving from the General Council on Finance and Administration a statement of the amount apportioned to the annual conference for the several general funds authorized by the General Conference, shall apportion the same to the several districts, charges, or churches by whatever method the conference may direct, but without reduction.

2. The council shall recommend to the annual conference for its action and determination whether the apportionments referred to in this paragraph shall be made by the council to the districts only or to the churches or charges of the conference. If the apportionments are made to the districts only, then the distribution to the churches or charges of each district shall be made as provided in ¶ 613.3. The conference may order that the entire distribution to all the churches or charges of the conference be made by the district superintendents.

3. Should the annual conference make the apportionments to the districts only, the distribution to the churches or charges of each district shall be made by its district board of stewards, composed of the district superintendent as chairperson and the district stewards elected by the several charge conferences (¶ 246.13). In that case, the board, meeting on call of the district superintendent as soon as practicable after the adjournment of the annual conference, shall make the distribution to the churches or charges of the district using such methods as it may determine, unless the annual conference shall have determined the method of distribution to the churches or charges.

4. If the council recommends an apportioned fund that combines two or more general apportioned funds with one another, or that combines one or more general apportioned funds with funds other than a general apportioned fund, the recommendation and consequent annual conference actions shall include: (1) a statement of the amount of each general fund apportionment included in the combined fund, and (2) a statement of the percentage of the combined fund total that corresponds to each general fund apportionment.

5. If an annual conference establishes an apportioned fund that combines funds subject to proportional payment under ¶ 620 with funds not subject to proportional payment, it shall establish procedures to ensure that the proportional payment provisions of ¶ 620 are observed.

6. If an annual conference establishes an apportioned fund that combines support for several distinct causes, it shall make available to local churches information identifying the causes supported by the fund.

¶ **614.** *Depository*—The council shall be responsible for designating a depository or depositories for conference funds.

¶ **615.** *Auditing*—The council shall have the following authority and responsibility with respect to the auditing of the financial records of the conference and its agencies:

1. To have the accounts of the conference treasurer for the preceding fiscal year audited by a certified public accountant within 120 days after the close of the conference fiscal year and to receive, review, and report such audit to the annual conference.[60]

As a part of the audit, the accountant shall confer with the presiding bishop of the annual conference and the president of the council.

2. To require and review at least annually audited reports, in such detail as it may direct, from all conference agencies and from all agencies, institutions, and organizations receiving any financial support from conference funds or from any authorized conference-wide appeal.

3. To require and review at least annually, in such detail as it may direct, compiled or audited reports of all funds received or administered by districts or district agencies, including funds held or administered by treasurers or officers other than the conference treasurer. Based on its review of such audits, the council may make such recommendations to the annual conference as it deems appropriate.

4. The council may establish an audit review committee to review all of the reports and audits required by ¶ 615.1, .2. If the council chooses to establish such a committee, at least half of its members should be persons who are not members of the council and who are chosen for their expertise in areas related to the work of the committee. Consideration shall be given to inclusiveness (¶¶ 124, 138) in the selection of persons to serve on the committee.

¶ **616.** *Bonding*—The council shall have the following authority and responsibility with respect to the bonding of conference and conference agency officers and staff whose responsibilities include the custody or handling of conference funds or other negotiable assets:

---

60. *See* Judicial Council Decision 334.

1. The council shall provide for the fidelity bonding of the conference treasurer and other staff under its authority and supervision in amounts it judges to be adequate.

2. In the case of those agencies, institutions, and organizations for which the conference treasurer does not serve as treasurer, the council shall have authority to require fidelity bonding of their treasurers in such amounts as it deems adequate and to withhold payment of the allocation of any such agency, institution, or organization until evidence of the required bonding has been submitted.

3. The council may provide, or require any conference agency to provide, directors' and officers' liability insurance in amounts it judges to be adequate.

4. The council shall require compliance with the policies established as provided by this paragraph and shall report annually to the annual conference on such compliance.

¶ 617. *Conference Treasurer/Director of Administrative Services*—Each annual conference, on nomination of its council on finance and administration, shall at the first session of the conference after the quadrennial session of the General Conference or jurisdictional conference, or at such other times as a vacancy exists, elect a **conference treasurer or conference treasurer/director of administrative services.**[61] The treasurer or treasurer/director shall serve for the quadrennium or until a successor shall be elected and qualify. If a vacancy should occur during the quadrennium, the council shall fill the vacancy until the next session of the annual conference. After consultation with the bishop in charge, the council may remove the treasurer or treasurer/director from office for cause and fill the vacancy until the next session of the conference. The treasurer/director shall be directly amenable to the council. The treasurer/director may sit with the council and its committees at all sessions and have the privilege of voice but not vote.

1. As conference treasurer, this officer shall have the following functions:

*a)* The conference treasurer shall receive and disburse, in accordance with the actions of the annual conference and the provisions of the *Book of Discipline*, remittances from local church treasurers for all duly authorized general, jurisdictional, annual conference, and district causes.[62]

---

61. *See* Judicial Council Decision 185.
62. *See* Judicial Council Decisions 456, 591.

(1) Local church treasurers shall remit monthly to the conference treasurer all amounts contributed in each local church for: *(a)* the World Service Fund and the Conference Benevolences fund, whether apportioned separately or as one combined fund; *(b)* all other funds authorized by the General Conference and apportioned to the annual conferences by the General Council on Finance and Administration; *(c)* all other jurisdictional, annual conference, and district funds or causes apportioned in accordance with ¶ 613, unless otherwise directed by the annual conference; *(d)* special Sunday offerings (¶ 262); *(e)* special appeals (¶¶ 612.5, 811.4); *(f)* Advance Special Gifts (¶ 814); *(g)* World Service Special Gifts (¶ 813); *(h)* Youth Service Fund (¶ 1209); and *(i)* all other general, jurisdictional, annual conference, and district funds not otherwise directed.

(2) *The World Service Fund and the Conference Benevolences Fund*—*(a)* If apportioned as one combined fund, the treasurer shall each month divide the total amount received from local churches for World Service and Conference Benevolences, setting aside the proper amount for World Service and the proper amount for conference benevolences, according to the ratio of each established by the annual conference in the total World Service and Conference Benevolences budget (¶ 612.3c).

*(b)* Whether apportioned separately or as one combined fund, the treasurer shall, from the share received for conference benevolences, credit monthly the accounts of the several agencies or causes included in the conference benevolences budget or make monthly remittances to the treasurers of such agencies or causes according to the rightful share and proportion of each (¶ 612.3a) or according to a payment schedule approved by the conference council on finance and administration, which shall provide that the total allocated to each agency or cause during the year shall be equal to the rightful share and proportion of each.

*(c)* Whether apportioned separately or as one combined fund, the treasurer shall remit each month to the treasurer of the General Council on Finance and Administration the total share received during the month for World Service. When the share so designated for World Service during a year exceeds the amount apportioned to the annual conference, the entire share contributed for World Service shall be remitted in regular order to the treasurer of the General Council on Finance and Administration before the end of the fiscal year.[63]

---

63. *See* Judicial Council Decisions 306, 332, 400, 521.

(*d*) If an annual conference establishes an apportioned fund which combines two or more general funds with one another, or which combines one or more general church funds with funds other than general church funds, the conference treasurer shall allocate to the general church funds amounts at least equal to the percentage of receipts set under ¶612.3–.5. Amounts so allocated shall be remitted at least monthly to the treasurer of the General Council on Finance and Administration.

(3) The treasurer shall, as far as practicable, remit monthly to the several district superintendents the amount due each of them (¶ 611.1*a*).

(4) The treasurer shall likewise credit or remit each month all funds received and payable for other jurisdictional, annual conference, and district causes in accordance with budgets adopted by the annual conference.

(5) The conference treasurer shall remit each month to the treasurer of the General Council on Finance and Administration the amounts received during the month for the General Administration Fund, the Episcopal Fund, the Interdenominational Cooperation Fund, the Black College Fund, the Ministerial Education Fund, World Service Special Gifts, Advance Special Gifts, general Church special Sunday offerings (¶ 262), special churchwide appeals (¶ 811.4), and all other general causes not otherwise directed.

*b)* The conference treasurer may serve as treasurer for any or all agencies served by a conference central treasury (¶ 611.11). The treasurer shall enter the proper credits to each at the end of each month's business. Disbursements from funds allocated to any conference agency shall be made only on proper order from the agency.[64]

*c)* The treasurer shall prepare at regular intervals such financial statements and reports as may be required for the bishop in charge, the district superintendents, the annual conference, the council, the agencies served by the conference central treasury and its officers, and the treasurer of the General Council on Finance and Administration.

(1) The treasurer shall make each month a full report of all general funds handled to the treasurer of the General Council on Finance and Administration and to the presiding bishop of the conference.

---

64. *See* Judicial Council Decisions 400, 521, 539.

(2) The treasurer shall prepare annually a report of all receipts, disbursements, and balances of all funds under his or her direction, which report shall be printed in the conference journal.

d) The treasurer may be authorized by the council to invest funds in accordance with policies and procedures established by the council (¶ 611.5). A listing of securities held shall be printed annually in the conference journal.

e) The treasurer shall provide counsel and guidance to local church business administrators, treasurers, financial secretaries, and committees on finance in the development of standardized financial recording and reporting systems (¶ 611.13).

f) The treasurer shall perform such other staff services as the council may require in the fulfillment of its functions and responsibilities.

2. As **director of administrative services,** this officer may have responsibility in one or more of the following areas: office management; payroll and personnel services; the provision of administrative services for annual conference officers and agencies; property management with respect to property owned by the annual conference or any of its agencies; and such other responsibilities of an administrative nature as the council, by mutual agreement with other annual conference officers and agencies, may assign. The director shall be present when the cabinet considers matters relating to conference administration related to the conference treasurer's or conference treasurer/director of administrative services' responsibilities, and other matters as the cabinet and director may determine. The director shall not be present during the cabinet discussions on matters related to the making of appointments.

3. The council shall have authority and supervision over the director and shall, after consultation with those annual conference officers and agencies for whom the director might be expected to perform services, define his or her specific responsibilities and do regular evaluation.

PASTORAL SUPPORT

¶ **618.** Assumption of the obligations of the itineracy, required to be made at the time of admission into the traveling connection, puts upon the Church the counter obligation of providing support for the itinerant ministry of the Church. In view of this, the claim for pastoral support in each pastoral charge shall include provisions for the support of pastors, district superintendents, bishops, and conference claimants.[65]

¶ 619. *Apportionment Distribution*—Each annual conference shall determine what plan and method shall be used in distributing the apportionments to its several districts and charges for the Episcopal Fund (¶ 821), for the support of district superintendents and conference claimants, and for the Equitable Compensation Fund (¶ 623).[66]

¶ 620. When the apportionments for bishops, district superintendents, conference claimants, and the Equitable Compensation Fund for the several districts and charges have been determined, payments made to the same in each pastoral charge shall be exactly proportional to the amount paid on the clergy base compensation (¶ 823). The treasurer or treasurers of each pastoral charge shall accordingly make proportional distribution of the funds raised in that charge for the support of the ordained ministry and shall remit monthly if practicable and quarterly at the latest the items for bishops, district superintendents, conference claimants, and the Equitable Compensation Fund to the proper treasurer or treasurers.[67]

¶ 621. *Base Compensation*—The several charge conferences shall determine the pastors' base compensation according to the provisions of ¶ 246.12.

¶ 622. *Payment Obligation*—Each church or charge has an obligation to pay the full compensation, as approved by the charge conference, to its pastor(s). If it becomes apparent that a church or charge will be unable to so provide the compensation approved by the charge conference, the church or charge shall immediately notify the district superintendent and may request consideration for a short-term emergency subsidy grant from the Equitable Compensation Fund (¶ 623.7).

¶ 623. *Equitable Compensation*—1. There shall be in each annual conference a **commission on equitable compensation** or other structure to provide for these functions and maintain the connectional relationships. It shall be composed of an equal number of lay and clergypersons, including at least one layperson and one clergyperson from churches of fewer than two hundred members, who are nomi-

---

65. *See* Judicial Council Decisions 306, 455, 551, 579.
66. *See* Judicial Council Decisions 208, 455.
67. *See* Judicial Council Decisions 320, 401.

nated by the conference nominating committee and elected by and amenable to the annual conference. It is recommended that in selection of commission members, consideration shall be given to inclusiveness. In addition, one district superintendent named by the cabinet shall be a member.

2. It is the purpose of the commission on equitable compensation to support full-time clergy serving as pastors in the charges of the annual conference by: *(a)* recommending conference standards for pastoral support; *(b)* administering funds to be used in base compensation supplementation; and *(c)* providing counsel and advisory material on pastoral support to district superintendents and committees on pastor-parish relations. Once the base compensation supplementation has been paid by the annual conference, the annual conference shall have no further obligation or responsibility to the pastor, the charge or anyone else regarding the pastor's compensation.

3. The commission shall carefully study the needs for additional support within the conference and the sources of income and shall recommend annually to the conference for its action a schedule of minimum base compensation for all full-time pastors or those clergy members of the annual conference appointed less than full-time to a local church, subject to such rules and regulations as the conference may adopt (¶ 329.1, .2).[68]

4. In some instances, for missional reasons, consideration may be given by the conference commission on equitable compensation to make funds available for the deacon in full connection when the primary appointment is to a local church.

5. Consistent with the provisions of this paragraph, the primary responsibility for the payment of pastoral base compensation remains with individual pastoral charges.[69]

6. On recommendation of the commission on equitable compensation, the annual conference may authorize the utilization of the Equitable Compensation Fund to provide for supplementing base compensation beyond the minimum base compensation schedule. Special attention shall be given to ethnic pastors serving ethnic ministries, with particular attention given to Native American pastors serving Native American ministries. In all cases (ethnic or nonethnic),

---

68. *See* Judicial Council Decisions 383, 579, 741.
69. *See* Judicial Council Decision 461.

emphasis shall be given to funding entry-level appointments in a teaching parish in a station church, circuit, or cooperative parish and/or equivalent, or to a cooperative parish.

7. In consultation with the commission on equitable compensation, the council on finance and administration shall recommend to the conference its estimate of the amount required to support the schedule of minimum base compensation and base compensation supplements for the pastors, as adopted by the conference. The conference council on finance and administration shall apportion the amount approved by the conference as an item of clergy support to the districts or the charges as the conference may direct (¶ 612.1e).[70]

8. The **Equitable Compensation Fund,** secured as described above in ¶¶ 612.1e and 623.7, shall be disbursed under the direction of the commission on equitable compensation.

9. The Equitable Compensation Fund, secured as described in 7, shall be used to provide each pastor who receives less than the minimum base compensation with an additional amount sufficient to make the base compensation approved by the pastoral charge plus the supplemental aid or income from other sources equal to the minimum base compensation approved by the conference. An annual conference may set a maximum amount to be used in attaining such minimum base compensation in any given case, and it may set its own policy regarding the number of years for which a pastoral charge is eligible to receive equitable base compensation funds, *provided* that no member in good standing who is appointed to a pastoral charge is denied the minimum base compensation (¶ 333).[71]

10. The commission shall assemble and distribute to the charges and the district superintendents advisory material for use in the process of negotiating the total of each pastoral support package, the schedule of minimum base compensation, and other information relevant to the establishment of more equitable base compensation by all the charges of the conference.

11. The guidelines of the annual conference program of equitable clergy support shall, insofar as possible, be observed by the bishops and district superintendents in arranging charges and making appointments. Each full-time pastor or those clergy members of the annual conference appointed less than full-time under episcopal

---

70. *See* Judicial Council Decisions 90, 179.
71. *See* Judicial Council Decisions 456, 492, 579, 587.

appointment to a local church are eligible for participation in the annual conference program of equitable base compensation (¶ 333.1, .2).

12. The commission may suggest to the annual conference for its consideration equitable base compensation ranges for the pastors and/or charges, and the annual conference may suggest such equitable base compensation ranges to the charges for their consideration.

¶ 624. *Sustentation Fund*—An annual conference may establish a **Sustentation Fund** for the purpose of providing emergency aid to the clergy of the conference who may be in special need. On recommendation of the conference council on finance and administration, the amount needed for this purpose may be apportioned to the pastoral charges as the conference may determine. The fund, if established, shall be administered jointly by the bishop, the appropriate district superintendent, and the chairperson of the commission on equitable compensation or the chairperson of such other agency as the annual conference may determine.

¶ 625. *Pastors' Expenses and Allowances*—Local churches shall report to the annual conference, in the manner indicated on the annual conference report form, expenditures for the following purposes: (1) amounts reimbursed to pastors for expenses incurred by them in the fulfillment of their professional responsibilities; (2) amounts paid to or for pastors as allowances (including housing allowance) in addition to base compensation. Local churches are encouraged to consider guidelines provided by the annual conference and/or the General Council on Finance and Administration in setting and reporting the amounts of such allowances and reimbursements.

¶ 626. *Compensation for Extension Ministries*—Every clergy member of an annual conference appointed to extension ministry shall furnish annually to the conference secretary at such time as the secretary shall direct a statement of his or her total compensation (including base compensation, travel, automobile, housing, and other expenses allowed and paid) for the year then ending, and said compensation of all clergy appointed to extension ministry shall be published in the journal of the annual conference.[72] When this information is not furnished, the appointment of the clergyperson shall be subject to review by the resident bishop and the cabinet.

---

72. *See* Judicial Council Decisions 345, 465.

OTHER CONFERENCE AGENCIES

¶ **627.** *Conference Board of Church and Society*—1. The annual conference shall organize a **board of church and society** or other structure to provide for the functions of this ministry and maintain the connectional relationship between the General Board of Church and Society and the conference, district, and local church, as well as for church and society responsibilities related to the objectives and scope of work of the General Board of Church and Society as set forth in ¶¶ 1002–1004.

2. The conference board of church and society or equivalent structure shall be composed of those persons as determined by the annual conference, including, by virtue of their offices, the mission coordinator for Mission Social Action of the conference United Methodist Women and members of the General Board of Church and Society from the annual conference who shall serve within limits set by ¶¶ 608.6 and 710.5. The conference board of church and society or equivalent structure shall also name a conference Peace with Justice Coordinator who will be responsible for administering the conference Peace with Justice Special Sunday Offering receipts and for coordinating peace and justice ministries. Guidelines for inclusiveness in the membership shall be followed (¶ 608.5).

3. The conference board, in cooperation with the General Board of Church and Society and the annual conference council on ministries, shall develop and promote programs on church and society within the bounds of the conference that include prison ministry and reform concerns. To this end, it may divide its membership into committees of approximately equal size patterned after the organization of the General Board of Church and Society. Committees of the board shall have responsibility to cooperate with one another to advance the respective and mutual concerns of their respective areas in social education, service, witness, and action.

4. The conference board of church and society shall serve to connect the General Board of Church and Society and the district and local churches in relating the gospel of Jesus Christ to the members of the Church and to the persons and structures of the communities, nation, and world in which they live. Program shall be developed that provides education and action on issues confronting the Church consistent with the Social Principles and the policies adopted by the General Conference.

5. The board shall estimate annually the amount necessary for support of its work and shall report this amount according to the procedure of the annual conference. The work of the board may be considered a benevolence interest of the Church within the conference.

6. The annual conference may employ a person or persons to further its purposes. Two or more annual conferences may cooperate in developing their programs and in employing one or more persons.

¶ 628. *Conference Board of Discipleship*—The annual conference shall organize a **board of discipleship** or other *equivalent* structure to provide for these functions and maintain the connectional relationship between the General Board of Discipleship and the conference, district, and local church, and to provide for discipleship functions related to the objectives and scope of work of the General Board of Discipleship as set forth in ¶¶ 1101, 1102. The person or persons serving as member(s) of the General Board of Discipleship shall be member(s) of the conference board of discipleship and may be granted voting privileges.

1. *General Responsibilities*—*a)* To lead and assist the congregations and districts in the conference in their efforts to communicate and celebrate the redeeming and reconciling love of God as revealed in Jesus Christ to persons of every age, ethnic background, and social condition; to invite persons to commit their lives to Christ and to his church; and to enable persons to live as Christian disciples in the world.

*b)* To foster and promote a holistic approach to the development of Christian disciples. This shall include such ministries as Christian education and other small-group ministries; camping, retreat, and outdoor activities; evangelism; stewardship; worship; lay development; Christian spiritual formation and devotional life; age-level, life-span, and family-life ministries; leadership education; and such other areas of work as the annual conference may determine.

*c)* To foster and promote camping experiences for persons with disabilities, including camps specifically designed for persons with disabilities, and the participation of persons with disabilities, when feasible, in camps sponsored by the district and conference.

*d)* To provide training for clergy and laity in ministries with persons with disabilities, including the areas of the Sunday school, camps and retreats, and faith development.

*e)* To provide guidance and training for related district leaders and agencies and for local church councils, officers, and committees.

*f)* To develop a unified and comprehensive program for leadership training to serve all age groups in the home, church, and community.

*g)* To provide continued training for pastors in effective ministry with children, child and faith development of children, and interpretation of curriculum resources.

*h)* To enable and strengthen the ministry with and to youth at all levels of the Church.

*i)* To determine the necessary directors, coordinators, or designated leaders for discipleship responsibilities at the annual conference level, including the maintenance of linkage with the General Board of Discipleship and related district committees within the annual conference.

2. *Responsibilities in the Area of Christian Education—a)* To develop and promote a conference program of Christian education for the whole life span, to lead, assist, and support congregations and districts in developing systems for educational and small-group ministries that give children, youth, young adults, adults, older adults, and families knowledge of and experience in the Christian faith and the spiritual disciplines as motivation for Christian service in the Church, the community, and the world. This may include guidance and training for district leaders responsible for Christian education and for local church ministry areas and commissions on education, superintendents of the church school, church school division superintendents, church school teachers, and other leaders in the educational ministry of local churches.

*b)* To develop and maintain an organized system for communicating and working with persons responsible for Christian education programs in local churches, districts, jurisdictions, and the General Board of Discipleship.

*c)* To provide training for confirmation leaders and to equip local congregations in confirmation experiences and in the use of approved resources.

*d)* To encourage the observance of the first Sunday of Christian Education Week, or some other day designated by the annual conference, in each local church as Christian Education Sunday for the purpose of emphasizing the importance of Christian education and for receiving an offering for the work of Christian education. (*See* ¶ 265.1.)

*e)* To develop and recommend to the annual conference plans for the acquisition or disposition of conference camps and/or retreat properties in accordance with standards of camping developed by the General Board of Discipleship (¶ 1108.10).

*f)* To promote church school extension by: (1) encouraging the development of new United Methodist church schools; (2) starting new classes; (3) expanding teaching and learning opportunities in the congregation and community.

*g)* To assist local congregations in initiating programs of teacher recruitment, development, training, and retraining in biblical, theological, and ethical thinking as well as in the procedures and methods of Christian education.

*h)* To cooperate in the promotion of knowledge about the support for all schools, colleges, universities, and seminaries related to the conference, the campus Christian movement, and the campus ministry of the conference, region, or area through the establishment and support of such programs as may be approved by the annual conference in harmony with the policies and procedures of the General Board of Higher Education and Ministry.

3. *Responsibilities in the Area of Evangelism—a)* To plan and promote an effective, comprehensive ministry of evangelism for people of all ages.

*b)* To create an understanding of, interest in, and commitment to evangelism throughout the conference.

*c)* To provide for the training of clergy and laypersons in leadership in ministries of evangelism, the distribution of promotional literature, the encouragement and enlistment of local church participation in an ongoing ministry of evangelism, and the support of church revitalization and new church development.

*d)* To give guidance to the groups responsible for the work of evangelism in the districts and to the ministry area of evangelism in the local church.

*e)* To give particular emphasis to the promotion of ministries of evangelism, which may include ministries in jails and prisons with offenders, victims, and their families, in order that all persons living in a community where there is a local United Methodist church, and who are without a church affiliation or who make no profession of faith, will be included within the nurturing and caring responsibility of that local church.

*f)* To recommend annually, in consultation with the board of ordained ministry, to the conference and to the bishop in charge the appointment of certain effective members of the conference as general evangelists, provided that such persons shall meet the standards set for general evangelists by the General Board of Discipleship. This person shall serve as an ex officio member of the conference board of discipleship area of evangelism. In the event that there is more than one general evangelist in said annual conference, at least one shall be selected by the conference committee on nominations.

*g)* To recommend and endorse the ministry of said general evangelist to the pastors and leadership of the annual conference.

4. *Responsibilities in the Area of Worship—a)* To be responsible for the concerns of worship for people of all ages within the annual conference.

*b)* To foster the use of the best resources for worship at conference meetings and in all the churches of the conference, promote the use of *The United Methodist Hymnal* (1989) and *The United Methodist Book of Worship* (1992) in all the churches of the conference. To plan and promote seminars and demonstrations on cooperative planning for worship involving pastors and musicians, forms of worship, and the use of music and other arts, with particular emphasis on congregational singing. This includes cooperating with the resident bishop, who has primary responsibility for planning all worship services at each annual conference.

*c)* To provide exhibits at the conference sessions, cooperate with the General Board of Discipleship, the conference council on ministries, the conference chapter of The Fellowship of United Methodists in Music and Worship Arts, and the Order of St. Luke in promoting seminars and training events in the area of worship, including music and other arts.

*d)* To assist local congregations in discovering and recruiting persons to serve as musicians (instrumentalists, singers, and song leaders) and in developing the skills of those serving in local congregations in cooperation with the General Board of Discipleship. This focus shall include persons who work full-time, part-time, and especially as volunteers in church music.

5. *Responsibilities in the Area of Stewardship—a)* To plan and promote a comprehensive program of stewardship for people of all ages throughout the conference in such areas as stewardship education, proportionate giving and tithing, funding the Church's ministries, planned giving, time and abilities, economics and money management, and lifestyle.

*b)* To interpret the biblical and theological basis for stewardship.

*c)* To promote giving consistent with a Christian lifestyle.

*d)* To develop funding concepts within annual conference, district, and local church consistent with sound stewardship principles and the doctrine of The United Methodist Church.

*e)* To educate the local church that tithing is the minimum goal of giving in The United Methodist Church.

*f)* To design and schedule training events, distribute promotional material, and enlist local church participation in a year-round program of stewardship.

*g)* To give guidance to the ministry area of stewardship in the districts and to the ministry area of stewardship and the committee on finance in the local church.

*h)* To develop a program that will create concern on the part of every local church for the ecological and environmental problems that confront the world and to motivate them to accept responsibility for aiding in the solution of such problems.

*i)* To participate in the work of national and jurisdictional organizations related to stewardship, such as the National Association of Stewardship Leaders and the National Association of United Methodist Foundations.

6. *Responsibilities in the Area of Spiritual Formation—a)* To promote spiritual formation and the development of the devotional life for families and people of all ages, *clergy and laity,* throughout the conference.

*b)* To conduct seminars and training events in the areas of private and corporate prayer.

*c)* To encourage and assist with the distribution and use of resources for spiritual formation as provided by The Upper Room and the General Board of Discipleship.

7. *Responsibilities in the Area of Ministry of the Laity—a)* To develop and promote programs to cultivate an adequate understanding of the theological and biblical basis for ministry of the laity among the members of the churches of the annual conference; to give special emphasis to programs and services that will enable laity of all ages to serve more effectively as leaders in both church and community.

*b)* To provide support and direction for such lay programs as lay speaking, the observance of Laity Day, and the work of lay leaders on the local and district levels.

*c)* To give support and direction to the conference and district program for local church leadership development, coordinating and developing training experiences that will enable persons of all ages to serve more effectively as members of local church councils on ministries, church councils, and the committees, commissions, and task forces related to these groups.

*d)* To organize a conference committee on lay speaking that will fulfill the requirements of ¶¶ 266–268 on behalf of the conference. This committee shall set guidelines and criteria to be used by district committees (*see* ¶ 662).

¶ **629.** *Conference Board of Laity*—1. There shall be in every annual conference a **conference board of laity** or other equivalent structure to provide for these functions and maintain connectional relationship.[73] It shall provide for the ministry of the laity related to the objectives of the General Board of Discipleship as set forth in ¶¶ 1101–1125.

2. The purpose of the conference board of laity shall be:

*a)* To foster an awareness of the role of the laity both within the local congregation and through their ministries in the home, workplace, community, and world in achieving the mission of the Church; to develop and promote programs to cultivate an adequate understanding of the theological and biblical basis for lay life and work among the members of the churches of the annual conference.

*b)* To develop and promote stewardship of time, talent, and possessions within the annual conference in cooperation with the conference council on ministries or other appropriate conference bodies.

*c)* To provide for the training of lay members of annual conference.

*d)* To provide support and direction for the ministry of the laity on the local, district, and annual conference levels and to promote the observance of Laity Sunday.

*e)* To provide organization, direction, and support for the development of local church leaders.

3. The following membership of the board is recommended: the conference lay leader, associate conference lay leaders, the conference director of Lay Speaking Ministries, and the presidents and two representatives elected by each of the conference organizations of United Methodist Men, United Methodist Women, United Methodist Young

---

73. *See* Judicial Council Decision 835.

Adults, and the conference council on youth ministries; and in addition, the district lay leaders, two laymen, two laywomen, and two youth elected by the annual conference upon nomination of the conference nominating committee, a district superintendent designated by the cabinet, the director of the conference council on ministries, and the presiding bishop. Special attention shall be given to the inclusion of people with disabilities and racial and ethnic persons.

4. The conference lay leader shall chair the board. Other officers shall be elected as the board shall deem necessary.

5. The board shall relate to Lay Speaking Ministries and other organized lay groups in the conference, such as United Methodist Men, United Methodist Women, United Methodist Young Adults, and United Methodist Youth and shall support their work and help them coordinate the activities of the organized laity of the conference.

6. *Conference Committee on Lay Speaking Ministries*—*a)* Every annual conference is encouraged to create a conference **committee on Lay Speaking Ministries** or other equivalent structure to fulfill the requirements of ¶¶ 266-268 and to relate to the conference board of laity and the General Board of Discipleship as per ¶ 1115 and others that might apply.

*b)* The purpose of a conference committee on Lay Speaking Ministries is to set criteria and guidelines for district committees on Lay Speaking Ministries, to develop lay speaking courses and approve courses developed by district committees, and to organize conference-wide lay speaking events.

*c)* A conference committee on Lay Speaking Ministries will consist, at a minimum, of the district directors of Lay Speaking Ministries or their equivalent.

*d)* There will be a **conference director of Lay Speaking Ministries.** This position will be filled in a manner to be determined by the annual conference. The conference director will chair the committee. Other officers will be elected by the committee as the committee deems necessary.

¶ 630. *Conference Board of Global Ministries*—1. The annual conference shall organize a **board of global ministries** or other structure to maintain the connectional relationship and provide for global ministries responsibilities related to the objectives and scope of work of the General Board of Global Ministries as set forth in ¶¶ 1302–1303.

2. The conference board of global ministries or equivalent structure shall be composed of those persons as determined by the annual

conference and shall fulfill those responsibilities as assigned. The
mission coordinator of Christian global concerns of the conference
United Methodist Women, by virtue of office, shall be a member of
the conference board of global ministries.

The chairperson of the conference board of global ministries shall
work with the conference secretary of global ministries to relate the
annual conference board of global ministries to the objectives and
scope of work of the General Board of Global Ministries. A person or
persons serving as member(s) of the General Board of Global Ministries from the annual conference shall, by virtue of their office, be
member(s) of the conference board of global ministries (*see* ¶¶ 608.6
and 710.5).

3. There shall be a **conference secretary of global ministries** who
shall be a member of the annual conference board and may be a
member of the annual conference council on ministries or equivalent
structure.

The conference secretary of global ministries shall work with the
chairperson of the conference board of global ministries to relate the
annual conference board of global ministries to the objectives and
scope of work of the General Board of Global Ministries.

4. *a)* The annual conference and the General Board of Global Ministries shall cooperate in carrying out the policies and promoting all
phases of the work as related to the scope of the board as set forth in
¶ 1302.

*b) Responsibilities*—(1) To designate the necessary committees,
sections, or commissions and individual secretaries, coordinators, or
other leaders for global ministries responsibilities at the annual conference level.

(2) To interpret to the annual conference the programs,
plans, and policies of the General Board of Global Ministries and to
plan and promote emphases on global ministries. To undergird with
education, constructive evaluation, communication, and cultivation
the total program of the General Board of Global Ministries.

(3) To receive reports of the liaison to the annual conference
from the General Board of Global Ministries.

(4) To interpret to the General Board of Global Ministries the
mission program, priorities, and concerns of the annual conference
and the local churches to enable the board to fulfill its responsibilities
as an extension of the local church.

(5) To plan and promote various kinds of meetings and

experiences throughout the conference for the purpose of developing a spirit of mission and participation in global ministries for training, education, and leadership development of mission leaders and persons in the field of human services and health and welfare ministries.

(6) To cooperate with the General Board of Global Ministries in its program outside the United States.

(7) To identify with all who are alienated and dispossessed and to assist them in achieving their full human development—body, mind, and spirit, including encouraging and implementing affirmative action programs.

(8) To engage in direct ministries to human need, both emergency and continuing institutional and noninstitutional, however caused.

(9) To cooperate with the conference organization of United Methodist Women in helping to equip all women for full participation in the mission of the Church.

(10) To cultivate, through the channels of the Church other than United Methodist Women, the Advance Special Gifts for ministries administered by designated units of the General Board of Global Ministries, including United Methodist Committee on Relief (UMCOR).

(11) To encourage, maintain, and strengthen the relationships between the annual conference and agencies related to the appropriate divisions and departments of the General Board of Global Ministries and provide a channel through which these agencies shall report to the annual conference.

(12) To develop and implement Church financial support of conference mission projects and programs, and health and welfare ministries, with particular emphasis on benevolent care and Golden Cross, education and social service ministries, and Crusade Scholarships.

(13) To enable, encourage, and support the development of congregations, cooperative parishes, community centers, education and human services, and health and welfare ministries so that they may be units of mission in urban and rural areas and partners with others in the worldwide mission of the Christian church.

(14) To encourage and support specialized urban and town and country ministries enabling comprehensive mission related to broad metropolitan and rural issues, services ministering to the needs of persons, and supportive programs strengthening the local church.

(15) To assist districts and local churches in exploring and developing new methods and direct service ministries as changing conditions and societal forms demand.

(16) To cooperate with Church and secular leaders at all levels in strategic planning, developing programs, and advocating legislation that impacts community and national issues.

(17) To envision and engage in imaginative new forms of mission appropriate to changing needs and to share the results of experimentation.

(18) To develop strategies in response to critical community issues, with special attention to the needs of ethnic and language groups, people with disabilities, people in transitional relationships, and those living under repressive systems.

(19) To support United Methodist Committee on Relief's refugee ministry by promoting an annual conference refugee committee that relates to the annual conference board of global ministries and encourages, advises, and assists churches with their refugee programs.

(20) To support the United Methodist Committee on Relief's World Hunger/Poverty Ministry by encouraging annual conferences to appoint an annual conference hunger coordinator and form an annual conference hunger committee that relates to the annual conference board of global ministries.

(21) To appoint annual conference disaster response coordinators to assist the United Methodist Committee on Relief by encouraging the formation of an annual conference disaster response committee that relates to the annual conference board of global ministries and includes, when possible, members of the General Board of Global Ministries from the annual conference. The membership of the Disaster Response Committee may include district disaster response coordinators and the conference director of communications or member of the commission on communications. Annual conference and district disaster response coordinators shall receive training at least once a quadrennium.

(22) To assist the program of Church and Community Ministry in setting goals, developing programs, providing funding, and evaluating the ministries.

(23) To cooperate with the General Board of Global Ministries in the recruitment of missionary personnel and to cooperate with the appropriate conference units in the promotion and recruit-

ment of persons for health and welfare service careers and other Church-related occupations.

(24) To review and certify applications to the General Board of Global Ministries for loans, donations, and grants; to administer such funds for their designated purposes in accordance with the established guidelines; and to participate with the General Board of Global Ministries in planning and evaluation processes related to these funds.

(25) To cultivate gifts for those special Sunday offerings that are administered through the General Board of Global Ministries.

(26) To work with health and welfare institutions and programs related to the annual conference to develop a mutual agreement between the annual conference and each institution concerning their relationships. The term *related to* shall mean any relationship defined by the annual conference.

The annual conference and each health and welfare institution shall have a clearly stated document that describes their legal and financial relationships; *provided* that no such document shall impose as a party to it The United Methodist Church and/or the General Board of Global Ministries.

The annual conference may consult with a health and welfare institution when that institution plans to establish a new facility, alter its major purpose or function, or make a plan for expansion of an existing facility. The purpose of such a consultation would be to review the mission of the annual conference in health and welfare ministries and to ensure that the new institution, the new facility, the new purpose, or the expansion be in harmony with the mission of the annual conference and that there not be unnecessary duplication of existing services. The consultation may include a discussion of proposed plans of development, financing, and types of services to be rendered.

(27) To strive to ensure mutual representation between the annual conference unit responsible for health and welfare ministries and each health and welfare institution related to the annual conference where such representation is called for by mutual agreement of the institution and the annual conference.

(28) To encourage the health and welfare institutions and programs within the annual conference related to a connectional unit of The United Methodist Church to utilize the programmatic standards, self-study, and peer review appropriate to Church-related

institutions and programs and available to them through organizations that will promote excellence in Christian ministry and mission and enhance the quality of services offered.

(29) To assist the annual conference in assessing needs in health and welfare ministries. To assist the annual conference in development of health and welfare services in local communities and within the annual conference.

(30) To work with the General Board of Global Ministries in leadership development programs and the promotion of health and welfare ministries, and to work with the United Methodist Association of Health and Welfare Ministries in leadership development programs and the promotion of health and welfare ministries.

(31) To promote Christian, financial, and professional standards in health and welfare ministries within the annual conference.

(32) To aid in planning and developing a religious ministry in annual conference-related institutions and programs and, wherever practical, in state and other institutions and programs not related to the conference where there is a need.

(33) To serve in an advisory capacity to the conference nominating processes where the annual conference participates in the selection of trustees for health and welfare institutions and programs related to the annual conference.

(34) To provide a channel through which health and welfare programs and institutions report to the annual conference.

(35) To promote an annual Golden Cross offering or other means of giving to be received in every local church on a day or days designated by the annual conference in support of the health and welfare ministries within the annual conference. This offering shall provide financial support to care for sick persons, older persons, children and youth, and people with disabilities. Special emphasis shall be given to aiding those ministries that provide direct financial assistance to persons in need. Promotion also should include all units of the General Board of Global Ministries related to health and welfare ministries.

(36) To make available program and other resources to local churches to help ensure physical accessibility of church buildings.

5. The annual conference shall establish a **committee on parish and community development** or assign this responsibility to an existing agency in the annual conference that will fulfill the responsibilities related to the objectives and scope of the General Board of

Global Ministries (¶ 1312). The committee shall initiate and develop programs with institutional and voluntary ministries related to the work of the board. The committee may form subcommittees for these areas. The committee shall be accountable to the conference board of global ministries, or to such other agency as the conference may determine. The chairperson of the committee and the chairpersons of the subcommittees shall be members of the conference board of global ministries or such body to which the committee shall be amenable.

*a)* The committee shall include persons involved in significant types of parish and community ministries, lay and clergy representatives of rural, town, and urban small-membership churches, the area or conference superintendent or director of parish development, representatives of related church agencies and groups, and at-large community representatives.

*b)* The general responsibilities of the committee shall include research, evaluation, planning and strategy development, policy formulation, program implementation, local and national liaison (denominational and ecumenical) related to parish and community development, and such other functions as the conference or agency to which the committee is accountable may determine.

*c)* Responsibilities of the subcommittee on institutional and voluntary ministries related to the General Board of Global Ministries may include developing a relationship to all such institutional and voluntary ministries within the annual conference; consulting with them in cooperative planning and strategy for the implementation of national mission concerns relative to needs in the area of social welfare as implemented through the ministries of community centers, residences, health-care agencies, schools, and other educational agencies; and working with funding sources to provide the support needed for effective service in such agencies.

*d)* In annual conferences where church and community workers are assigned through the General Board of Global Ministries, responsibilities of the subcommittee on church and community ministry shall include reviewing and evaluating projects; serving as liaison between projects and the General Board of Global Ministries; and securing consultative and financial support for workers.

*e)* Responsibilities of the subcommittee on congregational development shall include encouraging and supporting the development of new and established congregations; conducting research studies and community surveys that plan for and assist with developing innovative strategies for mission; and reviewing, evaluating, and making recommendations for loans, donations, and grants from the General Board of Global Ministries. The subcommittee also shall encourage greater use of such pastoral ministry models as tentmaking/bi-vocational ministries, part-time local pastors, and cooperative ministries by advocating for the removal of impediments to their use and emphasizing the pastors' proven ability to produce effective nurture, outreach, and witness ministries as the primary criterion for appointment.

*f)* Responsibilities of the subcommittee on town and country ministries shall include mission development and ministry in rural and town areas with a population of less than 50,000. These shall include small cities of 10,000 to 50,000 and rural areas under 2,500, fulfilling the functions outlined in ¶ 630.5*h.*

*g)* Responsibilities of the subcommittee on urban ministries shall include long-range mission strategy development and ministry for metropolitan communities with a population of more than 50,000, fulfilling the functions outlined in ¶ 630.5*h.*

*h)* Responsibilities of the subcommittees on town and country ministries and urban ministries shall include the following:

(1) consulting with the bishop, cabinet, area or conference superintendent/director of parish development, district representatives of town and country ministries and urban ministries, and the conference agencies in the development of policies for cooperative parish ministries, securing of funding for staff, and in initiating and strengthening these ministries;

(2) developing a comprehensive related missional strategy for the mission of the annual conference, the districts, and the local churches and reporting this plan to the annual conference for consideration, with the understanding that the plan may relate to a regional mission organization for purposes of larger geographical coordination; and

(3) initiating and/or assisting with programs to deal with needs such as:

(*a*) local church and community outreach organization and development;

(*b*) ministries with specialized constituencies and sectors of community life, agricultural and industrial production, and other issue-oriented ministries;

(c) the development and strengthening of regional and/or national networks and/or associations;

(d) ethnic and language groups;

(e) churches in transitional communities;

(f) small membership churches;

(g) the impact of oppressive systems on town and country and urban people and their communities; and

(h) to fulfill other functions as related to the objectives and scope of work of the General Board of Global Ministries as set forth in ¶ 1312.

i) Responsibilities of the subcommittee on the small membership church shall include the following: (1) being informed about needs and opportunities of the small membership church in rural, town, and urban settings in the total life of the conference; (2) calling for representation by small membership churches in the decision-making structures of the annual conference; (3) informing and sensitizing leadership at all levels of the conference on issues that affect small membership churches; (4) enlisting the support of the bishop, cabinet, council on ministries, and conference staff on policies, plans, and practices that affect small membership churches; (5) working with the subcommittees on town and country ministries and urban ministries within the parish and with the community development committee to develop and implement strategies for the nurturing, outreach, and witness ministries of small membership churches.

j) In metropolitan areas with a population of more than 50,000, consideration shall be given to the establishment of a **metropolitan commission** whose purpose shall be to promote long-range planning and to provide a coordinating framework for United Methodism's mission strategy for that metropolitan area. The membership may include the bishop or bishop's representative, the district superintendents involved, a selected group of clergy and laypersons representing the annual conference board of global ministries and the annual conference committee on urban ministry, the conference commission on religion and race, the annual conference United Methodist Women and United Methodist Men, representatives from community-based ministries, representatives from district council(s) on ministries, representatives from other boards and agencies deemed appropriate, and groups and individuals who have skills and experience enabling them to fulfill creative planning and strategy functions for United Methodism in the metropolitan area.

When the metropolitan area includes more than one annual conference, representatives shall be elected from each conference's constituent boards and agencies to the metropolitan commission.

6. There may be a **volunteer-in-mission coordinator** who will coordinate the volunteer-in-mission ministries of the annual conference in cooperation with the General Board of Global Ministries' mission volunteers office and the jurisdictional volunteer-in-mission office.

*a)* The coordinator shall be elected annually and shall be a member of the annual conference board of global ministries.

*b)* The coordinator will be responsible to:

(1) match volunteers with mission opportunities;

(2) be responsive to volunteers' desire to serve;

(3) train and mobilize volunteers for mission volunteer service;

(4) disseminate information on what is happening in the area of short-term volunteer-in-mission programs.

¶ 631. *Conference Board of Higher Education and Campus Ministry—* 1. There shall be in each annual conference a **board of higher education and campus ministry** or other structure to provide for these functions and maintain the connectional relationships. The number of members shall be determined by the annual conference, including representation from appropriate constituencies.

2. The annual conference board of higher education and campus ministry or equivalent structure shall provide for the connectional relationship between the Division of Higher Education of the General Board of Higher Education and Ministry and the conference, district, and local church and shall provide for a ministry in higher education related to the objectives and scope of work of the General Board of Higher Education and Ministry and the Division of Higher Education. A person serving as a member of the General Board of Higher Education and Ministry from that annual conference shall, by virtue of his or her office, be a member of the conference board of higher education and campus ministry or equivalent structure (*see* ¶¶ 608.6 and 710.5).

3. The annual conference chairperson of higher education and campus ministry or equivalent structure shall be a member of the annual conference council on ministries.

4. The responsibilities of an annual conference board of higher education and campus ministry or equivalent structure include:

*a) General Responsibilities*—(1) To interpret and promote the United Methodist ministries in higher education that are supported by the general Church and those specifically related to the annual conference.

(2) To recommend the policies guiding the annual conference in its program of ministry in higher education.

(3) To train and provide resources for district committees and local church ministry areas of higher education and campus ministry.

(4) To apprise United Methodists of their historic commitment to and present mission in higher education.

(5) To work with the annual conference council on ministries and with districts and local churches to interpret and promote higher education ministries supported by special days and funds: Black College Fund; Hispanic, Asian, and Native Americans (HANA) Educational Ministries; United Methodist Student Day; World Communion Sunday; and other funds and special days related to higher education ordered by the General Conference or annual conference.

(6) To promote use of the United Methodist Loan Fund and to designate appropriate persons to represent the United Methodist Loan Fund on campuses, such persons normally being Wesley Foundation directors or ecumenical campus ministers supported by the annual conference; to provide the Office of Loans and Scholarships with the names and addresses of those persons; and to apprise students of alternative ways to apply for loans in the event there is no campus minister.

(7) To evaluate schools, colleges, universities, and campus ministries related to the annual conference, with concern for the quality of their performance, the integrity of their mission, and their response to the missional goals of the general Church and the annual conference.

(8) To promote the education award programs provided by The United Methodist Church, including the United Methodist Higher Education Foundation's award programs.

(9) To confer at once with representatives of the General Board of Higher Education and Ministry to determine what resources and aid the board may be able to provide and to enable the Division of Higher Education to carry out its responsibilities in the event that any educational institution, Wesley Foundation, or other campus ministry moves to sever or modify its connection with the Church or

violates the rules adopted by the division in accordance with
¶ 1413.3.

(10) To provide that two or more annual conferences may, on
recommendation of their boards of higher education and campus
ministry or equivalent structures, join in constituting an area or
regional committee or commission on higher education and campus
ministry, the membership, scope, and functions of which shall be
determined by the cooperating conferences in consultation with their
bishop or bishops. The area committee or commission shall include a
majority of its members from the participating annual conference
boards of higher education and campus ministry or equivalent structure with appropriate representation of college presidents, campus
ministers, students, and ethnic persons.

*b) Fiscal Responsibilities*—In addition to its general responsibilities, the annual conference board of higher education and campus
ministry shall carry out the following fiscal duties:

(1) To present to the council on ministries and then to the
council on finance and administration of the annual conference the
financial needs for adequate support of the schools, colleges, universities, theological schools, campus Christian movements, Wesley
Foundations,[74] and other campus ministries related to the annual
conference for apportionment to the churches within the conference.

(2) To determine the distribution of the funds received from
undesignated gifts, returns from special days, annual conference and
district Advance Specials for higher education and scholarships of
the United Methodist Higher Education Foundation.

(3) To establish, where appropriate, foundations or other
means to ensure the ongoing support of the annual conference program of ministry in higher education.

(4) To counsel United Methodist schools, colleges, universities, and campus ministries related to the annual conference with
regard to their charters and constitutions, reversionary clauses, and
liability.

(5) To counsel United Methodist institutions about property
and endowments entrusted to the institutions and to maintain and
enforce trust and reversionary clauses in accordance with the provisions of the Division of Higher Education under ¶ 1413.3c.

---

74. *See* Judicial Council Decision 191.

(6) To monitor fiduciary and legal relationships with United Methodist schools, colleges, universities, and campus ministries and to assist annual conferences in their responsibilities in these matters.

(7) To administer the scholarship funds rebated to the annual conference by the Office of Loans and Scholarships in accordance with the guidelines of that office.

(8) To encourage the establishment of loan and scholarship funds in the annual conference and local churches and to administer the loan and scholarship funds of the annual conference.

c) *Responsibilities with Schools, Colleges, and Universities*—In addition to its general responsibilities, the annual conference board of higher education and campus ministry or equivalent structure shall carry out the following duties with regard to United Methodist schools, colleges, and universities:

(1) To make known to the district, subdistricts, and all local churches the names and location of all United Methodist educational institutions and, wherever possible, provide resources interpreting their work and special missions.

(2) To assist institutions related specifically to the annual conference in their efforts to raise funds, scholarships, recruit students, and extend services to the annual conference.

(3) To assume responsibility, after consultation with the annual conference committee on nominations and the nominating committee of the institution's board of trustees, for the nomination of those trustees who are to be nominated and elected by the annual conference to the boards of trustees of United Methodist schools, colleges, and universities. In the event that the annual conference confirms or elects trustees nominated by trustee-nominating committees, to consult with those committees, having special concern for the selection of persons who will appropriately address the financial, missional, and educational progress of the institution.

(4) To provide for interpretation of the programs of United Methodist schools, colleges, and universities throughout the educational program of the annual conference, especially in cooperation with those committees and persons responsible for youth and young adult ministries.

(5) To interpret systematically to the districts, subdistricts, and local churches the conference program with United Methodist schools, colleges, and universities, encouraging their support and participation.

(6) To represent the annual conference in its relationship to United Methodist schools, colleges, and universities, especially those related to the annual conference.

*d) Responsibilities with Campus Ministries*—In addition to the general responsibilities listed above, the annual conference board of higher education and campus ministry or equivalent structure shall have the following responsibilities with regard to campus ministry:

(1) To have available the names and addresses of all campus ministries supported by The United Methodist Church and to supply the names and addresses of campus ministries supported by the annual conference to all districts and local churches.

(2) To ensure representation of the annual conference board or equivalent structure on the boards of all campus ministries supported by the annual conference.

(3) To interpret systematically to the districts, subdistricts, and local churches the conference program of campus ministry as a ministry to the whole campus (students, faculty, staff, and administration), encouraging their support and urging United Methodist students of all ages to participate.

(4) To hold the Wesley Foundation board of directors responsible for the direction and administration of the foundation in accordance with the policies and objectives of the annual conference board of higher education and campus ministry or equivalent structure and the standards of the Division of Higher Education of the General Board of Higher Education and Ministry.

(5) To ensure that the Wesley Foundation board is related functionally and cooperatively to the United Methodist local church or churches in the immediate vicinity of the college or university and to the council on ministries or other organization of the district in which it is located.

(6) To determine whether or not Wesley Foundation boards, when incorporated, may hold property and to ensure such property is held and administered according to *The Book of Discipline of The United Methodist Church* and the laws of the state in which the foundation is located.

(7) To determine the policies for nomination and election by the annual conference of Wesley Foundation boards of directors.

(8) To determine, in consultation with local boards, the personnel needs of Wesley Foundations; to establish procedures for selection and termination of professional staff; and to consult with

the bishop and cabinet when securing the appointment of ministerial staff members.

(9) To establish and review covenants and agreements for ecumenical campus ministry and to ensure that they are in harmony with the policies, standards, and goals of the Division of Higher Education and the annual conference board of higher education and campus ministry or equivalent structure.

(10) To oversee the management of the annual conference program of campus ministry in Wesley Foundations, local churches, and ecumenical campus ministries; to determine where new campus ministries are needed, and to plan for their establishment and financial support.

(11) To provide resources for local churches and districts with programs of ministry with students or to campuses and, where those programs receive financial support from or are designated as ministries on behalf of the annual conference, to ensure that the policies, standards, and goals of the conference board of higher education and campus ministry or equivalent structure are observed.

(12) To establish the procedures for the nomination and election of United Methodist college students as lay members to annual conference.

*e) Public Policy*—In addition to its general responsibilities, the annual conference board of higher education and campus ministry shall have the following duties with regard to public policy and relationships to the state:

(1) To provide counsel, guidance, and assistance to United Methodist schools, colleges, universities, and campus ministries within the annual conference regarding their relationships to the state.

(2) To interact with public higher education as it reflects on the wholeness of persons and the meaning of life.

(3) To identify and work with the annual conference, church-related colleges, and campus ministries on issues of public policy that bear on higher education, such as issues bearing on access, equity, academic freedom, peace, and justice.

¶ 632. *Conference Board of Ordained Ministry*—1. Each annual conference at the first session following the General Conference, shall elect for a term of four years a **board of ordained ministry**.[75] At least

---

75. *See* Judicial Council Decision 887.

six ordained elders and deacons in full connection and, when possible, at least two associate members or local pastors who have completed the course of study shall be included as members of the board with voice but no vote. Each annual conference shall elect at least one-fifth laypersons, which may include diaconal ministers, and may at its discretion elect further lay members, up to one-third of the membership of the board. The board membership shall include women and ethnic persons, at least one ordained clergyperson in the retired relationship, at least one ordained clergyperson in extension ministry, and a district superintendent named by the bishop to represent the cabinet. Two-thirds of the members who are elders shall be graduates of seminaries listed by the University Senate.

*a)* Members shall be nominated by the presiding bishop after consultation with the chairperson of the board, the executive committee, or a committee elected by the board of the previous quadrennium, and with the cabinet. To ensure adequate board membership, consultation shall include an evaluation of the workload of the board in meeting disciplinary and annual conference responsibilities. Vacancies shall be filled by the bishop after consultation with the chairperson of the board. An elected board member may serve a maximum of three consecutive four-year terms. The chairpersons of the Orders of Deacons and of Elders shall be members of the board of ordained ministry (§ 1c) and its executive committee.

*b)* This board shall be directly amenable to the annual conference, notwithstanding its organizational relationship within any other program or administrative unit of the annual conference. The annual conference council on finance and administration shall recommend adequate administrative funds for the board and its staff in light of its workload.

*c)* The board shall organize by electing from its membership a chairperson, registrars, and such other officers as it may deem necessary. The board shall designate its executive committee, which shall include elders, deacons, and laity. The board shall organize in such manner as to care for its responsibilities, including the needs of certified persons, diaconal ministers, local pastors, deacons, and elders. The organization of the board shall include a committee to fulfill the governance responsibilities for diaconal ministers and those in process of becoming diaconal ministers (*see The Book of Discipline,* 1992, ¶¶ 301–317 and 734) and shall provide for certification in specialized ministry careers under the guidelines of the General Board of Higher Education and Ministry (*see* ¶ 1421). The board may include in its organization a division of deacons and a division of elders.

*d)* To ensure maximum contact with and support of persons in appointments beyond the local church, the board shall maintain relationships with all general agencies that have responsibility for persons in such appointments.

*e)* The board shall meet at least once prior to its meeting at the time of the annual conference session and may set a deadline prior to annual conference for transacting its business.

*f)* The board shall select from its own membership an official representative to serve as a member of each district committee on ordained ministry, which shall function as subcommittees of the board.

*g)* The board shall provide orientation for new members, including distribution of any available written guidelines.

2. The duties of the annual conference board of ordained ministry shall be:

*a)* To assume the primary responsibility for the enlistment and recruitment of ordained clergy by working in consultation with the cabinet and the General Board of Higher Education and Ministry to study and interpret the clergy needs and resources of the annual conference, with due regard to the inclusive nature of the Church. It shall, with the assistance of the local church committee on pastor-parish relations, conference agencies, and every ordained minister of the conference, enlist women and men of all races and ethnic origins for the ordained ministry and guide those persons in the process of education, training, and ordination, recommending colleges and schools of theology listed by the University Senate. Persons recruited should have an understanding of and appreciation for persons of different racial and ethnic heritages.

*b)* To seek from a school of theology information about the personal and professional qualities of an applicant for probationary membership or of a probationary member; *provided,* however, that the applicant or member consent to the provision of such information.

*c)* To receive annual reports on the progress made by each ministerial student enrolled in a theological school and to record credit for work satisfactorily completed.

*d)* It shall require a transcript of credits from each applicant before recognizing any of the applicant's educational claims. In case of doubt, the board may submit a transcript to the General Board of Higher Education and Ministry for evaluation.

*e)* The board shall annually appoint and train a sufficient number of mentors in each district in consultation with the district superintendent.

*f)* To guide the candidate for ordained ministry who is not enrolled in a theological school and who is pursuing the Course of Study as adopted by the General Board of Higher Education and Ministry.

*g)* To examine all applicants as to their fitness for the ordained ministry and make full inquiry as to the fitness of the candidate for: (1) annual election as local pastor; (2) election to probationary membership; and (3) election to full conference membership.

*h)* To provide all candidates for ordained ministry a written statement on the disciplinary and annual conference requirements for the local pastor, probationary, and full membership.

*i)* To interview and report recommendation concerning: (1) student local pastors; (2) certified candidates for ordination as deacons; and (3) certified candidates for ordination as elders.[76]

*j)* To assign a board member to serve as liaison to retired clergy in the conference.

*k)* To interview applicants and make recommendation concerning: (1) changes from the effective relation to a leave of absence or retirement; (2) return to the effective relation from other relations; (3) honorable location; (4) readmission of located persons and persons discontinued from probationary membership; (5) sabbatical leave; (6) incapacity leave; (7) appointment as a student; (8) termination; and (9) changes to or from less than full-time ministry.

The board shall keep a record of these changes and the reason behind them and place a copy in the permanent records of the annual conference maintained by the secretary of the conference.

*l)* To ensure confidentiality in relation to the interview and reporting process. The personal data and private information provided through the examinations of and by the board of ordained ministry will not be available for distribution and publication. There are occasions when the board of ordained ministry would not report privileged information, which in the judgment of the board, if revealed in the executive session of clergy members in full connection with the annual conference, would be an undue invasion of privacy without adding measurably to the conference's information about the

---

76. *See* Judicial Council Decision 405.

person's qualifications for ordained ministry. However, it is the right of the executive session of the clergy members in full connection with an annual conference to receive all pertinent information, confidential or otherwise, related to the qualifications and/or character of any candidate or clergy member of the conference.[77]

*m)* To be in consultation with the bishop through the chairperson or the executive committee regarding transfers. This consultation is to be at the bishop's initiative and, where possible, to take place prior to transfers into the annual conference.

*n)* To provide support services for the ordained minister's career development, including personal and career counseling, continuing education, formation in servant leadership and continuing spiritual growth in Christ, assistance in preparation for retirement, and all matters pertaining to clergy morale. In providing such support, the board, in cooperation with the cabinet, shall give training and guidance to each local committee on pastor-parish relations regarding its work and role.

*o)* To work with and support the Order of Deacon and the Order of Elder, including receiving reports, offering financial support, and coordinating the Order's activity with the continuing formation offerings of the board. The board may delegate continuing formation responsibility to the Orders by mutual agreement, with final approval, evaluation, and budgeting remaining with the board.

*p)* To work with and support the ordering of local pastors, including receiving reports, offering financial support, and coordinating their continuing formation.

*q)* To provide a means of evaluating the effectiveness of ordained ministers in the annual conference (¶¶ 604.4, 348). Suggested guidelines will be provided by the General Board of Higher Education and Ministry, Division of Ordained Ministry. In cooperation with the cabinet, the board shall develop standards of effectiveness for clergy serving as pastors of congregations in that annual conference.

*r)* To interpret the high ethical standards of ordained ministry set forth in the *Discipline* and to study matters pertaining to character (¶ 605.6).

*s)* To recommend to the full members of the annual conference for validation special ministries for which members seek appointment.

---

77. *See* Judicial Council Decisions 406, 751.

The appointment to such ministries is the prerogative of the bishop and the cabinet.

*t)* To care for the administration of professional certification established by the General Board of Higher Education and Ministry through (1) enlisting and recruiting clergy and laity to become certified in Christian education, music, youth, evangelism, and other areas established by the General Board of Higher Education and Ministry; (2) determining whether applicants meet the standards established by the General Board of Higher Education and Ministry; (3) to recommend to the annual conference board and the General Board of Higher Education and Ministry; (4) to renew or discontinue professional certification biannually based on a review of their ministry; and (5) to report annually to the annual conference for publication in the conference journal a roster of all persons certified in professional careers for which they have received certification, including places of service address.

*u)* To administer the portion of the Ministerial Education Fund for use by the annual conference in its programs of enlistment, basic professional educational aid, continuing formation, ethnic ministry and language training, and professional growth of ordained ministers. Priority shall be given to scholarships for seminary students preparing for ordination.

*v)* To cooperate with the General Board of Higher Education and Ministry and assist in: (1) the interpretation of current legislation concerning ordained ministry; (2) the interpretation and promotion of the Ministerial Education Fund; (3) the promotion and observance of Ministry Sunday; and (4) the supplying of a record of all information, recommendations, and action on each candidate for ordained ministry after each session of the annual conference; (5) the promotion and addition of standards required for certification in specialized ministry careers.

*w)* To promote in the annual conference and/or jurisdictional conference a system of financial aid to ministerial students. A conference transferring a person with less than three years of active service into another conference may require reimbursement either from the person or from the receiving conference for outstanding obligations for theological education financed through conference funds.

3. The board shall elect a **registrar** and such associate registrars as it may determine; one such associate registrar to be given responsibility for candidacy, including giving leadership to the training and

guidance of mentors in each district. A staff executive may be named by the board to fulfill the functions of registrar.

*a)* The registrar shall keep full personnel records for all candidates for ordained ministry under the care of the board, including essential biographical data, transcripts of academic credit, instruments of evaluation, and, where it applies, psychological and medical test records, sermons, theological statements, and other pertinent data.

*b)* Pertinent information and recommendations concerning each candidate shall be certified to the annual conference in duplicate; one copy of this record shall be kept by the registrar and one copy shall be mailed after each conference session to the General Board of Higher Education and Ministry. The registrar shall forward an acknowledgment of transfer to the pastor of the local church where each newly elected probationary and associate member held membership.

*c)* The registrar shall keep a record of the standing of the students in the Course of Study and report to the conference when required. This record shall include the credits allowed students for work done in accredited schools of theology, in approved Course of Study schools, or Course of Study correspondence.

*d)* The registrar shall file in the bishop's office for permanent record a copy of circumstances involving the discontinuance of probationary membership or termination of the local pastor status.

*e)* The records and files of the board of ordained ministry are kept on behalf of the annual conference and shall be maintained under guidelines provided by the General Council on Finance and Administration in consultation with the General Board of Higher Education and Ministry and the General Board of Pensions.

4. Administrative costs of the board of ordained ministry shall be a claim on the conference operating budget. The board of ordained ministry shall have direct access to the conference council on finance and administration in support of its program.

¶ **633.** *Conference Administrative Review Committee*—There will be an **administrative review committee** composed of three clergy in full connection and two alternates who are not members of the cabinet or the board of ordained ministry. The committee shall be nominated by the bishop and elected quadrennially by the clergy session of members in full connection with the annual conference. Its only purpose shall be to ensure that the disciplinary procedures for involuntary leave of absence (¶ 352.1*b*), involuntary retirement (¶ 356.3), or administrative location (¶ 359.3*c*) are properly followed. The entire administrative process leading to the action for change in conference relationship shall be reviewed by the administrative review committee, and it shall report its findings to the clergy session of members in full connection with the annual conference prior to any action of the annual conference. The administrative fair process hearing procedures (¶ 359.2) should be followed by the administrative review committee. Prior to its report, if the committee determines that any error has occurred, it may recommend to the appropriate person or body that action be taken promptly to remedy the error, decide the error is harmless, or take other action.

¶ **634.** *Conference Committee on Episcopacy*—1. There shall be a **conference committee on episcopacy** elected quadrennially by the annual conference at the session following the General Conference. The committee's membership shall number at least seven, but no more than seventeen. One-fifth of the committee's membership shall be appointed by the bishop. In addition to the lay and clergy members of the jurisdictional committee on episcopacy, who shall be ex officio members with vote, it is recommended that the committee consist of the following: one-third laywomen, one-third laymen, and one-third clergypersons, *provided* that one layperson shall be the conference lay leader. Special attention shall be given to the inclusion of racial and ethnic persons, youth (¶ 255.2), young adults, older adults, and people with disabilities. No member of the staff of the annual conference or any of its agencies, nor an immediate family member of such staff, shall serve as a member of the committee, except that a member of the jurisdictional committee on episcopacy or the conference lay leader shall not be disqualified from membership as a result of this provision.[78]

Two or more conferences under the presidency of a single bishop may decide to have one committee on episcopacy, in which case each annual conference shall be represented as stated in the preceding paragraph and shall each elect its own representatives.

2. The committee shall meet at least annually. It shall be convened by the bishop and shall elect a chairperson, a vice chairperson, and a secretary. The bishop and/or chairperson are authorized to call additional meetings when desired.

---

78. *See* Judicial Council Decisions 711, 778.

3. The functions of the conference committee on episcopacy shall be:

*a)* To support the bishop of the area in the oversight of the spiritual and temporal affairs of the Church, with special reference to the area where the bishop has presidential responsibility.

*b)* To be available to the bishop for counsel.

*c)* To assist in the determination of the episcopal needs of the area and to make recommendations to appropriate bodies.

*d)* To keep the bishop advised concerning conditions within the area as they affect relationships between the bishop and the people of the conference agencies.

*e)* To interpret to the people of the area and to conference agencies the nature and function of the episcopal office.

*f)* To engage in annual consultation and appraisal of the balance of the bishop's relationship and responsibilities to the area and annual conferences, the jurisdiction, general Church boards and agencies, and other areas of specialized ministry, including, at all levels, concern for the inclusiveness of the Church and its ministry with respect to sex, race, and national origin, and understanding and implementation of the consultation process in appointment-making.

*g)* To report needs for episcopal leadership to the jurisdictional committee on episcopacy through the duly elected conference members of that committee.

4. The conference council on finance and administration shall make provision in its budget for the expenses of this committee.

¶ **635.** *Episcopal Residence Committee*—1. The provision of housing for effective bishops in the jurisdictional conferences shall be the responsibility of the annual conference or conferences comprising the episcopal area to which the bishop is assigned.

2. In each episcopal area in the jurisdictional conferences there shall be an **episcopal residence committee** or other structure to provide for this function and maintain the connectional relationship. The committee shall be composed of the following persons:

*a)* The chairperson or designate of the conference committee on episcopacy from each conference.

*b)* The president or designate of the conference council on finance and administration from each annual conference.

*c)* The president or designate of the conference board of trustees from each annual conference.

*d)* Consultants without vote, with specific expertise related to the tasks of the committee, may be utilized.

3. The chairperson of the episcopal residence committee shall be the representative of the committee on episcopacy of the annual conference in which the episcopal residence is currently located.

4. It shall be the responsibility of the episcopal residence committee:

*a)* To make recommendations to the annual conference(s) regarding the purchase, sale, or rental of an episcopal residence.

*b)* To prepare an annual budget covering the cost of providing the episcopal residence, which may also include utilities, insurance, and normal costs of upkeep in maintaining the residence.

*c)* To forward the proposed budget annually to the General Council on Finance and Administration for its action as to that portion of the episcopal residence expense that shall be paid from the Episcopal Fund (*see* ¶ 825).

*d)* To forward the proposed budget annually and recommend to each conference council on finance and administration the proportionate share of the proposed budget to be borne by that annual conference, such proportionate share to be approved by each annual conference as it acts on budget recommendations (¶ 612).

*e)* To supervise the expenditure of funds allocated from all sources for expenses related to the provision of the episcopal residence and to account for such expenditures annually to each annual conference in the episcopal area and to the General Council on Finance and Administration.

*f)* To give oversight in all matters related to upkeep, maintenance, improvements, and appropriate insurance coverages for the episcopal residence.

5. Titles to properties held as episcopal residences shall be held in accordance with ¶ 2514.

¶ **636.** *Conference Board of Pensions*—1. *Authorization*—There shall be organized in each annual conference a conference board, auxiliary to the General Board of Pension and Health Benefits, to be known as the **conference board of pensions,** hereinafter called the board, that shall have charge of the interests and work of providing for and contributing to the support, relief, assistance, and pensioning of clergy and their families, other church workers, and lay employees of The United Methodist Church, its institutions, organizations, and agencies within the annual conference, except as otherwise provided for by the general board.

2. *Membership*—*a)* It is recommended that the board be composed of not less than twelve members not indebted to pension and benefit

funds, plans, and programs; one-third laywomen, one-third laymen, and one-third clergy; and in accordance with ¶ 605.3 elected for a term of eight years and arranged in classes as determined by the annual conference; and in addition thereto, any clergy member of the conference or lay member of a church within the conference who is a member of the General Board of Pension and Health Benefits. A vacancy in the membership of the board may be filled by the board for the remainder of the conference year in which the vacancy occurs, subject to the same qualifications before provided; and at its next session the conference shall fill the vacancy for the remainder of the unexpired term.

*b)* The members shall assume their duties at the adjournment of the conference session at which they were elected.

3. *Organization*—The board shall organize by electing a chairperson, vice chairperson, secretary, and treasurer, who shall serve during the ensuing quadrennium or until their successors shall have been elected and qualified. These officers shall constitute an executive committee; *provided,* however, that three members may be added thereto by the board. The duty of the executive committee shall be to administer the work of the board during the conference year in the interim between regular or special meetings of the board. The office of secretary may be combined with that of treasurer. The treasurer may be a person who is not a member of the board, in which case the person shall be an ex officio member of the executive committee, without vote. Calls for special meetings of the board shall be issued by the secretary on request of the chairperson, or the vice chairperson when the chairperson is unable to act.

4. *Proportional Payment*—The board shall compare the records of the amounts paid by each pastoral charge for the support of pastors and for pension and benefit programs, computing the proportional distribution thereof and keeping a permanent record of defaults of the churches of the conference that have failed to observe the following provisions pertaining to proportional payment, and shall render annually to each church that is in default a statement of the amounts in default for that and preceding years.[79]

*a)* When the apportionment to the pastoral charges for the pension and benefit program of the annual conference has been determined, payments made thereon by each pastoral charge shall be

---

79. *See* Judicial Council Decisions 50, 390, 401, 471.

exactly proportionate to payments made on the salary or salaries of the ordained minister or clergy serving it.

*b)* The treasurer of the pastoral charge shall be primarily responsible for the application of proportional payment; but in the event of the treasurer's failure to apply it, the pastor shall adjust cash salary and payment according to the proper ratio, as provided above, before the pastor enters the respective amounts in the statistical report to the annual conference.

*c)* The conference statistical tables shall provide separate columns for reporting the amount apportioned to each pastoral charge for pension and benefit purposes and the amount paid thereon.

*d)* It shall not be permissible for a pastor to receive a bonus or other supplementary compensation tending to defeat proportional payment.

5. *Reports to the General Board*—The board shall report to the General Board of Pension and Health Benefits immediately following the session of the conference, in such form as required by the general board, the names and years of service approved for pre-1982 pension credit for each eligible person and the names and addresses of clergy who are members of funds, plans, or programs administered by the general board.

¶ **637.** Each annual conference shall have a **board of trustees,** whose membership and duties are detailed in ¶ 2512.1–7.

¶ **638.** 1. In each annual conference there shall be a **conference commission on archives and history** or other structure to provide for these functions and maintain the connnectional relationships. The number of members of the commission and their terms of office shall be as the conference may determine and may include an ex officio representative of each United Methodist heritage landmark in its bounds. It shall be the duty of the commission to collect and preserve the historically significant records of the annual conference and its agencies, including data relating to the origin and history of the conference and its antecedents; to encourage and assist the local churches in preserving their records, compiling their histories, and celebrating their heritage; to provide for the permanent safekeeping of the historical records of all abandoned or discontinued churches in the bounds of the annual conference and its antecedents (*see* ¶ 2548.3); to maintain a fire-safe historical and archival depository and to see that all items that obviously will have value for future history are properly preserved therein; to provide for the ownership of real property and to receive gifts and bequests; to nominate to the General Commission on Archives and History buildings, locations, or structures within the annual conference for designation as historic sites or heritage landmarks; to maintain contact with officially designated historic sites and heritage landmarks in their bounds; to assist the bishop or the appropriate conference committee in planning for the historical hour and other appropriate historical observances at annual conference sessions; to establish retention and disposition schedules for annual conference and local church records under standards or guidelines developed by the General Commission on Archives and History; to cooperate with and report, when requested, to the general and jurisdictional commissions on archives and history; and to engage with other Wesleyan, Methodist, or Evangelical United Brethren-related denominations in lifting up our joint heritage.

2. The commission may organize a **conference historical society** and encourage membership therein for the purpose of promoting interest in the study and preservation of the history of the conference and its antecedents. The officers of the conference commission on archives and history may be the officers of the conference historical society. Membership in the historical society shall be established as the society may determine. Membership may include the payment of dues as the society may direct, and in return, members shall receive official publications and publicity materials issued by the commission and the society and other such benefits as may be deemed suitable.

3. Each annual conference may have a historian to undertake specific duties as may be designated by the commission. The **annual conference historian** may be a member of the annual conference commission on archives and history.

4. The annual conference commission on archives and history shall work with the ethnic congregations of the conference to develop and preserve the historical records of those congregations and antecedent conferences.

¶ **639.** 1. Each annual conference shall create a **conference commission or committee on Christian unity and interreligious concerns** or other structure to provide for these functions and maintain the connectional relationships with the General Commission on Christian Unity and Interreligious Concerns. The commission or committee will report each year to the conference in such manner as the conference may direct. The responsibilities of the commission on

397

Christian unity and interreligious concerns may be assigned to an existing or newly created multifunctional agency.

2. It is recommended that this commission or committee be composed of two United Methodists from each district (complying with ¶ 608.5), one of whom shall be district coordinator for Christian unity and interreligious concerns and shall serve as liaison with local church ministry areas on Christian unity and interreligious concerns. Additional members may include persons from The United Methodist Church or other member churches of the Consultation on Church Union as directed by the conference to ensure ecumenical expertise and interchange with other agencies. Laypersons from The United Methodist Church shall be full members of local churches. Ex officio members of the annual conference commission on Christian unity and interreligious concerns shall include the conference ecumenical officer(s), if elected, and any United Methodists residing within the conference bounds who are members of the following: the General Commission on Christian Unity and Interreligious Concerns, the governing board of the National Council of the Churches of Christ in the U.S.A., the World Methodist Council, the United Methodist delegation to the most recent World Council of Churches Assembly, and the United Methodist delegation to the most recent plenary meeting of the Consultation on Church Union.

3. There shall be a representative of the commission who serves as one of the conference representatives to state councils or conferences of churches.

4. The duties of the commission or committee shall be to act in cooperation with the annual conference council on ministries, in coordination with the duties of the General Commission on Christian Unity and Interreligious Concerns, as outlined in ¶¶ 1902–1903, and as it may recommend, and to take initiative in ecumenical and interreligious concerns as follows:

*a)* To interpret, advocate, and work for the unity of the Christian church in every aspect of the life of the conference and its churches and to encourage dialogue and cooperation with persons of other living faiths.

*b)* To recommend to the conference the goals, objectives, and strategies and to assist the conference, in cooperation with the bishop and the cabinet, in the development of ecumenical relationships and planning for mission with other judicatories, particularly in the establishment of new churches, yoked congregations, and in the process of local church union efforts.

*c)* To stimulate participation in and evaluation of mission programs ecumenically planned and implemented, such as experimental parishes, ecumenical parish clusters, ecumenical task forces, and united ministries in higher education, and in other issue-oriented tasks.

*d)* To stimulate conference, district, and congregational participation in councils, conferences, or associations of churches, in coalition task forces, and in interreligious groups through ecumenical educational or shared-time programs, jointly approved curriculum resources, interreligious study programs, or ecumenical community action projects such as institutional ministries and media communications, and various other modes of interchurch cooperation.

*e)* To participate in the selection of conference delegates to state councils or conferences of churches, which participation may include nomination, in cooperation with the conference nominating committee, for conference election the delegates to these bodies; to select representatives to district, area, and regional ecumenical and interreligious task groups and workshops; and to act as the body to which such delegates are accountable by receiving and acting on their reports and recommendations.

*f)* To promote and interpret the work of national and world ecumenical bodies such as the National Council of the Churches of Christ in the U.S.A., the World Council of Churches, the Consultation on Church Union, and the World Methodist Council; and to cooperate in and provide leadership for specific ecumenical experiences of worship and celebration such as the Week of Prayer for Christian Unity, Pentecost Sunday, World Communion Sunday, Reformation Sunday, and other appropriate occasions.

*g)* To stimulate understanding and conversations with all Christian bodies, to encourage continuing dialogue with Jewish and other living-faith communities, and to encourage an openness of mind toward an understanding of other major world religions.

*h)* To fulfill other functions assigned by the annual conference and to respond to such requests as may be made by its leadership.

¶ **640. 1.** There shall be in each annual conference a **conference commission on religion and race** or other structure to provide for these functions and maintain the connectional relationships. It shall follow the general guidelines and structure of the General Commission on Religion and Race as outlined in ¶¶ 2002 and 2008, where applicable.

2. The basic membership of the annual conference commission shall be nominated and elected by established procedure of the respective annual conferences. Each annual conference shall determine the number and composition of the total membership, which shall consist of a minimum of twelve. The commission membership shall include representation from each district. One of the district representatives shall be the district director of religion and race. Care shall be taken to ensure that the total membership represents an equitable balance in the number of laymen, laywomen, and clergypersons. It is strongly urged that the annual conference commissions be constituted so that the majority of the membership be represented by racial and ethnic minority persons (Asian Americans, African Americans, Hispanic Americans, Pacific Islanders, and Native Americans) reflecting the racial and ethnic minority constituency of the annual conference. Selection of commission members shall ensure adequate representation of women, youth, young adults, older adults, and people with disabilities. Members of the General Commission on Religion and Race residing in the annual conference shall be ex officio members of the annual conference commission on religion and race with vote.

3. The annual conference commission will assume responsibility for such matters as:

a) Providing resources and training to enable the work of the local church ministry area of religion and race as specified in ¶ 251.2b.

b) Examining ethnic representation on all of the conference boards, agencies, commissions, and committees, as well as the governing boards of related institutions. After such an examination, appropriate recommendations for total inclusiveness should be made to the annual conference.

c) Working with annual conference boards and agencies as they seek to develop programs and policies of racial inclusiveness.

d) Providing a channel of assistance to racial and ethnic groups as they seek to develop programs of empowerment and ministry to their communities.

e) Consulting with the board of ordained ministry and the cabinet to determine what provisions are made for the recruitment and itineracy of racial and ethnic minority clergy. The executive committee of the board of ordained ministry and cabinet are encouraged to meet at least once per year in joint sessions with the conference commission on religion and race.

*f)* Serving as a resource and support group to promote understanding between pastors appointed to local congregations across racial and ethnic lines and such congregations.

*g)* Consulting with local churches that are seeking to establish multiracial fellowships, and encouraging and supporting local churches in maintaining a Christian ministry in racially changing neighborhoods.

*h)* Coordinating the conference support and cooperation with various movements for racial and social justice in consultation with the conference board of church and society, as appropriate.

*i)* Providing opportunities for multiracial and interethnic dialogue and meetings throughout the conference.

*j)* Providing programs of sensitization and education at every level of the conference on the nature and meaning of racism—attitudinal, behavioral, and institutional.

*k)* Coordinating, in consultation with the General Commission on Christian Unity and Interreligious Concerns, the conference programs of cooperation with African American and other racial and ethnic denominations, especially those of the Methodist family.

*l)* Evaluating the priorities of the annual conference in light of the needs in the area of race relations. The commission shall develop recommendations to present to the appropriate agencies and report directly to the annual conference session. These recommendations shall lift up the need to deal with the pressing issue of racism, racial and ethnic group empowerment, and reconciliation among the races.

*m)* Evaluating the effects of merger and making appropriate recommendations to the annual conference session.

*n)* Reviewing the annual conference practices of employment, of annual conference program, business and administration, and office personnel, and reporting and recommending to the annual conference steps to be taken to actualize racial and ethnic inclusiveness; reviewing the annual conference-related institutions such as colleges, hospitals, homes for the aged, childcare agencies, and so forth concerning their practices of racial and ethnic inclusiveness in clientele and employment, and reporting to the annual conference session.

*o)* Serving in consultation with the bishop and other appropriate conference leadership to investigate and assist in resolution of complaints of racial discrimination made by clergy or laity.

*p)* Maintaining a close relationship with the General Commission on Religion and Race, seeking its guidance, utilizing its training and resources, and interpreting to the annual conference the programs, plans, and policies of the General Commission on Religion and Race.

4. The annual conference commission on religion and race shall develop an adequate budget for its operation as a commission for inclusion in the annual conference budget.

5. The annual conference commission on religion and race, or other structure to provide for its function and connectional relationship, shall have vote and voice in the decision-making unit of the conference such as the annual conference council on ministries, or equivalent structure.

¶ 641. There shall be in each annual conference, including the central conferences, a **conference commission on the status and role of women** or other structure to provide for these functions and maintain the connectional relationships.[80]

1. The responsibility of this commission shall be in harmony with the responsibility of the general commission (*see* ¶ 2103), with the following objectives established as guidelines for adaptation to the needs of the respective annual conferences:

*a)* To be informed about the status and role of all women in the total life of the conference. Data shall be gathered that relate to all structural levels of the conference, including the local church. Such information will be regularly updated and disseminated.

*b)* To initiate cooperation with United Methodist Women at the annual conference level and other levels as appropriate in order to achieve full participation of women in the decision-making structures.

*c)* To develop ways to inform and sensitize the leadership within the conference at all levels on issues that affect women, which shall be projected into and through all districts within the conference by the commission.

*d)* To focus on major priorities of issues related to women, which may include sexual harassment policies and procedures, and to enlist the support of the bishop, cabinet, and conference staff in policies, plans, and practices related to those priorities.

*e)* To advise the general commission about the progress and effectiveness of efforts to achieve full participation of women in the life of the Church.

---

80. *See* Judicial Council Decision 712.

*f)* To participate in connectional programs and plans initiated or recommended by the general commission, and to utilize the resources available from the general commission as needed.

2. The basic membership of the conference commission shall be nominated and elected by established procedures of the respective annual conferences. Each annual conference shall determine the number and composition of the total membership, which shall consist of not fewer than twelve nor more than thirty-six. All must be members of The United Methodist Church. Special consultants without vote may be used as resource persons. Among the basic members of the commission shall be representatives from each district. There shall be at least six members at large. It is recommended that the addition of the at-large membership ensure that the total membership maintain a balance of one-third laywomen, one-third laymen, and one-third clergy. The majority of the commission shall be women, including both clergy and lay. In an annual conference where there is not a sufficient number of clergywomen to meet the recommended balance, additional laywomen shall be elected beyond the one-third proportion to bring the total membership to a majority of women. A person or persons serving as member(s) of the General Commission on the Status and Role of Women from that annual conference shall, by virtue of their office, be member(s) of the conference commission on the status and role of women (*see* ¶¶ 608.6 and 710.5). Selection of commission members shall ensure adequate representation of racial and ethnic groups, youth, young adults, older adults, and persons of varying lifestyles.

At least one member shall be named by the conference United Methodist Women.

3. The chairperson of the commission shall be a woman.

4. The commission shall propose a budget and submit it for inclusion in the budget of the annual conference according to procedures for funding of all boards, commissions, and agencies of the annual conference.

¶ 642. There shall be in each annual conference a **conference commission on the small membership church,** or the responsibilities of the small membership church commission may be assigned to an existing or newly created multifunctional agency of the council or other structure that cares for the functions of support, nurture, and growth of small membership churches and their relationships to the conference, districts, and other local churches. Where these responsibilities are assigned to new or existing agencies within the conference, the individual(s) responsible for the functioning of the commission shall be designated by the annual conference and included in the listing of conference officers.

1. The responsibility of this commission shall be in harmony with the responsibility of the general commission, with the following objectives established as guidelines for adaptation to the needs of the respective annual conference:

a) To be informed about the needs and opportunities of the small membership church in rural, suburban, and urban settings in the total life of the conference. Specific data shall be gathered that relate to all structural levels of the conference, including the local church. This data shall include, but not be limited to, demographics, membership, information on the formation and effectiveness of cooperative ministries, information about pastoral tenure, compensation, and other factors that affect the vitality of the small membership churches. Such information will be regularly updated and disseminated to bishops, district superintendents, and to relating conference boards and agencies, the General Board of Global Ministries, and the General Board of Discipleship.

b) To ensure representation from small membership churches in the decision-making structures of the annual conference.

c) To develop ways to inform and sensitize the leadership within the annual conference at all levels on issues that affect small membership churches, which shall be projected into and through all districts within the annual conference by the commission.

d) To focus on major issues related to small membership churches and to enlist the support of the bishop, cabinet, and conference staff in policies, plans, and practices impacting those issues.

e) To advise the general commission on the progress and effectiveness of efforts to achieve full participation of laity and clergy from small membership churches in the life of the Church.

f) To participate in connectional programs and plans initiated or recommended by the general commission as needed.

2. The basic membership of the conference commission shall be nominated and elected by established procedures of the annual conferences. All must be members of The United Methodist Church. Special consultants without vote may be used as resource persons. Among the basic members of the commission shall be representatives of small membership churches from each district.

3. The commission shall propose a budget and submit it for inclu-

sion in the budget of the annual conference according to procedures for funding of all boards, commissions, and agencies of the annual conference.

¶ 643. In each annual conference there shall be a **commission on communications** or other structure to provide for these functions and maintain the connectional relationship. It shall include persons with skills in communications nominated for membership in a manner determined by the conference in accordance with ¶ 608.5.

The commission shall be a service agency to meet the communication, publication, multimedia, public and media relations, interpretation, and promotional needs of the annual conference. It may be responsible for providing resources and services to conference agencies, districts, and local churches in the field of communication. The commission shall have a consultative relationship with agencies and bodies within the conference structure.

¶ 644. **United Methodist Women**—*Constitution of United Methodist Women in the Conference—Article 1. Name*—In each annual conference there shall be a conference organization named United Methodist Women, auxiliary to the jurisdictional organization of United Methodist Women and to the Women's Division of the General Board of Global Ministries.

*Article 2. Function*—The function of the conference organization of United Methodist Women shall be to work with the district organizations and the local units of United Methodist Women in developing programs to meet the needs and interests of women and the concerns and responsibilities of the global Church; to encourage and support spiritual growth, missionary outreach, and Christian social action; and to promote the plans and responsibilities of the Women's Division.

*Article 3. Authority*—Each conference organization of United Methodist Women shall have authority to promote its work in accordance with the plans, responsibilities, and policies of the Women's Division of the General Board of Global Ministries.

*Article 4. Membership*—The conference organization of United Methodist Women shall be composed of all members of local units within the bounds of the conference. The resident bishop shall be a member of the conference organization of United Methodist Women and of its executive committee.

*Article 5. Officers and Committees*—The conference organization shall elect a president, a vice president, a secretary, a treasurer, and a committee on nominations. Additional officers and committees shall be elected or appointed in accordance with the plans of the Women's Division as set forth in the bylaws of the conference organizations of United Methodist Women.

Article 6. *Meetings and Elections—a)* There shall be an annual meeting of the conference organization of United Methodist Women, at which time there shall be presented a program designed to meet the needs of the women of the conference in harmony with the purpose, plans, and responsibilities of the Women's Division of the General Board of Global Ministries. Officers and the committee on nominations shall be elected, the necessary business transacted, and pledges made for the ensuing year.

*b)* The voting body of the annual meeting of the conference organization shall be composed of representatives from units in local churches as determined by the conference organization; such district officers as the conference organization may determine; the conference officers and chairpersons of committees; members of the Women's Division and officers of the jurisdictional organization residing within the bounds of the conference.

*c)* At the annual meeting of the conference organization prior to the quadrennial meeting of the jurisdictional organization, six conference officers shall be elected according to provisions in ¶ 533.3 for membership in the jurisdictional organization.

*d)* At the annual meeting of the conference organization prior to the quadrennial meeting of the jurisdictional organization, the conference organization shall nominate three women for membership on the Women's Division, the names to be sent to the jurisdiction organization according to ¶ 533.4.

Article 7. *Relationships—a)* The president of the conference organization of United Methodist Women is a member of the annual conference, as set forth in ¶ 30.

*b)* Designated officers shall represent the conference organization on the various agencies, councils, commissions, and committees of the conference as the constitutions and bylaws of such agencies provide.

*c)* The conference organization shall encourage women to participate in the total life and work of the Church and shall support them in assuming positions of responsibility and leadership.

Article 8. *Amendments*—Proposed amendments to this constitution may be sent to the recording secretary of the Women's Division prior to the last annual meeting of the division in the quadrennium.

¶ 645. United Methodist Men—*Constitution of United Methodist Men in the Conference—Article 1. Name*—In each annual conference there shall be a conference organization named United Methodist Men, auxiliary to the jurisdictional committee on United Methodist Men and to the General Commission on United Methodist Men (¶2301).

*Article 2. Function*—The function of the conference organization of United Methodist Men shall be to build and support the district organizations of United Methodist Men in developing resources to meet the needs and interests of men and the responsibilities of discipleship; to empower personal witness and evangelism; to enable outreach in individual and group mission and ministry; to encourage and support spiritual growth and faith development; and to promote the objectives and responsibilities of the General Commission on United Methodist Men. In the absence of a district organization, the conference organization, in consultation with the district superintendent, shall fulfill the district responsibilities (¶ 666).

*Article 3. Authority*—Each conference organization of United Methodist Men shall have the authority to promote its work in accordance with the plans, responsibilities, and policies of the General Commission on United Methodist Men.

*Article 4. Membership*—The conference organization of United Methodist Men shall be composed of all men of local churches or charges (chartered or unchartered) within the bounds of the conference and all clergy.

*Article 5. Officers and Committees*—*a)* The conference organization shall elect a president, at least one vice president, a secretary, and a treasurer.

*b)* The resident bishop shall serve as the honorary president and be a member of the conference organization and its executive committee.

*c)* The conference lay leader (or designated representative) shall be a member of the conference organization and its executive committee.

*d)* Additional officers (including civic youth-serving agencies/Scouting coordinator) and committees shall be elected or appointed in accordance with the guidelines of the General Commission on United Methodist Men and/or the bylaws of the conference organization of United Methodist Men.

*Article 6. Meetings and Elections*—*a)* There shall be an annual meeting of the conference organization of United Methodist Men, at which time there shall be presented an annual report and a program plan designed to meet the needs of the men of the conference. Officers and committees shall be elected in accordance with the requirements of the organization's bylaws.

b) The voting body of the annual meeting of the conference shall be determined by the organization's bylaws but shall include conference and district officers and committee chairpersons as determined, members of the General Commission on United Methodist Men, and members of the jurisdictional committee on United Methodist Men residing within the bounds of the conference.

*Article 7. Relationships—a)* The president of the conference organization of United Methodist Men is a member of the annual conference, as set forth in ¶ 30.

b) The president of the conference organization of United Methodist Men shall represent the conference organization on the jurisdictional committee on United Methodist Men. In the absence of the president a designated vice president may represent the conference organization.

c) Designated officers or members shall represent the conference organization on the various agencies, councils, commissions, and committees of the annual conference as the constitutions, bylaws, and rules of such agencies provide.

d) The conference organization shall encourage men to participate in the total life and work of the Church and shall encourage them to assume positions of responsibility and leadership as part of their discipleship.

*Article 8. Amendments*—Proposed amendments to this constitution may be sent to the recording secretary of the General Commission on United Methodist Men prior to the last annual meeting of the commission in the third year of the quadrennium.

*Article 9. Connectional Reporting—a)* Each annual conference shall file a current copy of their constitution with the General Commission on United Methodist Men.

b) Each annual conference shall submit an annual report to the General Commission on United Methodist Men for its spring meeting.

¶ **646.** 1. In each annual conference there shall be a **conference council on youth ministry** or other equivalent structure to provide for these functions and maintain the connectional relationships, or

the responsibilities outlined below may be assigned to such organization that follows the same membership requirements as the annual
conference provides pursuant to ¶ 608.1. Its purpose shall be to
strengthen the youth ministry in the local churches and districts of
the annual conference. For administrative purposes, the council shall
be related to the annual conference council on ministries. (See
¶ 1210 for the United Methodist Youth Organization Convocation
and the United Methodist Youth Organization Steering Committee.)

2. *Membership*—No more than one-third of the membership of the
council shall be adults, one of whom may be the conference lay leader
or his or her representative. It is recommended that the council be composed of 50 percent racial and ethnic group members. (It is suggested
that members at large may be added toward achieving fifty-fifty ethnic
and white membership in a manner to be determined by the conference council on youth ministry.) Where ethnic or language conferences
overlap nonethnic conferences, provision shall be made for the inclusion of members of the ethnic or language conferences and vice-versa.
Those serving on the conference council on youth ministry shall be
members (full or preparatory) of The United Methodist Church.

3. *Responsibilities*—*a)* To initiate and support plans, activities, and
projects that are of particular interest to youth.

*b)* To be an advocate for the free expression of the convictions
of youth on issues vital to them.

*c)* To support and facilitate, where deemed needed, the formation of youth caucuses.

*d)* To cooperate with the boards and agencies of the annual
conference, receiving recommendations from and making recommendations to the same.

*e)* To recommend to the annual conference committee on nominations qualified youth for membership on boards and agencies.

*f)* To elect and certify annual conference representatives to the
jurisdictional youth ministry organization convocation and the
United Methodist Youth Organization Convocation in keeping with
the provisions of ¶¶ 531 and 1205.

*g)* To receive and set the policy and criteria for its portion of the
Youth Service Fund (¶ 1209). No more than one-third shall be used
for administrative purposes; at least one-third shall be used for projects within the geographic bounds of the annual conference; and at
least one-third shall be used for projects outside the geographic
bounds of the annual conference.

*h)* To establish the policy for Youth Service Fund education and be responsible for its promotion throughout the annual conference, in cooperation with the United Methodist Youth Organization Steering Committee.

*i)* To establish a project review committee as an advisory committee with regard to the use of the Youth Service Fund receipts for projects. It is recommended that the committee be composed of at least 50 percent racial and ethnic group persons.

*j)* To participate with the appropriate conference agencies in the nomination of the conference coordinator of youth ministry, who shall serve as its adviser.

¶ **647.** 1. In each annual conference there may be a **conference council on young adult ministry.** Its purpose shall be to strengthen the young adult ministry in the local churches and districts of the annual conference. For administrative purposes, the council shall be related to the annual conference council on ministries or alternative structure.

2. *Membership*—The membership of the council shall be young adults (age nineteen to thirty). There shall be one young adult elected by each district of the conference selected by the district council on ministries. There may also be members at large nominated by the conference nominating committee. It is strongly recommended that the council include racial and ethnic minority members and persons of both genders to ensure inclusiveness. Those serving on the conference council on young adult ministry shall be members of The United Methodist Church. At least one-half of the members shall be laypersons. Members should represent the diversity of young adults in the general population, including college students, working persons, single, and married.

3. *Responsibilities*—*a)* To initiate and support plans and activities and projects that are of particular interest to young adults who are college students, working persons, single, and married.

*b)* To be an advocate for the free expression of the convictions of young adults on issues vital to them.

*c)* To support and facilitate, where deemed needed, the formation of young adult caucuses.

*d)* To cooperate with the boards and agencies of the annual conference, including the Wesley Foundations, receiving recommendations from and making recommendations to the same to provide for the needs of young adults in The United Methodist Church.

*e)* To recommend to the annual conference committee on nominations qualified young adults for membership on boards and agencies.

*f)* To participate with the conference council on ministries in the nomination of the conference coordinator of young adult ministry, who shall serve as its adviser.

¶ 648. There shall be a **joint committee on incapacity** in each annual conference. It shall be composed of a minimum of two representatives each from the board of ordained ministry and the conference board of pensions, who may be elected by those boards at the beginning of each quadrennium and at other times when vacancies occur, and a district superintendent appointed from time to time by the bishop to represent the cabinet. Unless and until other members are elected, the chairperson and registrar of the board of ordained ministry and the chairperson and secretary of the conference board of pensions, or others designated by them, shall be authorized to represent their respective boards. The committee shall organize at the beginning of each quadrennium by the election of a chairperson and a secretary. The duties of the joint committee on incapacity shall be:

*a)* To study the problems of incapacity in the annual conference.

*b)* To provide for a continuing personal ministry to any disabled clergy of the conference and to aid them in maintaining fellowship with the members of the conference.

*c)* To determine what medical doctor or doctors it will approve for medical examinations and reports regarding disabled clergy, and what medical doctor or doctors it will recommend to the General Board of Pension and Health Benefits for that purpose.

*d)* To make recommendations to the board of ordained ministry, the conference board of pensions, and the cabinet on matters related to incapacity, including steps for its prevention, incapacity leave, benefits, and programs of rehabilitation.

*e)* To cooperate with and give assistance to the General Board of Pension and Health Benefits in its administration of incapacity benefits through the Ministers Reserve Pension Fund or the Comprehensive Protection Plan.

¶ 649. There shall be in each annual conference a **committee on disability concerns** or other structure to provide for the functions of this ministry and maintain the connectional relationships.

1. The basic membership of the committee shall be nominated

and elected by established procedures of the respective annual conference. Each annual conference shall determine the number and composition of the total membership. Membership shall include persons with physical disabilities and persons with mental disabilities.

2. It shall be the responsibility of this committee:

*a)* To be aware of, and advocate for, the role of persons with disabilities in ministry, including ordained and diaconal ministries and local church and annual conference leadership positions.

*b)* To advocate for and help develop programs within the annual conference that meet the needs of persons with disabilities.

*c)* To be informed about current ministries within the annual conference that are related to persons with disabilities.

*d)* To develop ways to sensitize persons in leadership positions on issues that affect persons with disabilities and therefore the entire Church.

*e)* To foster cooperation among ministries within the annual conference that focus on specific disabilities (deaf, deafened, hard of hearing, development disabilities, mental retardation, mental illness, visual impairment, physical disabilities, etc.).

*f)* To be a resource for local churches who are attempting to develop ministries that are attitudinally and architecturally accessible.

*g)* To promote the full inclusion of persons with disabilities in the life of the local church and the annual conference.

*h)* To participate in jurisdictional accessibility associations in the sharing of knowledge and resources.

¶ 650. There shall be an annual conference **committee on Native American ministry** or other structure to provide for these ministries and maintain the connectional relationships. The basic membership of the committee shall be nominated and elected by established procedure of the respective annual conferences. Each annual conference shall determine the number and composition of the total membership. Where possible, the membership shall consist of a majority of Native Americans. It shall be the responsibility of this committee to determine the distribution of the Native American Ministries Sunday offering, coordinate the promotion of Native American Ministries Sunday, and monitor Native American ministries within the annual conference. Each committee shall report on how the offering funds have benefited Native Americans in their annual conference. Annual reports, including the amount of the total receipts from the Native

American Ministries Sunday offerings, should be forwarded to the conference council on ministries and to the General Council on Ministries.

Every local church at charge conference shall designate by nomination and election a minimum of one person per charge (without regard to race or ethnic origin) or a designated member of an established church committee to represent the need for better awareness of Native American contributions in the local church. These names are to be submitted to the district superintendent at charge conference to be given to the annual conference committee on Native American ministry.

¶ 651. 1. There may be a **conference Advance program,** established and carried out in the same spirit of partnership as the general Advance program.

2. A conference Advance Special Gift is one made to a conference Advance Special project within bounds of the annual conference or episcopal area authorized by an annual conference upon recommendation by the conference board of global ministries or its equivalent structure and consistent with the goals of the Advance. The funds as received shall be administered by the conference board of global ministries or such structure as designated by the conference.

3. An annual conference may undertake a conference-wide campaign for a lump sum to be applied to its missionary and church extension. The funds so received shall be designated as conference Advance Specials and shall be administered by the conference board of global ministries or equivalent structure. Local churches shall report their contributions as conference Advance Specials.

4. With the approval of the annual conference, a district within the conference may authorize and promote Advance Specials for church extension and missionary needs within the district, such funds to be administered by a district missionary society organized for that purpose or by a similar body set up by the district. Such special funds secured and administered on a district level shall be reported by each local church to the annual conference as conference Advance Specials.

5. Local churches shall report their contributions to general Advance Specials and conference Advance Specials to the charge conference and in the manner indicated on the annual conference report form.

¶ 652. The annual conference is encouraged to establish a **committee on criminal justice and mercy ministries** (CJAMM) to accomplish the following: (1) raise awareness and generate local church involvement; (2) identify existing programs; (3) promote criminal justice ministries; and (4) serve as a resource and connectional link with local churches, general program agencies, and ecumenical groups, and use prison ministry and prison reform resources made available through the general agencies. The purpose is to promote a ministry to persons of all genders and ages who are in prison, to the families of those in prison, and to the victims of crime and their families and to be an advocate for prison concerns. The CJAMM committee may relate to the board of global ministries and/or the board of church and society, which shares social justice concerns. The results of the work in this area will be reported to the annual conference.

**Section X. The District Conference**

Upon approval of the annual conference, the term *subdistrict* may be used in the references to district in ¶¶ 652–663.

¶ **653.** A **district conference** shall be held if directed by the annual conference of which it is a part and may be held upon the call of the district superintendent, which call shall specify the time and place.

¶ **654.** 1. A district conference shall be composed of members as determined and specified by the annual conference, giving attention to inclusiveness (*see* ¶¶ 124, 138).

2. The district conference may choose its own order of business. The secretary duly elected shall keep an accurate record of the proceedings and submit it to the annual conference for examination.

3. The district conference shall issue certificates of candidacy for the ordained ministry on recommendation of the district committee on ordained ministry and shall consider for approval the reports of this committee.

4. The district conference may incorporate a **district union,** under the laws of the state in which it is located, to hold and administer district real and personal property, receive and administer church extension and mission funds for use within the district, and exercise such other powers and duties as may be set forth in its charter or articles of incorporation as authorized by the annual conference having jurisdiction over said district. All such district unions chartered or incorporated by districts of the churches that joined and united in adopting the Constitution of The United Methodist Church are declared to be

disciplinary agencies of The United Methodist Church as though originally created and authorized by that Constitution and may act for or as a district conference when convened for that purpose by the district superintendent, who shall be its executive secretary, or by its president or other executive officer.

5. If any district or conference initiates, joins, monitors, or terminates a boycott, the guidelines in *The Book of Resolutions*, 2000, should be followed. The General Conference is the only body that can initiate, empower, or join a boycott in the name of The United Methodist Church.

¶ **655.** 1. The **district lay leader** is the elected leader of the district laity. The district lay leader shall provide for the training of local church lay leaders for their ministries in the local churches in relation to ¶ 248. The district lay leader shall have responsibility for fostering awareness of the role of the laity both within congregations and through their ministries in the home, workplace, community, and world in achieving the mission of the Church, and supporting and enabling lay participation in the planning and decision-making processes of the district and the local churches in cooperation with the district superintendent and pastors. The district lay leader is a member of the district conference and shall be a member of the district council on ministries or alternative structure and its executive committee. The district lay leader shall also be a member of the committee on district superintendency of his or her district.

2. There may be an associate district lay leader within a district. The associate lay leader shall be elected as determined by the annual conference. The method of nomination and term of office shall be determined by the annual conference.

3. The district lay leader shall relate to the organized lay groups in the district such as United Methodist Women, United Methodist Men, and United Methodist Youth and support their work and help them coordinate their activities.

4. The district lay leader may designate persons to serve as proxy in any of the above groups except the district conference, district council on ministries, and the district council on ministries executive committee.

5. The district lay leader shall be elected as determined by the annual conference. The method of nomination and term of office shall be determined by the annual conference.

6. The district lay leader shall serve on the district committee on Lay Speaking Ministries.

7. The district lay leader is a member of annual conference (*see* ¶ 30).

8. The district lay leader shall be a member of the conference board of laity or equivalent structure.

¶ 656. Each district of an annual conference may organize to develop, administer, and evaluate the missional life, advocacy needs, and ministries of the Church in and through the district. It shall maintain connectional relationships, organize to develop and strengthen ethnic ministries, including ethnic local churches and concerns, and provide encouragement, coordination, and support for local churches in their ministries of nurture, outreach, and witness in accordance with the mission of The United Methodist Church.

¶ 657. The district superintendent, after consultation with the conference board, may appoint a **district director of church and society.** Also, if desirable, a district may create a committee on church and society of laypersons and clergy, to work with the district superintendent to further the purposes of the conference board. The coordinator of the area of Christian social involvement of the district United Methodist Women shall be an ex officio member.

¶ 658. The district superintendent, after consultation with the annual conference on ethnic local church concerns committee, may appoint a **district director of ethnic local church concerns.** This director would become a member of the district council on ministries or its structural counterpart. A district may establish a committee on ethnic local church concerns comprised of laypersons and clergy to work with the district superintendent to implement the annual conference's comprehensive plan as it relates to that district and to further the purposes of the annual conference committee.

¶ 659. The district superintendent, after consultation with the annual conference commission on religion and race, may appoint a **district director of religion and race.** A district may establish a committee on religion and race to work with the district superintendent to further the purposes of the annual conference commission in the district. The district director, if appointed, shall be a member of the annual conference commission on religion and race. (*See* ¶ 640.2.)

¶ 660. There shall be a **district committee on ordained ministry.**

1. The district committee on ordained ministry shall be amenable to the annual conference through the board of ordained ministry. It shall be composed of a representative from the board of ordained ministry, named by the board after consultation with the district

superintendent, who may be named chairperson; the district superintendent, who may serve as the executive secretary; and at least six other clergy in the district, including women and ethnic clergy, wherever possible, nominated annually by the district superintendent in consultation with the chairperson or executive committee of the board of ordained ministry and approved by the annual conference. The committee shall include elders in full connection and, whenever possible, deacons in full connection and at least one elder who has taken the course of study. Interim vacancies may be filled by the district superintendent. The conference board of ordained ministry shall provide orientation for new members, including education regarding the ministry and roles of all clergy and distribution of any available written guidelines.

At least three members of local churches shall be members of the committee with vote, except on matters prohibited by ¶ 31, Article II, in the Constitution, nominated annually by the district superintendent and approved by the annual conference.

2. The district committee on ordained ministry shall elect its officers at the first meeting following the annual conference session when the members are elected.

3. The committee shall maintain a list of all persons who have declared their candidacy for the ordained ministry and are pursuing candidacy studies under a supervising pastor. A duplicate list shall be forwarded to the annual conference registrar for candidacy; such list being made current at least prior to each session of the annual conference.

4. The committee shall offer counsel to candidates regarding pretheological studies.

5. The committee shall supervise all matters dealing with candidacy for the ordained ministry and with the license for local pastor.

6. The vote of the committee on all matters of candidacy shall be by individual written ballot, with a three-fourths majority vote of the committee present required for certification or approval or recommendation.

7. The committee shall maintain a service record and file on every local pastor and candidate for the ordained ministry until the individual becomes an associate or probationary member of the annual conference, at which time a copy of the files shall be forwarded to the registrar of the board of ordained ministry. The records and files of the committee are kept on behalf of the annual conference and shall

be maintained under guidelines provided by the General Council on Finance and Administration in consultation with the General Board of Higher Education and Ministry and the General Board of Pension and Health Benefits.

8. The committee shall recommend to the board of ordained ministry those persons who qualify for associate and probationary membership, for license or continuance as local pastors, and for restoration of credentials. All persons shall have been current members of The United Methodist Church for at least one year immediately preceding certification, shall have been recommended by their charge conference, and shall, in the judgment of the committee, show evidence that their gifts, evidence of God's grace, and usefulness warrant such recommendation.[81]

9. The committee shall examine all persons who apply in writing for certification or renewal of certificate. Where there is evidence that their gifts, evidence of God's grace, and usefulness warrant and that they are qualified under ¶¶ 340–344, and on recommendation of their charge conference or the conference board of ordained ministry, the committee shall issue or renew their certificate.

10. All persons interviewed by the district committee shall be informed of decisions and recommendations as soon as possible, both orally and in writing.

11. The committee shall assist the conference board of ordained ministry in providing support services for all clergy under appointment within the district.

¶ **661.** Each district of an annual conference may organize a **district board of laity** or alternative structure.

1. The purpose of the district board of laity shall be:

*a)* To foster an awareness of the role of laity both within the local congregation and through their ministries in the home, workplace, community, and world in achieving the mission of the Church.

*b)* To work with the district lay leader in: (1) developing and promoting an increased role for laity in the life of the local church, (2) increasing the participation of laity in the sessions and programs of the district and local churches in cooperation with the district superintendent and pastors, and (3) encouraging laypersons to participate in the general ministry of the Church in the world. (*See* ¶ 656.)

---

81. *See* Judicial Council Decision 586.

*c)* To develop and promote stewardship of time, talent, and possessions within the district in cooperation with the district council on ministries.

2. The membership of the board shall include the district lay leader, associate district lay leader(s), district director of Lay Speaking Ministries, and may include the district superintendent, district president of United Methodist Women, district president of United Methodist Men, district president of United Methodist Youth, district president of United Methodist Young Adults, and, where organized, the district president of the Older Adult Council, and others as deemed necessary. Special attention shall be given to the inclusion of women, men, youth, young adults, and older adults; people with disabilities; and racial and ethnic group persons.

3. The district lay leader shall chair the board. Other officers shall be elected as the board shall deem necessary.

4. The board shall relate to the lay speaking program and to the organized groups in the district such as the United Methodist Women, United Methodist Men, United Methodist Youth, and United Methodist Young Adults and shall support their work and help them coordinate their activities.

¶ **662.** *District Committee on Lay Speaking Ministries*— Districts are encouraged to create a **district committee on Lay Speaking Ministries** related to the annual conference through the conference committee on lay speaking ministries.

1. The purpose of the district committee on Lay Speaking Ministries is to plan and supervise the program within the district.

2. The committee is chaired by the district director of Lay Speaking Ministries. In addition to the director, membership of the committee will include the district lay leader, the district superintendent, and an instructor of lay speaking courses. Other resource people may be added as needed.

3. The responsibilities of a district committee on Lay Speaking Ministries are to provide basic training for local church lay speakers and advanced courses for certified lay speakers as recommended by the General Board of Discipleship, or as approved by the conference committee on Lay Speaking Ministries; to decide who will be recognized as certified lay speakers; to help match lay speakers with service opportunities; and to support and affirm lay speakers as they serve.

4. The district committee shall plan advanced courses for lay

speaking that will enable certified lay speakers to maintain that recognition.

5. The district committee will report to the pastor and charge conference of each certified lay speaker the courses that have been satisfactorily completed by the certified lay speaker.

¶ **663.** *Committee on District Superintendency*—There shall be a **committee on district superintendency.**

1. *Membership*—This committee shall be composed of eleven members, including the district lay leader, and two persons appointed by the district superintendent. It is recommended that the remaining members of the committee consist of two laywomen, two laymen, two clergy, and two at-large members, all of whom should be selected with special attention to the representation of racial and ethnic persons, youth (¶ 255.2), young adults, older adults, and people with disabilities. At least three of the eleven persons shall be clergy, and seven shall be laypersons.

2. *Selection*—The members shall be selected in such manner as may be determined by the district conference or, where there is no district conference, by the annual conference. The district committee shall be authorized to co-opt members as advisory members who have expertise in areas of special need. The bishop of the area, or his or her authorized representative, shall be an ex officio member of said committee.

3. *Meeting*—The district committee shall meet at least annually and upon call of the district superintendent and/or the chairperson of the committee. The committee shall elect a chairperson, vice chairperson, and secretary.

4. *Purpose*—The purpose of the committee on district superintendency shall be to support the district superintendent of the district in the oversight of the spiritual and temporal affairs of the Church, with special reference to the district where the superintendent has responsibilities. In fulfilling this purpose, the committee shall give attention to the following responsibilities:

*a)* To advocate for adequate budget-support services for the district superintendent, such as adequate secretarial support, travel, continuing education, and parsonage needs (¶¶ 23.2, 612.1*a*).

*b)* To be available for counsel.

*c)* To keep the district superintendent advised concerning conditions within the district as they affect relations among the district superintendent, the laity, the clergy, and the district agencies.

*d)* To establish a clearly understood process for observing the district superintendent's ministry with direct evaluation and feedback, with special concern for the inclusiveness of the Church and its ministry with respect to sex, race, and national origin, and implementation of the consultative process in appointment-making.

*e)* To consult with the district superintendent concerning continuing education and to arrange with the cabinet and bishop for the necessary time and financial assistance for the attendance of the district superintendent at such continuing education events as may serve his or her professional and spiritual growth.

*f)* To interpret to the people of the district and to the district boards and agencies the nature and function of the district superintendency.

5. *Consultation*—The district committee and the district superintendent shall engage in an annual consultation and appraisal of the work of the district superintendent in the district and shall serve in an advisory relationship with the bishop of the area.

¶ **664. United Methodist Women**—*Constitution of United Methodist Women in the District*—*Article 1. Name*—In each district there shall be a district organization named United Methodist Women, auxiliary to the conference organization of United Methodist Women and the Women's Division of the General Board of Global Ministries.

*Article 2. Responsibilities*—The responsibilities of the district organization of United Methodist Women shall be to work with local units in developing programs to meet the needs and interests of women and the concerns and responsibilities of the global Church; to encourage and support spiritual growth, missionary outreach, and Christian social action; and to promote the plans and responsibilities of the Women's Division and the conference organization of United Methodist Women.

*Article 3. Authority*—Each district organization of United Methodist Women shall have authority to promote its work in accordance with the plans, responsibilities, and policies of the conference organization and the Women's Division of the General Board of Global Ministries.

*Article 4. Membership*—All members of organized units of United Methodist Women in the local churches of the district shall be considered members of the district organization. The district superintendent shall be a member of the district organization of United Methodist Women and of its executive committee.

*Article 5. Officers and Committees*—The district organization shall elect a president, a vice president, a secretary, a treasurer, and a committee on nominations. Additional officers and committees shall be elected or appointed in accordance with the plans of the Women's Division as set forth in the bylaws for the district organization of United Methodist Women.

*Article 6. Meetings and Elections*—There shall be an annual meeting of the district organization of United Methodist Women, at which time there shall be presented a program designed to meet the needs of the women of the district in harmony with the purpose, plans, and responsibilities of the conference organization and the Women's Division of the General Board of Global Ministries. Officers and the committee on nominations shall be elected, the necessary business transacted, and pledges made for the ensuing year.

*Article 7. Relationships—a)* Designated officers shall represent the district organization of United Methodist Women on the various boards, councils, commissions, and committees of the district as the constitution and bylaws of such agencies provide.

*b)* The district president shall be the only district representative with vote on the conference executive committee.

*c)* The district organization shall encourage women to participate in the total life and work of the Church and shall support them in assuming positions of responsibility and leadership.

*Article 8. Amendments*—Proposed amendments to this constitution may be sent to the recording secretary of the Women's Division of the General Board of Global Ministries prior to the last annual meeting of the division in the quadrennium.

¶ **665. United Methodist Men**—*Constitution of United Methodist Men in the District—Article 1. Name*—In each district there shall be a district organization named United Methodist Men, auxiliary to the conference organization of United Methodist Men and the General Commission on United Methodist Men (¶ 2301).

*Article 2. Responsibilities*—The responsibilities of the district organization of United Methodist Men shall be to work with local units of United Methodist Men in developing resources to meet the needs and interests of men and the responsibilities of discipleship; to empower personal witness and evangelism; to enable outreach in individual and group mission and ministry; to encourage and support spiritual growth and faith development; and to promote the objectives and responsibilities of the conference organization and the General Commission on United Methodist Men. The district organization shall also encourage and promote the chartering and annual recertification of local units through the General Commission on United Methodist Men (¶ 2302 and ¶ 256).

*Article 3. Authority*—Each district organization of United Methodist Men shall have the authority to promote its work in accordance with the plans, responsibilities, and policies of the conference organization and the General Commission on United Methodist Men.

*Article 4. Membership*—All men and clergy of local churches or charges (chartered and unchartered) of the district shall be considered members of the district organization.

*Article 5. Officers and Committees*—*a)* The district organization shall elect a president, at least one vice president, a secretary, and a treasurer.

*b)* Additional officers (including civic youth-serving agencies/Scouting coordinator) and committees shall be elected or appointed in accordance with the guidelines of the General Commission on United Methodist Men and/or the bylaws of the district organization of United Methodist Men.

*c)* The district superintendent shall be a member of the district organization and of its executive committee.

*d)* The district lay leader (or designated representative) shall be a member of the district organization and of its executive committee.

*Article 6. Meetings and Elections*—There shall be an annual meeting of the district organization of United Methodist Men, at which time there shall be presented an annual report as well as a program plan designed to meet the needs of the men of the district. Officers and committees shall be elected in accordance with the requirements of the organization's bylaws.

*Article 7. Relationships*—*a)* Designated officers or members shall represent the district organization of United Methodist Men on the various boards, councils, commissions, and committees of the district as the constitutions, bylaws and rules of such agencies provide.

*b)* The district president shall be a member of the conference executive committee.

*c)* The district organization shall encourage men to participate in the total life and work of the Church and shall encourage them to assume positions of leadership as part of their discipleship.

*Article 8. Amendments*—Proposed amendments to this constitution may be sent to the recording secretary of the General Commission on United Methodist Men prior to the last annual meeting of the commission in the third year of the quadrennium.

*Article 9. Connectional Reporting—a)* Each district shall file a current copy of their constitution with the conference organization of United Methodist Men.

*b)* Each district shall submit an annual report to the conference organization of United Methodist Men prior to its annual meeting.

**¶ 666.** Each district of an annual conference may organize a **district council on youth ministry.**

1. *Purpose*—The purpose of the district council on youth ministry is defined as follows: to assist local churches in ministry for, with, and by junior high and senior high youth more effectively; to serve as a channel of communication and involvement among the youth ministry in the local churches, the conference council on youth ministry, and the general agencies of the Church; to initiate youth programs for the district to influence the total programming of the district and conference as it relates to the concerns and needs of youth; and to take primary responsibility for promoting and raising money for the Youth Service Fund.

2. *Membership*—Each district may determine the membership and the method of election of its district council on youth ministry in consultation with the conference council on youth ministry. It is recommended that the membership include the following: *a)* no more than one-third of the membership shall be adults; *b)* at least a 50 percent ratio of nonwhite persons, if possible; *c)* the district youth coordinator, to be a member by virtue of his or her office; and *d)* representatives on the conference council on youth ministry.

3. *Functions*—The functions of the district council on youth ministry may be determined by the annual conference council on youth ministry and/or the district council on youth ministry. The following functions may be incorporated in its work:

*a)* To study the needs of the junior high and senior high youth ministry of the local churches in the district and help them establish and provide more effective ministry in and through the district.

*b)* To keep local churches informed of the work of the whole Church in youth ministry and to challenge each church to full participation.

*c)* To serve as a two-way channel of communications between the local church youth and the annual conference and to assist local church youth in communication with one another.

*d)* To cooperate with the programming and ministry of the district council on ministries as it serves to provide leadership training to persons in the district.

*e)* To assist in the implementation of the program of the annual conference and particularly of the annual conference council on youth ministry.

*f)* To serve as an advocate for the free expression of youth in the district and local churches of the district.

*g)* To provide leadership training.

*h)* To promote, educate, and be a resource to local churches on Youth Service Fund.

*i)* To participate with the district superintendent and the conference coordinator of youth ministry, who shall serve as its adviser. The district council on youth ministry's responsibilities shall include organizing, programming, consulting with local churches, and nurturing adult workers with youth in the district.

4. *Finances*—Each district council on youth ministries, in consultation with the conference council on ministries and the district council on ministries, shall determine the method by which it will be financed.

## Chapter Five

# ADMINISTRATIVE ORDER

## Section I. General Provisions

¶ 701. *Agencies and General Agencies*—1. Connectionalism is an important part of our identity as United Methodists. It provides us with wonderful opportunities to carry out our mission in unity and strength. We experience this connection in many ways, including our systems of episcopacy, itineracy, property, and mutual cooperation and support. Our connectional system performs at least three essential tasks: embracing God's mission for the church as making disciples for Jesus Christ; organizing our whole Church to enable local congregations, the primary arena for mission, faithfully and fruitfully to make disciples for Jesus Christ; and ensuring that all components in the connection carry out their appropriate responsibilities in ways that enable the whole United Methodist Church to be faithful in its mission. General agencies, in particular, are important to our common vision, mission, and ministry. They provide essential services and ministries beyond the scope of individual local congregations and annual conferences through services and ministries that are highly focused, flexible, and capable of rapid response.

The term *agency*, wherever it appears in the *Book of Discipline*, is a term used to describe the various councils, boards, commissions, committees, divisions, or other units constituted within the various levels of Church organization (general, jurisdictional, central, annual, district, and charge conferences) under authority granted by the *Book of Discipline*; the term does not and is not meant to imply a master-servant or principal-agent relationship between these bodies and the conference or other body that creates them, except where the authority is specifically granted.

2. The general agencies of The United Methodist Church are the regularly established councils, boards, commissions, committees, or other units with ongoing responsibilities that have been constituted by the General Conference. Not included are such commissions and committees as are created by the General Conference to fulfill a special function within the ensuing quadrennium, ecumenical groups on

which The United Methodist Church is represented, or committees related to the quadrennial sessions of the General Conference.[1] The term general agency or agency, wherever it appears in the *Book of Discipline* in reference to a general agency, does not and is not meant to imply a master-servant or principal-agent relationship between such a body and the General Conference or any other unit of the denomination, or the denomination as a whole.

¶ **702.** *Amenability and Program Accountability*—1. All the general agencies of The United Methodist Church that have been constituted by the General Conference are amenable to the General Conference, except as otherwise provided.

2. Between sessions of the General Conference, the following general agencies are accountable to the General Council on Ministries: the General Board of Church and Society, the General Board of Discipleship, the General Board of Global Ministries, the General Board of Higher Education and Ministry, the General Commission on Christian Unity and Interreligious Concerns, the General Commission on Religion and Race, the General Commission on the Status and Role of Women, the General Commission on Archives and History, the General Commission on United Methodist Men, and the General Commission on Communications in matters pertaining to their program responsibilities.[2]

3. Evaluation of general agencies by the General Council on Ministries shall be part of the accountability relationship (¶ 906.14). The evaluation process and its results shall be reported to each General Conference. The purpose for agency evaluation is to assist the agency in the process of fulfilling and supporting its ministry. Local church groups, district, and annual conference organizations may receive an explanation of the evaluation process by requesting it from the General Council on Ministries.

4. Questions and concerns about programs, projects, or decisions of a particular agency may be addressed to that agency, with copies to the General Council on Ministries. Agencies shall acknowledge receipt of requests for information within ten days and provide information requested within thirty days or as soon thereafter as it is available.

---

1. *See* Judicial Council Decision 139.
2. *See* Judicial Council Decisions 429, 496.

5. If any district, annual conference, or general agency initiates, joins, monitors, or terminates a boycott, the guidelines in the 2000 *Book of Resolutions* should be followed. The General Conference is the only body that can initiate, empower, or join a boycott in the name of The United Methodist Church.

6. In all matters of accountability episcopal oversight as provided in ¶ 427 is assumed.

¶ **703.** *Definitions, Structures, and Titles*—1. *General Council*—An organization created by the General Conference to perform defined responsibilities of review and oversight on behalf of the General Conference in relation to the other general agencies and to perform other assigned functions shall be designated as a general council. General councils are amenable and accountable to the General Conference and report to it. These councils are the General Council on Finance and Administration and the General Council on Ministries.[3]

(Note: The Council of Bishops and Judicial Council are authorized by the Constitution and are not created by the General Conference.)

2. *General Board*—A continuing body of the Church created by the General Conference to carry out assigned functions of program, administration, and/or service shall be designated as a general board.

3. *General Commission*—An organization created by the General Conference for the fulfillment of a specific function for an indefinite period of time.

4. *Study Committee*—An organization created by the General Conference for a limited period of time for the purpose of making a study ordered by the General Conference. The General Council on Ministries shall provide for coordination with and among the study committees except where General Conference otherwise designates.

5. *Program-Related General Agencies*—The general boards and commissions that have program and/or advocacy functions shall be designated as program-related general agencies. These agencies are amenable to the General Conference and between sessions of the General Conference are accountable to the General Council on Ministries: the General Board of Church and Society, the General Board of Discipleship, the General Board of Global Ministries, the General Board of Higher Education and Ministry, the General Commission on

---

3. *See* Judicial Council Decision 496.

Christian Unity and Interreligious Concerns, the General Commission on Religion and Race, the General Commission on United Methodist Men, and the General Commission on the Status and Role of Women.[4] In all matters of accountability, episcopal oversight as provided in ¶ 427 is assumed.

6. *Administrative General Agencies*—The general boards and commissions that have primarily administrative and service functions shall be designated as administrative general agencies. These agencies are the General Board of Pension and Health Benefits, The United Methodist Publishing House, and the General Commission on Archives and History and General Commission on Communication, both of which also carry program-related responsibilities for which they are accountable to the General Council on Ministries.

7. Each general agency, unless otherwise provided, shall adopt the following executive staff titles:

*a) General Secretary*—the chief staff officer of a general agency. Each general agency is entitled to only one general secretary, who is its chief administrative officer.

*b) Deputy General Secretary*—the chief staff officer assigned to oversight of a major programmatic or administrative unit(s), or with major programmatic or administrative responsibilities with a general board or council.

*c) Associate General Secretary*—the associate staff officer of a general agency or the chief staff officer of a division or a department of a general agency.

*d) Assistant General Secretary*—the assistant staff officer of a general agency or the chief staff officer of a section or office of a general agency.

*e) Treasurer*—the staff financial officer of a general agency, entrusted with the receipt, care, and disbursement of agency funds. In some general agencies there may be associate and/or assistant treasurers. There are general agencies in which "treasurer" is not a staff title but is an officer elected from the voting membership of the agency.

8. *Theme*—A theme is a theological focus, missional emphasis, prophetic statement, or program catalyst for ministry. A theme enhances programs or ministries basic to the life of the Church and serves as a rallying point for constituents involved in those programs.

---

4. *See* Judicial Council Decision 496.

9. *Missional Priority*—A missional priority is a response to a critical need in God's world that calls The United Methodist Church to a massive and sustained effort through primary attention and ordering or reordering of program and budget at every level of the Church, as adopted by the General Conference or in accord with ¶ 906.1. This need is evidenced by research or other supporting data, and the required response is beyond the capacity of any single general agency or annual conference. However, the ongoing priority of The United Methodist Church both in program and budget is to proclaim the good news that salvation comes through Jesus Christ.

10. *Special Program*—A special program is a quadrennial emphasis initiated by a general program-related agency in accordance with ¶¶ 906.1, .2, and .4, approved by General Conference, and assigned to a general program-related agency. The program shall be designed in response to a distinct opportunity or need in God's world that is evidenced by research or other supporting data and shall propose achievable goals within the quadrennium.

11. *Program*—A program is an ongoing or special activity designed and implemented to fulfill a basic disciplinary responsibility of a general agency accountable to the General Council on Ministries.

12. *Association or Fellowship*—Organizations not created by nor officially related to the General Conference and intended to provide professional relationships conducive to sharing professional techniques and information for groups within the denomination shall be designated as associations or fellowships.

¶ **704.** *Financial Accountability of General Agencies*—All general agencies receiving general church funds (*see* ¶ 810.2) shall account for receipts and expenditures of funds in a format designed by the General Council on Finance and Administration. A quadrennial report of such accounting shall be included in the report of the General Council on Finance and Administration to the General Conference. The report will include, in fully descriptive form, the amount of remuneration, in cash, and in cash value of any in-kind benefits provided to all executive employees, clergy and lay, of all general agencies, where executives shall include at least those persons in positions described in ¶ 703.7. No information in the report will be considered to be confidential, and in keeping with the spirit of ¶ 702.4, all information therein will be made available upon request.

Annual reports shall be made available by the respective agencies upon the request of annual conferences and local church councils or boards. The annual reports prepared by the agencies shall include a listing of organizations, individuals, associations, fellowships, coalitions, consultants, programs, and entities not formally part of the Church, and the amount (expended annually) of monetary and in-kind contributions. The listing shall include, but not be limited to, office space, printing, staff assistance, purchases, travel expense, and other forms of financial assistance that have been granted to such entities.

¶ 705. *General Agency Membership*—The people of God are called to faithful discipleship in the name of Jesus Christ. "The gifts he gave were that some would be apostles, some prophets, some evangelists, some pastors and teachers, to equip the saints for the work of ministry, for building up the body of Christ" (Ephesians 4:11-12). In response to God's call, some are called forth from local congregations to fulfill the common mission of The United Methodist Church as an expression of the Church made visible in the world. This call includes the invitation to some to be in ministry with others who together seek to fulfill the vision for the Church as members of general agencies. Such persons come to this ministry as servants of the whole Church.

The following provisions shall govern the nomination and election of the voting membership of those general agencies to which the jurisdictional conferences elect and central conferences nominate members.[5] All provisions pertaining to the nomination and election of general agency members shall take effect immediately upon the adjournment of the General Conference that enacts them. The secretary of the General Conference shall coordinate the processes pertaining to nominations and elections of general agency members.

1. *Nominations by Conferences—a)* Each annual and missionary conference in the United States, upon recommendation from a committee composed of the bishop and the general and jurisdictional conference delegation, and having allowed opportunity for nominations from the floor, shall elect persons to be submitted to a jurisdictional pool. The jurisdictional nominating committee shall select persons for election to the following general agencies: General Council on Ministries; General Board of Church and Society; General Board of Discipleship; General Board of Global Ministries; General Board of Higher Education and Ministry; General Board of Pension

---

5. *See* Judicial Council Decision 467.

and Health Benefits; The United Methodist Publishing House; General Commission on Christian Unity and Interreligious Concerns; General Commission on Communication; General Commission on Religion and Race; and the General Commission on the Status and Role of Women. Jurisdictional conferences may decide that persons elected by the annual and missionary conferences in the United States for inclusion in the jurisdictional pool shall not serve as members of the jurisdictional nominating committee.

*b)* Each annual and missionary conference in the United States shall nominate the persons most recently elected as delegates to the General Conference to the jurisdictional pool. In addition, it shall nominate at least fifteen and not more than forty-five persons to the jurisdictional pool, including, where available, at least two racial and ethnic persons from each of the ethnic groups Asian American, African American, Hispanic American, Native American, Pacific Islanders; and where available at least one and not more than five persons in each of the following seven categories: (1) clergy (including at least one woman), (2) laywomen, (3) laymen, (4) youth (¶ 258.2), (5) young adults, (6) older adults, and (7) persons with disabilities. Eligibility to be nominated in one category does not preclude being nominated in another category as long as the nominee is nominated only once.

*c)* Each central conference or a body authorized by it shall nominate to each general program board membership at least one person from each of the following three categories: (1) clergy, (2) laymen, and (3) laywomen to form a pool from which each board is to elect the additional members that are to come from the central conferences pursuant to ¶ 705.5.c. These lists shall be sent to the General Council on Ministries for use by the general agencies in electing additional members.

*d)* All nominees shall list one to three preferences for agency membership. In addition all nominees shall prepare an up to one-hundred-word biographical statement listing experience, gifts, training, and other qualifications for general agency membership. Biographical statements for all persons in the central and jurisdictional conference pools shall be available to the nominating committee members in the meeting at which they make their nominations. Names and biographical data of all persons nominated by the annual and missionary conferences in the United States or the central conferences, but not elected, shall be forwarded by the jurisdictional or central conference secretary to the General Council on Ministries to be used by the general agencies as a pool from which additional members may be elected (§§ 5e, 6b).[6]

2. *Additional Nominations*—In addition to the foregoing provisions (¶ 705.1), the United Methodist Youth Organization shall nominate ten youth to each jurisdictional pool, inclusive of race, ethnicity, gender, size of church, and persons with disabilities.

3. Members of the general agencies shall be elected using the following formula:

*a)* Five persons from each annual and missionary conference in the United States. At least thirty of these persons will be women elected by the Women's Division process as members on the General Board of Global Ministries.

*b)* Five persons from each central conference.

*c) Supplemental members*—Each annual and missionary conference whose membership exceeds 75,000 (as determined by the official records of the denomination on December 31 of the year immediately preceding the General Conference) shall have the following supplemental members of general agencies:

75,001–150,000: one supplemental member;

150,001–225,000: a total of two supplemental members; and

225,001 or more: a total of three supplemental members.

*d)* Seven persons from the Iglesia Metodista Autónoma Afiliada de Puerto Rico.

*e)* A total of 124 additional at-large members for inclusiveness and expertise.

*f)* Fifty-three effective episcopal leaders.

*g)* The total membership of all general agencies shall not exceed 667.

*h)* Each general agency shall elect at least one, but not more than three, member(s) with vote and voice from among the member churches of the Commission on Pan Methodist Cooperation. In addition, it is recommended that each general agency elect at least one member without vote from among the other member churches of the Consultation on Church Union. These members would be in addition to those otherwise specified in ¶ 705.3(*a-g*) above. The General Commission on Christian Unity and Interreligious Concerns shall assist general agencies in their compliance with this provision.

---

6. *See* Judicial Council Decisions 520, 538.

*i)* It is recommended that the membership of general agencies include both youth (¶ 255.2) and young adults. It is recommended that, wherever possible, at least 10 percent of the membership of each general agency be equally divided between youth and young adults. The youth and young adult membership of each general agency should be inclusive (consistent with ¶ 705.3 *j*).

*j)* It is recommended that the membership of each of the general agencies seeks to be inclusive based on gender, racial and ethnic persons, age, persons with disabilities, and size of church. In order to ensure adequate representation of racial and ethnic persons (Asian American, African Americans, Hispanic Americans, Native Americans, Pacific Islanders), it is recommended that a jurisdiction's membership on each general agency be at least 30 percent racial and ethnic persons and incorporate one-third clergy, one-third laymen, and one-third laywomen (except as provided in ¶¶ 1104, 1311). The episcopal members shall not be counted in the computation of the clergy membership.

*k)* The membership of the General Commission on United Methodist Men shall be elected in accordance with ¶ 534 and ¶ 2303.1. This legislation shall take effect upon the adjournment of the 2000 General Conference.

4. Members identified in § 3*a–f* will be elected as follows:

*a)* categories *a* and *c* (as applicable) shall be elected by the jurisdictional and central conferences, except for the members elected by the Women's Division process;

*b)* categories *b* and *c* (as applicable) shall be elected by the central conferences;

*c)* category *d* shall be elected by the Iglesia Metodista Autónoma Afiliada de Puerto Rico; and

*d)* category *e* shall be elected by the general agencies for inclusiveness and expertise.

*e)* The secretary of the General Conference shall assign the number of members to be elected to each general agency by each jurisdictional conference and the central conferences. The number of members will be determined on an equitable basis taking into consideration the total number to be elected by each jurisdiction and central conference.

5. *General Program Board Membership—a)* Each general program board shall have the number of members specified in ¶¶ 1006, 1104, 1311, and 1407, or as determined by the secretary of the General Conference (see ¶ 705.4*e*).

*b) Jurisdictional Membership*—Each jurisdiction shall elect the number of persons listed in the specific legislation for membership on each of the four general program boards. In the jurisdictional nominating process for membership on those boards, special attention shall be given to the inclusion of clergywomen, youth, (¶ 255.2), young adults, older adults, people with disabilities, and persons from small membership churches. In order to ensure adequate representation of racial and ethnic persons (Asian Americans, African Americans, Hispanic Americans, Native Americans, Pacific Islanders), it is recommended that at least 30 percent of a jurisdiction's membership on each general program board be racial and ethnic persons. It is further recommended that the jurisdiction membership on each program board incorporate one-third clergy, one-third laymen, and one-third laywomen (except as provided in ¶¶ 1104.1, 1311.2; *see also* ¶¶ 1311.6, 1407). The episcopal members shall not be counted in the computation of the clergy membership.[7]

*c) Central Conference Membership*—Each general program board shall elect at least four persons from the central conferences and one alternate for each who may attend if the elected member cannot attend. In the election of the central conference members, it is recommended that at least one clergy, one layman, and one laywoman be elected as specified in general agency paragraphs.

*d) Episcopal Membership*—The episcopal membership of the general program boards shall be not less than six nor more than eight members nominated by the Council of Bishops and elected by the General Conference (*see* exception, ¶ 1311.6). At least one of the episcopal members of each general program board shall be a central conference bishop.

*e) Additional Membership*—(1) Additional members shall be elected by each general program board in order to bring into the board persons with special knowledge or background that will aid in the work of the agency, to consider differing theological perspectives, and to perfect the representation of racial and ethnic persons, youth (¶ 255.2), young adults, older adults, women and men, people with disabilities, and persons from small-membership churches, and distribution by geographic area. Each general program board shall elect additional members as specified in general program board membership paragraphs. Insofar as possible, no more than one person shall

---

7. *See* Judicial Council Decisions 451, 467.

435

be elected from each episcopal area. It is recommended that such additional membership shall maintain the one-third laymen, one-third laywomen, and one-third clergy balance.[8]

(2) *Consultation Membership*—It is recommended that each general program board elect at least one member without vote from among the member churches of the Consultation on Church Union, other than The United Methodist Church, as an additional member.

6. *Other General Agencies*—*a*) Each jurisdictional conference shall elect members from the jurisdictional pool nominated by the annual and missionary conferences in the United States (¶ 705.1) in accordance with the specific membership provisions of those agencies as set forth in the *Book of Discipline:* General Council on Ministries (¶ 907), General Board of Pension and Health Benefits (¶ 1502.1*a*), The United Methodist Publishing House (¶ 1602), General Commission on Christian Unity and Interreligious Concerns (¶ 1906), General Commission on Communication (¶ 1807), General Commission on the Status and Role of Women (¶ 2104), and General Commission on Religion and Race (¶ 2003).

*b*) Episcopal and additional members, if any, of the general agencies listed in ¶ 205.5*a* shall be nominated and elected by the procedures specified in the paragraphs listed in ¶¶ 705.1*b*, 705.1*d*, and 705.5*a*. The agencies shall consider names forwarded to them by the General Council on Ministries as having been nominated by the annual and missionary conferences in the United States or in the central conferences, but not elected by these conferences to general agency membership. Additional names may be considered in order to perfect the representation as provided in ¶ 705.5*e*.

¶ **706.** *Nomination of Additional Board Members*—1. Giving due consideration to inclusiveness (see ¶¶ 124, 138), each jurisdiction shall designate one clergy, one laywoman, and one layman whom it has elected to a general program agency or to the General Council on Ministries to nominate the additional members of that program agency or council (¶ 705.5). The fifteen members thus designated by the five jurisdictions in each general program agency and in the General Council on Ministries shall constitute a committee to nominate additional members for that agency and shall be convened as provided in ¶ 706.2.

---

8. *See* Judicial Council Decisions 377, 446, 520.

2. A bishop designated by the president of the Council of Bishops shall convene the committee as soon as practical after jurisdictional elections have been completed. The committee shall consider, but not be limited to, names forwarded to it by the jurisdictions as having been nominated by the annual and missionary conferences in the United States and Puerto Rico to their jurisdictional pool as well as names from caucuses and other appropriate groups. To aid the committee, biographical data submitted by the annual conferences (¶ 705.1*d*) shall be made available from the jurisdictional conference secretaries. In addition, general agencies shall submit to the committee names and biographical data of persons eligible for reelection who are willing to serve. The provisions of the paragraph shall become effective immediately upon adjournment of the General Conference.

3. The committee shall complete its work prior to the organizational meeting (¶ 707) of any of the agencies listed in ¶ 703.5 and report by mail to the previously elected members of each of those agencies the names of persons nominated as additional members of that agency. All members shall be elected and seated before an agency proceeds to the election of officers or any other business.

¶ 707. *Meetings*—1. In those years in which the General Conference holds its regular session, all general program agencies shall meet, organize, and conduct such business as may properly come before the agency not later than ninety days after the close of the jurisdictional conferences. Each organizational meeting shall be convened by a bishop designated by the president of the Council of Bishops.

2. All councils, boards, commissions, and committees established by a general, jurisdictional, central, annual, or other conference shall meet and organize as promptly as feasible following the selection of their members.

3. Unless otherwise specified in the *Discipline* or by the establishing conference, every council, board, commission, and committee shall continue in responsibility until its successor council, board, commission, or committee is organized.

¶ 708. *Organization*—1. Each program board shall elect a president and one or more vice presidents from the voting membership of the board, and a secretary, treasurer, and such other officers as it deems appropriate, giving consideration to inclusiveness (¶¶ 124, 138); *provided* that all officers shall be members of The United Methodist Church.

2. Each program board shall elect chairpersons for its divisions, departments, or other subunits from the voting membership of the board. The divisions, departments, or other subunits shall elect a vice chairperson, a secretary, and such other officers as it deems appropriate.

3. Terms of officers of boards, divisions, and departments, or other subunits shall be for the quadrennium or until their successors are elected.

4. No person shall serve as president or chairperson of more than one general agency or division, department, or the structural counterpart thereof.

5. Staff of program boards shall not be eligible to serve as officers of corresponding General Conference legislative committees.

¶ 709. *Divisions and Subunits*—The membership of each program board shall be divided among the divisions or other subunits of the board in such number as the board determines.

¶ 710. *Membership Qualifications*—1. Members of all general agencies shall be full members of The United Methodist Church except as provided in ¶ 705.2j.

2. Members of all general agencies shall be persons of genuine Christian character who love the Church, are morally disciplined and loyal to the ethical standards of The United Methodist Church as set forth in the Social Principles, and are otherwise competent to serve as members of general agencies.

3. A voting member of a general agency shall be eligible for membership on that agency for no more than two consecutive four-year terms. The four-year term shall begin at the first organizational meeting of that agency following General Conference. Service of more than one year in fulfilling an unexpired or vacated position shall be considered as a full four-year term. To provide a continuing membership on these agencies, it is recommended that each nominating and electing body give special attention to continuing and effective membership on these agencies. If a general agency is merged with another agency, the years served by members prior to the merger shall be counted as part of the maximum specified above.[9]

A person who has been a voting member of general agencies for four consecutive quadrenniums shall be ineligible for election to a general agency in the succeeding quadrennium. The foregoing shall not apply to episcopal members.

---

9. *See* Judicial Council Decision 495.

4. No person shall serve at the same time on more than one general agency or any part thereof, except where the *Discipline* specifically provides for such interagency representation; provided, however, that if this limitation would deprive a jurisdiction of its full episcopal representation on an agency, it may be suspended to the extent necessary to permit such representation.[10] (*See* ¶ 907.1*b*.)

5. A voting member of a general agency, by virtue of such membership, shall become an ex officio (voting) member of the corresponding agency or its equivalent structure, if any, in the annual conference in accordance with the provisions of ¶ 607.6; unless such membership would conflict with ¶ 609.2*b*(2). Elected lay members of the General Board of Higher Education and Ministry may serve as lay observers in their annual conference board of ordained ministry (¶ 633.1) if so nominated by the resident bishop.

6. No person who receives compensation for services rendered or commissions of any kind from an agency shall be eligible for voting membership on that agency.[11]

7. No elected member, officer, or other employee shall vote on or take part in deliberations on significant matters directly or indirectly affecting his or her business, income, or employment, or the business, income, or employment of a member of his or her immediate family.

8. *a*) If any clergy member of a general or jurisdictional agency who was elected to represent a certain annual conference ceases to be a member of that annual conference, or if any lay member so elected changes permanent residence to a place outside the bounds of that annual conference, that member's place shall automatically become vacant.

*b*) If any clergy member of a general agency who was chosen to represent a certain jurisdiction ceases to be a member of an annual conference in that jurisdiction, or if any lay member so elected changes permanent residence to a place outside the bounds of that jurisdiction, that member's place shall automatically become vacant.

*c*) If any clergy member of a jurisdictional agency ceases to be a member of an annual conference in that jurisdiction, or if any lay member so elected changes permanent residence to a place outside the bounds of the jurisdiction, that member's place shall automatically become vacant.

---

10. *See* Judicial Council Decision 224.
11. *See* Judicial Council Decision 139.

9. If a member of a general agency is absent from two consecutive meetings of the agency without a reason acceptable to the agency, that person shall cease to be a member thereof. In that case the person shall be so notified, and that place shall be filled in accordance with the appropriate provisions of the *Discipline*.

10. When a bishop is unable to attend a meeting of an agency of which that bishop is a member, that bishop may name another bishop to attend that meeting with the privilege of vote. When an alternate to a central conference bishop must be named, that alternate shall be another central conference bishop.

¶ 711. *Dismissal of Members and Employees*—The councils, boards, committees, or commissions elected, authorized, or provided for by the General Conference shall have full power and authority to remove and dismiss at their discretion any member, officer, or employee thereof:

1. Who has become incapacitated so as to be unable to perform official duties.

2. Who is guilty of immoral conduct or breach of trust.

3. Who for any reason is unable to or who fails to perform the duties of the office or for other misconduct that any council, board, committee, or commission may deem sufficient to warrant such dismissal and removal.

In the event that any member, officer, or employee of such council, board, committee, or commission, elected, authorized, or provided for by the General Conference, is found guilty of any crime involving moral turpitude by any federal, state, or county court or pleads guilty thereto, then the council, board, committee, or commission of which that person is a member, officer, or employee shall be and is hereby authorized to remove such member, officer, or employee so convicted; and the place so vacated shall be filled as provided in the *Discipline*.

¶ 712. *Vacancies*—Unless otherwise specified, vacancies on general agencies occurring during the quadrennium shall be filled as follows: an episcopal vacancy shall be filled by the Council of Bishops; a vacancy in the jurisdictional or central conference membership shall be filled by the corresponding College of Bishops, with notice of the vacancy sent by the agency to the secretary of the Council of Bishops; a vacancy in the additional membership shall be filled by the agency itself. When the vacancy has been filled, the secretary of the agency will immediately notify the new member's annual conference secretary.

¶ **713.** *Accountability of General Secretaries to the General Council on Ministries*—The general secretary of each general program agency that is accountable to the General Council on Ministries shall be elected annually by ballot of the General Council on Ministries upon the nomination of the agency involved. Any general secretary of a general program agency who has not been elected by the General Council on Ministries shall not serve in such capacity beyond the end of that calendar year. Each general program agency shall elect annually by ballot its deputy and associate general secretary(ies) and may elect or appoint such other staff as may be necessary.[12]

¶ **714.** *Provisions Pertaining to Staff*—1. No elected general program agency staff shall hold the same position more than twelve years. Years of service prior to January 1, 1989, are not counted. The agency responsible for the election of such staff may annually suspend this provision by a two-thirds ballot vote.[13]

2. Official travel of the staffs of agencies shall be interpreted to include all travel that is necessary in the performance of official duties directly related to the agency functions. No staff person shall accept honoraria for such official duties. A staff member may accept an engagement not related to the functions of the employing agency when such an engagement does not interfere with official duties; the staff member may accept an honorarium for services rendered in connection with such engagements.

3. Normal retirement for all general agency staff personnel shall be at age sixty-five or the completion of forty years of service to The United Methodist Church in an elective, appointive, or employed capacity. Mandatory retirement for elective and appointive staff shall be at age seventy. There shall be no mandatory retirement age for other employed staff. All general agency staff personnel may elect to retire from the employing general agency at any time in accordance with the policy in place at the general agency or, if the general agency has a voting representative on the Committee on Personnel Policies and Practices of the General Council on Finance and Administration, with the policy established by the General Council on Finance and Administration upon recommendation of the Committee on Personnel Policies and Practices.

---

12. *See* Judicial Council Decisions 499, 567.
13. *See* Judicial Council Decisions 567, 858.

4. Provisions of the Staff Retirement Benefits Program shall be reviewed, with recommendations, by the Committee on Personnel Policies and Practices (¶ 807.11*b*).

5. The general secretary of the General Council on Ministries and/or the general secretary of the General Council on Finance and Administration may convene the general secretaries of the general agencies as necessary for the purpose of obtaining opinion and recommendations to assist the councils in discharging their functions.

6. All general secretaries, deputy general secretaries, associate general secretaries, and assistant general secretaries of all general agencies shall be members of The United Methodist Church. This provision shall not apply to persons employed prior to the 1992 General Conference.[14]

7. No member of the staff of a general agency shall be eligible for voting membership on any general or jurisdictional agency of The United Methodist Church, except where the *Discipline* specifically provides for such interagency representation.

8. Elected staff shall be allowed voice, but not vote in the agency and its subunits.

9. All management staff persons of general agencies shall be persons who model themselves after the servanthood of Jesus Christ. They shall be persons of genuine Christian character who love the Church and are committed to the oneness of the body of Christ, are morally disciplined and loyal to the ethical standards of The United Methodist Church as set forth in the Social Principles, and are competent to administer the affairs of a general agency.

10. Prior to any interviews of clergypersons for general board or agency staff positions, the bishop of the clergyperson under consideration shall be consulted at the initiative of the board or agency.

¶ 715. *Nondiscrimination Policies*—1. It shall be the policy of The United Methodist Church that all agencies and institutions, including hospitals, homes, and educational institutions, shall: *(a)* recruit, employ, utilize, recompense, and promote their professional staff and other personnel in a manner consistent with the commitment of The United Methodist Church to women and men of all races and ethnic origins, including persons with disabilities; *(b)* fulfill their duties and responsibilities in a manner that does not involve segregation or discrimination on the basis of race, color, age, sex, or disability, including HIV status; and *(c)* provide for adequate representation by laity.

---

14. *See* Judicial Council Decision 426.

2. All agencies and institutions shall, insofar as reasonably possible, schedule and hold all events, including designated places of lodging and meals for the events, in accessible settings that adequately accommodate persons with disabilities.

If for any reason whatsoever any event is scheduled or held in a facility that does not so conform, all notices of the meeting will include plainly stated advice to that effect, or alternatively may bear a logo consisting of the international symbol for access placed inside a slashed circle. The term *event* shall be given a broad interpretation and shall include, by way of example, scheduled conferences, seminars, and other meetings to which persons are invited or called to attend as representatives of the Church or its various institutions and agencies.

¶ **716.** *Socially Responsible Investments*—It shall be the policy of The United Methodist Church that all general boards and agencies, including the General Board of Pension and Health Benefits, and all administrative agencies and institutions, including hospitals, homes, educational institutions, annual conferences, foundations, and local churches, shall, in the investment of money, make a conscious effort to invest in institutions, companies, corporations, or funds whose practices are consistent with the goals outlined in the Social Principles; and shall endeavor to avoid investments that appear likely, directly or indirectly, to support racial discrimination, violation of human rights, sweatshop or forced labor, gambling, or the production of nuclear armaments, alcoholic beverages or tobacco, or companies dealing in pornography. The boards and agencies are to give careful consideration to shareholder advocacy, including advocacy of corporate disinvestment.

¶ **717.** *Record Maintenance*—Each general agency shall keep a continuous record of its advocacy roles, coalitions, and other organizations supported by membership or funds, and endorsement or opposition of federal or state legislation. Information concerning these activities shall be available to United Methodist churches upon written request. Organizations not officially related to the General Conference may take positions only in their own names and may not speak for a general agency or the denomination as a whole (¶ 509.1).

¶ **718.** *Decisions for Program Expenditures*—All programs or general funds administered by any general agency of The United Methodist Church (¶ 701) that are proposed to be used within an annual conference shall be implemented or disbursed only after consultation with the presiding bishop, the director of connectional ministries or equivalent, the Council on Ministries, and the appropriate district superintendent(s) of that annual conference. Consultation in matters of program implementation, funding, and relationships among various agencies, conferences, and other bodies of the Church requires communication, including written documentation, in which each party reveals plans and intents in such a way as to assure dialogue and mutual awareness, even if not agreement.[15]

¶ **719.** *International and Ecumenical Settings*—The General Board of Global Ministries shall facilitate and coordinate the program relationships of other program agencies of The United Methodist Church with colleague churches and agencies in nations other than the United States. The resources of the General Board of Global Ministries shall also be available to the Council of Bishops in the implementation of its responsibilities as defined in ¶ 416.2, .3. Central conferences of The United Methodist Church may request program and other assistance through direct relationships with the program agencies of The United Methodist Church.

¶ **720.** *Program and Fiscal Year*—1. The program and fiscal year for The United Methodist Church shall be the calendar year.

2. Unless otherwise specified in the *Discipline* for a specific purpose, the term *quadrennium* shall be deemed to be the four-year period beginning January 1 following the adjournment of the regular session of the General Conference.[16]

¶ **721.** *Restrictions on Closed Meetings*—In the spirit of openness and accountability, all meetings of councils, boards, agencies, commissions, and committees of the Church, including subunit meetings and teleconferences, shall be open. Portions of a meeting may be closed for consideration of specific subjects if such a closed session is authorized by an affirmative public vote with at least three-fourths of the voting members present. The vote shall be taken in public session and recorded in the minutes. Documents distributed in open meetings shall be considered public.

Great restraint should be used in closing meetings; closed sessions should be used as seldom as possible. Subjects that may be considered in closed session are limited to real estate matters; negotiations, when general knowledge could be harmful to the negotiation process;

---

15. *See* Judicial Council Decision 518.
16. *See* Judicial Council Decision 559.

personnel matters;[17] issues related to the accreditation or approval of institutions; discussions relating to pending or potential litigation or collective bargaining; communications with attorneys or accountants; deployment of security personnel or devices and negotiations involving confidential third-party information. While it is expected that the General Conference, the Judicial Council and the Council of Bishops will live by the spirit of this paragraph, each of these constitutional bodies is governed by its own rules of procedure.

A report on the results of a closed session shall be made immediately upon its conclusion or as soon thereafter as is practicable.

¶ 722. *Evangelical United Brethren Council of Administration*—The General Council on Finance and Administration shall preserve the corporate existence of the Evangelical United Brethren Council of Administration until such time as attorneys shall advise its dissolution. The General Council on Finance and Administration shall nominate for election the Board of Trustees of the Evangelical United Brethren Council of Administration.

¶ 723. *Translation of Church Name*—The name of The United Methodist Church may be translated by any central conference into languages other than English. The United Methodist Church in the Central and Southern Europe Central Conference and the Germany Central Conference may use the name *Evangelisch-methodistische Kirche.*

¶ 724. *Church Founding Date*—The United Methodist Church (¶ 118) has become the successor to all rights, powers, and privileges of The Evangelical United Brethren Church and The Methodist Church. The two churches, from their beginnings, have had a close relationship.

The Methodist Church, the first of the two churches to organize, dates from the Christmas Conference of 1784. Therefore, The United Methodist Church recognizes as its founding date the year 1784.

All General Conferences shall be designated not in numerical sequence from any particular date, but merely by the calendar years in which they are respectively held. An annual conference, local church, or other body within The United Methodist Church that is composed of uniting units with differing dates of origin shall use as the date of its founding the date of founding of the older or oldest of the uniting units while remaining sensitive to the recording of the

17. *See* Judicial Council Decision 751.

entirety of the Church's history, including all information regarding the younger unit.

### Section II. General Council on Finance and Administration

¶ 801. The work of the Church requires the support of our people. Participation through service and gifts is a Christian duty, a means of grace, and an expression of our love to God. In order that all members of The United Methodist Church may share in its manifold ministries at home and abroad and that the work committed to us may prosper, the following financial plan has been duly approved and adopted.

¶ 802. *Name*—There shall be a General Council on Finance and Administration of The United Methodist Church, hereinafter called the council.

¶ 803. *Incorporation*—The council shall be incorporated in such state or states as the council shall determine. This corporation shall be the successor corporation and organization to the Council on World Service and Finance (including the Council on World Service and Finance of The United Methodist Church, an Illinois corporation; the World Service Commission of the Methodist Episcopal Church, an Illinois corporation; the General Council of Administration of The Evangelical United Brethren Church, an Ohio corporation; the Board of Administration, Church of the United Brethren in Christ, an Ohio corporation) and the Board of Trustees.

This corporation shall receive and administer new trusts and funds, and so far as may be legal be the successor in trust of: The Board of Trustees of The United Methodist Church; The Board of Trustees of The Evangelical United Brethren Church, incorporated under the laws of Ohio; The Board of Trustees of the Church of the United Brethren in Christ, incorporated under the laws of Ohio; The Board of Trustees of The Evangelical Church, an unincorporated body; The Board of Trustees of The Methodist Church, incorporated under the laws of Ohio; The Trustees of The Methodist Episcopal Church, incorporated under the laws of Ohio; The Board of Trustees of The Methodist Episcopal Church, South, incorporated under the laws of Tennessee; and The Board of Trustees of The Methodist Protestant Church, incorporated under the laws of Maryland; and so far as may be legal, as such successor in trust, it is authorized to receive from any of its said predecessor corporations all trust funds and assets of every kind and character—real, personal, or mixed— held by them or any one of them, or to merge into itself any one or more of its said predecessor corporations. Any such trusts and funds coming to it as successor corporation, either by transfer or by merger, shall be administered in accordance with the conditions under which they have been previously received and administered by said predecessor corporations or unincorporated body.

¶ 804. *Amenability*—The council shall report to and be amenable to the General Conference, and it shall cooperate with the General Council on Ministries in the compilation of budgets for program agencies participating in World Service Funds, as defined in ¶ 806.1.

¶ 805. *Organization*—1. *Membership*—*a)* The voting members of the Council shall be elected quadrennially by the General Conference and shall consist of forty persons nominated as follows:

(1) three bishops, nominated by the Council of Bishops;

(2) six persons from each jurisdiction, nominated by the bishops of that jurisdiction;

(3) one person from an annual conference in the central conferences, nominated by the Council of Bishops; and

(4) six members at large, at least one of whom shall be a young person between the ages of twelve and seventeen and at least one of whom shall not be over thirty years of age at the time of election, and most of whom shall be elected for special skills. The members at large shall be nominated by the Council of Bishops without reference to jurisdictions.

*b)* It is recommended that attention be given to ensuring adequate representation of racial and ethnic groups, with at least two of the at-large members to be racial and ethnic persons. It is further recommended that in the membership from each of the jurisdictions and the at-large members, one-third be clergy in full connection, one-third be laymen, and one-third be laywomen.

*c)* The general secretaries who serve as the chief executive officers of the general agencies and the publisher of The United Methodist Church may sit with the council and shall have the right to the floor without the privilege of voting.

*d)* The voting members, including bishops, shall not be eligible for membership on, or employment by, any other general agency of The United Methodist Church (¶ 701.2), except where the *Book of Discipline* specifically provides for such interagency representation. Members shall also be guided by such conflict-of-interest policies and

447

provisions as may from time to time be adopted by the General Conference or by the council itself.

*e)* Members shall serve until their successors are elected and qualified.

*f)* Vacancies occurring between sessions of the General Conference shall be filled by the council on nomination of the College of Bishops of the jurisdiction concerned (*see* ¶ 712) if the vacancy is among members chosen to represent a jurisdiction, or, in the event of a vacancy among the episcopal, central conference, or at-large members, on nomination of the Council of Bishops.

2. *Meetings*—The council shall meet at least annually and at such other times as are necessary on call of the president or on written request of one-fifth of the members. Twenty-one voting members shall constitute a quorum.

3. *Officers*—The officers of the council shall be a president, a vice president, a recording secretary, and a general secretary, who shall also be the treasurer of the council, all of whom shall be elected by the council (*see* § 5). They shall serve until the adjournment of the next succeeding quadrennial session of the General Conference after their election and until their successors are duly elected and qualified. The president, vice president, and recording secretary shall be elected from the membership of the council. The general secretary shall sit with the council and its executive committee at all sessions and shall have the right to the floor without the privilege of voting.

4. *Committees*—*a) Executive Committee*—There shall be an executive committee of the council, consisting of the episcopal members, the officers of the council, chairpersons of the committees on services as defined in the council bylaws, the chairperson of the Committee on Council Operations, and up to three members at large to assure that, in addition to the episcopal members, there is at least one member from each jurisdiction and there is racial and ethnic participation. The executive committee shall meet on call of the president or of a majority of the membership and shall act for the council and exercise its powers in the interim between the meetings of the council, but it shall not take any action contrary to or in conflict with any action or policy of the council. A copy of the minutes of each meeting of the executive committee shall be sent from the central office to each member of the council as soon after the meeting as practicable.

*b) Committee on Audit and Review*—The executive committee of the council shall appoint a **Committee on Audit and Review**, no members of which shall be officers or members of the executive committee of the council, and at least half of whom shall not be members of the council, whose duty it shall be to review audits of all treasuries receiving general Church funds (*see* ¶ 810.2), including the funds of the council, and related policies with financial implications. Not included are the audits of the General Board of Pension and Health Benefits and The United Methodist Publishing House. In any matter of possible or potential financial impropriety reported to the committee by the auditors, the committee chair shall immediately inform the president and general secretary of the General Council on Finance and Administration and the president and general secretary of the applicable agency. The committee shall report its findings to the annual meeting of the council.

*c) Committee on Official Forms and Records*—The council shall maintain and supervise under the direction of its general secretary a **Committee on Official Forms and Records**, which shall have the duty of preparing and editing all official statistical forms, record forms, and record books for use in the Church. The committee shall consist of one bishop elected by the Council of Bishops and nine persons elected by the General Council on Finance and Administration, as follows: one member of the council from each jurisdiction, one conference secretary, one conference treasurer, one conference statistician, and one district superintendent. The following persons shall be consultants to this committee ex officio, without vote: a staff representative of the council, the director of the Department of Statistics, a staff representative of the General Council on Ministries, a representative of The United Methodist Publishing House, and representatives of other general agencies when their programs are directly involved. All official record forms, record books, and certificates designed by the committee for use in The United Methodist Church and available for sale shall be printed and published through The United Methodist Publishing House.

*d) Committee on Personnel Policies and Practices*—The council shall organize a committee consisting of three representatives from the General Council on Finance and Administration, one of whom shall serve as chairperson, two representatives from the General Council on Ministries, and one representative of each of the following agencies: the General Board of Church and Society, the General Board of Discipleship, the General Board of Global Ministries, the General

Board of Higher Education and Ministry, the General Commission on Archives and History, the General Commission on Christian Unity and Interreligious Concerns, the General Commission on Communication, the General Commission on Religion and Race, the General Commission on the Status and Role of Women, and the General Commission on United Methodist Men. Each of the aforementioned representatives shall be selected by the council, board, or commission represented from its membership. The committee shall have duties and responsibilities as defined in ¶ 807.11*b*.

*e) Committee on Legal Responsibilities*—The council shall organize a committee composed of six persons, three of whom shall be members of the council. The committee shall be amenable to the council and shall make recommendations to the council regarding the fulfillment of the responsibilities defined in ¶ 807.7.

*f) Other Committees*—The council shall elect or appoint such other committees and task forces as needed for the performance of its duties.

5. *Staff*—The council shall elect a general secretary as provided in § 3 above. On nomination of the general secretary, the council may elect deputy and/or associate general secretaries, who shall work under the direction of the general secretary. The general secretary shall be the chief administrative officer of the council.

6. *Financial Support*—*a)* Financial support from general church funds for the work of the council shall be from the following sources: (1) an on-ratio allocation from the General Administration Fund, in an amount determined by the General Conference; (2) fixed charges against the World Service Fund, the Episcopal Fund, the Interdenominational Cooperation Fund, and such other general funds as the General Conference may authorize, on recommendation of the council. Fixed charges shall be in proportion to the funds' receipts.

*b)* The council shall submit to each quadrennial session of the General Conference budgets of estimated income and expense for the four years of the ensuing quadrennium. Prior to the beginning of each fiscal year, the council shall approve a budget for its operation for the following year. In the event of unanticipated circumstances, the council may, by a two-thirds vote, amend a budget it had previously approved for its own operation.

*c)* The council shall report to each quadrennial session of the General Conference the amounts of its actual income and expenditures for the four preceding years.

¶ **806.** *Fiscal Responsibilities*—All monies contributed by a local church to any of the general funds of the Church, as listed or defined in ¶ 810.1, and such other funds as may have been authorized by the General Conference shall be held in trust by the council and distributed only in support of the ministries of the respective funds. The council shall be accountable to The United Methodist Church through the General Conference in all matters relating to the receiving, disbursing, and reporting of such funds, and agencies receiving such funds shall be fiscally accountable to the council. In the exercise of its fiscal accountability role, the council shall have the authority and responsibility to perform the following functions:

1. It shall submit to each quadrennial session of the General Conference, for its action and determination, budgets of expense for each of the general funds of the Church, as listed or defined in ¶ 810.1, and such other general funds as the General Conference may establish. It shall also make recommendations regarding all other funding considerations to come before General Conference. Actual receipts for each fund for the quadrennium then ending shall be the basis for all budgeting procedures and comparisons for the coming quadrennium.

*a)* The council shall make recommendations to the General Conference as to the amount and distribution of all funds provided for in § 1 above.

*b)* In the case of the World Service Fund, the General Council on Finance and Administration and the General Council on Ministries shall proceed in the following manner in developing budget recommendations as they relate to allocations to the general program agencies of the Church:

(1) The General Council on Ministries shall, in consultation with the General Council on Finance and Administration and the general program agencies, develop recommendations to the General Council on Finance and Administration on needs of the general program agencies for the programs, missional priorities, and special programs.

(2) The General Council on Finance and Administration shall then establish and communicate to the General Council on Ministries the total sum proposed for distribution from the World Service Fund among the general program agencies.

(3) The General Council on Ministries, after reviewing both the program priorities and the total funds available to the general program agencies, shall recommend to the General Council on

Finance and Administration the amount of the annual World Service allocation to each of those agencies, within the total sum proposed by the General Council on Finance and Administration for distribution among such agencies.

(4) Only when the General Council on Finance and Administration and the General Council on Ministries agree on the allocations to the several general program agencies shall these allocations be included in the World Service budget to be recommended to the General Conference by the General Council on Finance and Administration.

(5) The General Council on Finance and Administration shall establish the total sum to be recommended to the General Conference for the annual budget of the World Service Fund.

(6) Before the beginning of each year, the General Council on Finance and Administration shall determine and communicate to the General Council on Ministries the sum available at that time from World Service contingency funds to meet requests for additional funding from the general program agencies. The General Council on Ministries shall be authorized to approve allocations to the general program agencies for additional program funding up to the limit so established. No money shall be allocated by the General Council on Ministries from this source for general administrative costs, fixed charges, or capital outlay without approval by the General Council on Finance and Administration.

(7) The General Council on Ministries shall receive from the General Council on Finance and Administration copies of the proposed annual budgets of the general program agencies, in order that it may review such budgets in relation to the program proposals made by those agencies in their quadrennial budget requests.

*c)* It shall recommend the formulas by which all apportionments to the annual conferences shall be determined, subject to the approval of the General Conference.

2. It shall receive and disburse in accordance with budgets and/or directives approved by the General Conference all funds raised throughout the Church for any of the general funds of the Church, as listed or defined in ¶ 810.1, and for any other fund or funds, as directed by the proper authority.

3. *Accounting and Reporting*—It shall require all agencies receiving general Church funds (*see* ¶ 810.2) to follow uniform accounting classifications and procedures for reporting. It shall include in its quad-

rennial report to the General Conference a fiscal report for each such agency receiving general Church funds.

4. *General Agency Budget Review*—It shall require annually one month in advance of its annual meeting, or as is deemed necessary, and in such form as the council may require, statements of proposed budgets of all treasuries or agencies receiving general Church funds (*see* ¶ 810.2). It shall review the budget of each agency receiving general Church funds in accordance with guidelines that it shall establish and communicate to the agencies, including the relationship between administration, service, and promotion. In the interest of sound fiscal management, the council will ensure that expenditures of agencies receiving general Church funds do not exceed receipts and available reserves, and this within a budget approved by the council.

5. *General Agency Audits*—It shall require an annual audit of all treasuries receiving general Church funds (*see* ¶ 810.2), following such auditing procedures as it may specify. It shall select the auditing firm for these annual audits based on a recommendation by the Committee on Audit and Review.

6. *Internal Audit Functions*—It shall establish and conduct the internal auditing functions for all agencies receiving general Church funds (*see* ¶ 810.2).

7. It shall establish policy governing the functions of banking, payroll, accounting, budget control, and internal auditing for all agencies receiving general Church funds (*see* ¶ 810.2). The council may, upon mutual consent of the agencies involved, perform the functions of banking, check preparation, and payroll on behalf of an agency in order to maximize efficiency of operation.

8. It shall review for approval plans for financing all international or national conferences and convocations to be held under the auspices of any general agency receiving general Church funds (*see* ¶ 810.2).

9. It shall be responsible for ensuring that no board, agency, committee, commission, or council shall give United Methodist funds to any gay caucus or group, or otherwise use such funds to promote the acceptance of homosexuality. The council shall have the right to stop such expenditures.[18] This restriction shall not limit the Church's ministry in response to the HIV epidemic.

---

18. *See* Judicial Council Decisions 491, 597.

10. In keeping with the Church's historic stand on total abstinence, the council shall seek to ensure that no apportioned general funds are expended for the use of alcoholic beverages.

11. It shall develop general investment policies and guidelines for all agencies receiving general Church funds (*see* ¶ 810.2), following consultation with those agencies. These guidelines are recommended for all Church organizations. The council shall provide consultation, advice, and assistance on the development and approval of specific investment policies for all agencies receiving general Church funds. The council shall provide consultation and advice on the selection of investment counselors and managers for, and review, at the council's discretion but on at least an annual basis, the performance of all invested funds of all agencies receiving general Church funds. The council shall have complete authority to manage any portfolio of less than $5,000,000 and may, upon request by the agency, manage larger portfolios. The council is encouraged to invest in institutions, companies, corporations, or funds that make a positive contribution toward the realization of the goals outlined in the Social Principles of The United Methodist Church (¶¶ 160–166).

12. The Committee on Audit and Review (¶ 805.4*b*), on behalf of the council, shall monitor the compliance of agencies receiving general Church funds (*see* ¶ 810.2) with the fiscal accountability policies and practices set forth in ¶ 806 and the general policies set forth in ¶ 811.1–4, .7, and with recommendations made by the independent and/or internal auditors under ¶ 805.4*b*, with respect to matters of possible or potential financial impropriety. The council shall have authority to implement actions which it may approve based on recommendations from the committee.

*a)* If the committee finds that there are violations of such policies, practices, or recommendations, it shall first notify the president and general secretary of the agency involved and the president and general secretary of the General Council on Finance and Administration of its findings, in writing. It shall also request from the agency, within a specified timeline, a written response to the committee's findings, with the written response to include additional information and/or proposed corrective action.

*b)* After receiving the agency's response, the committee may take one or more of the following actions:

(1) It may determine that the response and any additional information supplied by the agency is sufficient to explain the issue

or situation that occasioned the initial finding, and that no further action in needed.

(2) It may determine that the corrective action proposed by the agency is sufficiently responsive to the issue or situation, and that, when implemented, no further action will be needed.

(3) It may determine that the agency's response is insufficient to address the issue or situation. In that case, it may recommend to the agency, for the agency's consideration, the type of corrective actions that it believes necessary to address the issue or situation adequately, along with a timeline for reporting corrective action taken.

(4) It may prepare an informational report on the matter for those members of the council who have been assigned responsibility for reviewing the annual budget of the agency.

*c)* It may recommend to the General Council on Finance and Administration for its action, with notice of the recommendation given to the president and general secretary of the agency involved, one or more of the following steps:

(1) Continuing monitoring by the council's internal audit department, at the expense of the agency involved, until the committee finds that the issue has been satisfactorily resolved.

(2) Withholding of an appropriate amount of funding from general fund receipts that would otherwise be payable to the agency, until the council, on recommendation of the committee, finds that the issue has been satisfactorily resolved.

(3) Reporting of any unresolved issues to the next session of the General Conference, along with recommendations for General Conference action.

¶ **807.** *Other Fiscal Responsibilities*—The council shall have the following additional fiscal responsibilities:

1. To receive, collect, and hold in trust for the benefit of The United Methodist Church, its general funds, or its general agencies any and all donations, bequests, and devises of any kind, real or personal, that may be given, devised, bequeathed, or conveyed to The United Methodist Church as such or to any general fund or agency of The United Methodist Church for any benevolent, charitable, or religious purposes, and to administer the same and the income there from in accordance with the directions of the donor, trustor, or testator; and, in cooperation with the Board of Discipleship, to take such action as is necessary to encourage United Methodists to provide for their continued participation in World Service, in one or more of the

World Service agencies, or in other general Church benevolence funds or interests, through wills and special gifts.

2. Where annual conferences, individually or in groups, have established United Methodist foundations, the council may provide staff leadership on request to advise in matters of financial management, to the end that foundation assets shall be wisely managed on behalf of the Church.

3. To make recommendations to the General Conference, in consultation with the General Council on Ministries and the Council of Bishops, regarding any offerings to be received in connection with special days observed on a churchwide basis. These recommendations shall include the number and timing of such special days with offerings, the amount, if any, to be established as a goal for each such offering, the causes to be benefited by each, the method by which the receipts on each such offering shall be distributed among the causes benefiting from it, and the method by which such receipts shall be remitted and reported by local churches. All such recommendations are subject to the approval of the General Conference.

4. To establish general policy governing the ownership, sale, rental, renovation, or purchase of property by a general agency in the United States or Puerto Rico. The council shall consider the plans of any general agency proposing to acquire or sell real estate or erect a building or enter into a lease in the continental United States and determine whether the proposed action is in the best interest of The United Methodist Church. On the basis of that determination it shall approve or disapprove all such proposed actions. In the case of such proposed action by a general program agency, it shall solicit and consider the recommendation of the General Council on Ministries. If either council disapproves, the agency shall delay the project until it can be considered by the next General Conference. Nothing in the foregoing shall include the operational requirements of The United Methodist Publishing House or the General Board of Pension and Health Benefits.

5. To act in concert with the General Council on Ministries to establish a procedure for making a quadrennial review, initiating proposals and/or responding to proposals by the general agencies regarding the location of headquarters and staff and reporting the same to the General Conference. (See ¶ 906.26.)

6. To exercise on behalf of the General Conference a property reporting function by receiving reports annually from general agen-

cies of the Church concerning property titles, values, debts, general maintenance, lease or rental costs, space usage, and such other information as the council may deem relevant. The council may consult and advise with the general agencies concerning any property problems that may arise. A summary of the property data shall be reported to each quadrennial General Conference. This provision shall apply to headquarters buildings but not to properties that are part of the program responsibilities of the General Board of Global Ministries or to any of the properties of The United Methodist Publishing House. Titles to historic sites and heritage landmarks, and such historical properties as may be acquired in the future, shall be held by the General Council on Finance and Administration.

7. To take all necessary legal steps to safeguard and protect the interests and rights of the denomination; to maintain a file of legal briefs related to cases involving the denominational interests of The United Methodist Church, and to make provisions for legal counsel where necessary to protect the interests and rights of the denomination. The council shall recommend to each general agency and unit thereof and to each annual conference council on finance and administration a uniform procedure to be followed by the aforesaid agencies and, where applicable, local churches, relative to the certification and payment of ordained ministers' housing allowances in accordance with provisions of the Internal Revenue Code of the United States. The council shall have the authority to pursue policies and procedures necessary to preserve the tax-exempt status of the denomination and its affiliated organizations.[19]

8. To supervise the use of the official United Methodist insignia and preserve the integrity of its design, in cooperation with the General Commission on Communication. It shall maintain appropriate registration to protect the insignia on behalf of the denomination. The insignia may be used by any official United Methodist agency, including local churches, to identify United Methodist work, programs, and materials. In order to preserve the integrity of its design, the insignia should not be altered or modified by those official United Methodist organizations that use it. Any commercial use of the design must be explicitly authorized in writing by an appropriate officer of the General Council on Finance and Administration.[20]

---

19. *See* Judicial Council Decision 458.
20. *See* Judicial Council Decision 828.

9. To supervise the use of the names "United Methodist" and "The United Methodist Church" and maintain the appropriate registrations of these names on behalf of the denomination.

10. To provide direction and coordination in the design and implementation of operating systems in order to maximize the efficiency of operating personnel, equipment, and resources between and within agencies. During the quadrennium, these agencies shall study their respective responsibilities, programs, and internal operations and institute such improvements and economies in their work as they find to be feasible and practicable. They shall cooperate with the council in working out, in advance of these studies, the general areas to be included and methods of carrying out this objective. They shall report their accomplishments in improvements and economies to the council before the close of the third fiscal year of each quadrennium, at a time determined by the council, which shall prepare from this information a combined report for the General Conference.

11. *a)* The council shall: (1) require each general agency as listed in ¶ 805.4*d*, including itself, to follow uniform policies and practices in the employment and remuneration of personnel, recognizing differences in local employment conditions (these policies and practices shall be consistent with the Social Principles and resolutions of The United Methodist Church); and (2) be authorized to gather from all general agencies, at such intervals and in such format as it may determine, information regarding salary remuneration and pay equity and the number of agency employees and staff. Information related to the remuneration of specific employees may be released only by the employing agency or employee.

*b)* The Committee on Personnel Policies and Practices (¶ 805.4*d*) shall: (1) prepare quadrennially, review annually, and recommend to the council an appropriate salary schedule, based upon responsibilities, for exempt staff personnel of the councils, boards, and commissions represented on the committee; (2) develop and recommend to the council a schedule of benefits for an employee benefit program for personnel of agencies represented on the committee and any changes required thereto from time to time; (3) receive from agencies and institutions receiving general Church funds (*see* ¶ 810.2) statements regarding their compliance with the policy stated in ¶ 811.1; and (4) receive from all general agencies information necessary to evaluate pay equity. Based on these statements, and in consultation with and upon the advice of the General Commission on

Religion and Race and the General Commission on the Status and Role of Women, the committee shall prepare for the General Council on Finance and Administration reports and recommendations deemed appropriate by the committee.

In the event it is determined by the council that an agency or institution receiving general Church funds is not in compliance with the equal employment opportunity policies and the salary and employee benefit schedules established by the committee, the council shall notify in writing the agency so named and suspend, after a three-month period of grace, an appropriate amount of future funding until the agency or institution complies.

12. To maintain a consultative service to assist general agencies in planning and making arrangements for national meetings, conferences, and convocations.

13. To maintain an accurate record of the mail addresses of all bishops; ordained and consecrated ministers in effective relation; local pastors, including retired ordained ministers serving charges; charges, local churches, parishes, fellowships, and new church starts; and such lists of general, jurisdictional, and conference boards, commissions, and committees, and officers of same, and of such other officers as the council may determine necessary. No one other than authorized bodies or officers of the Church shall be permitted to use these records.

14. To prepare the important statistics relating to The United Methodist Church for the General Minutes or such other publications and releases as may be approved by the council. It shall provide for the distribution of statistical information to annual conferences, the general planning and research agencies of the Church, and other interested parties. The council may establish an appropriate schedule of fees and charges to defray the cost of such information distribution services.

15. To assist and advise the jurisdictions, annual conferences, districts, and local churches in all matters relating to the work of the council. These matters shall include, but shall not be limited to, business administration, investment and property management, information technology, and auditing. Matters related to resourcing the development and implementation of financial programs within the local church committee on finance shall be the responsibility of the General Board of Discipleship. The council may perform certain functions for the jurisdictions, annual conferences, districts, or local

churches if the particular organization so elects and a suitable plan of operation can be determined.

16. To provide guidance and consultation in the area of local church business administration, including establishment of professional standards, a training program, certification of church business administrators and associate church business administrators; and to provide assistance to the **United Methodist Association of Church Business Administrators.**

17. To provide guidance and consultation for continuing education of church secretaries, including establishment of training and certification programs, and to provide assistance to the **Professional Association of United Methodist Church Secretaries.**

18. To provide guidance and consultation to the **National Association of Commissions on Equitable Compensation of The United Methodist Church.** The association shall provide guidance and counsel to annual conference commissions on equitable compensation in their areas of responsibility (¶ 623) by means of consultations, workshops, development of educational materials and informational resources, and other appropriate means. The council may provide such staff and in-kind services to the association as it deems appropriate.

19. To provide guidance and consultation and to encourage general agency participation in the **United Methodist Association of Annual Conference Computer Administrators.** The council may provide such staff and in-kind services to the association as it deems appropriate.

20. To institute, manage, and maintain an insurance program available, where approved by regulatory agencies, to all United Methodist local churches in the United States and Puerto Rico and, where acceptable on an underwriting basis, to all United Methodist annual conferences, agencies, and institutions in the United States and Puerto Rico.

21. To designate a staff member who, in cooperation with the general secretary, will fulfill such responsibilities as may be needed to assist the Commission on the General Conference with preparation for sessions of the General Conference. In fulfilling this role, the staff member will function as the commission's **business manager** and shall be related operationally to the Commission.

¶ **808.** *Conference Payments of Apportioned Funds*—1. The treasurer of the General Council on Finance and Administration shall, not less than ninety days prior to the session of each annual conference or as soon thereafter as practical, transmit to the presiding bishop thereof, to the president of the conference council on finance and administration, and to the conference treasurer a statement of the apportionments to the conference for the World Service Fund, the General Administration Fund, the Episcopal Fund, the Interdenominational Cooperation Fund, the Ministerial Education Fund, the Black College Fund, the Africa University Fund, and such other funds as may have been apportioned by the General Conference.

2. The treasurer shall keep an account of all amounts remitted by the conference treasurers and from other sources intended for the funds listed in ¶ 810.1 and any other fund so directed by the proper authority, and shall disburse the same as authorized by the General Conference and directed by the council. A separate account shall be kept of each such fund, and none of them shall be drawn on for the benefit of another fund.

3. If more than the amount approved by the General Conference for a fund total, or for a line item within a fund total, is received in any given year, the excess funds shall be held in trust by the council in an apportionment stabilization fund. All monies placed in such a fund shall be considered as fund balances restricted by the General Conference to the fund(s) or line item(s) in which the surplus occurred. They shall be held by the council until such time as shortfalls in such receipts occur during the same quadrennium, at which time they shall be released to compensate for the shortfalls. If undistributed funds remain in an apportionment stabilization fund at the end of the quadrennium, the council shall recommend, for action by the next General Conference, the disposition of any remaining fund balances, provided that those recommendations shall be consistent with the purposes for which the funds were raised.

¶ 809. *Annual Reports by the General Treasurer to the Annual Conferences of All General Church Expenditures*—The treasurer shall report annually to the council and to the respective conference councils as to all amounts received and disbursed during the year. The treasurer shall also make to each quadrennial session of the General Conference a full report of the financial transactions of the council for the previous four fiscal years. The treasurer shall be bonded for such an amount as may be determined by the council. The books of the treasurer shall be audited annually by a certified public accountant selected by the General Council on Finance and Administration upon recommendation by the Committee on Audit and Review (¶ 805.4*b*).

GENERAL FUNDS

¶ **810.** *Definition of General Funds*—1. The terms *general fund(s)* and *general Church fund(s),* wherever they appear in the *Book of Discipline,* refer to: the World Service Fund; the General Administration Fund; the Episcopal Fund; the Interdenominational Cooperation Fund; the Ministerial Education Fund; the Black College Fund; the Africa University Fund; World Service Special Gifts; general Advance Special Gifts; the World Communion Fund; the Human Relations Day Fund; the United Methodist Student Day Fund; the One Great Hour of Sharing Fund; Peace with Justice Sunday Fund; Native American Ministries Sunday Fund; the Youth Service Fund; and such other funds as may have been established by the General Conference and have been specifically authorized by the General Conference to be raised on a churchwide basis. They are restricted assets and are not funds of local churches, annual or jurisdictional conferences, or other units of the denomination. Such general funds are to be disbursed for the purpose or purposes set forth in ¶¶ 812–828 and budgets or similar directives adopted for the respective funds by the General Conference. The General Council on Finance and Administration, in the fulfillment of its fiscal responsibilities pursuant to ¶ 806, shall only have authority to disburse monies contributed to any of these funds in a manner specifically authorized by the *Book of Discipline* or for a purpose set forth in the budget or directives adopted by the preceding General Conference for that particular fund.

2. The terms *agency(ies) receiving general Church funds* and *treasury(ies) receiving general Church funds,* as used in ¶¶ 701–830 of the *Book of Discipline,* refer to agencies whose operational or administrative budgets are directly supported, in whole or in part, by allocations from one or more general Church funds. For the purposes of ¶¶ 701–830, the General Board of Pension and Health Benefits and The United Methodist Publishing House shall be deemed not to be agencies or treasuries whose operational or administrative budgets are directly supported, in whole or in part, by allocations from one or more general Church funds.

¶ **811.** *General Policies*—1. The General Council on Finance and Administration is authorized to withhold approval of a portion or all of the budget of any agency or any Church-related institution receiving general Church funds (see ¶ 810.2) until such agency or Church-related institution certifies to the council in writing that it has established and complied with a policy of: (a) recruiting, employing, utilizing, recompensing, and promoting professional staff and other personnel without regard to race, color, age, or sex; (b) fulfilling its duties and responsibilities in a manner that does not involve segregation or discrimination on the basis of race, age, or sex; and (c) insofar as possible, purchasing goods and services from vendors who are in compliance with such policies as are described in sections (a) and (b) of this paragraph. In the fulfillment of this directive, the council shall take the following steps to ensure that concerns of the General Commission on Religion and Race and the General Commission on the Status and Role of Women are represented: (1) consult with the two commissions in the development of a certification form to be submitted to the council by agencies and institutions receiving general Church funds; (2) share copies of such certifications with the two commissions; and (3) receive and consider recommendations from either of the two commissions regarding possible noncompliance with these policies by agencies and institutions receiving general Church funds.

2. It may withhold approval of any item or items in the budget or budgets receiving general Church funds (see ¶ 810.2) that in its judgment represent unnecessary duplication of administrative function; in cooperation with and on recommendation of the General Council on Ministries, it may withhold approval of any such item that represents unnecessary duplication of program within an agency or between two or more agencies. If the council finds that there is such duplication in existing activities, it shall promptly direct the attention of the agencies involved to the situation and shall cooperate with them in correcting the same, and it may decline to supply from general fund receipts money to continue activities that have been held to duplicate each other unnecessarily or plainly violate the principle of correlation as applied to the total benevolence program of the Church.

3. An agency of The United Methodist Church receiving general Church funds (see ¶ 810.2) proposing to borrow funds for a period in excess of twelve months or in an amount in excess of 25 percent of its annual budget or five hundred thousand dollars, whichever amount is smaller, whether for building or current expense purposes, shall

submit such proposal, accompanied by a plan for amortization, to the council for approval. If the council disapproves, the agency shall delay such borrowing until it can be considered by the next General Conference.

4. *Special Churchwide Financial Appeals—a)* Any general appeal to the Church at large for financial support for any cause, agency, institution, or purpose shall be subject to the provisions of this paragraph. Appeals to special or limited groups such as alumni or an educational institution are not included.

*b)* Any general board, cause, agency, or institution or any organization, group, officer, or individual of The United Methodist Church or to which The United Methodist Church contributes financial support desiring or proposing to make a special churchwide financial appeal during the quadrennium shall present a request for authorization to make such appeal to the General Council on Finance and Administration at the time budgets for the ensuing quadrennium are being considered. All such appeals shall be reviewed by the General Council on Ministries, and its actions shall be reported to the General Council on Finance and Administration. The council shall then report such request to the General Conference with a recommendation for its action thereon.

*c)* In the interim between the quadrennial sessions of the General Conference, such proposed churchwide financial appeal shall require the approval of the General Council on Finance and Administration and the Council of Bishops. In case of emergency, the executive committee of either of these bodies may act in such matter for the body itself, but only by a three-fourths vote.

*d)* All requests for approval of a special churchwide financial appeal, whether as a request for General Conference action or in the interim between sessions of General Conference, shall include a proposed budget for a promotion of the appeal, including proposed promotional expenditures and the sources of funding (*see* ¶ 1806.12).

*e)* Any individual or agency authorized to make a churchwide appeal for funds shall channel all gifts through the General Council on Finance and Administration.

*f)* The General Council on Finance and Administration may withhold payment of the allocation from any general fund to any agency or institution that it finds to be in violation of the provisions of this paragraph.

5. The apportionments for all apportioned general Church funds,

as approved by the General Conference, shall not be subject to reduction either by the annual conference or by the charge or local church (¶ 613.1).[21]

6. Individual donors or local churches may make contributions to the support of any cause or project that is a part of the work of any general Church agency. Such miscellaneous gifts shall be sent to the General Council on Finance and Administration, which shall then forward the gift to the agency for which it is intended. Agencies receiving miscellaneous gifts shall acknowledge receipt of the gift to the donor. No agency shall solicit or cultivate gifts for any cause or project that has not been approved for support through World Service Special Gifts (¶ 813), general Advance Special Gifts (¶184), or a special appeal (¶ 811.4).

7. No general council, board, commission, or committee receiving general Church funds (see ¶ 810.2) shall initiate or cause to be organized without approval of the General Council on Finance and Administration a foundation, endowment fund, or similar organization for the purpose of securing, conserving, or expending funds for the direct or indirect benefit or support of any general agency or any of its programs or work. Foundations, endowment funds, and similar organizations related directly or indirectly to any general Church agency receiving general Church funds shall report annually to the council in a manner determined by the council.

¶ 812. *The World Service Fund*—The **World Service Fund** is basic in the financial program of The United Methodist Church. World Service on apportionment represents the minimum needs of the general agencies of the Church. Payment in full of these apportionments by local churches and annual conferences is the first benevolent responsibility of the Church.

1. The council shall recommend to each quadrennial session of the General Conference the amount of the annual World Service budget for the ensuing quadrennium and the method by which it shall be apportioned to the annual conferences. In cooperation with the General Council on Ministries, it shall prepare and recommend a plan of distribution of World Service receipts among the World Service agencies, in accordance with the procedures described in ¶ 806.1b. In the planning of the World Service budget, it shall be the role of the General Council on Finance and Administration to facilitate sound fiscal

---

21. *See* Judicial Council Decision 818.

and administrative policies and practices within and among the general agencies of the Church. It shall be the role of the General Council on Ministries to relate the budget askings of the program agencies to one another in such a way as to implement the program and missional priorities of the Church.

2. The general secretary or other duly authorized representative of each agency of The United Methodist Church requesting support from the World Service Fund and the authorized representative of any other agency for which askings are authorized by the General Conference shall have the right to appear before the council at a designated time and place to represent the cause for which each is responsible, provided that such representation has been previously made to the General Council on Ministries.

3. The World Service agencies shall not solicit additional or special gifts from individual donors or special groups, other than foundations, unless approval for such solicitation is first secured from the council.

¶ 813. *World Service Special Gifts*—1. A World Service Special Gift is a designated financial contribution made by an individual, local church, organization, district, or annual conference to a project authorized as a World Service Special project by the General Council on Ministries. General agencies that qualify under the provisions of ¶ 907.6b(1) shall be eligible to recommend projects for approval by the General Council on Ministries as World Service Special projects.

2. General guidelines governing the types of projects that may be recommended for approval as World Service Special projects shall be approved by the General Conference on recommendation of the General Council on Ministries and the General Council on Finance and Administration.

3. The World Service Special Gifts program shall be under the supervision of the General Council on Ministries, which shall be responsible for: (a) establishing project approval criteria consistent with the guidelines adopted by the General Conference; (b) establishing the process by which projects may be recommended and approved; (c) approving projects to receive World Service Special Gift support; and (d) providing adequate staff administration and program accountability.

4. Churches and individuals shall give priority to the support of World Service and conference benevolences and other apportioned

funds. World Service Special Gift giving shall be voluntary and in addition to the support of apportioned funds. World Service Special Gifts shall not be raised as a part of a fund apportioned by an annual conference.

5. World Service Special Gifts shall be remitted in full by local church treasurers to annual conference treasurers, who shall remit each month to the General Council on Finance and Administration the total amounts received during the month as World Service Special Gifts. The council shall remit such gifts in full to the administering agencies, which shall acknowledge the receipt of every gift to the donor or the local church.

6. The promotion of this program may include general promotion, for purposes of name identification and visibility, which shall be the responsibility of United Methodist Communications.

7. Specific cultivation of approved projects shall be done by the administering agencies to specific audiences that have demonstrated previously their interest and concern for the ministry contained in the approved project. Expenses for specific cultivation shall be borne by the administering agencies. No promotional or cultivation expenses shall be paid from World Service Special Gifts receipts. Such expenses shall not exceed amounts approved by the General Council on Finance and Administration and the General Council on Ministries under guidelines approved by the General Conference.

¶ 814. *The Advance*—1. **The Advance for Christ and His Church** (hereafter referred to as the **Advance**) is an official program within The United Methodist Church through which support may be designated for projects approved by the Advance Committee of the General Council on Ministries. (*See* ¶ 1310.3*b*.)

2. A general Advance Special Gift is a designated financial contribution made by an individual, local church, organization, district, or conference to a project authorized for this purpose by the Advance Committee.

*a)* Gifts as Advance Specials may be made for specific projects or purposes authorized by the Advance Committee.

*b)* Gifts as Advance Specials may be made for broadly designated causes (such as a type of work, a country, or a region) or for use as block grants to a certain country or administrative unit, provided such causes are authorized by the Advance Committee. In such case the administering agency shall provide the donor with information

467

about the area to which the funds have been given and, where practicable, establish communication with a person or group representative of that type of work.

c) An Advance Special Gift may be given to an authorized agency (¶ 907.5d) rather than to a specific project, in which case the agency shall determine the Advance Special project or projects to which such a gift shall be allocated, inform the donor where the gift has been invested, and, as far as practicable, establish communication between donor and recipient.

3. Funds given and received as a part of the general Advance shall be subject to the following conditions:

a) Churches and individuals shall give priority to the support of the World Service and conference benevolences and other apportioned funds. Advance giving shall be voluntary and in addition to the support of apportioned funds.

b) Funds shall be solicited or received only for authorized projects. Programs and institutions having general Advance Special projects shall promote only for the projects approved and shall ask that gifts be remitted in the manner described in ¶ 814.4 below.

c) Funds received through the Advance shall be used solely for project support and are not to be used for administration or promotional costs.

d) Advance Special Gifts shall not be raised as a part of a fund apportioned by an annual conference. (For conference Advance Special Gifts, see ¶ 651.)

e) Upon receipt of funds for a general Advance Special, each administering agency shall communicate promptly with the donor, acknowledging receipt of the gift and suggesting avenues for communication if communication has not already been established.

4. Receipts for general Advance Specials shall be remitted by the local church treasurer to the conference treasurer, who shall make remittance each month to the participating agencies in a manner determined by the treasurer of the General Council on Finance and Administration. Individuals may remit directly to respective agencies in a manner determined by the treasurer of the General Council on Finance and Administration, with these remittances reported to the annual conference treasurer by the respective agencies.

¶ 815. *General Directives*—The following general directives shall be observed in the promotion and administration of the Advance and **One Great Hour of Sharing:**

1. In the appeal and promotion of Advance Specials and One Great Hour of Sharing offerings, there shall be no goals or quotas except as they may be set by the annual conferences for themselves.

2. The treasurer of the General Council on Finance and Administration shall be treasurer of the Advance and One Great Hour of Sharing.

3. The expense of promotion for Advance Specials shall be borne by the respective participating agencies in proportion to the amount received by each in Advance Specials. The causes of the Advance shall be coordinated with other financial appeals and shall be promoted by the Division of Program and Benevolence Interpretation of the General Commission on Communication.

4. The appeal for Advance Specials shall be channeled through bishops, district superintendents, and pastors, the details of the procedure to be determined by the Division of Program and Benevolence Interpretation of the General Commission on Communication in consultation with the designated mission cultivation unit of the General Board of Global Ministries and the Advance Committee.

5. In each annual conference the conference board of global ministries (if any; see ¶ 630), in cooperation with the General Board of Global Ministries, shall promote Advance Specials and One Great Hour of Sharing offerings through conference and district secretaries of global ministries, conference and district mission events, and other effective means as it may determine.

6. Should a clear emergency arise, any feature of the structure and administration of the Advance may be altered on the approval of a majority of the Council of Bishops and of the General Council on Finance and Administration.

¶ 816. *General Church Special-Day Offerings*—The following are the special days with offerings to be used in support of general Church causes:

1. *Human Relations Day*—A **Human Relations Day** shall be observed during the season of Epiphany, preferably on the Sunday before the observance of Martin Luther King Jr.'s birthday, with an offering goal recommended by the General Council on Finance and Administration and adopted by the General Conference. The purpose of the goal is to further the development of better human relations through funding programs determined by the General Conference upon recommendation of the General Council on Finance and Administration after consultation with the General Council on Ministries. Net receipts from this observance shall be

allocated as predetermined on ratio (*see* ¶ 263.1), with the funds being administered by the general boards under which approved programs are lodged.

2. *One Great Hour of Sharing*—There shall be an annual observance of the **One Great Hour of Sharing** as a special offering for relief (¶ 263.2). The observance shall be under the general supervision of the General Commission on Communication (¶ 1806.12), in accordance with the following directives:

*a)* The One Great Hour of Sharing shall be observed each year, preferably on the Fourth Sunday in Lent. All local churches shall be fully informed and encouraged to receive a freewill offering in behalf of the relief program.

*b)* Insofar as possible, the planning and promotion of the One Great Hour of Sharing shall be done cooperatively with other denominations through the National Council of the Churches of Christ in the U.S.A., it being understood, however, that receipts of the offerings shall be administered by The United Methodist Church.

*c)* Receipts from the offering, after payment of the expenses of promotion, shall be remitted by the treasurer of the General Council on Finance and Administration to the United Methodist Committee on Relief (¶ 1326.2) to be administered by that committee.

3. *United Methodist Student Day*—The **United Methodist Student Day** offering, taken each year, preferably on the last Sunday in November, shall be received for the support of United Methodist scholarships and the United Methodist Student Loan Fund (¶ 263.4). Receipts from the offering, after payment of the expenses of promotion, shall be remitted by the treasurer of the General Council on Finance and Administration to the General Board of Higher Education and Ministry to be administered by that board.

4. *World Communion Offering*—In connection with **World Communion Sunday,** there shall be a churchwide appeal conducted by the General Commission on Communication in accord with the following directives:

*a)* Each local church shall be requested to remit as provided in ¶ 816.8 all the Communion offering received on World Communion Sunday—preferably on the first Sunday of October—and such portion of the Communion offering received at other observances of the sacrament of the Lord's Supper as the local church may designate.

*b)* The net receipts, after payment of promotional costs, shall be divided as follows: 50 percent to the Crusade Scholarship Committee,

35 percent to the Ethnic Scholarship Program, and 15 percent to the Ethnic In-Service Training Program, the last two administered by the General Board of Higher Education and Ministry in consultation with the various ethnic groups (¶ 263.3).

5. *Peace with Justice Sunday*—**Peace with Justice Sunday** shall be observed, preferably on the First Sunday After Pentecost. The observance shall be under the general supervision of the General Board of Church and Society (*see* ¶ 263.5). There shall be a churchwide appeal and offering. The net receipts from the offering will be distributed as follows:

*a)* The annual conference treasurer shall retain 50 percent of the monies for Peace with Justice Ministries in the annual conference, to be administered by the annual conference board of church and society or equivalent structure.

*b)* The annual conference treasurer shall remit the remaining 50 percent of the monies to the General Council on Finance and Administration.

*c)* Net receipts from the offering, after payment of the expenses of promotion, shall be remitted by the treasurer of the General Council on Finance and Administration to the General Board of Church and Society for Peace with Justice Ministries.

6. *Native American Ministries Sunday*—**Native American Ministries Sunday** shall be observed with an offering, preferably on the Third Sunday of Easter. The purpose of the churchwide appeal is to develop and strengthen Native American ministries in the annual conferences, in target cities of the Native American Urban Initiative of the General Board of Global Ministries, and for scholarships for Native Americans attending United Methodist schools of theology (¶ 263.6).

7. Promotion of all authorized general Church special Sunday offerings shall be by the General Commission on Communication in consultation with the participating agencies. Expenses of promotion for each offering shall be a prior claim against the receipts of the offering promoted. In each case, such expenses shall be within a budget approved by the General Council on Finance and Administration upon recommendation of the General Commission on Communication after consultation with the participating agencies. In the promotion of these offerings there shall be an emphasis on the spiritual implications of Christian stewardship.

8. Receipts from all authorized general Church special Sunday offerings shall be remitted promptly by the local church treasurer to the annual conference treasurer, who shall remit monthly to the trea-

surer of the General Council on Finance and Administration. A special-gift voucher for contributions to the offerings will be issued when appropriate. Local churches shall report the amount of the offerings in the manner indicated on the annual conference report form.

¶ **817.** *General Administration Fund*—1. **The General Administration Fund** shall provide for the expenses of the sessions of the General Conference, the Judicial Council, such special commissions and committees as may be constituted by the General Conference, and such other administrative agencies and activities as may be recommended for inclusion in the general administration budget by the General Council on Finance and Administration and approved by the General Conference. Any agency or institution requiring or desiring support from the General Administration Fund shall present its case for the same to the council at a time and place that shall be indicated by the officers of the council. The council, having heard such requests, shall report the same to the General Conference with recommendations for its action and determination.

2. The treasurer of the council shall disburse the funds received for the General Administration Fund as authorized by the General Conference and as directed by the council. Where the General Conference has not allocated definite sums to agencies receiving money from the General Administration Fund, the council or its executive committee shall have authority to determine the amount to be allocated to each.

3. The expenses of the Judicial Council shall be paid from the General Administration Fund, within a budget submitted annually by the Judicial Council to the General Council on Finance and Administration for its approval and subject to the requirement of ¶ 817.4 .

4. The General Administration Fund, and all payments made from this fund, shall be subject to the financial, accounting, and auditing requirements of ¶ 806.

¶ **818.** *Interdenominational Cooperation Fund*—1. The General Commission on Christian Unity and Interreligious Concerns, in consultation with the Council of Bishops, shall recommend to the General Council on Finance and Administration the amount of the annual **Interdenominational Cooperation Fund** allocation to each of the recipients of the fund. The council shall recommend to the General Conference the amounts to be included in the annual Interdenominational Cooperation Fund budget.

2. This fund shall provide the United Methodist share of the basic budgets of those organizations that relate to the ecumenical responsibilities of the Council of Bishops and of the General Commission on Christian Unity and Interreligious Concerns. Such organizations shall include the Consultation on Church Union and the Church of Christ Uniting, the National Council of the Churches of Christ in the U.S.A., and the World Council of Churches. The fund shall also provide for the expenses of representatives chosen by the Council of Bishops or by the General Commission on Christian Unity and Interreligious Concerns to attend meetings and committees of such ecumenical agencies. The General Council on Finance and Administration shall reimburse such expenses from vouchers approved by persons designated by the general secretary of the General Commission on Christian Unity and Interreligious Concerns or by the general secretary of the General Council on Finance and Administration.

3. Before the beginning of each calendar year, the General Council on Finance and Administration shall determine and communicate to the General Commission on Christian Unity and Interreligious Concerns the sum available from the Interdenominational Cooperation Fund Contingency Reserve to be allocated by the commission to meet emerging needs of ecumenical agencies.

¶ 819. *Black College Fund*—The General Council on Finance and Administration shall recommend to the General Conference the sum that the Church shall undertake for the Black colleges and the method by which it shall be apportioned to the annual conferences. The purpose of the fund is to provide financial support for current operating budgets and capital improvements of the Black colleges related administratively to the Church.

1. The current funds received annually shall be distributed to those Black colleges whose eligibility under adopted guidelines of management, educational quality, and measurement by announced objectives shall be the precondition of participation. These guidelines shall be revised and administered by the Division of Higher Education of the General Board of Higher Education and Ministry, in consultation with the Council of Presidents of the Black Colleges. The Division of Higher Education of the General Board of Higher Education and Ministry shall administer the fund according to the guidelines for support and a formula approved by the General Conference.

2. In the interim between sessions of the General Conference, the guidelines for support and formula for distribution may be changed

as necessary upon recommendation of the Council of Presidents of the Black Colleges and the General Board of Higher Education and Ministry and with the consent of the General Council on Finance and Administration.

3. Promotion of the **Black College Fund** shall be by the Division of Higher Education and in consultation with the Council of Presidents of the Black Colleges, in cooperation with and with the assistance of the Division of Program and Benevolence Interpretation of the General Commission on Communication, the cost being a prior claim against the Black College Fund receipts and within a budget approved by the Division of Higher Education and the General Council on Finance and Administration.

¶ **820.** *The Ministerial Education Fund*—The council shall recommend to the General Conference the sum that the Church shall undertake for the **Ministerial Education Fund** and the method by which it shall be apportioned to the annual conferences, in accordance with the provisions adopted by the 1968 General Conference in establishing the Ministerial Education Fund. The purpose of the fund is to enable the Church to unify and expand its program of financial support for the recruitment and education of ordained and diaconal ministers and to equip the annual conferences to meet increased demands in this area.[22] The maximum amount possible from this fund shall go directly for programs and services in theological education, the enlistment and continuing education of ordained and diaconal ministers, and the courses of study. When these funds are used to finance continuing education events sponsored by the board of ordained ministry of an annual conference, such events may be open to laity for their attendance and participation at the option of the board of ordained ministry of each annual conference.

1. Of the total money raised in each annual conference for the Ministerial Education Fund, 25 percent shall be retained by the annual conference that raised it, to be used in its program of ministerial education as approved by the annual conference and administered through its board of ordained ministry. The board of ordained ministry will confer concerning use of the ministerial education fund. Administrative costs of the board of ordained ministry shall be a claim on the conference operating budget. No annual conference that

---

22. *See* Judicial Council Decision 545.

had been participating in a 1 percent plan or other conference program of ministerial student scholarships and loan grants prior to the establishment of this fund shall receive less for this purpose than it received in the last year of the quadrennium preceding the establishment of the fund, provided the giving from that conference for ministerial education does not fall below the level achieved in the quadrennium preceding the establishment of the fund.

*a)* "Service Loans" from the various conferences' portion of the Ministerial Education Fund may be considered repaid if the recipients served five years in the connection in appointments approved by their bishop.

*b)* In case the recipients of these loans do not satisfy the terms of the "Service Loans" by service in the "connection," they would make arrangements to repay the loans with the conferences from which they received their loans.

2. Of the total money raised in each annual conference for the Ministerial Education Fund, 75 percent shall be remitted by the conference treasurer to the treasurer of the council for distribution to the General Board of Higher Education and Ministry for support of ministerial education and shall be administered by that board. It shall be distributed as follows:

*a)* At least 75 percent of the amount received by the divisions shall be distributed to the theological schools of The United Methodist Church on a formula established by the General Board of Higher Education and Ministry after consultation with the theological schools. All the money allocated to the theological schools shall be used for current operations, not for physical expansion.

*b)* The remaining portion of the amount received shall be used for supplemental distributions to the theological schools and for board use in its program of ministerial enlistment and development. The General Board of Higher Education and Ministry will recommend to the general secretary of the General Board of Higher Education and Ministry appropriate funding for divisional programs of ministerial enlistment and development.

3. This fund shall be regarded by annual conferences as a priority to be met before any additional benevolences, grants, or funds are allocated to a theological school or school of religion.

## The Episcopal Fund

¶ **821.** The **Episcopal Fund,** raised in accordance with ¶ 823, shall provide for the salary and expenses of effective bishops[23] from the date of their consecration and for the support of retired bishops and surviving spouses and minor children of deceased bishops. Subject to the approval of the General Council on Finance and Administration, the treasurer shall have authority to borrow for the benefit of the Episcopal Fund such amounts as may be necessary for the proper execution of the orders of the General Conference.

¶ **822.** *Requirements*—The council shall recommend to each quadrennial session of the General Conference for its action and determination: (1) the amounts to be fixed as salaries of the effective bishops or a formula by which the council shall fix the salaries; (2) a schedule of such amounts as may be judged adequate to provide for their office expense; (3) provision for an annual operating budget for the Council of Bishops, including the offices of the secretary and the ecumenical officer of the Council of Bishops; (4) guidelines governing the payment of bishops' travel expenses, including all travel authorized by the Council of Bishops; (5) the minimum amounts to be fixed as annual pensions for the support of retired bishops and/or the method by which their annual pensions shall be determined; and (6) provisions for allowance for the surviving spouses and for the support of minor children of deceased bishops. From the facts in hand, the council shall estimate the approximate total amount required annually during the ensuing quadrennium to provide for the items of episcopal support mentioned above and shall report the same to the General Conference. This amount as finally determined shall be the estimated episcopal budget. The administration of the Episcopal Fund budget as determined by the General Conference shall be under the direction and authority of the General Council on Finance and Administration, including annual fiscal statements and audits. Nothing in this paragraph shall preclude the annual conference or conferences of an episcopal area from including in their budgets amounts for an area expense fund.

¶ **823.** *Proportionality*—The amount apportioned to a charge for the Episcopal Fund shall be paid in the same proportion as the charge pays its pastor (*see also* ¶ 620).

---

23. *See* Judicial Council Decision 781.

¶ 824. *Bishops' Salaries*—The treasurer of the General Council on Finance and Administration shall remit monthly to each effective bishop one-twelfth of the annual salary as determined by the General Conference, less such deductions or reductions from the salary as each bishop may authorize. Allowances for retired bishops and for the surviving spouses and minor children of deceased bishops shall be paid in equal monthly installments.

¶ 825. *Housing Expenses*—Upon receipt of a budget from the episcopal residence committee, the general Council on Finance and Administration shall provide funds from the Episcopal Fund to share in the costs of providing an episcopal residence, the amount of such funds to be set by the council in accordance with a policy approved by the General Conference on recommendation of the council. The treasurer of the General Council on Finance and Administration shall remit regularly, at such intervals as the council may determine, equal installments of the share approved for payment from the Episcopal Fund to the person or office designated by the episcopal residence committee to receive such housing payments. (*See also* ¶ 636.) The treasurer shall also remit regular equal installments of the amount approved by the council as office expenses to each bishop, or to the person or office designated by the bishop to receive such payments.

¶ 826. *Episcopal Expense Reimbursement and Honoraria Policies*—The treasurer of the council shall pay monthly the claim for the official travel of each bishop upon presentation of an itemized voucher with such supporting data as may be required by the General Council on Finance and Administration. *Official travel* of an effective bishop shall be interpreted to include: (1) all visitations to local churches and to institutions or enterprises of The United Methodist Church within the area; (2) such travel outside the area, but within the jurisdiction, as is approved by the College of Bishops; and (3) such other travel as may be consistent with guidelines approved by the General Conference as being within the meaning of *official travel*. No part of the expense and no honoraria for any such visitations shall be accepted from local churches or enterprises or institutions of The United Methodist Church, such expense being a proper claim against the Episcopal Fund. Nothing in this interpretation is intended to preclude special or nonofficial engagements of a bishop other than the oversight of the temporal and spiritual affairs of the Church, such as series of lectures in educational institutions, baccalaureate addresses, and preaching missions for several days' duration when such engagements do not interfere with official duties, nor does it preclude the acceptance of honoraria for such services.

¶ 827. *Audit of Episcopal Area Offices*—Fiscal reporting and audit procedures of each area office shall be determined according to a schedule as set forth by the council upon recommendation of the Committee on Episcopal Services.

¶ 828. *Episcopal Pensions*—The pensions for the support of retired bishops elected by general, jurisdictional, or central conferences and the surviving spouses and minor dependent children of such deceased bishops shall be administered by the General Council on Finance and Administration in consultation with the General Board of Pension and Health Benefits and in accordance with such program and procedures as may from time to time be determined by the General Council on Finance and Administration with the approval of the General Conference. For service years beginning January 1, 1982, and thereafter, the pensions for the support of bishops elected by jurisdictional conferences and those of their surviving spouses and dependent children shall include the benefits provided by the Ministerial Pension Plan and the Comprehensive Protection Plan of the General Board of Pension and Health Benefits.

¶ 829. *Bishops Whose Service Is Interrupted*—Should any effective bishop in the interim of the quadrennial sessions of the jurisdictional conference be relieved by the College of Bishops of the jurisdiction from the performance of regular episcopal duties on account of ill health or for any other reason, the president of the said College of Bishops shall so notify the treasurer of the Episcopal Fund. Beginning ninety days after such notification, the said bishop shall receive at least the minimum regular pension allowance of a retired bishop; the amount of such benefit for which the Episcopal Fund is responsible shall be reduced by the amount of any disability benefit payable from the Comprehensive Protection Plan of the General Board of Pension and Health Benefits. Such pension allowance shall continue until the regular duties of an effective bishop are resumed or until the bishop's status shall have been determined by the jurisdictional conference. Assignment of another bishop or bishops to perform the regular episcopal duties of a bishop so disabled or otherwise incapacitated, for a period of sixty days or more, shall be interpreted as a release of the said bishop from the performance of regular episcopal duties.

¶ 830. *Retired Bishops Appointed to Ad Interim Service*—Should any retired bishop, in the interim of the quadrennial sessions of the jurisdictional conference, be called into active service and assigned to active episcopal duty (¶ 407.3), that bishop shall be entitled to remuneration for such service. The Episcopal Fund shall be responsible for the difference between the pension of the retired bishop and the remuneration of an active bishop. In the event of such assignment of a retired bishop to active episcopal duty, the president or secretary of the Council of Bishops shall notify the treasurer of the Episcopal Fund. The treasurer of the Episcopal Fund shall make remittance accordingly.

### Section III. General Council on Ministries

¶ 901. *Name*—There shall be a **General Council on Ministries** of The United Methodist Church, hereinafter called the council.

¶ 902. *Incorporation*—The council shall be incorporated in such state or states as the General Council on Ministries shall determine. This corporation shall be the successor corporation and organization to the Program Council of The United Methodist Church.

¶ 903. *Amenability*—The council shall report to and be amenable to the General Conference.

¶ 904. *Purpose*—The purpose of the council, as a part of the total mission of the Church, is to facilitate the Church's program life as determined by the General Conference. The council's task is to encourage, coordinate, and support the general agencies as they serve on behalf of the denomination.

¶ 905. *Objectives*—The objectives of the General Council on Ministries are:

1. To study missional needs and propose priorities of the general Church; and, when necessary, to adjust emphases between sessions of the General Conference.

2. To establish the processes and relationships pertaining to the coordination and funding of the ministries and program emphases of the denomination through its general agencies and to minimize unnecessary overlapping or conflicting approaches to the local church and the annual conferences.

3. To enhance the effectiveness of our total ministries by reviewing and evaluating the performance of the general program agencies and their responsiveness to the needs of the local churches and annual conferences.

4. To facilitate informed decision-making at all levels of the

Church by engaging in research and planning in cooperation with the general agencies and the annual conferences.

¶ **906.** *Responsibilities*—The responsibilities of the council shall include, but not be limited to, the following:

1. Upon a two-thirds vote of the members of the General Council on Ministries present and voting, and upon a two-thirds vote of the Council of Bishops present and voting, to make changes in missional priorities or special programs necessitated by emergencies or by other significant developments between General Conferences that substantially affect the life of the Church, and to make adjustments in program budget allocations accordingly; *provided* that such adjustments are made within the total budget set by the previous General Conference; and *provided*, further, that such adjustments are made after consultation with the affected boards and agencies and approval by a two-thirds vote of the General Council on Finance and Administration.

2. To take the following actions, in sequence, with respect to recommendations to the General Council on Finance and Administration for the allocation of World Service funds to general program agencies:

*a)* The General Council on Ministries shall, in consultation with the General Council on Finance and Administration and the general program agencies, develop recommendations to the General Council on Finance and Administration on needs of the general program agencies for the programs, missional priorities, and special programs.

*b)* The General Council on Ministries shall receive the recommendation the General Council on Finance and Administration proposes to make to the General Conference as to that portion of the total World Service budget to be available for distribution among the general program agencies.

*c)* The General Council on Ministries, after reviewing both the program priorities and the total funds available to the general program agencies, shall recommend to the General Council on Finance and Administration the amount of the annual World Service allocation to each of those agencies, within the total sum proposed by the General Council on Finance and Administration for distribution among such agencies.

*d)* Only when the General Council on Ministries and the General Council on Finance and Administration agree on the allocations to several general agencies shall these allocations be included in the

World Service budget to be recommended to the General Conference by the General Council on Finance and Administration.

*e)* Before the beginning of each year, the General Council on Finance and Administration shall determine and communicate to the General Council on Ministries the sum available at that time from World Service contingency funds to meet requests for additional funding from the general program agencies. The General Council on Ministries shall be authorized to approve allocations to the general program agencies for such additional program funding up to the limit so established. No money shall be allocated by the General Council on Ministries from this source for general administrative costs, fixed charges, or capital outlay without approval by the General Council on Finance and Administration.

*f)* The General Council on Ministries shall receive from the General Council on Finance and Administration copies of the proposed annual budgets of the general program agencies, in order that it may review such budgets in relation to the program proposals made by those agencies in their quadrennial budget requests.

3. To designate, in cooperation with the General Council on Finance and Administration, the general agency to undertake a special study ordered by the General Conference when the conference fails to make such a designation.

4. To assign responsibilities for implementation of themes, missional priorities, and/or special programs initiated between sessions of the General Conference to the general program agencies or to special task forces created by the General Council on Ministries.

5. To coordinate the denomination's efforts to incorporate the contributions and concerns of the ethnic local church into all programs, budgets, agenda, and resources.

6. To ensure the development of a unified and coordinated program for the promoting of the connectional ministries of the Church, the General Council on Ministries shall:

*a)* Approve the scheduling and timing of all national conferences, convocations, and/or major consultations of general program agencies subject to the approval of the General Council on Finance and Administration of plans for financing such meetings;

*b)* Maintain a calendar of meetings on behalf of all agencies of The United Methodist Church as an aid to the agencies in regulating the number and the timing of such meetings; and

*c)* Review all plans of the general program agencies for the production, distribution, and timing of the release of free literature and promotional resource materials (except church school literature), avoiding duplication of both materials and activities.

7. To recommend to the General Conference, after consultation with the Council of Bishops, the number and timing of special days that are to be observed on a churchwide basis; *provided* that the General Council on Finance and Administration shall make recommendations to the General Conference as set forth in ¶ 807.3 regarding the special days to be observed with offering; and *provided*, further, that the Council of Bishops and the General Council on Finance and Administration may authorize a special financial appeal in an emergency.

8. To relate to annual conferences, their councils on ministries, or other corresponding structures:

*a)* To provide resources for them related to their basic tasks;

*b)* To enhance two-way communication with them;

*c)* To assist the conference councils in developing comprehensive approaches to planning, research, evaluation, and coordination; and

*d)* To inform conference councils of significant issues identified through the monitoring of trends in the world and the Church.

9. To consider the plans of any general program agency to publish a new periodical (except church school literature). Any general program agency proposing to publish such a new periodical shall submit its request to the council. If the council disapproves, the agency shall delay such publication until the proposal can be submitted to the General Conference for determination.

10. To consult with the general program agencies, the General Commission on Communication, and the president and publisher of The United Methodist Publishing House with regard to their publishing and communication policies in order to avoid unnecessary overlapping and duplication.

11. To resolve any overlapping in structure or functions or lack of cooperation among the general program agencies and/or interagency task force to minimize overlapping in structure and functions:

*a)* coordinating interagency programs where two or more general program agencies are involved, unless otherwise specified by the General Conference;

*b)* approving the creation of any ongoing interagency committee or task force;

*c)* receiving reports and recommendations from such committees or task forces;

*d)* appointing, when appropriate, observers to attend the meetings of any interagency group, including those that are part of the structure of program agencies; and

*e)* sponsoring, in cooperation with the general program-related agencies through the general secretaries, a quadrennial joint training event for annual conference program-related agencies.

12. To study the connectional structures of The United Methodist Church and, after consultation with the general agencies, recommend to the General Conference such legislative changes as may be appropriate to effect desirable modifications of existing connectional structures. Any such proposed legislative changes that would affect general fund budget allocations shall be studied in connection with the General Council on Finance and Administration and shall be recommended to the General Conference by these two councils acting in concert.

13. To provide for the training of the annual conference council on ministries directors or equivalent, to provide jointly with the General Board of Higher Education and Ministry and the Council of Bishops the training of district superintendents, and to consult with Central Conferences concerning comparable training sessions.

14. To review and evaluate the effectiveness of the general program agencies in fulfilling the ministries assigned to them (*see* ¶ 702.3).

15. To keep under review the concurrence of general program agencies with the Social Principles (¶¶ 160–166) of The United Methodist Church.

16. The general secretary of each general program agency that is accountable to the General Council on Ministries shall be elected annually by ballot of the General Council on Ministries upon the nomination of the agency involved. Any general secretary of a general program agency who has not been elected by the General Council on Ministries shall not serve in such capacity beyond the end of that calendar year. Each program agency shall elect annually by ballot its deputy and associate general secretary(ies) and may elect or appoint such other staff as may be necessary.[24]

---

24. *See* Judicial Council Decisions 499, 567.

17. To give leadership to and participate in planning and research for The United Methodist Church, thereby helping all levels of the Church to evaluate needs, set goals, and plan strategy; to coordinate planning and research for the denomination in cooperation with the general program agencies of The United Methodist Church; and to maintain a list of research and planning documents received from the general program agencies and the annual conferences.

18. To determine the need for and to develop and implement plans for themes, missional priorities, and/or special programs for the ministry of the Church for any particular quadrennium and, after consultation with the Council of Bishops, to recommend them to the General Conference for consideration.

19. To devise and implement measures to assure full, effective representation and participation of central conference members in the work of The United Methodist Church.

20. To report to the General Conference for its approval a summary of all decisions and recommendations made dealing with program changes and structure overlap.

21. To review, with the program agencies, all valid resolutions and positions adopted by the General Conference and recommend to the General Conference the removal of time-dated materials.

22. To receive reports from and refer matters to the General Commission on Christian Unity and Interreligious Concerns on the participation of The United Methodist Church in the various aspects of ecumenism.

23. To organize the Advance Committee, which shall have general oversight of the Advance program.

24. To organize the World Service Special Gifts Committee, which shall have general oversight of the World Service Special Gifts program.

25. To relate to and cooperate with the National Association of Conference Council Directors.

26. To act in concert with the General Council on Finance and Administration to establish a procedure for making a quadrennial review, initiating proposals, and/or responding to proposals by the general agencies regarding the location of headquarters and staff and report the same to the General Conference. (*See* ¶ 807.5.)

¶ **907.** *Organization*—1. *Membership*—*a*) The membership of the council shall consist of sixty-four members constituted in accordance with ¶ 705.6*a* of the General Provisions. The membership shall be constituted as follows:

(1) Jurisdictional members—Clergy, laywomen, and laymen shall be elected to the council by the jurisdictional conference upon nomination from the annual conference in accordance with ¶ 705.6*b*, based on the following formula: North Central—6, Northeastern—7, South Central—9, Southeastern—10, and Western—3.

These members shall be elected by the jurisdictional conference from a list of nominees submitted by each annual conference and each missionary conference that shall include at least one laywoman, one layman, and one from the clergy, with special attention to the inclusion of clergywomen and racial and ethnic persons. The nominations from the jurisdictions shall be made from the General Conference delegates. If there is not an adequate number of persons from the nominees, additional nominees may be selected from the jurisdictional delegates, and if additional nominees are further required, they may be selected from the membership of the jurisdiction. The above members shall consist, so far as possible, of one-third laywomen, one-third laymen, and one-third clergy;

(2) Supplemental members—One central conference member from the North Katanga Annual Conference and one member from the Nigeria Annual Conference as supplemental members according to the provisions of ¶ 705.4*c*;

(3) Five persons from central conferences, at least two clergy, two laywomen, one layman, and one alternate for each (who may attend if the elected member for whom he or she is the alternate cannot attend) nominated by the Council of Bishops and elected by the General Council on Ministries.

(4) A bishop from each jurisdiction and one bishop from the central conferences selected by the Council of Bishops (*see* ¶ 710.10).

(5) One additional youth from the Northeastern and Western jurisdictions, between the ages of twelve and seventeen at the time of his or her election, nominated by the jurisdictional youth ministry organization and elected by the jurisdictional conference.

(6) One young person between the ages of seventeen and twenty-seven at the time of his or her election, from the North Central, South Central, and Southeastern jurisdictions elected by the jurisdictional conference.

(7) Ten additional members to be elected by the council.

(*a*) Of the additional members elected by the council, in order to ensure that one fourth of the council's membership may represent racial and ethnic groups, it is recommended that there shall be not less than two representatives from each of the following groups: Asian Americans, African Americans, Hispanic Americans, Native Americans, and Pacific Islanders. (The council shall receive nominations from the racial and ethnic caucuses and ethnic annual conferences of these respective groups prior to the report of their nominating committee.) Insofar as possible, these additional members should be one-third laywomen, one-third laymen, and one-third clergy, with special attention to the inclusion of at least one clergywoman from each jurisdiction. Insofar as possible, these additional members will come from annual conferences not currently represented.

(b) It is further recommended that the council elect at least one member without vote from among the member churches of the Consultation on Church Union other than The United Methodist Church, as an additional member.

(8) One member elected by the Iglesia Metodista Autónoma Afiliada de Puerto Rico.

(9) The Council shall also include the general secretaries who serve as the chief executive officers of the general program agencies, the president and publisher of The United Methodist Publishing House, the general secretary of the General Commission on Archives and History, and the general secretary of the General Commission on Communication, all with voice but without vote.[25]

The agency may provide additional representatives with voice at the expense of the agency.

(10) The chairperson of the National Association of Conference Council Directors.

(11) If not otherwise provided at the beginning of the quadrennium, one conference council director or equivalent per jurisdiction shall be elected as a voting member of the council.

(12) The elected staff shall sit with the council with voice but without vote.

b) No members of the council shall serve on any boards or commissions or the divisions thereof having representation on the General Council on Ministries.

c) In order to ensure representation of older adults, it is recommended that at least one clergy member, one layman member, and one laywoman member be over sixty-five years of age.

---

25. See Judicial Council Decision 423.

*d)* In order to ensure representation of young people, it is recommended that the total membership be constituted by at least 10 percent youth and 10 percent young adults.

*e)* It is recommended that each jurisdictional conference give consideration to electing to membership on the council at least one third of the same persons elected to the council by the preceding jurisdictional conference.

*f)* When the committee selected to nominate the additional members of the General Council on Ministries meets prior to the organizational meeting, it shall determine the number of persons nominated by the annual conference and elected by the jurisdictional conference who were members of the council the previous quadrennium. If the number is less than ten, the nominating committee is encouraged to nominate enough persons from the eligible membership of the council in the previous quadrennium to bring this number to ten.

*g)* The members of the council shall serve for four years or until the convening of the organizational meeting. No voting member shall be eligible to serve for more than two consecutive four-year terms.

*h)* If a bishop is unable to attend a meeting of the council, that bishop may designate an alternate bishop from the same jurisdiction.

2. *Meetings*—Before the end of the calendar year in which regular sessions of the jurisdictional conferences are held, all persons who have been elected to membership on the council, including additional members nominated, shall be convened by an active bishop designated by the president of the Council of Bishops for the purpose of organizing.

The council shall meet at least once during each calendar year. It may meet in special session or at other times upon the call of the president or upon the written request of one-fifth of its members.

3. *Officers*—The council shall have a president, one or more vice presidents, a recording secretary, and a treasurer elected from the membership of the council. The president of the council shall be its presiding officer. Officers shall be elected for terms of four years and shall continue until their successors are duly elected.

4. *Internal Structure*—The council shall determine its internal structure as it deems necessary for the performance of its duties.

5. *Advance Committee*—There shall be an **Advance Committee,** which shall have general oversight of the Advance for Christ and His

Church (¶ 814). It shall be organized under the authority and direction of the General Council on Ministries. It shall consist of twenty members of the General Council on Ministries.

*a) Director of the Advance*—(1) There shall be a **Director of the Advance,** nominated by the Advance Committee from the staff of one of the participating agencies and elected by the General Council on Ministries. The participating agencies are the General Board of Global Ministries; the Division of Program and Benevolence Interpretation of the General Commission on Communication; the General Council on Ministries; and the General Council on Finance and Administration.

(2) The salary and related benefits of the director shall be paid by the participating agency. Other administrative costs of the Advance shall be borne by the General Council on Ministries.

(3) While continuing as a staff member of the participating agency, the director shall be a staff member of the General Council on Ministries related to the Advance Committee.

*b) Responsibilities of Director*—The responsibilities of the director of the Advance shall be:

(1) To coordinate the total program of the Advance, including its promotion, cultivation, and administration;

(2) To coordinate the staff work required of the participating agencies within the Advance;

(3) To report directly to the Advance Committee concerning the program and progress of the Advance; and

(4) To keep a record of all general Advance Special projects.

*c) General Advance Special Projects*—It shall be the responsibility of the Advance Committee to determine which projects are approved to receive general Advance Special Gifts (¶ 814.2). The Advance fosters partnership between those who give and those who receive, and it affirms the right of persons to determine the priority of their own needs. Projects shall therefore be proposed by authorized persons closely related to the project and shall be recommended to the Advance Committee by the administering agency. The Advance Committee may consider and approve proposals for either specific projects or broadly designated causes, such as a type of work, a country, a region, or an administrative unit.

*d) Administering Agencies*—Agencies authorized to recommend projects and receive and administer funds for general Advance Special projects shall be the following designated programmatic units of the General Board of Global Ministries: Evangelization and Church

Growth Program Area, Community and Institutional Ministries Program Area, Mission Contexts and Relationships Program Area, Mission Personnel Program Area, United Methodist Committee on Relief, and such other agencies as are designated by the General Council on Ministries. The administering agencies shall report annually to the Advance Committee on the financial progress of projects and assist in providing programmatic information as requested.

No project within the boundaries of an annual conference shall be approved by the Advance Committee for promotion, cultivation, and administration as a mission Advance Special without consultation with the annual conference council on ministries and the board or agency delegated responsibility for missions by the annual conference.

6. *World Service Special Gifts Committee—a)* There shall be a **World Service Special Gifts Committee** within the council to give administrative oversight to the World Service Special Gifts program, including establishing the procedure and criteria for approving specific projects, providing for staff administration of the program, and ensuring program accountability to the council by the administering agencies. The council shall make provisions for the General Council on Finance and Administration and administering agencies to have representation with voice but not vote. Any costs related to such representation shall be borne by the respective agencies.

*b)* In the World Service Special Gifts program, it shall be the responsibility of the General Council on Ministries to determine which projects are approved to receive World Service Special Gifts (¶ 813) under guidelines approved by the General Conference.

(1) All general boards and commissions except those units of general agencies authorized to receive general Advance Special Gifts are authorized to recommend World Service Special Gift projects for approval by the council, provided the project is specifically related to one or more of the disciplinary functions of the recommending agency.

(2) The participating agencies shall report annually to the council on the financial progress of World Service Special Gift projects and assist in providing programmatic information as requested.

(3) No World Service Special Gift project within the boundaries of an annual conference shall be approved by the council without consultation with the director of the annual conference council on ministries.

7. *Staff*—The council shall elect annually a general secretary and

489

associate general secretaries as needed. The elected staff shall sit with the council with voice but without vote.

### Section IV. General Board of Church and Society

¶ **1001.** *Name*—There shall be a **General Board of Church and Society** in The United Methodist Church, as an expression of the mission of the Church.

¶ **1002.** *Purpose*—The purpose of the board shall be to relate the gospel of Jesus Christ to the members of the Church and to the persons and structures of the communities and world in which they live. It shall seek to bring the whole of human life, activities, possessions, use of resources, and community and world relationships into conformity with the will of God. It shall show the members of the Church and the society that the reconciliation that God effected through Christ involves personal, social, and civic righteousness.[26]

¶ **1003.** *Objectives*—To achieve its purpose, the board shall:

1. Project plans and programs that challenge the members of The United Methodist Church to work through their own local churches, ecumenical channels, and society toward personal, social, and civic righteousness;

2. Assist the district and annual conferences with needed resources in areas of such concerns;

3. Analyze the issues that confront persons, communities, nations, and the world; and

4. Encourage Christian lines of action that assist humankind to move toward a world where peace and justice are achieved.

¶ **1004.** *Responsibilities*—The prime responsibility of the board is to seek the implementation of the Social Principles and other policy statements of the General Conference on Christian social concerns. Furthermore, the board and its executives shall provide forthright witness and action on issues of human well-being, justice, peace, and the integrity of creation that call Christians to respond as forgiven people for whom Christ died. In particular, the board shall conduct a program of research, education, and action on the wide range of issues that confront the Church.

The board shall analyze long-range social trends and their underlying ethical values. It shall explore systemic strategies for social

---

26. *See* Judicial Council Decision 387.

change and alternative futures. It shall speak its convictions, interpretations, and concerns to the Church and to the world.

The board shall develop, promote, and distribute resources and conduct programs to inform, motivate, train, organize, and build networks for action toward social justice throughout society, particularly on the specific issues prioritized by the board. Special attention shall be given to the nurture of the active constituency of the board. The board will encourage an exchange of ideas on strategy and methodology for social change. Through conferences, districts, coalitions, and networks, it will assist Church members as they identify and respond to critical social issues at community, regional, national, and international levels.

All the above shall be consistent with the Social Principles and policies adopted by the General Conference.

The board shall maintain close relationships with the General Commission on Religion and Race, the General Commission on the Status and Role of Women, and the Appalachian Development Committee as they seek to coordinate denominational support and cooperation with various movements for racial, sexual, and social justice, according to guidelines stated in the *Book of Discipline*. In cooperation with ecumenical agencies and other appropriate boards and agencies, the board shall encourage and promote ministries and models of mediation and conflict resolution, both ecumenically and within the agencies and institutions of The United Methodist Church.[27]

¶ **1005.** *Incorporation*—The General Board of Church and Society shall be a corporation existing under the laws of the District of Columbia and shall be the legal successor and successor in trust of the corporations, boards, departments, or entities known as the General Board of Christian Social Concerns of The United Methodist Church; the Department of Christian Social Action of The Evangelical United Brethren Church; the Board of Christian Social Concerns of The Methodist Church; the Division of General Welfare of the General Board of Church and Society of The United Methodist Church; the Division of General Welfare of the General Board of Christian Social Concerns of The United Methodist Church; the Division of Alcohol Problems and General Welfare of the Board of Christian Social Concerns of The Methodist Church; the Division of Temperance and General Welfare of the Board of Christian Social Concerns of The Methodist

---

27. *See* Judicial Council Decision 387.

Church; the Board of Temperance of The Methodist Church; the Board of Temperance, Prohibition, and Public Morals of The Methodist Episcopal Church; the Board of World Peace of The Methodist Church; the Commission on World Peace of The Methodist Church; the Commission on World Peace of The Methodist Episcopal Church; the Division of World Peace of the General Board of Church and Society of The United Methodist Church; the Board of Social and Economic Relations of The Methodist Church; the Division of Human Relations of the General Board of Church and Society of The United Methodist Church.

¶ **1006.** *Organization*—1. The General Board of Church and Society shall have sixty-three members, constituted in accordance with ¶ 704.3*e*, and shall be organized as specified in its bylaws and in harmony with ¶¶ 702–710 of the General Provisions. The membership shall be constituted as follows:

*a) Jurisdictional Members*—Clergy, laywomen, and laymen shall be elected to the board by the jurisdictional conference upon nomination from the annual conference in accordance with ¶ 705.6*b*, based on the following formula: North Central—7, Northeastern—8, South Central—11, Southeastern—12, and Western—3.

*b) Supplemental Members*—One member from Central Congo Annual Conference and one member from North Katanga Annual Conference.

*c) Central Conference Members*—Four central conference members shall be elected to the board on nomination by the Council of Bishops, according to the provisions in ¶ 705.5*c*.

*d) Episcopal Members*—Six episcopal members, including at least one from the central conferences, shall be named by the Council of Bishops.

*e)* One member elected by Iglesia Metodista Autónoma Afiliada de Puerto Rico.

*f) Additional Members*—1. *United Methodist*—Additional members are nominated by a committee composed of three persons from each jurisdiction (one clergy, one laywoman, and one layman) elected by the jurisdictional conference. They shall elect up to nine additional members to ensure inclusivity and expertise.

2. It is recommended that the board elect at least one of the additional members without vote from among the other churches of the Consultation on Church Union.

¶ **1007.** *Vacancies*—Vacancies in the board membership shall be filled by the procedure defined in ¶ 712.

¶ **1008.** *Financial Support*—1. The General Conference shall determine and provide the funding for the board in accord with policies and procedures of ¶ 806.

2. Either on behalf of its total work or on behalf of one of its programs, the board may solicit and create special funds, receive gifts and bequests, hold properties and securities in trust, and administer all its financial affairs in accordance with its own rules and provisions of the *Book of Discipline*. Funds vested in any of the predecessor boards shall be conserved for the specific purposes for which such funds have been given.

¶ **1009.** *Staff*—1. The general secretary shall be the chief administrative officer of the board, responsible for the coordination of the total program of the board, the supervision of staff, and the administration of the headquarters office. The general secretary shall be an ex officio member of the executive committee without vote and shall sit with the board when it is in session, with voice but without vote.

2. All other staff are to be elected or appointed in a manner prescribed by the board consistent with the affirmative action policies of the Church and the board.

¶ **1010.** *Headquarters*—The headquarters location shall be determined in accordance with ¶ 807.5. A United Nations Office shall be maintained in cooperation with the Women's Division of the General Board of Global Ministries.

¶ **1011.** *Bylaws*—The General Board of Church and Society shall provide its own bylaws, which shall not violate any provisions of the Constitution or the *Book of Discipline*. The bylaws may be amended by a two-thirds vote of the members present and voting thereon at a regular or special meeting; *provided* that notice of such amendment has previously been given to the members.

### Section V. General Board of Discipleship

¶ **1101.** *Purpose*—1. There shall be a **General Board of Discipleship,** the purpose of which is found within the expression of the total mission of the Church. Its primary purpose shall be to assist annual conferences, districts, and local churches of all membership sizes in their efforts to win persons to Jesus Christ as his disciples and to help these persons to grow in their understanding of God that they may respond in faith and love, to the end that they may know who they are and what their human situation means, increasingly identifying themselves as children of God and members of the Christian community, to live in the Spirit of God in every relationship, to fulfill their common discipleship in the world, and to abide in the Christian hope.

2. The board shall use its resources to enhance the meaning of membership as defined in ¶¶ 216–220, which emphasizes the importance of the identification of church membership with discipleship to Jesus Christ. The board shall seek to enable congregations to carry out their primary task and shall provide resources that support growth in Christian discipleship. In doing its work, the board shall listen to the needs and requests of the Church, conduct research, design and produce resources, offer training, and deliver resources. All of this is to support congregations in their primary task of reaching out and receiving all who will respond, encouraging people in their relationship with God and inviting them to commitment to God's love made known in Jesus Christ, providing opportunities for them to be nurtured and formed in the Christian faith, and supporting them to live lovingly and justly in the power of the Holy Spirit as faithful disciples. The board, through all activities, shall lead and assist congregations in becoming inclusive communities of growing Christians, celebrating and communicating to persons of every age, racial and ethnic background, and social condition the redeeming and reconciling love of God as revealed in Jesus Christ.

¶ **1102.** *Responsibilities*—All the responsibilities assigned to the units within the board shall be considered to be the responsibilities of the board. In addition to these, the board shall have authority to:

1. Provide for special publications directed toward the local church nurture, outreach, witness ministries, age-level and family ministries, ministry group representatives, the ministry group chairpersons, the pastor, and the other local church officers for whom the board has primary responsibility.

2. Manage and produce *The Upper Room* daily devotional guide and a wide range of other resources to help people grow in their relationship with God.

3. Provide systems of resources and support to users of resources that will assist people in the historic disciplines of the Church, i.e., Christian education, evangelism, lay ministries, spiritual growth,

stewardship, and worship. These resources will address ministry concerns across children, youth, and adult ages and family groupings and across programmatic and administrative functions of the congregation in order to improve ministry and the quality of Christian leadership for the future ministry of the Church.

4. Develop and provide resources, training, and consultation for pastors of congregations. These resources will focus on equipping pastors for their spiritual and visioning leadership role with their congregations and their role as partners with the laity.

5. Develop and provide resources, training, and consultation for pastors and congregational leaders as they enhance and evaluate the ministries of the laity and initiate new forms of ministry that nurture faith, build Christian community, and equip people for ministry in daily life.

6. Provide resources and training that will assist annual conference leaders in building, improving, and sustaining systems that develop spiritual leaders for congregations.

7. Provide resources and training that will assist leaders in planning and administering comprehensive children, youth, young-adult, adult, and older-adult ministries that encourage lifelong learning and growth in faith, that strengthen understanding of God and relationship with God and other people, and that lead to spiritual maturity in faith and in practice.

8. Provide representation in ecumenical and interdenominational agencies as they relate to the work of the board.

9. Respond to requests and needs for ministries throughout the world, in consultation with conferences and appropriate agencies.

10. Engage in research, experimentation, innovation, and the testing and evaluation of programs, resources, and methods to discover more effective ways to help persons achieve the purpose set forth in ¶ 1101. This responsibility will include authority for experimentation and research in all areas of ministry assigned to the General Board of Discipleship and will encourage cooperation with other agencies in the conduct of such research and experimentation. This research and experimentation may be assigned to appropriate units within the board.

11. Ensure that ethnic local church concerns shall be an integral part of the total life of the board, providing guidance, resourcing, and training so that these concerns are incorporated in all areas of discipleship in the local church.

¶ **1103.** *Incorporation*—The General Board of Discipleship shall be a corporation existing under the laws of Tennessee and shall be the legal successor and successor in trust of the corporations known as the General Board of Evangelism of The United Methodist Church and the General Board of Laity of The United Methodist Church, and it shall further be responsible for the performance of the functions previously conducted by the Commission on Worship of The United Methodist Church, the Division of the Local Church, and the Division of Curriculum Resources of the General Board of Education of The United Methodist Church.

The General Board of Discipleship is authorized to take such action as is appropriate under the corporation laws of Tennessee so as to accomplish the end result stated above, and under which the General Board of Discipleship shall be one legal entity.

The divisions of the General Board of Education were not incorporated separately; it is the intent, however, that responsibility for the functions delegated to the divisions by prior legislative action be transferred consistent with the separation of the divisions between the General Board of Discipleship and the General Board of Higher Education and Ministry. In the division of the assets of the General Board of Education, it is the intent that all assets be used in keeping with the original intent and purpose for which they were established or acquired, and so be assigned as appropriate to the General Boards of Discipleship and Higher Education and Ministry, respectively. It is further intended that the annuities, bequests, trusts, and estates formerly held by the General Board of Education be used for the benefit and use of the General Boards of Discipleship and Higher Education and Ministry (in accord with their purposes as defined in the *Discipline*), respectively, as their interests may appear, and that real estate titles be authorized to be conveyed as appropriate and apportioned where indicated.

In the event that the intent of the original donor of existing annuities, bequests, trusts, and estates cannot clearly be determined in relation to the interests of the two boards, such assets shall be divided equally between the two boards.

It is further intended that should additional assets accrue to the former General Board of Education by reason of annuities, bequests, trusts, and estates not now known and where the intent of the donor can be clearly ascertained, the assets shall be used in keeping with the original intent and purpose for which they were established or acquired and so be assigned as appropriate to the General Boards of Discipleship and Higher Education and Ministry, respectively.

It is further intended that should additional assets accrue to the former General Board of Education by reason of annuities, bequests, trusts, and estates not now known and where the intent of the original donor cannot be clearly determined in relation to the interests of the two boards, such assets shall be divided equally between the two boards.

The president of the board, the general secretary, and the treasurer shall have the power to execute on behalf of the board legal paper such as conveyances of real estate, releases on mortgages, transfer of securities, contracts, and all other legal documents.

¶ 1104. *Organization*—1. The board shall consist of fifty-eight members constituted in accordance with ¶ 705.3 of the General Provisions. It shall be organized to accomplish its work through elected officers as prescribed in ¶ 708. The membership shall be constituted as follows:

*a)* Jurisdictional members, clergy, laywomen, and laymen shall be elected to the board by the jurisdictional conference upon nomination from the annual conference in accordance with ¶ 705.4e and 705.4a based on the following formula: North Central—6, Northeastern—7, South Central—10, Southeastern—11, and Western—2.

*b) Supplemental Members*—One member from the southern Congo Annual Conference and one member from the Nigeria Annual Conference as supplemental members according to the provisions of ¶ 705.5e.

*c) Central Conference Members*—Five central conference members shall be elected to the board on nomination by the Council of Bishops, according to the provisions in ¶ 705.5c.

*d) Episcopal Members*—Six episcopal members, including at least one from the central conferences, shall be named by the Council of Bishops.

*e)* One member elected by Iglesia Metodista Autónoma Afiliada de Puerto Rico.

*f) Additional Members*—(1) *United Methodist*—Additional members are nominated by a committee composed of three persons from each jurisdiction (one clergy, one laywoman, and one layman) elected by the jurisdictional conference. They shall elect up to eight additional members to ensure inclusivity and expertise. (2) It is recommended that the board elect at least one of the additional members without vote, from among the other churches of the Consultation on Church Union.

2. The board may elect an executive committee and establish such rules as necessary for the carrying out of its duties.

3. The board shall determine and establish the appropriate organization of the board and its staff, and it may create or discontinue as deemed necessary divisions, sections, committees, task forces, and consultations in order to carry out the regular or special duties of the board.

4. The board shall provide such bylaws as necessary to facilitate the work of the board, which shall not violate any provisions of the *Discipline* and which may be amended by a two-thirds vote of the members present and voting thereon at a regular or special meeting; *provided* that written notice to such amendment has been given to the members and the vote thereon shall be delayed at least one day.

5. Adequate provisions shall be made in its organizational structure for all responsibilities assigned to the board. These organizational units shall be amenable to and report regularly to the board and its executive committee.

¶ **1105.** *Organizational Units*—The organizational units shall be organized by the board so as to fulfill the objectives and the responsibilities assigned to them within the mandate of the board (*see* ¶ 1104.3). The basic organization of these units shall be as follows:

1. *Membership*—The units shall be composed of board members as provided in ¶ 705. In order to provide for unit members with special knowledge and experience, the board shall have authority to elect members at large to the units on nomination of the units and in accord with ¶ 705.

2. *Meetings*—The units shall meet in conjunction with the meetings of the board. Special meetings may be called in a manner prescribed by the board. The presence of one-third of the members of a unit shall constitute a quorum.

3. *Officers*—Each unit shall have a chairperson, elected by the board; such vice chairpersons as necessary; and a recording secretary, elected by the unit.

4. *Executive Committee*—Each unit may elect an executive committee and establish such rules as necessary for the carrying out of its duties.

5. *Unit Staff*—The administrative officer of each unit shall be elected by the board and shall sit with the unit and all its regular committees. In all of these relationships, he or she shall have the right of the floor without the power to vote. All other staff persons are to be elected or appointed in a manner prescribed by the board (¶ 714).

¶ **1106.** *Financial Support*—1. The financial support of the board shall be determined as follows: the General Conference shall determine and provide the budget for the board in accord with procedures defined in ¶ 806.

2. The board shall have authority to receive and administer funds, gifts, or bequests that may be committed to it for any portion of its work and to solicit, establish, and administer any special funds that may be found necessary for the carrying out of its plans and policies in accordance with ¶ 811.3. In the investment of any funds, the board shall adhere to the specific investment guidelines adopted by the General Conference.

3. No funds, property, or other investments either now in hand or hereafter accumulated by *The Upper Room* or other devotional and related literature hereafter produced by *The Upper Room* shall be used for the support of other features of the board's work, but all funds from the sale of such publications shall be conserved by the board for the purpose of preparing and circulating such literature and cultivating the devotional life; *provided,* however, that this shall not prevent the setting up of a reserve fund out of such income as a protection against unforeseen emergencies.

4. When special missions are conducted or special projects are undertaken by the board, offerings and contributions may be received toward defraying expenses.

5. In the discharge of its responsibility for Christian education in The United Methodist Church, the board may establish and provide for participation by church school groups in a fund (or funds) for missions and Christian education in the United States and overseas. Plans for the allocation of, administration of, and education for this fund(s) shall be developed cooperatively by such means as the board shall determine in consultation with the General Board of Global Ministries.

¶ **1107.** *Christian Education*—1. The board shall have general oversight of the educational interests of the Church as directed by the General Conference. The board shall be responsible for the development of a clear statement of the biblical and theological foundations of Christian education, consistent with the doctrines of The United Methodist Church and the mission of the board. The board shall devote itself to strengthening and extending the teaching ministry of the Church through research; testing new approaches, methods, and resources; evaluation; and consultation.

2. Through the ministry of Christian education, United Methodist

congregations shall reach out to people of all ages as they are, encourage them to commit themselves to Christ and membership in his church, provide opportunities for them to grow in faith and to connect that faith with their daily lives, and equip them to live as God's people in the world. Opportunities for Christian education shall include educational aspects of all the general areas and interests of the denomination, such as evangelism, stewardship, missions, Christian social action, and Bible instruction. The ministry of Christian education shall be developed as a comprehensive, unified, and coordinated program for children, youth, adults, and families in local churches. It shall be promoted and administered by the board in cooperation with those agencies responsible for Christian education in jurisdictions, annual conferences, districts, and local churches. It shall give careful consideration to the needs of all churches, such as small and large membership churches, rural and urban settings, and ethnic populations.

¶ **1108.** *Education Responsibilities and Standards*—The board shall organize as may be necessary for carrying on the educational ministry throughout the whole life span of persons. The board shall:

1. Formulate and interpret the philosophy of Christian education based on biblical, theological, and educational foundations (consistent with the Doctrinal Standards and General Rules of The United Methodist Church, ¶ 103) as they relate to the church school and related activities; individual or group study; fellowship, education, and action groups for children, youth, and adults; related educational programs provided by civic youth-serving agencies; weekday nurseries and kindergartens; daycare centers; choirs, drama groups, mission studies; education for leisure; outdoor education; camping; education of persons with developmental disabilities and others of special need; special Bible study groups; confirmation and church membership training.

2. Develop educational approaches in a variety of settings that appeal to persons of different ages, lifestyles, learning needs, and theological perspectives.

3. Develop educational approaches that will enable persons of different racial, ethnic, and cultural groups to appropriate the gospel for their own life situations.

4. Promote church school extension in a variety of ways, such as providing resources and training that help persons in sponsoring new church schools, starting new church school classes, and expanding teaching and learning opportunities in the congregation and the community.

5. Provide resources and support services for pastors, parents, educational leaders, teachers, and others responsible for teaching and learning with persons across the life span at the local church, district, and conference levels.

6. Provide resources and support services for teacher recruitment, development, and training in biblical, theological, and ethical thinking, as well as in procedures and methods; work with the colleges and seminaries of the Church wherever possible to forward the common interest in the training of professional Christian educators and the training of ministerial students in local church Christian education; provide national camp training events and assist jurisdictions and annual conferences in designing, guiding, and resourcing camp training programs and outdoor Christian education.

7. Set standards and provide guidance concerning programming, leadership, and grouping for the various educational settings of the Church, including the church school.

8. Establish guidelines for the organization and administration of the church school, for recording and reporting membership and attendance of the church school, and for the equipment, arrangement, and design for church school buildings and rooms, with particular attention given to the needs of persons with disabilities.

9. Provide resources and services related to the training and work of local church directors, ordained and diaconal ministers, and associates of Christian education and educational assistants.

10. Develop standards governing all types of camping in regard to physical facilities, program, and leadership. To the extent possible, all camps shall be accessible to persons with disabilities.

11. Cooperate with the General Board of Higher Education and Ministry as they develop standards for certifying professional ministry careers as provided in ¶ 1424.1 and promote the continuing growth of local church staff related to educational ministries.

12. Provide resources, models, and training to support annual conferences and local churches as they help people make decisions related to their general Christian vocation as well as their specific occupations or careers.

13. Review and recommend for approval the curriculum plans developed in cooperation with the other boards and agencies in the Curriculum Resources Committee and interpret and support the curriculum developed by the committee.

14. Promote the observance of Christian Education Sunday (¶¶ 265.1, 1806.12).

¶ **1109.** *Cooperation*—1. The board shall cooperate with other general boards and agencies in the promotion of stewardship, evangelism, worship, mission education, and social action, and in the evaluation of these ministries from the perspective of sound educational procedure.

2. The board, in cooperation with the General Board of Global Ministries, shall be responsible for developing a unified program of mission education for all age groups in the local church. The mission education program shall include provisions for the following:

*a)* Linking emerging philosophies of mission and of education through information flow and cooperative work of the respective staffs and boards;

*b)* Developing and interpreting varied styles of mission education appropriate to different groups, including age groupings and the various racial and ethnic cultures;

*c)* Curriculum planning for education in mission, providing mission information about projects supported by The United Methodist Church (including ecumenical projects) through the church school resources, and preparing curricular and other materials for mission education;

*d)* Participating with various agencies in the design, development, and promotion of ecumenical mission education resources;

*e)* Developing and interpreting educational approaches and channels for mission giving of children, youth, and adults, such as the Children's Fund for Christian Mission;

*f)* Developing and interpreting models for new approaches to mission study and educational participation in mission;

*g)* Providing information regarding educational criteria to the staff of the General Board of Global Ministries for use in certifying leaders for schools of mission;

*h)* Disseminating a comprehensive listing of mission resources for leaders;

*i)* Cooperating with the General Board of Higher Education and Ministry and the General Board of Global Ministries in providing an emphasis on mission education in the schools of theology through United Methodist courses on history, polity, and doctrine now required for candidates considering ordination or consecration.

3. The board shall have authority to cooperate with other agencies of the Church, with defined organizations, and with ecumenical agencies to promote the ministry of Christian education.

4. The board is authorized to cooperate with the General Board of Global Ministries in the planning and execution of programs for the strengthening and development of the town and country, urban, and ethnic local church ministries of The United Methodist Church and of interdenominational cooperation in these fields.

¶ 1110. *Evangelism*—The board shall have general oversight of the evangelism ministries of the Church as directed by the General Conference. Evangelism is central to the mission of the Church. *Evangelism* is defined in the *Book of Discipline*, ¶ 628.1.

The board shall share the blessing of the gospel of the Lord Jesus Christ with people of all ages by the development, promotion, and support of all phases of evangelism throughout The United Methodist Church.

¶ 1111. *Evangelism Responsibilities*—In response to God's love in Jesus Christ, the board shall have general oversight of the evangelism ministries of The United Methodist Church by the envisioning and developing of resources and by training and consultation in various settings. The board shall:

1. Set forth an adequate biblical and theological basis and understanding for the personal, corporate, and social aspects of evangelism, consistent with the doctrine and tradition of The United Methodist Church, and it shall communicate and interpret the same to the membership of the Church.

2. Give emphasis to the development, interpretation, and promotion of ministries of evangelism at the conference, district, and local church levels so that persons who are not active Christian disciples through any local church will be invited and cared for by a United Methodist church.

3. Provide resources and training for strategies, ministries, and programs in evangelism, including resources for the local church ministry of evangelism (¶ 253).

4. Cooperate with other program agencies of the Church in supporting and equipping both clergy and laity at all levels in involvement in evangelism, church growth, and new congregational development.

5. Provide and encourage research in what creative congregations of various membership sizes and settings are doing in effective evangelism that can serve as models for other churches, and foster experi-

mentation and demonstration of additional evangelistic approaches, consistent with the nature of the Christian gospel and the Church, at all levels of the Church's life, including new congregations and all racial and cultural groups.

6. Provide resources and services for those serving as pastors, diaconal ministers, directors of evangelism, general evangelists, and other professionals in evangelism in local churches.

7. Set standards for elders desiring to serve as general evangelists. The board shall send copies of these standards quadrennially to the bishops, district superintendents, conference boards of discipleship, and general evangelists. An elder who feels called by God to be a general evangelist should prepare definitely for such service under the guidance of the annual conference to which that person belongs.

8. Relate and provide liaison services to denominational and ecumenical associations and fellowships of evangelism.

9. Seek mutual cooperation among and with the seminaries of the Church and the General Board of Higher Education and Ministry in the training and nurturing of persons for ministry and in continuing education where the responsibilities intersect.

10. Communicate with other agencies in whose programs the subject matter of evangelism would be included, and provide counsel, guidance, and resources for the implementation of such programs.

11. Participate in and cooperate with the work of the Curriculum Resources Committee of the board for the inclusion of evangelism concepts and resources in local church study curriculum.

12. Provide consultation with conferences, districts, local congregations, and other agencies to develop strategies in evangelism for outreach, church revitalization, and new congregational development.

13. Work with the General Board of Global Ministries for the extension of the Church. To this end there shall be a Joint Committee on Congregational Development with equal representation of members from the General Board of Discipleship and the General Board of Global Ministries, which shall meet regularly for mutual learning, developing strategies for Church extension, and providing resources and assistance to conferences and districts in the field of new congregational development and congregational revitalization.

¶ **1112.** *Worship Responsibilities*—The board shall: 1. Set forth and interpret the biblical and theological basis for corporate worship with people of all ages through resources, programs, and training materials consistent with the doctrines of The United Methodist Church, and cultivate the fullest possible meaning in the corporate worship celebrations of the Church to the glory of God, including liturgy, preaching, the sacraments, music, related arts, and the observance of the liturgical seasons of the Christian Year.

2. Develop standards and resources for the conduct of public worship in the churches, including liturgy, preaching, the sacraments, music, and related arts.

3. Make recommendations to the General Conference regarding future editions of a book of worship and a hymnal and, as ordered, provide editorial supervision of the contents of these publications, which shall be published by The United Methodist Publishing House. The hymnals of The United Methodist Church are *The United Methodist Hymnal* (1989), *Mil Voces Para Celebrar: Himnario Metodista* (1996), and *Come, Let Us Worship: The Korean-English United Methodist Hymnal* (2000). The ritual of the Church is that contained in *The United Methodist Hymnal* (1989), *The United Methodist Book of Worship* (1992), *Mil Voces Para Celebrar: Himnario Metodista* (1996), and *Come, Let Us Worship: The Korean-English United Methodist Hymnal* (2000).

4. Prepare revisions of the Ritual of the Church and approved orders of worship for recommendation to the General Conference for adoption.

5. Work with other North American Christian denominations through the Consultation on Common Texts in the continuing development of a common calendar and lectionary, and encourage the voluntary use of the *Revised Common Lectionary* and resources based upon it.

6. Prepare and sponsor the publication of supplemental orders and texts of worship.[28]

7. Maintain a cooperative but not exclusive relationship with The United Methodist Publishing House in the preparation and publication of worship resources.

8. Advise the general agencies of the Church in the preparation, publication, and circulation of orders of service and other liturgical materials bearing the imprint of The United Methodist Church, encouraging use of racial and ethnic worship resources and incorporation of language that recognizes the several constituencies of the Church. (*See* ¶ 4.)

---

28. *See* Judicial Council Decision 445.

9. Counsel with the editors of the periodicals and publications of The United Methodist Church concerning material offered in the fields of worship, including preaching, music, and the other liturgical arts.

10. Participate in and cooperate with the Curriculum Resources Committee of the board for the inclusion of worship concepts and resources in local church study curriculum.

11. Encourage in the schools of theology and pastors' schools, and other settings, the offering of instruction in the meaning and conduct of worship. This should include the worship practices and expressions of the various racial cultures.

12. Counsel with those responsible for planning and conducting the worship services of the General Conference and other general assemblies of the Church.

13. Give guidance to, provide resources for, and encourage the continuing growth of those persons responsible for music leadership in the local church, i.e., directors, ordained ministers, associates, music assistants, and those volunteering in music and the other worship arts. (See ¶ 1405.7.)

14. Cooperate with the Fellowship of United Methodists in Music and Worship Arts and The Order of St. Luke in affirming the sacramental life embracing liturgy, preaching, music, and other arts appropriate for the inclusive worship life of the Church.

15. Develop performance standards for associates, directors, and ministers of music in cooperation with the General Board of Higher Education and Ministry, and cooperate with the General Board of Higher Education and Ministry in the development of standards and requirements for certification of directors, associates, and ministers of music as provided in ¶ 1405.6.

¶ 1113. *Stewardship Responsibilities*—1. To interpret the biblical and theological basis for stewardship through programs, resources, and training materials for people of all ages consistent with the doctrines of The United Methodist Church.

2. To provide education, counsel, resourcing, and training for the local church stewardship ministry group chairperson, commission on stewardship, board of trustees, endowment and permanent fund committees, wills and estate planning committees, memorial committees, committee on finance, committee on finance chairperson, financial secretaries, and treasurers, and to develop program resources and training materials for use with and by the above-named persons and/or groups (*see* ¶ 807.15). Matters relating to procedures involv-

ing official records, forms, and reporting of finances shall be the responsibility of the General Council on Finance and Administration.

3. To create within The United Methodist Church a deepening commitment to personal and corporate Christian stewardship, which includes the use and sharing of talents and resources and the practice of a Christian lifestyle.

4. To develop strategies, provide resources, and implement actions that lead to a continuing improvement in the level of giving of United Methodists in providing adequate support for the mission of the Church.

5. To counsel in the area of stewardship and finance with jurisdictional and annual conference program agencies relative to their organizational structure and program responsibilities and assist them in their interpretation of program and resources.

6. To provide counsel, resources, and guidance to conference and area foundations as they fulfill their stewardship functions and to associations such as the National Association of United Methodist Foundations and the National Association of Stewardship Leaders.

7. To call together regularly United Methodist general agency leaders whose programs include the subject matter of stewardship to work toward common language, consistent stewardship theology, and cooperative efforts.

¶ 1114. *Spiritual Formation Responsibilities of* The Upper Room—To develop resources that foster an international community of people and congregations who are seeking God, building a vision of new life in Christ, nurturing one another by sharing experiences of God's love and guidance, and encouraging one another in Christian action to transform the world.

2. To explore and communicate a biblically and theologically informed vision of the spiritual life that encourages and supports spiritual leaders in the church who can guide people of all ages into a more vital, intimate, and transforming relationship with God through Christ.

3. To maintain and extend the worldwide ministry of *The Upper Room* and other resources, which are available in an increasing number of languages and which address the spiritual needs of people throughout their life and continue to embody the interdenominational character of the ministry of *The Upper Room.*

4. To cooperate with all other units within the board, as well as other groups within United Methodism, and other denominations whose concerns are related to the spiritual life.

¶ **1115.** *Ministry of the Laity*—The board shall interpret and spread through the Church all the rich meanings of the universal priesthood of believers, of Christian vocation, and of the ministry of the laity in daily life.

The United Methodist Church has the responsibility of training and enabling the *laos*—the whole body of its membership—to enter into mission and to minister and witness in the name of Jesus Christ, the Head of the Church. Although all units of the Church have some responsibility for this imperative, the General Board of Discipleship has a preeminent responsibility in that it is charged with developing discipleship. To this end, the board shall:

1. Help develop an adequate understanding of the theological and biblical basis for ministry of the laity.

2. Develop and interpret ministry of the laity both inside and outside the institutional Church.

3. Provide resources and support services for the development and improvement of leadership in the local church, except as specifically delegated to other agencies, and especially for those persons who serve as members of charge conferences, church councils, councils on ministries, committees on pastor-parish relations, personnel committees, committees on lay leadership, those who serve as lay leaders, lay members of annual conferences, and leaders of related organizations in local churches, districts, annual conferences, and jurisdictions.

4. Assist congregations, districts, and annual conferences in equipping persons for leadership in community ministries.

5. Provide resources and suggested plans for the observance of Laity Sunday in the local church.

6. Provide support to conference and district directors of Lay Speaking Ministries and to conference and district committees on Lay Speaking Ministries. In consultation with the conference directors, set standards for local church and certified lay speakers and provide teaching resources for use by annual conference and district committees.

7. Provide support services to conference and district lay leaders and conference and district boards of laity, to the National Association of Annual Conference Lay Leaders, and to other appropriate conference and district officers and agencies.

8. Initiate a process of coordination and collaboration in developing a comprehensive approach to leadership development and training within all program areas for which the General Board of Discipleship has responsibility.

9. Encourage ordained elders to select and train laity to distribute the consecrated Communion elements as soon as feasible to sick or homebound persons following a service of Word and Table. This distribution also may apply to laypersons who have been assigned pastoral roles in a church or in more than one church by the district superintendent.

¶ **1116.** *Christian Discipleship Formation Responsibilities*—The board shall interpret and promote group ministries in local congregations in order to support the formation of Christian disciples focused on the transformation of the world.

1. *Small Group Ministries*—Recognizing the diverse means of grace necessary in forming Christian disciples, the General Board of Discipleship shall assist local congregations in developing a comprehensive system of small-group ministries by:

*a*) providing resources, training, and support services for leaders of small-group ministries that support people in their search for God, in their yearning for community, and in their desire to be formed as Christian disciples;

*b*) providing resources and support services that equip people throughout the life span for faithful Christian living in the world, and especially those areas for which the General Board of Discipleship has responsibility. When developing resources, attention should be given to the impact of the oral and visual cultures in which we live and to the importance of story.

2. *Accountable Discipleship*—Affirming that our Wesleyan heritage embraces a distinct emphasis of mutual accountability, the General Board of Discipleship shall encourage accountability in congregations by:

*a*) promoting the General Rule of Discipleship: "To witness to Jesus Christ in the world, and to follow his teachings through acts of compassion, justice, worship, and devotion, under the guidance of the Holy Spirit"[29];

*b*) advocating the formation of Covenant Discipleship Groups for all ages throughout the church by providing resources, training, and support services that ground leadership in the richness of our Wesleyan tradition;

---

29. Adapted version of Wesley's General Rules; *see* Gayle Turner Watson's *A Guide to Covenant Discipleship Groups* (Discipleship Resources, 2000), p. 12.

*c)* providing resources, training, and support services for revitalizing the role of class leaders so that they may interpret the General Rule of Discipleship to all church members and assist the pastor in fostering mutual accountability throughout the congregation;

*d)* providing consultative services to jurisdictions, conferences, and districts in the introduction and development of Covenant Discipleship Groups and class leaders in congregations.

¶ **1117.** *Ethnic Local Church Concerns*—The board shall function as an advocate for programs and concerns of ethnic local churches. It shall coordinate efforts to keep the needs of the membership of ethnic churches uppermost in the minds of its membership. The board will ensure that adequate resources—fiscal, human, and programmatic— are used to support and encourage the ministries of the ethnic local churches.

¶ **1118.** *Age-Level, Life-Span, and Family Ministries*—The board will provide for an integrated and coordinated approach in development of resources and service support for ministries with children, youth, adults of all ages, and families. Through its services to administrative and coordinating leaders, the board will assist congregations and conferences to:

*a)* Build knowledge for development of ministries that support the primary task of the local congregation;

*b)* Provide for the development and nurture of persons at all age levels and stages of growth and for families in diverse configurations;

*c)* Assist individuals and families in spiritual development and growth; and

*d)* Promote the making and keeping of covenants as foundations for family living.

The board will also engage in research and testing, consultation and training, and collaborative planning so as to enhance the delivery of resources and services to leaders with age-level and family ministries responsibilities.

1. *Comprehensive Children's Ministries*—The board will assist congregations and conferences in developing comprehensive ministries for and with children. Such ministries may include, but shall not be limited to, the following: Sunday school and vacation Bible school, weekday ministries for preschool and elementary ages, fellowship and neighborhood groups, Scouting ministries, and short-term studies and activities within and outside the church facilities. Ministries

should focus on biblical foundations, prayer and spiritual formation, community service, personal worth through Jesus Christ, human sexuality, values, United Methodist studies, creative and fine arts, multicultural awareness, outreach to others, and celebration of significant moments in children's lives.

Responsibilities may include such supportive tasks as: assisting congregations to be advocates on behalf of children; identifying the needs and concerns of children, their families and congregations; assessing the status of ministries with children in The United Methodist Church; collecting and disseminating pertinent data on issues, models, and programs that inform the leaders in congregations and church structures to strengthen the quality of life of children.

2. *Comprehensive Youth Ministry*—There shall be a comprehensive approach to development and implementation of youth ministry programming at all levels of the Church. The comprehensive approach is based on the understanding of the primary task of youth ministry: to love youth where they are, to encourage them in developing their relationship to God, to provide them with opportunities for nurture and growth, and to challenge them to respond to God's call to serve in their communities. Four component parts undergird this comprehensive ministry:

*a) Curriculum*—Through the Curriculum Resources Committee (¶ 1120), the General Board of Discipleship shall ensure the availability of curriculum and leaders' guides for use in a variety of settings suitable for the specific needs of all persons in the twelve- to eighteen-year-old age group;

*b) Program Resources*—Additional and supplemental guidebooks and other program aids shall be developed and promoted for effective youth ministry programs in the local church and at the district, conference, jurisdictional, and general Church levels;

*c) Leadership Training and Networking*—Leadership training shall be provided to encourage and support adult workers with youth and youth leaders in their roles as teachers, counselors, advisers, and enablers at all levels of the Church. Networking shall be developed to maintain ongoing communication through workshops, special mailings, and publications between leaders in youth ministries across the denomination for the enhancement of skills and the sharing of effective models and resources;

*d) Structures*—Active and effective structures for youth ministry programming shall be promoted and maintained at the local church, district, conference, jurisdictional, and general Church levels for the full involvement of youth in leadership and membership and for the advocacy of youth concerns in all areas of Church life, planning, and administration.

3. *Comprehensive Adult Ministries*—The board will assist congregations and conferences in developing comprehensive ministries by, with, and for adults. In keeping with the primary task of the board, adult ministries may include but need not be limited to: education and ministries with young adults, middle adults, older adults, and single adults (i.e., widowed, always single, separated, and divorced), and intergenerational programs involving adults. Such a plan would include biblical foundation and study, developmental stages and tasks of adults, faith development and spiritual formation, and leadership training in various models of adult educational ministries.

Responsibilities may include such supportive tasks as: identifying the needs and concerns of adults (i.e., young adults, middle adults, older adults, and single adults); assessing the status of ministries by, with, and for adults in The United Methodist Church; collecting and disseminating pertinent data on issues, models, and programs that inform the leaders in local congregations, districts, conferences, boards, and agencies to strengthen the quality of faith and life of adults.

4. *Comprehensive Family Ministries*—The board will assist congregations and conferences in developing comprehensive ministries with families. In alignment with the primary task, the ministries may assist families in the following areas: spiritual formation and development, marital growth ministries, parenting, human sexuality, care giving, and issues affecting the quality of family life. Such a plan would include: biblical exploration and study, as well as theological and experiential understandings of family life and the evolving patterns of family living. Ministries with families will focus on persons rather than structures.

The board may organize and administer a Committee on Family Life. The committee will provide an arena for information sharing, collaborative planning, and/or cooperative programming in alignment with the purpose and responsibilities of representative participants. The committee will serve as advocates for ministries with families in all boards and agencies.

Responsibilities may include such supportive tasks as: identifying the needs and concerns of families and of congregations, assessing the status of ministries with families in The United Methodist

Church, collecting and disseminating pertinent data on issues, models, and programs that inform the work of the boards and agencies to strengthen the quality of family life. The committee will relate to and provide liaison services to ecumenical and interdenominational agencies in the area of family life.

¶ **1119.** *General Provisions for the Committee on Older Adult Ministries*—1. There shall be a **Committee on Older Adult Ministries,** which shall be administratively related to the General Board of Discipleship.

2. *Purpose*—The committee will provide a forum for information sharing, cooperative planning, and joint program endeavors as determined in accordance with the responsibilities and objectives of the participating agencies. The committee shall serve as an advocate for older adult concerns and issues and shall serve to support ministries by, with, and for older adults throughout The United Methodist Church and in the larger society.

3. *Responsibilities*—The responsibilities of the committee shall include the following:

*a*) Identify the needs, concerns, and potential contributions of older adults.

*b*) Promote a plan of comprehensive ministry by, with, and for older adults in local churches that includes spiritual growth, education, training, mission, service, and fellowship.

*c*) Support the development of resources that will undergird local church ministries by, with, and for older adults.

*d*) Advocate development and implementation of policies and service designed to impact systems and concepts that adversely affect older adults.

*e*) Educate and keep before the Church the lifelong process of aging, with emphasis on the quality of life, intergenerational understanding, and faith development.

*f*) Encourage the development of resources and programs that can be used by annual conferences, jurisdictions, and the denomination at large in training and equipping older adults for new roles in the ministry and mission of the Church.

*g*) Serve as focal point for supplying information and guidelines on older adult ministries to local churches.

*h*) Encourage coordination among agencies responsible for the development of resources, programs, and policies relating to older adult ministries.

4. *Membership*—The committee shall be composed of one board member and one staff member from each of the following agencies: the General Board of Discipleship, the General Board of Global Ministries, the General Board of Church and Society, the General Board of Higher Education and Ministry, and the General Council on Ministries; one member (board or staff) from the Commission on the Status and Role of Women, one from the Commission on Religion and Race, and one from the Commission on United Methodist Men; one retired bishop representing the Council of Bishops; one central conference representative; five older adults, one to be selected by each jurisdictional College of Bishops; and no more than five additional members to be selected by the committee for expertise, professional qualifications, and/or inclusiveness (racial and ethnic, disability, age, gender, laity, clergy, or geographic distribution). Staff members will provide appropriate liaison and reports to their respective agencies. They will have voice but not vote.

5. *Meetings*—The committee will meet at least once a year in conjunction with a meeting of the General Board of Discipleship.

¶ **1120.** *Duties and Responsibilities of the Curriculum Resources Committee*—There shall be a Curriculum Resources Committee, organized and administered by the General Board of Discipleship, which shall be responsible for the construction of plans for curriculum and curriculum resources to be used in the Christian educational ministry of the Church and other study settings. (*See* ¶ 258.1.)

1. The Curriculum Resources Committee shall carefully review and act on the plans constructed and proposed by the staff of Church School Publications based upon research, including ideas from the Curriculum Resources Committee and other persons in United Methodist educational ministries.

2. The plans for curriculum and curriculum resources shall be designed to help local churches carry out the Church's educational ministry with children, youth, young adults, adults, and families and to meet the needs of various racial, ethnic, age, cultural, and language constituencies, as well as the needs of persons of various learning capacities, backgrounds, levels of psychological development, sight and hearing impairments, and Christian maturity. Plans for curriculum shall give particular attention to the characteristics and needs of small membership congregations. They shall be for use in a variety of settings, both formal and informal, including Sunday schools; fellowship groups; outdoor experiences; family life; leadership education;

campus ministries; preparation with parent(s), guardian(s), and sponsor(s) or godparent(s) who are presenting children to be baptized; and classes preparing youth for their profession of faith and their confirmation.

3. The plans for curriculum and curriculum resources shall be consistent with the educational philosophy and approach formulated for the educational ministry of the Church by the General Board of Discipleship and shall reflect a unity of purpose and a planned comprehensiveness of scope. They shall be designed to support the total life and work of the Church, shall teach Christian truth consistent with the Doctrinal Standards and General Rules of The United Methodist Church (¶ 103), and shall reflect the official positions of The United Methodist Church as authorized by the General Conference.

4. Plans for major new curriculum resources and new series that have been approved by the General Board of Discipleship shall be circulated by staff among appropriate persons and groups in the Church for review, suggestions for improvement, and additional ideas. In all matters, staff shall be responsible for bringing the review results into unity and harmony with the intent of the Curriculum Resources Committee.

*a*) The purpose of the review process shall be to improve the resource plans in order to fulfill ¶ 1120.

*b*) Opportunity for timely review shall be offered to teachers, leaders, and pastors in local churches of various sizes, locations, and racial, ethnic, and cultural constituencies; general secretaries of the General Boards of Discipleship, Global Ministries, Church and Society, and Higher Education and Ministry, and the General Commissions on History and Archives, Christian Unity and Interreligious Concerns, the Status and Role of Women, United Methodist Men, and Religion and Race; professors of educational ministries in United Methodist colleges and seminaries; professional Christian educators; and others who may have interest, experience, and skills to aid the perfection of the plans.

¶ **1121.** *Curriculum Requirements*—When the plans for curriculum and curriculum resources have been approved by the General Board of Discipleship, the editorial staff of Church School Publications shall be responsible for the development of curriculum resources based on the approved plans. The curriculum resources shall be based on the Bible, shall reflect the universal gospel of the living Christ, shall use the traditional calendar year designations of B.C. (Before Christ) and A.D. (*Anno Domini*, or Year[s] of the Lord) as a reflection of and witness to the Christian understanding of the centrality of Jesus Christ in the history of humankind, shall be in agreement with United Methodist doctrine as delineated in ¶¶ 103 and 104 of the *Book of Discipline*, and shall be designed for use in the various settings that are defined by the board.

¶ **1122.** *Authority of the Curriculum Resources Committee to Review Teaching Resources of General Agencies*—The Curriculum Resources Committee shall review and may approve and recommend existing or projected resources from other agencies. The committee shall make certain that all approved materials conform to United Methodist doctrine as delineated in ¶¶ 103 and 104 of the *Book of Discipline*. All curriculum resources that are approved by the General Board of Discipleship shall be authorized for use in the church school.

¶ **1123.** *Relationship of the Curriculum Resources Committee to the General Board of Discipleship and to The United Methodist Publishing House*—1. The Curriculum Resources Committee shall be related to the General Board of Discipleship as follows:

*a)* The committee shall be responsible to the board with respect to educational philosophy and approaches and shall seek to maintain the standards set by the board.

*b)* The committee shall work with the General Board of Discipleship in setting policies for interpreting and promoting the use of approved curriculum resources.

*c)* The chairperson of the Curriculum Resources Committee shall serve as a member of the executive committee of the General Board of Discipleship.

*d)* In preparation of the budget for presentation to the board of The United Methodist Publishing House (¶ 1636), the editor of Church School Publications shall consult with the general secretary of the General Board of Discipleship.

2. The Curriculum Resources Committee shall be related to The United Methodist Publishing House as follows:

*a)* The publisher of The United Methodist Publishing House or the chairperson of the board of The United Methodist Publishing House may sit with the General Board of Discipleship for consideration of matters pertaining to joint interests of the Curriculum Resources Committee and The United Methodist Publishing House and shall have the privilege of the floor without vote.

*b)* The United Methodist Publishing House shall publish, manufacture, and distribute the curriculum resources prepared by the editorial staff of Church School Publications. The United Methodist Publishing House and the General Board of Discipleship shall be responsible jointly for interpretation and support of these resources.

c) The United Methodist Publishing House shall cooperate with the editor of Church School Publications in developing formats and types of curriculum resources, such as periodicals, books, booklets, graphics, recordings, and other audiovisual materials. The publishing house shall have final responsibility in relation to publishing and financial matters, and in these matters the editor of Church School Publications shall recommend changes in formats of publications to be produced and shall work cooperatively with the publisher in the design, layout, and handling of proofs and in equivalent steps in the case of non-printed resources.

d) The work of the Curriculum Resources Committee shall be financed by The United Methodist Publishing House.

3. The committee shall exercise these additional relationships:

a) The committee shall cooperate with other agencies of The United Methodist Church so that their assigned concerns are reflected in and supported by the church school resources.

b) The committee may explore and implement opportunities at home and overseas for cooperative planning and publishing wherever such cooperation seems best for all concerned and when it is found to be practicable and in harmony with editorial and publishing policies.

c) The committee may cooperate with The United Methodist Publishing House and the General Board of Discipleship in educational research, in the development of experimental resources, and in the evaluation of resources that are provided for the church school.

¶ 1124. *Editor of Church School Publications*—1. The **editor of Church School Publications** shall be responsible for the administration of the work of the Curriculum Resources Committee and the editorial staff of Church School Publications, the general editorial policy, and the final determination of editorial content of the church school publications.

2. The editor shall be elected by the General Board of Discipleship upon nomination by a joint committee composed of the president of the General Board of Discipleship, the chairperson of the Curriculum Resources Committee, one other member of the General Board of Discipleship representing educational concerns, the chairperson and two

other members of The United Methodist Publishing House. The election of the editor shall be subject to confirmation by the board of The United Methodist Publishing House.

3. The editor shall be responsible to the General Board of Discipleship for seeing that the content of church school publications is consistent with the educational philosophy formulated by the board.

¶ **1125.** *Membership of the Curriculum Resources Committee*—1. The Curriculum Resources Committee shall consist of twenty-one voting members elected quadrennially by the General Board of Discipleship as follows:

*a)* A bishop who is a voting member of the General Board of Discipleship, to be nominated by the executive committee of the board.

*b)* Twenty members, nominated by the executive committee of the board, at least seven of whom shall be pastors, at least three of whom shall be voting members of the board, and at least one of whom shall be at the time of election serving a church of two hundred members or less; at least seven shall be laypersons actively participating as member, leader, or teacher in the educational ministry in the local church; at least three of whom shall be voting members of the board; at least one of whom shall be at the time of election a member of a church of two hundred members or fewer; six additional members shall be nominated, three of whom shall be members of the board, with due consideration to the diversity in theological perspectives, educational attainments, sex, age, racial, and ethnic differences, and sizes of local churches, and in consultation with the directors of councils on ministries or boards of discipleship in each of the annual conferences.

*c)* Twenty persons from the program boards shall participate in Curriculum Resources Committee meetings with the privilege of the floor without vote. These persons shall be: the general secretaries of the General Board of Discipleship, the General Board of Global Ministries, the General Board of Church and Society, and the General Board of Higher Education and Ministry, or someone designated by them; the editor of Church School Publications; the president and publisher and the vice president in charge of publishing of The United Methodist Publishing House; and with due consideration to providing for diversity in sex, age, racial, and ethnic differences, five staff members of Church School Publications and eight other staff members representing the broad concerns of the General Board of Discipleship.

*d)* The chairperson of the committee shall be a member of the General Board of Discipleship.

2. The Curriculum Resources Committee may select other persons to assist in its work, including persons nominated by the boards, agencies, and general commissions of the Church.

The committee may prepare such bylaws and operating guidelines as are necessary to facilitate the work of the committee.

### Section VI. United Methodist Youth Organization

¶ **1201.** There shall be a **United Methodist Youth Organization.**

¶ **1202.** *Purpose*—The purpose of the United Methodist Youth Organization is to make The United Methodist Church a community of mutual respect and understanding between youth and adults, resulting in ministry where influence and worth are not limited by age or experience.

1. *Mission*—The mission of the United Methodist Youth Organization is to respond to God's call as Disciples: Here and Now.

2. *Core Values*—The core values of United Methodist Youth Organization are:

*a)* Compassion: Actively listen to issues and concerns of youth.

*b)* Advocacy: Affirm and witness to the gifts and graces of youth.

*c)* Partnership: Emphasize youth and adult unity in ministry.

*d)* Outreach: Inspire youth to commit to meaningful service.

*e)* Leadership: Serve as followers of Jesus Christ.

¶ **1203.** *Accountability*—United Methodist Youth Organization shall be accountable to the General Board of Discipleship. The accountability will involve evaluation by the General Board of Discipleship of the United Methodist Youth Organization's disciplinary mandates.

¶ **1204.** *Structure*—United Methodist Youth Organization shall be composed of three basic units: Steering Committee, Youth Service Fund, and Convocation.

¶ **1205.** *United Methodist Youth Organization Convocation*—
1. *Focus*—The United Methodist Youth Convocation shall be consistent with the core values of the United Methodist Youth Organization.

2. *Expenses*—The jurisdictional council on ministries or equivalent body shall provide funding for expenses for the jurisdictional chairperson and coordinator. It is strongly recommended that the annual

conference councils on youth ministry secure scholarships for Convocation participants, giving special attention to economic factors, inclusiveness, and expressed interest in the United Methodist Youth Organization and in attending the Convocation.

3. *Legislation.* During the Convocation there shall be opportunities for conference delegations and individuals to propose legislation in a forum within the Convocation known as the **United Methodist Youth Legislative Assembly.** Legislation brought to the Legislative Assembly shall relate to the United Methodist Youth Organization or youth-related issues.

4. The membership of the United Methodist Youth Legislative Assembly shall be:

a) *Voting Members*—Four representatives selected from each annual conference council on youth ministry. Of those selected, three are to be youth and one of whom is the conference council on youth president or designate and one of whom is recommended to be a junior high youth; and one adult, who shall be the conference youth coordinator or designate. It is strongly recommended that at least one of the conference representatives, preferably a youth, shall be a person from one of the five racial and ethnic minority groups: Asian Americans, African Americans, Hispanic Americans, Native Americans, and Pacific Islanders. An annual conference must have a youth present in order to exercise voting privileges. Voting members shall be members of The United Methodist Church. The youth chairpersons from each jurisdiction shall be in addition to the three youth and one adult from their annual conferences.

b) *Nonvoting Members*—(1) Youth members of the general agencies; and (2) members of the United Methodist Youth Organization Steering Committee shall have the right to participate in the United Methodist Youth Convocation Legislative Assembly with voice but without vote.

¶ **1206.** *Steering Committee*—There shall be a **United Methodist Youth Organization Steering Committee.**

1. *Membership*—The United Methodist Youth Organization Steering Committee shall consist of youth and adults who are preparatory or full members of The United Methodist Church. All youth elected to the steering committee shall be at the time of their election entering into the eleventh grade or under, or their age shall be sixteen or younger. It is strongly recommended that at least one-half of these youth shall be from these racial and ethnic minority groups: Asian

Americans, African Americans, Hispanic Americans, Native Americans, and Pacific Islanders, so elected that each racial and ethnic minority group is represented. It is strongly recommended that at least one youth with a disability be elected. In addition, there shall be on the United Methodist Youth Organization Steering Committee one adult involved in youth ministry on the annual conference level from each jurisdiction; a bishop chosen by the Council of Bishops; two elected members (one youth and one adult) and a staff member related to youth ministry of the General Board of Discipleship; a General Board of Discipleship, Church School Publications youth editor; and one elected youth member from each of the program-related general agencies (¶ 703.5) and the General Council on Ministries, each chosen by their respective agencies. All will serve with voice and vote. Additional board or staff representatives may be added at the discretion of the steering committee. In addition, as many as two elected youth members may be selected to serve a third contiguous year as ex-officio member(s) with vote.

2. *Election—a)* Each jurisdiction shall elect three youth and one adult worker with youth to the United Methodist Youth Organization Steering Committee, with at least one youth being a racial and ethnic minority youth (¶ 531). There shall be elected at large five youth, one from each of the minority ethnic groups, a youth with disability, as well as one racial and ethnic adult. Each of the five racial and ethnic national caucuses (Black Methodists for Church Renewal, Metodistas Asociados Representando la Causa de Hispano-Americanos, National Federation of Asian American United Methodists, Native American International Caucus, Pacific Islander National Caucus of United Methodists) may recommend one youth to serve on the Steering Committee as an at-large member. The Steering Committee will select the youth with disability and the racial and ethnic adult by process of application. The youth recommended by the caucuses and elected to the Steering Committee, and the members selected by the Steering Committee will be full members of the Steering Committee, entitled to the same rights as members elected from their jurisdictions.

*b)* As many as two elected youth members may be added for a third contiguous year as ex-officio members (with vote) nominated by the Administration Committee and approved by the UMYO Executive Committee.

*c)* Any vacancy that occurs due to an unfulfilled term shall be filled as follows:

(1) The jurisdictional convocation shall determine the definition of vacancy and the process for filling jurisdictional vacancies.

(2) The steering committee shall fill vacancies to maintain racial and ethnic minority representation as required by 2*a* above.

(3) Youth shall be elected to fill youth vacancies, and adults shall be elected to fill vacancies in adult positions.

3. *Term*—The term for steering committee members (with the exception of general board and agency representatives) shall be two years.

*a)* Members cannot serve two consecutive terms, and they shall begin their term immediately upon adjournment of the jurisdictional convocation legislative assembly at which they were elected and shall conclude upon the adjournment of the next respective jurisdictional convocation or legislative assembly.

*b)* The term for board and agency representatives begins immediately following the organizational meeting of their respective board or agency and concludes at the end of the steering committee meeting following the next General Conference.

4. *Responsibilities*—The United Methodist Youth Organization Steering Committee shall have the responsibility:

*a)* To maintain the core values (¶ 1202) of the United Methodist Youth Organization.

*b)* To plan the United Methodist Youth Convocation.

*c)* To convene the United Methodist Youth Legislative Assembly and implement its decisions.

*d)* To recommend action goals and issues to the United Methodist Youth Legislative Assembly.

*e)* To encourage participation of youth in appropriate denominational and interreligious enterprises and deliberations.

*f)* To recommend youth to nomination committees of general boards and agencies, considering suggestions from annual conference councils on youth ministry (¶ 646) and other appropriate youth organizations.

*g)* To communicate the work of the United Methodist Youth Organization to the General Board of Discipleship for its information and evaluative response.

¶ **1207.** *Executive Director and Staff*—The United Methodist Youth Organization shall have an executive director.

1. The executive director shall provide managerial oversight of the United Methodist Youth Organization and staff, communicate the decisions of the United Methodist Youth Organization, communicate

the concerns of youth to the general boards and agencies, and interpret the actions of the United Methodist Youth Organization to The United Methodist Church.

2. Administrative staff persons shall be nominated by the United Methodist Youth Organization Steering Committee and elected by the General Board of Discipleship.

3. The United Methodist Youth Organization Steering Committee shall also determine the need for and responsibilities of additional staff.

4. In all meetings of the United Methodist Youth Organization Steering Committee, United Methodist Youth Organization Convocation, and United Methodist Youth Organization Legislative Assembly the staff shall have the right of voice without vote.

5. The General Board of Discipleship, in consultation with the United Methodist Youth Organization Steering Committee, shall provide access to office space and support service to the staff of United Methodist Youth Organization. The staff shall be governed by the personnel policies and guidelines of the Committee on Personnel Policies and Practices (¶ 805.4*d*) and the United Methodist Youth Organization Steering Committee.

¶ **1208.** *Funding*—The United Methodist Youth Organization shall be responsible for administering its own budget. The operating funds shall be derived from two main sources: general Church funds and the national portion of the Youth Service Fund. A minimum of 70 percent of the general portion of the Youth Service Fund shall be used for projects, and 30 percent shall be used for resource promotion and interpretation. United Methodist Communications shall assist United Methodist Youth Organization in promotion and interpretation of the Youth Service Fund.

¶ **1209.** *Youth Service Fund*—There shall be a **Youth Service Fund.** 1. *Organization*—There shall be a Youth Service Fund, which shall be a means of stewardship education and mission support of youth within The United Methodist Church. As a part of its cultivation, the youth shall have been challenged to assume their financial responsibilities in connection with the total program and budget of the church of which they are members. Local church treasurers shall send the full amount of Youth Service Fund offerings to the treasurer of the annual conference, who shall retain 70 percent of the amount for the annual conference council on youth ministry. The annual conference treasurer shall send monthly the remaining 30

percent to the treasurer of the General Council on Finance and
Administration to be forwarded to the United Methodist Youth
Organization. All other Youth Service Fund money raised in the
annual conference shall be divided in the same manner and distributed in the same way.

2. *Project Selection*—The steering committee shall constitute a Project Review Committee to advise them in the selection of projects. The
Project Review Committee shall be composed of five youth from the
Steering Committee and one adult who is an elected member of the
Steering Committee. The projects shall be chosen according to the
policies and criteria established by the United Methodist Youth Organization Steering Committee.

### Section VII. General Board of Global Ministries

¶ **1301.**—There shall be a **General Board of Global Ministries,**
hereinafter referred to as the board, the purpose of which is found
within the expression of the total mission of the Church. It is a missional instrument of The United Methodist Church, its annual conferences, missionary conferences, and local congregations in the context
of a global setting.

The Church in mission is a sign of God's presence in the world.
By the authority of God and the power of the Holy Spirit, the Church:

1. Joins God's mission to reclaim, restore, and redeem the life of
all creation to its divine intention;

2. Confesses by word and deed the redeeming activity of God in
Christ among the whole human family;

3. Seeks to embody and realize the potential of new life in Christ
among all human beings; and

4. Looks forward in faith and hope for the fulfillment of God's
reign and the completion of God's mission.

¶ **1302.** *Responsibilities*—1. To discern those places where the
gospel has not been heard or heeded and to witness to its meaning
throughout the world, inviting all persons to newness of life in Jesus
Christ through a program of global ministries.

2. To encourage and support the development of leadership in
mission for both the Church and society.

3. To challenge all United Methodists with the New Testament
imperative to proclaim the gospel to the ends of the earth, expressing
the mission of the Church; and to recruit, send, and receive mission-

aries, enabling them to dedicate all or a portion of their lives in service across racial, cultural, national, and political boundaries.

4. To plan with others and to establish and strengthen Christian congregations where opportunities and needs are found, so that these congregations may be units of mission in their places and partners with others in the worldwide mission of the Christian church.

5. To advocate the work for the unity of Christ's church through witness and service with other Christian churches and through ecumenical councils.

6. To engage in dialogue with all persons, including those of other faiths, and to join with them where possible in action on common concerns.

7. To assist local congregations and annual conferences in mission both in their own communities and across the globe by raising awareness of the claims of global mission and by providing channels for participation.

8. To express the concerns of women organized for mission and to help equip women for full participation both locally and globally in Church and world.

9. To engage in direct ministries to human need, both emergency and continuing, institutional and noninstitutional, however caused.

10. To work within societies and systems so that full human potential is liberated and to work toward the transformation of demonic forces that distort life.

11. To identify with all who are alienated and dispossessed and to assist them in achieving their full human development—body, mind, and spirit.

12. To envision and engage in imaginative new forms of mission appropriate to changing human needs and to share the results of experimentation with the entire Church.

13. To facilitate the development of cooperative patterns of ministry so that the unified strength of local congregations and other units of the Church in designated areas can respond with more effective ministries of justice, advocacy, compassion, and nurture.

14. To affirm Volunteers in Mission as an authentic form of personal missionary involvement and devise appropriate structure to interpret and implement opportunities for mission volunteers in the global community.

15. To facilitate the receiving and assignment of missionaries from

churches in nations other than the United States in cooperation with the other general agencies and with annual conferences.

**¶ 1303.** *Objectives*—1. The objectives of the board shall be:

*a)* To plan for the implementation of the responsibilities of the board in the missional outreach of The United Methodist Church.

*b)* To establish the appropriate organization of the board and staff to accomplish its program and fulfill the responsibilities of the board.

*c)* To determine, in cooperation with mission constituencies, the areas to be served and the nature of the work to be undertaken.

*d)* To determine policy and program, to establish goals and priorities, to project long-range plans, to evaluate the program and services of the board as to the progress made in fulfilling its purpose in accordance with ¶¶ 1301 and 1302, and to seek to achieve its objectives through the programs of the board.

*e)* To coordinate and harmonize the work of the board.

*f)* To elect or appoint, according to the bylaws, the staff of the board.

*g)* To assign responsibility and delegate authority to staff and to provide oversight of the staff.

*h)* To receive and properly administer all properties, trust funds, permanent funds, annuity funds, and other special funds.

*i)* To receive, secure, appropriate, and expend funds to underwrite its program and fulfill its responsibilities.

*j)* To receive and act upon the reports of its units, committees, and their staff.

*k)* To make a report of its activities during the quadrennium to the General Conference.

*l)* To develop and maintain cooperative relations with other general agencies and with jurisdictional, central, annual, and missionary conferences.

*m)* To be responsible for implementing a policy stating that The United Methodist Church is not a party to any comity agreement that limits the ability of any annual conference in any jurisdiction to develop and resource programs of ministry of any kind among Native Americans, including the organization of local churches where necessary.

2. The board shall develop and maintain cooperative working relationships with churches and ecumenical agencies on matters of mutual concern in the implementation of disciplinary responsibilities.

3. The board shall facilitate and coordinate the program relationships of other program agencies of The United Methodist Church with churches and agencies in nations other than the United States.

¶ **1304.** *Authority*—The board shall have authority to make bylaws and regulate its proceedings in harmony with the *Book of Discipline*. Bylaws may be amended by a two-thirds vote of the members present and voting thereon at a regular or special meeting, *provided* that required notice of such amendment has previously been given to the members. The board shall have the power and right to do any and all things that shall be authorized by its charter. It shall have authority to develop and carry out its responsibilities as described in ¶ 1302; to buy, acquire, or receive by gift, devise, or bequest property—real, personal, and mixed; to hold, mortgage, sell, and dispose of property; to sue and be sued; to borrow money in case of necessity in a manner harmonious with ¶¶ 806–807; to develop and maintain ecumenical relations to carry out its responsibilities; and to administer its affairs through the board and its various units and committees.

¶ **1305.** *Incorporation*—1. The General Board of Global Ministries shall be incorporated and shall function through the board and its units.

2. The General Board of Global Ministries of The United Methodist Church shall be the successor to the following corporations: the Board of Missions of The Evangelical United Brethren Church, the Home Missions and Church Erection Society of the Church of the United Brethren in Christ, the Foreign Missionary Society of the United Brethren in Christ, the Women's Missionary Association of the Church of the United Brethren in Christ, the Missionary Society of The Evangelical Church, and the Board of Church Extension of The Evangelical Church, and as such successor it shall be and is authorized and empowered to receive from its said predecessor corporations all trust funds and assets of every kind and character—real, personal, or mixed—held by them, and it shall and hereby is authorized to administer such trusts and funds in accordance with the conditions under which they have been previously received and administered by the said predecessor corporations.

3. It shall have control of all the work formerly controlled and administered by the following: the Board of Health and Welfare Ministries; the Board of Missions of The United Methodist Church; the Board of Missions and Church Extension of The Methodist Church; the Missionary Society, the Board of Foreign Missions, the Board of

Home Missions and Church Extension, the Woman's Foreign Missionary Society, the Woman's Home Missionary Society, the Wesleyan Service Guild, and the Ladies' Aid Societies of The Methodist Episcopal Church; the Board of Missions, including the Woman's Missionary Society, the Woman's Board of Foreign Missions, the Woman's Board of Home Missions, the Woman's Missionary Council, and the Board of Church Extension of The Methodist Episcopal Church, South; the Board of Missions of The Methodist Protestant Church; the Board of Missions of The Methodist Church; such other incorporated or unincorporated divisions and departments and their predecessors as may have been merged into the board; and such other corporations or agencies of the General Conference as do similar work; but this list shall not be construed as exclusive.

4. Subject to the limitations hereinafter specified, any corporations within the board shall be subject to the supervision and control of the General Conference of The United Methodist Church in all things not inconsistent with the Constitution and laws of the United States and of the states of incorporation.

5. The board shall have the power to create those subsidiary units or sections needed in the fulfillment of designated functions, upon approval of the board.

¶ **1306.** *Executive Committee*—There shall be an executive committee, which shall exercise the powers of the board *ad interim*, and whose membership and responsibilities shall be determined by the bylaws of the board.

¶ **1307.** *Corporate Officers*—The board shall elect as its corporate officers a president, three vice presidents, a treasurer, a recording secretary, and such other officers as it shall deem necessary. The board shall determine the powers and duties of its officers.

The president, general secretary, and treasurer of the board are ex officio members of all units and their executive committees, and standing committees of the board, without vote. The Women's Division shall elect its president, who shall be one of the three vice presidents of the board.

¶ **1308.** *Elected Staff*—1. *Board Cabinet*—*a)* The board, through a personnel committee, shall make nominations to the General Council on Ministries for the office of general secretary. As chief staff officer of the board, the general secretary shall have direct involvement in staff selections.

*b)* The board shall elect a deputy general secretary for administration, a maximum of five other deputy general secretaries, and a board treasurer. In addition, the Women's Division shall nominate its deputy general secretary for election by the division and the board after consultation with the president and the general secretary of the board.

c) The board personnel committee, in consultation with the general secretary of the board, shall recommend candidates for the positions of deputy general secretaries and board treasurer for election by the board. The deputy general secretaries shall have administrative responsibility as assigned by the general secretary and shall be responsible to the general secretary.

d) The general secretary may add positions to the cabinet.

2. *Unit Staff*—a) The Women's Division shall nominate for election by the board such other staff persons of the Women's Division as are deemed necessary to carry out the work assigned.

b) The board shall elect additional staff as needed.

3. The board shall elect, on nomination of the board personnel committee and in consultation with the general secretary, one or more associate treasurers of the General Board of Global Ministries, one of whom shall be the treasurer of the Women's Division and nominated by the Women's Division. The associate treasurer(s) will be responsible to the treasurer of the General Board of Global Ministries for board fiscal procedures and to the assigned deputy general secretary for administrative procedures (¶ 703.7e).

¶ **1309.** *Personnel Policies*—1. *Selection*—The staff of the board shall be selected on the basis of competency and with representation of ethnic and racial groups, young adults, and women, in accordance with policies in ¶ 714.

2. *Staff Participation of Women*—a) Of the cabinet-level staff positions within the board, a minimum of 40 percent shall be occupied by women.

b) A minimum of 40 percent of all elected staff, as well as a minimum of 40 percent of the appointed staff, shall be women.

¶ **1310.** *Properties, Trusts, and Annuities*—1. All properties, trust funds, annuity funds, permanent funds, and endowments now or formerly held and administered by the Board of Missions, the Board of Health and Welfare Ministries, and the United Methodist Committee on Relief of The United Methodist Church; the Board of Missions of The Methodist Church; the Board of Missions of The Evangelical United Brethren Church or their successors; and their respective divisions and departments or their successors shall be carefully safeguarded. The General Board of Global Ministries of The United Methodist Church shall endeavor to invest in institutions, companies, corporations, or funds that make a positive contribution toward the realization of the goals outlined in the Social Principles of The United Methodist Church and to administer such investments in the interest of those persons and causes for which said funds were established. Such properties, trust funds, annuity funds, permanent funds, and endowments shall be transferred to the General Board of Global Ministries of The United Methodist Church from merged boards and societies only when such transfers can be made in accordance with the laws of the states where the several boards and societies are chartered and on the recommendation of the board and the approval of such boards and societies. Funds of the board and its preceding corporations and societies that are subject to appropriation shall be appropriated only on recommendation of the board. (*See* ¶ 806.11.)

2. **Former Evangelical United Brethren** mission agencies located within the United States not directly owned by the General Board of Global Ministries or the Women's Division of the board and which receive more than 50 percent of their charitable donations through United Methodist channels of giving shall be governed by a board of trustees or directors of whom two-thirds of its elected voting membership shall be members of The United Methodist Church.

3. The financial affairs of the board shall be as follows:

*a)* The income of the board, exclusive of the Women's Division, shall be derived from apportionments, assessments, or askings distributed to jurisdictions, annual conferences, and pastoral charges by the budget-making process of the General Conference in such manner as the General Conference may prescribe, and from church schools, gifts, donations, freewill offerings, annuities, bequests, specials, and other sources from which missionary and benevolence funds are usually derived, in harmony with *The Book of Discipline* and actions of the General Conference. Funds for the fulfillment of the responsibilities of the Women's Division shall be derived from annual voluntary pledges, offerings, gifts, devises, bequests, annuities, or money received through special emphases and from meetings held in the interest of the division.

*b)* Cultivation for the Advance shall be through channels of the Church other than United Methodist Women.

*c)* All contributions to and income on all funds of the board should be used for current expenses and annual appropriations unless otherwise designated by the donor.

4. Askings shall be received from the fields, and budgets shall be prepared by the board, consistent with its constitution and charter, and the budget shall be presented to the General Council on Ministries in accordance with ¶ 806.

¶ 1311. *Membership*—The policies, plans of work, management, business, and all affairs of the General Board of Global Ministries of The United Methodist Church shall be governed and administered by the board, which shall be composed according to the following conditions:

1. The basic members (clergy, laymen, and laywomen) are elected by the jurisdiction upon the nomination of the annual conferences in accord with ¶ 705.4*e* and 705.5*a*. Each annual conference shall have representation from this category on the General Board of Global Ministries at least once within a three-quadrennia period.

The jurisdictions shall use the following formula when electing members: Northeastern Jurisdiction—7; Southeastern Jurisdiction—8; Western Jurisdiction—4; North Central Jurisdiction—7; and South Central Jurisdiction—9 (at least one of whom shall be from either the Oklahoma Indian Missionary Conference or the Rio Grande Annual Conference). Each central conference shall elect one member to the basic membership of the board for a total of seven. The additional members of the board are nominated by a committee composed of three persons from each jurisdiction—a clergy member, a layman, and a laywoman—elected within each jurisdiction. The committee is to be convened by the president of the board, or if there be none, the secretary of the Council of Bishops. There shall be one additional member from each of the five jurisdictions (the member from the South Central Jurisdiction shall be from either the Oklahoma Indian Missionary Conference or the Rio Grande Annual Conference, unless they are already represented in the basic membership of the board). There shall be five additional members from the central conferences elected from those nominated according to ¶ 705.1*c*, 705.5*e*. An intentional effort shall be made to rotate representation among the central conferences.

2. The Women's Division membership procedures are an exception to those described in ¶¶ 705, 709 of the General Provisions. Women's Division membership is defined in ¶ 1324. Members of the Women's Division who are members of the board shall also serve on the membership of other units and committees of the board.

3. The composition of the board and its units should reflect the major recognized categories of Church members. (*See* ¶ 705.) A minimum of one-half of the membership should be women.

4. Members of the board shall be distributed across the component units and standing committees of the board in accord with board bylaws.

5. The term of office of all members whose election is provided for in this paragraph shall begin and the board shall organize at a meeting to be held within ninety days after the adjournment of the last meeting of the several jurisdictional conferences held after the adjournment of the General Conference.

6. On nomination of the Council of Bishops, the General Conference shall elect to the board one bishop from each jurisdiction and three central conference bishops.

7. The general secretary, the treasurer of the board, and the deputy general secretaries shall be members without vote.

8. Salaried members of staff of any agency receiving appropriation funds from the board shall not be eligible to serve as voting members of said board, except in order to fulfill the provisions of ¶ 705.

### MISSION PROGRAM AREAS

¶ 1312. *Program Areas*—Six program areas shall be assigned responsibilities within the General Board of Global Ministries as it seeks to enhance the involvement of all United Methodists in Christian mission and develop ways to facilitate their mission involvement. The membership of the program areas shall be constituted in accord with the bylaws of the General Board of Global Ministries.

1. The Evangelization and Church Growth Program Area exists to facilitate the proclamation and witness to the saving grace of Jesus Christ through word, deed, and sacrament in every sphere of human existence, the establishment of faith communities or new churches, and the strengthening of existing congregations. The responsibilities of Evangelization and Church Growth shall be:

*a*) To support evangelization among people who have not heard or heeded the gospel.

*b*) To undertake strategic new mission initiatives and to establish new congregations where United Methodism and/or cooperative church relationships do not exist.

*c)* To identify, prepare, train, and empower persons for leadership in the church and community so that vital mission-oriented congregations may be developed.

*d)* To prepare persons to share their Christian faith and witness among persons of other faiths.

*e)* To revitalize existing congregations and faith communities.

*f)* To provide technical and architectural services to support mission programs and church extension.

*g)* To assist congregations with the development of financial stewardship.

*h)* To work with the General Board of Discipleship for the extension of the Church through a Joint Committee on Congregational Development composed of equal representation from the General Board of Global Ministries and the General Board of Discipleship, which shall meet at least annually to expedite cooperation between these two boards in the field of congregational development of both new congregations as well as the revitalization of existing congregations.

*i)* To administer the United Methodist Development Fund in accord with policies set by the General Board of Global Ministries for the purpose of making first mortgage loans to United Methodist churches, districts, city societies, district unions, mission institutions, or conference church extension agencies for the purchase of sites and for the purchase, construction, expansion, or major improvement of churches, parsonages, or mission buildings.

2. The Community and Institutional Ministries Program Area exists to facilitate, resource, and support missional outreach to meet human needs, with special emphasis on ministries with women, children, youth, and older adults through the following: direct services; specialized ministries; community organizing and development, including economic development; and community justice advocacy. The responsibilities of Community and Institutional Ministries shall be:

*a)* To develop strategies for church and community development, including grants, loans and technical assistance for programs of self-development and self-determination pertaining to social needs arising from concerns for ethnic and cultural pluralism, economic and sexual exploitation, and political and racial oppression.

*b)* To develop community-based programs in areas such as agricultural mission, communications, student and youth ministries.

*c)* To provide funding, consultation, training, resources, and coordinated mission strategy to new and historically related community centers, residences, health-care agencies, multiservice mission complexes, special regional agencies, childcare institutions, schools, and other educational institutions.

*d)* To use institutions as places to develop new models of community transformation.

*e)* To develop strong local and regional organizations and the capacity to network and become part of an internationally related program.

*f)* To foster and facilitate cooperative patterns of ministry such as cooperative parishes, metropolitan ministries, rural and town and country ministries; to work with denominational, ecumenical, and secular coalitions; and, as appropriate, to develop new patterns of joint mission.

*g)* To facilitate and coordinate program relationships of other agencies of The United Methodist Church with community and institutional ministries.

3. The Mission Contexts and Relationships Program Area exists to analyze and evaluate the context in which the Church is called to Christian ministry, including factors such as culture, religion, history, politics, economics, environment, and demographics; to develop and sustain covenant relationships and mission partnerships; to explore dialogues with persons of other faiths and engage in ecumenical cooperation; and to develop concerted actions and advocacy for global justice, peace, and freedom. The responsibilities of Mission Contexts and Relationships shall be:

*a)* To identify and analyze the missional concerns that shape the conditions under which the Church is called to minister.

*b)* To develop and sustain covenant relationships and mission partnerships that include sharing of opportunities and resources, networking, and cooperation. This includes maintaining and fulfilling the connectional relationships with annual conferences, missionary conferences, and central conferences; autonomous, affiliated autonomous, and united churches; and ecumenical church bodies.

*c)* To develop missional relationships in countries and communities where The United Methodist Church has no commitments by pursuing a working agreement with the church, churches, a united mission organization, or ecumenical bodies related to the area. If these approaches are not available, the board may participate in the formation of a new United Methodist denominational structure, in which case it may request the Council of Bishops to provide any necessary episcopal oversight.

*d)* To request each central conference and its conferences, both annual and provisional, and each affiliated autonomous Methodist church or united church, where applicable, to make provision for liaison functions with the board.

*e)* To provide information and assist in developing action and advocacy for global justice, peace, and freedom through working cooperatively with other agencies of the Church; other denominations; and ecumenical, interfaith, and secular coalitions.

*f)* To foster interaction of churches and ecumenical groups for the purpose of mutuality in the definition and implementation of Christian mission and international concerns.

*g)* To administer funding and other forms of resource sharing for projects and programs—especially those serving women, children, and youth—of partner churches and ecumenical bodies.

*h)* To relate to persons in mission of partner churches.

*i)* To resource leadership training programs and administer scholarships, including the Crusade Scholarship Program.

4. The Mission Education Program Area exists to develop a mission education philosophy for the General Board of Global Ministries that is rooted in a biblical and theological understanding of Christian global mission and to undergird the total program of the board through mission education. The responsibilities of Mission Education shall be:

*a)* To provide opportunities for United Methodists to understand the global mission of The United Methodist Church and for personal and corporate witness through involvement in and support of the mission.

*b)* To initiate and develop, in consultation with appropriate units of the board, programs, and resources that will encourage persons of particular cultures to become receivers and bearers of the gospel across boundaries and to live faithfully within a multicultural world.

*c)* To provide for mission interpreters a specific period of training and assistance in effective communication, including audiovisual techniques, public speaking, briefings on current issues, and an overview of the board's work.

*d)* To tell the story of global mission throughout the Church, including its relationship to the World Service funds and other apportioned funds and special offerings.

*e)* To train mission leaders, in cooperation with other units of the board and others in the Church, to fulfill their responsibilities.

*f)* To work with schools of theology and professors of mission in providing an emphasis on education for mission, in cooperation with the General Board of Higher Education and Ministry.

*g)* To cooperate with the General Board of Discipleship, especially the Curriculum Resources Committee, in providing opportunities for mission involvement and understanding of all age levels.

*h)* To initiate and develop special programs and resources through which children and youth may understand the mission of the Church.

*i)* To work with ecumenical agencies in fulfilling mission education responsibilities.

*j)* To provide opportunities for United Methodists to gather and witness as a global church.

5. The Mission Volunteers Program Area exists to enable the participation of persons from throughout the world in global mission volunteer programs and projects so that affirming, empowering, and trusting relationships are established. The responsibilities of the program area, Mission Volunteers, shall be:

*a)* To plan for and develop a broad range of mission volunteer opportunities for short-term assignments.

*b)* To promote and interpret the need for volunteers with a variety of skills and abilities.

*c)* To work in close relationship with conference and jurisdictional officers to assist in identifying, developing, and supporting opportunities for mission volunteer service (i.e., Volunteers in Mission, disaster response volunteers, and special volunteer programs).

*d)* To provide information enabling the relationship between volunteers and projects.

*e)* To provide, in cooperation with jurisdictions and conferences, guidelines and procedures for participation and training of mission volunteers.

*f)* To develop, in cooperation with jurisdictions and conferences, standards by which projects qualify for mission volunteers and to evaluate a project upon request.

*g)* To encourage local churches, districts, central conferences, and annual conferences to provide funds and/or materials and spiritual support for those who offer their skills, talents, and commitment.

*h)* To work cooperatively with agencies of the Church, other denominations, and coalitions, both ecumenical and secular.

6. The Mission Personnel Program Area exists to serve the Church in the identification, recruitment, selection, preparation, training, assignment, supervision, and support of mission personnel for short- and long-term assignments. It also exists to assist in the identification of opportunities for Christian service in representing mission personnel concerns before the General Board of Global Ministries. The responsibilities of Mission Personnel shall be:

*a)* To promote the opportunities for mission service related to the General Board of Global Ministries throughout the constituencies of the Church.

*b)* To recruit, select, prepare, and assign mission personnel, including, but not limited to, missionaries, deaconesses, US-2s, mission interns, and church and community workers.

*c)* To provide all mission personnel with preparation and training for effective service in mission.

*d)* To evaluate mission personnel for appropriate placement.

*e)* To recommend persons as candidates for commissioning as deaconesses and missionaries, and to supervise and confirm the completion of all requirements for commissioning.

*f)* To engage in supervision and support of mission personnel through referral, transfer procedures, career counseling, missionary wellness, and personnel development, assisting them in the fulfillment of their missional vocation.

*g)* To administer a diverse program of remuneration and benefits for personnel service.

*h)* To offer training for mission service throughout the global church.

*i)* To work with ecumenical agencies in fulfilling mission personnel responsibilities.

*j)* To facilitate the receiving and assigning of missionaries—lay and clergy—from central conferences and from autonomous, affiliated autonomous, and united churches, in cooperation with other boards and agencies and with annual conferences.

OFFICE OF DEACONESS

**¶ 1313.** *General Provisions*—1. There shall be in The United Methodist Church the **Office of Deaconess.** The purpose of the office of deaconess shall be to express representatively the love and concern of the believing community for the needs in the world and to enable, through education and involvement, the full ministry and mission of the people of God. Deaconesses function through diverse forms of service directed toward the world to make Jesus Christ known in the fullness of his ministry and mission, which mandate that his followers:

*a)* Alleviate suffering;

*b)* Eradicate causes of injustice and all that robs life of dignity and worth;

*c)* Facilitate the development of full human potential; and

*d)* Share in building global community through the church universal.

2. Deaconesses are persons who have been led by the Holy Spirit to devote their lives to Christlike service under the authority of the Church. They are approved by the General Board of Global Ministries and commissioned by a bishop at a session of the board or at a setting approved by the board. They shall have a continuing relationship to The United Methodist Church through the General Board of Global Ministries.

Deaconesses are available for service with any agency or program of The United Methodist Church. Deaconesses may also serve in other than United Methodist Church agencies or programs, provided that approval be given by the board in consultation with the bishop of the receiving area.

3. Full-time service is the norm for the ministry of a deaconess, meaning that the person's entire vocational time is devoted to work of ministry in the field of labor to which one is appointed by the bishop.

*a)* The program office shall process appointments for deaconesses in consultation with the bishop of the area, in accordance with the policies and procedures of the General Board of Global Ministries.

*b)* The appointment shall be fixed by the bishop (¶ 415.5) at the session of annual conference and printed in the list of appointments in the annual conference journal.

*c)* The annual conference secretary shall:

(1) Keep a record of all persons in the annual conference who have been commissioned to the office of deaconess.

(2) Publish annually in the annual conference journal the list of appointments of deaconesses.

4. A deaconess shall hold church membership in a local church within the conference where her appointment is located and shall be a voting member of the charge conference of that church. Those holding staff positions with a general board or connectional agency of The United Methodist Church may hold church membership in an annual conference within reasonable distance of the headquarters of the board or agency served.

5. Deaconesses shall be seated at the sessions of the annual conference with voice.[30]

6. A deaconess may become a member of the annual conference when elected in accordance with ¶¶ 30 and 250.2.

7. Deaconesses shall be subject to the administrative authority of the program or agency to which they are appointed. In matters of their assignment they are subject to the authority of the General Board of Global Ministries and may not contract for service that would nullify this authority.

8. Each deaconess shall enroll in a pension plan. The rights of any deaconess in any prior or existing agreement or pension plan shall be fully protected.

9. A deaconess may request an honorable location when:

*a)* no longer available for appointment as a deaconess of The United Methodist Church; or

*b)* not eligible for appointment as determined by the General Board of Global Ministries; or

*c)* for any reason the person decides to suspend the commissioned relationship.

10. Involuntary termination for a deaconess shall follow the procedural guidelines as set forth in ¶ 2702.

11. Persons on honorable location may be reactivated with approval of the General Board of Global Ministries.

¶ **1314.** *Home Missionaries*—All persons commissioned to the office of **home missionary** shall retain that office with all of the rights and privileges pertaining thereto.

---

30. *See* Judicial Council Decision 718.

¶ **1315.** *Committee on Deaconess Service*—1. There shall be a **Committee on Deaconess Service,** which shall be advisory to the General Board of Global Ministries.

2. The Committee on Deaconess Service shall be composed of one bishop who is a member of the General Board of Global Ministries; four active deaconesses and two active home missionaries selected by vote of the active deaconesses and home missionaries who relate to the board; and four directors of the General Board of Global Ministries, at least two of whom shall also be directors of the Women's Division.

Additional members may be co-opted as deemed necessary by the Committee on Deaconess Service.

3. There shall be an executive committee and other committees as necessary for carrying out the duties of the Committee on Deaconess Service.

4. The work of the committee shall be carried out in accordance with the bylaws as approved by the General Board of Global Ministries.

¶ **1316.** *Deaconess Program Office*—There shall be a **program office for deaconesses** to represent the deaconess relationship on a national level and to maintain a community of professionally competent persons who are committed to service under authority of the Church. The executive secretary of the program office shall be a deaconess.

1. All administrative policies and procedures that pertain to the office of deaconess shall also apply to the office of home missionary and be administered by the Deaconess Program Office (¶¶ 1313–1316).

2. The General Board of Global Ministries shall assign the administration of the program office to the Mission Personnel Program Area or another unit as it may determine (¶ 1303.1*b*).

3. There may be a national organization of deaconesses, which shall operate according to policies approved by the General Board of Global Ministries.

4. There may be jurisdictional organizations of deaconesses and home missionaries and their support constituencies, which shall operate according to policies approved by the General Board of Global Ministries.

WOMEN'S DIVISION

¶ **1317.** The Women's Division shall be actively engaged in fulfilling the mission of Christ and the Church and shall interpret the purpose of United Methodist Women. With continuing awareness of the concerns and responsibilities of the Church in today's world, the Women's Division shall be an advocate for the oppressed and dispossessed with special attention to the needs of women and children; shall work to build a supportive community among women; and shall engage in activities that foster growth in the Christian faith, mission education, and Christian social involvement throughout the organization.

¶ 1318. *Responsibilities*—The responsibilities of the Women's Division shall be:

1. To recommend program and policies to United Methodist Women.

2. To interpret the role and responsibility of the division in fulfilling the mission of Christ and the Church.

3. To provide resources and opportunities for women that enrich their spiritual life and increase their knowledge and understanding of the needs of the world and their responsibility in meeting those needs.

4. To secure funds through the channels of United Methodist Women for the support of the program of the Church through the General Board of Global Ministries, with special concern for the needs and responsibilities of women.

5. To project plans specially directed toward leadership development of women through appropriate planning with the other units of the board.

6. To strengthen the Church's challenge to women to enlist in the diaconate as missionaries and deaconesses.

7. To enlist women in activities that have a moral and religious significance for the public welfare and that contribute to the establishment of a just global society.

8. To work with the other agencies of the Church and community in areas of common concern and responsibility. A United Nations Office shall be conducted in cooperation with the General Board of Church and Society.

9. To give visible evidence of oneness in Christ by uniting in fellowship and service with other Christians, including the World Federation of Methodist Women, Church Women United, and other similar groups, thereby strengthening the ecumenical witness and program of the Church.

10. To formulate concepts of contemporary mission.

**¶ 1319.** *Authority*—1. The Women's Division shall have the authority to make its bylaws and to regulate its proceedings in harmony with the charter of the board, and with its approval, to develop and carry out the functions of the board as described in ¶ 1302; to buy and sell property; to solicit and accept contributions, subject to annuity under the board's regulations; and to appropriate its funds.

2. The division shall meet annually at the time of the meeting of the board and at such other times as it shall deem necessary.

3. The Women's Division shall include in its responsibilities:

*a)* Those formerly carried by the Woman's Society of Christian Service of The Methodist Church, and the Women's Society of World Service of The Evangelical United Brethren Church, the Women's Society of Christian Service of The United Methodist Church, and those other organizations of women of similar purposes that have operated in the churches forming the United Methodist tradition, including the Women's Missionary Association of the Church of the United Brethren in Christ; the Woman's Missionary Society of The Evangelical Church; the Woman's Foreign Missionary Society, the Woman's Home Missionary Society, the Wesleyan Service Guild, and the Ladies' Aid Societies of The Methodist Episcopal Church; the Woman's Missionary Society, the Woman's Board of Foreign Missions, the Woman's Board of Home Missions, and the Woman's Missionary Council of The Methodist Episcopal Church, South; and the Woman's Convention of the Board of Missions of The Methodist Protestant Church. This list shall not be construed as exclusive.

*b)* All policy matters pertaining to the homes for retired workers owned by the Women's Division.

4. The Women's Division shall have the authority:

*a)* To organize jurisdictional, conference, district, and local church organizations of United Methodist Women, which shall be auxiliary to the General Board of Global Ministries, through the Women's Division, of The United Methodist Church.

*b)* To recommend constitutions and make bylaws for United Methodist Women.

*c)* To appropriate funds received through United Methodist Women.

*d)* To serve as the national official policy-making body of United Methodist Women, with the officers of the Women's Division designated as the national officers.

**¶ 1320.** *Organization*—The Women's Division shall elect an executive committee of nineteen members, which shall exercise the powers of the division *ad interim*. The Women's Division shall name members of its executive committee to serve on the board executive committee. The number named shall be at least one-third of the board executive committee membership. Members of the Women's Division executive committee shall be elected by the Women's Division to serve on executive committees of board units and committees as defined in board bylaws. The president, general secretary, and treasurer of the board (¶ 1307) and the deputy general secretary, treasurer, and assistant general secretaries of the Women's Division shall be members ex officio without vote.

¶ **1321.** *Structure*—The Women's Division shall be organized into such sections as the division shall determine.

¶ **1322.** *Assembly*—There may be an assembly of United Methodist Women, including a delegated body termed the Assembly. The division shall determine the time and place of meeting and the purpose, composition, functions, and powers of the Assembly.

¶ **1323.** *Financial Relationship to the General Board of Global Ministries*—The funds for the fulfillment of the responsibilities of the Women's Division shall be derived from annual voluntary pledges, offerings, gifts, devises, bequests, annuities, or money received through special emphases and meetings held in the interest of the division. All funds, except those designated for local purposes, shall be forwarded through the channels of finance of United Methodist Women to the treasurer of the division. Undesignated funds received by the Women's Division shall be allocated by the division, on recommendation of the appropriate section or committee, for the work of the several sections of the Women's Division and to such other units of the General Board of Global Ministries as the division shall determine for the fulfillment of the responsibilities of the division. Funds appropriated for the work of the other units of the board may be given with specific designations and time limits, after which unspent funds are to be returned to the division.

¶ **1324.** *Membership*—The Women's Division shall be composed of fifty members as follows: forty shall be laywomen elected by the jurisdiction organizations of United Methodist Women at quadrennial meetings (¶ 533.4); five shall be the jurisdiction presidents of United Methodist Women; and five shall be elected by the Women's Division. The president, general secretary, and treasurer of the board (¶ 1307) and the deputy general secretary, treasurer, and assistant general secretaries of the Women's Division shall be members ex officio. The Women's Division shall elect from its membership to board membership a number equivalent to one-third of total board membership but not less than thirty. It shall also elect members to units and committees of the board as defined in board bylaws.

¶ 1325. *Constitution of United Methodist Women*—For the Constitution of United Methodist Women in the jurisdiction, *see* ¶ 533; for the Constitution of United Methodist Women in the conference, *see* ¶ 644; for the Constitution of United Methodist Women in the district, *see* ¶ 664; for the Constitution of United Methodist Women in the local church, *see* ¶ 255.

### HEALTH AND RELIEF

¶ 1326. 1. *General Provisions—a) Purpose*—The **Health and Relief Unit** exists to assist United Methodists and churches to become involved globally in health and welfare ministries and in direct ministry to persons in need through programs of relief, rehabilitation, and service, including issues of refugees, hunger and poverty, and disaster response; and to assist organizations, institutions, and programs related to annual conferences and other units of The United Methodist Church in their involvement in direct service to persons in need through both residential and nonresidential ministries.

*b) Authority*—The Health and Relief Unit, a single administrative unit with two functional areas—United Methodist Committee on Relief, and Health and Welfare Ministries—shall operate under policies set by the General Board of Global Ministries.

*c) Membership*—The membership of Health and Relief shall be constituted in accord with the bylaws of the General Board of Global Ministries.

2. *United Methodist Committee on Relief—a) Responsibilities*—The responsibilities of the United Methodist Committee on Relief shall be:

(1) To provide immediate relief of acute human need and to respond to the suffering of persons in the world caused by natural, ecological, political turmoil and civil disaster.

(2) To work cooperatively with the appropriate conference units, ecumenical bodies, and interdenominational agencies in the identification of, advocacy for, and assistance with ministries with refugees, hunger and poverty, and disaster response.

(3) To work cooperatively with United Methodist Communications in promotion of the One Great Hour of Sharing offering.

(4) To initiate printed, audiovisual, electronic, and other resources to interpret, support, and communicate with conferences and churches concerning appeals for help and information related to ministries with refugees, hunger and poverty, and disaster response.

(5) To assist and train conference coordinators to address emerging and ongoing issues related to refugee ministries, root causes of hunger and poverty, disaster relief, and rehabilitation.

*b) Financial Support*—Sources of funds shall include: voluntary gifts, One Great Hour of Sharing offering, Advance Special Gifts, supplementary gifts of United Methodist Women, churchwide appeals made by authority of the Council of Bishops and the General Council on Finance and Administration, and designated benevolence funds. Sources of funds for administrative functions of the General Board of Global Ministries shall be other than designated funds to the United Methodist Committee on Relief.

*c) Consultation*—The response of United Methodist Committee on Relief growing out of natural or civil disaster shall be made at the request of the appropriate body related to The United Methodist Church. Repair and reconstruction of local church property and other church-related property shall be included in the funding response of the United Methodist Committee on Relief only when such response has been included in the appeal made for funds or the Advance Special Gifts made for this purpose. When this condition has been met, the United Methodist Committee on Relief shall respond in cooperation with the General Board of Global Ministries as follows:

(1) UMCOR, in consultation with conference disaster response coordinators, bishops, and district superintendents, shall identify specific locations where local church property and church-related properties have suffered damage.

(2) This information shall be relayed to the General Board of Global Ministries, which shall contact the conference disaster response coordinator to arrange an on-site visit to evaluate damages and initiate an ongoing consultative process.

3. *Health and Welfare Ministries—a) Responsibilities*—The responsibilities of Health and Welfare Ministries shall be:

(1) To assist conference units in addressing emerging and ongoing global health issues, including comprehensive community-based primary health care, HIV/AIDS, ministries with persons with

physically and mentally challenging conditions, environmental health, and particularly the health needs of women, children, youth, the communities of color in the United States, and racial and ethnic communities globally.

(2) To provide upon request of the appropriate conference unit consultation services to existing and emerging health and welfare institutions and programs, and to jurisdictional, conference, district, and local church units.

(3) To assist local churches, districts, and annual conferences to develop ministries of health, healing, and wholeness.

(4) To provide help to conferences and health and welfare institutions to clarify their relationship with one another, including matters of legal and financial responsibility, and to help health and welfare institutions to become involved in outreach ministry globally.

(5) To provide programs for annual conferences, districts, and local churches that encourage awareness of the gifts and needs of persons with disabilities and to promote the leadership and employment throughout the connectional system of persons with disabilities.

(6) To initiate printed, audiovisual, electronic, and other resources to interpret, support, and communicate with conferences and churches concerning development of health and welfare ministries and promotion of Golden Cross and similar offerings.

*b) Financial Support*—Sources of funds shall include financial support from World Service and other funds designated for the program of health and welfare ministries, including such proportion of undesignated gifts as may be determined by the board, and from gifts, wills, and trust funds given especially to Health and Welfare Ministries. Health and Welfare Ministries is authorized to receive financial grants and trusts from private foundations and funds from public agencies and is empowered to act as trustee for the administration of bequests.

*c) Relationship with the United Methodist Association of Health and Welfare Ministries*—Health and Welfare Ministries shall work with the United Methodist Association of Health and Welfare Ministries in leadership development and may make services available to the association.

*d) Limitation of Responsibility*—Health and Welfare Ministries shall not be responsible, legally or morally, for the debts, contracts, or obligations or for any other financial commitments of any character or description created, undertaken, or assumed by any institution or interest related to a unit of The United Methodist Church, whether or not such institution or interest shall be approved, accepted, or recognized by Health and Welfare Ministries or shall be affiliated with Health and Welfare Ministries, or whether or not the promotion or establishment of the same shall be approved by the constitution of Health and Welfare Ministries. No such institution or interest related to a unit of The United Methodist Church and no officer or member of Health and Welfare Ministries shall have any authority whatsoever to take any action directly or by implication at variance with, or deviating from, the limitation contained in the preceding sentence hereof, except as Health and Welfare Ministries may directly own and manage an institution in its own name.

## Section VIII. General Board of Higher Education and Ministry

¶ 1401. There shall be a **General Board of Higher Education and Ministry,** hereinafter referred to as the board.

¶ 1402. *Incorporation*—The General Board of Higher Education and Ministry shall be a corporation under the laws of Tennessee and shall be responsible for the functions previously conducted by the Division of Higher Education of the General Board of Education and the Commission on Chaplains and Related Ministries of The United Methodist Church.

The General Board of Higher Education and Ministry is authorized to take such action as is appropriate under the corporation laws of Tennessee so as to accomplish the end result stated above, and under which the General Board of Higher Education and Ministry shall be one legal entity.

The divisions of the General Board of Education were not incorporated separately; it is the intent, however, that responsibility for the functions delegated to the divisions by prior legislative action be transferred consistent with the separation of the divisions between the General Board of Discipleship and the General Board of Higher Education and Ministry. In the division of the assets of the General Board of Education, it is the intent that all assets be used in keeping with the original intent and purpose for which they were established or acquired, and so be assigned as appropriate to the General Boards of Discipleship and Higher Education and Ministry, respectively. It is further intended that the annuities, bequests, trusts, and estates formerly held by the General Board of Education be used for the benefit and use of the General Boards of Discipleship and Higher Education and Ministry (in accord with their purposes as defined in the *Discipline*), respectively, as their interests may appear, and that real estate titles be authorized to be conveyed as appropriate and apportioned where indicated.

In the event that the intent of the original donor of existing annuities, bequests, trusts, and estates cannot be clearly determined in relation to the interests of the two boards, such assets shall be divided equally between the two boards.

It is further intended that should additional assets accrue to the former General Board of Education by reason of annuities, bequests, trusts, and estates not now known and where the intent of the donor can be clearly ascertained, the assets shall be used in keeping with the original intent and purpose for which they were established or acquired and so be assigned as appropriate to the General Boards of Discipleship and Higher Education and Ministry, respectively.

It is further intended that should additional assets accrue to the former General Board of Education by reason of annuities, bequests, trusts, and estates not now known and where the intent of the original donor cannot be clearly determined in relation to the interests of the two boards, such assets shall be divided equally between the two boards.

¶ **1403.** *Amenability and Accountability*—The board shall be amenable to the General Conference, and between sessions of the General Conference it shall be accountable to the General Council on Ministries.

¶ **1404.** *Purpose*—The board exists, within the expression of the total mission of the Church, for the specific purpose of preparing and assisting persons to fulfill their ministry in Christ in the several special ministries, ordained and diaconal; and to provide general oversight and care for campus ministries and institutions of higher education, including schools, colleges, universities, and theological schools.

¶ **1405.** *Objectives*—All the objectives assigned to the divisions shall be considered to be the objectives of the board. In summary, the board shall have authority:

1. To maintain the historic mission of The United Methodist Church in higher education and to serve as advocate for the intellectual life of the Church.

2. To seek to understand and communicate the significance of the

Christian mission in higher education and ministry throughout the world as the context in which values and Christian lifestyle are shaped.

3. To ensure that the board's programs and policies address the needs and concerns for ministry with racial and ethnic persons and people with disabilities.

4. To provide counsel, guidance, and assistance to annual conferences through their boards of ordained ministry and higher education and campus ministry, and other such program units as may be organized in the annual conferences.

5. To study needs and resources for ordained and diaconal ministries, including identification of new types of ministry.

6. To develop and maintain standards and procedures for certification in professional ministerial careers and for ordination into the ordained ministry.[31]

7. To promote and give direction to work among racial and ethnic groups, and people with disabilities for enlistment, training, and placement of persons in the professional Church-related ministries.

8. To coordinate and make visible information about career assessment opportunities and continuing education that will assist persons in professional Church-related ministries with their professional growth and development.

9. To recruit, endorse, and provide general oversight of United Methodist ordained ministers, including persons who speak languages in addition to English, who desire to serve as chaplains in specialized institutional ministry settings in both private and governmental sectors.

10. To represent The United Methodist Church in, and provide liaison with, United Methodist ordained ministers certified by professional certifying and accrediting organizations related to ministry in specialized settings.

11. To plan and implement a continuing ministry to United Methodist laity in institutions and armed forces who are separated from their local churches.

12. To develop and provide services directed to enlistment for specialized Church-related ministries, professional growth and development, and counseling.

---

31. *See* Judicial Council Decision 507.

13. To offer personnel and placement assistance for persons involved in professional Church-related ministries.

14. To conduct research on human needs to be met by the Church through its resources in higher education.

15. To provide for the allocation of funds to institutions and to programs related to the board.

16. To maintain adequate fiduciary and legal relationships with institutions and ministries and to assist annual conferences and other judicatories in their responsibilities in these matters.

17. To provide counsel, guidance, and assistance to institutions of higher education in their relationships with governmental agencies.

18. To guard property and endowments entrusted to the institutions and to maintain and enforce adequate trust and reversionary clauses.

19. To monitor and interact with public higher education in terms of its reflection on the wholeness of persons and the meaning of life, and to study and inform constituencies of public policy issues related to higher education, both independent and public.

20. To promote, in cooperation with the General Commission on Communication, special days and funds: Black College Fund, Ministerial Education Fund, United Methodist Student Day, World Communion Sunday, and other funds and special days ordered by the General Conference.

21. To evaluate United Methodist higher education and professional Church-related ministries with concern for the quality of their performance and the integrity of their mission.

22. To provide standards and support for and interpretation of the work of United Methodist theological schools.

23. To analyze needs of those in Church-related ministries for continuing education, including assessment of effectiveness, professional growth and development, and funding.

24. To provide professional ministerial courses of study for orderly entrance into ordained ministry. In providing these courses of study, consideration shall be given to languages other than English and to persons with disabilities.

25. To provide for a continuing discussion of the theological bases for professional Church-related ministries and higher education.

26. To provide such services as will create a climate of acceptance and empowerment for women, racial and ethnic persons, and people with disabilities in higher education and professional Church-related

ministries, and to be alert to the necessity of advocacy in behalf of these professional ministries in questions of equity and justice.

27. To provide counsel, guidance, and assistance to professional associations and fellowships related to diaconal and other Church-related special ministries.

28. To interpret, promote, and administer the loan and scholarship programs of the board, and to cooperate with the General Board of Global Ministries in matters related to the Crusade Scholarship Program.

29. To engage in research related to personnel needs and interpretation of occupational opportunities in the Church.

30. To provide such support agencies as are deemed necessary to carry out the functions of the board.

31. To give priority to the planning and policy development functions of the board on behalf of the Church.

¶ 1406. *Responsibilities*—The responsibilities of the General Board of Higher Education and Ministry shall be:

1. To establish and review the objectives of the General Board of Higher Education and Ministry within the wider mission of The United Methodist Church.

2. To establish appropriate organizational structures within the board and staff to achieve established objectives, including writing bylaws, electing officers, establishing committees, electing staff, and filling vacancies in accord with ¶ 712.

3. To determine policy and program, establish goals and priorities, project long-range plans, and evaluate program and services of the board.

4. To give direction to the staff and to delegate authority to board executives through general oversight of the administration.

5. To report the activities of the board to The United Methodist Church through appropriate agencies of the general and jurisdictional conferences.

6. To develop and maintain cooperative relationships with ecumenical agencies and other denominations for the full discharge of the objectives of the board.

7. To cooperate with other agencies in The United Methodist Church in the fulfillment of the programs of the General Conference.

8. To develop and maintain cooperative relationships with higher educational institutions, campus ministries, chaplains and related ministries, and diaconal ministries throughout the world in collaboration with the General Board of Global Ministries.

9. Upon request, to provide resources and technical assistance in higher education throughout the world in collaboration with churches of the Wesleyan tradition.

10. In cooperation with the General Council on Finance and Administration, to develop long-range investments and fundraising projects within the Church that shall guarantee, insofar as possible, the continuous flow of resources for United Methodist higher education for the decades and the centuries to come. In developing such long-range investments, the board shall adhere to the specific investment guidelines adopted by the General Conference.

11. To promote awareness of and concurrence with "Policies Relative to Socially Responsible Investments" (¶ 716), the Social Principles (¶¶ 160–166), and *The Book of Resolutions of The United Methodist Church.*

¶ 1407. *Organization*—1. The membership shall be sixty-four persons constituted in accordance with ¶ 705.4e and 705.5 of the General Provisions.

2. The membership shall be constituted as follows:

*a) Jurisdictional Members*—Clergy, laywomen, and laymen shall be elected to the board by the jurisdictional conference upon nomination from the annual conference in accordance with ¶ 705.5, based on the following formula: North Central—8, Northeastern—8, South Central—11, Southeastern—12, and Western—3.

*b) Supplemental Members*—One member from North Katanga Annual Conference and one member from Southern Congo Annual Conference shall be elected as supplemental members according to the provisions of ¶ 705.5e.

*c) Central Conference Members*—Four Central Conference members shall be elected to the board on nomination by the Council of Bishops according to the provisions in ¶ 705.5c.

*d) Episcopal Members*—Six episcopal members shall be named by the Council of Bishops, including at least one from the central conferences (*see* ¶ 710.10).

*e)* One member elected by Iglesia Metodista Autónoma Afiliada de Puerto Rico.

*f) Additional Members*—(1) *United Methodist*—Additional members are nominated by a committee composed of three persons from each jurisdiction (one clergy, one laywoman, and one layman) elected by the jurisdictional conference. They shall elect up to nine additional members to ensure inclusivity and expertise. (2) It is recommended that the board elect at least one of the additional members without vote from among the other churches of the Consultation on Church Union.

g) If a vacancy occurs in the board, it shall be filled in accordance with ¶ 712.

¶ 1408. 1. *Divisions*—The board shall provide for a Division of Higher Education, and a Division of Ordained Ministry providing support for ordained clergy, local pastors, and diaconal ministers. Further, the board is authorized to alter its organization to adjust to changing circumstances, within the parameters of responsibility established by *The Book of Discipline*.

2. *Offices*—The board, in implementing the objectives (¶¶ 1403, 1405), shall have authority to establish and maintain the following offices: (a) Interpretation; and (b) Loans and Scholarships.

¶ 1409. *Provision for Funding*—1. The work and program of the board shall be supported from the general benevolences of the Church and the Ministerial Education Fund. Funds received by the board for the divisions from the Ministerial Education Fund shall be restricted to the support of theological schools and the Division of Ordained Ministry in the development of their programs of enlistment, basic professional degree programs, and continuing education (in accordance with ¶ 820.2a and b).

2. Administration and other programs of the divisions shall be supported solely from World Service moneys. The associate general secretaries shall recommend through the general secretary of the board to the General Council on Finance and Administration the amount of financial support that should be allocated for the divisions.

### DIVISION OF HIGHER EDUCATION

¶ 1410. *Duties and Responsibilities*—1. Higher education is a significant part of our Wesleyan heritage, our present task, and our future responsibility. The Church continues its historic mission of uniting knowledge and vital piety by maintaining educational institutions and a campus ministry, and through them an intellectual, spiritual, and material ministry to all persons within the academic community without respect to sex, race, creed, or national origin.

2. There shall be a **Division of Higher Education** representing The United Methodist Church in its relationships with educational

institutions and the campus ministry. The division shall have an advisory relationship to all United Methodist-affiliated institutions, including universities, colleges, secondary and special schools, Wesley Foundations, and similar organizations as well as ecumenical campus ministry groups. The division will, on request, serve in an advisory and consultative capacity to all agencies of the Church owning or administering educational institutions and campus ministry units.

3. The nominating committee of the board shall, insofar as possible, provide representation for nomination as members of the Division of Higher Education an equitable number of persons directly related to the areas of concern of the division.

4. Principal objectives of the division are:

*a)* To determine the nature of the United Methodist mission in and through its elementary, secondary, and higher educational institutions and campus ministries.

*b)* To develop policy that enables The United Methodist Church to engage effectively in higher education throughout the world.

*c)* To encourage the Church in programs designed to nurture and sustain educational institutions and campus ministry units as invaluable assets in the ongoing life of the Church.

*d)* To promote a campus Christian movement and a concerned Christian ministry of the educational community; to witness in the campus community to the mission, message, and life of Jesus Christ; to deepen, enrich, and mature the Christian faith of college and university students, faculty, and staff through commitment to Jesus Christ and the Church and to assist them in their service and leadership to the world, in and through the Church.

*e)* To interpret both the Church and its educational institutions and campus ministry to each other; to help the agencies of the Church and higher education participate in the greater realization of a fully humane society committed to freedom and truth, love, justice, peace, and personal integrity.

*f)* To foster within educational institutions the highest educational standards, effective programs of Church relationships, the soundest business practices, the finest ethical and moral principles, and especially Christian ideals; to help people experience release from enslavement, fear, and violence; and to help people live in love.

*g)* To preserve and protect resources, property, and investments of The United Methodist Church or any conference, agency, or institution thereof, in any educational institution, Wesley Foundation, or other campus ministry unit founded, organized, developed, or assisted under the direction or with the cooperation of The United Methodist Church.

*h)* To relate to professional organizations of higher education and campus ministry on behalf of The United Methodist Church.

*i)* To enable the division's constituencies to develop an interest in and response to public policies bearing on higher education, both independent and public.

*j)* To provide resources and suggest guidelines for annual conference boards of higher education and campus ministry.

5. The division shall appoint personnel, including an assistant general secretary for campus ministry, an assistant general secretary for schools, colleges, and universities, and an assistant general secretary for the Black College Fund, and it shall establish such committees and commissions as may be necessary for effective fulfillment of its objectives. It may adopt such rules and regulations as may be required for the conduct of its business.

¶ **1411.** *Responsibilities to General and Annual Conferences*—The Division of Higher Education will cooperate with and assist the General and annual conferences and their respective boards and area commissions organized in behalf of educational institutions and the campus ministry. (For annual conference boards, *see* ¶ 631.2.)

1. The division shall:

*a)* Provide for the cooperative study of plans for maximum coordination of the work of United Methodist higher education with the Church's mission in Christian education.

*b)* Direct attention of Church members to the contribution of United Methodist educational institutions and campus ministry units to the life and character of students, faculty, and staff and to the place the institutions and campus ministry have in the preservation and propagation of the Christian faith for our time.

2. The division shall assess institutional and campus ministry relationships with and responsibilities to the Church, and it shall aid in the determination of the degree of active accord between institutional and campus ministry policies and practices and the policies of the Church as expressed in the *Discipline* and in General Conference enactments.

3. The division shall assist educational societies and foundations

related to the annual conferences for the promotion of Christian higher education and the campus ministry, and it shall recognize such societies and foundations as auxiliaries of the division when their objectives and purposes, articles of incorporation, and administrative policies shall have been approved by the annual conference within whose boundaries they have been incorporated.

4. The division should provide the connectional relationship whenever agencies of the General Church wish to enter into discussion with or make inquiry into United Methodist-related schools, colleges, and universities.

5. The division shall direct attention to the work and needs of those educational institutions that stand in special relationship to The United Methodist Church and shall request support for them. Due recognition shall be given to the needs of the Black colleges historically related to The United Methodist Church. (*See* ¶¶ 819, 1420.)

6. The division shall approve changes in institutional sponsorship and relationships to the general or annual conferences, including separation from United Methodist program boards, from the general or one or more annual conferences, or from the University Senate as the certifying agency of The United Methodist Church.

¶ **1412.** *Responsibilities to Educational Institutions*—The Division of Higher Education shall establish policy and practice providing for consultation with and support of United Methodist educational institutions, campus ministry units, and annual conference boards of higher education and campus ministry in matters of institutional study and evaluation, promotion, interpretation, management, program, and finance.

1. The division shall, in cooperation with the University Senate:

*a)* Study trends in higher education, the needs of the Church, and public and private educational opportunities and requirements and make recommendations to the educational institutions and state commissions or other bodies or publics concerned with higher education.

*b)* Recommend and approve plans for institutional cooperation, consolidation, or merger between or among United Methodist-related colleges and/or between them and institutions of other denominations that ensure that the interests of The United Methodist Church are adequately protected.

*c)* Investigate the objectives, academic programs, educational standards, personnel policies, plant and equipment, business and management practices, financial program, public relations, student personnel services, student development programs, religious life, and Church relations of any educational institution claiming or adjudged to be related to The United Methodist Church.

*d)* Evaluate and classify institutions in order to authenticate relatedness to the Church and determine eligibility for Church financial support.

2. The division shall, in regard to campus ministry, Wesley Foundations, and ecumenical campus ministry groups, provide a structure within the division in order to:

*a)* Assist in development of plans for the systematic evaluation of these units in cooperation with their regularly constituted boards of directors or trustees and with conference, area, or regional committees or commissions on Christian higher education and campus ministry or appropriate ecumenical agencies.

*b)* Study the trends in programming and funding in campus ministry, review reports from conference agencies and local units, and interpret these findings to the constituency as appropriate.

*c)* Affirm its commitment to an ecumenical approach to campus ministry; encourage local, campus, state, and regional units of that ministry to work toward ecumenical programming and structures where appropriate to provide counsel and support to conference boards and agencies in reviewing, evaluating, and strengthening existing and proposed local and regional ecumenical covenants for campus ministry; and ensure that ecumenical covenants and procedures for these units are on file with the annual conference boards of higher education and campus ministry.

*d)* Recognize and cooperate with agencies with whom relationships may serve to further the objectives of the division.

*e)* Provide for representation and participation, as deemed necessary, with other national ecumenical campus ministry agencies.

*f)* Provide services to meet specific denominational needs.

*g)* Relate college and university students of The United Methodist Church to a national United Methodist student organization and such ecumenical student organizations as may be appropriate.

3. The division shall, as it seeks to interpret higher education:

*a)* Promote the Church's mission in higher education, including the special missions and educational ministries to ethnic groups, people with disabilities, and other peoples disadvantaged by world conditions.

*b)* Promote Christian instruction and provide opportunity for Christian service.

*c)* Encourage educational institutions and campus ministry units to inculcate human and humane values consistent with the gospel and the public good.

*d)* Foster the development of Christian community within the life of educational institutions and campus ministry units.

*e)* Make use of the existing Church organization and publications for interpreting the mission of higher education.

*f)* Participate in the Crusade Scholarship program.

*g)* Design and organize the promotion of United Methodist Student Day to recognize United Methodist students in higher education.

¶ **1413.** *Financial Support of Higher Education*—1. In recognition of its heritage and the mandate to maintain its mission in higher education and in light of emergent fiscal concerns, The United Methodist Church affirms its commitment to higher education and to the means by which it can be continuously supported and renewed.

2. The Division of Higher Education shall be empowered to take such action as may be necessary to:

*a)* Promote the financial support of Christian higher education within the Church.

*b)* Create arrangements that shall provide for the flow of supporting funds from the whole Church to the institutions affiliated with the Church as affirmed by the University Senate (¶ 1416).

*c)* Develop corporations, or other fiscal or fiduciary agencies, for the purpose of financing, creating, recycling, managing, or otherwise caring for institutions and campus ministry units or their assets and liabilities.

3. The division, in regard to fiscal matters, shall:

*a)* Study the financial status of United Methodist educational institutions and campus ministry units, encourage the Church to give them continuous support, and provide consultative services in fiscal affairs and other aspects of institutional management. The division shall study all appropriate related data and may recommend to each conference or agency the support levels appropriate for each related institution or institutions.

*b)* Appropriate such funds as are available for the support of educational institutions, Wesley Foundations, or other campus ministry units related to The United Methodist Church under such rules as the board may adopt.

*c)* Take such action as is necessary to protect or recover resources, property, and investments of The United Methodist Church or any conference, agency, or institution thereof, in capital or endowment funds of any educational institution, Wesley Foundation, or other campus ministry unit founded, organized, developed, or assisted under the direction or with the cooperation of The United Methodist Church should any such institution discontinue operation or move to sever or modify its connection with the Church or violate the terms of any rules adopted by the board or the terms of any such grant of new capital or endowment funds made by The United Methodist Church or any conference, agency, or institution thereof. In order to carry out its duties under this paragraph, the division shall, at its discretion, investigate, audit, and review all necessary records and documents of any educational institution claiming or adjudged by the division to be related to The United Methodist Church. In the event any such educational institution, Wesley Foundation, or other campus ministry unit shall endeavor to discontinue operation or move to sever or modify its connection with the Church or violate the rules adopted by the division in accordance with ¶ 1413.3*b*, it shall be the duty of the trustees and the administrators of such institutions, along with the conference agency on higher education and the resident bishop of the conference in which such institution is located, to confer at the earliest possible opportunity with appropriate representatives of the division to determine what resources and aid the division may be able to provide and to permit the division to carry out its responsibilities under this paragraph.

*d)* (1) Foster and aid through a special apportionment the United Methodist institutions historically related to education for African Americans. It shall have authority to institute plans by which colleges sponsored by the division may cooperate with or may unite with colleges of other denominations or under independent control; *provided* that the interests of The United Methodist Church are adequately protected. (2) Encourage such Black colleges to secure adequate endowments for their support and maintenance. Whenever the division is assured that their support will be adequate and the property will be conserved and perpetuated for Christian education under the auspices and control of The United Methodist Church, it may transfer the colleges to boards of trustees under such conditions as the General Board of Higher Education and Ministry may prescribe, which shall include the right of reversion to the board under conditions prescribed by the board.

UNIVERSITY SENATE

¶ **1414.** *Organization and Membership*—1. The University Senate is an elected body of professionals in higher education created by the General Conference to determine which schools, colleges, universities, and theological schools meet the criteria for listing as institutions affiliated with The United Methodist Church.[32]

2. The senate shall be composed of twenty-five voting members who, at the time of election, are actively engaged in the work of education through employment in an educational institution and are fitted by training and experience for the technical work of evaluating educational institutions. Election is for the quadrennium, except in cases where conflict of interest arises as a result of change in employment. Nine of these members shall be elected quadrennially by the National Association of Schools and Colleges of The United Methodist Church—seven of whom shall be chief executive officers of United Methodist-related educational institutions, the other two holding other positions relevant to academic or financial affairs or Church relationships; four by the General Board of Higher Education and Ministry—two of whom shall be chief executive officers of United Methodist-related higher educational institutions, the other two holding other positions relevant to academic or financial affairs or Church relationships; four by the General Conference—two of whom shall be chief executive officers of United Methodist-related educational institutions at the time of their election, the other two holding other positions relevant to academic or financial affairs or Church relationships; four by the senate itself, without limitation other than the general provisions of this paragraph; and four shall be appointed by the Council of Bishops—two of whom shall be chief executive officers of United Methodist-related educational institutions, the other two holding other positions relevant to academic or financial affairs or Church relationships. Each of the five electing bodies shall elect at least one woman.

Members elected by the General Conference shall be nominated and elected by the following procedure: Twelve persons shall be nominated by the Council of Bishops, six of whom shall be chief executive officers of United Methodist-related educational institutions, the other six holding other positions relevant to academic or financial

---

32. *See* Judicial Council Decision 589.

affairs or Church relationships. At the same daily session at which the above nominations are announced, additional nominations may be made from the floor but at no other time. From these nominations, the General Conference shall elect without discussion, by ballot and by plurality vote, the four persons to serve on the senate, two from each of the two categories of nominees. Should a vacancy occur in the members elected by General Conference in the interim prior to the next General Conference, the Council of Bishops shall appoint a replacement taken from the remaining nominees. The election process shall be repeated at each succeeding General Conference. Care should be taken that women, racial and ethnic persons, and representatives from the United Methodist-related Black colleges and graduate theological seminaries shall be members of the senate. If a member (other than the four elected by the General Conference) retires from educational work, or for any other cause a vacancy occurs during the quadrennium, it shall be filled by the agency by which the retiring member was elected at its next meeting. The general secretary of the General Board of Higher Education and Ministry and the associate general secretaries of the Divisions of Higher Education and Ordained Ministry (Section of Elders and Local Pastors and Section of Deacons and Diaconal Ministers) of that board shall serve as ex officio members of the senate, with voice but without vote. There shall be one staff representative on the senate from the General Board of Global Ministries, with voice but without vote, named by the general secretary of the General Board of Global Ministries.

3. The associate general secretary of the Division of Higher Education shall be the executive secretary of the senate. The general secretary of the board shall convene it for organization at the beginning of each quadrennium. The senate shall elect its own officers, including a president, a vice president, and a recording secretary, and it may appoint such committees and commissions and delegate to them such powers as are incident to its work. Thereafter, it shall meet semiannually at such time and place as it may determine. Special meetings may be called on the written request of five members or at the discretion of the president and the executive secretary.

4. After consultation with the officers of the senate, the Division of Higher Education shall provide in its annual budget for the expense of the senate as it may deem sufficient, except that expenses incurred by the senate on behalf of any other board of the Church shall be borne by that board.

**¶ 1415.** *Purposes and Objectives*—1. To establish the criteria that must be met by schools, colleges, universities, and theological schools to achieve and retain listing as institutions affiliated with The United Methodist Church.

2. To support the development of institutions whose aims are to address and whose programs reflect significant educational, cultural, social, and human issues in a manner reflecting the values held in common by the institutions and the Church.

3. To provide an effective review process to ensure that schools, colleges, universities, and theological schools listed by the University Senate and qualifying for Church support have institutional integrity, well-structured programs, sound management, and clearly defined Church relationships.[33]

4. To establish effective annual reporting procedures that will provide the senate with the data necessary to complete its review of the institutional viability and program integrity of member institutions.

**¶ 1416.** *Institutional Affiliation*[34]—1. Approval by the senate is prerequisite to institutional claim of affiliation with The United Methodist Church.

2. Every effort shall be made by both the annual conferences and institutions to sustain and support each other, but identification of an institution with The United Methodist Church shall depend upon its approval by the senate. The senate shall provide adequate guidelines and counsel to assist institutions seeking initial or renewed affiliation.

3. Only institutions affiliated with The United Methodist Church through approval by the senate shall be eligible for funding by annual conferences, General Conference, general boards, or other agencies of The United Methodist Church.

4. To qualify for affiliation with The United Methodist Church, institutions must maintain appropriate academic accreditation.

5. Assessment of Church relationships shall be a part of the process for those institutions seeking approval of the senate for affiliation with The United Methodist Church. Inasmuch as declarations of Church relationships are expected to differ one from the other, and because of the diversity in heritage and other aspects of institutional life, declarations of Church relationship will necessarily be of institutional design.

---

33. *See* Judicial Council Decision 589.
34. *See* Judicial Council Decision 589.

¶ **1417.** *Annual Reports of Approved Institutions*—1. Each year the senate shall publish a list classifying United Methodist-affiliated institutions. These institutions shall include secondary schools, colleges, universities, graduate theological seminaries, and special schools.

2. The senate shall also prepare annually a list of approved schools, colleges, universities, and graduate theological seminaries for use by annual conference boards of ordained ministry in determining candidate educational eligibility for admission into full connection.

3. An institution that chooses to disaffiliate with The United Methodist Church for any reason shall: *a)* inform the University Senate as soon as possible after discussions begin concerning disaffiliation; *b)* inform all appropriate United Methodist judicatories; and *c)* seek technical and legal assistance from the Division of Higher Education regarding fiduciary issues.

4. The senate shall publish annually, with its list of United Methodist-affiliated institutions, the names of institutions of other historic Methodist Churches that wish to participate in research projects, the insurance program, and technical services of the General Board of Higher Education and Ministry. Such institutions shall be designated as "associate" institutions.

¶ **1418.** *Consultative Services*—1. Support for approved institutions shall include, through the appropriate divisions of the General Board of Higher Education and Ministry, consulting teams with skills in comprehensive institutional design, management, governance, and program.

2. Support for approved institutions shall include an interpretation of and consultation on data in the annual institutional reports.

3. The Division of Higher Education shall report annually to the senate on the level and types of institutional support rendered by related conferences and agencies and shall evaluate such support, including specific responses of conferences and agencies to recommended levels.

UNITED METHODIST HIGHER EDUCATION FOUNDATION

¶ **1419.** The **United Methodist Higher Education Foundation** is incorporated in the State of Tennessee as a nonprofit, charitable organization with permanent ties to the Division of Higher Education, which elects its board of trustees. The general purpose of the foundation is to foster the growth and development of institutions of higher education by encouraging persons and corporations to provide financial support and by acting as a foundation for such support. The foundation is also authorized to serve as a trustee and administrator of gifts and bequests designated by donors to specific institutions.

## COUNCIL OF PRESIDENTS OF THE BLACK COLLEGES

¶ **1420.** *Council of Presidents of the Black Colleges*—1. There shall be an organization known as the **Council of Presidents of the Black Colleges.** It shall be composed of all the presidents of the United Methodist institutions historically related to the education of African Americans and with a current relationship to The United Methodist Church.

2. *Purposes and Objectives*—The purpose of the council shall be to:

*a)* Help identify and clarify the roles of these colleges in higher education and in The United Methodist Church.

*b)* Promote fundraising efforts through the Church.

*c)* Study, review, and discuss programs of member institutions.

The council shall have a minimum of two regular meetings in each calendar year and shall be amenable to the Division of Higher Education in the implementation of its responsibilities.

## DIVISION OF ORDAINED MINISTRY

¶ **1421.** *Duties and Responsibilities*—**The Division of Ordained Ministry** shall be responsible for leading and serving the church in inviting, equipping, and supporting faithful and effective spiritual leaders who serve as ordained deacons and elders, licensed local pastors, diaconal ministers, certified persons in specialized ministries, and clergy endorsed for extension ministries in order to fulfill the mission of The United Methodist Church and the proclamation of the gospel of Jesus Christ. The division's work includes all who are serving in categories of appointment by a bishop. This responsibility shall be discharged in active relation with schools of theology, annual conference boards of ordained ministry, cabinets, jurisdictional boards or committees on ordained ministry, central conferences, and other appropriate bodies. This division shall be responsible for the promotion of theological education and its support for the whole church.

In fulfillment of this responsibility and in accordance with the disciplinary requirements established for each region of the church in the world, the division will:

1. Study ministerial needs and resources in The United Methodist Church and cooperate with appropriate groups in the interpretation of ministry as a vocation, in an effort to enlist suitable persons for ordained ministry.

2. Provide for the enlistment, training, continuing education and formation, and career development of faithful and effective spiritual leaders of all races and ethnic origins in the ordained ministry serving in local churches, extension ministries, and other appointed ministries in the church and world. Provision shall be made for special resources in training for ministry in distinctive ethnic minority groups. Attention shall be given to the specific needs of persons with disabilities.

3. Provide resources for enlisting and supporting women in ordained, licensed, and certified ministry.

4. Work with boards of ordained ministry, district committees on ordained ministry, and other appropriate agencies by: a) developing guidelines, training, and resources for their work; b) providing guidance and counseling in the examination of ministerial students; c) assisting in the training of mentors; and d) interpreting current disciplinary legislation concerning ordained and licensed ministry.

5. Maintain the educational standards of the ordained ministry of The United Methodist Church; certify the course offerings in all seminaries for meeting the requirements in United Methodist history, doctrine, and polity specified in ¶326.(3); provide boards of ordained ministry with a list of the courses approved; and monitor the implementation of ¶ 1425.

6. Provide educational programs and standards for the training of local pastors.

7. Identify the areas of need for specialized ministries and provide standards and educational programs for candidates for certification.

8. Provide guidance and resources for a system of support for clergy in their work, for ongoing formation in ministry subsequent to ordination, including continuing education and spiritual growth, giving attention to the needs of all racial, cultural, and special needs groups within the denomination. This will include resources for bishops and annual conferences in the development of the Order of Deacon and Order of Elder.

9. Support and cooperate with bishops and district superintendents in the fulfillment of their ministry of superintending by *a)* providing jointly with the General Council on Ministries and the Council of Bishops for the training of new district superintendents; *b)* providing ongoing training and support for bishops and superintendents in their work; and *c)* developing resources to assist clergy, superintendents, and local churches in assessment and evaluation of ministry.

10. Study and coordinate mutual ministry between United Methodist schools of theology and annual conferences in fulfillment of ¶ 1426.

11. Lead in the churchwide interpretation and promotion of the Ministerial Education Fund and support other funds and programs that assist in training persons for ordained ministry.

12. Work with other bishops, cabinets, boards of ordained ministry, and other church agencies in maintaining the professional and ethical standards of the United Methodist ordained ministry for all persons within the covenant of conference membership.

13. Provide the connectional relationship whenever agencies of the general Church wish to enter into discussion with or make inquiry into the work of United Methodist seminaries.

14. Relate to the University Senate and its Commission on Theological Education in the review and approval on non-United Methodist seminaries for candidates for ordination.

## SECTION OF CHAPLAINS AND RELATED MINISTRIES

**¶ 1422.** *Duties*—**The Section of Chaplains and Related Ministries** (SCRM) supports chaplains and clergy in endorsed extension ministries and the mission and ministry of The United Methodist Church locally and globally through programs and activities that:

1. Identify, assess, and support clergymen and clergywomen who serve in pastoral care, making the church visible for persons in health-care settings, retirement homes, prisons, workplaces, counseling centers, and the armed forces.

2. Establish standards calling for endorsed persons to have special education, training and skills, and, when required, professional certification, in order to ensure that The United Methodist Church provides quality pastoral care to prisoners, patients, counselees, armed forces personnel, and workers.

3. Carry out procedures for providing Ecclesiastical Endorsement

for elders and, when required, for deacons under appointment to ministries of chaplaincy and pastoral care.

*a)* The Section of Chaplains and Related Ministries, through its endorsing committee, shall have the authority to grant and remove endorsement and to adopt appropriate rules of procedure for such, providing that the rights of appeal shall be adequately safeguarded.

*b)* An endorsing committee, consisting of elected members of the section and representation from the other sections of the division and chaired by a bishop, shall represent The United Methodist Church in all endorsing procedures.

*c)* Endorsement is affirmation that a person is performing a valid ministry of The United Methodist Church and has presented evidence of having the special education, training, skills, and, when required, professional certification necessary to perform that ministry. Endorsement is authority granted by the denomination to be appointed to and provide ministry in a specific setting. When such authority is no longer required, the endorsement ceases to exist.

4. Carry out procedures for Ecclesiastical Approval for persons in the armed forces student chaplain candidate programs, intermittent chaplaincy with the Department of Veterans Affairs, certain volunteer chaplaincy settings such as those relating to the Civil Air Patrol, the International Conference of Police Chaplains, and other entities.

5. Maintain programs for the oversight, support, and advocacy of endorsed/approved persons

*General Oversight*—The section shall provide general oversight for all those under endorsement, particularly for those serving outside the bounds of their annual conferences. The section shall assure conference boards of ordained ministry of the validity of ministry of clergy serving under its endorsement. The section shall verify annually to bishops and conference boards of ordained ministry those clergy under its endorsement and request their reappointment.

6. Establish and maintain standards for ecclesiastical endorsement and professional certification.

*a)* The section shall establish standards for endorsements for all ministry settings in ¶335.1*b*. In addition, it shall provide standards for use by annual conference boards of ordained ministry in determining the appropriateness of other extension ministry settings not identified in ¶335.1 and will assist, as requested, in evaluating specific settings. It shall provide advocacy for persons appointed under ¶335.1*d* and encourage new efforts to enrich the missional emphases of our denomination through the development of new extension ministry settings.

*b)* The section shall work with certifying bodies in the development of standards for pastoral care certification in a variety of ministry settings.

7. Link congregations, conferences, and church structures with those persons in specialized ministry settings.

8. Resource congregations, conferences, and church structures in the development of programs of pastoral care in specialized settings.

9. Interpret these specialized ministries to the church and serve as an advocate for persons in extension ministries under its endorsement. Such advocacy may include: representing their interests within the non-church institutional systems where they serve; representing their interests within the connectional system of The United Methodist Church in conferences and boards and agencies; being in dialogue with the various professional and certifying agencies; helping to facilitate, as an agent on their behalf, the transition into or out of extension ministries; and giving attention to the needs for continuing education and ongoing spiritual formation for those under endorsement.

10. Assist in providing a ministry to United Methodist laity in or associated with the armed forces, particularly those stationed in locations outside the United States. The General Board of Higher Education and Ministry, through the section, shall cooperate with the General Board of Discipleship, the General Board of Global Ministries, and other agencies of the Church in preparing materials, planning programs, and providing a continuing ministry that includes such activities as retreats, confirmation classes, and other pastoral functions. Basic to all such ministry will be involvement in the life of the local United Methodist community and existing ecumenical and interreligious programs. These shall take into account the language and cultural needs of the persons involved.

SECTION OF DEACONS AND DIACONAL MINISTRIES

¶ 1423. *Duties*—**The Section of Deacons and Diaconal Ministries** (SDDM) shall be responsible for the work of the Division of Ordained Ministry relating to the clergy order of deacon and persons who are preparing to serve as deacons in full connection, diaconal ministers (under provision of *The Book of Discipline*, 1992); persons certified in various specialized ministries for which an agency has set professional standards; and persons in professional ministry careers as their vocation.

In fulfillment of this responsibility, the section will:

1. Cooperate with other sections in the Division of Ordained Ministry and groups and agencies in the church in the study of the needs of United Methodist ministry; especially regarding the order of deacon, diaconal ministry, and certification in specialized areas of ministry and to make recommendations accordingly;

2. Provide resources and training to conference boards of ordained ministry and similar recognized bodies in their responsibility for administering the standards, requirements, examination, and interviews for the order of deacon and certification in ministry careers;

3. Provide guidance and standards for preparation for the ordination as deacon in full connection;

4. Work with the graduate theological seminaries and other graduate schools in development of curricula for the academic preparation of deacons;

5. Lead in the interpretation of the ministry of the deacon and other diaconal careers and work with cabinets and bishops on the interpretation of the Order of Deacon;

6. Encourage and resource conference boards of ordained ministry and other similar bodies for the on-going support of deacons, diaconal ministers, and persons in professional careers;

7. Study needs and recommend to GBHEM and General Conference the requirements and standards that shall be minimal for certification in professional ministry careers after consultation with the agencies responsible for programs and areas of work related to the careers;

8. Work with conference boards of ordained ministry regarding their responsibility for recruitment and administration of the standards and requirements for certification in professional ministry careers. Particular emphasis will be given to the recruitment of ethnic minority persons to strengthen the church;

9. Review the conference boards of ordained ministry recommendations of persons to be approved for professional certification;

10. Work with seminaries, graduate schools, universities, and colleges by providing guidance and standards for the academic preparation for professional ministry careers;

11. Provide guidance through the Division of Ordained Ministry for continuing education of ordained deacons, diaconal ministers, and certified persons;

12. Provide guidance to cabinets and other annual conference agencies to ensure conditions of employment, support, and benefits commensurate with their training, ability, and experience for the deacon in full connection, diaconal ministers, and certified persons;

13. Foster cooperative relationships among persons in the diaconate in The United Methodist Church, including the Central Conferences, and with their colleagues in other denominations and faiths and participate in the continuing study of ministry related to the diaconate;

14. Cooperate with professional associations and fellowships of The United Methodist Church in ways that will be supportive of their professional ministry careers;

15. Cooperate with other United Methodist agencies and general boards in their resourcing members of professional associations and fellowships;

16. Provide leadership to Diakonia of the America and Caribbean (DOTAC), DIAKONIA (World Federation of Diaconal Associations), the North American Association of the Diaconate, and other emerging ecumenical and international groups to support the ongoing development of the diaconate;

17. Consult with United Methodist seminaries and all University Senate approved seminaries regarding the requirements for ordination as a deacon and the development of curriculum and other programs related to the training of the deacon;

18. Relate to the University Senate Commission on Theological Education regarding the review and approval of non–United Methodist seminaries for candidates for ordination as deacon;

19. Promote the Ministerial Education Fund as a primary means of assuring well educated, effective, and faithful certified persons in specialized ministries and deacons in full connection to serve the church.

SECTION OF ELDERS AND LOCAL PASTORS

¶ 1424. *Duties*—The mission of the **Section of Elders and Local Pastors** shall be the calling, training, and supporting of pastoral leadership by elders and local pastors, to the end that the gospel of Christ might be proclaimed and the mission of The United Methodist Church accomplished. The section will provide leadership and resources for the church in interpreting the ministry of the elder and local pastor as pastor in charge in local congregations and the elder in extension ministries.

To accomplish this mission, the section will cooperate with schools of theology, boards of ordained ministry, cabinets, and other agencies in interpreting the pastoral needs of the church in ways that are appropriate to each region of the church in the world. The section will:

1. Study the needs of the annual conferences in terms of pastoral leadership, including retirement trends, retention of clergy, and shifting pastoral needs in annual conferences, and lead the church in the enlistment of persons to serve as elders and local pastors.

2. Lead the church in lifting up God's call to pastoral ministry in the local congregation and, in cooperation with the Section of Chaplains and Related Ministries, interpret and encourage the ministry of elders serving in extension ministries.

3. Work with ethnic centers related to the United Methodist seminaries, general church initiatives, and the ethnic caucuses to enlist ethnic minority candidates for pastoral ministry.

4. Prescribe the Course of Study for local pastors and an advanced Course of Study for local pastors who seek to qualify for full membership and ordination as an elder (¶ 315.6). The Course of Study shall include studies for license as local pastor, the basic five-year curriculum, and the advanced Course of Study. All work in the Course of Study shall be taken in programs approved by the section. The section will be responsible for the requirements of the Course of Study and will consult with annual conference boards of ordained ministry and seminaries in the organizing, funding, and managing of Course of Study schools (¶ 343.1).

5. Maintain the educational standards and requirements of *The Book of Discipline* for full membership and ordination as elder.

6. Consult with the United Methodist seminaries and all University Senate approved seminaries concerning the requirements for ordination as an elder, the development of the M.Div. curriculum, and other programs related to the training of the elder and local pastor.

7. Relate to the University Senate Commission on Theological Education regarding the review and approval of non–United Methodist seminaries for candidates for ordination as elder.

8. Consult with the schools of theology and programs of pastoral

training in the Central Conferences concerning the pastoral needs, the relationship between United Methodist seminaries in the Central Conferences and the United States, and other resources for training pastors to serve in the Central Conferences.

9. Promote the importance of theological training in the Wesleyan tradition for all pastors in the United Methodist seminaries and in the whole church. The section will work with the Office of Loans and Scholarships, the Foundation for Christian Higher Education, the Crusade Scholarship Program, and other funding agencies in regard to scholarship assistance for persons preparing for ordination as an elder with a particular concern for financial assistance for ethnic minority students.

10. Lead the church in the acceptance and support of women in pastoral ministry, particularly in annual conferences where 10 percent or fewer of the elders in full connection are women.

11. Cooperate with the other sections of the division in the training and resourcing of boards of ordained ministry, particularly in regard to the enlistment, review, and examination of candidates for ordination as elder or licensing as local pastor, the probationary process, and the mentoring of new clergy.

12. Consult with the Council of Bishops and cabinets with regard to issues of itinerant ministry and the appointive system of The United Methodist Church, the ministry of the district superintendent, and supervision of itinerant elders and local pastors. The section will provide resources for bishops and district superintendents, particularly in regard to the supervision and evaluation of effective pastoral leadership in local churches.

13. Provide guidance regarding the ongoing needs of elders and local pastors for continuing education, spiritual growth, vocational development, and career assessment. The section will give leadership to the development of support systems for elders and local pastors, resources for the Order of Elders, and support for the associations of local pastors, including women, ethnic minority persons, and clergy with disabilities.

14. Cooperate with the GCFA and boards of ordained ministry concerning legal issues, policies of professional ethics for pastors, and other matters related to clergy practice.

15. Promote the Ministerial Education Fund as a primary means of assuring well-educated, faithful, and effective pastoral leadership for the church.

16. Cooperate with ecumenical groups and other agencies of The United Methodist Church in matters related to the calling, training, and supporting of pastoral leadership throughout the church.

SCHOOLS OF THEOLOGY OF THE UNITED METHODIST CHURCH

¶ **1425.** *Goals*—1. United Methodist schools of theology share a common mission of preparing persons for leadership in the ministry of The United Methodist Church; of leading in the ongoing reflection on Wesleyan theology; and of assisting the church in fulfilling its mission to make disciples of Jesus Christ. They contribute to the life of the global United Methodist connection through theological education for the sake of the worldwide mission of the church. These schools of theology are maintained for the education of ordained and lay leadership, for the interpretation of the Christian faith and United Methodist tradition through biblical and theological research, and for prophetic leadership. The General Board of Higher Education and Ministry provides leadership and support in this common mission and in the development of relationships among the schools of theology in the U.S.A. and the central conferences and the various agencies of the General Church.

2. All candidates for ordination as deacon or elder in The United Methodist Church are strongly encouraged to attend United Methodist schools of theology since these schools share with the General Board of Higher Education and Ministry and the conference Boards of Ordained Ministry in the work of preparing persons for ordination and leadership in The United Methodist Church.

3. *Schools of theology of The United Methodist Church located in the U.S.A.*—*a)* Schools of theology of The United Methodist Church located in the U.S.A. exist to serve The United Methodist Church, primarily in the United States, but with concern for the witness of the church around the world. In addition to their commitment to United Methodism, they also serve students of other denominations in witness to United Methodism's ecumenical relationships. As denominational schools, they have a historic relationship to the denomination and are officially related to The United Methodist Church through the Board of Higher Education and Ministry and the approval of the University Senate. The following schools comprise this network of United Methodist schools of theology in the U.S.A.: Boston University School

of Theology, Claremont School of Theology, Duke Divinity School, Candler School of Theology, the Theological School—Drew University, Gammon Theological Seminary (ITC), Garrett–Evangelical Theological Seminary, Iliff School of Theology, Methodist Theological School in Ohio, Perkins School of Theology, Saint Paul School of Theology, United Theological Seminary (Dayton, Ohio), and Wesley Theological Seminary. They are accountable to the church through the General Board of Higher Education and Ministry and the University Senate. Therefore, agencies of the church seeking to monitor the use of the schools will do so in cooperation with the General Board of Higher Education and Ministry, Division of Ordained Ministry.

*b)* These schools of theology shall receive financial support for the current operating expenses from the annual conferences in the USA through the Ministerial Education Fund, administered by the Division of Ordained Ministry, General Board of Higher Education and Ministry. (*See* ¶ 820.2.) The Ministerial Education Fund shall be regarded by the annual conferences in the USA as a priority to be met before any additional benevolence, grants, or funds are allocated to other theological schools or schools of religion.[35]

*c)* In fulfilling their task of preparing persons for effective service for Christ and the church, The United Methodist schools of theology located in the USA shall acquaint students with the current polity, theology and programs of The United Methodist Church and shall offer practical experience in administration, evangelism, stewardship, and other areas which will prepare them for effective Christian ministry in a multi-cultural society. Each school of theology, in consultation with the General Board of Higher Education and Ministry, Division of Ordained Ministry, shall provide the courses in United Methodist history, doctrine, and polity specified in ¶ 326.(3) and seek to form persons for ministry in the Wesleyan tradition.

*d)* Any institution seeking affiliation with The United Methodist Church for the preparation of candidates for ordination must first present its plan to the General Board of Higher Education and Ministry, Division of Ordained Ministry for approval and recommendation to the University Senate, which alone can grant affiliation and listing as a United Methodist school of theology. A select number of non-United Methodist schools of theology may be granted

---

35. *See* Judicial Council Decision 545.

approval for the preparation of candidates for ordination under the criteria of the University Senate.

4. *Schools of Theology of The United Methodist Church located in the Central Conferences—a)* In order to meet the needs for theological education and clergy training in their regions, the central conferences establish schools of theology to serve the United Methodists in their distinct cultural, social, and linguistic context. Schools of theology and programs of clergy training are also established by General Board of Global Ministries and the General Board of Higher Education and Ministry to serve the needs of the central conferences. These schools may be supported through the central conference and/or the General Board of Global Ministries and/or the General Board of Higher Education and Ministry and are accountable to the appropriate bodies for their program and their relationship to the denomination.

*b)* Additional schools of theology and pastoral training may be established by the central conference, General Conference, General Board of Higher Education and Ministry, or the General Board of Global Ministries and accountability depends on the founding documents of the institutions.

5. The United Methodist Church also shares in global theological education through ecumenical schools of theology where The United Methodist Church is a partner. Though not United Methodist–related, these institutions serve on behalf of United Methodists in those regions and may relate to the General Board of Global Ministries and/or General Board of Higher Education and Ministry, in accordance with their charter and mission.

¶ **1426.** *Education of Ordination Candidates*—The United Methodist schools of theology share with the conference boards of ordained ministry the responsibility for the education and formation of candidates for admission to the annual conferences.

## Section IX. General Board of Pension and Health Benefits

GENERAL ADMINISTRATION

¶ **1501.** *Establishment*—1. *a)* There shall be a **General Board of Pension and Health Benefits** of The United Methodist Church, hereinafter called the general board, having the general supervision and administration of the support, relief, and assistance and pensioning of clergy of this denomination, lay workers of the various units of the Church, and their families.

*b)* The general board shall be the successor to the General Board of Pensions of The United Methodist Church, the Board of Pensions of The Evangelical United Brethren Church, and the General Board of Pensions of The Methodist Church.

2. The general board shall have authority to establish, maintain, and discontinue the location of its headquarters office and such auxiliary offices as it shall deem proper and advisable.

3. The general board shall report to and be amenable to the General Conference. As a result of the work performed by the Connectional Process Team and the report prepared by the Connectional Process Team, the general Church may experience a period of transition. During any such transition in the general structure of the general Church and in order to discharge its fiduciary duties solely in the interest of participants and their beneficiaries and for the exclusive purpose of providing benefits to participants and their beneficiaries as required by ¶1504.14 of the *Discipline,* all matters related to the work of the General Board of Pension and Health Benefits shall be conducted in accordance with the provisions of *The Book of Discipline,* 1996, until the General Conference adopts specific provisions amending the provisions which exist in *The Book of Discipline,* 1996. The effective date of this subparagraph shall be the close of the 2000 General Conference.

¶ **1502.** 1. *Membership—a)* The membership of the general board shall be composed of two bishops, elected by the Council of Bishops; sixteen members elected by the jurisdictional conferences from the annual conference nominations on a ratio providing for an equitable distribution among the various jurisdictions, based on the combined clergy and laity membership thereof, as determined by the secretary of the General Conference, provided that no jurisdiction shall be represented by fewer than two such members; six members, with not more than two from the same jurisdiction, elected by the General Conference on nomination of the Council of Bishops; and eight additional members for the purpose of bringing to the general board special knowledge or background, not more than two from the same jurisdiction, nominated and elected by the general board in such manner as it shall provide in its bylaws.

*b)* The aforementioned electing bodies shall give consideration during the nominating process to equitable representation on the basis of race, color, age, gender, and people with disabilities.

*c)* The general secretary of the general board shall be an ex officio member thereof, without vote.

*d)* The terms of all members so elected shall be four years, to take effect at the first meeting of the general board following the General Conference, hereinafter referred to as the organizational meeting.

(1) Members shall serve during the terms for which they are elected and until their successors shall have been elected and qualified.

(2) Other paragraphs of the *Discipline* notwithstanding, members of the general board may serve a maximum of three consecutive terms.

(3) In case a vacancy occurs between regular sessions of the jurisdictional conferences for any cause, the general board shall fill the vacancy for the unexpired term from that jurisdiction in the representation of which the vacancy occurs, except in the case of members elected by the General Conference or the general board where such vacancies would be filled by the general board in the manner prescribed by its bylaws without regard to geographic or jurisdictional representation.

2. *Officers*—*a)* The general board shall elect from its membership at its organizational meeting a chairperson, a vice chairperson, and a recording secretary whose duties shall be prescribed in its bylaws.

*b)* The general board shall elect quadrennially at its organizational meeting a general secretary, who shall be the chief executive officer of the general board.

*c)* Other offices that are deemed desirable and in the best interest of the general board for carrying out its purposes may be created by the general board, and persons may be elected or appointed to fill such offices.

*d)* A vacancy in any of these offices shall be filled by the general board for the remainder of the unexpired term in a manner prescribed in its bylaws.

3. *Meetings*—The general board shall hold at least one meeting in each calendar year.

*a)* The place and time of all meetings shall be designated by the general board, but if it fails to do so, then the time and place shall be designated by the chairperson.

*b)* It shall convene at such other times on call of the chairperson, on written request by one-fifth of its members, or on written request by a majority of its executive committee.

*c)* A majority of the members of the general board shall constitute a quorum.

4. *Committees*—The general board shall establish the following committees:

*a) Executive Committee*—An executive committee shall be elected by the general board from its membership. During the periods between the meetings of the general board, its business and affairs shall be managed by the executive committee.

*b) Committee on Audit and Review*—A committee on audit and review shall be elected by the general board. At least one half of the members of this committee shall not be members of the general board. The committee on audit and review shall be responsible for reviewing the financial audits and related policies of the general board and its constituent legal entities.

*c) Committee on Appeals*—A committee on appeals shall be elected by the general board. The committee on appeals shall hear appeals from participants in the funds, plans, and programs administered by the general board. Decisions of the committee on appeals shall be final and not reviewed by the full general board.

*d) Other Committees*—The general board shall have the authority to establish, from time to time, such other standing committees or special committees as provided in its bylaws.

*e) Committee Membership*—The general board shall elect the membership of its standing committees in accordance with its bylaws. The membership of any special committees shall be selected in accordance with the resolution establishing such special committee.

*f) Committee Members at Large*—The general board shall have the authority to elect additional members to its committees, not to exceed a majority of the committee membership, for the purpose of bringing to those committees special knowledge or background. These committee members at large shall have full voice and vote on the committee, but they shall have voice, but not voting privileges, on the general board.

¶ **1503.** *Legal Entities*—1. Subject to the continuing control and direction of the General Conference of The United Methodist Church as set forth from time to time in the *Discipline,* the general board is authorized and empowered to cause the operations of the General

Board of Pension and Health Benefits to be carried on and the general authorizations defined in ¶ 1504 to be achieved in such manner, through or by means of such agencies or instrumentalities, and by use of such procedures as the general board may from time to time determine to be necessary, advisable, or appropriate, with full power and authority in the premises to take all such action and to do all such other acts and things as may be required or found to be advisable. In particular, and without limiting the generality of the foregoing, the general board is authorized and empowered, for the purposes of this paragraph:

*a)* To use, manage, operate, and otherwise utilize all property and assets of every kind, character, and description of any corporation(s) created by the general board pursuant to ¶ 1503.2 below, as well as all income from such property and assets and the avails thereof, all with liability or obligation to account for such property and assets, the use thereof, the income therefrom, and avails thereof only to the General Conference of The United Methodist Church.

*b)* To cause a corporation(s) created by the general board pursuant to ¶ 1503.2 to take all such action and to do all such things as the general board may deem necessary or advisable to carry out the intent and purposes of this paragraph. The governing body of said corporation(s) from time to time shall take all action that the general board deems necessary or advisable to carry out the intent and purpose of this paragraph, unless local law would require such governing bodies to make independent decisions with respect to particular actions.

2. The general board is authorized and empowered in its discretion at any time it may deem such action to be desirable or convenient to create corporations or other legal entities through which it shall fulfill its responsibilities described hereunder.

*a)* The general board is authorized and empowered in its discretion to cause its general administrative operations to be conducted through a corporation, the name of which shall be the General Board of Pension and Health Benefits of The United Methodist Church, Incorporated in Illinois.

*b)* The general board is authorized and empowered in its discretion to cause its general trust operations to be conducted through a corporation, the name of which shall be the General Board of Pension and Health Benefits of The United Methodist Church, Incorporated in Missouri.

*c)* The Board of Pensions of The Evangelical United Brethren Church, which is incorporated under the laws of the State of Ohio in that name, and the Board of Pensions of The Methodist Church, which is incorporated under the laws of the State of Illinois in that name, and the Board of Pensions of The Methodist Church, which is incorporated under the laws of the State of Maryland in that name, and the Board of Pensions of The Methodist Church, which is incorporated under the laws of the State of Missouri in that name, may be continued at the general board's discretion, subject to the direction, supervision, and control of the General Board of Pension and Health Benefits of The United Methodist Church, but with their corporate names changed to and to be known as the Board of Pensions of The United Methodist Church, Incorporated in Ohio, and the General Board of Pension and Health Benefits of The United Methodist Church, Incorporated in Illinois, and The Board of Pensions of The United Methodist Church, Incorporated in Maryland, and The General Board of Pension and Health Benefits of The United Methodist Church, Incorporated in Missouri, respectively, or other names as determined by the general board.

*d)* If the general board creates and directs more than one legal entity, it is authorized and empowered at its discretion at any time it may deem such action desirable or convenient to take action in the name of said legal entities to surrender the charter or charters of one or several or all of said legal entities or to merge, consolidate, or affiliate such corporations, or any of them, in compliance with appropriate state or federal laws.

*e)* The governing bodies of such legal entities shall be determined by the general board in conformance with applicable local law. A majority of the members of the governing bodies shall be elected from the membership of the general board.

*f)* The legal entities created under this paragraph are agencies or instrumentalities through which the denomination known as The United Methodist Church provides benefits, investment services, and other services outlined in ¶ 1504 below in the name of the General Board of Pension and Health Benefits.

**¶ 1504.** *Authorizations*—The General Board of Pension and Health Benefits is authorized and empowered to provide administrative, trust, and investment support to The United Methodist Church and its constituent boards, agencies, conferences, organizations, and other institutions in their efforts to provide support, relief, and assistance, and pension, welfare, and other benefits for clergy of this denomination, lay workers of the various units of the Church, and their families. Subject to the provisions of ¶ 2506 herein the general board shall perform its duties and responsibilities in the spirit of the Church's mandate for inclusiveness and racial and social justice. In particular, and without limiting the generality of the foregoing, the general board, directly or through any entity created by it, is authorized and empowered:

1. To operate, manage, and administer the mandatory benefit funds, plans, and programs established by the General Conference: (a) the Ministerial Pension Plan; (b) the Staff Retirement Benefits Program; and (c) the Comprehensive Protection Plan. The provisions of these mandatory benefit programs shall be incorporated by reference into the *Discipline* and shall have the full force of law as if printed in the *Discipline*. No proposal shall be made to the General Conference that changes a benefit presently in effect without first securing through the General Board of Pension and Health Benefits an actuarial opinion concerning the cost and other related aspects of the proposed change.

2. To create, amend, operate, manage, administer, and terminate nonmandatory relief, assistance, and benefit funds, plans, and programs for interested conferences, local churches, boards, agencies, institutions, and other affiliated units of The United Methodist Church.

3. To continue the operation, management, and administration of relief, assistance, and benefit funds, plans, and programs created prior to 1981, including but not limited to: the Lay Pension Plan; Joint Contributory Annuity Fund; Staff Pension Fund; the Pension Plan for Lay Employees; Lay Employees Pension Fund; Bishops Reserve Pension and Benefit Fund, in consultation with the General Council on Finance and Administration; the Chaplains Supplemental Pension Grant Fund, in consultation with the Division of Chaplains and Related Ministries; the Printing Establishment of the United Brethren in Christ Fund; and the Retirement Allowance for Bishops, General Church Officers, and Staff Personnel Plan of the former Evangelical United Brethren Church, with funds to be provided by the General Council on Finance and Administration.

4. To make reports to the General Conference with respect to the support, relief, assistance, and pension, welfare, and other benefits for clergy of this denomination, lay workers of the various units of the Church, and their families.

5. To adopt rules, regulations, and policies for the administration of the relief, assistance, and benefit funds, plans, and programs that the general board administers, in all matters not specifically covered by General Conference legislation or by reasonable implication, and to prescribe such forms and records as are needed for the administration of such funds, plans, and programs.

6. To prepare and publish benefit summaries, manuals, and other publications or media related to the funds, plans, and programs administered by the general board.

7. To compile and maintain complete service records of clergy members in full connection, associate members, and probationary members, and of local pastors whose service may be related to potential annuity claims of the annual conferences of The United Methodist Church situated within the boundaries of the United States and Puerto Rico. Such service records shall be based on answers to the Business of the Annual Conference questions as published in the journals of the annual conferences situated within the boundaries of the United States and Puerto Rico and in the General Minutes of The United Methodist Church, or in comparable publications of either or both of the uniting churches, and from information provided by annual conference boards of pensions. The conference boards of pensions shall be responsible for providing census data when requested by the general board on participants and their families, including but not limited to such data as birth dates, marriage dates, divorce dates, and dates of death.

8. To administer a clearinghouse for the allocation of pension responsibility among the annual conferences situated within the boundaries of the United States and Puerto Rico, in accordance with the principle of divided annuity responsibility, and for the collection and distribution of pension funds related to such responsibility.

*a)* For each beneficiary involved in the operation of the clearinghouse, the general board shall determine the division of responsibility on account of approved service rendered.

*b)* The general board shall have authority to determine the pension responsibility of each annual conference, in accordance with the principle of divided annuity responsibility, and to collect from each annual conference, as determined on the basis of their respective pension programs, the amount required by the clearinghouse to provide the pension benefits related thereto. Each annual conference shall provide funds to meet its annuity responsibility to beneficiaries of other annual conferences on the same basis as it provides pension payments for beneficiaries related directly to itself.

*c)* The general board is authorized and empowered to make all the rules concerning details that may be necessary for the operation of the clearinghouse.

9. On request of an annual conference or conference organization or agency of The United Methodist Church, to receive therefrom distributable and reserve pension funds and to make the periodic pension payments to the beneficiaries of such annual conference, conference organization, board, or agency, in accordance with a schedule of distribution, which shall be provided for the guidance of the general board in making such payments. The general board shall report annually the details of transactions under this provision. The general board shall be entitled to recover the cost of performing such services.

10. To administer the Chartered Fund for the benefit of all the annual and provisional annual conferences in The United Methodist Church, the boundaries of which are within the United States, its territorial and insular possessions, and Cuba, unless the General Conference shall order otherwise. Once a year the net earnings of the fund, after provision for depreciation, shall be divided equally among such annual and provisional annual conferences in accordance with the restrictive rule contained in ¶ 20.

11. To order and direct that the income from the General Endowment Fund for Conference Claimants (formerly known as the General Endowment Fund for Superannuates of The Methodist Episcopal Church, South) held by the General Board of Pension and Health Benefits of The United Methodist Church, Incorporated in Missouri, shall be distributed on account of service of conference claimants rendered in an annual conference of The United Methodist Church; provided, however, that such distribution shall be restricted to annual conferences that, directly or through their predecessor annual conferences, participated in raising this fund, in proportion to the number of approved years of annuity responsibility of each annual conference as shall be determined by the General Board of Pension and Health Benefits.

12. To distribute on the basis it determines the appropriations from the net earnings of the publishing interests that are contributed to the pension programs of The United Methodist Church and of the several annual conferences.

13. To create such legal entities in order to obtain, accept, receive, manage, and administer any and all assets or property, absolute or in trust, for the purpose of providing for, aiding in, and contributing to the support, relief, assistance, and pension, welfare, and other benefits for clergy of this denomination, lay workers of the various units of the Church, and their families and for other purposes stated in the trust instrument.

14. To discharge its fiduciary duties with respect to a benefit fund, plan, or program solely in the interest of the participants and beneficiaries and for the exclusive purpose of providing benefits to participants and their beneficiaries and defraying reasonable expenses of administering the plan, with the care, skill, prudence, and diligence under the circumstances then prevailing that a prudent person acting in a like capacity and familiar with such matters would use in the conduct of an enterprise of a like character and with like aims.

15. To receive, hold, manage, merge, consolidate, administer, invest, and reinvest all connectional relief, support, and benefit funds. The general board is encouraged to invest in institutions, companies, corporations, or funds that make a positive contribution toward the realization of the goals outlined in the Social Principles of the Church, subject to other provisions of the *Discipline,* and with due regard to any and all special contracts, agreements, and laws applicable thereto. Among the tools the general board may use are shareholder advocacy, selective divestment, and advocacy of corporate disinvestment from certain countries or fields of business.[36]

16. To receive, hold, manage, administer, and invest and reinvest, by and through its constituent corporations, endowment funds or other funds of an annual conference, local church, board, agency, or other unit affiliated with The United Methodist Church that have been designated for the funding of relief, support, or benefit funds, plans, or programs, and endowment funds or other funds of such units not so designated. The general board is encouraged to invest in institutions, companies, corporations, or funds that make a positive contribution toward the realization of the goals outlined in the Social Principles of the Church; *provided,* however, that at no time shall any part of the principal of the endowment funds be appropriated by the general board for any other purpose. The general board shall annually provide to such units an accounting of such funds.

---

36. *See* Judicial Council Decision 720.

17. To receive any gift, devise, or bequest made or intended for beneficiaries of The United Methodist Church, being the legal successor to and vested with the legal title to any and all such gifts, devises, and bequests. If the language or terms of any gift, devise, or bequest are inexact or ambiguous, the general board shall dispose of or administer the same in the manner deemed most equitable according to the apparent intent of the donor as determined by the general board after careful inquiry into the circumstances in connection with the making of such gift, devise, or bequest, and after granting full opportunity to all interested parties to be heard, after due and timely written notice of the time and place of hearing. Such notice shall be mailed to each and all interested parties through their respectively known representatives, at their last known addresses.

18. To collect, receive, and administer such gifts, devises, and bequests, and other funds as may be specifically designated to any constituent corporation of the general board by donors, subject to the rules, regulations, and policies of the general board with respect thereto. All undesignated gifts, devises, bequests, and donations shall be collected, received, and administered under the direction of the general board.

19. To charge the various trusts, funds, plans, and programs for which it is responsible an administrative fee for its general services and to charge reasonable and appropriate transactional fees for specific services provided to a unit of the Church or to a participant or beneficiary. The general board shall not use for operational or administrative purposes moneys allocated from any of the general Church funds of The United Methodist Church.

20. To cause its operations to be carried on and the objectives defined above to be achieved in such manner by use of such procedures as the general board may from time to time determine to be necessary, advisable, or appropriate, with full power and authority in the premises to take all such action and to do all such other acts and things as may be required or found to be advisable.

¶ 1505. *General Agency Pension Credit*—Pension for service approved for pension credit by an agency of The United Methodist Church receiving financial support from the general Church funds shall be provided by the employing agency in uniformity with that provided by other agencies under one of the pension funds, plans, or programs administered by the General Board of Pension and Health Benefits of The United Methodist Church; *provided*, however, that where service has been rendered in two or more agencies, the total pension benefit shall be calculated as if all such service had been with one agency, and the final agency shall provide any additional pension benefits necessary to accomplish this; furthermore, such agency may not make any arrangement with a life insurance company or any other entity for the purchase of annuities for the benefit of individual effective or retired employees or take any steps to nullify, in whole or in part, the pension plans or program of The United Methodist Church by making contracts with outside parties.

ANNUAL CONFERENCE ADMINISTRATION

¶ **1506.** *Powers, Duties, and Responsibilities of Annual Conferences—* 1. The annual conference, on recommendation of the conference Board of Pensions, shall determine the admissibility and validity of service approved, or compensation entering the contribution base, for pension credit and the payments, disallowances, and deductions thereunder, subject to the provisions of the *Discipline* and the rules and regulations of the pension and benefit funds, plans, and programs of The United Methodist Church.[37]

2. *a)* Service rendered prior to January 1, 1982, by a clergyperson in The United Methodist Church, including service rendered in either or both of the uniting churches prior to Church union, shall be approved for pension credit in accordance with provisions of the *Discipline* in effect and applicable thereto, or as subsequently amended, at the time such service was rendered. Pension for such service shall be provided in accordance with the past service provisions of the Ministerial Pension Plan.

*b)* Pension for full-time service rendered by a clergyperson in The United Methodist Church prior to January 1, 1982, shall be not less than an amount based upon pension credit for service prior to January 1, 1982, and the benefit levels in effect on December 31, 1981; *provided,* however, that the pension of a clergyperson whose membership was terminated prior to January 1, 1982, shall be determined in accordance with the provisions of the *Discipline,* pension funds, plans, and programs in effect at the time of such termination.

*c)* Pensions earned by bishops (elected by a jurisdictional conference) and other clergy, and protection benefits for such bishops

---

37. *See* Judicial Council Decisions 81, 360, 379.

and other clergy in The United Methodist Church after December 31, 1981, shall be provided in accordance with the provisions of the Ministerial Pension Plan and the Comprehensive Protection Plan.[38]

3. For service rendered prior to January 1, 1982, the following years of approved service in an annual conference of The United Methodist Church shall be counted for pension credit subject to the conditions stated in this paragraph:

*a)* By a clergyperson who is a probationary member or who is in the effective relation as an associate member or a member in full connection in the annual conference: (1) as pastor, associate or assistant pastor, or other clergyperson in a pastoral charge; (2) as district superintendent, presiding elder, conference president, conference superintendent, or other full-time salaried official of the conference; (3) under appointment beyond the local church to an institution, organization, or agency that in the judgment of the annual conference rendered to it some form of service, direct or indirect, sufficient to warrant pension credit, or to a community church, or as a conference-approved evangelist; *provided,* however, that such institution, organization, agency, community church, or evangelist accepts and pays such apportionments as the conference may require, with the recommendation that this apportionment shall be not less than twelve times the annuity rate of the conference; and *provided* further, that pension related to such service may be arranged through one of the pension funds or plans administered by the General Board of Pension and Health Benefits; (4) as a student appointed to attend school, but only if the clergyperson serves subsequently with pension credit in an annual conference or conferences for three or more years under appointment other than to attend school, such credit as a student not to exceed three years; *provided,* however, that all years for which pension credit was given under legislation in effect prior to the 1972 General Conference, on account of appointment to attend school, shall be counted in determining the pension claim thereon; and *provided* further, that if a clergyperson is again appointed to attend school after having served under appointment for six consecutive years as a clergy member in full connection with pension credit in an annual conference or conferences other than under appointment to attend school, pension credit shall be given for up to but not more than three additional years under appointment to attend school if the clergy-

---

38. *See* Judicial Council Decision 502.

person serves subsequently with pension credit in an annual conference or conferences for three or more additional years under appointment other than to attend school; (5) as a clergyperson on sabbatical leave, *provided* that not less than five of the ten years just preceding the granting of such leave were served with pension credit in the annual conference that grants the sabbatical leave; and (6) as a clergyperson on disability leave subsequent to the 1968 Uniting Conference, not to exceed fifteen years.[39]

*b)* By a person classified by the board of ordained ministry as eligible to be appointed as a full-time local pastor, and by an approved supply pastor prior to Church union in 1968, as a pastor or assistant pastor of a pastoral charge in full-time service under appointment; *provided,* however, that such credit shall be conditional and subject to provisions hereinafter stated in this paragraph.[40]

*c)* By an ordained minister from another Christian denomination who has not attained the age of mandatory retirement for a conference clergy member, who has not retired from the denomination, and who is approved by the annual conference on recommendation of the board of ordained ministry as provided in ¶ 337.2 who renders full-time service under appointment as a pastor or assistant pastor subject to provisions hereinafter stated in this paragraph.

*d)* In calculating fractions of years of service for pension credit earned prior to January 1, 1982, the following formula shall be used:

(1) Any period of up to and including forty-five days shall not be counted.

(2) Forty-six days up to and including 136 days shall be counted as one quarter of a year.

(3) One hundred thirty-seven days up to and including 228 days shall be counted as one half of a year.

(4) Two hundred twenty-nine days up to and including 319 days shall be counted as three quarters of a year.

(5) Three hundred twenty days up to and including 365 days shall be counted as one year.

4. Concerning the normal conditions for pension credit and pro rata pension credit, the following provisions shall apply for service rendered prior to January 1, 1982, in determining approval for pension credit, eligibility for pension, and allocation of responsibility:

---

39. *See* Judicial Council Decision 180.
40. *See* Judicial Council Decisions 73, 206.

*a) Normal Conditions*—The normal conditions required of a clergyperson for full pension credit shall be:

(1) That full-time service is rendered by a person appointed to a field of labor under provisions of ¶ 329.1;

(2) That this person not be attending school as a regular student except as provided in ¶ 1506.3*a*(4);

(3) That this person not be on leave of absence;

(4) That this person not be substantially employed in work other than that to which he or she is appointed by the bishop; and

(5) That this person receive not less cash support per annum from all Church and/or conference-related sources than that provided in the schedule of equitable salaries adopted by the annual conference for those in this person's classification.

*b) Proportional Pension Credit*—Effective as of the closing day of the 1980 annual conference session, pro rata pension credit may be granted to persons appointed to less than full-time service under the provisions of ¶ 329.2 by a three-fourths vote of those present and voting in the annual conference session on recommendation of the conference board of pensions. Such pension credit shall be in one-quarter year increments; *provided,* however, that no one individual receives in excess of one year of pension credit per annum.

*c) Full Pension Credit*—Full pension credit may be granted for persons not meeting some or all of the above conditions by a three-fourths vote of those present and voting in the annual conference on recommendation of the conference board of pensions.[41]

*d)* Service as a chaplain on full-time duty prior to January 1, 1947, which previous legislation includes as eligible to be counted in determining the annuity claim on an annual conference, shall be so recognized.

*e)* Pension responsibility on account of the appointment of a clergy member of an annual conference to attend school prior to 1982 shall be allocated to the conference or conferences in which the clergy member shall first thereafter render six years of service under appointment to a local church, to conference staff, as a district superintendent, or to an appointment beyond the local church normally considered to be eligible for pension by the annual conference. This allocation procedure shall continue through December 31, 1987, at which time any unallocated years shall be assigned on a pro rata

---

41. *See* Judicial Council Decision 386.

basis to the conference or conferences in which service under appointment to a local church, to conference staff, as a district superintendent, or to an appointment beyond the local church normally considered to be eligible for pension coverage by the annual conference totaled less than six years; *provided,* however, that such allocation shall not apply in cases where pension payments were in effect prior to January 1, 1985, on the basis of the allocation of responsibility under previous legislation.

*f)* Service of a local pastor prior to 1982 may be approved for pension credit only by vote of the annual conference, on recommendation of the conference board of pensions, after consultation with the district superintendents. If such credit is granted, it should be included under the *Discipline* question, "What other personal notation should be made?"

*g)* Upon recommendation of the conference board of pensions and by a three-fourths vote of those present and voting in the annual conference, pension credit may be granted to a clergy member in full connection, probationary member, or associate member of the conference on account of full-time service previously rendered as an approved local pastor or approved supply pastor to an institution, organization, or agency, which in the judgment of the annual conference rendered to it some form of service sufficient to warrant pension credit; *provided,* however, that such institution, organization, or agency shall accept and pay such apportionment as the conference may require.

*h)* On recommendation of the conference board of pensions and approval by the annual conference, appointments beyond the local church shall be listed in the conference journal as follows: (1) with pension responsibilities on the annual conference, or (2) with pension responsibility on the institution or agency served. If at any session the conference fails to make such listing, it may be done subsequently, whenever desirable, under the Business of the Annual Conference question, "What other personal notation should be made?"[42]

*i)* In the event of retirement under ¶ 355.2b, the pension or subsequent pension resulting from annuity rate increases for service rendered prior to January 1, 1982, shall be determined by reducing the

---

42. *See* Judicial Council Decision 95.

pension (years times rate) by the lesser of: (1) one-half percent per month or fraction of a month of age less than sixty-five years attained on the date the actuarially reduced pension is to commence (or the date of such annuity rate increase), or (2) one-half percent per month for each month of difference between the assumed date at which forty years of service under appointment would have been completed and the actual date the actuarially reduced pension or annuity rate increase is to commence under ¶ 356.2b. Effective at the close of the 1988 General Conference, if retirement is granted in accordance with ¶ 356.2e, the actuarially reduced pension shall be calculated from the deferred retirement date. Such actuarially reduced pension shall be calculated by the General Board of Pension and Health Benefits and allocated pro rata to the annual conference or conferences that are charged with the pension responsibility.[43]

5. *a)* A pension shall be payable on account of pension credit for service prior to 1982 as a full-time local pastor or supply pastor if: (1) the local pastor shall have been admitted as an associate or probationary member or member in full connection in an annual conference and has subsequently been placed in the retired relation by the conference, or (2) the local pastor shall have rendered no less than four consecutive years of full-time service with pension credit for service prior to 1982 or with full participation in the Comprehensive Protection Plan since 1981, or a combination thereof, in one annual conference.

*b)* On recommendation of the conference board of pensions, a pension shall be payable on account of pension credit for service prior to 1982 for an ordained minister from another Christian denomination who shall have rendered not less than four consecutive years of full-time service with pension credit for service prior to 1982 or with full participation in the Comprehensive Protection Plan since 1981, or a combination thereof, in one annual conference while qualified under ¶ 337.2, who has attained the age of voluntary retirement for a conference clergy member. (*See also* § 3c above.)

6. The annual conference, on recommendation of the conference board of pensions, shall have the power to revise, correct, or adjust a clergyperson's record of pension credit as set forth in his or her service record. Prior to the revision of such record, the General Board of Pension and Health Benefits may be requested to review relevant

---

43. *See* Judicial Council Decision 428.

data and report its findings thereon. Such revisions, corrections, and adjustments shall be published in the journal of the annual conference in answer to Business of the Annual Conference questions and shall be reported to the General Board of Pension and Health Benefits by the conference board of pensions.[44]

7. The annual conference shall review annually the annuity rate for service rendered in the annual conference prior to January 1, 1982, for the purpose of adjusting the rate as appropriate, taking into account changes in economic conditions. Such annuity rate may remain the same or be increased without restriction. It is recommended that such rate be not less than 1 percent of the average compensation of the conference as computed by the General Board of Pension and Health Benefits. However, for plan years beginning after December 31, 1998, in no case may the annuity rate be less than eight-tenths of one percent of the average compensation of the conference. The annuity rate for approved service of local pastors shall also be determined by the conference each year and shall be the same as the rate for service of clergy members in full connection, probationary members, and associate members. A successor conference resulting from a merger involving a former Central Jurisdictional conference shall establish for all for whom it has pension responsibility the same rate for past service of clergy members in full connection, probationary members, and associate members in the Central Jurisdiction as for service in a geographic former Methodist jurisdiction and the same rate for past service of local pastors regardless of the jurisdiction in which the service was rendered.[45]

8. On or before July 15, 2002, each annual conference shall develop, adopt and implement a formal funding plan for retiring its pre–1982 pension obligations. This funding plan must result in the retirement of its pre–1982 pension obligations on or before December 31, 2021. The funding plan shall identify any funds which have been designated by the annual conference and protected for the exclusive purpose of retiring its pre–1982 pension obligations. The funding plan shall: (a) address the funding for both the existing and incremental liabilities incurred by future increases in the past service rate, (b) be approved annually by the annual conference, following the receipt and inclusion of a written opinion from the General Board of

---

44. *See* Judicial Council Decision 386.
45. *See* Judicial Council Decisions 360, 389.

Pension and Health Benefits, and *(c)* be published along with the written opinion of the General Board of Pension and Health Benefits in the journal of the annual conference. In addition, the General Board of Pension and Health Benefits shall present a report to General Conference 2004 concerning the retiree medical issues of the denomination. In order to prepare this report, each annual conference shall provide to the General Board of Pension and Health Benefits information requested by the General Board of Pension and Health Benefits concerning the retiree medical obligations of the particular annual conference.

9. Persons who have served full-time appointments beyond the local church under endorsement by the Division of Chaplains and Related Ministries are eligible for pension support for those years of service so served for which no other pension is provided. Such pension support shall be in accordance with the Chaplains Supplemental Pension Grant Fund or the Ministerial Pension Plan under arrangements agreed to by the General Board of Higher Education and Ministry through its Division on Chaplains and Related Ministries and the General Board of Pension and Health Benefits.

10. The responsibility for pension for service approved for pension credit shall rest with the annual conference in which the service was rendered; *provided,* however, that in the event of mergers, unions, boundary changes, or transfers of churches, such responsibility shall rest with the successor annual conference within whose geographical boundaries the charge is located.[46]

11. Pension for service approved for pension credit by an annual conference shall be provided by the annual conference under one of the pension funds, plans, or programs administered by the General Board of Pension and Health Benefits of The United Methodist Church.

12. An annual conference may not make any arrangement with a life insurance company for the purchase of annuities for the benefit of individual effective or retired clergy or take any steps to nullify, in whole or in part, the pension plans and programs of The United Methodist Church by making contracts with outside parties.[47]

---

46. *See* Judicial Council Decisions 203, 389, 523.
47. *See* Judicial Council Decision 716.

13. *Other Annual Conference Organizations—a)* Annual conferences, hereinafter called conferences, are authorized to establish, incorporate, and maintain investment funds, preachers' aid societies, and organizations and funds of similar character, under such names, plans, rules, and regulations as they may determine, the directors of which shall be elected or otherwise designated by the conference, where permissible under the laws of the state of incorporation, and the income from which shall be applied to the support of the pension program through the conference board of pensions.[48]

*b)* Distributable pension funds from all sources shall be disbursed by or under the direction of the conference board of pensions, excepting only such funds as are otherwise restricted by specific provisions or limitations in gifts, devises, bequests, trusts, pledges, deeds, or other similar instruments, which restrictions and limitations shall be observed.

*c)* It shall not be permissible for any conference or permanent fund organization thereof to deprive its beneficiaries who are beneficiaries in other conferences of the privilege of sharing in the distribution of the earned income of such funds through the clearinghouse administered by the General Board of Pension and Health Benefits.

*d)* (1) Prior to January 1, 1982, a conference subject to the laws of the state in which it is incorporated shall have power to require from its clergy who are serving with pension credit from the conference an annual contribution to either its permanent or reserve fund or for current distribution or to a preachers aid society for the benefit of its beneficiaries, subject to the following provisions:[49]

*(a)* The annual payment may be made in installments as provided by the conference.

*(b)* The making of such payment shall not be used as the ground of contractual obligations upon the part of the conference or as the ground of any special or additional annuity claim of a clergyperson against the conference; neither shall it prevent disallowance of a clergyperson's annuity claim by conference action.

*(c)* The conference may fix a financial penalty for failure of the clergyperson to pay.

*(d)* In case membership in the conference is terminated under the provisions of the *Discipline,* the conference may refund the

---

48. *See* Judicial Council Decision 218.
49. *See* Judicial Council Decision 181.

amount so paid, in whole or in part, after hearing has been given to the clergyperson, in case such hearing is requested.

(e) Clergy entering a conference shall not be charged an initial entry fee by any organization mentioned in § a above; furthermore, the annual contribution required from a clergyperson shall not exceed an amount equal to 3 percent of the clergyperson's support.

(2) If a clergyperson is participating in one of the pension funds, plans, or programs administered by the General Board of Pension and Health Benefits, that individual shall not be required by the conference or by an organization thereof related to the support of beneficiaries to make any other contribution for pension purposes.

e) Each conference, on recommendation of its conference board of pensions or one of the organizations mentioned in § a above, may select a Sunday in each year to be observed in the churches as Retired Ministers Day, in honor of the retired clergy, their spouses, and the surviving spouses of clergy in recognition of the Church's responsibility for their support. The bishop may request each conference in the area to insert a Retired Ministers Day in its calendar.

14. A conference board of pensions may make special grants to clergy or former clergy of an annual conference who have served under appointment in that conference; or to their spouses, former spouses, surviving former spouses, or surviving dependent children (including adult dependent children). A report of such special grants shall be made annually to the annual conference.

15. a) A former clergy member in full connection, probationary member, or associate member of an annual conference whose membership was terminated on or after January 1, 1973, and prior to January 1, 1982, after the completion of ten or more years of service with pension credit in an annual conference or conferences, shall retain the right to receive a pension beginning the first of any month following the date the former clergyperson attains age sixty-two, based on the years of service approved for pension credit.[50] Such former clergyperson's pension shall be based on all years of service with pension credit if the former clergyperson had twenty or more such years. If less than twenty such years but at least ten years, the years used in the calculation of the benefit shall be a percentage of the approved service years; such percentage shall be determined by multiplying the credited whole years by 5 percent, resulting in 50 percent of such

---

50. *See* Judicial Council Decision 717.

years for ten years of credited service and 100 percent for twenty years of such service. If pension begins prior to the age at which retirement under ¶ 356.2c could have occurred, then the provisions of ¶ 1506.4i shall apply.

*b)* A former clergy member in full connection, probationary member, or associate member of an annual conference whose membership was terminated on or after January 1, 1982, after the completion of ten or more years of service under appointment in an annual conference or conferences, shall retain the right to receive a pension beginning the first day of any month coinciding with or following the date the former clergyperson attains age sixty-two, based on the years of service prior to January 1, 1982, approved for pension credit.[51] If pension begins prior to the age at which retirement under ¶ 356.2c could have occurred, then the provisions of ¶ 1506.4i shall apply.

*c)* Effective at the close of the 1976 General Conference, former clergy members in full connection, probationary members, and associate members of the annual conference whose membership was terminated on or after such date shall have any vested pension benefits calculated at the annuity rate in effect on the date such person's membership is terminated.

*d)* Clergy members in full connection, probationary members, and associate members in an annual conference who voluntarily withdraw from the ministry of The United Methodist Church to enter the ministry of another church or denomination, on the attainment of age sixty-two and on recommendation of the conference board of pensions and a three-fourths vote of those present and voting in any annual conference in which approved service was rendered prior to January 1, 1982, or the legal successor, may be recognized and granted pensions on account of approved service rendered in that conference. If pension begins prior to the age at which retirement under ¶ 356.2c could have occurred, then the provisions of ¶ 1506.4i shall apply.

16. The responsibility for providing pension on account of service rendered prior to January 1, 1982, in a missionary conference, provisional annual conference, or former mission within the United States or Puerto Rico that has been approved for pension credit shall rest jointly with: *(a)* the missionary conference, provisional annual confer-

---

51. *See* Judicial Council Decision 717.

ence, or former mission concerned, *(b)* the General Board of Pension and Health Benefits with funds provided by the General Council on Finance and Administration, and *(c)* the General Board of Global Ministries. The revenue for pension purposes covering such service shall be provided by the aforesaid parties in accordance with such plan or plans as may be mutually agreed to by them.

17. *a)* A clergyperson who has been granted the retired relation in a central conference or an affiliated autonomous church shall be entitled to a pension from a conference or conferences in the United States or Puerto Rico for the years of approved service rendered therein upon attainment of the required age or the completion of the required years of approved service. Such clergyperson shall notify the General Board of Pension and Health Benefits upon his or her retirement. The General Board of Pension and Health Benefits shall certify the years of approved service to each annual conference concerned. Payments due thereunder shall be collected from the conference concerned and forwarded to the claimant by the General Board of Pension and Health Benefits in such manner as it may deem most expedient and economical.

*b)* In the event of the death of such clergyperson prior to the annuity starting date, the spouse shall be eligible for a benefit equal to 70 percent (75, 85, or 100 percent if elected by the applicable conference) of the clergyperson's formula benefit. If no spouse survives, the Service Annuity Accumulation will be paid in accordance with the provision of the Ministerial Pension Plan.

18. Pension and benefit contributions are the responsibility of the Plan Sponsor, if not remitted by the salary-paying unit of a participant in the Ministerial Pension Plan and the Comprehensive Protection Plan. Unless otherwise determined by vote of the annual, missionary, or provisional conference, the treasurer of a local church or pastoral charge shall remit such contributions to the General Board of Pension and Health Benefits related to the participant's compensation that is provided from local church funds. If compensation from the local church or pastoral charge is supplemented from other church sources, pension and benefit contributions related to such supplements shall be paid from that same source. If the entire compensation for a participant is from a salary-paying unit other than a local church or a pastoral charge, the unit responsible for compensation shall remit the pension and benefit contributions to the General Board of Pension and Health Benefits. Nothing in this paragraph shall be understood as preventing an annual, missionary, or provi-

sional conference from raising part or all of the annual contributions for the pension program of its pastors by an apportionment to the churches of the conference, remitting payments to the General Board of Pension and Health Benefits on behalf of all the pastors covered; there is no time limit on this provision.

19. Actual compensation, limited by the denominational average compensation, is the basic contribution base of the Ministerial Pension Plan. Other options setting the contribution base as actual compensation limited by 150 percent of the denominational average compensation, or actual compensation, may be elected by the annual conference or other participating groups as they may determine. Actual compensation, limited by 200 percent of the denominational average compensation, is the basic contribution base of the Comprehensive Protection Plan.

20. An annual conference may establish a pension support fund to be administered by the conference board of pensions. Local churches may request pension assistance from this fund when special circumstances arise that result in nonpayment of pension contributions and/or apportionments for pension and benefit purposes. The board shall present its estimate of the amount required to the conference council on finance and administration, which shall include it in its recommendation to the conference. If the amount is approved by the conference, it shall be apportioned as an item of clergy support.

21. The annual conference board of pensions, in consultation with the General Board of Pension and Health Benefits, shall have the responsibility to enroll clergy of the annual conference in the Ministerial Pension Plan and the Comprehensive Protection Plan in accordance with the provisions of such plans.

22. Optional provisions contained in the Ministerial Pension Plan and Comprehensive Protection Plan may be adopted by vote of the annual conference subsequent to the receipt of a recommendation from the conference board of pensions.

The recommended contribution rate for service rendered after December 31, 1985, for the Ministerial Pension Plan is 12 percent of the contribution base. However, for service rendered after December 31, 1985, the percentage of the contribution base that may be paid to fund the Ministerial Pension Plan in any one year will be limited to:

a) Twelve percent, if the then current annuity rate is at least nine-tenths of 1 percent of the conference average compensation, as computed by the General Board of Pension and Health Benefits.

*b)* For the period January 1, 1986, through December 31, 1989, not more than 11 percent, if the then current annuity rate is at least eight tenths of 1 percent, but less than nine-tenths of 1 percent of the conference average compensation as computed by the General Board of Pension and Health Benefits.

*c)* For the period January 1, 1986, through December 31, 1989, not more than 10 percent, if the then current annuity rate is less than eight-tenths of one percent of the conference average compensation as computed by the General Board of Pension and Health Benefits.

*d)* Effective January 1, 1990, 11 percent, if the then current annuity rate is less than nine-tenths of one percent of the conference average compensation as computed by the General Board of Pension and Health Benefits.

¶ **1507.** *Financing Pension and Benefit Programs*—The annual conference shall be responsible for annually providing moneys in the amount necessary to meet the requirements of the pension and benefit funds, plans, and programs of the conference.

1. The board shall compute the amount to be apportioned annually to meet the requirements of the pension and benefit programs of the conference.

2. After consultation with the board, the conference council on finance and administration shall report to the annual conference the amounts computed by the board that are required to meet the needs of the pension, benefit, and relief programs of the conference.

3. Distributable pension funds from all sources, unless restricted by specific provisions or limitations, shall be disbursed by, or under the direction of, the conference board of pensions.

4. The board may accumulate a fund from the income for pension purposes in order to stabilize the pension program of the conference.[52]

¶ **1508.** *Policies Related to Conflict of Interest and Investment Management*—The following rules shall apply to the financial administration of annual conference pension and pension-related funds:

1. A member of the board connected or interested in any way with the securities, real estate, or other forms of investment sold to or purchased from such funds, or with an insurance program or a contract under consideration by the board, shall be ineligible to participate in the deliberation of the investment committee or of the board or to vote in connection therewith.

---

52. *See* Judicial Council Decision 50.

2. No officer or member of a conference agency handling such funds shall receive a personal commission, bonus, or remuneration, direct or indirect, in connection with the purchase or sale of any property the loan of any money, the letting of any annuity or insurance contract, the making or acceptance of any assignment, pledge, or mortgage to secure the payment of any loan, or for the purchase or sale of any securities or other properties from or to that agency, or be eligible to obtain a loan in any amount from funds committed to the care of that agency. No investment shall be purchased from or sold to any member of the board or any member of the family of a member of the board.

3. To prevent development of any conflict of interest or preferential treatment and to preserve goodwill and confidence throughout the Church, no local church, Church-related institution, or organization thereof shall be eligible to obtain a loan in any amount from such funds.[53]

4. The principle of diversification of investments shall be observed, with the agency encouraged to invest in institutions, companies, corporations, or funds that make a positive contribution toward the realization of the goals outlined in the Social Principles of our Church, however with primary consideration given to the soundness and safety of such investments.

5. Real property may hereafter be accepted as consideration for gift annuity agreements only with the stipulation that the annuity shall not exceed the net income from the property until such property shall have been liquidated. Upon liquidation, the annuity shall be paid upon the net proceeds at the established annuity rate.

6. An annual conference agency handling such funds shall not offer higher rates of annuity than those listed in the annuity schedule approved by the General Board of Pension and Health Benefits.

7. a) There shall be printed in the annual conference journal a list of the investments held by each agency handling such funds directly or indirectly under the control of the annual conference, or such list may be distributed directly to the members of the annual conference at their request. A copy of all such lists of investments shall be filed annually with the General Board of Pension and Health Benefits.

b) The conference board of pensions shall require an annual audit of pension and pension-related funds setting forth the total asset value of such funds and the distribution of income from such

---

53. See Judicial Council Decision 145.

funds from persons and organizations appointed or employed for the management of these funds.

8. The borrowing of money in any conference year by a conference corporation or organization to enable the conference board of pensions to meet the requirements of the pension and benefit programs shall be done only on authority of the conference granted by three-fourths vote of the members present and voting.

9. *Depositories and Bonding*—*a)* The conference board of pensions shall designate a bank or banks or other depository or depositories for deposit of the funds held by the board and may require a depository bond from such depository or depositories.

*b)* The board, through the conference council on finance and administration, shall provide a fidelity bond in suitable amount for all persons handling its funds.

¶ **1509.** *Joint Distributing Committees*—1. *Authorizations*—Whenever two or more annual or provisional annual conferences are to be merged, in whole or in part, there shall be elected by each conference affected a distributing committee of three members and three alternates, which shall act jointly with similar committees from the other conference or conferences. The joint distributing committee thus formed shall have power and authority: *(a)* to allocate the pension responsibility involved; *(b)* to distribute equitably the permanent funds and all other pension assets of the conference or conferences affected, taking into consideration the pension responsibility involved, such distribution to be made within twelve months of the date of the dissolution of the committee as provided in ¶ 1509.3*d; (c)* to the extent not otherwise previously provided for by the conference or conferences involved, to apportion or distribute equitably any other assets or property and any other liabilities or obligations. It shall be governed by the legal restrictions or limitations of any contract, trust agreement, pledge, deed, will, or other legal instrument.

2. *Organization*—The committee shall be convened by the general secretary of the General Board of Pension and Health Benefits, or by some other officer of that board designated by the general secretary in writing, and shall elect from its membership a chairperson, a vice chairperson, and a secretary.

3. *Powers, Duties, and Responsibilities*—*a)* The committee shall determine the number of years of service approved for pension credit rendered in the conferences that will lose their identity in the merging of conference territories, and the findings of the committee shall

be final unless substantial evidence to the contrary is presented, and the annuity payments by the continuing conference or conferences shall be made accordingly. The determination of pension benefits in The United Methodist Church shall recognize all pension rights to which clergy are entitled under the pension plans in existence at the time of Church union and shall recognize all approved service that has been rendered in The Evangelical United Brethren Church and The Methodist Church prior to the date of Church union.

*b)* The committee shall keep complete minutes of its transactions, and a copy thereof shall be filed with the secretary of each annual conference involved and with the General Board of Pension and Health Benefits.

*c)* Until the committee's work shall have been completed, the corporate organization of each conference in the process of merger shall be maintained. After the committee shall have completed its work, the officers of such corporation, subject to the completion of its business, shall dissolve or merge it, in accordance with applicable corporate laws, after being authorized to do so by the conference involved.

*d)* The committee, having completed its work in connection with the merger or mergers for which it was organized and having filed copies of its findings and actions with the secretaries of the conferences involved for publication in the respective conference journals, and with the General Board of Pension and Health Benefits, shall be dissolved; subject, however, to recall by the general secretary of the General Board of Pension and Health Benefits in the event of the discovery and presentation to the general board of data substantially at variance with those previously submitted, for the purpose of reviewing such data and possible revision of its previous actions.

4. Whenever a single annual conference or provisional annual conference is to be divided into two or more conferences, the provisions of ¶ 1509 shall be applied; *provided* the distributing committee members of each resulting conference shall be named subsequent to the effective date of the division and no later than the first regular annual session of such conferences.

### Section X. The United Methodist Publishing House

¶ **1601.** *Authorization and Establishment*—The United Methodist Publishing House comprises the publishing interests of The United

Methodist Church. It shall have responsibility for and supervision of the publishing and distribution for The United Methodist Church. The United Methodist Publishing House shall, through agencies or instrumentalities it deems necessary, achieve the objectives set forth in ¶ 1613. The United Methodist Publishing House shall provide publishing and distribution services for other agencies of The United Methodist Church and shall share with other agencies of The United Methodist Church in the total program of The United Methodist Church, as well as share in the total ecumenical program in the area of publishing for the advancement of the cause of Christ and his Kingdom as The United Methodist Publishing House shall determine to be appropriate. All matters related to the work of The United Methodist Publishing House shall be under the direction of the Board of The United Methodist Publishing House in accordance with the provisions of the 1996 *Book of Discipline* and the Restrictive Rules (¶ 20, section III, article VI, of the Constitution) until and unless the General Conference takes specific action amending these provisions. The effective date of this subparagraph shall be the close of 2000 General Conference.

¶ **1602.** *Membership*—1. The board of The United Methodist Publishing House, hereinafter called the board, shall consist of up to forty-three members as follows:

*a) Episcopal members*—Two bishops selected by the Council of Bishops.

*b) Jurisdictional members*—Thirty members elected by the jurisdictional conferences based on the following formula: North Central—6, Northeastern—6, South Central—7, Southeastern—9, and Western—2; *provided* that no jurisdiction shall be represented by fewer than two members.

*c) Additional members*—Up to ten additional members may be elected by the board, with consideration given to representation of women and racial and ethnic groups not elected by the jurisdictions, and to special knowledge or background in publishing, marketing, graphic arts manufacturing, production of audiovisuals or electronic media, or other business fields. It is recommended that persons elected by each jurisdiction be inclusive of women and ethnic groups—Asian Americans, African Americans, Hispanic Americans, Native Americans, and Pacific Islanders.

*d) Central Conference Members*—One central conference member elected by the Council of Bishops.

*e)* At least two persons who are young adults at the time of election shall be elected each quadrennium.

*f)* Membership on the board shall be equally divided, as far as practicable, between ordained ministers and laypersons.

*g)* Other paragraphs of the *Discipline* notwithstanding, membership shall also be by classes based on term of office for one, two, or three quadrenniums, attention being given to the principle of rotation so that, as far as practicable, one third of the membership shall be elected each quadrennium.[54] The principle of rotation is also applicable to the executive committee.

*h)* In case a vacancy occurs between sessions of the jurisdictional conferences for any cause, the board shall fill the vacancy for the unexpired term from that jurisdiction in the representation of which the vacancy occurs, except in the case of members elected by the board where such vacancies would be filled by the board in the prescribed manner without regard to geographic or jurisdictional relationship.

*i)* The publisher of The United Methodist Church (¶ 1614) shall be an ex officio member of the board without vote.

¶ **1603.** *Annual Meeting*—The board shall hold at least one meeting in each calendar year. The place and time of all meetings shall be designated by the board, but if it fails to do so, then the time and place shall be designated by the chairperson. It shall convene at such other times on call of the chairperson or by the board or by the executive committee. At all meetings of the board, a majority of the members shall constitute a quorum.

¶ **1604.** *Record of Proceedings*—The board shall keep a correct record of its proceedings and make written report thereof to the Church through the General Conference.

¶ **1605.** *Tenure of Board Members and Officers*—The members of the board and all officers of the board elected by it shall hold office until their successors are chosen and the new board is duly organized.

¶ **1606.** *Executive Committee*—The board is authorized to perfect its organization from its membership, including the offices of chairperson, vice chairperson, and secretary. The board shall elect from its membership an executive committee of eleven members, including the chairperson, vice chairperson, and secretary of the board, who shall serve, respectively, as chairperson, vice chairperson, and secre-

---

54. *See* Judicial Council Decision 593.

tary of the committee. Special attention shall be given to representation of racial and ethnic groups and women. Not more than three members of the executive committee shall be from any one jurisdiction. The bishops serving on the board shall be ex officio members, and the publisher of The United Methodist Church (¶ 1614) shall be an ex officio member without vote. Any vacancy occurring in the membership of the executive committee shall be filled by it, subject to confirmation by the board at its next meeting.

¶ **1607.** *Powers and Duties of the Executive Committee*—The executive committee shall have and may exercise all the powers of the board except those expressly reserved by the board and/or by the *Discipline* for board action. It shall meet quarterly to examine the affairs under its charge and shall keep and submit to the board correct records of its proceedings. Special meetings may be called by the chairperson on his or her own initiative and shall be called on the written request of four members of the executive committee. A majority of the members shall constitute a quorum.

¶ **1608.** *Successor in Interest*—The board shall be the successor in interest to and carry on the work of the Board of Publication of The Evangelical United Brethren Church and the General Board of Publication of The Methodist Church.

¶ **1609.** *Powers and Duties of the Board*—1. The board is empowered and authorized in its discretion to carry out its general operations under the name of The United Methodist Publishing House.

2. The board is authorized and empowered in its discretion at any time it may deem such action to be desirable or convenient to create an additional corporation(s), in compliance with appropriate state corporation laws.

3. If the board creates and directs more than one corporate entity, it is authorized and empowered in its discretion at any time it may deem such action desirable or convenient to take corporate action in the name of said corporations to surrender the charter or charters of one or several or all of said corporations or to merge, consolidate, or affiliate such corporations, or any of them, in compliance with appropriate state laws.

¶ **1610.** *Board Members as Trustees*—The members of the board shall serve and act as directors or trustees of the corporation(s) named in ¶ 1609.

¶ **1611.** *Agency Status*—The corporation(s) named in ¶ 1609 is an agency or instrumentality through which The United Methodist Church conducts its publishing, printing, and distribution in the

name of The United Methodist Publishing House in accordance with
the objectives set forth in ¶ 1613. The corporation(s) shall comply
with the policies set forth in ¶ 715.

¶ **1612.** *Report to General Conference*—The board shall examine carefully the affairs of The United Methodist Publishing House and make
written report thereof to the Church through the General Conference.

¶ **1613.** *Objectives*—The objectives of The United Methodist Publishing House shall be: the advancement of the cause of Christianity
throughout the world by disseminating religious knowledge and useful literary, scientific, and educational information in the form of
books, tracts, multimedia, electronic media, and periodicals; the promotion of Christian education; the implementation of any and all
activities properly connected with the publishing, manufacturing in a
variety of media, and distribution of books, tracts, periodicals, materials, and supplies for churches and church schools, including the
ecumenical outreach of Christianity, and such other activities as the
General Conference may direct.

¶ **1614.** *Direction and Control*—The United Methodist Publishing
House shall be under the direction and control of the board, acting
through an executive officer elected quadrennially by the board, who
shall be the publisher of The United Methodist Church, and such
other officers as the board may determine.

¶ **1615.** *Appropriation of Net Income*—The net income from the operations of The United Methodist Publishing House, after providing
adequate reserves for its efficient operation and allowing for reasonable growth and expansion, shall be appropriated by the board and
distributed annually on the basis of a just plan provided by the General Board of Pension and Health Benefits to the several annual conferences for the persons who are and shall be conference claimants.
The just plan may encompass disproportionate allocations to annual
conferences where there is a desperate need relative to other annual
conferences, as, for example, in underdeveloped nations relative to
developed nations.

¶ **1616.** *Designation of Net Income*—The net income from the operations of The United Methodist Publishing House shall be appropriated to no other purpose than its own operating requirements and for
persons who are or shall be conference claimants as provided in ¶ 20
and ¶ 1615.[55]

---

55. *See* Judicial Council Decisions 322, 330.

¶ **1617.** *Board Members as Successors*—The members of the board and their successors in office are declared to be the successors of the incorporators named in the charters of The Methodist Book Concern issued by the States of New York and Ohio and in the charter of the Board of Publication of the Methodist Protestant Church issued by the State of Pennsylvania. The executive officer of the board, elected from time to time under this or any subsequent *Discipline,* is declared to be the successor in office of the Book Agents of The Methodist Episcopal Church, South, named in the charter issued to the corporation of that name by the State of Tennessee.

¶ **1618.** *Powers and Duties of the Board*—Subject to the provisions of ¶ 1614 and to the continuing control and direction of the General Conference of The United Methodist Church as set forth from time to time in the *Discipline,* the board is authorized and empowered to cause the operations of The United Methodist Publishing House to be carried on and the objectives defined in ¶ 1613 to be achieved in such manner, through or by means of such agencies or instrumentalities and by use of such procedures as the board may from time to time determine to be necessary, advisable, or appropriate, with full power and authority in the premises to take all such action and to do all such other acts and things as may be required or found to be advisable. In particular, and without limiting the generality of the foregoing, the board is authorized and empowered, for the purposes of this section:

1. To use, manage, operate, and otherwise utilize all property and assets of every kind, character, and description of any corporation(s) created by the board pursuant to ¶ 1609.2, as well as all income from such property and assets and the avails thereof, all with liability or obligation to account for such property and assets, the use thereof, the income therefrom, and avails thereof, only to the General Conference of The United Methodist Church or as it shall direct.

2. To cause a corporation(s) created by the board pursuant to ¶ 1609.2 to take all such action and to do all such things as the board may deem necessary or advisable to carry out the intent and purposes of this paragraph. The governing body of said corporation(s) from time to time shall take all action that the board deems necessary or advisable to carry out the intent and purposes of this paragraph. The board shall cause all legal obligations of said corporation(s) to be met, fulfilled, and performed.

3. To continue to exercise the powers and administer the duties and responsibilities conferred on it as an agency of The United

Methodist Church through the corporation named The United Methodist Publishing House, incorporated under the laws of the State of Illinois in accord with authority delegated to it by the General Conference of 1952, or through such other means and agencies as it may from time to time determine to be expedient and necessary in order to give full effect to the purposes expressed in this section.[56]

¶ **1619.** *Ownership and Control of Assets*—1. The property, assets, and income of the Illinois corporation shall be held by it, under the direction of the board, as an agency of The United Methodist Church and shall at all times be subject to the control and direction of the General Conference of The United Methodist Church as set forth from time to time in the *Discipline*.

2. In carrying out and executing its operations and functions, the board of The United Methodist Publishing House shall be entitled to hold, use, manage, operate, and otherwise utilize all property and assets of every kind, character, and description of the corporation(s) identified in ¶ 1618.1 (other than its corporate powers and franchises) and all income therefrom and avails thereof for the purposes and objectives defined in this section.

3. The Illinois corporation and any corporation(s) created by the board pursuant to ¶ 1609.2 shall from time to time take all such action as the board deems necessary or advisable to carry out the intent and purposes of this paragraph and section.

4. The board of The United Methodist Publishing House shall be liable for and shall execute and satisfy all legal obligations of the corporation(s) created by the board pursuant to ¶ 1609.2, but neither it nor the board shall have or be under any obligation to account for principal and income to any such other corporation or to otherwise report to any of them.

¶ **1620.** *Dissolution of The Evangelical Press and Otterbein Press*— Pursuant to the Declaration of Union of The Evangelical United Brethren Church and The Methodist Church and under the authority of ¶¶ 939, 950–954 of *The Book of Discipline* of The United Methodist Church, 1968, The Otterbein Press, an Ohio corporation, and The Evangelical Press, a Pennsylvania corporation, have been legally dissolved and their charters have been surrendered. The proceeds of their corporate assets have been and are being administered pursuant to said disciplinary provisions.

_____
56. *See* Judicial Council Decision 330.

¶ **1621.** *Corporate Officers*—The officers of the corporation(s) under the direction of the board shall be elected annually in accordance with its charter and bylaws.

¶ **1622.** *Corporate President*—The executive officer (publisher) elected pursuant to ¶ 1614 shall also be elected the president of the corporation(s) under the direction of the board.

¶ **1623.** *Salaries for Corporate Officers*—The board shall fix the salaries of the officers of the corporation(s) and shall report the same quadrennially to the General Conference.

¶ **1624.** *Quarterly Financial Reports*—The board shall require the president to submit quarterly to the executive committee and annually to the board written reports of the financial condition and operating results of The United Methodist Publishing House.

¶ **1625.** *Authority to Extend Activities*—The president (publisher) and the board shall have authority to extend the activities of The United Methodist Publishing House in such manner as they may judge to be for the best interests of the Church.

¶ **1626.** *Fidelity Bonding of President and Corporate Officers*—The board shall require the president and other corporate officers to give bond conditioned on the faithful discharge of their respective duties. It also shall authorize the execution of a blanket bond covering all staff personnel whose responsibilities justify such coverage. The amount of the bonds shall be fixed by the board, and the bonds shall be subject to the approval of the board. The premiums shall be paid by The United Methodist Publishing House, and the chairperson of the board shall be the custodian of the bonds.

¶ **1627.** *Power to Suspend Officers*—The board shall have power to suspend, after hearing, and to remove, after hearing, the president or any of the officers for misconduct or failure to perform the duties of their offices.

¶ **1628.** *Book Editor*—The board shall elect annually a book editor, who shall be designated editorial director of general publishing. The book editor shall have joint responsibility with the publisher for approving manuscripts considered for publication. The book editor shall edit or supervise the editing of all books and materials of our publication. In the case of church school publications and official forms and records, the book editor shall collaborate with the editor of Church School Publications and the Committee on Official Forms and Records whenever such collaboration is mutually desirable and beneficial. The book editor shall perform such other editorial duties as may be required by the board.

¶ **1629.** Quarterly Review—The board, at its discretion, may continue the publication of the periodical *Quarterly Review,* with the book editor responsible for its editorial content.

¶ **1630.** *Salary of Book Editor*—The board shall fix the salary of the book editor.

¶ **1631.** *Suspension of Book Editor*—The board shall have power to suspend or remove, after hearing, the book editor for misconduct or failure to perform the duties of the office.

¶ **1632.** *Editor of Church School Publications*—There shall be an editor of Church School Publications, elected as set forth in ¶ 1124.

¶ **1633.** *Duties of Editor of Church School Publications*—The editor of Church School Publications shall be responsible for the preparation of all curriculum materials as set forth in ¶ 1124.

¶ **1634.** *Church-School Curriculum*—The curriculum of the church school shall be determined by the Curriculum Resources Committee, which shall include in its membership the vice president in charge of publishing and the publisher, as set forth in ¶ 1125.1c.

¶ **1635.** *Salary of Editor of Church School Publications*—The board shall fix the salary of the editor of Church School Publications and shall have full financial responsibility for all expenses connected with this work.

¶ **1636.** *Publications of the Curriculum Resources Committee*—The publications of the Curriculum Resources Committee shall be manufactured, published, and distributed through The United Methodist Publishing House. In matters involving financial responsibility, the final determination in every case shall lie with the board. After consultation with the publisher, the editor of Church School Publications shall prepare a complete budget for this work, including salaries of assistants and office secretaries and travel, etc., to be effective when approved by the board, and shall direct its operation from year to year.

¶ **1637.** *Service of the Entire United Methodist Church*—There shall be one complete, coordinated system of literature published by the board for the entire United Methodist Church. This literature is to be of such type and variety as to meet the needs of all groups of our people. The board president and publisher shall consult with the general program agencies, the General Commission on Communication, and the General Council on Ministries with regard to their publishing needs in order to avoid unnecessary overlapping and duplication.

¶ **1638.** *Financial Feasibility*—The board and the publisher shall have authority to decline to publish any item of literature when in their judgment the cost would be greater than should be borne by The United Methodist Publishing House.

¶ **1639.** *Board Participation*—The editor of Church School Publications (¶ 1124) and a member of the General Board of Discipleship designated by the president shall have the right to sit with the board and shall have the privilege of the floor without vote for the consideration of matters pertaining to their joint interests.

¶ **1640.** *Cooperative Publications*—The United Methodist Publishing House shall explore and engage in cooperative publication of United Methodist church school curriculum resources wherever both The United Methodist Publishing House and the Curriculum Resources Committee of the General Board of Discipleship find this to be practicable and in harmony with related editorial and publishing policies.

¶ **1641.** *Use of Distribution System by General Agencies*—It is recommended that all general agencies of The United Methodist Church use the distribution system of The United Methodist Publishing House for distribution of resources, materials, and supplies needed for use in the local church.

¶ **1642.** *Real Estate Purchases*—The United Methodist Publishing House shall not buy any real estate costing in excess of $500,000 and shall not sell or exchange any real estate having a fair market value in excess of $500,000 except by the order of the General Conference or, between sessions of the General Conference, by a two-thirds vote of all the members of the board. In either case, such vote shall be taken at a regular or called meeting of the board, and if at a called meeting, the purpose of this meeting shall have been stated in the call. The erection of a new building or improvement, alteration, or repair of an existing building or the purchase of real estate for retail purposes involving an expenditure of not more than $500,000, or the sale or exchange of real estate used by the publishing house for retail purposes that has a fair market value of not more than $500,000, may be authorized by the vote of a majority of the executive committee. These provisions shall not prevent the making of investments on mortgage security or the protection of the same or the collection of claims and adjustments.

## Section XI. General Commission on Archives and History

¶ **1701.** *Authorization and Establishment*—The name of the official historical agency of The United Methodist Church shall be the **General Commission on Archives and History.**

¶ **1702.** *Incorporation*—The General Commission on Archives and History shall be incorporated under the laws of whatever state the commission may determine.

¶ **1703.** *Purpose*—1. The purpose of the commission shall be to promote and care for the historical interests of The United Methodist Church at every level. It shall gather, preserve, and hold title to library and archival materials, and it shall disseminate interpretive materials on the history of The United Methodist Church and its antecedents. It shall cooperate with other bodies, especially the Historical Society of The United Methodist Church, the World Methodist Historical Society, and the World Methodist Council in areas of mutual concern. It shall maintain archives and libraries in which shall be preserved historical records and materials of every kind relating to The United Methodist Church and shall see that such holdings are available for responsible public and scholarly use. It shall provide guidance for the proper creation, maintenance, and disposition of documentary record material at all levels of The United Methodist Church (*see* ¶ 1711.1*b*). It shall provide support, direction, and encouragement for the work of annual conference and jurisdictional historical agencies and organizations by developing and making available historical, interpretive, and training media. It shall develop policies and resources for the designated United Methodist Historic Sites and United Methodist Heritage Landmarks. It shall provide general supervision for the observance of Heritage Sunday (*see* ¶ 264.1). It shall engage with other Wesleyan, Methodist, or Evangelical United Brethren-related denominations in lifting up our joint heritage.

2. The commission shall be accountable to the General Council on Ministries for all programmatic assignments.

3. The commission shall have responsibility for and supervision of its archives and historical libraries and other depositories of similar character, if any, established by The United Methodist Church.

4. The commission shall promote collection and dissemination of information and materials concerning the historic witness made individually and collectively by women, racial and ethnic peoples, and other constituencies not covered extensively in traditional historical documentation in the worldwide life of The United Methodist Church and its antecedents.

5. The commission shall develop and make available interpretive materials such as handbooks, services of worship and celebrations of

historical events, training films, and other media helpful to annual conferences and local churches.

6. Once each quadrennium, the commission may hold a historical convocation, to which may be invited members of jurisdictional and annual conference historical agencies and organizations; appropriate faculty and students in institutions of higher education related to The United Methodist Church; members of the Historical Society of The United Methodist Church; members of other Wesleyan, Methodist, and Evangelical United Brethren-related historical organizations; and such other persons, groups, or organizations as may be interested.

¶ 1704. *Membership*—1. The commission shall be constituted quadrennially, and its members and all officers elected by it shall hold office until their successors have been chosen. The commission may fill interim vacancies during a quadrennium where not otherwise provided by the *Discipline*.

2. The commission shall be composed of twenty-four members in the following manner: ten members elected by the General Conference on nomination of the Council of Bishops, in which number it is recommended that at least one shall be from the central conferences; two bishops (one of whom shall come from the central conferences); five presidents of the jurisdictional commissions on archives and history, or where no commission exists or any disciplinary conflict arises, a person designated by the jurisdictional College of Bishops; and seven additional members elected by the general commission ensuring that all three regions of the central conferences are represented. It is recommended that careful consideration be given to people with special interests and skills in the history of United Methodism and that careful consideration be given to inclusiveness, including representation from men, women, age levels, all racial and ethnic groups, and central conferences.

¶ 1705. *Meetings*—The commission shall meet annually at such time and place as it may determine, subject to the provisions of the act of incorporation. The commission may hold special meetings on the call of the president. A majority of the members of the commission shall constitute a quorum.

¶ 1706. *Officers*—The commission shall elect from its membership a president, vice president, secretary, and such other officers as may be needed. The president shall be a bishop. The officers shall perform the duties usually incident to their positions.

¶ 1707. *Staff*—The commission shall elect a general secretary and such other staff officers as may be needed. The general secretary shall be the executive and administrative officer and shall carry on the work of the commission, keep the records and minutes, serve as editor of official publications of the commission, supervise the depositories, make an annual report to the commission, and furnish such reports as are required to the General Conference and General Conference agencies. The general secretary shall attend meetings of the commission and the executive committee and shall have the privilege of the floor without vote. Archivists, curators, and librarians employed by the commission shall be responsible to the general secretary. They shall attend meetings of the commission and the executive committee when it is deemed necessary by the general secretary. When in attendance, they shall have the privilege of the floor without vote.

¶ 1708. *Executive Committee*—There shall be an executive committee, composed of the president, vice president, secretary, and two members from each of the three standing committees—Heritage Landmarks, Archives and Library, and History and Interpretation. The executive committee shall perform the duties and exercise the authority of the commission between meetings. Its minutes shall be submitted to the commission for approval. The executive committee and the commission may vote on any matter by mail. Mail polls shall be directed by the general secretary, who shall state clearly the propositions to be voted on and announce the results to all the members.

¶ 1709. *Finances*—The commission shall be financed by appropriations of the General Conference; the sale of literature and historical materials; subscriptions to the commission's official publications; dues from associate members; and gifts, grants, and bequests of interested individuals and organizations.

¶ 1710. *Historical Society of The United Methodist Church*—1. The general commission shall endorse and encourage the **Historical Society of The United Methodist Church** and encourage membership therein for the purpose of promoting interest in the study, preservation, and dissemination of the history and heritage of The United Methodist Church and its antecedents. The Historical Society shall be encouraged to enlist the support and cooperation of commission on archives and history (or equivalent) at the annual conference, jurisdictional conference, and general Church levels as well as other interested agencies and organizations in the promotion of the historical interests of the Church. The society shall be financially self-supporting through dues and other sources, except for such services as may be provided by the General Conference Commission on Archives and History.

2. Membership in the Historical Society shall be established as the society may determine. Membership shall entail the payment of such dues as the society may direct, in return for which members shall receive publications and other benefits as are deemed suitable.

¶ **1711.** 1. *Archival Definitions—a) Archives,* as distinguished from libraries, house not primarily books, but documentary record material.

*b) Documentary record material* shall mean all documents, minutes, journals, diaries, reports, pamphlets, letters, papers, manuscripts, maps, photographs, books, audiovisuals, sound recordings, magnetic or other tapes, electronic data processing records, artifacts, or any other documentary material, regardless of physical form or characteristics, made or received pursuant to any provisions of *The Discipline* in connection with the transaction of Church business by any general agency of The United Methodist Church or of any of its constituent predecessors.

*c) General agency* of The United Methodist Church or of its constituent predecessors shall, in turn, mean and include every Church office, Church officer, or official (elected or appointed)—including bishop, institution, board, commission, bureau, council, or conference—at the national level.

2. *Custodianship of Records*—The church official in charge of an office having documentary record material shall be the custodian thereof, unless otherwise provided.

3. *Procedures—a)* The general commission shall establish a central archives of The United Methodist Church and such regional archives and record centers as in its judgment may be needed.

*b)* The bishops, General Conference officers, general boards, commissions, committees, and agencies of The United Methodist Church shall deposit official minutes or journals, or copies of the same, in the archives quadrennially and shall transfer correspondence, records, papers, and other archival materials described above from their offices when they no longer have operational usefulness. No records shall be destroyed until a disposal schedule has been agreed upon by the General Commission on Archives and History and the agency. When the custodian of any official documentary record material of a general agency certifies to the General Commission on Archives and History that such records have no further use or value for official and administrative purposes and when the commission certifies that such records appear to have no further use or value for research or reference, then such records may be destroyed or otherwise disposed of by the agency or official having custody of them. A record of such certification and authorization shall be entered in the minutes or records of both the commission and the agency. The General Commission on Archives and History is hereby authorized and empowered to make such provisions as may be necessary and proper to carry this paragraph into effect.

*c)* The commission shall have the right to examine the condition of documentary record material and shall, subject to the availability of staff and funds, give advice and assistance to Church officials and agencies in regard to preserving and disposing of documentary record material in their custody. Officials of general agencies shall assist the commission in the preparation of an inventory of records in their custody. To this inventory shall be attached a schedule, approved by the head of the agency having custody of the records and the commission, establishing a time period for the retention and disposal of each series of records. So long as such approved schedule remains in effect, destruction or disposal of documentary record material in accordance with its provisions shall be deemed to have met the requirements of ¶ 1711.3*b.*

*d)* The commission is authorized and directed to conduct a program of inventorying, repairing, and microfilming among all general agencies of The United Methodist Church for security purposes that documentary record material which the commission determines has permanent value and to provide safe storage for microfilm copies of such material. Subject to the availability of funds, such program may be extended to material of permanent value of all agencies of The United Methodist Church.

*e)* The general boards, commissions, committees, and agencies of The United Methodist Church shall place two copies, as they are issued, of all their publications, of whatever kind, in the archives or in lieu thereof shall file a statement with the archivist affirming that they are preserving copies of all such items in their own libraries or depositories.

*f)* Official documents, or copies thereof, such as articles of incorporation, constitutions, bylaws, and other official papers of the boards and agencies of The United Methodist Church shall be deposited in the archives.

*g)* Whoever has the custody of any general agency records shall, at the expiration of the term of office, deliver to the successor, custodian, or, if there be none, to the commission all records, books, writings, letters, and documents kept or received in the transaction of official general agency business. This will also apply to the papers of temporary and special general Church committees.

*h)* The bishops, General Conference officers, and the general boards, commissions, committees, and agencies of The United Methodist Church are urged to counsel with the central archivist concerning the preservation of all materials.

*i)* Jurisdictional and annual conference secretaries shall deposit two copies of their respective conference journals quadrennially or annually, as the case may be, in the central archives and in the appropriate regional archives.

*j)* Secretaries of jurisdictional and annual conference boards, commissions, committees, and agencies shall deposit annually, or as often as they meet, copies of their minutes (as distinguished from reports that are printed separately or in the jurisdictional and annual conference journals) in the central archives or in the appropriate regional archives.

*k)* Bishops, General Conference officers, general agency staff personnel, missionaries, and those ordained ministers and laypersons in positions of leadership and influence at any level of the Church are urged to deposit or bequeath their personal papers to the archives of the general commission.

*l)* Organizations and individuals may negotiate appropriate restrictions on the use of materials that they deposit in the archives.

*m)* Upon recommendation of its executive committee, the commission may authorize the transfer of materials to an organization, agency, or family.

*n)* All materials in the archives shall be available for research and exhibition, subject to such restrictions as may be placed on them.

¶ **1712.** *Historic Sites and Heritage Landmarks*—1. *a) Historic Sites*—*Historic sites* are buildings, locations, or structures that are specifically related to a significant event, development, or personality in the history of an annual, central, or jurisdictional conference (or its antecedents). Historic sites are designated by formal action of the annual, central, or jurisdictional conference within whose regions the site is located. Such designation shall first be considered and reviewed by the respective commission on archives and history (or equivalent). After action by the annual, central, or jurisdictional conference to designate a building, structure, or location as a historic site, the president or chairperson of the commission on archives and history (or equivalent) shall advise the General Commission on Archives and History of the action taken and provide such documentation as may be required. The general commission in turn shall provide an official historic site marker, keep a register of all historic sites, and maintain an ongoing file of pertinent information concerning them.

*b) Heritage Landmarks—Heritage landmarks* of The United Methodist Church are buildings, locations, or structures that are specifically related to significant events, developments, or personalities in the overall history of The United Methodist Church or its antecedents. They must have distinctive historic interest and value for the denomination as a whole, as contrasted with local or regional historic significance. Ordinarily, buildings, locations, or structures that have achieved historic significance within the preceding fifty years shall not be considered for designation as a heritage landmark.

*c) Designation of Heritage Landmarks—*All nominations for the designation of buildings, locations, and structures as United Methodist heritage landmarks shall be made by the annual, central, or jurisdictional conference commission on archives and history (or equivalent) within whose regions they are located. Such nominations shall be referred for consideration to the General Commission on Archives and History, in accord with guidelines established by the commission. Through its Committee on Heritage Landmarks, the commission shall consider the merits of each nomination and shall make such recommendation as it deems appropriate to the ensuing General Conference for its action and determination.

The commission shall recommend only a building, location, or structure for designation as a heritage landmark that has been registered as a historic site by an annual, central, or jurisdictional conference and has met the requirements established by the commission. The commission shall keep a register of all duly designated heritage landmarks and maintain an ongoing file of pertinent information concerning them.

*d) Quadrennial Review—*The commission shall be responsible for making a quadrennial review of the existing duly designated heritage landmarks, according to the criteria that it shall prepare and which shall be compatible with *The Book of Discipline.* The commission shall further be responsible for recommending to the General Conference the redesignation or reclassification of the designated heritage landmarks as such action may be appropriate in keeping with such criteria.

2. *Present Heritage Landmarks*—The present heritage landmarks of The United Methodist Church (and the year of their designation by General Conference) are: Acuff's Chapel, between Blountville and Kingsport, TN (1968); Albright Memorial Chapel, Kleinfeltersville, PA (1968); Asbury Manual Labor School and Mission, Ft. Mitchell, AL (1984); Barratt's Chapel, near Frederica, DE (1968); Bethune-Cookman College, Daytona Beach, FL (1984); Bishop John Seybert/Flat Rock Cluster, Flat Rock and Bellevue, OH (1992); Boehm's Chapel, Willow Street, PA (1984); Cokesbury College, Abingdon, MD (1984); Cox Memorial United Methodist Church, Hallowell, ME (1992); Deadwood Cluster, Deadwood, SD (1984); Edward Cox House, near Bluff City, TN (1968); First Evangelical Association Church Building and Publishing House, New Berlin, PA (1988); First United Methodist Church, Johnstown, PA (1996); Green Hill House, Louisburg, NC (1968); Hanby House, Westerville, OH (1988); John Street Church, New York City (1968); John Wesley's American Parish, Savannah, GA (1976); Keywood Marker, Glade Spring, VA (1988); Lovely Lane Chapel, Baltimore, MD (1972); McMahan's Chapel, Bronson, TX (1972); Methodist Hospital, Brooklyn, NY (1972); Old McKendree Chapel, Jackson, MO (1968); Old Otterbein Church, Baltimore, MD (1968); Old Stone Church Cemetery and Site, Leesburg, VA (1968); Organization of The Methodist Episcopal Church, South, Louisville, KY (1984); Peter Cartwright United Methodist Church, Pleasant Plains, IL (1976); Rehobeth Church, near Union, WV (1968); Robert Strawbridge's Log House, near New Windsor, MD (1968); Rutersville Cluster, Rutersville, TX (1988); St. George's Church, Philadelphia, PA (1968); St. Simon's Island, Brunswick, GA (1968); Wesley Foundation, University of Illinois, Champaign, IL (1996); Town of Oxford, GA (1972); United Brethren Founding Sites Cluster, Frederick, Keedysville, and Beaver Creek, MD (2000); Wesleyan College Cluster, Macon, GA (1992); Whitaker's Chapel, near Enfield, Halifax County, NC (1972); Willamette Mission, near Salem, OR (1992); Wyandot Indian Mission, Upper Sandusky, OH (1968); and Zoar United Methodist Church, Philadelphia, PA (1984).

## Section XII. General Commission on Communication

¶ **1801.** As United Methodists, our theological understanding obligates us, as members of the body of Christ, to communicate our faith by speaking and listening to persons both within and outside the Church throughout the world, and to utilize all appropriate means of communication.

The responsibility to communicate is laid upon every church member, every pastor, every congregation, every annual conference, every institution, and every agency of the Church. Within this total responsibility, there are certain functions that the General Conference has assigned to the General Commission on Communication, to be performed in behalf of all through the talents and resources at its command.

¶ **1802.** *Name*—There shall be a **General Commission on Communication** of The United Methodist Church, which for communication and public relations purposes may be designated as United Methodist Communications (UMCom).

¶ **1803.** *Incorporation*—The General Commission on Communication is successor to the Joint Committee on Communications, incorporated in the State of Ohio, and shall be authorized to do business as United Methodist Communications (UMCom). It is authorized to create such other corporate substructures as the commission deems appropriate to carry out its functions.

¶ **1804.** *Amenability and Accountability*—The General Commission on Communication shall be amenable to the General Conference. As an administrative general agency that carries significant program functions in addition to its many service and support responsibilities, the commission shall be accountable to, report to, and be evaluated by the General Council on Ministries in program matters and shall be accountable to and report to the General Council on Finance and Administration for matters of finance.

¶ **1805.** *Purpose*—The General Commission on Communication shall give leadership to the Church in the field of communication in a holistic way. It shall serve in meeting the communication, public relations, and promotional needs of the entire Church, reflecting the cultural and racial diversity within The United Methodist Church. It shall be responsible for providing resources and services to local churches and annual conferences in the field of communication. It shall have a consultative relationship to all general agencies of the Church and to any structures for communication and public relations at the jurisdictional, episcopal area, annual conference, district, or local church level.

¶ **1806.** *Responsibilities*—Specific responsibilities and functions of the General Commission on Communication and its staff are as follows:

1. It shall be the official news-gathering and distributing agency for The United Methodist Church and its general agencies. In discharging its responsibilities, in keeping with the historic freedom of the press, it shall operate with editorial freedom as an independent news bureau serving all segments of church life and society, making available to both religious and public news media information concerning the Church at large.

2. It shall have major responsibility on behalf of The United Methodist Church in the United States to relate to the public media in presenting the Christian faith and work of the Church to the general public through broadcast, the press, and audiovisual media. It may develop such structures for broadcast and audiovisual communication purposes as are deemed helpful to the Church in its witness through the media. It shall serve in unifying and coordinating public media messages and programs of United Methodist general agencies.

3. It shall give special attention to television, including broadcast television, cable, videotape, videodisc, and satellite. It shall provide counsel and resources to annual conferences—and through conferences, to districts and local churches—to develop and strengthen their television ministries. Responsibilities of the commission shall include program production and placement, and relationships to commercial broadcasters at the national level in the U.S.A.

4. It shall represent The United Methodist Church in the Department of Communication of the National Council of the Churches of Christ in the U.S.A. and in other national and international interdenominational agencies working in the area of mass communications. Budget allocations and other funds granted to these ecumenical agencies shall be administered in accordance with ¶ 818.

5. It shall have responsibility to work toward promotion and protection of the historic freedoms of religion and the press, and it shall seek to increase the ethical, moral, and human values of media structures and programs.

6. It shall have general supervision over the conduct of public relations activities for The United Methodist Church in the United States, planning and carrying out public relations work at the denomination-wide level, and giving counsel to the various units of the Church in regard to their public relations needs. It shall interpret to

the constituency of the Church the significance of the denomination and its various programs.

7. It shall develop and oversee a unified and comprehensive program of audiovisual materials for the Church. It shall plan, create, produce or cause to be produced, and distribute or cause to be distributed audiovisual materials that are informative and vital to the religious life of all United Methodists. It shall unify and coordinate the audiovisual programs of all United Methodist agencies dealing with projected pictures, recordings, videotape, and other audiovisual or electronic materials.

8. It shall give oversight to a comprehensive communication system for the Church, providing a total view of communication structure and practices, including telecommunications. It shall create networks of communicators at all levels, including local church, district, conference, jurisdiction, and general. These networks may include periodic consultations for such purposes as idea exchange, information sharing, joint planning, and monitoring and evaluating the total Church's communication enterprises. With respect to the use of computers for communication purposes, the agency shall cooperate with the General Council on Finance and Administration (*see* ¶ 807.7).

9. It shall provide guidance, resources, and training for the local church coordinator of communications (¶ 254[3]), provided that training at the local level shall be through and in cooperation with annual conferences.

10. It shall be responsible for education and training in the principles and skills of communication, including the following: (*a*) national workshops and training experiences in communication skills related to the various media; (*b*) consultation with and assistance to annual conferences, districts, and racial and ethnic groups in the training of local church persons, especially the local church coordinator of communications; (*c*) training experiences for bishops, personnel of general Church agencies, and other groups on request; (*d*) providing and facilitating apprenticeship, internship, and scholarship programs for church communicators; and (*e*) counseling schools of theology and other institutions of higher education about the training of faculty, candidates for the ordained ministry, and laypersons in the principles and skills of communication, media resource development, and media evaluation.

11. It shall determine and implement, after consultation with the

Council on Finance and Administration, policy for the interpretation, promotion, and cultivation of all financial causes demanding church-wide promotion or publicity. The General Commission on Communication shall assist episcopal areas, annual conferences, and districts by means of a field service program providing counsel and resources in communication, program interpretation, and the promotion of benevolence and administrative funds.

12. It shall be the central promotional agency for the purpose of promoting throughout the Church the following general Church funds: World Service Fund (¶ 812.1), World Service Special Gifts (¶ 813), the Advance (¶ 814), One Great Hour of Sharing (¶¶ 816.2 and 263.2), World Communion Sunday (¶¶ 816.4 and 263.3), General Administration Fund (¶ 817), Interdenominational Cooperation Fund (¶ 818), Ministerial Education Fund (¶ 820), Episcopal Fund (¶ 821), Human Relations Day (¶¶ 816.1 and 263.1), Black College Fund (¶ 819), United Methodist Student Day (¶¶ 816.3 and 263.4), Christian Education Sunday (¶ 265.1), Peace with Justice Sunday (¶¶ 816.5 and 263.5), Golden Cross Sunday (¶ 265.2), Youth Service Fund (¶ 1209), Native American Ministries Sunday (¶¶ 816.6 and 263.6), Africa University Fund (¶ 806.2), and all other general Church funds approved by the General Conference, as well as any emergency appeals that may be authorized by the Council of Bishops and the General Council on Finance and Administration (¶ 811.4). In the interpretation, promotion, and cultivation of these causes, this agency shall consult with and is encouraged to utilize content material provided by the program agency responsible for the area and with the agency responsible for the administration of the funds. Budgets for the above promoted funds shall be developed in cooperation with the General Council on Finance and Administration. In cases where the General Conference assigns a portion of the promotional responsibility to some other agency, such promotional work shall be subject to coordination by the General Commission on Communication. The cost of promotion of the funds, as set in the approved promotional budget, shall be a charge against receipts, except that the cost of promotion for general Advance Specials shall be billed to the recipient agencies in proportion to the amount of general Advance Special funds received by each (¶ 815.3), and the promotion of World Service Special Gifts shall be borne by administering agencies (¶ 813.6). The administration of the money thus set aside for promotion shall be the responsibility of the General Commission on Communication.

13. It shall undertake the promotion of any cause or undertaking, financial or otherwise, not herein mentioned demanding churchwide promotion or publicity; *provided* that such action shall have been previously approved by the Council of Bishops and the General Council on Finance and Administration, or their respective executive committees. The General Council on Finance and Administration shall determine the source of the funding for any such authorized promotions.

14. Appeals for giving that are made to United Methodists shall be consistent with the aims of Christian stewardship. There shall be cooperation between this agency and the General Board of Discipleship in order that programs and resource materials of the two agencies may be in harmony in their presentation of Christian stewardship.

15. It shall publish a program journal for pastors and other church leaders that shall present the program and promotional materials of the general agencies in a coordinated manner and shall be in lieu of general agency promotional periodicals. This agency shall determine the manner of selecting the principal editors, who shall be responsible for the content of the journal. This agency shall obtain from the churches or district superintendents the names of church officials entitled to receive the journal so as to compile a subscription list compatible with regulations of the U.S. Postal Service.

16. It shall give leadership in study and research in the field of communication, applying research findings from the professional and academic communities to the work of the Church, and in evaluative research in the field of communication. It shall cooperate with other agencies and other levels of the Church in research and development work in the field of communication and share the findings of study and research.

17. It shall represent United Methodist interests in new technological developments in the field of communication, including research, the evaluation of new devices and methods, and the application of technological developments to the communication services of the Church.

18. It may develop information services and other innovative services that provide channels of communication to and from all levels of the Church.

19. It shall provide resources, counsel, and staff training for area, conference, and district communication programs and develop guidelines in consultation with persons working in areas, conferences, and districts.

20. It shall produce materials for program interpretation in cooperation with the General Council on Ministries and the general program boards, including the official program calendar of the denomination.

21. The General Commission on Communication shall be charged with planning and implementation of the official United Methodist presence on and use of the Internet, the World Wide Web, or other computer services that can connect United Methodist conferences, agencies, and local churches with one another and with the larger world.

¶ **1807.** *Organization*—1. *Membership*—The membership of the General Commission on Communication shall be composed of twenty-six members as follows:

*a)* Two bishops elected by the Council of Bishops.

*b)* Sixteen members elected by the jurisdictional conferences based on the following formula: North Central—3, Northeastern—3, South Central—4, Southeastern—4, and Western—2. It is recommended that at least one of the persons elected by the jurisdictional conferences be a racial or ethnic minority person.

*c)* One member of the central conferences elected by the Council of Bishops.

*d)* Seven additional members elected by the commission to ensure membership of persons with expertise in the field of communication.

*e)* The additional members shall be nominated by a committee composed of one commission member designated from each jurisdiction and one of the member bishops.

*f)* In order to ensure inclusiveness, the composition of the commission shall reflect the major recognized categories of Church members (*see* ¶ 705.3*i*).

2. *Meetings*—The commission shall hold at least one meeting in each calendar year. Fifteen members shall constitute a quorum.

3. *Officers*—The commission shall elect a president, at least one vice president, a recording secretary, and such other officers as it determines.

There may be an executive committee comprised of not more than one-third of the total membership of the commission and elected by the commission. The membership of the executive committee shall be representative of the composition of the commission.

4. *Internal Organization*—The General Commission on Communi-

cation is empowered to create internal structures as it deems appropriate for effective operation.

5. *Staff*—The commission shall elect annually a general secretary upon nomination by the executive committee or a nominating committee and shall elect such associate general secretaries as needed, and it shall provide for election or appointment of other staff. The general secretary shall cooperate with the General Council on Ministries for program services and with the general secretary of the General Council on Finance and Administration for financial services.

¶ 1808. *Finance*—The General Conference shall provide for the financial needs of the General Commission on Communication upon recommendation by the General Council on Finance and Administration. The commission shall consult with the General Council on Ministries in the area of program matters in development of an annual budget, which shall be reported to the General Council on Finance and Administration for approval.

¶ 1809. *Religion in American Life, Incorporated,* is recognized as an interdenominational and interfaith agency through which the denomination may work to direct attention to church attendance and religious values. United Methodist Communications shall nominate United Methodist representatives to be elected to its board of directors by Religion in American Life. In consultation with the General Council on Finance and Administration, United Methodist Communications shall determine the amount of the annual contribution to this program in behalf of The United Methodist Church, such funds being made available through the budget of United Methodist Communications.

## Section XIII. General Commission on Christian Unity and Interreligious Concerns

¶ 1901. The name of this agency shall be the **General Commission on Christian Unity and Interreligious Concerns.**

¶ 1902. *Purpose*—The General Commission on Christian Unity and Interreligious Concerns shall exercise its ecumenical leadership role in seeking to fulfill two major responsibilities in the context of the search for the unity of the human community and the renewal of creation:

1. To advocate and work toward the full reception of the gift of Christian unity in every aspect of the Church's life and to foster

approaches to ministry and mission that more fully reflect the oneness of Christ's church in the human community.

2. To advocate and work for the establishment and strengthening of relationships with other living faith communities, and to further dialogue with persons of other faiths, cultures, and ideologies.

¶ 1903. *Responsibilities*—The responsibilities of the General Commission on Christian Unity and Interreligious Concerns shall be:

1. To enable ecumenical and interreligious understanding and experience among all United Methodists, including assistance to all United Methodist agencies.

2. To recruit and provide ecumenical leadership training and opportunities for all United Methodists, with special attention to youth, young adults, and racial and ethnic minority persons.

3. To provide resources and counsel to conference commissions or committees on Christian unity and interreligious concerns and to local church leadership.

4. To develop or assist in the development of resources and other educational materials that will stimulate understanding and experience in ecumenical and interreligious relationships.

5. To develop and interpret the primary relationships of The United Methodist Church to ecumenical and interreligious organizations (such as the World Council of Churches, regional councils of churches, the National Council of the Churches of Christ in the U.S.A., the World Methodist Council, the Consultation on Church Union, and the World Conference on Religion and Peace); to united churches, which include a church formerly related to The United Methodist Church or its predecessors; to churches with which a concordat of exchange of voting delegates has been established by General Conference; and to churches that have entered into a formal covenanting act with The United Methodist Church. We further encourage dialogue with other organizations such as the National Association of Evangelicals and the World Evangelical Fellowship.

6. To pursue or initiate relationships and conversations with Christian ministries, organizations, and denominations that are not a part of the National Council of the Churches of Christ in the U.S.A., to seek areas of cooperation and common cause in the advancement of the cause of Christ.

7. To pursue or initiate relationships and conversations with other Christian churches on possible church unions and in general bilateral or multilateral dialogues.

8. To develop and engage in dialogue, cooperation, and unity discussions with the historic members of the Methodist denominational family in the United States—namely, the African Methodist Episcopal, the African Methodist Episcopal Zion, and the Christian Methodist Episcopal churches, and all those Wesleyan bodies in the United States related to the World Methodist Council. (*See* ¶ 2405.)

9. To work toward unity and greater understanding within The United Methodist Church.

10. To report to General Conference on developments in Christian unity and interreligious issues and to make recommendations on any specific proposals for church union.

11. To continue or initiate relationships, conversations, and cooperative efforts with other religious faith communities.

12. To consider resolutions, pronouncements, and actions of ecumenical and interreligious councils and agencies, to be responsible for appropriate United Methodist responses, and to initiate or to channel counsel to ecumenical and interreligious bodies.

13. To receive reports from the Consultation on Church Union, the National Council of the Churches of Christ in the U.S.A., the World Methodist Council, and the World Council of Churches on their work, such reports to include relevant financial information.

14. To maintain a close relationship with the General Board of Church and Society and the General Commission on Religion and Race as they seek to coordinate denominational support and cooperation in eradicating racism, promoting social justice, and enhancing Christian unity.

15. To receive copies of all requests for funds from ecumenical and interreligious bodies to all United Methodist agencies and to review for possible recommendations to both the ecumenical and United Methodist agencies.

16. To enable and review the ecumenical and interreligious involvements, programming, and funding of all United Methodist program agencies; to review funding of ecumenical agencies by United Methodist program agencies through examination of the disclosure records annually provided to the General Council on Finance and Administration; and to report findings and make recommendations to those agencies and to the General Council on Ministries and the General Council on Finance and Administration as requested.

17. To advocate for appropriate funding and oversee disbursement of United Methodist funds provided in support of the major ecumenical and interreligious agencies (*see* ¶ 818).

18. To advocate for adequate funding for the core budgets of the major ecumenical and interreligious agencies.

19. To provide from its own budget, where possible, supplementary funding for cognate units in ecumenical agencies and ad hoc ecumenical and interreligious enterprises.

20. To report to the General Council on Ministries and recommend to the General Council on Finance and Administration the total goal and constituent allocations of the Interdenominational Cooperation Fund for submission to General Conference and to administer all aspects of the fund in accordance with guidelines established in consultation with the General Council on Finance and Administration and with the Council of Bishops. (*See* ¶ 818.)

21. To receive and administer funds allocated to it through the General Conference or the General Council on Finance and Administration and other sources.

22. To report annually to the Council of Bishops on aspects of Christian unity and interreligious developments, issues, and trends.

23. To channel and recommend to the Council of Bishops qualified United Methodists for service as representatives on ecumenical councils or agencies and to special meeting or assemblies, and to name such representatives to councils, agencies, or assemblies not named by the Council of Bishops.

24. To work as partners with agencies of The United Methodist Church on matters of mutual concern.

25. To care for other matters as may be deemed necessary by the commission or requested by the General Conference, the Council of Bishops (*see* ¶ 2401), or the General Council on Ministries.

¶ **1904.** *Authority and Powers*—The General Commission on Christian Unity and Interreligious Concerns shall have the authority and power to fulfill all the responsibilities noted in ¶ 1903 and to fulfill other functions that may be requested of it by the Council of Bishops, the General Council on Ministries, or the General Council on Finance and Administration and General Conference. (*See* ¶ 2401 on relationships with the Council of Bishops.)

¶ **1905.** *Organization*—The General Commission on Christian Unity and Interreligious Concerns shall be organized quadrennially in conformity with ¶¶ 705–710. In addition:

1. The commission shall elect from its membership a chairperson and other officers as it may determine.

2. There shall be an executive committee of the commission with powers as determined by the commission. It shall be composed of the chairperson of the commission, other officers of the commission, and additional elected directors for a total voting membership of not less than eight nor more than ten persons.

3. The general secretary shall be a member of the commission executive committee without vote.

4. The general secretary, in relationships with other churches, shall be referred to as the ecumenical staff officer for The United Methodist Church, in conformity with common practice in other churches.

5. The commission shall meet annually and at such other times as it shall deem necessary. A majority of the members of the commission shall constitute a quorum.

6. The general commission shall nominate annually, according to approved process in ¶ 713, its general secretary and shall elect annually by ballot its associate general secretary(ies). Other staff may be elected or appointed as the general commission shall determine.[57]

7. The responsibilities of the general secretary are to be defined by the commission.

¶ **1906.** 1. The General Commission on Christian Unity and Interreligious Concerns shall be composed of thirty-eight United Methodists as follows:

*a)* Four bishops appointed by the Council of Bishops, one of whom shall be the ecumenical officer of the Council of Bishops and one of whom shall be from a central conference.

*b)* Persons from each jurisdiction, based on the following formula: North Central—5, Northeastern—4, South Central—6, Southeastern—5, and Western—2, elected by the jurisdictional conferences (*see* ¶ 705).

*c)* One person from the central conferences, elected by the Council of Bishops.

*d)* Nine additional members with vote selected by the elected commission at the organizational meeting. It is recommended that persons elected by each jurisdiction and by the General Commission on Christian Unity and Interreligious Concerns be inclusive of ethnic

---

57. *See* Judicial Council Decisions 496, 499.

representation—Asian American, African American, Hispanic American, Native American, and Pacific Islander—and youth and young adults. Two additional members with vote may include persons from the other churches in the Consultation on Church Union.

2. All members shall be selected with a view to balances envisioned in ¶ 705 and may well include persons from administration or faculty of United Methodist schools of theology and undergraduate colleges, campus ministers, seminarians, members of conference commissions on Christian unity and interreligious concerns, delegates to or members of central or executive committees of the World Council of Churches and the National Council of the Churches of Christ in the U.S.A., the Consultation on Church Union, the World Methodist Council, and staff of regional and local cooperative agencies.

3. The general commission shall be authorized to fill vacancies in its membership during the quadrennium according to the three categories of membership: (a) by requesting appointment by the Council of Bishops; (b) by requesting replacement appointment by the appropriate jurisdictional College of Bishops (see ¶ 712); (c) by its own nomination and election process for the other directors.

### Section XIV. General Commission on Religion and Race

¶ **2001.** *Authorization and Establishment*—There shall be a **General Commission on Religion and Race.**

1. *Amenability and Accountability*—The general commission shall be amenable to the General Conference of the United Methodist Church. Between sessions of the General Conference, the commission shall be accountable to the General Council on Ministries by reporting and interpreting activities designed to fulfill the purpose of the commission and by cooperating with the council in the fulfillment of its legislated responsibilities.

¶ **2002.** *Purpose*—The primary purpose of the General Commission on Religion and Race shall be to challenge the general agencies, institutions, and connectional structures of The United Methodist Church to a full and equal participation of the racial and ethnic constituency in the total life and mission of the Church through advocacy and by reviewing and monitoring the practices of the entire Church so as to further ensure racial inclusiveness.

¶ **2003.** *Membership*—The total membership of the commission shall be forty-three, composed of:

*a)* Two bishops appointed by the Council of Bishops.

*b)* Twenty-seven persons elected by the jurisdictions from the annual conference nominations, based on the following formula: North Central—5, Northeastern—7, South Central—6, Southeastern—6, and Western—3. It is recommended that persons elected by each jurisdiction include persons from each ethnic group—Asian American, African American, Hispanic American, Native American, and Pacific Islanders. At least two shall be women, and at least one under the age of thirty.

*c)* Thirteen additional members to be elected by the commission. One member shall be elected by Iglesia Metodista Autónoma Afiliada de Puerto Rico. It is recommended that of the additional members, at least two members shall be elected from each of the five racial and ethnic groups (Asian American, African American, Hispanic American, Native American, and Pacific Islanders). There shall be four young people, two between the ages of eighteen and thirty and two between the ages of twelve and seventeen.[58]

¶ 2004. *Vacancies*—Vacancies in the commission membership shall be filled by the procedure defined in ¶ 712 of the General Provisions.

¶ 2005. *Officers*—The General Commission on Religion and Race shall elect as its officers a president, a vice president, a secretary, and such other officers as it shall deem necessary.

¶ 2006. *Staff*—The General Commission on Religion and Race shall nominate its general secretary for election by the General Council on Ministries (¶ 713). The commission shall select by whatever process it chooses the additional staff needed to assist the general secretary in carrying out the commission's responsibilities.

¶ 2007. *Finances*—The General Council on Finance and Administration shall make provision for the support of the work of the commission, including provision for a general secretary and associated staff and an office for the commission.

¶ 2008. *Responsibilities*—The general commission will assume general Church responsibility for such matters as:

1. Coordinating the denominational concern and providing a channel of assistance to ensure that ethnic and racial group members of The United Methodist Church will have equal opportunities for service, representation, and voice on every level of the Church's life and ministry.

---

58. *See* Decision 5, Interim Judicial Council.

2. Reviewing, evaluating, and assisting agencies and institutions of the Church as they seek to develop programs and policies to implement the mandate for racial inclusiveness, including equality of compensation for racial and ethnic clergy and lay staff at all levels of the Church.

3. Reviewing, evaluating, and assisting annual conferences and their appointive cabinets as they seek to develop appointments, programs, and policies designed to achieve racial and ethnic inclusiveness.

4. Providing channels of assistance to racial and ethnic groups as they seek to develop programs of empowerment and ministry to their local churches and communities.

5. Relating to and coordinating the concerns of the racial and ethnic groups as they relate to minority group empowerment and ministry within the Church.

6. Reviewing, investigating, and conducting hearings where necessary in response to written allegations of violation of the Church's policy of racial and ethnic inclusiveness that have not been satisfactorily resolved in the annual conference, any general agency, or other institution of the Church. All involved parties shall meet with the General Commission on Religion and Race or its designated representatives, presenting their briefs, arguments, and evidence related to said allegations. The commission will submit its findings and recommendations to the appropriate parties, conferences, general agencies, or institutions concerned, for the purpose of securing a satisfactory resolution to the case at hand.

7. Administering the Minority Group Self-Determination Fund. The Minority Group Self-Determination Fund is established by the General Conference of The United Methodist Church for the empowerment of racial and ethnic minority persons within and outside the Church. The fund is available through grants to racial and ethnic minority congregations, community agencies, and other groups for the purposes established by the General Conference. The Fund shall be administered by the General Commission on Religion and Race on behalf of The United Methodist Church guided by the principle of self-determination. The General Commission shall be responsible for developing guidelines and policies regarding grants, and for evaluation of projects receiving support.

8. Providing resources for the local church ministry group on religion and race, enabling them to address the different situations in

which they find themselves: inner city, suburbia, metropolitan, and rural communities.

9. Counseling local churches that are seeking to establish multiracial fellowships, and encouraging and supporting local churches in maintaining a Christian ministry in racially changing neighborhoods.

10. Maintaining a close relationship with the General Board of Church and Society in seeking to coordinate the denominational support and cooperation with various movements for racial and social justice.

11. Being available to assist central conferences, autonomous and affiliated autonomous Methodist and united churches, and Methodist bodies in countries other than the United States as they address the issues of racism and ethnocentric tribalism and ethnocentrism.

12. Providing opportunities for multiracial and interethnic dialogue and meetings throughout the Church.

13. Working directly with the Council of Bishops and the related annual conferences to plan workshops, seminars, and consultations on racism based on biblical and theological grounds.

14. Providing programs of sensitization and education at every level of the Church's life on the nature and meaning of racism—attitudinal, behavioral, and institutional.

15. Relating to and assisting the annual conference commissions on religion and race, enabling them to address their different communities and situations: inner city, suburbia, metropolitan, and rural communities.

16. Advising the General Council on Finance and Administration (¶ 811.1) with regard to the policies and practices of agencies and Church-related institutions receiving general Church funds concerning their implementation of the denomination's policy of inclusiveness and nondiscrimination on the basis of race and ethnic heritage. This shall be done by: (1) consulting with the council in development, review, and maintenance of the certification form to be submitted to the council by agencies and institutions receiving general Church funds; (2) reviewing annually the submissions of certifications of compliance with ¶ 811.1*a, b,* and *c;* and (3) recommending to the council acceptance of the certifications, or other appropriate action, including withholding approval of the entire budget of an agency or institution because of noncompliance with ¶ 811.1*a, b,* or *c.*

17. Developing leadership among racial and ethnic groups for the total ministry in the life of the Church.

18. Facilitating the delivery of program services and information to racial and ethnic local churches.

19. Maintaining a close relationship with the General Board of Church and Society and the General Commission on Christian Unity and Interreligious Concerns, as they seek to coordinate denominational support and cooperation in eradicating racism, promoting social justice, and enhancing Christian unity.

20. Reporting to the General Conference on the status of racial and ethnic minority groups within The United Methodist Church and on the progress of the denomination's journey toward racial inclusiveness.

### Section XV. General Commission on the Status and Role of Women

¶ **2101.** There shall be a **General Commission on the Status and Role of Women** in The United Methodist Church.

¶ **2102.** *Purpose*—The primary purpose of the General Commission on the Status and Role of Women shall be to challenge The United Methodist Church, including its general agencies, institutions, and connectional structures, to a continuing commitment to the full and equal responsibility and participation of women in the total life and mission of the Church, sharing fully in the power and in the policy-making at all levels of the Church's life.

Such commitment will confirm anew recognition of the fact that The United Methodist Church is part of the universal church, rooted in the liberating message of Jesus Christ, that recognizes every person, woman or man, as a full and equal part of God's human family.

The general commission shall function as an advocate with and on behalf of women individually and collectively within The United Methodist Church; as a catalyst for the initiation of creative methods to redress inequities of the past and to prevent further inequities against women within The United Methodist Church; and as a monitor to ensure inclusiveness in the programmatic and administrative functioning of The United Methodist Church.

¶ **2103.** *Responsibility*—The general commission shall be charged with the responsibility of fostering an awareness of issues, problems, and concerns related to the status and role of women, with special reference to their full participation in the total life of the Church at least commensurate with the total membership of women in The United Methodist Church.

1. In the fulfillment of its mandate, this commission shall have the authority to initiate and utilize such channels, develop such plans and strategies, and assign staff as may be required in the implementation of the following primary needs across The United Methodist Church: leadership enablement, resources and communication, affirmative action and advocacy roles, and interagency coordination.

Such plans and strategies related to these needs shall be directed toward the elimination of sexism in all its manifestations from the total life of The United Methodist Church, including general agencies as well as the various connectional channels and structures that reach the local church. The commission shall work with the respective agencies as needs may determine in achieving and safeguarding representation and participation of women, including racial and ethnic groups.

2. The commission, through its various research and monitoring processes, shall continue to gather data, make recommendations, and suggest guidelines for action as appropriate to eradicate discriminatory policies and practices in any form or discriminatory language and images wherever found in documents, pronouncements, publications, and general resources.

3. The commission shall stimulate ongoing evaluation procedures and receive progress reports toward the end of effecting the guidelines in § 2 above in all responsible bodies of the Church.

4. The commission shall establish and maintain a working relationship with annual conference commissions, taking into account the objectives and guidelines for conferences in ¶ 641.1 and seeking to develop and strengthen the leadership of the conference for the realization of these objectives within the general context of the responsibilities of the general commission (¶ 2103.1).

5. The commission shall recommend plans and curricula for new understanding of theology and biblical history affecting the status of women. The commission shall also be encouraged to explore the relationships between spiritual gifts and women in the Bible.

6. The commission shall create needed policies and recommendations and program for immediate and long-range implementation related to the enhancement of the role of women in professional and voluntary leadership in the Church.

7. The commission shall serve in an advocacy role to ensure openness and receptivity in matters related to women's role in the Church's life, with particular attention to the contributions of clergy

and lay professional women, racial and ethnic women, and those experiencing changing lifestyles. The commission in its role as advocate shall assist the local church, annual conferences, the councils, boards, commissions, schools of theology, and other related institutions on eradicating the problems of sexual harassment by developing policies and procedures for addressing these problems.

8. The commission shall generate active concern and give full support toward immediate efforts in the fulfillment of the following directive: Councils, boards, commissions, committees, personnel recruitment agencies, schools of theology, and other related institutions are directed to establish guidelines and policies for specific recruitment, training, and full utilization of women in total employment, which includes but is not limited to pastoral and related ministries, health and welfare ministries, and faculties and staffs of seminaries and other educational institutions.

9. Advise the General Council on Finance and Administration (¶ 811.1) with regard to the policies and practices of agencies and Church-related institutions receiving general Church funds concerning their implementation of the denomination's policy of inclusiveness and nondiscrimination on the basis of gender. This shall be done by: (1) consulting with the council in development, review, and maintenance of the certification form to be submitted to the council by agencies and institutions receiving general Church funds; (2) reviewing annually the submissions of certifications of compliance with ¶ 811.1*a, b,* and *c;* and (3) recommending to the council acceptance of the certifications, or other appropriate action, including withholding approval of the entire budget of an agency or institution because of noncompliance with ¶ 811.1*a, b,* or *c.*

10. The commission shall provide resources for the local church ministry group on the status and role of women.

¶ **2104.** *Membership*—1. The policies, plans, and administration of the work of the general commission shall be determined by its membership, which shall be composed of forty-three persons in accord with the following guidelines:

*a)* Jurisdictional membership shall be nominated and elected by the jurisdictional conferences, ensuring that the pluralism and diversity of the Church's membership is reflected in the representation of racial and ethnic minorities and various age categories. Each jurisdiction shall elect persons for membership based on the following formula: North Central—5, Northeastern—5, South Central—7,

Southeastern—7, Western—3. It is recommended that where possible, the members include at least one laywoman, one layman, one clergywoman, and one clergyman. Of the persons elected by each jurisdictional conference, at least one should be from a racial and ethnic group and at least one shall be under thirty-one years of age at the time of election.

*b)* There shall be ten additional members elected by the general commission, in accord with the provisions of ¶ 705.4*e*. The election of the additional members shall take into account the need to provide adequate representation of racial and ethnic groups and of the various age categories, and to include persons of special competence. It is recommended that the addition of the at-large membership ensure that the total membership maintains the one-third laymen, one-third laywomen, one-third clergy balance as well as majority membership of women. It is further recommended that such additional members shall maintain a membership total of at least 10 percent youth and 10 percent young adults.

*c)* There shall be three women named by the Women's Division from its members or staff to serve as ex officio members with vote.

*d)* There shall be two bishops named by the Council of Bishops.

*e)* There shall be one member elected by Iglesia Metodista Autónoma Afiliada de Puerto Rico.

*f)* In the total membership: (1) Persons over sixty-five years of age shall be included. (2) There should be no less than four persons (two women and two men) from each of these five racial and ethnic groups: Asian Americans, African Americans, Hispanic Americans, Native Americans, and Pacific Islanders. (3) There shall be at least one member who is a diaconal minister.

*g)* The general commission shall be authorized to fill vacancies in its membership during the quadrennium.

¶ **2105.** *Officers*—The president of the general commission shall be a woman elected by the total commission from its membership. Other officers shall be elected as the commission determines.

¶ **2106.** *Meetings*—The general commission shall meet annually, with such additional meetings as needs demand.

¶ **2107.** *Funding*—The funds for carrying out the general commission's purpose shall be authorized by the General Conference.

¶ **2108.** *Staff*—The general commission shall nominate for election by the General Council on Ministries its general secretariat or general secretary who shall provide executive, administrative, and program staff leadership (¶ 713). The commission shall elect such other staff members as needs require within the General Conference mandates and the authority vested in the commission to develop policies and programs directed toward the realization of its purpose.

¶ **2109.** *Relationships*—In order to fulfill its responsibilities and the directives of the General Conference, the general commission shall work with the Council of Bishops, the general agencies, institutions, and other appropriate structures and channels at all levels of the Church.

## Section XVI. Commission on Central Conference Affairs

¶ **2201.** *General Provisions*—1. Recognizing the differences in conditions that exist in various areas of the world and the changes taking place in those areas, there shall be a **Commission on Central Conference Affairs** to study the structure and supervision of The United Methodist Church in its work outside the United States and its territories and its relationships to other Church bodies. The commission shall prepare such recommendations as it considers necessary for presentation directly to the General Conference. All resolutions and petitions related to central conferences presented to the General Conference shall be referred to the commission for consideration, and the commission shall report its recommendations directly to the General Conference.

2. The commission shall be composed of one bishop, one ordained minister, and one layperson from each jurisdiction who are delegates to the General Conference and named by the Council of Bishops; one bishop, one ordained minister, and one layperson from each central conference who are delegates to the General Conference and named by the Council of Bishops; one bishop, one ordained minister, and one layperson who are elected members of the General Board of Global Ministries and named by the Council of Bishops. Special attention shall be given to the inclusion of women, clergy and lay.

The chairperson of the commission shall be a bishop.

The commission shall meet at the seat of the General Conference.

3. The episcopal members of the commission, plus one layman and one laywoman, shall act as the executive committee between sessions of the General Conference. The executive committee shall have authority to take necessary actions on behalf of the commission,

including submitting petitions to General Conference under the provisions of ¶ 507.6.

4. The General Council on Finance and Administration shall recommend to the General Conference for its action and determination a provision in the budget of an appropriate general Church fund for the expenses incurred by the commission and its executive committee in the interim between sessions of the General Conference.

### Section XVII. General Commission on United Methodist Men

¶ **2301.** There shall be a **General Commission on United Methodist Men** in The United Methodist Church.

The general commission shall be amenable to the General Conference of The United Methodist Church. Between sessions of the General Conference, the general commission shall be accountable to the General Council on Ministries by reporting and interpreting activities in its purpose (¶ 702.2).

¶ **2302.** *Purpose*—The General Commission on United Methodist Men shall have primary oversight for the coordination and resourcing of men's ministry within The United Methodist Church.

1. United Methodist Men exists to declare the centrality of Christ in every man's life. Men's ministry leads to the spiritual growth of men and effective discipleship. This purpose is served as men are called to model the servant leadership of Jesus Christ.

2. Individual and group strategies form the foundation of UMMen ministry:

*a*) enhance Evangelism, Mission, and Spiritual Life (EMS), as men become servant leaders.

*b*) advocate programs that train men within local churches to promote specific ministries including prayer, missions, stewardship, and civic/youth serving ministries.

*c*) forge pastoral partnerships by men committed to the effective support and service of clergy and local congregations.

*d*) enhance organizational strength by effective leadership, resources, membership growth, and financial accountability.

*e*) assist men in their ever-changing relationships, roles and responsibilities in their family setting, workplace, and society.

*f*) understand the organization, doctrines, and beliefs of The United Methodist Church.

*g)* fulfill the membership vows through commitment to prayer, presence, gifts, and service in congregational life.

*h)* fulfill the Great Commission with and through The United Methodist Church as one part of the body of Christ.

3. To provide support services to promote the ministry and growth of United Methodist Men:

*a)* provide specific and optional models for men in the local church, district, annual conference, and jurisdiction;

*b)* maintain effective communications and cooperation with the National Association of Conference Presidents of United Methodist Men and other national organizations representing the central conferences and other worldwide Methodist liaisons;

*c)* promote the chartering and annual recertification of local church men's units (¶ 256) with the General Commission on United Methodist Men.

4. To provide resources that assist men in their growing relationship with the Lord Jesus Christ and his church:

*a)* programs of evangelism that are geared to men's needs in cooperation with all areas of the Church dealing with the area of evangelism that model to men that witness is an integral part of daily life in the workplace, the community, the parish, and the home;

*b)* programs of mission in cooperation with all areas of the Church dealing with missional opportunities enabling men for outreach and service as an integral part of their Christian discipleship;

*c)* programs of spiritual life in cooperation with areas of faith development will assist men to realize that witness and outreach, with mission and ministry, become extensions of their faith development and their personal relationship to God through Jesus Christ;

*d)* programs of stewardship in cooperation with the area of stewardship that will lead men to an understanding of their responsibility as stewards of God's creation and personal stewardship of time, talent, money, and prayer;

*e)* programs that affirm the role of men in their family situations;

*f)* to advocate, research, and develop programs for The United Methodist Church to minister to and through men;

*g)* program partnership with The Upper Room in the Living Prayer Center ministry, including support for WATS telephone service and promotion. At all levels of the United Methodist Men's network there shall be prayer advocates;

There shall be a program in partnership with local churches

called Moving United Methodists to assist United Methodist members who are moving from one congregation to another (see ¶235).

5. The General Commission will provide resources and support for the office of Civic Youth-Serving Agencies/Scouting Ministries:

*a*) to provide training of local church, district, annual conference, and jurisdictional Scouting coordinators;

*b*) to provide advocacy, cooperation, and relationship in partnership with the National (USA) Association of United Methodist Scouters, the General Board of Discipleship, the Council of Bishops, and the civic youth-serving agencies (Boy Scouts of America, Girl Scouts of the USA, Camp Fire Boys and Girls, 4-H, and such appropriate organizations within the Central Conferences) for the promotion of youth-serving/Scouting ministries within The United Methodist Church;

*c*) to coordinate, promote, and resource as needed annual conference Bishop's Dinners for Scouting.

6. This legislation shall take effect upon the adjournment of the 2000 General Conference.

¶ **2303.** *Membership*—1. The commission shall consist of thirty-nine voting members as defined in ¶ 705. 3 in the General Provisions and ¶ 534. The membership shall be composed of:

*a*) two bishops elected by the Council of Bishops;

*b*) twenty members elected by the various jurisdictional conferences upon nomination by the jurisdictional committee on United Methodist Men (¶ 534). Each jurisdiction shall elect four persons. Included among the four per jurisdiction shall be at least one clergy, one woman, ethnic representation, and the jurisdictional president of United Methodist Men;

*c*) six members elected by the National Association of Conference Presidents of United Methodist Men, including the national president and five members at large (including at least two members of the commission from the previous quadrennium, for continuity) chosen for expertise and jurisdictional balance if possible;

*d*) three elected presidents from a national organization of United Methodist Men of central conferences, representing each of the three central conference regions, selected by the central conference members of the College of Bishops;

*e*) the president of the United Methodist Men Foundation;

*f*) two members elected by the National Association of United Methodist Scouters, including the president and one youth who is a current member of a civic youth-serving/Scouting ministry;

*g)* five members at large elected by the commission, including at least two young people between ages nineteen and thirty;

*(h)* In addition, the GCUMM welcomes participation from persons representing men's ministry in Pan-Methodist and concordat youth organizations.

This legislation shall take effect upon the adjournment of the 2000 General Conference.

2. *Vacancies*—Vacancies in the general commission membership shall be filled by procedures defined in ¶ 712 of the General Provisions.

3. *Officers*—The General Commission on United Methodist Men shall elect as its officers a president, vice president, secretary, treasurer, and other such officers as it shall deem necessary. In addition, the president of the National Association of Conference Presidents of United Methodist Men and the Presidents of the Central Conference Organizations shall also be considered officers.

4. *Staff*—The General Commission on United Methodist Men shall nominate for election by the General Council on Ministries its general secretary, who shall provide executive, administrative, and programmatic leadership (¶ 713). The commission shall elect such other staff members as needs require within the General Conference mandates and the authority vested in the commission to develop policies and programs directed toward the realization of its purpose.

5. *Meetings*—The general commission shall meet annually, with such additional meetings as needs demand.

6. *Funding*—The General Council on Finance and Administration shall make provision for the necessary support of the work of the commission by providing World Service Funds to complement the direct revenue and contributions from United Methodist Men. This shall include meeting and related expenses for the central conference presidents.

## Section XVIII. Ecumenical Organizations

¶ **2401.** *Liaison Role of the Council of Bishops*—1. In formal relations with other churches and/or ecclesial bodies, the Council of Bishops shall be the primary liaison for The United Methodist Church. The ecumenical officer of the Council of Bishops shall be responsible for these relationships and shall work in cooperation with the General Commission on Christian Unity and Interreligious Concerns in the fulfillment of these functions.

2. The General Commission on Christian Unity and Interreligious Concerns shall consult with the Council of Bishops in establishing the guidelines for the administration of the Interdenominational Cooperation Fund (*see* ¶¶ 818 and 1903.15).

3. The United Methodist representatives to ecumenical organizations in the following paragraphs shall be selected by the Council of Bishops from nominations reviewed by the General Commission on Christian Unity and Interreligious Concerns. Such representatives shall be inclusive in terms of gender, race and ethnicity, age, persons with disabilities, and region. Representatives shall reflect consideration of balances required both by The United Methodist Church and the respective ecumenical organization. Consideration shall be given to persons named to jurisdictional and central conference pools (*see* ¶ 705.1.*b*, *c*).

When proxies are needed to substitute for United Methodist representatives to a specific ecumenical organization, the general secretary of the General Commission on Christian Unity and Interreligious Concerns, in consultation with the ecumenical officer of the Council of Bishops, is authorized to name such proxies. Consideration shall be given to United Methodists residing in the area of the ecumenical organization's meeting, and to the inclusivity of the delegation. The names of proxies shall be reported at the next meeting of the Council of Bishops.

Representatives and proxies from The United Methodist Church to various working groups of any of the ecumenical organizations in the following paragraphs shall be named by the general secretary of the General Commission on Christian Unity and Interreligious Concerns, in consultation with the ecumenical officer of the Council of Bishops.

4. Notwithstanding the other provisions of this section, should structural changes be voted between sessions of the General Conference by any of the ecumenical organizations in the following paragraphs, necessitating election of a new group of United Methodist delegates, the Council of Bishops is authorized to elect, based on recommendations from the General Commission on Christian Unity and Interreligious Concerns, such delegates as may be required.

¶ **2402**. *Financial Support*—United Methodist financial support of the ecumenical organizations in the following paragraphs shall be remitted from the Interdenominational Cooperation Fund through the General Council on Finance and Administration in accordance with ¶ 818. The general agencies of the Church may make such payments to these ecumenical organizations as they deem to be their responsibility and proportionate share in the cooperative programs. Such payments shall be reported to the General Council on Finance and Administration, and that Council shall include a summary report of United Methodist financial support in its annual financial report to the Church. United Methodist financial support of ecumenical dialogues and multilateral conversations, approved by the General Commission on Christian Unity and Interreligious Concerns, shall also be remitted from the Interdenominational Cooperation Fund in the same manner.

¶ 2403. *Methodist Unity*—1. *World Methodist Council—a)* The United Methodist Church is a member of the World Methodist Council, its predecessor Methodist and Evangelical United Brethren churches having been charter members of such body. The council is a significant channel for United Methodist relationships with other Methodist churches and with autonomous Methodist churches, affiliated autonomous Methodist churches, affiliated united churches formerly part of The United Methodist Church or its predecessor denominations, and other churches with a Wesleyan heritage.

*b)* Each affiliated autonomous Methodist church and each affiliated united church that is a member of the World Methodist Council may choose to send delegates either to the General Conference as proposed in ¶¶ 547.3 and 550 or to the World Methodist Council (receiving from the General Administration Fund the expense of travel and per diem allowances thereto). But no such church shall be entitled to send delegations at the expense of the General Administration Fund to both the World Methodist Council and the General Conference.

2. *Commission on Pan-Methodist Cooperation*—Given the historical relationship and shared traditions of the denominations of the Wesleyan tradition called Methodists in America, there shall be a Commission on Pan-Methodist Cooperation developed jointly among The African Methodist Episcopal Church, The African Methodist Episcopal Zion Church, The Christian Methodist Episcopal Church, and The United Methodist Church. The membership of the commission shall consist of six persons from each member denomination, with each denomination naming two bishops, two clergypersons, one layman, and one laywoman, to include at least one young adult.

The commission shall work to define, determine, plan, and, in cooperation with established agencies of the several denominations, execute activities to foster meaningful cooperation among the four Methodist denominations in the collaboration. Such cooperation shall include, but not be limited to, evangelism, missions, publications, social concerns, and higher education. Each denomination will pay the expenses of its delegation to participate in commission affairs. The commission may develop one or more Pan-Methodist coalitions to further meaningful cooperation on a particular activity or issue.

Each quadrennium, the commission shall plan and convene a Consultation of Methodist Bishops. The commission shall report to each of its member denominations through their General Conferences. The commission may be expanded by the inclusion of other denominations of the Wesleyan tradition called Methodists in America, and the commission shall establish guidelines to provide for such expansion. Before another Wesleyan or American Methodist denomination may become a part of the commission, it must have the approval of its general conference.

3. *Commission on Union*—Growing from the continuing work of the Commission on Pan-Methodist Cooperation and the Consultations of the Methodist Bishops, the Commission on Union was formed by the General Conferences of The African Methodist Episcopal Church, The African Methodist Episcopal Zion Church, and The Christian Methodist Episcopal Church, and The United Methodist Church, to explore possible union and related issues. These churches commit themselves to the goal of full reconciliation and union and to continued participation in the commission. The membership of the commission shall consist of six persons from each member denomination, with each denomination naming two bishops, two clergypersons, one layman, and one laywoman, to include at least one young adult. Each denomination will pay the expenses of its members in the work of the commission. The commission shall report to each of its member denominations through their General Conferences.

4. *Striving Toward Union*—As a result of our heritage as a part of a people called Methodist, The United Methodist Church commits itself to strive toward closer relationship with other Methodist or Wesleyan churches wherever they may be found (¶ 5).

¶ **2404.** *Covenantal or Conciliar Relationships*—The United Methodist Church strives toward greater Christian unity through its participation in councils of churches and/or covenantal relationships. The United Methodist Church may establish covenants with other Christian churches through bilateral or multilateral efforts.

1. *The Consultation on Church Union (Churches Uniting in Christ)*— The United Methodist Church is a member of the Consultation on Church Union (Churches Uniting in Christ), its predecessor Methodist and Evangelical United Brethren churches having been involved in its very beginnings and in all its committees and plenary consultations. The United Methodist Church is in covenantal relationship with other churches in the Consultation on Church Union (Churches Uniting in Christ).

2. *National or Regional Ecumenical Organizations—a) The National Council of the Churches of Christ in the U.S.A.*—The United Methodist Church is a member of the National Council of the Churches of Christ in the U.S.A., its predecessor Methodist and Evangelical United Brethren churches having been charter members of such body.

*b) Other National or Regional Ecumenical Organizations*—The General Commission on Christian Unity and Interreligious Concerns, in consultation with the Council of Bishops, shall be in dialogue with United Methodists in whatever countries they may reside, and shall coordinate, explore, and advocate United Methodist participation in regional ecumenical and interfaith organizations and shall address the Interdenominational Cooperation Fund funding committee of the GCCUIC on financial needs and the advisability of support of these organizations.

*c)* The United Methodist Church shall seek observer status in the National Association of Evangelicals. United Methodist observers to these bodies shall be appointed by the Council of Bishops.

3. *The World Council of Churches and Other International Ecumenical Organizations—a) World Council of Churches*—The United Methodist Church is a member of the World Council of Churches, its predecessor Methodist and Evangelical United Brethren churches having been charter members of such body.

*b) Other International Ecumenical Organizations*—The General Commission on Christian Unity and Interreligious Concerns, in consultation with the Council of Bishops, shall be in dialogue with United Methodists in whatever countries they may reside, and shall coordinate, explore, and advocate United Methodist participation in international ecumenical and interfaith organizations and shall address the Interdenominational Cooperation Fund funding committee of the GCCUIC on financial needs and the advisability of support of these organizations.

*c)* The United Methodist Church shall seek observer status in the World Evangelical Fellowship. United Methodist observers to these bodies shall be appointed by the Council of Bishops.

¶ **2405.** *The American Bible Society*—To encourage the wider circulation and use of the Holy Scriptures throughout the world and to provide for the translation, printing, and distribution essential thereto, the American Bible Society shall be recognized as a means of mission outreach for The United Methodist Church, for which appropriate entities of The United Methodist Church shall offer means for seeking the financial support needed for this program.

*Chapter Six*

# CHURCH PROPERTY

## Section I. All Titles—In Trust

¶ **2501.** *Requirement of the Trust Clause for All Property*—In consonance with the legal definition and self-understanding of The United Methodist Church (*see* ¶ 139), and with particular reference to its lack of capacity to hold title to property, The United Methodist Church is organized as a **connectional structure,** and titles to all real and personal, tangible and intangible property held at general, jurisdictional, annual, or district conference levels, or by a local church or charge, or by an agency or institution of the Church, shall be held in trust for The United Methodist Church and subject to the provisions of its *Discipline*. Titles are not held by The United Methodist Church (*see* ¶ 807.1) or by the General Conference of The United Methodist Church, but instead by the incorporated conferences, agencies, or organizations of the denomination, or in the case of unincorporated bodies of the denomination, by boards of trustees established for the purpose of holding and administering real and personal, tangible and intangible property.

¶ **2502.** *Registration of the Names* United Methodist *and* The United Methodist Church—The words *Methodist* or *United Methodist* are not to be used as, or as a part of, a trade name or trademark or as a part of the name of any business firm or organization, except by corporations or other business units created for the administration of work undertaken directly by The United Methodist Church. The General Council on Finance and Administration is directed to register as a service mark the names *United Methodist* and *The United Methodist Church*.

¶ **2503.** *Trust Clauses in Deeds*—1. Except in conveyances that require that the real property so conveyed shall revert to the grantor if and when its use as a place of divine worship has been terminated, all written instruments of conveyance by which premises are held or hereafter acquired for use as a place of divine worship or other activities for members of The United Methodist Church shall contain the following trust clause:[1]

---

1. *See* Judicial Council Decision 688.

*In trust, that said premises shall be used, kept, and maintained as a place of divine worship of the United Methodist ministry and members of The United Methodist Church; subject to the* Discipline, *usage, and ministerial appointments of said Church as from time to time authorized and declared by the General Conference and by the annual conference within whose bounds the said premises are situated. This provision is solely for the benefit of the grantee, and the grantor reserves no right or interest in said premises.*

2. All written instruments by which premises are held or hereafter acquired as a parsonage for the use and occupancy of the ministers of The United Methodist Church shall contain the following trust clause:

*In trust, that such premises shall be held, kept, and maintained as a place of residence for the use and occupancy of the ordained ministers of The United Methodist Church who may from time to time be entitled to occupy the same by appointment; subject to the* Discipline *and usage of said Church as from time to time authorized and declared by the General Conference and by the annual conference within whose bounds the said premises are situated. This provision is solely for the benefit of the grantee, and the grantor reserves no right or interest in said premises.*

3. In case the property so acquired is to be used for both a house of worship and a parsonage, the provisions of both trust clauses specified in §§ 1 and 2 above shall be inserted in the conveyance.

4. In case the property so acquired is not to be used exclusively for a place of worship, or a parsonage, or both, all written instruments by which such premises are held or hereafter acquired shall contain the following trust clause:

*In trust, that said premises shall be kept, maintained, and disposed of for the benefit of The United Methodist Church and subject to the usages and the* Discipline *of The United Methodist Church. This provision is solely for the benefit of the grantee, and the grantor reserves no right or interest in said premises.*

5. When property is acquired from another United Methodist entity or organization, whether it is to be used as a place of divine worship, parsonage, or other use, all written instruments by which such premises are held or hereafter acquired shall contain the following trust clause:

*In trust, that said premises shall be held, kept, maintained, and disposed of for the benefit of The United Methodist Church and subject to the usages and the* Discipline *of The United Methodist Church.*

6. However, the absence of a trust clause stipulated in §§ 1, 2, 3, 4, or 5 above in deeds and conveyances executed previously or in the future shall in no way exclude a local church or church agency, or the board of trustees of either, from or relieve it of its connectional responsibilities to The United Methodist Church. Nor shall it absolve a local church or church agency or the board of trustees of either, of its responsibility and accountability to The United Methodist Church, including the responsibility to hold all of its property in trust for The United Methodist Church; *provided* that the intent of the founders and/or a later local church or church agency, or the board of trustees of either, is shown by any or all of the following:

*a)* the conveyance of the property to a local church or church agency (or the board of trustees of either) of The United Methodist Church or any predecessor to The United Methodist Church;

*b)* the use of the name, customs, and polity of The United Methodist Church or any predecessor to The United Methodist Church in such a way as to be thus known to the community as a part of such denomination; or

*c)* the acceptance of the pastorate of ordained ministers appointed by a bishop or employed by the superintendent of the district or annual conference of The United Methodist Church or any predecessor to The United Methodist Church.

¶ **2504.** *Effect of Union*—Nothing in the Plan of Union at any time after the union is to be construed so as to require any existing local church of any predecessor denomination to The United Methodist Church to alienate or in any way to change the title to property contained in its deed or deeds at the time of union, and lapse of time or usage shall not affect said title or control. Title to all property of a local church, or charge, or agency of the Church shall be held subject to the provisions of the *Discipline,* whether title to the same is taken in the name of the local church trustees, or charge trustees, or in the name of a corporation organized for the purpose, or otherwise.

¶ **2505.** *Oil, Gas, and Mineral Leases*—Subject to and in accordance with the laws of the state, province, or country, the governing body of any church unit or agency owning land in trust for The United Methodist Church as provided in this *Discipline* may lease said land for the production of oil, gas, coal, and other minerals, upon such terms as it may deem best; *provided,* however, that such production shall not interfere with the purpose for which said land is held. The moneys received from such leases as rentals, royalties, or otherwise shall be used so far as practicable for the benefit of the church unit and for the promotion of the interests of The United Methodist Church. The lessee shall have no control over or responsibility for the payments made under such lease.

### Section II. Compliance with Law

¶ **2506.** *Conformity of* Discipline *with Local Law*—All provisions of the *Discipline* relating to property, both real and personal, and relating to the formation and operation of any corporation, and relating to mergers are conditioned upon their being in conformity with the local laws, and in the event of conflict therewith the local laws shall prevail; *provided,* however, that this requirement shall not be construed to give the consent of The United Methodist Church to deprivation of its property without due process of law or to the regulation of its affairs by state statute where such regulation violates the constitutional guarantee of freedom of religion and separation of church and state or violates the right of the Church to maintain connectional structure; and *provided* further, that the services of worship of every local church of The United Methodist Church shall be open to all persons without regard to race, color, or national origin. *Local laws* shall be construed to mean the laws of the country, state, or other like political unit within the geographical bounds of which the church property is located.[2]

¶ **2507.** *The Terms* Trustee, Trustees, *and* Board of Trustees— *Trustee, trustees,* and *board of trustees,* as used herein or elsewhere in the *Discipline,* may be construed to be synonymous with *director, directors,* and *board of directors* applied to corporations when required to comply with law.

¶ **2508.** *Conformity of Deeds and Conveyances with Local Law*—In order to secure the right of property, with the appurtenances thereof, of the churches and parsonages of The United Methodist Church, care shall be taken that all conveyances and deeds be drawn and executed in due conformity to the laws of the respective states, provinces, and countries in which the property is situated and also in due conformity to the laws of The United Methodist Church. Deeds shall be registered or recorded directly upon their execution.

---

2. *See* Judicial Council Decisions 11, 315.

¶ **2509.** *Instituting and Defending Civil Action*—Because of the nature of The United Methodist Church (¶ 139), no individual or affiliated church body or unit, nor any official thereof, may commence or participate in any suit or proceeding in the name of or on behalf of The United Methodist Church, excepting, however, the following:

1. Any person or church unit served with legal process in the name of The United Methodist Church may appear for the purpose of presenting to the court the nonjural nature of The United Methodist Church and to raise issues of lack of jurisdiction of the court, lack of capacity of such individual or unit to be served with process, and related constitutional issues in defense of denominational interests.

2. Any denominational unit authorized to hold title to property and to enforce trusts for the benefit of the denomination may bring suit in its own name to protect denominational interests.

¶ **2510.** *Limitation of Financial Obligations*—No conference, council, board, agency, local church, or other unit can financially obligate the denomination or, without prior specific consent, any other organizational unit thereof.

## Section III. Audits and Bonding of Church Officers

¶ **2511.** All persons holding trust funds, securities, or moneys of any kind belonging to the general, jurisdictional, annual, or provisional annual conferences or to organizations under the control of the general, jurisdictional, annual, or provisional annual conferences shall be bonded by a reliable company in such good and sufficient sum as the conference may direct. The accounts of such persons shall be audited at least annually by a recognized public or certified public accountant. A report to an annual conference containing a financial statement that the *Discipline* requires to be audited shall not be approved until the audit is made and the financial statement is shown to be correct. Other parts of the report may be approved pending such audit.

## Section IV. Annual Conference Property[3]

¶ **2512.** 1. *Conference Trustees*—Each annual conference shall have a **board of trustees**, which shall be incorporated unless the conference is

---

3. For authority regarding property held by general agencies of the Church, *see* ¶ 807.4, .6.

incorporated in its own name. In either case, the board shall consist of twelve persons, and it is recommended that one-third be clergy, one third laywomen, and one-third laymen, in accordance with the provisions of ¶ 608.5. Said persons must be of legal age as determined by law, and lay members shall be members in good standing of local churches within the bounds of the conference. Such persons shall be the directors of the corporation. They shall be elected by the conference for terms of four years, except for the first board, one-fourth of whom shall be elected for a term of one year, one-fourth for a term of two years, one-fourth for a term of three years, and one-fourth for a term of four years, and shall serve until their successors have been elected; *provided,* however, that existing incorporated trustees of any annual conference may continue unaffected while the charter or articles of incorporation are amended to bring them into conformity with this paragraph.

2. The board of trustees shall meet at least annually and organize by electing a president, vice president, secretary, and treasurer, whose duties shall be those usually pertaining to such offices. They shall be amenable to the annual conference. Vacancies occurring between sessions of an annual conference shall be filled as follows: Upon nomination by the conference committee on nominations, the district superintendents shall, by majority vote, elect a trustee to serve until the next annual meeting of the trustees. Vacancies shall be filled by the annual conference for the unexpired term.

3. The board of trustees shall have the following authority with respect to the properties of the annual conference and its agencies:

*a)* The said corporation shall receive, collect, and hold in trust for the benefit of the annual conference any and all donations, bequests, and devises of any kind or character, real or personal, that may be given, devised, bequeathed, or conveyed to the said board or to the annual conference as such for any benevolent, charitable, or religious purpose, and shall administer the same and the income therefrom in accordance with the directions of the donor, trustor, or testator and in the interest of the church, society, institution, or agency contemplated by such donor, trustor, or testator, under the direction of the annual conference. When the use to be made of any such donation, bequest, or devise is not otherwise designated, the same shall be used as directed by the annual conference.

*b)* When so directed by the annual conference, the said corporation may receive and hold in trust for and on behalf of the annual conference, its districts, or any of its agencies any real or personal property previously acquired by the conference, its districts, or its agencies to be used in carrying out their mission, ministry, and program. With respect to such properties, the board shall take no action that would alter or interfere with their missional or programmatic use or function unless such action is specifically directed by the annual conference. The provisions of this subsection shall not apply to educational or health and welfare institutions whose properties are held in their own name or in the name of their own duly elected boards of trustees or directors; nor shall they apply to the property of local churches except as such local church property may have been declared discontinued or abandoned under the provisions of ¶ 2548.

*c)* Except as restricted in § 3*b*, the board shall have the power to invest, reinvest, buy, sell, transfer, and convey any and all funds and properties that it may hold in trust, subject always to the terms of the legacy, devise, or donation.

*d)* The annual conference may include in any resolution authorizing proposed action regarding annual conference property a direction that any contract, deed, bill of sale, mortgage, or other necessary written instrument be executed by and on behalf of the annual conference board of trustees by any two of its officers, who thereupon shall be duly authorized to carry out the direction of the annual conference; and any written instrument so executed shall be binding and effective as the action of the annual conference.

*e)* The conference board of trustees is encouraged to invest in institutions, companies, corporations, or funds that make a positive contribution toward the realization of the goals of the Social Principles of our Church. The board of trustees shall act as a socially responsible investor and report annually to the annual conference regarding its carrying out of this responsibility. Among the tools the board may use are shareholder advocacy, selective divestment, advocacy of corporate disinvestment from certain countries or fields of business, and affirmative investments (as in affordable housing, care of the environment, minority business and banks, and so forth), as well as other appropriate strategies.

*f)* Funds committed to this board may be invested by it only in collateral that is amply secured and after such investments have been approved by the said board or its agency or committee charged with such investment, unless otherwise directed by the annual conference.[4]

---

4. *See* Judicial Council Decisions 135, 160, 190.

4. The board may intervene and take all necessary legal steps to safeguard and protect the interests and rights of the annual conference anywhere and in all matters relating to property and rights to property whether arising by gift, devise, or otherwise, or where held in trust or established for the benefit of the annual conference or its membership.

5. It shall be the duty of the pastor within the bounds of whose charge any such gift, bequest, or devise is made to give prompt notice thereof to said board, which shall proceed to take such steps as are necessary and proper to conserve, protect, and administer the same; *provided*, however, that the board may decline to receive or administer any such gift, devise, or bequest for any reason satisfactory to the board. It shall also be the duty of the pastor to report annually to the board of trustees of the annual conference a list of all property, including real, personal, or mixed, within the charge belonging to or which should be under the control or jurisdiction of the said board.

6. The board shall make to each session of the annual conference a full, true, and faithful report of its doings, of all funds, monies, securities, and property held in trust by it, and of its receipts and disbursements during the conference year. The beneficiary of a fund held in trust by the board shall also be entitled to a report at least annually on the condition of such fund and on the transactions affecting it.

7. *Establishment of Annual Conference Policy with Regard to Government Efforts to Designate Church-Owned Property as Landmarks*— The board, after consultation with the conference commission on archives and history, or alternate structure, shall develop a policy for an annual conference response, on behalf of any local church, church-related agency, or district or annual conference board of trustees located within the bounds of the annual conference, to any governmental effort to designate a property held in trust for the benefit of The United Methodist Church (¶ 2503) by any such board of trustees as a cultural, historical, or architectural landmark.

¶ **2513.** *United Methodist Foundations*—An annual conference or conferences may establish a United Methodist Foundation. The purposes for establishing such a foundation may include:

1. Providing the services described in ¶ 2512.3 as designated by the donor or at the direction of the conference board of trustees;

2. The promotion of planned-giving programs on behalf of local churches, conferences, and general Church boards and agencies;

3. Furnishing counsel and guidance to local churches with regard to promotion and management of permanent funds; and

4. Other responsibilities as determined by the annual conference. The United Methodist Foundation shall have a governing board as determined by the annual conference. The governing board will establish policies upon which the foundation will operate.

¶ 2514. *Jointly Owned Episcopal Residences*—When authorized by two-thirds of the annual conferences comprising an episcopal area, an episcopal residence for the resident bishop may be acquired, the title to which shall be held in trust by the trustees of the annual conference within which the residence is located. Any such property so acquired and held shall not be sold or disposed of except with the consent of a majority of the conferences that participate in the ownership. Whenever there is a plan to sell an episcopal residence or to transfer an annual conference from one episcopal area to another, that plan shall include provision for safeguarding each conference's equity, if any, in an episcopal residence; except that an annual conference, by its own decision, may relinquish its claims to an equity interest in an episcopal residence.[5]

¶ 2515. *Sale, Transfer, Lease, Mortgage, or Purchase of Annual Conference Property*—No annual conference property shall be sold, transferred, or leased for a term that exceeds twenty years, or mortgaged or purchased without the consent of the annual conference or, *ad interim, (a)* the consent of the presiding bishop and of a majority of the district superintendents, and, in the case of discontinued or abandoned local church property or property to be purchased, the consent of a majority of the district board of church location and building (*see* ¶ 2548); and *(b)* the bishop's determination that such transfer or encumbrance conforms to the *Discipline*. The bishop's written statement evidencing the satisfaction of this condition shall be affixed to or included in any instrument of transfer or encumbrance. Any required written instrument necessary to carry out the action so authorized shall be executed in the name of the conference corporation by any two of its officers or, where the conference is unincorporated, by any two officers of its board of trustees, and any written instrument so executed shall be binding and effective as the action of the conference.

---

5. *See* Judicial Council Decision 194.

¶ **2516.** *Camps, Conference Grounds, and Retreat Centers*—Title to annual conference or district camps, conference grounds, and retreat centers held in trust by an incorporated board or agency of an annual conference or district, or by an unincorporated board, commission, society, or similar body of the conference or district, can be mortgaged or sold and conveyed by such corporation or unincorporated body only after authorization by the annual or district conference to which such body is related.

### Section V. District Property

¶ **2517.** *District Parsonages and Boards of Trustees*—1. **A district parsonage** for the district superintendent may be acquired when authorized by the charge conferences of two-thirds of the charges in the district or when authorized by a two-thirds vote of the district conference, subject to the advice and approval of the district board of church location and building as provided in ¶¶ 2518–2523.

2. The title of district property may be held in trust by a **district board of trustees.** Unless the district union is incorporated in its own name, each district shall have a district board of trustees, which shall be incorporated. The board shall consist of not fewer than three nor more than nine members in accordance with ¶ 608.5, having the same qualifications provided for trustees of local churches (¶ 2524), who shall be nominated by the district superintendent in consultation with the district nominating committee, if one exists, and elected by the district conference. Where there is no district conference, they may be elected by the district board of stewards or by the annual conference on nomination of the district superintendent. They shall be elected for a term of one year and serve until their successors shall have been elected, and they shall report annually to the district conference or annual conference. Title to district property may be held in trust by the district board of trustees. If the title to the district parsonage is not held in trust by the district board of trustees, the same shall be held in trust by the trustees of the annual conference of which such district is a part, and such trustees shall report annually to the annual conference. Except as the laws of the state, territory, or country prescribe otherwise, district property held in trust by a district board of trustees may be mortgaged or sold and conveyed by them only by authority of the district conference or annual conference, or if such property is held in trust by the trustees of the annual conference, it

may be mortgaged or sold and conveyed by such trustees only by authority of the annual conference. The district conference, or annual conference in the case of property held in trust by the trustees of the annual conference, may include in the resolution authorizing such proposed action a direction that any contract, deed, bill of sale, mortgage, or other necessary written instrument may be executed by and on behalf of the respective board of trustees by any two of its officers, who thereupon shall be duly authorized to carry out the direction of the district conference or annual conference; and any written instrument so executed shall be binding and effective as the action of the district conference or annual conference. The purchase price and maintenance cost of a district parsonage may be equitably distributed among the charges of the district by the district board of stewards. Where there is an incorporated district union (¶ 654.4), the board of directors of the district union shall have the same duties and responsibilities with respect to district property as are described here for the district board of trustees.

3. When district boundaries are changed by division, rearrangement, or consolidation so that a district parsonage purchased, owned, and maintained by one district is included within the bounds of another district, each such district shall be entitled to receive its just share of the then-reasonable value of the parsonage in which it has invested funds; and the amount of such value and just share shall be determined by a committee of three persons, appointed by the bishop of the area, who shall not be residents of any of the said districts. The committee shall hear claims of each district regarding its interest therein before making a decision. From any such determination, there is reserved unto each of the interested districts the right of appeal to the next succeeding annual conference. Any sum received as or from such share shall be used for no other purpose than purchase or building of a parsonage in the district. The same procedure shall be followed in determining equities of a district in any other property that may be included in another district by changes in district boundaries.

¶ **2518.** *Authorization and Establishment of District Boards of Church Location and Building*—There shall be in each district of an annual conference a **district board of church location and building.** The board shall consist of the district superintendent and a minimum of six and a maximum of nine additional persons nominated by the district superintendent in consultation with the district nominating committee, if one exists, and elected annually by the annual conference; *pro-*

659

*vided* that in a district of great geographical extent an additional board may be so elected. It is recommended that the membership include one-third clergy, one-third laymen, one-third laywomen, and, where possible, should be inclusive of sex, race, age, and people with disabilities. The members of the board, excluding the district superintendent, shall be divided into three classes. One third shall be elected annually for a three-year term. A chairperson and a secretary shall be elected annually at the first meeting following annual conference. The board shall file a report of any actions taken with the charge conference of each local church involved, and the report so filed shall become a part of the minutes of the said conference or conferences. The board shall also make a written report to the district conference (or, if there is no district conference, to the district superintendent), and this report shall become a part of the records of that conference.

¶ **2519.** *Duties and Responsibilities of the District Boards of Church Location and Building*—1. *Local Church Building Sites and Plans*—The board of church location and building shall investigate all proposed local church building sites, ascertaining that such sites are properly located for the community to be served and adequate in size to provide space for future expansion and parking facilities. (*See* ¶¶ 259.1, 2543.2.)

2. If there is a district strategy committee for parish development or a metropolitan commission (¶ 630.5*j*) in the district, the board shall consider its recommendations in planning a strategy for continuing the service of The United Methodist Church in changing neighborhoods. If no parish development committee or commission is operative, the board shall study the duties assigned to each and seek ways to provide continuity of service in parishes where there is a change in the racial, ethnic, or cultural character of the residents, to the end that the resolutions of the General Conference involving such neighborhoods be given careful consideration. One member of the board shall also have membership on the strategy committee or on the commission.

3. The board of church location and building shall investigate all proposed local church or parsonage buildings to determine the best method to make the structure energy-efficient.

¶ **2520.** *Standards for the Approval of Building Proposals*—1. The board shall require any local church in its district, before beginning or contracting for construction or purchase of a new church or educational building or a parsonage, or remodeling of such a building if the cost will exceed 10 percent of its value, to submit for consideration and approval a statement of the need for the proposed facilities, preliminary architectural plans, an estimate of the cost, and a financial plan for defraying such costs, as provided in ¶ 2543.4–.5. Before finally approving the building project, the board shall ascertain whether the preliminary architectural design and financial programs have been reviewed, evaluated, and approved by proper authorities (¶ 2543.5). The design for renovation shall provide for equal access to people with disabilities where readily achievable and financially feasible.

2. When the local church has secured final architectural plans and specifications and a reliable and detailed estimate of the cost of the proposed undertaking as provided in ¶ 2543.7, the board shall require their submission for consideration and approval. The board shall study carefully the feasibility and financial soundness of the undertaking and ascertain whether the financial plan will provide funds necessary to ensure prompt payment of all proposed contractual obligations, and it shall report its conclusions to the church in writing.

3. A final decision of the board approving purchase, building, or remodeling shall automatically terminate after a period of one year where no action has been taken by the local church to carry out such decision.

¶ **2521.** *Appeals of District Boards of Church Location and Building Decisions*—A decision of the board disapproving such purchase, building, or remodeling shall be final unless overruled by the annual conference, to which there is reserved unto the local church the right of appeal.

¶ **2522.** *Application of Standards to the Acquisition of a District Parsonage*—The above provisions shall apply to the acquisition of a district parsonage.

¶ **2523.** *Sale, Transfer, Lease, or Mortgage of District Property*—No district property shall be sold, transferred, or leased for a term that exceeds twenty years, or mortgaged, without: (*a*) the consent of the presiding district superintendent; and (*b*) the district superintendent's determination that such transfer or encumbrance conforms to the *Discipline*. The district superintendent's written statement evidencing the satisfaction of this condition shall be affixed to any instrument or transfer or encumbrance. Any required written instrument necessary to carry out the action so authorized shall be executed in the name of the corporation by any two of its officers, or any two officers of its board of trustees, and any written instrument so executed shall be binding and effective as the action of the corporation.

## Section VI. Local Church Property

¶ **2524.** *Local Church Board of Trustees' Qualifications*—In each pastoral charge consisting of one local church, there shall be a **board of trustees,** consisting of not fewer than three nor more than nine persons, and it is recommended that at least one-third be laywomen and that at least one-third be laymen. The trustees shall be of legal age as determined by law, and at least two-thirds shall be members of The United Methodist Church (*see* ¶¶ 258.1, .3; 2529). No pastor is a voting member of the board of trustees unless elected as a member.

¶ **2525.** *Local Church Board of Trustees' Election*—The members of the board of trustees shall be divided into three classes, and each class shall as nearly as possible consist of an equal number of members. At the charge conference, on recommendation by the committee on lay leadership or from the floor, it shall elect, to take office at the beginning of the ensuing calendar year or at such other times as the charge or church conference may set, to serve for a term of three years or until their successors have been duly elected and qualified, the required number of trustees to succeed those of the class whose terms then expire; *provided,* however, that nothing herein shall be construed to prevent the election of a trustee to self-succession.[6] The charge conference may assign the responsibility for electing trustees to a church conference.

¶ **2526.** *Church Local Conference—Duties, Authority, and Membership*—1. In a pastoral charge consisting of two or more local churches, a **church local conference,** constituted and organized under the *Discipline* of The United Methodist Church in each local church therein, shall be vested with authority and power in matters relating to the real and personal property of the local church concerned. Such church local conference shall elect the board of trustees of such local church in number and manner described in ¶ 2525, and the duties of such trustees, duly elected, shall be the same as and identical with the duties described in ¶ 2527. The duties, authority, and power vested in the church local conference, insofar as

---

6. *See* Judicial Council Decision 130.

they relate to the property, real and personal, of the local church concerned, are the same as and identical with the authority and power vested in the charge conference of a pastoral charge of one local church (¶ 2528); and the authority, power, and limitations therein set forth shall be applicable to the church local conference as fully and to the same extent as if incorporated herein. The effect of the provisions for a church local conference is to give to each local church in a charge of two or more churches, rather than to the pastoral charge conference, supervision over and control of its own property, subject to the limitations prescribed in the *Discipline* with regard to local church property.

2. Whenever required under the *Discipline* of The United Methodist Church for matters relating to real or personal property of the local church or to mergers of churches, a local church in a pastoral charge consisting of two or more local churches shall organize a church local conference. The membership of the church local conference shall consist of the persons specified for membership of the charge conference (¶ 248.2) so far as the officers and relationships exist within the local church, except that the pastor shall be a member of each church local conference. The provisions of ¶ 248.2–.10 relating to membership qualification and procedures of a charge conference shall be applicable to membership qualifications and procedures of a church local conference.

¶ **2527.** *Charge or Cooperative Parish Board of Trustees*—1. A pastoral charge composed of two or more churches, each having a local board of trustees, may have, in addition, **a board of trustees** for the charge as a whole. This board shall hold title to and manage the property belonging to the entire charge, such as parsonage, campground, burial ground, and such other property as may be committed to it. It shall receive and administer funds for the charge in conformity with the laws of the state, province, or country in which the property is located. This board shall consist of not less than three persons, at least two-thirds of whom shall be members of The United Methodist Church and of legal age as determined by law. These trustees shall be elected by the charge conference for three years or until their successors are elected.

2. A cooperative parish composed of two or more charges may have, in addition to its charge trustees and local church trustees, a board of trustees for the cooperative parish as a whole. This board shall hold title to and manage the property belonging to the coopera-

tive parish in accordance with ¶¶ 2503, 2526, and 2527. These trustees shall be elected by the charge conference and/or church local conference related to the cooperative parish and shall be representative of each congregation that composes the cooperative parish.

3. The board of trustees of a charge shall provide for the security of its funds, keep an accurate record of its proceedings, and report to the charge conference to which it is amenable.

4. When two or more local churches compose a single pastoral charge having a parsonage and one or more thereof is separated from such charge and established as a pastoral charge or united with another pastoral charge, each such local church shall be entitled to receive its just share of the then reasonable value of the parsonage in which it has invested funds, with the exception that those churches departing from a circuit who had joined the circuit after the parsonage was acquired would have no claim on any value of the parsonage. The amount of such value and just share shall be determined by a committee of three persons, appointed by the district superintendent, who shall be members of The United Methodist Church but not of any of the interested local churches. Such committee shall hear all interested parties and shall take into account the investment of any church in any such property before arriving at a final determination. From any such determination there is reserved to each of the interested churches the right of appeal to the next succeeding annual conference, the decision of which shall be final and binding. Any sum received as or from such share shall not be applied to current expense or current budget.

¶ **2528.** *Charge Conference Authority*—In a pastoral charge consisting of one local church, the charge conference, constituted as set forth in ¶¶ 245–246, shall be vested with power and authority as hereinafter set forth in connection with the property, both real and personal, of the said local church, namely:

1. If it so elects, to direct the board of trustees to incorporate the local church, expressly subject, however, to the *Discipline* of The United Methodist Church and in accordance with the pertinent local laws and in such manner as will fully protect and exempt from any and all legal liability the individual officials and members, jointly and severally, of the local church and the charge, annual, jurisdictional, and general conferences of The United Methodist Church, and each of them, for and on account of the debts and other obligations of every kind and description of the local church.

2. To direct the board of trustees with respect to the purchase, sale, mortgage, encumbrance, construction, repairing, remodeling, and maintenance of any and all property of the local church.

3. To direct the board of trustees with respect to the acceptance or rejection of any and all conveyances, grants, gifts, donations, legacies, bequests, or devises, absolute or in trust, for the use and benefit of the local church, and to require the administration of any such trust in accordance with the terms and provisions thereof and with the local laws appertaining thereto. (*See* ¶ 2532.5.)

4. To do any and all things necessary to exercise such other powers and duties relating to the property, real and personal, of the local church concerned as may be committed to it by the *Discipline*.

¶ **2529.** *Local Church Board of Trustees' Organization and Membership*—The board of trustees shall organize as follows:

1. Within thirty days after the beginning of the ensuing calendar or conference year (whichever applies to the term of office), each board of trustees shall convene at a time and place designated by the chairperson, or by the vice chairperson in the event that the chairperson is not reelected a trustee or because of absence or disability is unable to act, for the purpose of electing officers of the said board for the ensuing year and transacting any other business properly brought before it.

2. The board of trustees shall elect from the membership thereof, to hold office for a term of one year or until their successors shall be elected, a chairperson, vice chairperson, secretary, and, if need requires, a treasurer; *provided*, however, that the chairperson and vice chairperson shall not be members of the same class; and *provided* further, that the offices of secretary and treasurer may be held by the same person; and *provided* further, that the chairperson shall be a member of the local church. The duties of each officer shall be the same as those generally connected with the office held and which are usually and commonly discharged by the holder thereof. The church local conference may, if it is necessary to conform to the local laws, substitute the designations *president* and *vice president* for and in place of *chairperson* and *vice chairperson*.

3. Where necessity requires, as a result of the incorporation of a local church, the corporation directors, in addition to electing officers as provided in § 2 above, shall ratify and confirm by appropriate action and, if necessary, elect as officers of the corporation the treasurer or treasurers, as the case may be, elected by the charge confer-

ence in accordance with the provisions of the *Discipline*, whose duties and responsibilities shall be as therein set forth. If more than one account is maintained in the name of the corporation in any financial institution or institutions, each such account and the treasurer thereof shall be appropriately designated.

¶ **2530.** *Removal of Local Church Trustees*—1. Should a trustee withdraw from the membership of The United Methodist Church or be excluded therefrom, trusteeship therein shall automatically cease from the date of such withdrawal or exclusion.

2. Should a trustee of a local church or a director of an incorporated local church refuse to execute properly a legal instrument relating to any property of the church when directed so to do by the charge conference and when all legal requirements have been satisfied in reference to such execution, the said charge conference may by majority vote declare the trustee's or director's membership on the board of trustees or board of directors vacated.

3. Vacancies occurring in a board of trustees shall be filled by election for the unexpired term. Such election shall be held in the same manner as for trustees.

¶ **2531.** *Meetings of Local Church Boards of Trustees*—The board of trustees shall meet at the call of the pastor or of its president at least annually at such times and places as shall be designated in a notice to each trustee and the pastor(s) at a reasonable time prior to the appointed time of the meeting. Waiver of notice may be used as a means to validate meetings legally where the usual notice is impracticable. A majority of the members of the board of trustees shall constitute a quorum.

¶ **2532.** *Board of Trustees' Powers and Limitations*—1. Subject to the direction of the charge conference, the board of trustees shall have the supervision, oversight, and care of all real property owned by the local church and of all property and equipment acquired directly by the local church or by any society, board, class, commission, or similar organization connected therewith; *provided* that the board of trustees shall not violate the rights of any local church organization elsewhere granted in the *Discipline; provided* further, that the board of trustees shall not prevent or interfere with the pastor in the use of any of the said property for religious services or other proper meetings or purposes recognized by the law, usages, and customs of The United Methodist Church, or permit the use of said property for religious or other meetings without the consent of the pastor or, in the pastor's absence, the consent of the district superintendent; and *provided* further, that pews in The United Methodist Church shall always be free; and *provided* further, that the church local conference may assign certain of these duties to a building committee as set forth in ¶ 2543 or the chairperson of the parsonage committee, if one exists.

2. The board of trustees shall review annually the adequacy of the property, liability, and crime insurance coverage on church-owned property, buildings, and equipment. The board of trustees shall also review annually the adequacy of personnel insurance. The purpose of these reviews is to ensure that the church, its properties, and its personnel are properly protected against risks. The board shall include in its report to the charge conference (¶ 2549.7) the results of its review and any recommendations it deems necessary.[7]

3. When a pastor and/or a board of trustees are asked to grant permission to an outside organization to use church facilities, permission can be granted only when such use is consistent with the Social Principles (¶¶ 166–166) and ecumenical objectives.

4. The chairperson of the board of trustees or the chairperson of the parsonage committee, if one exists, the chairperson of the committee on pastor-parish relations, and the pastor shall make an annual review of the church-owned parsonage to ensure proper maintenance.

5. Subject to the direction of the charge conference as hereinbefore provided, the board of trustees shall receive and administer all bequests made to the local church; shall receive and administer all trusts; and shall invest all trust funds of the local church in conformity with laws of the country, state, or like political unit in which the local church is located. Nevertheless, upon notice to the board of trustees, the charge conference may delegate the power, duty, and authority to receive, administer, and invest bequests, trusts, and trust funds to the permanent endowment committee or to a local church foundation and shall do so in the case of bequests, trusts, or trust funds for which the donor has designated the committee or the local church foundation to receive, administer, or invest the same.

The board of trustees is encouraged to invest in institutions, companies, corporations, or funds that make a positive contribution toward the realization of the goals outlined in the Social Principles of our Church. The board of trustees is to act as a socially responsible

---

7. *See* Judicial Council Decision 866.

investor and to report annually to the charge conference regarding its carrying out of this responsibility.

6. The board of trustees, in cooperation with the health and welfare ministries representative, shall conduct or cause to be conducted an annual accessibility audit of their buildings, grounds, and facilities to discover and identify what physical, architectural, and communication barriers exist that impede the full participation of people with disabilities and shall make plans and determine priorities for the elimination of all such barriers. The Accessibility Audit for churches shall be used in filling out the annual church and/or charge conference reports.

¶ **2533.** *Permanent Endowment Fund Committee*—A charge conference may establish a local church **permanent endowment fund committee.** The purposes for establishing such a committee include the responsibilities to:

1. Provide the services described in ¶ 2532.5 as designated by the donor or at the direction of the charge conference upon notice to the board of trustees. Consideration shall be given to the placement of funds with the conference or area United Methodist foundation, or local church foundation, for administration and investment.

When the charge conference has designated the committee to provide the services described in ¶ 2532.5, the committee shall have the same investment and reporting duties as are imposed on the board of trustees in that paragraph.

2. The charge conference shall adopt guidelines for action by the committee on planned giving and/or permanent endowment fund. Subject to the direction and supervision of the charge conference, the committee shall fulfill its responsibilities in administering the planned-giving and/or permanent endowment fund.

Following each General Conference, the charge conference shall update any required changes in the planned-giving and/or permanent endowment fund documents.

3. Emphasize the need for adults of all ages to have a will and an estate plan and provide information on the preparation of these to the members of the congregation.

4. Stress the opportunities for church members and constituents to make provisions for giving through United Methodist churches, institutions, agencies, and causes by means of wills, annuities, trusts, life insurance, memorials, and various types of property.

5. Arrange for the dissemination of information that will be help-

ful in preretirement planning, including such considerations as establishing a living will, a living trust, and the need for each person to designate someone to serve as a responsible advocate should independent decision-making ability be lost.

6. Permanent Endowment Fund trustees are directed by the charge conference to follow the guidelines and actions initiated by the charge conference, overturn any transaction that the charge conference may deem excessive, and remove any trustee who does not carry out the directions of the charge conference. Careful attention will be given to the election of trustees to ensure that there is no conflict of interest. Following each General Conference, the permanent endowment document shall be brought into line with any changes in the *Discipline*.

7. Other responsibilities as determined by the charge conference.

8. Resources for these tasks may be secured from conference and/or area United Methodist foundations and development offices, the National Association of United Methodist Foundations, the General Board of Discipleship, the General Council on Finance and Administration, and other appropriate sources for program assistance and direction.

¶ 2534. *Local Church Foundations*—After securing the written consent of the pastor and of the district superintendent, local churches may, by charge conference action, establish local church foundations whose trustees, directors, or governing body shall be elected by the charge conference. Such foundations shall be incorporated, organized, and function in compliance with state law and subject to the provisions of the *Discipline*. Any such foundation shall not violate the rights of any other local church organization and shall be subject to the direction of the charge conference. The charge conference may delegate to the foundation the power and authority to receive, invest, and administer in trust for the local church bequests, trusts, and trust funds upon notice to the board of trustees as provided in ¶ 2532.5, in which event the foundation shall have the same investment and reporting duties as are imposed on the board of trustees. No such delegation of authority shall be construed to be a violation of the rights of any other local church organization.

¶ 2535. *Unincorporated Local Church Property—Title and Purchase—* Unless otherwise required by local law (¶ 2506), title to all property now owned or hereafter acquired by an unincorporated local church, and any organization, board, commission, society, or similar body connected therewith, shall be held by and/or conveyed and transferred to its duly elected trustees, their successors and assigns, in trust for the use and benefit of such local church and of The United Methodist Church. The trustees shall be named as the board of trustees of the local church in the written instrument conveying or transferring title. Every instrument of conveyance of real estate shall contain the appropriate trust clause as set forth in the *Discipline* (¶ 2503).

¶ **2536.** *Unincorporated Local Church Property—Notice and Authorization*—Prior to the purchase by an unincorporated local church of any real estate, a resolution authorizing such action shall be passed at a meeting of the charge conference by a majority vote of its members present and voting at a regular meeting or a special meeting of the charge conference called for that purpose; *provided,* however, that not less than ten days' notice of such meeting and the proposed action shall have been given from the pulpit or in the weekly bulletin of the church; and *provided* further, that written consent to such action shall be given by the pastor and the district superintendent. (*See* ¶ 2543.)

¶ **2537.** *Incorporated Local Church Property—Title and Purchase*—Unless otherwise required by local law (¶ 2506), the title to all property now owned or hereafter acquired by an incorporated local church, and any organization, board, commission, society, or similar body connected therewith, shall be held by and/or conveyed to the corporate body in its corporate name, in trust for the use and benefit of such local church and of The United Methodist Church. Every instrument of conveyance of real estate shall contain the appropriate trust clause as set forth in the *Discipline* (¶ 2503).

¶ **2538.** *Incorporated Local Church Property—Notice and Authorization*—Prior to the purchase by a local church corporation of any real estate, a resolution authorizing such action shall be passed by the charge conference in corporate session, or such other corporate body as the local laws may require, with the members thereof acting in their capacity as members of the corporate body, by a majority vote of those present and voting at any regular or special meeting called for that purpose; *provided* that not less than ten days' notice of such meeting and the proposed action shall have been given from the pulpit or in the weekly bulletin of the local church; and *provided* further, that written consent to such action shall be given by the pastor and the district superintendent; and *provided* further, that all such transactions shall have the approval of the charge conference.

¶ **2539.** *Unincorporated Local Church Property—Sale, Transfer, Lease,* *or Mortgage*—Any real property owned by or in which an unincorporated local church has any interest may be sold, transferred, leased for a term of thirty days or more (which shall include leases for less than thirty days if such a lease is consecutive with the same lessee), or mortgaged subject to the following procedure and conditions:

1. Notice of the proposed action and the date and time of the regular or special meeting of the charge conference at which it is to be considered shall be given at least ten days prior thereto (except as local laws may otherwise provide) from the pulpit of the church or in its weekly bulletin.

2. A resolution authorizing the proposed action shall be passed by a majority vote of the charge conference members (in a pastoral charge consisting of two or more local churches, the church local conference; *see* ¶ 2526) present and voting at a special meeting called to consider such action.

3. The written consent of the pastor of the local church and the district superintendent to the proposed action shall be necessary and shall be affixed to or included in the instrument of sale, transfer, lease, or mortgage. Prior to consenting to any proposed action required under this paragraph involving any United Methodist church property, the pastor, district superintendent, and the district board of church location and building shall ensure that: *(a)* full investigation shall be made and an appropriate plan of action shall be developed for the future missional needs of the community; *(b)* the transfer or encumbrance shall conform to the *Discipline;* and *(c)* the congregation, if no longer to continue as an organized local United Methodist Church, does not sell but may transfer title of its facilities to another United Methodist church or agency. Certification by the district superintendent shall be conclusive evidence that the transfer or encumbrance conforms to the *Discipline.* The requirements of investigation and the development of a plan of action, however, shall not affect the merchantability of the title to the real estate or the legal effect of the instruments of sale or transfer to any congregation.

4. The resolution authorizing such proposed action shall direct that any contract, deed, bill of sale, mortgage, or other necessary written instrument be executed by and on behalf of the local church by any two of the officers of its board of trustees, who thereupon shall be duly authorized to carry out the direction of the charge conference; and any written instrument so executed shall be binding and effective as the action of the local church.

¶ **2540.** *Incorporated Local Church Property—Sale, Transfer, Lease, or Mortgage*—Any real property owned by or in which an incorporated local church has any interest may be sold, transferred, leased for a term of thirty days or more (which shall include leases for less than thirty days if such a lease is consecutive with the same lessee), or mortgaged subject to the following procedure and conditions:

1. Notice of the proposed action and the date and time of the regular or special meeting of the members of the corporate body—i.e., members of the charge conference at which it is to be considered—shall be given at least ten days prior thereto (except as local laws may otherwise provide) from the pulpit of the church or in its weekly bulletin.

2. A resolution authorizing the proposed action shall be passed by a majority vote of the members of the corporate body present and voting at any regular or special meeting thereof called to consider such action and a majority vote of the members of the charge conference, if the corporate members are different than the charge conference members.

3. The written consent of the pastor of the local church and the district superintendent to the proposed action shall be necessary and shall be affixed to or included in the instrument of sale, conveyance, transfer, lease, or mortgage. Prior to consenting to any proposed action required under this paragraph involving any United Methodist church property, the pastor, the district superintendent, and the district board of church location and building shall ensure that— *(a)* a full investigation shall be made and an appropriate plan of action shall be developed for the future missional needs of the community; *(b)* the transfer or encumbrance shall conform to the *Discipline; (c)* the congregation, if no longer to continue as an organized United Methodist church, does not sell but may transfer title of its facilities to another United Methodist church or agency; and *(d)* the congregation, in case of relocation, first offers its property to a United Methodist congregation or agency at a price not to exceed fair market value. The district strategies or other missional strategies should include the ministries of both United Methodist congregations and the community where the existing facility is located. Certification by the district superintendent shall be conclusive evidence that the transfer or encumbrance conforms to the *Discipline.* The requirements of investigation and the development of a plan of action shall not affect the merchantability of the title to the real estate or the legal effect of the instruments of sale or transfer.

4. The resolution authorizing such proposed action shall direct and authorize the corporation's board of directors to take all neces-

sary steps to carry out the action and to cause to be executed, as hereinafter provided, any necessary contract, deed, bill of sale, mortgage, or other written instrument.

5. The board of directors at any regular or special meeting shall take such action and adopt such resolutions as may be necessary or required by the local laws.

6. Any required contract, deed, bill of sale, mortgage, or other written instrument necessary to carry out the action so authorized shall be executed in the name of the corporation by any two of its officers, and any written instrument so executed shall be binding and effective as the action of the corporation.

¶ **2541.** *Disposition and Mortgage of Church Building or Parsonage*— Real property acquired by a conveyance subject to the trust clause may be sold in conformity with the provisions of the *Discipline* of The United Methodist Church when its use as a church building or parsonage, as the case may be, has been, or is intended to be, terminated; and when such real estate is sold or mortgaged in accordance with the provisions of the *Discipline* of The United Methodist Church, the written acknowledged consent of the proper district superintendent representing The United Methodist Church to the action taken shall constitute a release and discharge of the real property so sold and conveyed from the trust clause or clauses; or in the event of the execution of a mortgage, such consent of the district superintendent shall constitute a formal recognition of the priority of such mortgage lien and the subordination of the foregoing trust provisions thereof; and no bona fide purchaser or mortgagee relying upon the foregoing record shall be charged with any responsibility with respect to the disposition by such local church of the proceeds of any such sale or mortgage; but the board of trustees receiving such proceeds shall manage, control, disburse, and expend the same in conformity to the order and direction of the charge conference or church local conference, subject to the provisions of the *Discipline* of The United Methodist Church with respect thereto.

¶ **2542.** *Restriction on Proceeds of Mortgage or Sale*[8]—1. No real property on which a church building or parsonage is located shall be mortgaged to provide for the current (or budget) expense of a local church, nor shall the principal proceeds of a sale of any such property be so used. This provision shall apply alike to unincorporated and incorporated local churches.[9]

---

8. *See* Judicial Council Decision 688.
9. *See* Judicial Council Decision 399.

2. A local church, whether or not incorporated, on complying with the provisions of the *Discipline* may mortgage its unencumbered real property as security for a loan to be made to a conference board of global ministries or a city or district missionary society; *provided* that the proceeds of such loan shall be used only for aiding in the construction of a new church.

3. Exception to this restriction may be granted in specifically designated instances to allow use of equity and/or accumulated assets from the sale of property to provide for congregational redevelopment efforts including program and staff. Such exception may be granted by the annual conference, the bishop, and the cabinet upon request of the local church in consultation with congregation development staff where applicable. A clear and detailed three-to-five-year redevelopment plan that projects a self-supporting ministry must accompany the request.

¶ **2543.** *Planning and Financing Requirements for Local Church Buildings*—If any local church desires to:

a) build a new church, a new educational building, or a new parsonage;

b) purchase a church, educational building, or parsonage; or

c) remodel an existing church, an existing educational building, or an existing parsonage where the cost of the remodeling will exceed 10 percent of the value of the existing structure, then the local church shall first establish a study committee to:

    (1) analyze the needs of the church and community;

    (2) project the potential membership with average attendance;

    (3) write up the church's program of ministry (¶¶ 201–204); and

    (4) develop an accessibility plan including chancel areas.

The information and findings obtained by the study committee shall:

    (a) form the basis of a report to be presented to the charge conference (¶ 2543.3);

    (b) be used by the building committee (¶ 2543.4); and

    (c) become a part of the report to the district board of church location and building (¶¶ 2543.5, 2520.1).

1. After the study committee finishes its work, the local church shall secure the written consent of the pastor and the district superintendent to the building project, purchase proposal, or remodeling project.

2. In the case of a building project or purchase proposal, the local church shall secure the approval of the proposed site by the district board of church location and building as provided in the *Discipline* (¶ 2519.1).

3. The charge conference of the local church shall authorize the building project, purchase proposal, or remodeling project at a regular or called meeting. Notice of the meeting and the proposed action shall have been given for not less than ten days prior to the charge conference (except as local laws may otherwise provide) from the pulpit or in the weekly bulletin.

*a)* After approving a building project or a remodeling project, the charge conference shall elect a building committee of not fewer than three members of the local church to serve in the development of the project as hereinafter set forth; *provided* that the charge conference may commit to its board of trustees the duties of the building committee.

*b)* After approving a purchase proposal, the charge conference shall be deemed to have authorized and directed the board of trustees to proceed with the purchase. In the case of the purchase of a parsonage, the board of trustees shall either:

(1) purchase a parsonage that has on the ground-floor level:

*(a)* one room that can be used as a bedroom by a person with a disability;

*(b)* one fully accessible bathroom; and

*(c)* fully accessible laundry facilities; or

(2) purchase a parsonage without the accessible features for persons with disabilities specified above and remodel it within one year's time, so that it does have those features.

4. The building committee shall:

*a)* use the information and findings of the study committee and any other relevant information to estimate carefully the building facilities needed, as the case may be, to house the church's program of worship, education, and fellowship or to provide for the present and future pastors and their families;

*b)* ascertain the cost of any property to be purchased; and

*c)* develop preliminary architectural plans that:

(1) comply with local building, fire, and accessibility codes;

(2) clearly outline the location on the site of all proposed present and future construction; and

(3) provide adequate facilities for parking, entrance, seating,

rest rooms, and accessibility for persons with disabilities, but providing for such adequate facilities shall not apply in the case of a minor remodeling project;

*d)* provide on the ground-floor level of a newly constructed parsonage:

(1) one room that can be used as a bedroom by a person with a disability;

(2) a fully accessible bathroom; and

(3) fully accessible laundry facilities;

*e)* secure an estimate of the cost of the proposed construction;

*f)* develop a financial plan for defraying the total cost, including an estimate of the amount the membership can contribute in cash and pledges and the amount the local church can borrow if necessary.

5. The building committee shall submit to the district board of church location and building for its consideration and preliminary approval:

*a)* a statement of the need for the proposed facilities;

*b)* the preliminary architectural plans, including accessibility plans;

*c)* the preliminary cost estimate; and

*d)* the preliminary financial plan.

6. After preliminary approval by the district board of church location and building, the pastor, with the written consent of the district superintendent, shall call a church conference, giving not less than ten days' notice (except as local laws may otherwise provide) of the meeting and the proposed action from the pulpit or in the weekly bulletin. At the church conference, the building committee shall present:

*a)* the preliminary architectural plans;

*b)* the preliminary cost estimate;

*c)* the preliminary financial plan; and

*d)* the building committee's recommendation.

A majority vote of the membership present and voting at the church conference shall be required to approve the preliminary architectural plans, cost estimate, and financial plan and the building committee's recommendation.

7. After approval by the church conference, the building committee shall develop detailed plans and specifications and secure a reliable and detailed estimate of cost, which shall be presented for approval to the charge conference and to the district board of church location and building.

8. After approval by the charge conference and district board of church location and building, the building committee may begin the building project or remodeling project. Written documentation substantiating the approvals of the charge conference and the district board of church location and building shall be lodged with the district superintendent and the secretary of the charge conference.

9. In metropolitan areas, the building committee shall ensure that adequate steps are taken to obtain the services of minority (nonwhite) and female skilled persons in the construction in proportion to the racial and ethnic balance in the area. In non-metropolitan areas, the building committee shall ensure that racial and ethnic persons are employed in the construction where available and in relation to the available workforce.

10. The local church shall acquire a fee simple title to the lot or lots on which any building is to be erected. The deed or conveyance shall be executed as provided in this chapter. It is recommended that contracts on property purchased by a local church be contingent upon the securing of a guaranteed title, and the property's meeting of basic environmental requirements of lending institutions and of local and state laws.

11. If a loan is needed, the local church shall comply with the provisions of ¶ 2539 or ¶ 2540.

12. The local church shall not enter into a building contract or, if using a plan for volunteer labor, incur obligations for materials until it has cash on hand, pledges payable during the construction period, and (if needed) a loan or written commitment therefor that will assure prompt payment of all contractual obligations and other accounts when due.

13. Neither the trustees nor any other members of a local church shall be required to guarantee personally any loan made to the church by any board created by or under the authority of the General Conference.

14. It is recommended that a local church not enter into a binding building contract without the contractor being properly bonded or furnishing other forms of security, such as an irrevocable letter of credit approved by the conference, district, or local church attorney.

¶ **2544.** *Consecration and Dedication of Local Church Buildings*—On acquisition or completion of any church building, parsonage, or other church unit, a service of consecration may be held. Before any church building, parsonage, or other church unit is formally dedicated, all indebtedness against the same shall be discharged.

¶ **2545.** *Merger of Local United Methodist Churches*—Two or more local churches, in order to more effectively fulfill their ministry (¶¶ 201–204), may merge and become a single church by pursuing the following procedure:

1. The merger must be proposed to the charge conference of each of the merging churches by a resolution stating the terms and conditions of the proposed merger.

2. The plan of the merger as proposed to the charge conference of each of the merging churches shall be approved by each of the charge conferences in order for the merger to be effected, except that for a charge conference that includes two or more local churches, the required approval shall be by the church local conference of each local church in accordance with the requirements of ¶ 2526.

3. The merger must be approved by the superintendent or superintendents of the district or districts in which the merging churches are located.

4. The requirements of any and all laws of the state or states in which the merging churches are located affecting or relating to the merger of such churches must be complied with, and in any case where there is a conflict between such laws and the procedure outlined in the *Discipline*, said laws shall prevail and the procedure outlined in the *Discipline* shall be modified to the extent necessary to eliminate such conflict.

5. All archives and records of churches involved in a merger shall become the responsibility of the successor church.

¶ **2546.** *Interdenominational Local Church Mergers*—One or more local United Methodist churches may merge with one or more churches of other denominations and become a single church by pursuing the following procedure:

1. Following appropriate dialogue, which shall include discussions with the United Methodist district superintendent of the district in which the merging churches are located and the corresponding officials of the other judicatories involved, a plan of merger reflecting the nature and ministry of the local church (¶¶ 201–204) shall be submitted to the charge conference of the local United Methodist church and must be approved by a resolution stating the terms and conditions and missional plans of the proposed merger, including the denominational connection of the merger church.

2. The plan of merger, as approved by the charge conference of the United Methodist church, in a charge conference including two or more local churches must be approved by the church local conference of each local church in accordance with the requirements of ¶ 2526.

3. The merger must be approved in writing by the superintendent of the district, a majority of the district superintendents, and the bishop of the area in which the merging churches are located.

4. The provisions of ¶ 2503 shall be included in the plan of merger where applicable.

5. The requirements of any and all laws of the state or states in which the merging churches are located affecting or relating to the merger of such churches must be complied with, and in any case where there is a conflict between such laws and the procedure outlined in the *Discipline*, said laws shall prevail and the procedure outlined in the *Discipline* shall be modified to the extent necessary to eliminate such conflict.

6. Where property is involved, the provisions of ¶ 2547 obtain.

¶ **2547.** *Deeding Church Property to Federated Churches or Other Evangelical Denominations*—1. With the consent of the presiding bishop and of a majority of the district superintendents and of the district board of church location and building and at the request of the charge conference or of a meeting of the membership of the church, where required by local law, and in accordance with the said law, the annual conference may instruct and direct the board of trustees of a local church to deed church property to a federated church.

2. With the consent of the presiding bishop and of a majority of the district superintendents and of the district board of church location and building and at the request of the charge conference or of a meeting of the membership of the local church, where required by local law, and in accordance with said law, the annual conference may instruct and direct the board of trustees of a local church to deed church property to one of the other denominations represented in the Commission on Pan-Methodist Cooperation and Union or to another evangelical denomination under an allocation, exchange of property, or comity agreement; *provided* that such agreement shall have been committed to writing and signed and approved by the duly qualified and authorized representatives of both parties concerned.

¶ **2548.** *Discontinuation or Abandonment of Local Church Property*— 1. Prior to a recommendation by a district superintendent to discontinue the use of church property as a local church pursuant to ¶ 2548.2 hereof, or before any action by the annual conference trustees with regard to the assumption of any local church property considered to be abandoned pursuant to ¶ 2548.3, the district superintendent should obtain and consider an opinion of legal counsel as to the existence of any reversion, possibility of reverter, right of reacquisition, or similar restrictions to the benefit of any party.

2. *Discontinuation*—*a)* Prior to a recommendation of the district superintendent, in consultation with the appropriate agency assigned the responsibility of the conference parish and community development strategy, that a local church be discontinued, the district superintendent shall guide the congregation in an assessment of its potential as outlined in ¶ 213. A recommendation of discontinuance shall include recommendations as to the future use of the property and where the membership (¶ 228) and the title to all the real and personal, tangible and intangible property of the local church shall be transferred. On such recommendation that a local church no longer serves the purpose for which it was organized and incorporated (¶¶ 201–204), with the consent of the presiding bishop and of a majority of the district superintendents and the district board of church location and building of the district in which the action is contemplated, the annual conference may declare any local church within its bounds discontinued.

*b)* If a church has been discontinued by the annual conference without direction concerning the disposition of property, the real and personal, tangible and intangible property shall be disposed of as if it were abandoned local church property (¶ 2548.3).

*c)* If the annual conference declares any local church discontinued, the failure to complete any of the prior steps will not invalidate such discontinuance.

3. *Abandonment*—When a local church property is no longer used, kept, or maintained by its membership as a place of divine worship, the property shall be considered abandoned, and when a local church no longer serves the purpose for which it was organized and incorporated (¶¶ 201–204), with the consent of the presiding bishop, a majority of the district superintendents, and of the district board of church location and building, the annual conference trustees may assume control of the real and personal, tangible and intangible property. If circumstances make immediate action necessary, the conference trustees, should give first option to the other denominations repre-

sented in the Commission on Pan-Methodist Cooperation and Union. The conference trustees may proceed to sell or lease said property, retain the proceeds in an interest-bearing account, and recommend the disposition of the proceeds in keeping with annual conference policy. It shall be the duty of the annual conference trustees to remove, insofar as reasonably possible, all Christian and church insignia and symbols from such property. In the event of loss, damage to, or destruction of such local church property, the trustees of the annual conference are authorized to collect and receipt for any insurance payable on account thereof as the duly and legally authorized representative of such local church.[10]

4. All the deeds, records, and other official and legal papers, including the contents of the cornerstone, of a church that is so declared to be abandoned or otherwise discontinued shall be collected by the district superintendent in whose district said church was located and shall be deposited for permanent safekeeping with the commission on archives and history of the annual conference.

5. All gifts held in trust, assets of any endowment funds, and assets of any foundation of the church, shall be reviewed as part of the discontinuance or abandonment. All such assets shall pass as directed by the annual conference, or, if there is no such direction, to the trustees of the annual conference, unless otherwise directed by operation of law.

6. Any gift, legacy, devise, annuity, or other benefit to a pastoral charge or local church that accrues or becomes available after said charge or church has been discontinued or abandoned shall become the property of the trustees of the annual conference within whose jurisdiction the said discontinued or abandoned church was located or shall pass as directed by vote of the annual conference.

¶ **2549.** *Board of Trustees Report to the Charge Conference*—The board of trustees shall annually make a written report to the charge conference, in which shall be included the following:

1. The legal description and the reasonable valuation of each parcel of real estate owned by the church;

2. The specific name of the grantee in each deed of conveyance of real estate to the local church;

3. An inventory and the reasonable valuation of all personal property owned by the local church;

---

10. *See* Judicial Council Decisions 119, 138, 143.

4. The amount of income received from any income-producing property and a detailed list of expenditures in connection therewith;

5. The amount received during the year for building, rebuilding, remodeling, and improving real estate, and an itemized statement of expenditures;

6. Outstanding capital debts and how contracted;

7. A detailed statement of the insurance carried on each parcel of real estate, indicating whether restricted by co-insurance or other limiting conditions and whether adequate insurance is carried;

8. The name of the custodian of all legal papers of the local church, and where they are kept;

9. A detailed list of all trusts in which the local church is the beneficiary, specifying where and how the funds are invested, clarifying the manner in which these investments made a positive contribution toward the realization of the goals outlined in the Social Principles of the Church, and in what manner the income therefrom is expended or applied.[11]

10. An evaluation of all church properties, including the chancel areas, to ensure accessibility to persons with disabilities; and when applicable, a plan and timeline for the development of accessible church properties.

¶ 2550. *Exceptions to Requirements of this Chapter*—The provisions herein written concerning the organization and administration of the local church, including the procedure for acquiring, holding, and transferring real property, shall not be mandatory in central conferences, provisional central conferences, provisional annual conferences, or missions; and in such instances, the legislation in ¶¶ 535–545 and 553–563 shall apply.

¶ 2551. *Covenant Relationships in Multi-Ethnic and Multi-Language Settings*—In situations where a local church or churches share a building with a congregation or with another group performing ministries in different languages and/or with different racial and ethnic groups, it shall be in accordance with ¶¶ 202, 206, and 212. The district superintendent must consent to any such action before implementation. The district board on church location and building must be informed of such action.

1. If the congregations are United Methodist, the following shall apply:

---

11. *See* Judicial Council Decision 420.

*a)* By action of the charge conference(s) involved, a covenant relationship shall be mutually agreed upon in written form and shall include a statement of purpose for sharing the facility and shall state whether the agreement is seen as temporary, long-term, or permanent. The covenant of relationship may provide for mutual representation on such bodies as church council and other committees and work groups. The board of trustees of the church that holds title to the property may form a property committee composed of representatives of each congregation. The purpose of this arrangement is to enhance communication between the two or more congregations, to coordinate schedules and building usage, to involve the congregations in building maintenance and care under supervision of the board of trustees, and to coordinate cooperative programs.

*b)* No United Methodist congregation shall pay rent to another United Methodist church. However, each congregation should be expected to pay a mutually agreed share of building expenses.

*c)* Congregations that share the same facility and other properties are encouraged to organize and share intentionally in some mutual ministries to strengthen their relationships and their effectiveness when focusing on the same objectives. Cooperative programs may be developed that enhance the ministry of both congregations and their witness to the love of Jesus Christ in the community. Such programs may include joint bilingual worship services and Christian education programs, fellowship meals, and community outreach ministries.

*d)* Each congregation in a shared facility is strongly encouraged to accept an interdependent relationship in reference to use of the facility. Such a relationship affirms cooperatively planned and executed programs and activities as well as independently planned and executed programs and activities. Thus, scheduling programs and using the facility will be implemented in a manner that contributes to the positive growth of each congregation.

*e)* In situations where local congregations and/or ministries that share facilities cannot negotiate decisions that are supportive mutually by each congregation or ministry, the district superintendent shall consult with the leadership of each congregation and/or ministry prior to the implementing of any decision that may adversely affect the future of either congregation or ministry.

2. If a United Methodist church is sharing with a congregation of another denomination, the following should apply:

*a)* Prior to agreeing to share facilities with a congregation that is not United Methodist and is of a different ethnic or language background, the United Methodist pastor and the district superintendent shall first contact district and conference congregational development agencies and ethnic leadership to explore the possibilities of organizing as an ecumenical shared ministry or a new United Methodist congregation with that ethnic or language group.

*b)* If it is decided that the United Methodist congregation and the congregation of another denomination should share facilities, as a part of the covenant of mission, a property-use agreement shall be negotiated in writing in accordance with ¶ 2503; this agreement shall have the consent of the district superintendent and shall be approved by the United Methodist charge or church conference. Shared activities may be entered into to enhance the ministry of both congregations. A liaison committee to both congregations may be appointed to resolve conflicts, clear schedules, and plan cooperative activities.

3. Ninety-day notification of intent to terminate the covenant relationship shall be made to the district superintendent and to the other parties in the covenant relationship. This termination shall require the consent of the district superintendent following consultation with the parties involved.

4. The district committee on religion and race shall monitor all consultations and plans related to the transfer or use of property to ensure fairness and equity in situations involving two or more local congregations or ministries.

## Section VII. Requirements—Trustees of Church Institutions

¶ **2552.** *Standards and Requirements*—Trustees of schools, colleges, universities, hospitals, homes, orphanages, institutes, and other institutions owned or controlled by any annual, jurisdictional, or central conference or any agency of The United Methodist Church shall be at least twenty-one years of age. At all times, not less than three-fifths of them shall be members of a local church and/or members of an annual conference or the Council of Bishops of The United Methodist Church, and all must be nominated, confirmed, or elected by such conference or agency of the Church or by some body or officer thereof to which or to whom this power has been delegated by such conference or agency; *provided* that the number of trustees of any such institution owned or controlled by any annual conference or conferences required to be members of a local church and/or annual conference or the Council of Bishops of The United Methodist Church may be reduced to not less than the majority by a three-fourths vote of such annual conference or conferences; and *provided* further, that when an institution is owned and operated jointly with some other religious organization, said requirement that three-fifths of the trustees shall be members of a local church and/or annual conference or the Council of Bishops of The United Methodist Church shall apply only to the portion of the trustees selected by the United Methodist agency or annual, jurisdictional, or central conference. It is recognized that there are numerous educational, health-care, and charitable organizations that traditionally have been affiliated with The United Methodist Church and its predecessor denominations, which are neither owned nor controlled by any unit of the denomination.

## Chapter Seven

# JUDICIAL ADMINISTRATION

### Section I. The Judicial Council

¶ **2601.** *Duties and Responsibilities of the Judicial Council*—The Judicial Council is the highest judicial body in The United Methodist Church. The Judicial Council shall have authority as specified in the Constitution, ¶¶53–55, and in ¶¶ 2609–2612.

¶ **2602.** *Members*—1. Composition and Term—The Judicial Council shall be composed of nine members and should reflect the racial, ethnic, and gender diversity of The United Methodist Church. In the year 2000 and each sixteen years thereafter, there shall be elected three laypersons and two ordained clergy other than bishops. In 2004 and each eight years thereafter, there shall be elected two ordained clergy other than bishops and two laypersons. In 2008 and each sixteen years thereafter, there shall be three ordained clergy other than bishops and two laypersons. They shall be members of The United Methodist Church. Elections shall be held at each session of the General Conference for only the number of members whose terms expire at such session. A member's term of office shall be eight years. A member may serve a maximum of two consecutive eight-year terms, with a minimum of four years before re-election to the council.

2. Nominations and Election—Members of the council shall be nominated and elected in the manner following: At each quadrennial session of the General Conference, the Council of Bishops shall nominate by majority vote three times the number of ordained ministers and laypersons to be elected at such session of the General Conference. The number to be elected shall correspond to the number of members whose terms expire at the conclusion of such session. Each of the jurisdictions and the central conferences as a group shall be represented by at least one nominee, but it shall not be a requirement that each of the jurisdictions or the central conferences as a group be represented by an elected member.[1] At the same daily session at which the above nominations are announced, nominations of both

---

1. *See* Judicial Council Decision 540.

ministers and laypersons may be made from the floor, but at no other time. The names of all nominees, identified with the conference to which each belongs, and a biographical sketch that does not exceed one hundred words shall be published by the *Daily Christian Advocate* at least forty-eight hours prior to the time of election, which shall be set by action of the General Conference at the session at which the nominations are made; and from these nominations the General Conference shall elect without discussion, by ballot and majority vote, the necessary number of ministerial and lay members.

¶ 2603. *Alternates*—There shall be six alternates for the clergy members and six alternates for the lay members, and their qualifications shall be the same as for membership on the Judicial Council. The term of the alternates shall be for four years.

The alternates shall be elected in the following manner: From the clergy and lay nominees remaining on the ballot after the election of the necessary number of members of the Judicial Council to be elected at sessions of the General Conference, the General Conference shall by separate ballot, without discussion and by majority vote, elect the number of clergy and lay alternates to be chosen at such session of the General Conference.

¶ 2604. *Vacancies*—1. If a vacancy in the membership of the council occurs during the interim between sessions of the General Conference, a clergy vacancy shall be filled by the first-elected clergy alternate and a lay vacancy by the first-elected lay alternate. The alternate filling such vacancy shall hold office as a member of the Judicial Council for the unexpired term of the member whom the alternate succeeds. In the event of any vacancy, it shall be the duty of the president and secretary of the council to notify the alternate entitled to fill it.

2. In the event of an absence of one or more members of the council during a session of the Judicial Council, such temporary vacancy among the clergy members may be filled for that session or the remainder thereof by the clergy alternates in order of election who can be present, and such temporary vacancy among the lay members by the lay alternates in order of election who can be present; but inability or failure to fill a vacancy does not affect the validity or any action of the council so long as a quorum is present.

¶ 2605. *Expiration of Term*—The term of office of the members of the council and of the alternates shall expire upon the adjournment of the General Conference at which their successors are elected.

¶ **2606.** *Ineligibility of Members*—Members of the council shall be ineligible to serve as delegates to the general, jurisdictional, or central conference or to serve in any general, jurisdictional, or central conference board or agency.[2]

¶ **2607.** *Confidentiality and Ex Parte Communication*—1. The members of the Judicial Council will not permit discussion with them on matters pending before them or that may be referred to them for determination, save and except before the Judicial Council in session. Questions of procedure may be raised with the presiding officer or secretary of the Judicial Council. While strictly observing the intent of the preceding paragraph, a member of the council to whom a case has been assigned by the president may request that the secretary secure from persons and agencies concerned directly or indirectly with the case pertinent facts, briefs, and statements shall be sent promptly by the secretary of the council to other members of the council as is deemed necessary.[3]

2. Prior to the decision of a case in question, members of the Judicial Council shall not discuss with any party matters of substance pending in the judicial process unless all parties are privy to the discussion.

The Judicial Council shall in all cases in which a decision or memorandum is issued set forth the specific provisions of the Constitution or the *Discipline* that provide the basis of the decision and the rationale that led to the conclusion.

¶ **2608.** *Organization and Procedure*—1. The Judicial Council shall provide its own method of organization and procedure, both with respect to hearings on appeals and petitions for declaratory decisions. All parties shall have the privilege of filing briefs and arguments and presenting evidence under such rules as the council may adopt from time to time; provided that at the time of filing, copies of such briefs are delivered to all parties of record.

2. Time and Place—The council shall meet at the time and place of the meeting of the General Conference and shall continue in session until the adjournment of that body, and at least one other time in each calendar year and at such other times as it may deem appropriate, at such places as it may select from time to time. Seven members shall constitute a quorum. An affirmative vote of at least six members

---

2. *See* Judicial Council Decision 196; and Decision 3, Interim Judicial Council.
3. *See* Judicial Council Decision 763.

of the council shall be necessary to declare any act of the General Conference unconstitutional. On other matters, a majority vote of the entire council shall be sufficient. The council may decline to entertain an appeal or a petition for a declaratory decision in any instance in which it determines that it does not have jurisdiction to decide the matter.

¶ **2609.** *Jurisdiction and Powers*—1. The Judicial Council shall determine the constitutionality of any act of the General Conference upon an appeal by a majority of the Council of Bishops or one-fifth of the members of the General Conference.

2. The Judicial Council shall have jurisdiction to determine the constitutionality of any proposed legislation when such declaratory decision is requested by the General Conference or by the Council of Bishops.

3. The Judicial Council shall determine the constitutionality of any act of a jurisdictional or central conference upon an appeal by a majority of the bishops of that jurisdictional or central conference or upon an appeal by one-fifth of the members of that jurisdictional or central conference.[4]

4. The Judicial Council shall hear and determine the legality of any action taken by any body created or authorized by the General Conference or any body created or authorized by a jurisdictional or central conference, upon appeal by one-third of the members thereof or upon request of the Council of Bishops or a majority of the bishops of the jurisdictional or central conference wherein the action was taken.

5. The Judicial Council shall hear and determine the legality of any action taken by any body created or authorized by a General Conference or any body created or authorized by the jurisidictional or central conference on a matter affecting an annual or a provisional annual conference, upon appeal by two-thirds of the members of the annual or provisional annual conference present and voting.[5]

6. The Judicial Council shall pass upon and affirm, modify, or reverse the decisions of law made by bishops in central, district, annual, or jurisdictional conferences upon questions of law submitted to them in writing in the regular business of a session; and in order to facilitate such review, each bishop shall report annually in writing to

---

4. *See* Judicial Council Decision 338.
5. *See* Judicial Council Decision 463.

the Judicial Council on forms provided by the council all the bishop's decisions of law. No such episcopal decision shall be authoritative, except in the case pending, until it has been passed upon by the Judicial Council, but thereafter it shall become the law of the Church to the extent that it is affirmed by the council. Normally, the bishop shall rule before the close of the annual conference session during which the question was submitted, but in no case later than thirty days after the close of the session. The annual conference secretary shall enter in the annual conference journal an exact statement of the question submitted and the ruling of the bishop.[6]

7. The Judicial Council shall hear and determine any appeal from a bishop's decision on a question of law made in a central, district, annual, or jurisdictional conference when said appeal has been made by one-fifth of that conference present and voting.[7]

8. The Judicial Council shall have power to review an opinion or decision of a committee on appeals of a jurisdictional or central conference if it should appear that such opinion or decision is at variance with the *Book of Discipline*, a prior decision of the Judicial Council, or an opinion or decision of a committee on appeals of another jurisdictional or central conference on a question of Church law. In the event the committee on appeals decision appears to be at variance with the decision of another committee on appeals, then the following procedure should be followed:

*a)* Any party to the opinion or decision may appeal the case to the Judicial Council on the ground of such conflict of decisions; or

*b)* The committee on appeals rendering the last of such opinions or decisions may certify the case to, and file it with, the Judicial Council on the ground of such conflict of decisions; or

*c)* The attention of the president of the Judicial Council being directed to such conflict or alleged conflict of decisions, the president may issue an order directing the secretaries of the committees on appeals involved to certify a copy of a sufficient portion of the record to disclose the nature of the case and the entire opinion and decision of the committee on appeals in each case to the Judicial Council for its consideration at its next meeting.

The Judicial Council shall hear and determine the question of Church law involved but shall not pass upon the facts in either case

---

6. *See* Judicial Council Decisions 747, 762, 763.
7. *See* Judicial Council Decision 153.

further than is necessary to decide the question of Church law involved. After deciding the question of Church law, the Judicial Council shall cause its decision to be certified to each of the committees on appeals involved, and such committees on appeals shall take such action, if any, as may be necessary under the law as determined by the Judicial Council.

*d)* All opinions and decisions of jurisdictional and central conference committees on appeal shall be sent to the secretary of the Judicial Council within thirty days after a decision. These decisions shall be made available to those who are involved in trials when needed and for those preparing for trial, but not otherwise.

9. The Judicial Council shall have other duties and powers as may be conferred upon it by the General Conference.

10. All decisions of the Judicial Council shall be final. However, when the Judicial Council shall declare any act of the General Conference then in session unconstitutional, that decision shall be reported to that General Conference immediately. This legislation shall take effect immediately upon passage by the General Conference.

¶ 2610. *Declaratory Decisions*—1. The Judicial Council, on petition as hereinafter provided, shall have jurisdiction to make a ruling in the nature of a declaratory decision as to the constitutionality, meaning, application, or effect of the *Discipline* or any portion thereof or of any act or legislation of a General Conference; and the decision of the Judicial Council thereon shall be as binding and effectual as a decision made by it on appeal.[8]

2. The following bodies in The United Methodist Church are hereby authorized to make such petitions to the Judicial Council for declaratory decisions: (a) the General Conference;[9] (b) the Council of Bishops; (c) any body created or authorized by the General Conference on matters relating to or affecting the work of such body; (d) a majority of the bishops assigned to any jurisdiction on matters relating to or affecting jurisdictions or the work therein; (e) a majority of the bishops assigned to any central conference on matters relating to or affecting the central conferences or the work therein; (f) any jurisdictional conference on matters relating to or affecting jurisdictions or jurisdictional conferences or the work therein; (g) any body created

---

8. *See* Judicial Council Decisions 106, 172, 301, 434, 443, 454, 463, 474, 566.
9. *See* Judicial Council Decision 889.

or authorized by the jurisdictional conference on matters relating to or affecting the work of such body; (h) any central conference on matters relating to or affecting central conference or the work therein; (i) any body authorized or created by a central conference on matters relating to or affecting the work of such body; and (j) any annual conference on matters relating to annual conferences or the work therein.[10]

3. When a declaratory decision is sought, all persons or bodies who have or claim any interest that would be affected by the declaration shall be parties to the proceeding, and the petition shall name such parties. Except for requests filed during the General conference, any party requesting a declaratory decision shall file a brief statement of the question involved with the secretary of the Judicial Council. After receiving such request, the secretary of the Judicial Council shall submit a brief statement of the question involved to *Newscope*, or any publication specified by notice in *Newscope*, to be included—without cost—in the next edition. The Judicial Council shall not hear and determine any such matter until thirty days after such publication in *Newscope*. The same information shall also be printed in *The Interpreter* and be published at the official United Methodist Web site (www.umc.org) or its successor. If the president of the council determines that other parties not named by the petition would be affected by such a decision, such additional parties shall also be added, and the petitioner or petitioners, upon direction of the secretary of the Judicial Council, shall then be required to serve all parties so joined with a copy of the petition within fifteen days after such direction by the secretary of the Judicial Council. In like manner, any interested party may, on the party's own motion, intervene and answer, plead, or interplead.[11]

¶ **2611.** *Precedential Value*—The decisions of the Judicial Council of The Methodist Church heretofore issued shall have the same authority in The United Methodist Church as they had in The Methodist Church, persuasive as precedents, except where their basis has been changed by the terms of the Plan of Union or other revisions of Church law.

¶ **2612.** *Notification and Publication*—The decisions of the Judicial Council on questions of Church law, with a summary of the facts of the opinion, shall be filed with the secretary of the General Confer-

---

10. *See* Judicial Council Decisions 29, 212, 255, 301, 309, 382, 452, 535.
11. *See* Judicial Council Decision 437.

ence and with the bishop, chancellor, and secretary of each annual conference. Publication of decisions shall be as follows:

1. Within ninety days following each session of the Judicial Council, the digest of decisions of the Judicial Council shall be published in *Newscope* and *The Interpreter* or their successor publications. This requirement for published notice may also be complied with by posting the digests of decisions on official United Methodist Internet Web Sites.

2. The decisions of the Judicial Council rendered during each year shall be published in the General Minutes.

3. The decisions of the Judicial Council shall be at the official United Methodist Web site (www.umc.org or its successor).

4. When the Judicial Council shall have declared unconstitutional any provision of the *Book of Discipline*, the secretary of the Judicial Council shall notify the chairperson of the Committee on Correlation and Editorial revision which phrase or sentence was found to violate the Constitution so that it will not appear in the next edition. All such deletions also shall appear in the *Advance Daily Christian Advocate* (or successor publication) of the next General Conference for information purposes.

## Section II. Investigations, Trials, and Appeals

¶ **2701.** *Fair Process in Judicial Proceedings*—The judicial process shall have as its purpose a just resolution of judicial complaints, in the hope that God's work of justice, reconciliation and healing may be realized in the body of Jesus Christ. The following procedures are presented for the protection of the rights of individuals guaranteed under Section III, Article IV, of our Constitution and for the protection of the Church. The presumption of innocence shall be maintained until the conclusion of the trial process. The judicial proceedings and the rights set forth in this paragraph commence upon referral of a matter as a judicial complaint from counsel for the Church to the committee on investigation. The judicial process terminates at the end of any appeal or right of appeal. Special attention should be given to ensuring racial, ethnic, and gender diversity of boards, committees, and courts and the timely disposition of all matters.[12]

1. The Right to be Heard—In any judicial proceeding, (a) the respondent (the person to whom the procedure is being applied) and

---

12. *See* Judicial Council Decision 695.

the Church shall have a right to be heard before any final action is taken, and (b) the complainant and the respondent have the right to be present.

2. Notice of Judicial Process Hearings—Notice of any judicial process hearing shall advise the respondent of the reason for the proposed procedures, with sufficient detail to allow the respondent to prepare a response. Notice shall be given not less than twenty days prior to the hearing.

3. Right to be Accompanied—The respondent shall have a right to be accompanied by a clergyperson in full connection to any judicial process hearing to which he or she is subject, in accordance with the appropriate disciplinary provisions (see ¶ 2706.2). The clergyperson accompanying the respondent shall have the right of advocacy.

4. Communications—In any judicial proceeding, under no circumstances shall one party or counsel, in the absence of the other party or counsel, discuss substantive matters with members of the pending hearing, trial, or appellate body while the case is pending. Questions of procedure may be raised with the presiding officer or secretary of the hearing or appellate body.

5. Double Jeopardy—No bill of charges shall be certified by any committee on investigation after an earlier bill of charges has been certified by a committee on investigation based on the same alleged occurrences.

6. Access to Records—The respondent and the Church shall have access to all records relied upon in the determination of the outcome of the committee on investigation, trial court, or appeal committee or body.[13]

7. Failure to Appear or Respond—In the event that a clergyperson fails to appear for supervisory interviews, refuses mail, refuses to communicate personally with the bishop or district superintendent, or otherwise fails to respond to supervisory requests or requests from official administrative or judicial committees, such actions or inactions shall not be used as an excuse to avoid or delay any Church processes, and such processes may continue without the participation of such individual.

8. Healing within the Congregation—As a part of the judicial process, the bishop and cabinet, in consultation with the presiding officer of the pending hearing, trial, or appellate body then sitting, shall provide for healing within the congregation if there has been significant disruption to congregational life by the judicial matter. This may

---

13. *See* Judicial Council Decisions 691, 765.

include a mediation process for unresolved conflicts, support for victims, and reconciliation for all who are involved. This process may also include the sharing of information by the bishop or a cabinet member about the nature of the complaint without disclosing alleged facts underlying the complaint that might compromise the judicial process.

9. Immunity of Participants—In order to preserve the integrity of the Church's judicial process and ensure full participation in it at all times, the resident bishop, the cabinet, the presiding officer of the trial, trial officers, trial court, witnesses, counsels, assistant counsels, advocates, complainant, committee on investigation and all others who participate in the Church's judicial process shall have immunity from prosecution of complaints brought against them related to their role in a particular judicial process, unless they have committed a chargeable offense in conscious and knowing bad faith. The complainant in any proceeding against any such person related to their role in a particular judicial process shall have the burden of proving, by clear and convincing evidence, that such person's actions constituted a chargeable offense committed knowingly in bad faith. The immunity set forth in this provision shall extend to civil court proceedings, to the fullest extent permissible by the civil laws.

¶ 2702. *Chargeable Offenses and the Statute of Limitations*—1. A bishop, clergy member of an annual conference (¶ 365), local pastor, clergy on honorable or administrative location, or diaconal minister may choose a trial when charged (subject to the statute of limitations in ¶ 2702.4)* with one or more of the following offenses: (a) immorality; (b) practices declared by The United Methodist Church to be incompatible with Christian teachings;[14] (c) crime; (d) failure to perform the work of the ministry; (e) disobedience to the Order and Discipline of The United Methodist Church; (f) dissemination of doctrines contrary to the established standards of doctrine of The United Methodist Church; (g) relationships and/or behavior that undermines the ministry of another pastor;[15] (h) racial harassment; (i) child abuse;** (j) sexual abuse;[16] (k) sexual misconduct** or (l) sexual harassment.

---

*The statute of limitations went into effect as law on a prospective basis starting on January 1, 1993. All alleged offenses that occurred prior to this date are time barred. *See* Judicial Council Decisions 691, 704, and 723.

14. *See* Judicial Council Decision 702.

15. *See* Judicial Council Decision 702.

** This offense was first listed as a separate chargeable offense in the 1996 *Book of Discipline* effective April 27, 1996. *See* Judicial Council Decision 691.

16. *See* Judicial Council Decisions 736, 768.

2. A bishop, clergy member of an annual conference, or diaconal minister may be brought to trial when the appropriate body recommends involuntary termination.[17]

3. A lay member of a local church may be charged with the following offenses, and, if so, may choose a trial: (a) immorality; (b) crime; (c) disobedience to the Order and Discipline of The United Methodist Church; (d) dissemination of doctrines contrary to the established standards of doctrine of The United Methodist Church; (e) racial harassment; (f) sexual abuse; (g) sexual misconduct;[‡] (h) sexual harassment; or (i) child abuse.[‡]

4. *Statute of Limitations*—No judicial complaint or charge shall be considered for any alleged occurrence that shall not have been committed within six years immediately preceding the filing of the original complaint, except in the case of sexual or child abuse (¶ 359.1*d*[1]).[*] In the case of sexual or child abuse there shall be no limitation. Time spent on leave of absence shall not be considered as part of the six years.

5. *Time of Offense*—A person shall not be charged with an offense that was not a chargeable offense at the time it is alleged to have been committed. Any charge filed shall be in the language of *The Book of Discipline* in effect at the time the offense is alleged to have occurred and must relate to an action listed as a chargeable offense in the *Discipline*.

PROCEDURES FOR REFERRAL AND INVESTIGATION OF A JUDICIAL COMPLAINT

¶ **2703.** *Composition of the Committee on Investigation*—

1. When respondent is a bishop—There shall be a committee on investigation elected by each jurisdictional or central conference on nomination of the College of Bishops in consultation with the jurisdictional episcopacy committee. The committee shall consist of seven clergy in full connection (with not more than one clergyperson from each annual conference, if possible), two lay observers, and six alternate members, five of whom shall be clergypersons in full connection (with not more than one clergyperson from each annual conference, if

---

17. *See* Judicial Council Decision 767.

‡This offense was first listed as a separate chargeable offense in the 2000 *Book of Discipline*, effective January 1, 2001. *See* Judicial Council Decision 691.

*See* note on p. 696.

possible) and one of whom shall be a layperson. Committee members shall be in good standing and should be deemed of good character. The committee should reflect racial, ethnic, and gender diversity. The committee shall elect a chairperson and organize at the jurisdictional or central conference. Seven clergy or alternates seated as members of the committee shall constitute a quorum.

2. When respondent is a clergy member of an annual conference, clergy on honorable or administrative location or a local pastor— There shall be a committee on investigation consisting of seven clergy in full connection, two laypersons, and six alternate members, five of whom shall be clergy in full connection and one of whom shall be a layperson. The committee shall be nominated by the presiding bishop in consultation with the board of ordained ministry and elected quadrennially by the annual conference. Committee members shall be in good standing and should be deemed of good character. The committee should reflect racial, ethnic, and gender diversity. The committee on investigation shall elect a chair and organize at the annual conference. None of the members or alternates shall be members of the board of ordained ministry, the cabinet, or immediate family members of the above. Should a member of the committee on investigation have been a party to any of the prior proceedings in a case that finally comes before the committee, he or she shall be disqualified from sitting on the committee during its consideration of that case, and his or her place shall be taken by an alternate member. Seven members or alternates seated as members of the committee shall constitute a quorum.

3. When respondent is a diaconal minister—In all cases, the pastor, district superintendent or bishop should take supervisory steps to resolve any grievances or complaints. There shall be a committee on investigation consisting of not fewer than three diaconal ministers or members of the Church who are not members of the board of ordained ministry, nominated by the presiding bishop and elected by the annual conference. Two alternate members shall be elected. Committee members shall be in good standing and should be deemed of good character. The committee should reflect racial, ethnic, and gender diversity. The committee on investigation shall elect a chair and organize at the annual conference. Three members or alternates seated as members of the committee shall constitute a quorum. When a conference does not have sufficient diaconal ministers to elect the required minimum committee and an investigation is needed, the

bishop, in consultation with the College of Bishops, shall request members of diaconal committees on investigation from other conferences in the jurisdiction in sufficient number to provide the required minimum committee for conducting the investigation.

4. <u>When respondent is a layperson</u>—In all cases, the pastor or district superintendent should take pastoral steps to resolve any complaints. If such pastoral response does not result in resolution and a written complaint is made against a layperson for any of the offenses in ¶ 2702.3, the pastor in charge or co-pastors (¶ 205.1) of the local church, in consultation with the district superintendent and the district lay leader, may appoint a committee on investigation consisting of seven lay members who come from other congregations, exclusive of the churches of the respondent or the complainant. Committee members shall be in good standing and should be deemed of good character. The committee should reflect racial, ethnic, and gender diversity. When the pastor in charge is (or co-pastors are) bringing the charge, the district superintendent, in consultation with the district lay leader, shall appoint the committee on investigation.

¶ **2704.** *Referral of Original Complaint to Counsel for the Church, Who Shall Prepare Judicial Complaint and Supporting Material for Consideration by Committee on Investigation—*

1. <u>When respondent is a bishop</u>—

*a)* If a written complaint is made against a bishop for any of the offenses in ¶ 2702.1, the counsel for the Church, as appointed under ¶ 413.3a, shall prepare, sign, and forward the judicial complaint and all documentary evidence under consideration to the chairperson of the committee on investigation, the person making the original complaint, and the bishop being charged (respondent). The respondent shall be given an opportunity to submit to the committee on investigation a written response to the judicial complaint within thirty days of receipt of the judicial complaint. The chairperson shall convene the committee on investigation within sixty days of receiving the judicial complaint.

*b)* If five or more members of the committee on investigation so recommend, the jurisdictional committee on the episcopacy may suspend the respondent pending the outcome of the judicial process.

*c)* For the purpose of this paragraph, the United Methodist bishops of the central conferences shall constitute one College of Bishops.

2. <u>When respondent is a clergy member of an annual conference, clergy on honorable or administrative location or a local pastor</u>—

*a)* If a written complaint is made against a clergyperson for any of the offenses in ¶ 2702.1, the bishop shall appoint a clergyperson in full connection as counsel for the Church (*see* ¶ 359.1 *d*[1]). Counsel for the Church shall prepare, sign, and refer the judicial complaint, with all relevant material, to the chairperson of the conference committee on investigation and represent the interests of the Church in pressing the claims of the person making the original complaint in any proceedings before the committee. A copy of the complaint and documentary evidence under consideration shall be sent to the respondent, the person making the original complaint, and the bishop. The respondent shall be given an opportunity to submit to the committee on investigation a written response to the judicial complaint within thirty days of receipt of the judicial complaint . The chairperson of the conference committee on investigation shall have sixty days to convene the committee on investigation after receiving the judicial complaint.

*b)* If five or more members of the committee on investigation so recommend, the bishop may suspend the person charged from all clergy responsibilities pending the outcome of the judicial process. The respondent retains all rights and privileges as stated in ¶ 325.

3. When respondent is a diaconal minister—

*a)* If a written complaint is made against a diaconal minister for any of the offenses in ¶ 2702.1, and the supervisory response does not result in resolution, the respondent's district superintendent may appoint a clergyperson in full connection or diaconal minister as counsel for the Church. Counsel for the Church shall prepare, sign, and refer the judicial complaint, with all relevant material, to the chairperson of the conference committee on investigation for diaconal ministers and represent the interests of the Church in pressing the claims of the person making the original complaint in any proceedings before the committee. A copy of the complaint and documentary evidence under consideration shall be sent to the respondent, the person making the original complaint, and the bishop. The respondent shall be given an opportunity to submit to the committee on investigation a written response to the judicial complaint within thirty days of receipt of the judicial complaint. The chairperson of the conference committee on investigation shall have sixty days to convene the committee on investigation after receiving the judicial complaint.

*b)* If at least two-thirds of the committee on investigation so recommend, the bishop may suspend the person charged from all professional responsibilities pending the outcome of the judicial process.

4. <u>When respondent is a layperson</u>—

*a)* In all cases, the pastor or district superintendent should take pastoral steps to resolve any grievances or complaints. If after such steps have been taken and have not resulted in a resolution and a written complaint is made against a layperson for any of the offenses in ¶ 2702.3, the pastor in charge or co-pastors (¶ 205.1) of the local church, in consultation with the district superintendent and the district lay leader, may appoint counsel for the Church, who shall be a United Methodist. Counsel for the Church shall prepare, sign, and refer the judicial complaint, with all relevant material, to the chairperson of committee on investigation.

*b)* If five or more members of the committee so recommend, the pastor may suspend the charged layperson from exercising any Church office pending outcome of the judicial process.

*c)* All complaints against a layperson under ¶ 2702.3 shall be submitted in writing, signed by the person(s) making the original complaint, and delivered to the pastor in charge of the local church of which the respondent is a member, and a copy shall be sent to the respondent.

*d)* The member shall be given an opportunity to submit to the committee on investigation a written response to the judicial complaint within thirty days of a receipt of the judicial complaint and the appointing of the committee and before consideration of the judicial complaint by the committee.

*e)* The district superintendent shall preside at all meetings of the committee, shall be given a copy of the judicial complaint and any response, and shall have the right to be present and to speak at all meetings of the committee.

¶ **2705.** *The Form of the Judicial Complaint*—The judicial complaint shall be prepared and signed by counsel for the Church. The complaint should explain to the committee on investigation the alleged events surrounding and relating to one or more chargeable offense(s). All relevant documents and other exhibits supporting the judicial complaint may be attached. The judicial complaint should include the appropriate chargeable offense(s) based on the list in ¶ 2702 and proposed specifications.

¶ **2706.** *Committee on Investigation—Procedures*—

1. <u>Introduction</u>—The role of the committee on investigation is to

conduct an investigation into the allegations made in the judicial complaint and to determine if reasonable grounds exist to bring a bill of charges and specifications to trial. If so, it shall prepare, sign and certify a bill of charges and specifications. The committee's duty is only to determine whether reasonable grounds exist to support the charges. It is not the committee's duty to determine guilt or innocence.

2. <u>Parties and counsel</u>—The parties are the respondent and the Church.

*a) Counsel for the Church*—Counsel for the Church shall be appointed as provided in ¶ 2708.7. Counsel for the Church shall be entitled to choose one assistant counsel without voice who may be an attorney.

*b) Committee on Investigation*—The committee on investigation may have legal counsel present, who shall not be the conference chancellor, for the sole purpose of providing advice to the committee.

*c) When respondent is a bishop, a clergy member of an annual conference, clergy on honorable or administrative location, a local pastor, a clergyperson, or a diaconal minister*—A respondent who is a bishop, a clergyperson, or a diaconal minister shall be entitled to select a clergyperson in full connection to serve as respondent's counsel. A respondent shall be entitled to choose one assistant counsel without voice who may be an attorney.

*d) Investigation of a respondent who is a layperson*—A lay respondent shall be entitled to select a lay member or clergyperson to serve as respondent's counsel. A respondent shall be entitled to choose one assistant counsel without voice who may be an attorney.

3. <u>Preliminary meeting</u>—Basic procedural decisions shall be made in a preliminary meeting. During this meeting, the respondent and the respondent's counsel, the person making the original complaint, and the counsel for the Church shall have the right to argue procedural points before a decision is made by the chair. All advance procedural decisions and such unanticipated decisions as may come in the course of the meeting of the committee on investigation shall be rendered in writing so as to be available for consideration in all further possible stages of the case.

4. <u>Hearing before the Committee on Investigation</u>—

*a)* If possible, the respondent and the person(s) bringing the original complaint shall be brought face to face, but the inability to do this shall not invalidate an investigation. Notice of the hearings shall be given to all parties, and the person(s) bringing the original complaint and they all shall be permitted to be present during testimony, but not during deliberations. Proceedings in the investigation shall be informal. No oaths shall be taken. All procedural decisions shall be made by the chairperson.

*b) Interview of witness prior to or outside of hearing*—The chairperson shall have the power, whenever it is appropriate in the committee's own discretion, to appoint a member(s) of the committee to interview any witness(es), provided that all parties may be present (without voice) and that three days notice of the time and place of such interview shall have been given to all parties. The person(s) so appointed shall create a verbatim record of the interview and certify the record by signature for transmittal to the chairperson.

*c) Examination of witnesses*—The committee on investigation may call and question such persons or request such written information, including but not limited to materials from the supervisory process, as it deems necessary to establish whether or not there are reasonable grounds for formulating a charge or charges. The committee may receive from the counsels suggested lists of persons to be questioned, sources of written material or questions. There shall be no right of cross-examination by either the respondent or the person(s) bringing the original complaint.

*d) Evidence*—The committee should only consider testimony or evidence which is relevant and reliable. The chairperson or presiding officer, after consultation with counsel for both parties, shall rule on challenges to relevance and reliability. The introduction of any material relating to events barred by the statute of limitations (¶ 2702.4) as evidence, as preface to evidence, or as build-up for evidence in the procedures of the committee on investigation or the trial proceedings shall be permitted when the presiding officer, after consultation with counsel for both parties, rules that such material is relevant and reliable.

*e) Verbatim transcript*—There shall be a verbatim record of all proceedings of the committee on investigation, except when the committee meets in executive session. The term *executive session* shall mean the committee meeting alone or with its legal counsel. If the complaint is dismissed or returned to the bishop, no verbatim record need be transcribed and the record that exists will be sent to the conference secretary for retention.

5. <u>Bill of Charges and Specifications, Deliberations, Vote, and Referral</u>—A vote on each charge and each specification shall be taken separately.

*a) Bill of Charges and Specifications*—A charge is one of the chargeable offenses listed in ¶ 2702. A charge shall not include more than one such chargeable offense. More than one charge against the same person may be presented and tried at the same time. Each charge must be written, with specifications that support the charge. Each charge must be accompanied by one or more specifications of fact. Each specification, standing alone, must allege a factual occurrence that, if found to be true, would support a finding of guilty on the related charge. The specifications should be as specific as possible with information such as date, place, and specific events alleged to have occurred. The bill of charges and specifications may contain other relevant and material background factual evidence as an introduction (separate and apart from the actual charges and specifications).

*b) Finding of reasonable grounds by committee and referral of bill of charges and specifications for trial*—

(1) *When respondent is a bishop*—A vote to adopt any charge or specification shall require five votes. Any bill of charges and specifications adopted shall be sent to the bishop charged, to the secretary of the jurisdictional or central conference, to the president and secretary of the College of Bishops, to counsel for the Church, and to the chairperson of the jurisdictional committee on the episcopacy.

(2) *When respondent is a clergyperson other than a bishop*—A vote to adopt any charge or specification shall require five votes. Any bill of charges and specifications adopted by the committee on investigations shall be sent by the chairperson within five days to the respondent, the person making the complaint, the secretary of the annual conference, the counsel for the Church, and the resident bishop.

(3) *When respondent is a diaconal minister*—A vote to adopt any charge or specification shall require two votes. Any bill of charges and specifications adopted shall be sent to the respondent within five days, the secretary of the annual conference, the chairperson of the board of ordained ministry, the respondent's district superintendent, counsel for the Church, and the resident bishop.

(4) *When respondent is a layperson*—A vote to adopt any charge or specification shall require five votes. Any bill of charges and specifications adopted by the committee shall be sent to the per-

son charged, the recording secretary of the charge conference, counsel for the Church, the pastor(s), and the district superintendent.

*c) Findings other than reasonable grounds by committee—*

(1) If the committee on investigation determines that there are no reasonable grounds for charges, it may dismiss the judicial complaint. When deemed appropriate, it may also refer matters of concern to the proper referring Church official (to the president or secretary of the College of Bishops in the case of bishop, to the resident bishop in the case of a clergyperson or diaconal minister, or to the pastor or co-pastors in the case of layperson) for administrative or other action. Notification of these actions, should be given to the respondent, the person making the original complaint, counsel for the Church and the proper referring Church officials.

(2) If the committee on investigation determines that the judicial complaint is not based upon chargeable offenses, or for other good cause, the committee may refer the complaint to the proper referring Church official (*see* ¶ 2706.5c[1] above) for administrative or other action. Such referral will not constitute a dismissal or double jeopardy under ¶ 2701.5. Notification of these actions should be given to the respondent, the person making the original complaint, counsel for the Church and the proper referring Church officials.

## Trials

¶ **2707.** *Fundamental Principles for Trials*—Church trials are to be regarded as an expedient of last resort. Only after every reasonable effort has been made to correct any wrong and adjust any existing difficulty should steps be taken to institute a trial. No such trial as herein provided shall be construed to deprive the respondent or the Church of legal civil rights, except to the extent that immunity is provided as in ¶ 2701.9. All trials shall be conducted according to *The Book of Discipline* in a consistent Christian manner by a properly constituted court after due investigation.

¶ **2708.** *General Organization and Pre-Trial Procedures—*

1. Officers of the Court—Officers shall consist of a presiding officer (*see* ¶¶ 2712.2, 2713.2, 2714.2), who shall appoint a secretary and such other officers as deemed necessary. The presiding officer may have legal counsel, who shall not be the conference chancellor, at the expense of the annual conference holding the trial, for the sole purpose of advice to the presiding officer during the trial.

2. <u>Time and Place of Trial</u>—The official charged with convening the trial shall also fix the time and place for the trial and will notify the presiding officer, the respondent, counsel for the Church and the person making the original complaint. In all cases, sufficient time shall be allowed for these persons to appear at the given place and time and for the respondent to prepare for the trial. The presiding officer shall decide what constitutes "sufficient time," but in no case shall this time be less than twenty days.

3. <u>Pre-Trial Motions</u>—All appeals of any procedural or substantive matters that have occurred prior to referral of the charges to trial must be appealed to the presiding officer of the trial court before the convening of the trial. Otherwise, the right to appeal on such matters is forfeited. All objections to and motions regarding the regularity of the proceedings and the form and substance of charges and specifications must be made before the convening of the trial court. The presiding officer may determine all such preliminary objections and motions; in furtherance of truth and justice may permit amendments to the specifications or charges not changing the general nature of the same; and may dismiss all or any part of the bill of charges upon a finding by the presiding officer (1) that all or such part is without legal or factual basis or (2) that, even assuming the specifications to be true, they do not constitute a basis for a chargeable offense.

4. <u>Change of Venue</u>—The respondent may request a change of venue. This shall be a written request to the presiding officer of the court within ten days of receipt of notice to appear for trial. The presiding officer shall rule upon the request after hearing arguments by the respondent and the Church. If the motion is approved, the presiding officer shall name the annual conference outside the episcopal area wherein the trial shall be held and shall notify the resident bishop of that conference, who shall convene the court. The cost of prosecution shall be borne by the conference where the case originated.

5. <u>Notice</u>—

*a)* All notices required or provided for in relationship to investigations, trials, and appeals shall be in writing, signed by or on behalf of the person or body giving or required to give such notice, and shall be addressed to the person or body to whom it is required to be given. Such notices shall be served by delivering a copy thereof to the party or chief officer of the body to whom it is addressed in person or sent by other delivery system to the last-known residence or address of such party. Proof of notice shall be provided and becomes a part of the record of the case.

*b)* In all cases wherein it is provided that notice shall be given to a bishop or district superintendent and the charges are against that particular person, then such notice (in addition to being given to the accused) shall be given, in the case of a bishop, to another bishop within the same jurisdiction and, in the case of a district superintendent, to the bishop in charge.

6. Trial Scheduling and Continuances—If in any case the respondent, after due notice (twenty days) has been given, shall refuse or neglect to appear at the time and place set forth for the hearing, the trial may proceed in the respondent's absence. However, if in the sole discretion of the presiding officer there is good and sufficient reason for the absence of the respondent or another essential person, the presiding officer may reschedule the trial to a later date.

7. Counsel—In all cases, a respondent shall be entitled to appear and to select and be represented by counsel, a clergyperson in full connection of The United Methodist Church if the respondent is a bishop, a clergyperson, or a diaconal minister; and a lay or clergy member of The United Methodist Church if the respondent is a lay member. The respondent and the Church shall be entitled to have counsel heard in oral or written argument or both. The official charged with convening the court (see ¶¶ 2712.1, 2713.1, 2714.1) shall, within thirty days after receiving a copy of the charges and specifications, appoint counsel for the Church, if counsel has not been previously appointed. In the case of a trial of a bishop, clergyperson, or local pastor, counsel for the Church shall be a clergyperson in full connection (¶¶ 359.1*d*[1], 2712.4) to represent the interests of the Church in pressing the claims of the person making the complaint.

No person who was a member of the cabinet, board of ordained ministry, or committee on investigation who earlier considered the case now before the trial court shall be appointed counsel for the Church or serve as counsel for the respondent or any of the persons bringing complaints in a case. In all cases of trial where counsel has not been chosen by the respondent, counsel shall be appointed by the presiding officer. The counsel for the Church and for the respondent each shall be entitled to choose one assistant counsel, who may be an attorney, without voice. "Without voice" means without the ability to speak to or within the hearing of the trial court.

8. Witnesses—Notice to appear shall be given to such witnesses

as either party may name and shall be issued in the name of the Church and be signed by the presiding officer of the trial. It shall be the duty of all clergy and lay members of The United Methodist Church to appear and testify when summoned. Refusal to appear or to answer questions ruled by the presiding officer to be relevant may be considered as disobedience to the Order and Discipline of The United Methodist Church except when refusal to answer is based on a good faith claim that answering might tend to incriminate the witness under state or federal criminal law or is based on a claim of confidential communication to a clergyperson under ¶ 332.5.

9. <u>Witness Qualifications</u>—A witness, to be qualified, need not be a member of The United Methodist Church.

10. <u>Commissioned Out-of-Court Testimony</u>—The presiding officer of any court before which a case may be pending shall have power, whenever the necessity of the parties or witnesses shall require, to appoint, on the application of either party, a commissioner or commissioners, either a clergy or a layperson or both, to examine the witnesses; provided that three days' notice of the time and place of taking such testimony shall have been given to the adverse party. The party making this request shall have the burden of showing good cause and shall bear the cost of such commissioned out-of-court testimony. Counsel for both parties shall be permitted to examine and cross-examine the witness or witnesses whose testimony is thus taken. The commissioners so appointed shall take such testimony in writing as may be offered by either party. The testimony properly certified by the signature of the commissioner or commissioners shall be transmitted to the presiding officer of the court before which the case is pending.

11. <u>Amendments to Bill of Charges and Specifications</u>—After consultation with counsels, the presiding officer of the trial may make amendments to the bill of charges, or request that the committee on investigation make amendments to the bill of charges; provided that they do not change the nature of the charges and specifications and do not introduce new matter of which the respondent has not had due notice. When an amendment or amendments to a bill of charges is or are denied by the presiding officer, it or they shall not be introduced in the form of testimony in the trial. Charges or specifications previously considered and dropped by the committee on investigation shall not be introduced in the trial in the form of evidence or otherwise.

12. <u>Open or Closed Trials</u>—The deliberations of the trial court shall be closed. All other sessions of the trial shall be closed, except upon written request to the presiding officer by counsel for the respondent, the trial shall be open. Also, the trial may be opened by the presiding officer, upon written request of either the counsel for the Church or the counsel for the person charged, to family of the person charged, or family of the person making the original complaint, and/or to other personally significant people. Any motions to open the trial should be presented and decided prior to the date of the trial. In addition, the presiding officer may, in his or her judgment on motion of counsel for either party or on the presiding officer's own motion, declare a particular session of the court to be closed. At all times, however, in the hearing portion of the trial, the presiding officer, the members of the trial court, the person(s) making the original complaint, the person representing the Church as well as counsel for the Church, the respondent, and counsel for the respondent shall have a right to be present.

13. <u>Combined Trials of Multiple Persons</u>—In cases in which a number of persons have allegedly engaged in the same offense at the same time and place, their trials may be combined into one trial for that same offense. The presiding officer shall make the determination on combination of trials.

**¶ 2709.** *Trial Convening and Organization*—

1. <u>Convening of the Trial</u>—The convenor shall notify the respondent in writing to appear at a fixed time and place no less than twenty days after service of such notice and within a reasonable time thereafter for selection of the members of the trial court.

2. <u>Trial Pool</u>—At the appointed time, in the presence of the respondent, counsel for the respondent, counsel for the Church, and the presiding officer, thirteen persons shall be selected as a trial court out of a pool of thirty-five or more persons selected according to ¶¶ 2712.3, 2713.4, and 2714.5. Special consideration should be given so that the pool includes persons representative of racial, ethnic, and gender diversity.

3. <u>Selection of the Trial Court</u>—No person shall serve as a member of the trial court who was a member of the cabinet, board of ordained ministry, or committee on investigation who considered the case in the process of coming to trial court. The counsel for the Church and the respondent shall each have up to four peremptory challenges and challenges for cause without limit. If by reason of

challenges for cause being sustained the number is reduced to below thirteen, additional appropriate persons shall be nominated in like manner as was the original panel to take the places of the numbers challenged, who likewise shall be subject to challenge for cause. This method of procedure shall be followed until a trial court of thirteen members and two alternate members has been selected.

4. Alternates—The two alternate members shall sit as observers of the trial. They shall replace members of the trial court who are not able to continue to serve, so that the trial court shall always consist of thirteen members, unless the respondent and counsel for the Church agree to a lesser number.

5. Trial Court Questions—The members of the trial court, including the alternate members, may, subject to the approval of the presiding officer of the court, ask questions on matters on which evidence has been presented.

¶ **2710.** *Trial Guidelines and Rules—*

1. Authority of Presiding Officer—After the trial is convened the authority of the presiding officer shall include the right to set reasonable time limits, after consultation with counsel for the Church and counsel for the person charged, for the presentation of the case, provided such time is equal for both. The authority of the presiding officer shall be limited to ruling upon proper representation of the Church and the person charged, admissibility of evidence, recessing, adjourning, and reconvening sessions of the trial, charging the members of the trial court as to the Church law involved in the case at the beginning of the trial and just before they retire to make up their verdict, and such other authority as is normally vested in a civil court judge sitting with a jury, but he or she shall not have authority to pronounce any judgment in favor of or against the person charged other than such verdict as may be returned by the trial court, which body shall have the exclusive right to determine the innocence or guilt of the person charged.

2. Order of Trial—After selection of the trial court, each counsel may make an opening statement to inform the trial court of what the evidence is expected to be. Evidence shall then be offered by questioning of witnesses and by documents shown to be reliable. Each counsel shall have opportunity to make closing arguments before the trial court begins deliberations. Deliberations of the trial court and receiving of the verdict shall follow.

3. Oaths—The administration of oaths shall not be required. At

the beginning of the trial, the presiding officer shall remind all parties of the duties and responsibilities of Church membership (¶ 218) and/or the clergy covenant (¶¶ 306.4 *f* and 325).

4. Entering of the Plea—At the beginning of the trial, the respondent shall be called upon by the presiding officer to plead to the charge, and the pleas shall be recorded. If the respondent pleads "guilty" to the charges preferred, no trial shall be necessary, but evidence may be taken with respect to the appropriate penalty, which shall thereupon be imposed. If the respondent pleads "not guilty" or if the respondent should neglect or refuse to plead, the plea of "not guilty" shall be entered, and the trial shall proceed. The respondent shall at all times during the trial, except as hereinafter provided, have the right to produce testimony and that of witnesses and to make defense.

5. Recess and Trial Procedures—The court may recess from time to time as convenience or necessity may require. During the time of recess, the members of the trial court shall be instructed that under no circumstance will they speak to one another or to others about the trial or observe media reports regarding the case. When, in consultation with counsel for both parties, the presiding officer finds it advisable, the members and reserves shall be sequestered. Threatening or tampering with the trial court or officers of the trial court shall be considered disobedience to the Order and Discipline of The United Methodist Church. The presiding officer shall remain and preside until the decision is rendered and the findings are completed and shall thereupon sign and certify them.

6. Objections—Objections of any party to the proceedings shall be entered on the record.

7. Exclusion of Witnesses—No witness afterward to be examined shall be present during the examination of another witness if the opposing party objects. Witnesses shall be examined first by the party producing them, then cross-examined by the opposite party and may be questioned by members of the trial court, with the approval of the presiding officer. The presiding officer of the court shall determine all questions of relevancy and competency of evidence.

8. Recording of Proceedings—A verbatim record of all proceedings of the trial shall be by stenograph or other appropriate means and reduced to writing and certified by the presiding officer or secretary. The record, including all exhibits, papers and evidence in the case, shall be the basis of any appeal that may be taken.

9. Evidence—The introduction of any material relating to events happening before the six-year statute of limitation period as evidence, as preface to evidence, or as build-up for evidence in the procedures of the trial proceedings may be permitted when the presiding officer, after consultation with counsel for both parties, rules that such material is relevant and reliable. Documentary evidence deemed by the presiding officer to be relevant and reliable may be in the physical possession of the trial court during deliberations.

10. Instructions and Charges—The presiding officer shall not deliver a charge reviewing or explaining the evidence or setting forth the merits of the case. The presiding officer shall express no opinion on the law or the facts while the court is deliberating. If requested by either party's counsel, the presiding officer shall instruct the trial court on Church law applicable to the case. Instructions may be given at the beginning of the trial, during the trial, before the trial court begins deliberations or a combination of any of these. If requested by the trial court, instructions may be given during deliberations. The presiding officer shall not review or explain the evidence or comment on the merits of the case.

¶ 2711. *Power of the Trial Court—*

1. Instruction, Disqualification, Voting and Verdicts—The trial court shall have full power to try the respondent. The trial court shall be a continuing body until the final disposition of the charge. If any regular or alternate member of the trial court fails to attend any part of any session at which evidence is received or oral argument is made to the trial court by counsel, that person shall not thereafter be a member of the trial court, but the rest of the trial court may proceed to judgment.

2. Votes—It shall require a vote of at least nine members of the trial court to sustain the charge(s) and nine votes also shall be required for conviction. Fewer than nine votes for conviction shall be considered an acquittal. The burden of proof for a vote to convict shall be clear and convincing. The trial court shall present to the presiding officer a decision on each charge and each individual specification under each charge. Its findings shall be final, subject to appeal to the committee on appeals of the jurisdictional conference or the central conference, as the case may be.

3. Penalties—

*a) If the Trial Results in Conviction.* Further testimony may be heard and arguments by counsel presented regarding what the penalty should be. The trial court shall determine the penalty, which shall require a vote of at least seven members. The trial court shall have the power to expel the respondent from the Church, terminate the conference membership and/or revoke the credentials of ordination or consecration of the respondent, suspend the respondent from the exercise of the functions of office, or to fix a lesser penalty. The penalty fixed by the trial court shall take effect immediately unless otherwise indicated by the trial court.

*b) Suspension After Trial.* The resident bishop may, with the unanimous concurrence of the district superintendents, suspend the person charged from all clergy responsibilities but not the related benefits, such as annuity and conference group medical and hospital insurance and life insurance, pending the outcome of the appeals process. If the person charged should be found innocent at the end of the judicial process, he or she shall be financially recompensed by his or her annual conference for the time lost under said suspension. Equitable recompense shall be determined by the conference council on finance and administration, taking into account service years, the loss of income during suspension, and loss of parsonage use, if any. In no case shall the recompense be less than the minimum salary. Time on a suspension imposed by the resident bishop may be applied to lessen the time of suspension fixed by the trial court and sustained or modified by the appeals process.

¶ 2712. *Trial of a Bishop—*

1. The president of the College of Bishops of the jurisdictional or central conference—or in case the person charged is the president, the secretary of the college—shall proceed to convene the court under the provisions of ¶ 2709.

2. The president of the College of Bishops (or in the case the person charged is the president, the secretary) may preside or designate another bishop to serve as presiding officer.

3. The trial shall be convened as provided in ¶ 2709 with the pool of thirty-five or more persons to consist of clergy in full connection named by the College of Bishops in approximately equal numbers from each episcopal area within the jurisdictional or central conference. Special consideration should be given so that the pool includes persons representative of racial, ethnic, and gender diversity.

4. Counsel for the Church shall be a bishop or another clergyperson in full connection.

5. The secretary of the court shall at the conclusion of the pro-

ceedings send all trial documents to the secretary of the jurisdictional or central conference, who shall keep them in custody. If an appeal is taken, the secretary shall forward the materials forthwith to the secretary of the Judicial Council. After the appeal has been heard, the records shall be returned to the secretary of the jurisdictional or central conference.

6. A bishop suspended from office shall have claim on the Episcopal Fund for salary, dwelling, pension, and other related benefits. A bishop removed from office shall have no claim upon the Episcopal Fund for salary, dwelling, pension and other related benefits from the date of such removal.

7. For the purpose of this paragraph, the United Methodist bishops outside of the United States shall constitute one College of Bishops.

¶ **2713.** *Trial of a Clergy Member of an Annual Conference, Local Pastor, Clergy on Honorable or Administrative Location, or Diaconal Minister—*

1. The resident bishop of the respondent shall proceed to convene the court under the provisions of ¶2709.

2. The resident bishop shall designate another bishop to be presiding officer.

3. *a)* The trial for a clergy member or a local pastor shall be convened as provided in ¶ 2709 with the pool of thirty-five or more persons to consist of clergy in full connection. If there are not enough persons in appropriate categories in an annual conference to complete the pool, additional persons may be appointed from other annual conferences. All appointments to the pool shall be made by the district superintendents. Special consideration should be given so that the pool includes persons representative of racial, ethnic, and gender diversity.

*b)* The trial for a diaconal minister shall be convened as provided in ¶2709 and shall consist of a pool of thirty-five or more persons who shall be diaconal ministers or, when necessary, members of the Church. Special consideration should be given so that the pool includes persons representative of racial, ethnic, and gender diversity.

4. Counsel for the Church shall be a clergyperson in full connection.

5. The secretary of the court shall at the conclusion of the proceedings send all trial documents to the secretary of the annual conference, who shall keep them in custody. Such documents are to be held in a confidential file and shall not be released for other than

appeal or new trial purposes without a signed release from both the clergyperson charged and the presiding officer of the trial that tried the case. If an appeal is taken, the secretary shall forward the materials forthwith to the president of the court of appeals of the jurisdictional or central conference. If a president has not been elected, the secretary shall send the materials to such members of the court of appeals as the president of the College of Bishops shall designate. After the appeal has been heard, the records shall be returned to the secretary of the annual conference unless a further appeal on a question of law has been made to the Judicial Council, in which case the relevant documents shall be forwarded to the secretary of that body.

¶ 2714. *Trial of Lay Member of a Local Church*—

1. The district superintendent of the person charged shall proceed to convene the court under the provisions of ¶ 2709.

2. The district superintendent may be the presiding officer or may designate another clergyperson in full connection to preside.

3. The trial shall be convened as provided in ¶2709, with the pool of thirty-five or more persons to consist of lay members of local churches other than the local church of the charged layperson within the same district. Appointments to the pool shall be made by the district superintendent, who may consult with the district lay leader. Special consideration should be given so that the pool includes persons representative of racial, ethnic, and gender diversity.

4. Counsel for the Church shall be a lay or clergyperson who is a member of The United Methodist Church.

5. The person charged may request a change of venue. This shall be a written request to the officers of the court within ten days of receipt of notice to appear for trial. The presiding officer shall rule upon the request after hearing argument for the defense and the Church. If the motion is approved, the presiding officer shall name another district wherein the trial shall be held and shall notify the district superintendent, who shall convene the court. The thirty-five—member pool shall consist of lay members from that district. The cost of prosecution shall be borne by the annual conference.

6. If the trial court finds that the charges are proven by clear and convincing evidence, then it may impose such penalties as it may determine, including that the membership of the charged layperson in The United Methodist Church be terminated; provided that the trial court shall first consider other remedies that would fulfill the provisions of ¶ 220.

7. The appropriate officer of the trial shall, at the conclusion of the proceeding, deposit all trial documents with the secretary of the charge conference. If an appeal is taken, the secretary shall deliver all documents to the district superintendent. After the appeal has been heard, the records shall be returned to the custody of the secretary of the charge conference.

## APPEALS

**¶ 2715.** *Appeal Procedures—General—*

1. In all cases of appeal, the appellant shall within thirty days give written notice of appeal and at the same time shall furnish to the officer receiving such notice (¶¶ 2716.2, 2717.1, 2718.2) and to the counsel a written statement of the grounds of the appeal, and the hearing in the appellate body shall be limited to the grounds set forth in such statement.[18]

2. When any appellate body shall reverse in whole or in part the findings of a committee on investigation or trial court, or remand the case for a new hearing or trial, or change the penalty imposed by the trial court, it shall return to the convening officer a statement of the grounds of its action.

3. An appeal shall not be allowed in any case in which the respondent has failed or refused to be present in person or by counsel at the investigation and the trial. Appeals shall be heard by the proper appellate body unless it shall appear to the said body that the appellant has forfeited the right to appeal by misconduct, such as refusal to abide by the findings of the trial court; or by withdrawal from the Church; or by failure to appear in person or by counsel to prosecute the appeal; or, prior to the final decision on appeal from conviction, by resorting to suit in the civil courts against the complainant or any of the parties connected with the ecclesiastical court in which the appellant was tried.[19]

4. The right of appeal, when once forfeited by neglect or otherwise, cannot be revived by any subsequent appellate body.

5. The right to prosecute an appeal shall not be affected by the death of the person entitled to such right. Heirs or legal representatives may prosecute such appeal as the appellant would be entitled to do if living.

---

18. *See* Judicial Council Memorandum 826.
19. *See* Judicial Council Decision 3.

6. The records and documents of the trial, including the evidence, and these only, shall be used in the hearing of any appeal.

7. The appellate body shall determine two questions only: (*a*) Does the weight of the evidence sustain the charge or charges? (*b*) Were there such errors of Church law as to vitiate the verdict and/or the penalty? These questions shall be determined by the records of the trial and the argument of counsel for the Church and for the respondent. The appellate body shall in no case hear witnesses. It may have legal counsel present, who shall not be the conference chancellor for the conference from which the appeal is taken, for the sole purpose of providing advice to the appellate body.

8. In all cases where an appeal is made and admitted by the appellate committee, after the charges, findings, and evidence have been read and the arguments conclude, the parties shall withdraw, and the appellate committee shall consider and decide the case. It may reverse in whole or in part the findings of the committee on investigation or the trial court, or it may remand the case for a new trial to determine verdict and/or penalty. It may determine what penalty, not higher than that affixed at the hearing or trial, may be imposed. If it neither reverses in whole or in part the judgment of the trial court, nor remands the case for a new trial, nor modifies the penalty, that judgment shall stand. The appellate committee shall not reverse the judgment nor remand the case for a new hearing or trial on account of errors plainly not affecting the result. All decisions of the appellate committee shall require a majority vote.

9. In all cases, the right to present evidence shall be exhausted when the case has been heard once on its merits in the proper court, but questions of Church law may be carried on appeal, step by step, to the Judicial Council.

10. The Church shall have no right of appeal from findings of the trial court. In regard to cases where there is an investigation under ¶ 2702, but no trial is held, egregious errors of Church law or administration may be appealed to the jurisdictional committee on appeals by counsel for the Church. The committee on investigation's decision not to certify a bill of charges does not alone constitute an egregious error of Church law or administration. When the committee on appeals shall find egregious errors of Church law or administration under this part, it may remand the case for a new hearing, in which event it shall return to the chair of the committee on investigation a statement of the grounds of its action. This is not to be double jeopardy.

11. Questions of procedure may be raised with the presiding officer or secretary of the appellate body. Under no circumstances shall one party in the absence of the other party discuss substantive matters with members of any appellate body while the case is pending (cf. ¶ 2701.4).

12. In all matters of judicial administration, the rights, duties, and responsibilities of clergy members and diaconal ministers of missionary conferences and provisional annual conferences are the same as those in annual conferences, and the procedure is the same.

13. Contacts with members of any appellate body shall be limited to matters of procedure and shall be directed only to the presiding officer or secretary of the appellate body. Under no circumstances shall matters of substance be discussed.

¶ **2716.** *Appeal of a Bishop, Clergy Member of an Annual Conference, Clergy on Honorable or Administrative Location, Local Pastor, or Diaconal Minister—*

1. Each jurisdictional and central conference, upon nomination of the College of Bishops, shall elect a committee on appeals composed of four clergy, one diaconal minister, one full-time local pastor, and three laypersons who have been at least six years successively members of The United Methodist Church, and an equal number of corresponding alternates. This committee shall serve until its successors have been elected. No member shall participate in the hearing of an appeal who is a member of a conference in the episcopal area of the appellant. Any vacancy shall be filled by the College of Bishops.

The committee on appeals shall have full power to hear and determine appeals of bishops, clergy members, clergy members on honorable or administrative location, local pastors, and diaconal ministers from any annual conference, provisional or missionary conference within the jurisdiction or central conference. The committee shall elect its own president and secretary and shall adopt its own rules of procedure, and its decisions shall be final, except that an appeal may be taken to the Judicial Council only upon questions of law related to procedures of the jurisdictional committee on appeals, central conference committee on appeals, or under the provisions of ¶ 2609.8. A bishop designated by the College of Bishops shall convene the committee at the site of jurisdictional or central conference for the purpose of electing officers.

2. In case of conviction by a trial court, a bishop, clergy member, local pastor, clergy on honorable or administrative location, or dia-

conal minister shall have the right of appeal to the jurisdictional or central conference committee on appeals above constituted; *provided* that within thirty days after the conviction, the appellant shall notify the presiding bishop of the conference (or, when the appellant is a bishop, the president and secretary of the College of Bishops) and the presiding officer of the court in writing of the intention to appeal.

3. When notice of an appeal has been given to the presiding officer of the court, the presiding officer shall give notice of the same to the secretary of the committee on appeals of the jurisdictional or central conference and submit the documents in the case, or in case the documents have been sent to the secretary of the annual conference, instruct the secretary to send the documents to the president of the committee on appeals. The jurisdictional or central conference committee on appeals shall within thirty days give notice to the presiding bishop of the conference from which the appeal is taken (or to the president and secretary of the College of Bishops when the appellant is a bishop) and to the appellant of the time and place where the appeal will be heard. Such hearing shall occur within 180 days following receipt of notice to the committee on appeals. Both the annual conference, missionary conference, or provisional conference and the appellant may be represented by counsel as specified in ¶ 2708.7. The presiding bishop of the conference or, in the appeal of a bishop, the president or secretary of the College of Bishops, shall appoint counsel for the Church.

4. All necessary traveling and sustenance expense incurred by the committee on appeals, including any cost for legal counsel retained to advise the committee, in the hearing of an appeal case coming from an annual conference and appearing before any jurisdictional or central conference committee on appeals, shall be paid out of the administrative fund of the central or jurisdictional conference in which the proceedings arise. The president of the committee on appeals shall approve all expenses. Expenses for counsel for the Church shall be paid by the annual conference. Such expenses for counsel for the respondent shall be paid by the respondent, unless in the interest of fairness, the committee on appeals orders the annual conference to reimburse the respondent.

¶ **2717.** *Appeal of a Lay Member—*

1. A lay member convicted by a trial court shall have the right of appeal and shall serve written notice of appeal with the pastor and the district superintendent within thirty days of conviction.

2. The district superintendent shall, on receipt of notice of appeal, give written notice to all concerned of the time and place of the convening of a committee on appeals not less than ten nor more than thirty days after such notice has been delivered.

3. The committee on appeals shall be constituted in the following manner: The district superintendent shall appoint eleven laypersons who are members of United Methodist Churches within the annual conference other than the appellant's local church, none of whom shall have been members of the trial court, and who hold office either as lay leader or lay member of the annual conference. At the convening of the committee on appeals, from seven to eleven of these shall be selected to serve on the committee. The counsel for the appellant and the counsel for the Church shall have the right to challenge for cause, and the decisions on the validity of such challenges shall be made by the presiding officer, who shall be the district superintendent.

4. The findings of the committee on appeals shall be certified by the district superintendent to the pastor of the church of which the accused is a member.

¶ **2718.** *Other Appeals—*

1. The order of appeals on questions of law shall be as follows: from the decision of the district superindent presiding in the charge or district conference to the bishop presiding in the annual conference, and from the decision of the bishop presiding in the annual conference to the Judicial Council, and from a central conference to the Judicial Council.

2. When an appeal is taken on a question of law, written notice of the same shall be served on the secretary of the body in which the decision has been rendered. It shall be the secretary's duty to see that an exact statement of the question submitted and the ruling of the chair thereon shall be entered on the journal. The secretary shall then make and certify a copy of the question and ruling and transmit the same to the secretary of the body to which the appeal is taken. The secretary who thus receives said certified copy shall present the same in open conference and as soon as practicable lay it before the presiding officer for a ruling thereon, which ruling must be rendered before the final adjournment of that body, that said ruling together with the original question and ruling may be entered on the journal of that conference. The same course shall be followed in all subsequent appeals.

**¶ 2719.** *Miscellaneous Provisions—*

1. Any clergy members residing beyond the bounds of the conference in which membership is held shall be subject to the procedures of ¶¶ 2701, 2618 exercised by the appropriate officers of the conference in which he or she is a member, unless the presiding bishops of the two annual conferences and the clergy member subject to the procedures agree that fairness will be better served by having the procedures carried out by the appropriate officers of the annual conference in which he or she is serving under appointment, or if retired, currently residing.

2. When a bishop, clergy member, local pastor, or diaconal minister is charged with an offense under ¶ 2702 and desires to withdraw from the Church, the jurisdictional or central conference in the case of a bishop, the annual conference in the case of a clergy member, or the district conference (where there is no district conference, the charge conference) in the case of a local pastor or diaconal minister will ask him or her to surrender his or her credentials and will remove his or her name from the roll of members; in which case the record shall be "Withdrawn under charges."

3. When a member of the Church is charged with an offense and desires to withdraw from the Church, the charge conference may permit such member to withdraw, in which case the record shall be "Withdrawn under complaints." If formal charges have been presented, such member may be permitted to withdraw, in which case the record shall be "Withdrawn under charges." In either case, the status shall be the same as if the member had been expelled.

4. In all matters of judicial administration, the rights, duties, and responsibilities of clergy members, local pastors, clergy on honorable or administrative location, and diaconal ministers of missions, missionary conferences, and provisional annual conferences are the same as those in annual conferences, and the procedure is the same.

# INDEX

The numbers, unless otherwise indicated, refer to paragraphs (¶) and to subparagraphs. Subparagraphs are indicated by the numerals following the decimal points.

Youth Ministry Organization
Convocation, ¶ 531
monitoring compliance by, ¶ 806.12
receiving general Church funds,
¶ 810.2
special appeals, ¶ 612.5
United Methodist Publishing House
as, ¶¶ 1611, 1618.3

**agenda of annual conference,**
¶¶ 605.2, 605.5

**aging**
Older Adult Ministries, Committee,
¶ 1119
rights, Social Principles, ¶ 162E

**agriculture**
Social Principles, ¶¶ 162N–O, 163H

**AIDS (Acquired Immune Deficiency
Syndrome)**
Social Principles, ¶ 162S

**air**
Social Principles, ¶ 160A

**Albright, Jacob,** ¶ 102 *(p. 56)*

**alcohol,** ¶ 611.17
Social Principles, ¶ 162J
use by ordained ministers, ¶ 306.4

**alcoholic beverages,** ¶ 806.10

**amendments**
to bill of charges and specifications,
¶ 2708.11

**Amendments to Constitution,**
¶¶ 57–59

**American Bible Society,** ¶ 2405

**American Methodism**
doctrinal standards, ¶ 102 *(p. 52– 55)*

**Americans with Disabilities accessi-
bility standards,** ¶ 138

**animal life**
Social Principles, ¶ 160C

**annual conference agencies**
administrative review committee,
¶ 633
Advance program, ¶ 651
annual conference responsibility for
structure, ¶ 608
archives and history, conference
commission, ¶¶ 638, 2548.4
Christian unity and interreligious
concerns, conference commission,
¶ 639
church and society, conference
board, ¶ 627
communications, conference commission, ¶¶ 611.4, 643
criminal justice and mercy ministries, ¶ 652
disability concerns, conference committee, ¶ 649
discipleship, conference board,
¶ 628. *See also* discipleship,
conference board.
episcopacy, conference committee,
¶ 634
episcopal residence committee,
¶¶ 612.1c, 635
finance and administration, conference council, ¶ 609–626. *See also*
finance and administration, conference council.
global ministries, conference board,
¶ 630
parish and community development, conference committee,
¶ 630.5
Higher Education and ministry, conference board, ¶ 631. *See also*
Higher Education and Ministry,
conference board.
incapacity, joint committee, ¶¶ 355,
648
laity, conference board, ¶¶ 603.9b,
629
meeting location, ¶ 608.4
membership, ¶¶ 608.3, 608.5
Native American ministry, conference committee, ¶ 650

**Boston University School of
Theology,** ¶ 1425.3*a*

**boundaries**
of annual conferences, central
conference adjustment,
¶ 537.10
constitutional provisions,
jurisdictional conferences,
¶ 35

**Boy Scouts,** ¶ 255.3

**boycott,** ¶ 702.5
annual conference action,
¶ 604.12
charge conference action on,
¶ 246.18
district conference action, ¶ 654.5

**British Methodist Conference**
delegates, ¶ 12

**budget.** *See also* Finance and
Administration.
of agencies, ¶ 806.4
of annual conference, ¶¶ 611.1, 612
for general funds of the Church,¶ 806.1
of local church
church council responsibility for,
¶ 251.4*c*
finance committee responsibility
for, ¶ 258.4
program agencies, ¶ 806.1*b*(7)
program expenditures, general
agency decisions, ¶ 718

**building committee, local church,**
¶ 2543
funding for plan, ¶¶ 2543.11–13
information to district board for
church location and building,
¶ 2543.6
presentation to church conference,
¶ 2543.6

**burial**
authority and duties of local pastors,
¶ 341

**C**

**cabinet,** ¶ 429
appointments to cooperative
ministries, ¶ 206.6
appointments to ecumenical shared
ministries, ¶ 211
immunity from prosecution of
complaints, ¶ 359.2*g*

**calendar,** ¶ 1112.5. *See also* Special
Sundays.
liturgical seasons, ¶ 1112.1
year designations in curriculum
resources, ¶ 1121

**calling,** ¶ 132

**Camp Fire Boys and Girls,** ¶ 255.3

**camping**
as conference board of discipleship
responsibility, ¶¶ 628.1*c*, 628.2*e*
as General Board of Discipleship
responsibility, ¶ 1108.10

**camps**
title to properties, ¶ 2516

**campus ministries**
evaluating those related to annual
conference, ¶ 631.4*a*(7)
funding, ¶ 1413.3*b*
Higher Education and Ministry,
conference board responsibilities,
¶ 631.4*b–d*
Higher Education Division
responsibilities, ¶¶ 1410.4*c–d*,
1412.2
properties and investments,
¶ 1413.3*c*

**campus pastor**
receiving new members, ¶ 221

**candidacy for licensed and ordained
ministry.** *See under* ordained
ministry.

training, ¶ 906.14

training in cooperative ministries,
¶ 206.5

written consent requirements for
engagement of evangelist, ¶ 332.1

**district union,** ¶ 654.4

**districts.** *See also* ordained ministry,
district committee.
Advance Special Gifts, ¶ 651.4
apportionments to, ¶¶ 613.2–3, 619
audit of funds, ¶ 423.14
church and society, director, ¶ 657
ethnic local church concerns,
director, ¶ 658
laity board, ¶ 661
religion and race, director, ¶ 659

**divorce**
Social Principles, ¶ 161*D*

**Doctrinal Heritage,** ¶ 101

**Doctrinal History,** ¶ 102

**Doctrinal Standards**
and curriculum content, ¶ 1124.3

**documentary record material**
definition, ¶ 1711.1*b*
inventorying, repairing,
microfilming, ¶ 1711.3*d*
preservation, ¶ 1711.3*c*

**double jeopardy**
and fair process in judicial proceedings, ¶ 2701.5

**Drew University Theological School,**
¶ 1425.3*a*

**drug use**
Social Principles, ¶ 162*J*

**Duke Divinity School,** ¶ 1425.3*a*

**dying, faithful care**
Social Principles, ¶ 161*L*

**E**

**Ecclesiastical Approval,** ¶ 1422.4

**Ecclesiastical Endorsement,** ¶ 1422.3
standards, ¶ 1422.6

**ecumenical campus ministries,**
¶ 631.4*d*(9)

**ecumenical organizations,**
¶¶ 2401–2405
American Bible Society, ¶ 2405
Christian Unity and Interreligious
Concerns, General Commission,
¶ 2404.3*b*. *See also* Christian Unity
and Interreligious Concerns,
General Commission.
Churches Uniting in Christ, ¶ 2404.1
Consultation on Church Union,
¶ 2404.1. *See also* Consultation on
Church Union.
Council of Bishops liaisons, ¶ 2401.1
elder appointment to, ¶ 335.1*a*(4)
financial support, ¶ 2402
National Association of
Evangelicals, ¶ 2404.2*c*
National Council of the Churches of
Christ in the U.S.A, ¶¶ 263.2,
639.2, 816.2, 818.2, 2404.2
Department of Communication,
¶ 1806.4
reports from, ¶ 1903.12
Pan-Methodist Cooperation,
Commission, ¶ 2403.2
relationships with Wesleyan
churches, ¶ 2403.4
Union, Commission on, ¶ 2403.3
United Methodist representative
selection, ¶ 2401.3
World Council of Churches,
¶¶ 818.2, 2404.3
reports from, ¶ 1903.12
World Evangelical Fellowship,
¶ 2404.3*c*
World Methodist Council, ¶¶ 639.2,
1903.8, 2403.1
reports from, ¶ 1903.12

**equitable base compensation**
council on finance and administration recommendations, ¶ 612.1*e*

**equitable compensation, conference commission,** ¶ 623

**Equitable Compensation Fund,**
¶¶ 333.1, 619, 620, 623.8–9
apportionments for, ¶ 620
short-term emergency subsidy grant, ¶ 622
utilization, ¶ 623.6

**Equitable Compensation of The United Methodist Church, National Association of Commissions on,** ¶ 807.18

**estates**
held by General Board of Education, ¶¶ 1103, 1402

**Ethnic In-Service Training Program,** ¶ 263.3

**ethnic local church concerns**
district director, ¶ 658
General Board of Discipleship responsibility, ¶ 1117

**ethnic persons.** *See also* inclusiveness.
collection of information and materials on historical witness, ¶ 1703.4
rights, Social Principles, ¶ 162*A*

**Ethnic Scholarship Program,** ¶ 263.3

**evaluation,** ¶ 348

**The Evangelical Church,** *p. 18*
Board of Church Extension, ¶ 1305.2
doctrinal traditions, ¶ 102 *(p. 55–58)*
Missionary Society, ¶ 1305.2

**evangelical denominations**
deeding church property to, ¶ 2547

**The Evangelical Press**
dissolution, ¶ 1620

**Evangelical United Brethren Church**
Board of Missions, ¶ 1305.2
Board of Pensions, ¶ 1503.2*c*
Board of Publication, ¶ 1608
Confession of Faith, ¶ 102 *(p. 58);*
¶ 103 *(p. 66–71)*
mission agencies of former, ¶ 1310.2
statement of social principles, *p. 95*
tradition, ¶ 101 *(p. 45)*
Women's Society of World Service, ¶ 1319.3*a*

**Evangelical United Brethren Council of Administration,** ¶ 722

**Evangelicals, National Association of,** ¶ 2404.2*c*

*Evangelischmethodistische Kirche,* ¶ 723

**evangelism**
as conference discipleship board responsibility, ¶¶ 628.1, 628.3
as General Board of Discipleship responsibility, ¶¶ 1110–1111
leadership as pastor's responsibility and duty, ¶ 331.1*g*

**evangelists**
district superintendent written consent requirements, ¶ 332.1

**Evangelization and Church Growth Program Area**
in General Board of Global Ministries, ¶ 1312.1

**evidence**
in judicial complaint, ¶ 2706.4*d*
in trial process, ¶ 2710.9

**examination**
of candidate for probationary membership, ¶ 315.9

**executive committee**
General Board of Global Ministries, ¶ 1306

**General Conference, Commission**
business manager, ¶ 807.21

**General Conference of 1808,** ¶ 102
(*p. 53*)

**General Conference of the United
Brethren in Christ (1815),** ¶ 102
(*p. 57*)

**General Council,** ¶ 703.1. *See also*
Finance and Administration,
General Council; and Ministries,
General Council.

**General Endowment Fund for Con-
ference Claimants,** ¶ 1504.11

**General Episcopal Fund**
central conference participation,
¶ 537.4

**general evangelists**
appointment as, ¶ 628.3*f–g*
standards, ¶ 1111.7

**General Funds**
The Advance, ¶¶ 651, 814, 1806.12
Advance Special Gifts ¶ 810
Africa University Fund, ¶ 810
Black College Fund, ¶ 819. *See also*
Black College Fund.
definition, ¶ 810
Episcopal Fund, ¶ 810
General Administration Fund,
¶¶ 810, 817
general directives, ¶ 815
Human Relations Day Fund, ¶ 810
Interdenominational Cooperation
Fund, ¶¶ 810, 818. *See also* Interde-
nominational Cooperation Fund.
Ministerial Education Fund, ¶ 820.
*See also* Ministerial Education
Fund.
Native American Ministries Sunday
Fund, ¶ 810
One Great Hour of Sharing Fund,
¶ 810
Peace with Justice Sunday Fund, ¶ 810
policies, ¶ 811

Special Sunday offerings, ¶ 816. *See
also* Special Sundays, with
offerings.
United Methodist Student Day
Fund, ¶ 810
World Communion Fund, ¶810
World Service Fund, ¶¶ 810, 812. *See
also* World Service Fund.
World Service Special Gifts, ¶ 813
Youth Service Fund, ¶ 810

**General Membership roll**
for new church start, ¶ 259.3

**General Rule of Discipleship,**
¶ 1116.2*a*

**General Rules,** ¶ 101 (*p. 48–49*); ¶ 135
constitutional provisions, General
Conference restrictive rules, ¶ 19
origin, *p. 12*

**general secretary,** ¶ 703.7*a*
accountability to General Council on
Ministries, ¶ 713
convening of all, ¶ 714.5
General Board of Global Ministries,
¶ 1307
General Board of Pension and
Health Benefits, ¶ 1502.2*b*
General Commission on Archives
and History, ¶ 1707
General Commission on Communication, ¶ 1807.5
General Council on Ministries membership, ¶ 907.1*a*(9)
relation to General Council on
Finance and Administration,
¶ 805.1*c*

**genetic technology**
Social Principles, ¶ 162M

**Germany Central Conference,**
¶ 535.3*d*
Church name, ¶ 723

**gifts**
to general agencies, ¶ 811.6
pastor's duty to notify trustees of,
¶ 2512.5

of local church
  election, ¶ 248
  responsibilities, ¶ 250.1

**lay leadership**
  pastor's responsibility for
    development, ¶ 331.2*b*

**lay leadership committee,**
  ¶¶ 243, 258.1
  election, ¶ 248
  lay leader membership, ¶ 250.1c

**lay members**
  annual conference, ¶¶ 2502, 602.4-7
  constitutional provisions
    delegate election to general and
      jurisdictional conference, ¶ 34
    election to annual conference, ¶ 30
  delegate to General Conference,
    ¶ 502
  judicial complaint, ¶ 2702.3
    finding of reasonable grounds and
      referral for trial, ¶ 2706.5*b*(4)
    investigation committee,
      ¶ 2703.4
    referral of complaint to counsel
      for the church, ¶ 2704.4
    right to appeal trial decision,
      ¶ 2717
    trial, ¶ 2714
  in provisional central conferences,
    ¶ 542

**lay missionaries in non-United
Methodist churches**
  church membership, ¶ 236

**lay missioners**
  provisions, ¶ 270

**lay speakers,** ¶ 266
  charge conference recommendations
    on, ¶ 246.11
  lay leader as, ¶ 250.1*f*
  local church, ¶ 267
  pastor-parish relations committee
    recommendations, ¶ 258.2*f*(7)
  training, ¶ 266.4

**Lay Speaking Ministries**
  conference committee, ¶ 629.6
  conference director, ¶ 629.6*d*
  conference lay leader relation to,
    ¶ 603.9*b*
  district committee, ¶ 662
  lay leader as member,
    ¶ 655.6
  General Board of Discipleship
    support, ¶ 1115.6

**leadership**
  bishops' responsibilities, ¶ 414
  district superintendents'
    responsibilities, ¶ 420
  style for superintendency, ¶ 402.1

**leadership development and
resourcing ministries of local
church,** ¶ 251.2

**leadership in local church.** *See also*
  administrative committees in local
    church; board of trustees.
  church historian, ¶ 246.5
  church-school superintendent, ¶ 254
  consecutive terms of office, ¶ 246.7
  coordinators
    communications, ¶ 254
    health-and-welfare ministries,
      ¶ 254
    for ministry groups, ¶ 253
    for specialized ministries, ¶ 252
  development as discipleship board
    responsibility, ¶ 628.7*c*
  duties, ¶ 250
  election, ¶ 248
  membership secretary, ¶ 233
  removal of officers and filling of
    vacancies, ¶ 249
  resources for developing, ¶ 1115.3
  for United Methodist Women,
    ¶ 255.4

**lease**
  of annual conference property,
    ¶ 2515
  of district property, ¶ 2523
  of incorporated local church
    property, ¶ 2540

of unincorporated local church property, ¶ 2539

**leave of absence,** ¶ 352
bishops, ¶ 411
for continuing education, ¶ 349.2
family, ¶ 353
for formation and spiritual growth, ¶ 349.3
incapacity leave resulting from health and disabling conditions, ¶ 355
appointment termination, ¶ 355.3
maternity or paternity, ¶ 354
ordained ministry, conference board responsibility, ¶ 632.2*k*
sabbatical, ¶ 350
termination, ¶ 352.4

**lectionary,** ¶ 1112.5

**legal briefs**
for cases involving denominational interests, ¶ 807.7

**legal counsel,** ¶ 807.7

**Legal Responsibilities committee**
of General Council on Finance and Administration, ¶ 805.4*e*

**leisure**
Social Principles, ¶ 163*C*

**less than full-time appointment,** ¶ 433.7
for deacon, ¶ 322.7
for ordained elders, ¶ 329.2
compensation, ¶ 333.2
ordained ministry, conference board responsibility, ¶ 632.2*k*

**license for pastoral ministry,** ¶¶ 340–346. *See also* local pastors.
authority and duties, ¶ 341
candidacy process, ¶ 306
entrance procedures, ¶ 305
surrender, ¶ 346.1

**life-span ministries,** ¶ 1118

**life-sustaining medical treatment**
Social Principles, ¶ 161*L*

**Living Prayer Center ministry,** ¶ 2302.2*g*

**living will,** ¶ 2533.5

**Loans and Scholarships, Office**
of annual conference, ¶ 631.4*a*(6)
of General Board of Higher Education and Ministry, ¶ 1408.2

**local church,** ¶¶ 201–270. *See also* charge conference; church council; church membership; pastoral charge.
accountability of, ¶ 1116.2
building accessibility, ¶ 630.4b(36)
business administration guidance, ¶ 807.16
care of members, ¶ 204
communications coordinator, training, ¶ 1806.9
congregation responsibility following baptism, ¶ 225.2
constitutional provisions
election of officers, ¶ 42
transfer between conferences, ¶ 39
contributions to Advance Specials, ¶ 651.5
cooperative parish, ¶ 205.2, 206
covenant relationships in multi-ethnic and multi-language settings, ¶ 2551
deaconess membership in, ¶ 1313.4
definition, ¶ 201
designation by located clergy members, ¶ 357.2
ecumenical shared ministries, ¶¶ 207–211
elder in extension ministries relation to, ¶ 335.3
elders' affiliate relation to, ¶ 335.3*b*
ethnic local church concerns district director, ¶ 658

in transitional communities,
¶¶ 212–213
assessment process for potential,
¶ 213

**local laws**
property provisions compliance
with, ¶¶ 2506–2510

**local pastor**
appointment as pastors, ¶ 328.2
authority and duties, ¶ 341
categories, ¶ 343
committee membership, ¶ 343.5
continuation as, ¶ 344
discontinuance, ¶ 346.1
Fellowship of Local Pastors and
Associate Members, ¶ 345
financial arrangements for
continuing education, ¶ 349.4
interim license, ¶ 342
judicial complaint, right to appeal
trial decision, ¶ 2716
licensing, ¶ 340.2
membership in annual conference,
¶¶ 365.1, 602.1
mentors, ¶ 347.1b
person on honorable location
appointed as, ¶ 357.2
probationary members classed as
after discontinuance, ¶ 318.6
records on termination, ¶ 632.3d
reinstatement of status, ¶ 346.4
requirements for probationary
membership, ¶ 315.6
restriction as lay member to annual
conference, ¶ 250.2
retirement, ¶ 346.5
service for pension credit,
¶ 1506.4f
student, ¶¶ 341.7, 343.3–4
training, ¶ 1421.6. *See also* Course of
Study curriculum.
trial, ¶¶ 346.3, 2713
voting rights in annual conference,
¶ 341.6
withdrawal under complaints and
charges, ¶ 346.2

**local preachers**
General Conference legislative
power, ¶ 15.2

**loose-leaf book**
for permanent church register,
¶ 232.2

**Lord's Supper**
elders in full connection, availability
for, ¶ 335.3
laity training in distribution to
homebound persons, ¶ 1115.9
licensed ministry authority and
duties, ¶ 341
as pastor's responsibility and duty,
¶ 331.1b

## M

**making disciples.** *See* mission of the
Church.

**mandatory retirement**
of bishop, ¶ 409.1
of clergy, ¶ 356.1
of general agency staff personnel,
¶ 714.3

**marriage**
central conferences adaptation of
rites and ceremonies, ¶ 537.18
licensed ministry authority and
duties, ¶ 341
as pastor's responsibility and duty,
¶ 331.1i
Social Principles, ¶ 161C

**Master of Divinity**, ¶ 315.4

**maternity leave**, ¶ 354

**media violence**
Social Principles, ¶ 162Q

**mediation**, ¶¶ 359.1e, 413.3

**medical experimentation**
Social Principles, ¶ 162L

# N

name of church
constitutional provision, ¶ 2

National Association of Annual Conference Lay Leaders, ¶ 1115.7

National Association of Commissions on Equitable Compensation of The United Methodist Church, ¶ 807.18

National Association of Conference Council Directors, ¶ 906.25
General Council on Ministries membership, ¶ 907.1*a*(10)

National Association of Conference Presidents of United Methodist Men, ¶¶ 2302.3*b*, 2303.1*c*

National Association of Evangelicals, ¶ 2404.2*c*

National Association of Schools and Colleges of The United Methodist Church, ¶ 1414.2

National Association of Stewardship Leaders, ¶ 628.5*i*, 1113.6

National Association of United Methodist Foundations, ¶¶ 628.5*i*, 1113.6

National (USA) Association of United Methodist Scouters, ¶ 2302.5*b*

National Council of the Churches of Christ in the U.S.A, ¶¶ 263.2, 639.2, 816.2, 818.2, 2404.2
Department of Communication, ¶ 1806.4
reports from, ¶ 1903.12

National Federation of Asian American United Methodists, ¶ 1206.2*a*

National Plan for Hispanic Ministries
lay missioners guidelines, ¶ 270

nations
Social Principles, ¶ 165*A*

Native American International Caucus, ¶ 1206.2*a*

Native American ministries
funding considerations, ¶ 623.6

Native American Ministries Sunday, ¶¶ 263.6, 650, 816.6

Native American ministry, conference committee, ¶ 650

networking leaders in youth ministry, ¶ 1118.2*c*

new churches
annual conference recognition, ¶ 604.10
organization method, ¶ 259
strategy development, ¶ 1111.13

news-gathering
General Commission on Communication, responsibility, ¶ 1806.1

*Newscope*
Judicial Council actions, ¶ 2612.1
Judicial Council notice, ¶ 2610.3

Nigeria Annual Conference
General Board of Discipleship membership, ¶ 1104.1*b*
General Council on Ministries membership, ¶ 907.1*a*(2)

nomination of bishops, ¶ 406.1

financing pension and benefit programs, ¶ 1507
joint distributing committees, ¶ 1509
membership, ¶ 636.2
organization, ¶ 636.3
policies related to conflict of interest and investment management, ¶ 1508
powers, duties and responsibilities, ¶ 1506
proportional payment, ¶ 636.4
responsibility for census data, ¶ 1504.7

**perfection,** ¶ 101, *p. 46*

**performance evaluations**
deacons, ¶ 322.14*d*
elders, ¶¶ 325.2.*c–d*

**periodicals,** ¶ 906.9

**Perkins School of Theology,** ¶ 1425.3*a*

**permanent church register,** ¶ 232.1

**permanent endowment fund committee**
in local church, ¶ 2533

**personal equality**
Social Principles, ¶ 162

**personal papers in archives,** ¶ 1711.3*k*

**personnel issues in local church.** *See* pastor-parish relations committee.

**personnel policies**
General Board of Global Ministries, ¶ 1309
for missions, ¶ 1312.6

**Personnel Policies and Practices committee**
of General Council on Finance and Administration, ¶¶ 805.4*d*, 807.11*b*

**personnel records**
access to, ¶ 606.9

**petitions to General Conference,** ¶ 507

**pews,** ¶ 2532.1

**Philippines Central Conference,** ¶ 535.3*f*

**planning**
General Council on Ministries role, ¶ 906.17
as pastor's responsibility and duty, ¶ 331.2*b*

**plants**
Social Principles, ¶ 160*A*

**plea**
entering, ¶ 2710.4

**"Policies Relative to Socially Responsible Investments,"** ¶¶ 611.5, 716, 1406.11

**political responsibility**
Social Principles, ¶ 164*B*

**pollution**
Social Principles, ¶ 160*A*

**population growth**
Social Principles, ¶ 162*I*

**poverty**
Social Principles, ¶ 163*E*
United Methodist Committee on Relief responsibilities, ¶ 1326.2*a*(2)

**power of nations**
Social Principles, ¶ 165*B*

**prayer advocates,** ¶ 2302.2*g*

**prayer in public schools**
Social Principles, ¶ 164*D*

**property ownership**
Social Principles, ¶ 163*A*

**proportional pension credit,** ¶ 1506.4*b*

**provisional annual conferences,**
¶¶ 554–557
board of global ministries, ¶ 557
delegates to General Conference,
¶ 502.1*a*
General Conference legislative
power, ¶ 15.3
organization, ¶ 556
provisions, ¶ 555

**provisional central conference,**
¶¶ 536.8, 538–545

**psychological testing of certified
candidate for licensing or
ordination,** ¶ 306.4*b*

**public media**
Communication, General
Commission responsibility to
relate to, ¶ 1806.2

**public policy**
Higher Education and Ministry,
conference board responsibilities,
¶ 631.4*d*

**public relations**
Communication, General Commission responsibility, ¶ 1806.6

**Publication, General Board,** ¶ 1608

**publishing.** *See also* General Commission on Communication; General
Board of Discipleship; United
Methodist Publishing House.
General Council on Ministries role,
¶ 906.10

**publishing houses.** *See also* United
Methodist Publishing House.
net income restrictive rule, ¶ 20

**purchase of annual conference
property,** ¶ 2515

## Q

**quadrennial review,** ¶ 807.5

**quadrennium**
term defined, ¶ 720.2

**qualifications for ordination,** ¶ 304

*Quarterly Review,* ¶ 1629

**questions for the examiners**
of candidate for deacons orders,
¶ 321.4
of candidate for elders orders, ¶ 326.7
historical examination for admission
to full connection, ¶ 327
from Wesley, ¶ 305

**quorum**
for charge conference, ¶ 245.6
for church council, ¶ 251.6
General Board of Pension and Health
Benefits meetings, ¶ 1502.3*c*
General Comission on Archives and
History, meetings, ¶ 1705
General Commission on Communication meetings,¶ 1807.2
for General Conference, ¶ 506
Judicial Council, ¶ 2608.2
United Methodist Publishing House
board executive committee, ¶ 1607
United Methodist Publishing House
board meetings, ¶ 1603

## R

**race discrimination**
policy on elimination, ¶ 604.1

**race relations**
religion and race, conference
commission, ¶ 639

**racism**
Social Principles, ¶ 162*A*

**re-baptism,** ¶ 331.1*c*

**religion and race, district director,** ¶ 659

**Religion and Race, General Commission,** ¶¶ 2001–2008
accountability, ¶ 702.2
amenability and accountability, ¶ 2001.1
finances, ¶ 2007
General Board of Church and Society relationship, ¶ 1004
General Comission on Christian Unity and Interreligious Concerns, relationship, ¶ 1903.13
and general funds availability, ¶ 811
members' election, ¶ 705.1
membership, ¶ 2003
officers, ¶ 2005
purpose, ¶ 2002
responsibilities, ¶ 2008
staff, ¶ 2006
vacancies, ¶ 2004

**Religion in American Life, Inc.,** ¶ 1809

**religious minorities' rights**
Social Principles, ¶ 162B

**remedial action**
in disposition of administrative complaint, ¶ 359.3a

**renewal leave**
bishops, ¶ 411.2
district superintendents, ¶ 425

**reprimand, private,** ¶ 359.3a(10)

**research**
archival materials available for, ¶ 1711.3n
General Board of Church and Society role, ¶ 1004
General Board of Discipleship role, ¶ 1102.10
General Board of Higher Education and Ministry role, ¶ 1405.14
General Council on Ministries role, ¶ 906.17

**reserve commission as armed forces chaplain**
leave of absence, ¶ 352.3

**resignation**
of bishop, ¶ 409.4

**resolutions of General Conference,** ¶ 510.2

**responsibility of nations**
Social Principles, ¶ 165B

**restorative justice**
Social Principles, ¶ 164F

**retired bishop,** ¶ 409
compensation
for assignment of churchwide responsibility, ¶ 409.1c
when appointed to ad interim service, ¶ 830
from former central conferences, ¶ 537.31
pension, ¶ 409.1b
status, ¶ 410

**retired clergy**
ordained ministry, conference board liaison, ¶ 632.2j

**Retired Ministers Day,** ¶ 1506

**retirement,** ¶ 356. See also pensions.
appointment of retired ordained ministers, ¶ 356.6
charge conference membership, ¶ 356.5
clergy affiliate membership in local annual conference, ¶ 325.4
of general agency staff personnel, ¶ 714.3
involuntary, ¶ 356.3
of local pastor, ¶¶ 346.1, 346.5
mandatory, ¶ 356.1
ordained ministry, conference board responsibility, ¶ 632.2k
preretirement counseling, ¶ 356.4

return to effective relationship, ¶ 356.7

status of honorable location, ¶ 357.3

voluntary, ¶ 356.2

**retirement homes**
chaplains, ¶ 1422

**retreat centers**
title to properties, ¶ 2516

*Revised Common Lectionary*, ¶ 1112.5

**right to be accompanied**
and fair process in judicial proceedings, ¶ 2701.3

**right to be heard**
and fair process in judicial proceedings, ¶ 2701.1

**Rio Grande Annual Conference**
General Board of Global Ministries membership, ¶ 1311.1

**Ritual**, ¶ 1112.3–4
central conferences adaptation of, ¶ 537.17
constitutional provisions, General Conference legislative power, ¶ 15.6

**Rules of Order**
for General Conference, ¶ 505
jurisdictional conferences, ¶ 517

**rural life**
Social Principles, ¶ 162N

**Rural Life Sunday**, ¶ 265.3

## S

**sabbatical**, ¶ 350
bishops, ¶ 411.3
clergy affiliate membership in local annual conference, ¶ 325.4
ordained ministry, conference board responsibility, ¶ 632.2k

**Sacraments**. *See also* baptism; Communion; Lord's Supper.
licensed ministry authority and duties, ¶ 341
as pastor's responsibility and duty, ¶ 331.1b

**Saint Paul School of Theology**, ¶ 1425.3a

**salaries**
bishops, ¶¶ 822, 824
bishops on special assignment, ¶ 407.3
for exempt staff of councils, boards and commissions, ¶ 807.11b
United Methodist Publishing House book editor, ¶ 1630
Church School Publications, editor, ¶ 1635
corporate officers, ¶ 1623

**salaries of pastors**
charge conference responsibility for, ¶ 246.12
during leave of absence, ¶ 352.1
local church responsibility for deacon's, ¶ 322.14b
during maternity/paternity leave, ¶ 354.4
support for elders appointed to pastoral charges, ¶ 333

**sale**
of annual conference property, ¶ 2515
of district property, ¶ 2523
of incorporated local church property, ¶ 2540
of unincorporated local church property, ¶ 2539

**sanctification**, ¶ 101 *(p. 46)*

**satellite congregation**
charge conference sponsorship, ¶ 246.20

**scholarships**, ¶¶ 816.3, 1312.3i
General Board of Higher Education and Ministry role, ¶ 1405.27

for persons preparing for ordination, ¶ 1424.9

**schools**
affiliation with The United
Methodist Church, ¶¶ 1415–1416
annual reports, ¶ 1417
disaffiliation, ¶ 1417.3
evaluating those related to annual
conference, ¶ 631.4*a*(7)
Higher Education and Ministry,
conference board
responsibilities, ¶ 631.4*b–c*
Higher Education Division
responsibilities to,
¶ 1411.6

**schools of theology**
affiliation with The United
Methodist Church, ¶ 1425.3*d*
cooperation with Mission Education
Program Area, ¶ 1312.4*f*
instruction in meaning and conduct
of worship, ¶ 1112.11
Ministerial Education Fund
distribution, ¶ 820.2
Ordained Ministry Division
relationship, ¶ 1421.10
Section of Elders and Local Pastors
relationship, ¶¶ 1424.6, 1424.8
of The United Methodist Church,
¶ 1425

**science and technology**
Social Principles, ¶ 160*E*

**Scouting ministries,** ¶¶ 255.3, 1118.1
United Methodist Men, General
Commission support, ¶ 2302.5

**Scripture**
basic affirmations, ¶ 101 *(p. 44)*
United Methodist views, ¶ 104
*(p. 78–79)*
Wesley's beliefs, ¶ 104 *(p. 78–79)*

**secretary-designate**
election at General Conference,
¶ 504.1

**secretary for charge conference,**
¶ 246.4

**secretary of annual conference,**
¶ 603.7
records for office of deaconess,
¶ 1313.3*c*

**secretary of General Conference**
assigned duties, ¶ 504.3
assumption of office, ¶ 504.2
calculation of number of delegates,
¶ 502.3
duties, ¶ 510
petitions sent to, ¶ 507.1

**self-control by ministers,** ¶ 306.4*f*

**self-examination**
by ordination candidate, ¶ 306.4*f*

**seminaries**
course offering certification, ¶ 1421.5
Section of Deacons and Diaconal
Ministries consultation with,
¶ 1423.17
United Methodist, ¶ 138

**seminary students**
scholarships, ¶ 632.2*u*

**separation of church and state**
Social Principles, ¶¶ 164*B*, 164*D*

**servant leadership,** ¶¶ 136–137

**servant ministry,** ¶¶ 131–135

**service**
as requirement for probationary
membership candidate, ¶ 315.2

**Service Loans**
from Ministerial Education Fund,
¶ 820.1*a–b*

**service records**
of ordained and diaconal ministers,
¶ 606.6

**Wesleyan churches**
relationships with, ¶ 2403.4

**Wesleyan Service Guild,** ¶¶ 1305.3,
1319.3*a*

**West Africa Central Conference,**
¶ 535.3*g*

**Western Jurisdiction**
constitutional provisions,
boundaries, ¶ 35
membership on general boards and
agencies
General Board of Church and
Society, ¶ 1006.1*a*
General Board of Global
Ministries, ¶ 1311.1
General Board of Higher Educa-
tion and Ministry, ¶ 1407.2*a*
General Commission on Christian
Unity and Interreligious Con-
cerns, ¶ 1906.1*b*
General Commission on Commu-
nication, ¶ 1807.1*b*
General Commission on Religion
and Race, ¶ 2003*b*
General Commission on the Status
and Role of Women, ¶ 2104.1*a*
General Council on Ministries,
¶ 907.1*a*(1)
United Methodist Publishing
House board, ¶ 1602.1*b*

**withdrawal from clergy membership,**
¶ 358

**withdrawal of membership,** ¶ 241
without notice, ¶ 240

**withdrawal under complaints,** ¶ 358.3

**witness ministries of local church,**
¶ 251.2

**witnesses**
in judicial complaint, ¶ 2708.8–9
examination, ¶ 2706.4*c*
exclusion, ¶ 2710.7
interview, ¶ 2706.4*b*

**Woman's Board of Foreign Missions,**
¶ 1319.3*a*

**Woman's Board of Home Missions,**
¶ 1319.3*a*

**Woman's Foreign Missionary Society,**
¶¶ 1305.3, 1319.3*a*

**Woman's Home Missionary Society,**
¶¶ 1305.3, 1319.3*a*

**Woman's Missionary Council,**
¶ 1319.3*a*

**Woman's Missionary Society,**
¶ 1319.3*a*

**women.** *See also* Status and Role of
Women, General Commission.
collection of information and materials on historical witness, ¶ 1703.4
enlistment and support in ministry,
¶¶ 1421.3, 1424.10
General Board of Global Ministries
responsibility for expressing
concerns, ¶ 1302.8
General Board of Global Ministries,
staff participation, ¶ 1309.2
General Commission on the Status
and Role of Women, ¶ 641
rights, Social Principles, ¶ 162*F*
United Methodist Women, ¶ 255.4.
*See also* United Methodist Women.

**women and men**
Social Principles, ¶ 161*F*

**Women's Division, General Board of
Global Ministries,** ¶¶ 533,
1317–1325
assembly, ¶ 1322
authority, ¶ 1319
deputy general secretary, ¶ 1308.1*b*
financial relationship to General
Board of Global Ministries, ¶ 1323
General Commission on the Status
and Role of Women, membership,
¶ 2404.1*c*